THE ADULT EXPERIENCE

THE ADULT EXPERIENCE

JANET BELSKY

Middle Tennessee State University

West Publishing Company

An International Thomson Publishing Company

Production Credits

Composition and Imaging: Carlisle Communications

Copyediting: Sherry Goldbecker

Cover Image: *Beach at Gloucester* (66.4130) by Maurice Prendergast. Hirshhorn Museum and Sculpture Garden, Smithsonian Institution, Gift of Joseph H. Hirshhorn Foundation, 1966. Photographed by Lee Stalsworth.

Interior Design: Kimberly Loscher and John Rokusek/Rokusek Design

Index: Sandi Schroeder

(Photo Credits follow the Index)

WEST'S COMMITMENT TO THE ENVIRONMENT

In 1906, West Publishing Company began recycling materials left over from the production of books. This began a tradition of efficient and responsible use of resources. Today, 100% of our legal bound volumes are printed on acid-free, recycled paper consisting of 50% new fibers. West recycles nearly 27,700,000 pounds of scrap paper annually—the equivalent of 229,300 trees. Since the 1960s, West has devised ways to capture and recycle waste inks, solvents, oils, and vapors created in the printing process. We also recycle plastics of all kinds, wood, glass, corrugated cardboard, and batteries, and have eliminated the use of polystyrene book packaging. We at West are proud of the longevity and the scope of our commitment to the environment.

West pocket parts and advance sheets are printed on recyclable paper and can be collected and recycled with newspapers. Staples do not have to be removed. Bound volumes can be recycled after removing the cover.

Production, Prepress, Printing and Binding by West Publishing Company.

COPYRIGHT ©1997   By WEST PUBLISHING COMPANY
610 Opperman Drive
P.O. Box 64526
St. Paul, MN 55164-0526

All rights reserved

Printed in the United States of America

04 03 02 01 00 99 98 97   8 7 6 5 4 3 2 1 0

Library of Congress Cataloging-in-Publication Data

Belsky, Janet, 1947–
      The Adult Experience / Janet Belsky.
         p.   cm.
      Includes bibliographical references and index.
      ISBN 0-314-20189-0 (alk. paper)
      1. Adulthood—United States.   2. Adulthood—United States-
-Psychological aspects.   3. Aging—United States.   4. Life cycle,
Human.   I. Title.
HQ799.97.U5B45   1997
305.24'0973—dc20
                                                                                96-9733
                                                                                CIP

For Muriel Kaplan and Lillian Sheerr, who made my adult development possible

For David and Thomas, who give meaning to my developing adult life

Contents in Brief

Contents

Preface

In 1990, I decided to write this book to fill a gap. I wanted a text that would highlight the personal experience of adult development and bring home to my students how what social scientists learn in an academic setting applies to the actual lives of adults. My ideal book would both be research-oriented and pay full attention to the applied side of adult development, demonstrating how research translates into concrete interventions to improve the quality of adult life. It would explore the salient issues that my students were personally grappling with, such as family relationships, parenting, and love and marriage, in depth. Most important, it would give full attention to the most pressing social concerns we Americans are grappling with as turn-of-the-century adults, issues such as intergenerational equity, health care for minorities and the elderly, and the dramatic changes in roles that have transformed family life.

Now, in 1996, at the end of a six-year-long writing effort, *The Adult Experience* remains unique. It is still the only book on the market to have these special features, the only text to fully emphasize "what is really happening" as adults develop in the contemporary United States.

The Adult Experience is more practical, more social-issue-oriented, and less abstract than other books. So it will be of special interest to students who do not plan to go on for an academic psychology Ph.D. Its comprehensive coverage of health care and family relationships makes this text an ideal choice for students considering careers in teaching, medicine, social work, clinical psychology, or allied health fields. This does not mean that my approach to adult development is unscholarly or that the book you are about to read gives basic research in physical aging, cognition, and personality short shrift. I have tried to write a book that is rigorous enough to appeal to the aspiring scholar as well as to engage the beginning student, one that appeals to all readers because it demonstrates the promise of behavioral science scholarship to address the *full range* of topics of interest to adults.

Specifically, this book has the following distinctive features:

1. **It highlights how basic research translates into real-life applications through a unique technique.** After a full exploration of the *behavioral science* findings, each chapter or major topic concludes with a section describing examples of applications and interventions. These examples are varied, including cognitive remediation studies, clinical trials designed to show that at-risk behavior can be changed, descriptions of relevant applied programs, public policy initiatives, and mental health treatments relating to the findings.

2. **It highlights adult roles and relationships.** A chapter each is devoted to marriage and parenthood. Another chapter describes family relations in later life. This book provides a more in-depth discussion of topics such as fatherhood, grandparenthood, adult child/elderly parent relationships, courtship, love, and marriage than any other book currently on the market.

3. **It highlights the salient social issues facing adults today.** Controversial topics, such as single parenthood, work force changes and discrimination, intergenerational equity, socioeconomic and ethnic differences in illness and access to health care, and ethical issues relating to terminal care, are forthrightly discussed. A research-based look at the compelling social issues facing American adults is one focal point of this book.

4. **It highlights ethnic, cohort, gender, socioeconomic, and individual variability.** Ongoing attention to the impact of gender, ethnicity, and socioeconomic status on adult development is another major theme that pervades this book. In this context, students are repeatedly reminded that individual diversity and individual differences are the hallmark of adult life.

5. **It highlights the "experience of adulthood" through a unique technique.** Instead of relying on secondhand accounts of exceptional older people, in order to emphasize the personal dimension of adult development I have conducted *interviews in which adults of every age reflect on their experiences and feelings.* When the topic is geriatric medicine, I interview a geriatric physician. I talk to a young adult coping with chronic illness, speak with a divorced father, and ask a researcher in applied gerontology to describe her experiences setting up a program in a nursing home.

6. **It offers students a coherent, well-organized view of the field.** The demographic changes described in the first chapter and their implications are expanded on throughout the book. In the theories and methods chapter, I introduce students to *specific* theories, research methods, and methodological issues that are repeatedly referred to throughout the book. Instead of superficially cataloging a disconnected array of facts, in this book salient topics and the most important studies are highlighted and explored in depth.

7. **It highlights how adulthood and research in adult development are continually evolving.** My goal is to offer students a larger framework for interpreting the contemporary research and social trends. So chapters describing the psychological research—for instance, in cognition and personality—begin with the early studies and then progress to current findings and conceptions. Chapters covering topics such as parenthood, work, retirement, sexuality, and family relations in later life also introduce these topics by providing the historical context. This allows students to put what is happening now in perspective, to gain an appreciation of adulthood as continually changing, and to see adult development as an evolving, dynamic field.

ACKNOWLEDGMENTS

During these years of writing and rewriting and changes of editors and publishers, many people believed in my work and encouraged me to persist. However, first and foremost, I want to thank Joan Gill, my main editor at West. Often an author will say, "This book would never have been published without such and such editor's help." In this case, the statement is absolutely true, as Joan rescued this manuscript from the brink of death, seeing its potential, steadfastly believing in its excellence, and making heroic efforts to put *The Adult Experience* into production before West merged with International Thomson Publishing this past summer. Laura Nelson, my accomplished production editor at West, also went above and beyond the requirements of her job to see this book to completion, petitioning to take my book with her and finish our work even though she left her full-time job with the company. It would have been natural and understandable for these women to have abandoned my book or given it short shrift during this stressful professional time. However, they continued to give it their utmost care. In my view, not only are Laura and Joan consummate professionals, but also they give meaning to the words "a true adult."

At West, I also was privileged to have an accomplished freelance copyeditor, Sherry Goldbecker, and a terrific editorial assistant, Angela Barnhart. Sherry made the manuscript grammatical and carefully checked references. Angela sifted through the reviews, decided on revisions, and offered advice at improving the content of the book. Tom Richardson, a graphic artist, created the charts and graphs. At Middle Tennessee State University, I was supported by a Faculty Research Grant, outstanding librarians and Psychology Department secretaries, and graduate assistants Pamela Ahrens and Amy Powell-Wirdzek.

I think you will agree that the people I interviewed in this book also serve as inspirations for what it means to be a true adult. Through telling me about their lives, they have not only made the research come alive, but also enriched my own life. I also want to thank the following reviewers for their thoughtful comments and helpful suggestions. A wonderful side benefit of having one's manuscript reviewed so often is to feel proud of one's colleagues, gratified by the high level of competence of the people who teach in this field:

Cheryl Anagnopoulos	Black Hills State University
Mel J. Ciena	University of San Francisco
Ruth Doyle	Casper College
John Fletcher	Southwest Texas State University
Mark Matthews	University of Kansas
Marc Potash	University of Wisconsin-Fox Valley
Sharon Ramsey-Swartz	Framingham State University
Alice Scheuer	University of Hawaii
Richard Sebby	Southeast Missouri State University
Matthew Sharps	California State University-Fresno
Ellen Strommen	Michigan State University
Robert Stowe, Jr.	Central Connecticut State University
Laura Thompson	New Mexico State University
Sandi Townley	University of Tennessee at Chattanooga
Margaret Young	Washington State University

Responsibility for this book also depends on what we developmental psychologists call the wider context, the life milieu that offers the underpinning for any of us to succeed. One critical component of my personal wider context has been the people here at Middle Tennessee State University. Six years ago, I was lucky enough to find the perfect academic job, one that offered the kind of supportive, collegial environment to allow my talents as a writer and teacher to flower. Not only do I have wonderful colleagues in this department, but also my students are an inspiration. Many are adult heroes in their own right, working 40 hours a week, going to school full-time, and trying to raise families. In fact, the life stories of several of these students are depicted in this book.

Then there is the family context that is responsible for this book: my husband, David, and son, Thomas, whogive my life purpose, and my parents and grandparents, who have nurtured me through life. While this book is also a tribute to the many adults that I have met over almost a half century of living, it is to these closest living relatives that I dedicate this book.

September 1996, Murfreesboro, Tennessee

PART I

THE FRAMEWORK

The People and the Field

Chapter Outline

In the spring semester of 1996, in my undergraduate class in Adult Development at Middle Tennessee State University, there are three students: Albert, age 71; Anocha, age 20; and Jan, age 45.

Al is paying close attention today, participating in the discussion, thrilled to be in class. What a wise decision it was to go to college after retirement! What a fulfilling way to spend the final decades of an interesting life! Born in rural Tennessee before the Depression, Al had a hard childhood. He remembers the harsh winters, the outdoor plumbing, the days there was barely enough to eat. As one of nine children, Al was the first person in his family to attend high school. He is proud of working his way up the ladder at Welgram to become a vice president, pleased at his 40 years of service to the company and his upper-middle-class life. He is happy about the person he has become in recent years—a more gentle man, more family-oriented, more able to relax. He has anxieties. For now the overall slowing—the need to spend more time memorizing material, to allow extra minutes to climb the stairs to class—is not so important. Al has no disabilities. He lives an active life. His main concern is the future, not for himself, but for his wife of 47 years. Margaret has arthritis. If Al becomes seriously ill, she will not be able to care for him alone. He does not want to leave his wife impoverished by medical bills or have her worry over the decision if he does need a nursing home. Will Al spend his final years as a burden? What will happen to Margaret in 10 or 15 years?

Anocha is daydreaming again today, an activity that has become standard behavior in recent months. Anocha is bored with school. She is tired of papers and multiple-choice tests. She has a more important concern. Anocha recently found out she is pregnant. She is excited about becoming a mother, but has no immediate plans to marry her boyfriend, John. The 15-year age difference is worrisome, as is the fact that at age 35 John seems to be in a different stage of life. On the positive side, John is African-American. When her Asian-American mother and African-American father divorced a few years ago, Anocha made the decision to only marry someone of her own race. Since they have been living together, it is apparent that she and John share many values. Anocha enjoys cooking and housework. She wants a large family. John makes a good living as a manager at the Saturn plant. By getting married, Anocha would have a husband who welcomes, and can financially afford, her "unusual" wish to be a stay-at-home mother and wife. If Anocha does get married, what will her life be like in 20 or 40 years?

Jan is also finding it difficult to focus, but not because she is not interested; she is tired. After working the night shift at the hospital, it is hard to come to any class at 8 A.M., even one so relevant to her life. Jan has her own concerns. Her main worry is her nine-year-old son. Shawn needs more attention than she can provide with her full-time school and work schedule. Luckily she has her mother to help with childcare. Jan was relieved to leave her husband. She has no feeling that she needs a man in her life. Jan wants to be a lawyer. This is her last chance for a career. Can she still perform well intellectually? Does she have the same capacity to learn or remember or to get a job as in her younger years?

Adult development is about these concerns and ours. It deals with the basic questions we have about our future: How do people change physically, cognitively, and in personality as they age? It probes the predictable **roles,** or major life activities, that punctuate adult life—retirement, parenthood, marriage, career. It concerns other, less expected transitions, such as divorcing, being unemployed, and entering a nursing home. How will Al change physically as he ages? Is Anocha making the right marital choice? Are Jan's fears about her memory and ability to learn realistic? What are her chances of successfully beginning a new career in midlife?

Adult development involves the search for universal patterns, exploring the ways we all develop and change. It also examines the different pathways we follow as adults. As we saw in these vignettes, apart from their age, Al, Jan, and Anocha differ along other basic dimensions, such as ethnicity, gender, and socioeconomic status, that may

role
Sociological term referring to the major life activities people engage in.

Socioeconomic Status (or SES, Social Class)
Definition: A person's social ranking, as defined by a combination of income, education, and occupation. While the classic sociological studies of class in the United States list more differentiated categories, typically Americans are labeled as *working class* or *blue collar* when they work in manual jobs and/or do not have a college education and as *middle class, upper middle class,* or *white collar* when they work in a professional or managerial job and have a college or higher degree.
Deficiencies: Social class is an ill-defined marker. For instance, one might be middle class in income, but work in a blue-collar job; one might have a Ph.D. and be on welfare. Moreover, the terms *working class* and *middle class* were always supposed to involve an implicit set of values (e.g., middle-class parents are interested in upward mobility and education). These generalizations may not be appropriate today.

Ethnicity
Definition: The group a person fits into, based on religion or, more often, country of origin and race.
Deficiencies: Americans are often a mixture of ethnicities, making it impossible to categorize people definitively. Categorizing people into broad groups, such as "Hispanic-American," can be misleading, as individuals lumped into this category are not alike in their customs, values, and country of origin.

Concluding comments: These markers are extremely useful in adult development, revealing a good deal about inequities in society and offering important information about everything from health status to parenting and marital trends. However, by using them, we also run the risk of stereotyping people.

greatly influence adult life (see Table 1-1). These students vary in another way that is certain to make their development unique, the historical time in which they were born.

Al, Jan, and Anocha are from different cohorts. In adult development, cohort is a crucial concept. **Cohort,** a word similar to generation, refers to any group of people born within a specified short period. Because Al is a member of the cohort born in 1925, Jan in 1950, and Anocha in 1976, each student will be exposed to different experiences, opportunities, and conditions not just when they reach adulthood, but also at every point during adult life.

For instance, being a young adult right after World War II, when jobs were plentiful and a college degree was not necessary to advance, Al had work experiences that are different than those he would have had if he had reached adulthood during the 1920s, the 1970s, or today. He has a different orientation to his retirement years. At this moment in history, because retirement lasts on average almost two decades, it is more likely to be the beginning of a new phase of life, rather than death. Jan might never have left her husband or might not be considering a career as a lawyer if she had been in her forties during the 1950s, when divorce was much less common and far fewer women considered a professional career. Anocha is entering adulthood during a time when women can decide *not* to get married when they become pregnant without much sense of shame. However, today marriages are more fragile, and making the "unusual" choice to be a full-time homemaker seems more risky than ever.

cohort
Group of people born within a specified short period of time who travel through life at the same point in history.

Al's cohort reaching adulthood at the triumphant end of the Second World War (photo A) faced a different set of life-conditions and expectations than Jan's cohort who came of age in the early 1970s at the height of the tumultuous women's movement (photo B). How do you think these different social conditions might shape each person's attitudes, relationships, and world view as they travel through adult life?

Throughout this book, we will see how our cohort, our gender, our ethnic group, and our social class affect our journey as adults. Despite this emphasis on diversity, this book is limited in one important respect. It is devoted to what social scientists study and know best: adulthood in our time and in this location of the world. The following chapters describe the adult experience as this remarkable century closes.

A DEMOGRAPHIC PERSPECTIVE ON ADULT DEVELOPMENT

demography
Statistical study of large populations.

Now we begin with a bird's-eye view of the terrain. **Demography,** the study of populations, offers a statistical picture of today's American adults, illustrates how adulthood in America has changed, and offers hints about adulthood in the future.

A Longer Adulthood: The Life-Expectancy Revolution

The first major change in adulthood concerns that basic dimension, age.[1] Americans as a group are older than ever. They will be even older in the next few decades. As Figure 1-1 shows, the median age of the U.S. population is expected to rise from its current age of about 35 to 43 by the middle of the twenty-first century.

This upward shift is due partly to the bulge in the population called the postwar baby boom. After World War II, the birth rate soared. This meant that, as Figure 1-1 shows, over the past 50 years the median age of the U.S. population first declined and then, as the baby boom cohort grew older, climbed. When this huge cohort turns 65, we will be a top-heavy society. By 2030, the proportion of people over 65 will swell from one in nine to one in five.

baby boom cohort
Group of people born during the period following World War II, from 1946 to 1964.

The members of the **baby boom cohort,** defined as people born from 1946 to 1964, have left an indelible imprint on the United States as they cut their swath through life. When these children dominated the population during the 1950s and early 1960s, deviations from the two-parent family were discouraged, gender roles were highly

[1]Information in this section is from U.S. Senate Special Committee on Aging, 1991a, unless otherwise noted.

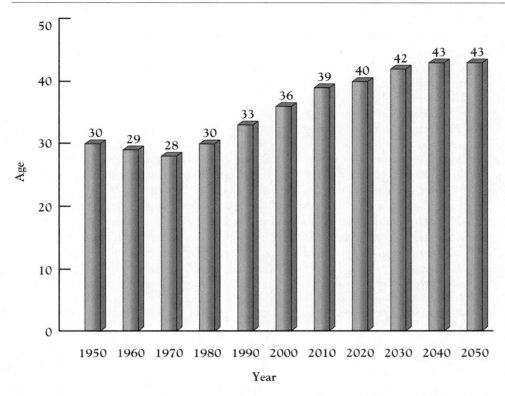

The changing age structure of the United States partly reflects the passage of the huge baby boom cohort through the life span. Notice how the median age of the population first declined and then has steadily risen since the mid-1970s as the baby boomers age.

Note: The median refers to the bisecting or middle point of a population—in this case, the age at which 50 percent of Americans are older and 50 percent younger.
Source: U.S. Senate Special Committee on Aging, 1991, *Aging America: Trends and Projections,* Washington, D.C.: Author.

traditional, and full-time mothering was expected to be a woman's job in life. Then, as rebellious adolescents during the 1960s and 1970s, this huge cohort helped engineer a radical transformation in these attitudes and roles. When the baby boomers settled down to working and having their own families during the 1970s and 1980s, career concerns and children once again assumed center stage as we entered a more conservative era in politics. Now that this cohort is middle-aged, the phenomenon demographers refer to as the **graying of America** is in full swing. The United States is bracing for a boom in senior citizens in the next few decades as the baby boomers begin to enter their retirement years.

graying of America
Phrase referring to the fact that a growing fraction of Americans are in the aging phase of life.

The baby boomers, however, are only partly responsible for the graying of America. The main reason for the growing numbers of older Americans is more enduring: an increase in life expectancy during the twentieth century unparalleled in human history.

In every culture, some people always lived to old age. However, the chance of reaching one's seventies or eighties used to be fairly small. In the Roman Empire, only

average life expectancy
Age to which an individual has a 50/50 probability of living from a specific age, most often birth.

life-expectancy revolution
Phrase referring to the dramatic increase in life expectancy that has taken place during the twentieth century.

infectious diseases
Category of illnesses that are transmitted by infectious agents or microorganisms.

chronic diseases
Category of illnesses that are long-lasting and not typically caused by infectious agents.

lifestyle movement
Change in health consciousness during the 1960s and 1970s, emphasizing good health practices as the key to disease prevention.

one-fifth of the population made it to middle age. The statistics were no different in Colonial America, where in the Chesapeake colonies only about 10 percent of white male children lived to age 60. Because the high rates of infant and childhood mortality dragged down this figure, in these cultures there was a remarkably low **average life expectancy,** one's chances at birth *on average* of living to a certain age. In the well-off New England colonies, average life expectancy was about age 30. In Maryland during that same time, it was *under* age 20, both for masters and for their slaves (Fischer, 1977).

During the eighteenth and especially the nineteenth centuries, life expectancy in America steadily improved. By 1900, it was 47.3. Then, in the next half century, it shot up. Today a U.S. baby can expect on average to live to about age 76. During the twentieth century, life expectancy increased by almost 30 years.

The twentieth-century **life-expectancy revolution** has two phases. In the earlier decades of the century, dramatic gains in life expectancy occurred at younger ages, allowing most people to live past youth. Now our main strides have been made in extending life expectancy in later life. For instance, Americans who turned 65 in 1987 could expect on average to live 16.9 more years. Today we can expect to be senior citizens for almost as long as we were children and adolescents.

This extension occurred because of a shift in the pattern of disease control. Earlier in the twentieth century, medical advances, such as immunization and antibiotics, wiped out deaths from many **infectious diseases,** such as diphtheria. Since these diseases killed both the young and the old, their eradication allowed most people to live past midlife. Now we have become better able to limit, but not cure, diseases that strike people in middle and later life. People reaching age 65 now live on for years because of declines in mortality from these illnesses of aging, called **chronic diseases** (heart disease, cancer, stroke).

While these advances are partly due to medical breakthroughs, such as improved medicines and better surgical techniques, much credit belongs to us. Many experts feel the **lifestyle movement,** which began in the 1960s and 1970s, with its emphasis on exercise and diet, is responsible for the striking decline in mortality from heart disease and stroke that has occurred over the past few decades (Fries, 1990; Lesnoff-Caravaglia and Klys, 1987). As we will see in Chapter 3, exercising, eating the right foods, and being concerned with our health earlier really do help slow the onset and pace of certain important age-related chronic diseases.

The rise in late-life life expectancy means unparalleled numbers of Americans are living to their ninth, tenth, or even eleventh decades of life. People over age 85 are now the fastest-growing part of the population. We can expect their numbers to dramatically rise in the next few decades. As Figure 1-2 shows, by the middle of the twenty-first century the percentage of the population aged 85 or older is expected to increase almost sixfold.

One consequence is that four-generation families are now common. People often have the joy of witnessing the birth of a great-grandchild. In their forties and fifties, they have the pleasure of seeing a parent or even a grandparent still alive. There are problems along with this good news. While we have added time to the end of the life span, we have not necessarily given these family patriarchs or, more likely, matriarchs a high-quality life. As we will see in Chapter 5, the increase in people living to their eighties and nineties means more sick elderly and thus an exploding need for medical and nursing care.

By about our ninth decade of life, the chance of being physically disabled by disease increases dramatically. In part because of this, researchers in adult development frequently make a distinction between two groups of older people: the young-old and the old-old. The **young-old,** defined as people aged 65 to 75, do not often have disabling diseases. They often look and feel middle-aged. They overwhelmingly reject the idea that

young-old
People in their mid-sixties to mid-seventies.

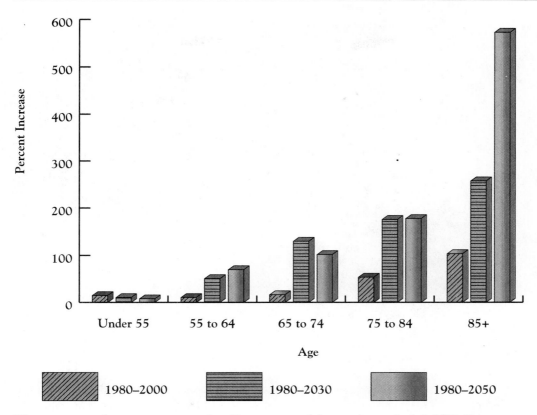

We can expect a dramatic increase in the oldest segment of the population through 2050. How will this transformation change society?

Source: U.S. Senate Special Committee on Aging, 1991, *Aging America: Trends and Projections*, Washington, D.C.: Author.

they are old (Palmore, 1990). The **old-old,** people in their late seventies and beyond, seem in a different class. Since they are more likely to have physical and mental disabilities, these people are more prone to fit the stereotype of the frail, dependent older adult.

old-old
People in their late seventies and beyond.

    We have many well-known demoralizing stereotypes about old age. Older people are supposed to be unattractive, unable to think clearly or move quickly, physically feeble, and mentally impaired (Butler, 1980; Palmore, 1990). These ideas are deeply ingrained and widespread. As Feature 1-1 shows, these stereotypes have been common throughout world and American history (Cohen and Kruschwitz, 1990) and reveal themselves remarkably early in life. From a very young age, children describe old people as dependent, unattractive, and weak. In far-flung locations, such as the Aleutian Islands of Alaska, Paraguay, and Australia, they view the elderly with distaste (Jantz, Seefeldt, Galper, and Serock, 1976; Miller, Blalock, and Ginsberg, 1984–1985).

    However, today these visions are far less accurate. In some respects, they do not even fit the old-old. Even over age 85, most Americans are able to function by

Like the runner in photo A, people who are young-old are often vigorous and actively engaged in life. The woman in photo B displays the physical frailties more likely to be present among the old-old.

themselves. Though they often do have disabilities, they do not need nursing-home care. Moreover, as we will see in Chapter 7, only a small minority of elderly Americans suffer from the intense cognitive impairments often seen as synonymous with being old. How have these stereotypes fared now that we are confronted with these millions of vital older adults?

There is encouraging evidence that our stereotypes are breaking down. Instead of applying to everyone over age 65, negative stereotypes only come into play when an older person appears to be ill and infirm (Gekoski and Knox, 1990). When researchers asked college students to list as many traits as possible linked with being old, they got a hodge-podge of responses. Older people were viewed as frail and incompetent, but also resilient and tough. They were labeled as quarrelsome and set in their ways, but also generous, loving, and wise (Schmidt and Boland, 1986). In other words, while we still think of older people in the traditional ways, these ideas have been supplemented by new perceptions. The strange outcome is a set of firmly held *contradictory* thoughts about what the elderly are like.

So reality is permeating the stereotype. Older people defy generalizations. Many are active, involved, and competent; some are ill and frail. Some are at the height of their powers; others are the embodiment of decline. The words *golden years* sometimes fit this stage of life. At other times, they are a cruel parody. More than in any previous time in history, diversity and individual differences are the hallmark of senior citizenhood today. In fact, contrary to our rosy ideas about how older people used to be treated, as Feature 1-1 reveals, today we may be living in one of the most *age-friendly* ages of all.

This new army of senior citizens is changing society. They are fighting against **ageism,** or prejudice on the basis of age. They have made inroads. Today we have laws prohibiting age discrimination in the work force and, with some exceptions, mandatory retirement on the basis of age. We have a different conception of what is possible in our older years. Running a marathon, beginning a new career, or carrying on a passionate romance is no longer viewed as just for the young. While we still may have a way to go

ageism
Any form of prejudice based on age.

The forehead scowls, the hair is grey. . . . The brows are gone, the eyes are blear. . . . The nose is hooked and far from fair. . . . The ears are rough and pendulous. . . . The face is sallow, dead and drear. . . . The chin is purs'd. . . . the lips hang loose. . . . Aye such is human beauty's lot! The arms are short. . . . The hands clench tight; the shoulders tangle in a knot. . . . The breasts in shame they shrink from sight. . . . the thighs are thin; As withered hams, and have a blight of freckles like a sausage-skin.

Thus we mourn for the good old days. Perch'd on our buttocks, wretched crones, huddled together by the blaze. . . . We who have sat on lovers' thrones! With many a man 'tis just the same. . . . (Excerpted from "Lament of the Fair Heaulmiere," or helmet-maker's girl, an Old English poem quoted in Minois, 1989, p. 230)

Many of us assume that people had better values and attitudes toward growing old in "the good old days." Poems such as the one above urge a closer look.[1]

In ancient times, many historians believe, old age was seen as a miracle of nature because it was so rare. Where there was no written language, older people were greatly valued for their knowledge. They were given an exalted place. Elders formed the governing bodies in ancient Rome and Greece. The elderly owned the land and resources and so had absolute control over their daughters and sons. However, this elevated status applied only to the elite—*if they were male.* For slaves, servants, and women, old age was often a cruel time. Moreover, when we look closely, a different picture emerges.

In some societies, the same person who had been lionized might be subjected to barbaric treatment once he had outlived his usefulness, that is, had become decrepit or senile. Tribes such as the Samoans killed their aged members outright in elaborate ceremonies in which the victim was required to participate. Others left their older people to die of neglect. Strong norms requiring "respect for one's elders" prevented this fate from happening to older people among other groups. However, even in cultures Westerners traditionally look up to as models of enlightenment, aging was deprecated and feared.

Sophocles and Michelangelo, who were revered as old men, stand out as supposedly typical of the age-accepting attitudes of the social milieu in which they lived. However, the images portrayed in their works of art celebrated youth and beauty. Even in these important cultures, Classical Greece and the Renaissance, old age was looked down on as the worst time of life.

As historian Georges Minois (1989) concludes in a survey of how Western civilization treated its elders: "It is the tendency of every society to live and go on living: it extols the strength and fecundity that are so closely linked to youth and it dreads the. . . . decrepitude of old age. Since the dawn of history, . . . young people have regretted the onset of old age— The fountain of youth has always constituted Western man's most irrational hope (p. 303)."

[1] *The material in this feature is from Fischer, 1977 and Minois, 1989.*

before reaching an **age-irrelevant society** (Neugarten, 1977), where everything is equally possible at any age, we have much less rigid rules about what is acceptable at age 70 or 85 than before.

A More Variable Adulthood: Changing Social Roles

The life-expectancy revolution paved the way for our liberated view of late life. With so many vigorous and healthy older people, the older years have come to be seen as a time of new possibilities as well as of decline. However, the real push for this new freedom

age-irrelevant society
Ideal society in which people can engage in any activity at any time in life.

Although she may not be fully aware of its importance, this elderly female mountaineer is a product of both the women's revolution and the revolution in the meaning of age.

arose from a revolution in attitudes and social norms. This change, which, as mentioned earlier, occurred when the baby boomers were adolescents in the 1960s and early 1970s, encouraged self-expression, not just for the elderly, but also for every adult.

The "Decade of Protest" began with the civil rights and women's movements and ended with the counterculture movement, which emphasized liberation in every area of life (Bengtson, 1989). Sexuality before marriage became acceptable. Alternatives to the traditional path of marriage for life were explored. While any joy attached to the mere process of exploring these new alternatives has evaporated, their legacy endures. Divorcing, living together, and having children without being married are now permanent parts of contemporary American life.

Divorce is not just a product of the 1960s. Divorce rates had been climbing steadily over the twentieth century. However, after this revolutionary decade, the divorce rate soared. Today, with more than one-half of all marriages ending in divorce, this event has become normal. Divorce is *more predictable* today than staying married for life (Furstenberg and Cherlin, 1991; Popenoe, 1988). The rise in divorce has been accompanied by a dramatic increase in the number of women who have children without being married. By the late 1980s, one out of four births was out of wedlock (Levitan and Conway, 1990). Among African Americans, 63.7 percent of births were to unmarried women (Hacker, 1992).

Because of these two changes, from 1970 to 1985 the proportion of single mothers doubled from 1 in 10 to 1 in 5. Even for married couples with children, the traditional homemaker wife and breadwinner husband are no longer typical. They are a victim of an even more basic change, women in the work force.

Some women always worked (Coonts, 1992). Even during the 1950s, more than a third of all women had paying jobs (Schor, 1991). During the late 1960s and 1970s, however, women entered the workplace in huge numbers, propelled by the push for self-fulfillment and, increasingly, by financial need. Today women make up 45 percent of the labor force. Nearly 60 percent of women are working full-time during their prime adult years. Even staying at home with very young children is no longer typical. As of 1988, more than half of all U.S. women with preschool-age children had paying jobs (Ferber, O'Farrell, and Allen, 1991; Levitan and Conway, 1990).

This shift in women's roles has transformed American society. Not only, as we will see in Chapter 10, is the increase in working women intimately tied to the decrease in two-parent families, but also it has changed the role of grandparent, making this job more central than before. It has profoundly affected men, changing their family relationships and work opportunities and affecting their personalities. Today there is no single accepted path, no clearly carved-out role or way of acting for women *or* for men. Both genders face an expanding range of choices as they travel through life.

This same diversity applies, not just to the paths we select based on gender or age, but also to other aspects of American life.

Immigration, Income, and Adult Life

Americans are becoming more ethnically diverse. The main reason is a new wave of immigration. In 1980, the foreign-born population reached 14.1 million people, 6.2 percent of all Americans. While this is far from the 13 percent it had been at turn of the century, during the past few decades our country has become a nation of immigrants again (Portes and Rumbaut, 1990).

The different origins of this immigrant flood are responsible for making the United States a genuinely "global" nation. Since 1960, immigration from Western Europe and Canada has slowed, while the number of immigrants from Asia, Africa, and Latin America has swelled. To one observer, this means: "In the San Jose telephone directory, the Nuguyens outnumber the Joneses fourteen columns to eight, while in Los Angeles a

Turn of the century immigrant families, such as the one pictured in photo A, escaping hunger and persecution in Europe imparted their own distinctive character to early 20th century America. Today's ethnically and economically diverse new U.S. citizens will leave their own imprint on the United States during the next few decades of this new century (photo B).

Korean restaurant serves Kosher burritos in a largely black neighborhood" (Rumbaut, 1991, p. 209). The United States lives up to its image of refuge for the world as never before.

The common stereotype is that these immigrants are poor and ill-educated. Like "the huddled masses" from Europe that preceded them, they are believed to be escaping hunger and persecution. Nothing could be farther from the truth. As Feature 1-2 illustrates, the new immigrants are as likely to be skilled professionals as refugees. The diversity of social and economic backgrounds and the reasons people migrate rival the diversity of countries from which they come (Portes and Rumbaut, 1990; Rumbaut, 1991).

Another shift involves a widening gap between the "haves" and the "have nots," which has gradually taken place during these same few decades. The increase in single mothers, taxation policies favoring the wealthy during the Reagan years, and especially the loss of well-paying blue-collar jobs have caused the income differences between Americans to grow. In a reversal of a trend toward greater equality that had been occurring since World War II, during the 1970s and especially the 1980s, the wealthiest one-fifth of the nation grew wealthier. Those less well off got a smaller slice of the nation's net worth (Peterson, 1993; Reich, 1992). We can make some generalizations about these poorest Americans. Women, if they live alone, and minorities, especially African Americans and Hispanic Americans, continue to be disproportionately found at the lower end of the socioeconomic totem pole.

Women, Minorities, and Adult Life

Women and minorities follow a different path compared to that of Caucasian men in a number of areas of adult life. As just suggested, one difference involves income. On average, full-time working women earn only about 72 percent of what men do (Gilbert, 1993). In a two-earner family, this wage difference may not present huge problems. However, if a woman is a single mother with children, the lack of parity can be

In China, the members of Anna's family were professionals. After the revolution in 1930, they fled and helped set up the new state in Taiwan. As a teenager, when Anna's father moved the family to the United States temporarily on business, she remembers how anxious she was to get back to Taiwan. Anna had no idea that she would end up living in a small town in Tennessee.

In Taiwan, there are only a few universities. When Anna married, she and her husband took the path followed by many friends: going to the United States to get a graduate degree. During her first months at Arizona State, Anna was too frightened to open the door or answer the phone. The language was unfamiliar. Even when she could understand others, no one had a clue as to what she said. An English teacher encouraged her and pushed her to get out of the house. Anna began to feel more comfortable. Her husband got an engineering degree. She gave birth to her son. There were very few jobs for engineers in Taiwan. Her husband's broken English was an impediment to getting a job in his field in the United States. Still, opportunities were more plentiful here. A relative lived in middle Tennessee, and Anna and her husband liked the area. Anna had worked in a restaurant, so they opened up a Chinese restaurant in our town.

During the first months, they almost lost everything. They would prepare the food night after night and then wait, but no one would come in. Today the Chinese restaurant is doing well. Anna and her husband are part owners of two others. Her family is scattered around the country. A sister lives in Seattle and a brother in Los Angeles. She has cousins in New York. She is happy to have these relatives, but not motivated to be with other immigrants from Taiwan. Nor does she care about congregating with other Asians in town. She and the Laotians do not speak the same language. Their cultures are very different, even though they have a shared history and language. In her words, Anna feels more comfortable with Americans, than the "aloof and guarded" mainland Chinese. Her son is an honor student at the local school. He is "an American boy." Fifteen years after immigrating, Anna feels the same way: "Now," she says, "I feel like a stranger when I return to Taiwan."

In their book, *Immigrant America,* Alejandro Portes and Ruben Rumbaut (1990) categorize the new immigrants into four types. Only one category fits our negative stereotypes. These are the illegal aliens who sneak across the border or overstay on tourist visas. The primary lure for this group is wages, which far exceed those they could earn in their countries of origin. A second, smaller group is comprised of genuine refugees, people given asylum from persecution. Another group is made up of small-business people who settle in ethnic sections in large cities, such as Koreatown in Los Angeles or Chinatown in New York, enclaves that offer security and economic mobility. Finally, there are the immigrants who come to improve their careers. These people are upwardly mobile professionals who often come to get further education and then stay. For instance, in 1987, more than one half of all of the doctorates in engineering awarded by U.S. universities were received by foreign-born students. Most of these immigrants, as was true of Anna's husband, decided not to return to their countries of origin, but to remain in the United States. While they do get work in their profession, as we saw in our interview, because of linguistic or cultural barriers, some have turned to new careers. Even so, the success of these new immigrants is remarkable. These new arrivals are numerous, but inconspicuous. As with Anna's family, they are rapidly assimilated, do not congregate in ethnic enclaves, and feel thoroughly American. In other words, Anna is not unusual. Her life is typical of a major strand of immigration that is transforming the United States.

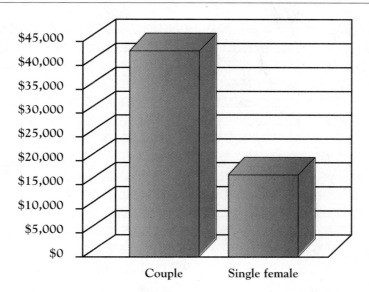

The median income of female-headed families in 1992 was about $17,000 a year—almost three times less than the approximately $45,000 annual combined income earned by married couples.

Source: U.S. Bureau of the Census, 1995, *Statistical Abstract of the U.S., Chartbook, 1995,* Washington, D.C.: U.S. Government Printing Office.

devastating. The income of *working* single mothers is only about one-third that of married couples. Approximately one-half of mother-headed families spend some time on welfare (Levitan and Conway, 1990; U.S. Bureau of the Census, 1995; see Figure 1-3).

Women also differ from men in life expectancy. However, here they are the winners. Today women outlive men by 6.9 years. A complex set of influences accounts for the gender differences in mortality that occur at every point in life. While more males are born, boys are more likely to die in infancy, childhood, and adolescence from accidents and diseases. During adulthood, women are much less likely to develop heart disease early on (Hazzard, 1990; Ory and Warner, 1990).

Since 1970, the male/female gap in life expectancy has narrowed by almost one year. It may decline further if the lifestyle factors contributing to these male death rates are reduced. Men tend more often to smoke or drink to excess. They have more hazardous jobs. These environmental differences are thought to partly explain why males have especially high mortality rates from preventable causes of death, such as accidents, heart disease and stroke, and lung cancer (U.S. Public Health Service, 1995). But, even if we eliminate the external reasons why men die sooner, experts agree the gender difference in longevity will persist because it has biological causes. Once modern medicine eliminated deaths from childhood illnesses and especially made pregnancy and childbirth safe, women began to outlive men. Today, as Figure 1-4 shows, in every developed country, women outlive men by at least three or more years (Nathanson, 1990). Because they must survive childbearing, women are the biologically hardier sex (Verbrugge, 1989, 1990).

Figure 1-4

Sex Difference in Life Expectancy at Birth in Developed Countries, 1975–1978

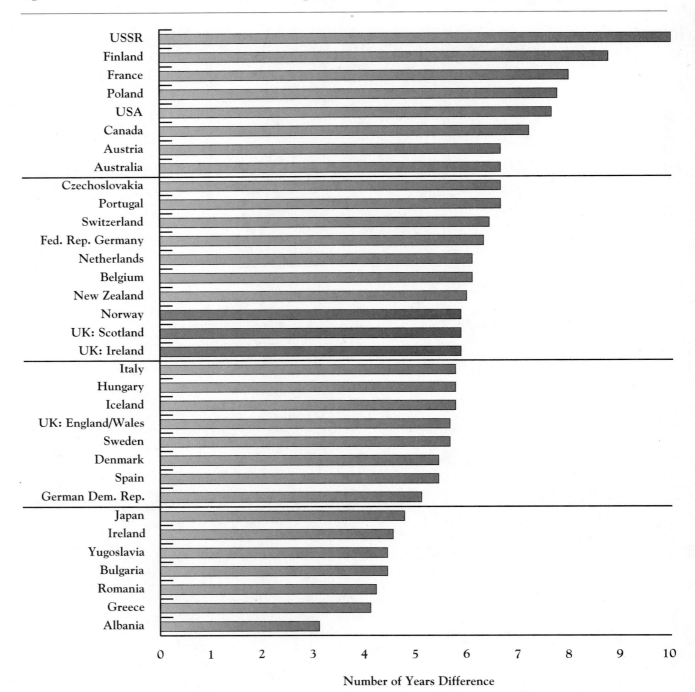

Number of Years Difference

Women outlive men in every developed country. The gap in life expectancy varies dramatically, for largely unknown reasons, from country to country.

Source: C. A. Nathanson, 1990, The Gender-Mortality Differential in Developed Countries: Demographic and Sociocultural Dimensions, in M. G. Ory and H. R. Warner (Eds.), *Gender, Health, and Longevity: Multidisciplinary perspectives.* New York: Springers.

This means that in most of the world the older population is mainly composed of women. The imbalance is especially startling at life's uppermost limits. In 1989, at age 65–69 for every 100 U.S. women, there were 84 men. In the age group over 85, there were only 39 (U.S. Senate Special Committee on Aging, 1991a). So most married women can expect to be widowed and to live as widows for years. Because there is also a trend not to live with children, older women often live their final years alone. They are more likely to enter a nursing home. Especially if old-old, widows are likely to be poor (Burkhauser, 1994). The earning differences between males and females ensure less assets for women to draw on in advanced old age.

The statistics on socioeconomic status and life expectancy among minorities are equally revealing because these comparisons, collected at each census, are our nation's main barometer of the progress we are making in ensuring that people of every ethnic group achieve the American Dream. While, as we saw in Feature 1-2, the practice of grouping minorities obscures the tremendous differences in national origin within each group, the more than one-quarter of Americans classified as racial/ethnic minorities in the 1990 census are grouped into four categories: African Americans (12.4 percent), Hispanic Americans (9.4 percent), Asians and Pacific Islanders (3.1 percent), and Eskimos and American Indians (.8 percent) (U.S. Bureau of the Census, 1993). While Asian Americans do better, Hispanic Americans and African Americans are more likely to be disadvantaged in a number of areas of life.

As is true for women, a major contrast is economic. In 1993 the average yearly income of an African-American family was less than three-fifths that of a white family. Hispanic Americans were only slightly better off (see Figure 1-5). In the early 1990s African Americans and Hispanic Americans were several times more likely to be living below the poverty line than whites (Jencks, 1992).

The encouraging news is that especially for African Americans the large gaps in education are narrowing. Today African-American young adults are almost as likely to graduate from high school as whites. They have higher college graduation rates than ever. However, income is not keeping pace with these educational gains. At each comparable educational level, Hispanic- and African-American heads of households still earn substantially less and are more likely to be living in poverty than whites (Hacker, 1992; Jencks, 1992).

The mortality statistics are equally disturbing. While Hispanic Americans and Asian Americans may actually outlive whites, this is not the case for men in our largest minority group. In 1990, African-American men had an average life expectancy of 65.2 years. White men outlived them by about seven years; white women survived on average almost 14 extra years. More distressing, while the racial gap in life expectancy had been declining for both sexes, starting in the mid-1980s the gap for men began to grow again. As Table 1-2 (see p. 19) shows, African Americans continue to have much higher death rates from 11 of the 15 top-ranking causes of death. Growing up in poverty, having poorer diets, having less access to medical care, and living in dangerous environments all make it more likely that African Americans, especially if they are male, will not survive to their later years (Jackson, Antonucci, and Gibson, 1990).

So adulthood in the United States continues to be more rocky for our nation's major minority groups. Hispanic Americans and African Americans are more likely to suffer from poverty. They are less likely to live within a two-parent family. If African-American and male, they are less likely to reap the benefits of our life-expectancy progress. These comparisons ignore the remarkable individual variability within every ethnic group. They also neglect the equally remarkable civil rights progress made over the last half of the twentieth century. However, they do suggest that the path of adult life continues to differ dramatically depending on ethnicity and race.

In describing how far we still have to go, it is easy to forget what conditions used to be like for African Americans a mere half century ago.

Figure 1-5

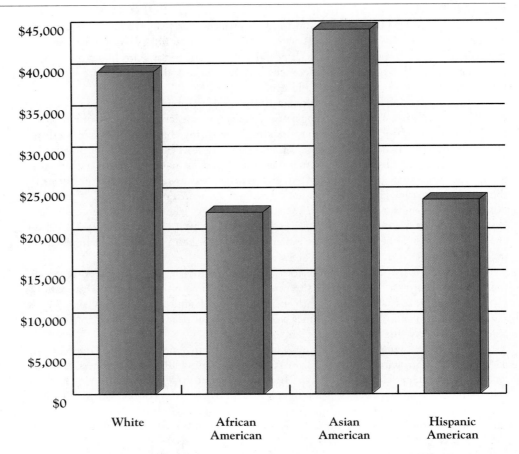

Notice that in 1993 the median income of Asian Americans exceeded that of whites, while the median income of African Americans and Hispanic Americans lagged well behind.

Source: U.S. Bureau of the Census, 1995, *Statistical Abstract of the United States*, Washington, D.C.: Government Printing Office.

A HISTORICAL PERSPECTIVE ON THE FIELD OF ADULT DEVELOPMENT

Statistics provide an external snapshot. They do not offer insights into the ways we behave and change over time. For these insights, we turn to the field called adult development, the scientific study of the phase of life called adulthood.

The effort to scientifically examine adulthood is surprisingly recent. Child development is one of psychology's oldest specialties. Among the research areas social scientists study, adult development ranks as a young child.

For the first half century of psychology's existence, developmental psychology meant child psychology. (Even when contemporary psychologists use the phase "developmental psychology," they may still be referring only to children.) While American research in this extremely popular area of psychology was under way as early as 1900,

Ratio of Age-Adjusted Death Rates for the 15 Leading Causes of Death for the Total U.S. Population by Race, 1992.

Table 1-2

Rank order	Cause of death (Ninth Revision, International Classification of Diseases, 1975)	Ratio of black to white
. . .	All causes	1.61
1	Diseases of heart	1.48
2	Malignant neoplasms, including neoplasms of lymphatic and hematopoietic tissues	1.37
3	Cerebrovascular diseases	1.86
4	Chronic obstructive pulmonary diseases and allied conditions	0.81
5	Accidents and adverse effects	1.27
. . .	Motor vehicle accidents	1.03
. . .	All other accidents and adverse effects	1.57
6	Pneumonia and influenza	1.44
7	Diabetes melitis	2.41
8	Human immunodeficiency virus infection	3.69
9	Suicide	0.58
10	Homicide and legal intervention	6.46
11	Chronic liver disease and cirrhosis	1.48
12	Nephritis, nephrotic syndrome, and nephrosis	2.76
13	Septicemia	2.71
14	Atherosclerosis	1.08
15	Certain conditions originating in the perinatal period	3.21

With the exception of lung conditions and suicide, African Americans suffer higher mortality rates from each top-ranking cause of death.

Source: U.S. Public Health Service, 1995, *Monthly Vital Statistics Report* (Vol. 43, Supplement No. 6), Atlanta: Centers for Disease Control and Prevention.

child psychology expanded dramatically between World Wars I and II. A few sporadic efforts to study adulthood were made by some leaders of the child development movement during this time. Still, in psychologists James Birren and Betty Birren's words, before the end of World War II, "it is easy to form the impression that most psychologists . . . regard[ed] the child as an end product rather than as part of an ongoing course of the human life span" (1990, p. 6).

The scientific study of adult development grew out of **gerontology,** the study of old age. Gerontology became an established field in the United States in the late 1940s, when an institute devoted to research on aging was sponsored by the National Institutes of Health and a variety of professional organizations, The Gerontological Society of America, the American Geriatrics Society, and a Division of Maturity and Aging, now called the Division of Adult Development and Aging, of the American Psychological Association were formed (see Table 1-3). In recent decades, spurred on by the increasing number of older people, these organizations have flourished, and gerontological research on memory, personality, and physical aging has accelerated (Riegel, 1977). However, it was only within the past quarter century that many researchers have begun to turn their attention to all of adult life.

During the 1970s, research by sociologists on life transitions, such as marriage, signaled an effort to pay attention to adulthood as a whole. At the same time, spurred on

gerontology
Study of the aging process and of older people.

Table 1-3   Some of the Major Professional Aging Organizations

Gerontological Society of America: The main American aging organization, a multidisciplinary group of mainly researchers interested in gerontology; publishes journals and books and has annual and regional meetings.

American Society on Aging: A newer organization that includes both researchers and gerontologists working in a wide variety of applied areas; publishes its own journal and has annual meetings; is more likely to highlight innovative practice than research.

American Psychological Association, Division of Adult Development and Aging: A special interest division of the American Psychological Association specifically for psychologists interested in adult development and aging; publishes a newsletter.

American Geriatrics Society: A special interest organization specifically for physicians specializing in geriatrics; publishes a journal and has meetings.

by the publication of an undergraduate textbook (Kimmel, 1974), adulthood and aging became the subject of a standard course in psychology departments.

Why did it take so long for social scientists to consider adult development worthy of studying? One reason lay in the climate in psychology. As we will see in the next chapter, the main theories influencing researchers and practitioners during the middle decades of the twentieth century, behaviorism and psychoanalytic theory, either considered age irrelevant to understanding human behavior or specifically stated that people did not change after the first few years of life. Jean Piaget, the most famous theorist who did believe in systematic developmental change, felt intellectual development reached its peak in adolescence. This idea that "stages end at adulthood" supported the biological idea that adolescence is the peak of development and the rest is decline. Furthermore, while studying development through childhood or during the older years seemed manageable, conducting research covering all of adult life was an awesome task. It was only in the 1970s that some studies in which subjects had been followed for decades began to bear fruit, offering a research portrait of how we change throughout adult life (Birren and Birren, 1990; see the next chapter).

The fact that adult development is in its infancy explains some gaps in the following pages. Because it is so new, adult development is still more of a fragmented collection of topics than a unified field. Furthermore, in many ways, this youthful field is dominated by its mother, gerontology, the study of later life. This definite aging or later-life orientation to the research will be especially noticeable in the chapters dealing with physical functioning and cognitive change. The irony is that, because *both* ends of the life span are easier to study, chart, and make generalizations about, we know more about what it is like to be age 70 or 80 than age 20 or 35.

THE PERSPECTIVE AND PLAN OF THIS BOOK

Now that we have a perspective on the people and on our developing field, I want you to know my own perspective in writing this book. While occasionally I will be discussing physical aging, this book basically concerns behavior. It describes what behavioral and social scientists know about adult life.

Within this framework, I will be offering a balanced look at the physiological, psychological, and social aspects of life. After these introductory chapters, Part 2 explores the physical dimension, providing an overview of normal aging and disease prevention (Chapter 3); then highlighting aging in two important areas of life, sexuality and sensory-motor functioning (Chapter 4); and then focusing on the end point of age-related physical change—disease, disability, and health care (Chapter 5). Part 3 concerns the psychology of adult life. This four-chapter sequence covers intelligence (Chapter 6); then once again spotlights two important topics in cognitive aging, memory and dementia (Chapter 7); and then explores personality (Chapter 8) and psychopathology (Chapter 9) during adult life. Part 4 concerns the social dimension, that is, our relationships and major roles as adults: love, marriage, and intimate relationships (Chapter 10); parenthood (Chapter 11); the older family (Chapter 12); and work and retirement (Chapter 13). The book concludes with Chapter 14, covering death and dying, and some end notes on the people and the field.

Throughout this book, as in this chapter, I will be putting information in its historical context, as I believe it is important for us to understand where we have come from in order to appreciate the current research and the world views we take for granted today. I also believe it is important to demonstrate how what is learned through scholarly research translates into real life. Therefore, I have planned each chapter or each major topic to end with an Applications and Interventions section, describing practical implications of the research. This same focus on practical issues pervades this book. In fact, my main goal is to write a book that speaks directly to the issues and concerns you and I are grappling with as American adults.

For this reason, in the following chapters I will be highlighting the salient social issues facing Americans today, focusing on issues such as health care for the elderly and minorities, the explosion of single parenthood, and discrimination in the work force. I will be paying special attention to how gender, ethnicity, and socioeconomic status shape the quality of our lives.

My background as a clinical psychologist has shaped another special feature of this book. In addition to surveying the literature, I have taken the step of surveying adults. The vignettes that introduce each chapter and that appear in the feature called The Adult Experience are based on the lives of real people. For the most part, they come from interviews I have conducted in preparing this book. While I hope these first-person accounts of adulthood in action make the research come alive, please do not read these experiences as though they represented *universal reactions* or even feelings typical of most adults. The same is true of every generalization I will be making in this book. I cannot emphasize strongly enough that diversity and individual differences are the essence and the beauty of adult life.

I hope that this book conveys the excitement of adult development, this new field that speaks directly to your developing life. Keep in mind that just as lives develop the field of adult development is continually evolving. Perhaps you will be inspired enough by the unfolding story in the following pages to decide to help our young field grow toward maturity.

KEY TERMS & CONCEPTS

role
cohort
socioeconomic status
ethnicity
demography

baby boom cohort
graying of America
average life expectancy
life-expectancy revolution
infectious diseases
chronic diseases
lifestyle movement
young-old
old-old
ageism
age-irrelevant society
gerontology

RECOMMENDED READINGS

Birren, J. E., and Schaie, K. W. (Eds.). (1996). *Handbook of the psychology of aging* (4th ed.). New York: Academic Press.
   This edited book, revised every five years or so, is the definitive reference on the psychology of aging. Glance through the chapters to get a sense of the topics social scientists study.

Fischer, D. H. (1977). *Growing old in America*. New York: New York University Press.
Minois, G. (1989). *History of old age*. Chicago: University of Chicago Press.
   These books offer interesting historical accounts of how the elderly used to be viewed and treated. Fischer covers old age in America; Minois deals with Western culture through the Renaissance.

Ory, M., and Warner, H. (Eds.). (1990). *Gender, health, and longevity*. New York: Springer.
   This edited book summarizes research relating to gender differences in health and longevity.

Portes, A., and Rumbaut, R. (1990). *Immigrant America*. Berkeley, Ca.: University of California Press.
   The authors discuss the new immigration.

U.S. Senate Special Committee on Aging. (1991). *Aging America: Trends and projections*. Washington, D.C.: Author.
   This comprehensive book is a good source for facts about older Americans, covering income, illness, disability, the utilization of health care services, living arrangements, minorities, and more through 1991.

Wolfe, A. (Ed.). (1991). *America at century's end*. Berkeley, Ca.: University of California Press.
   This edited collection of essays focuses on contemporary America and its status and problems as the twentieth century draws to a close.

Theories and Research Methods

Chapter Outline

"As we age, we grow more spiritual." "My unhappy childhood caused the problems I'm having now." "That nursing home resident is getting attention when she yells. That is why she acts in this way." Each time we make these statements, we are using an important theory developed to explain adult behavior.

theories
Systematic efforts to explain behavior within a coherent framework.

Theories are attempts to organize and explain the "raw data" of behavior. They make sense of the observations we make about adults. A good theory is clear, is broad in scope, provides new insights, and fits in well with observations. It explains why past events occurred, makes definite predictions about the future, and offers concrete suggestions about how to intervene to improve the quality of adult life (Thomas, 1996). Determining the accuracy of any theory demands research. In this chapter, we survey the two cornerstones of adult development, theories and research methods.

Throughout this book, you will be introduced to many theories. In this chapter, I offer a preview of some broad theoretical approaches and concepts we will be repeatedly encountering in the following chapters and sample a few ways psychologists have conceptualized how we develop as adults. I will be using the same selective strategy in describing research, focusing on techniques to measure development during adulthood, and bringing up issues that loom large in conducting research in our field.

In exploring theories, I have chosen a down-to-earth approach. First, we look at four theories that do not focus specifically on adulthood. According to these broad, non-adult-centered perspectives, the same principles are used to understand behavior at ages 18 and 75. Then we explore four theories specifically addressing changes that occur during our adult years.

THEORIES

Emphasis on Age Irrelevance in Adult Development

A BEHAVIORAL PERSPECTIVE ON ADULTHOOD. Behaviorism, the most influential theory shaping psychology (Kimble, 1993), has a clear position about change during adult life. Behaviorists reject the idea that there is *any* defined, age-related process of development. They believe that the forces motivating a one-year-old are identical to those that motivate a person of 65. After exploring some basic concepts of this theory, we will look at the interesting insights this *anti*-developmental stance offers on development during our adult years.

Behaviorists emphasize *nurture* (the environment), not *nature* (genetics). They believe that our actions are determined by our outer-world experiences, not by what we are born with, that is, inherited traits. Behaviorists believe behavior is predictable and obeys simple laws. According to **traditional behaviorism,** all learning occurs through two basic mechanisms called classical and operant conditioning.

traditional behaviorism
Original theory that all learning occurs by operant and classical conditioning and that behavior can be understood and predicted by referring to external stimuli and reinforcers alone.

classical conditioning
Behavioral process by which humans and animals learn emotions and physiological reactions in new situations.

Classical conditioning, the most primitive type of learning, involves involuntary responses, actions or physiological reactions outside of conscious control. In this type of learning, a stimulus automatically evoking a particular emotion or physiological reaction (the unconditioned stimulus) occurs in conjunction with a neutral stimulus (the conditioned stimulus). After a number of pairings or even one association, a connection is formed, and the response is now elicited by the new stimulus alone.

Classical conditioning explains why we salivate when we smell a steak sizzling on the grill. It accounts for that happy feeling that (hopefully) wells up when we approach this class in the morning or turn into our driveway in the evening to see our family. In practice, however, behaviorists most often use classical conditioning to explain why we learn negative emotions in certain situations, such as specific fears. Once we have had an inherently frightening experience, such as being in a car accident, fear gets connected to the initially neutral stimulus situation of being in the car. When we next put our key in the ignition, anxiety automatically wells up.

When this experience causes us to change our behavior, perhaps to give up driving and take the bus to work, the second type of learning, operant conditioning, has occurred. **Operant conditioning,** or *instrumental conditioning,* is the major mechanism explaining conscious or voluntary actions. Here the principle is simple. Responses that are rewarded, or **reinforced,** will tend to recur. Responses that are not reinforced will **extinguish,** or disappear. In this case, relief from the anxiety that wells up as we approach our car would be a potent reinforcer, propelling us to avoid the object of our fear.

According to behaviorists, reinforcement drives all behavior. It explains why an 85-year-old widow calls her children daily, complaining of chest pains even though there is nothing physically wrong. It makes sense of why her 50-year-old daughter, having finally enrolled in college after her children are grown, works long and hard to excel. For the old-old widow, the reinforcer motivating her actions seems to be attention. Only by acting ill can this lonely, isolated woman get the caring contact she craves. For the middle-aged woman, the reinforcer might be a different kind of attention: "proving to my family that I am capable intellectually or, possibly, getting the grades that will demonstrate that I can go to graduate school." Still, in order to prove that these specific reinforcers might be motivating each woman's behavior, we would have to chart the conditions surrounding each person's actions. According to behaviorists, we can only determine what is reinforcing by carefully measuring the outcomes linked to performing each response.

We also would want to chart when reinforcement occurs because different *schedules of reinforcement,* such as being rewarded after every response, at predictable intervals, or irregularly, produce different patterns of behavior. For instance, if their actions were resistant to extinction, continuing for some time without a current reward, both women should be under some type of *variable reinforcement schedule.* In this common pattern, reinforcement occurs at unpredictable times, so people learn persistence, the idea that if they continue responding, at some point they will be reinforced. We would imagine that, while some days her children might be more unresponsive, at other times the old-old widow's children gathered around. They worried about her, told her they loved her, and rushed to her side. We would imagine the middle-aged student is having experience with the hit-or-miss quality of grades. This would teach her a lesson of a superficially different type: "I have to keep studying, even when I do not get A's. Eventually, my efforts will pay off." In both cases, while the actual content of the learned behavior (industriousness versus incompetence) appears antithetical, the process is the same. Learning is occurring through the identical principle or law.

These simple concepts offer an unusual perspective on important questions in adult development. Why is it that behavior stays stable over the years? What accounts for age-related change? To explain why we can see much of the older person in the young adult, a traditional behaviorist would invoke operant conditioning and reinforcement. Repeated reinforcement explains why motivated, high-achieving young adults tend to be unusually accomplished in middle age, why they often become increasingly more successful compared to other people in their field or cohort as the years pass (see Chapter 13). Reinforcement would account for the persistence of negative traits, such as hostility. The angry young man provokes a hostile response in other people, solidifying his ill temper. The disagreeable college student is transformed into the hostile, bitter man of 75 (see Chapter 8).

The same behaviorist would use extinction to explain age-related change. Extinction offers insights into many age losses described in this book. Since men no longer see them as sexually attractive, many elderly women report no longer having sexual feelings

operant conditioning
Behavioral process by which humans and animals acquire voluntary behavior; also called instrumental conditioning.

reinforce
Behavioral term for reward.

extinguish
Behavioral term for disappear.

(see Chapter 4). When people are working in routine jobs, their intellectual flexibility declines over the years (see Chapter 6). Extinction also explains why, because she is no longer reinforced for acting independent and healthy, the aged widow described above finds that her only chance for human contact lies in acting ill.

Behaviorism's New Face: The Cognitive/Social Learning Approach. For much of the twentieth century, behaviorists were satisfied that classical conditioning and operant conditioning were sufficient to explain all learning. They believed that it was not necessary to make inferences about internal processes, such as feelings and thoughts. In fact, behaviorists believed that only by studying stimuli and responses that could be objectively measured would they ensure that psychology was a true "science" of human beings. During the 1960s and early 1970s, a shift occurred. Many behaviorists realized that operant conditioning and classical conditioning could not adequately explain all behavior. Accounting for why people acted as they did required widening one's focus, venturing beyond what could be externally observed.

The theorist most responsible for this widened focus was Albert Bandura. In an influential set of studies conducted during the 1960s and early 1970s, Bandura (1977) and his Stanford University colleagues demonstrated that learning often can and does occur without getting concrete rewards. There is another way we learn; by **modeling,** or *observational learning,* watching and then imitating what others do. According to **Bandura's social learning theory,** most learning occurs in an interpersonal context, from observing people. Moreover, we actively *choose* the models and bits of behavior we wish to imitate.

Bandura's ideas were accompanied by other evidence that contradicted traditional behavioral thinking. Some people might continue to act in the same way for months or years when reinforcements seemed minimal, when there appeared to be no reason why extinction did not occur. The same reinforcing experience, such as repeatedly being praised, might dramatically change the behavior of one individual, but have little effect on another. Once again, just focusing on what was objectively happening *to* the person seemed inadequate. It seemed necessary to look internally, to examine the individual's cognitions or thoughts *about* the world. The *cognitive behavioral movement* had begun.

Cognitive behaviorists still follow many principles of traditional behaviorism. They believe behavior obeys predictable laws and must be systematically charted in order to be understood and changed. Although admitting that inherited or biological predispositions to act in certain ways exist, cognitive behaviorists are still great advocates of nurture. They look to the environment to explain behavior and believe people can change quite easily as a result of environmental interventions. However, there is a central philosophical difference between the ways cognitive behaviorists and their traditional counterparts approach human behavior. As implied earlier, rather than viewing human beings as *reactive,* our behavior passively determined by the stimuli and reinforcers that happen to exist, cognitive behaviorists view us as *active* agents who shape our own reinforcers (Bandura, 1989). Instead of examining only external events and observable responses, cognitive behaviorists concentrate on identifying, understanding, and changing our perceptions about the world.

Now it is time to introduce two cognitive behavioral concepts we will be repeatedly encountering in this book: self-efficacy and explanatory style. **Self-efficacy** refers to our belief in our competence, our conviction that we can perform a given task successfully. According to Bandura (1989, 1992), who also developed this concept, efficacy feelings powerfully motivate behavior. They determine the goals people set. They predict which activities we engage in as we travel through life. When efficacy expectations are low, we shy away from acting. We choose not to ask a beautiful stranger for a date. We decide that going to medical school is just too difficult. When self-efficacy is high, we not only

modeling
Learning that occurs through watching and imitating others; also called observational learning.

Bandura's social learning theory
Theory that learning occurs in a social context, by observing others.

cognitive behaviorism
Movement in behaviorism stressing the central role that cognitions, perceptions, and thoughts play in behavior.

self-efficacy
An internal conviction that one is able to perform a task successfully.

take action, but also persist in acting long after the traditional behavioral approach suggests extinction should occur. Self-efficacy makes sense of why James Joyce tried repeatedly after his manuscript was rejected by dozens of publishers. It tells us why the Beatles went on to fame and fortune after Decca Records turned down their recordings, saying "We don't like their sound." As Bandura (1992, p. 22) states: "Ordinary social realities are strewn with difficulties. They are full of impediments, failures, adversities, set-backs, frustrations, and inequities. People must have a robust sense of personal efficacy to sustain the . . . effort needed to succeed." If we looked just to standard reinforcement, he argues, many of man's highest achievements would never have occurred.

Explanatory style refers specifically to the lens that people adopt for viewing non-reinforcing or reinforcing events. Do we see failures or disappointments as enduring, global, and internal; as signs of incompetence; as permanent states that will always occur? Or do we view setbacks as temporary, single cases having an external cause? "True, my creative work was rejected, but this was chance. I happened to choose a publisher or record company without vision. This event says little about my competence or ultimate success." Do we see successes as permanent, global, and internal or pass them off as temporary, single events? "I got published or had that hit record because I happened to get lucky this time." (Using the example of a young author, these contrasting ways of viewing the world are spelled out in Table 2–1.)

Let's illustrate by returning to the 50-year-old female college student discussed previously in the context of reinforcement. Bandura would say that feelings of

explanatory style
Specific way a person perceives positive and negative events.

How Young Writers with Different Explanatory Styles Would Interpret the Acceptance or Rejection of Their First Novel	Table 2-1

Negative event: Novel gets rejected by a publisher
Optimistic explanatory style: Event is (1) temporary, (2) a single case, (3) situational or extrinsic to the self. *Sample cognitions:* (1) This will change. (2) Every other publisher will love my work. (3) This editor was uninformed. I am a gifted writer. I have written and will continue to write terrific books.
Pessimistic Explanatory style: Event is (1) permanent, (2) global, or covering all cases, (3) internal or basic to the self. *Sample cognitions:* (1) This will never change. (2) Other publishers will feel the same way. (3) This editor's judgment was accurate. I am an untalented writer. I have written and will continue to write poor books.

Positive event: Novel gets accepted by a publisher
Optimistic explanatory style: Event is (1) permanent, (2) global, or covering all cases, (3) internal or basic to the self. *Sample cognitions:* (1) This will never change. (2) I will have success repeatedly throughout my career. (3) This editor's judgment was accurate. I have real talent. I am a gifted writer. I have written and will continue to write terrific books.
Pessimistic Explanatory style: Event is (1) temporary, (2) a single case, (3) situational or extrinsic to self. *Sample cognitions:* (1) This will change. (2) I just happened to get lucky with this particular publisher. (3) This has little to do with my real talent. The editor just happened to be looking for a book with this theme.

Notice that these different explanatory styles not only should affect each novelist's subsequent writing efforts, but also may have an impact on overall physical and mental health.

self-efficacy—that is, a conviction that she is competent and intelligent—are underlying her drive to study so hard. Furthermore, by examining the strength of these feelings, we can predict what will happen if in one semester her hopes for making A's are dashed. If feelings of self-efficacy are weak, this lack of reinforcement might cause extinction. If robust, the student will work even harder, spending more hours in the library than before.

Explanatory style refers to how the student interprets the disappointing grades. Does she see this failure as global, internal, and stable, reasoning that "this shows I will always perform poorly as I am incapable of doing well"? Does she view this event as a temporary, single case, extrinsic to the self? "That semester I had an unusually difficult set of professors. I happened to do poorly because so much was on my mind."

APPLICATIONS
AND
INTERVENTIONS

Traditional behavioral concepts have been used in almost every area of adult development—to make sense of why marriages fail or succeed, to explain why people become depressed, to understand why memory and physical capacities may deteriorate when people enter long-term care. According to the theory, any time reinforcing experiences are lacking, responses, such as love for one's partner or interest in life, extinguish or erode. In nursing homes, physical disability and memory impairment are predictable because in these settings the reinforcers tend to promote disability, rather than a competent life (see Baltes and Werner-Wahl, 1992; Feature 2–1).

The same is true of self-efficacy and explanatory style. These cognitive behavioral perceptions not only have been used by researchers to predict behaviors as different as longevity and love, but also offer their own unique perspective on age-related decline. When older people believe that memory problems or illnesses are inevitable at their age, cognitive behaviorists argue, these age-linked changes in efficacy feelings might lead to retiring early, avoiding physical or mental activity, or retreating to a rocking chair (Lachman, 1991). The same is true of age-associated shifts in explanatory style. When the younger person loses his keys or develops a pain, we see the event as temporary and passing, reasoning: "He has too much on his mind. He is not feeling well *today.*" In an older person, we interpret these events in an internal, permanent, global way: "That individual is suffering from old age."

Now that we have this framework, we can summarize behaviorism's appeal, particularly for people who work in applied settings with adults and the elderly:

1. **Behaviorism is optimistic.** The theory offers an "easily reversible" perspective on deficits that occur in any situation and at any age. When behaviorists see a person who is disagreeable, abrasive, or unable to effectively love and work, they look not to that individual's basic character, but to the reinforcing experiences and perceptions maintaining the behavior. When behaviorists find memory problems or impaired physical functioning in an older adult, they think: "How is this problem being maintained by the current reinforcements or lack of reinforcing experiences in the person's life? How can I rearrange the reinforcements to reverse what *seems* to be decline intrinsic to advancing age? How can I change the cognitions that are keeping this individual from living a productive life?"

2. **Behaviorism has wide scope.** Rather than just being a theory of personality, cognition, or physical functioning, behaviorism has global applicability. The principles of learning offer a framework for understanding everything from emotional problems, to memory deficits, to end-of-life disabilities, such as incontinence (see Feature 2-1).

3. **Behaviorism is action-oriented.** Behaviorism offers a clear blueprint for change. By using the principles of learning, not only can we understand why behavior is acquired, but also we can immediately intervene to improve the quality of life.

2-1 The Adult Experience: A Behaviorist in the Nursing Home

How is the behavioral approach used with disabled older adults? What are some issues psychologists face in using traditional behavioral techniques in applied settings such as nursing homes? We can get insights from this interview I conducted with a geriatric behavioral researcher:

"I decided to be a clinical psychologist because I wanted to help people. Behavioral approaches, because they are so well documented, were attractive to me. I liked the precision of behaviorism, the idea that by changing the reinforcement contingencies you could make a difference in people's lives.

My interest is in the iatrogenic effects of institutional care—that means the negative effect that the environment has on residents, even when 'good care' is being provided. As my definition of the environment includes the social world, my main focus is the staff. I became interested in care in nursing homes. When you do applied research, you pick a problem that the staff is interested in. I was more interested in deteriorating cognition as a function of being in the institution, but the staff was concerned about incontinence. So I ran a project to determine the reinforcers controlling incontinence. I was convinced that residents were being incontinent in order to receive attention from the staff because if you looked at the staff-resident interactions, most social contact was occurring around dressing and changing the person.

My colleague and I set up a procedure whereby residents would be regularly given the chance to go to the toilet and attention would be applied as a consequence of requesting assistance and withheld when the person was wet. An aide went into residents' rooms every hour, asking if the person wanted to go the bathroom. Residents were only taken to the toilet if they requested to go. The purpose of this strategy, which we called prompted voiding, was to put control back in the hands of the residents so they would get assistance only when they wanted it. *Over half—and I emphasize half—of the incidents of incontinence are eradicated within two days if you do that.* Incontinence is a multibillion dollar problem, and our idea was that, if you could reduce incontinent episodes, you could significantly reduce nursing home costs.

The problem we encountered is that the nursing home aides; while well meaning, are overworked. So a person arrives one day and a coworker is absent and that individual has 12 people to change and dress rather than 8. Prompted voiding has to be done on the resident's schedule, not the staff's. If there is no reinforcement for asking the resident, the temptation is not to ask. I remain convinced that our techniques are effective. The real need is to shift focus to the powers higher up. We need to change the industrywide reinforcement contingencies that inadvertently can operate to foster less-than-optimal care.*"

*I will be expanding on the issues this gerontologist is addressing when we discuss nursing homes in Chapter 5.

So, to return to the criteria of good theory at the beginning of this chapter, behaviorism gets high marks for its broad scope, ability to provide new insights, clarity of predictions, and practical implications. However, despite these attractive features, questions remain. Can the principles of reinforcement really explain why our personality, interests, and methods of coping with stress are often so enduring, despite the many changes in the external conditions or reinforcers in our lives? Why is it that adults vary so greatly in self-efficacy and explanatory style? Where do these differences in world views really come from, and can't they be more resistant to change than behaviorists assume? Perhaps there is more to personality than a collection of isolated, easily charted behaviors and thoughts. These are the issues this next theory addresses.

If behaviorism has been the most influential theory historically in psychology, **psychoanalytic theory,** developed by Sigmund Freud during the early decades of the twentieth century, is the model of human behavior that has triumphed in the wider world. Every time we hear statements such as "My problems are caused by traumatic childhood experiences" or "I must have done that unconsciously," we are listening to ideas loosely based on Freud's writings. In fact, although psychoanalytic theory has been heavily criticized in recent decades, Freud, who wrote prolifically from 1900 to the brink of World War II, clearly qualifies as a world-class genius. This man powerfully shaped modern Western culture. He profoundly altered the way people think about human motivations and actions.

Freud believed that our basic personality is formed by early childhood and then remains relatively stable. He thought that personality has conscious and unconscious aspects. The deepest layer of personality, the unconscious, is the most important determinant of behavior. He also believed that personality has three facets: the id, ego, and superego.

The *id*, present at birth, is the mass of instincts, wishes, and needs we have when entering the world. The *ego*, the largely conscious, reality-oriented "executive" of personality, is formed when as children we realize that our needs cannot be immediately satisfied. Ego functions involve logic, reasoning, and planning, that is, getting what we desire in an appropriate way. Next the *superego*, the unconscious internalization of parental and societal prohibitions, norms, and ideals, develops. In other words, during early childhood, Freud believed, we learn the requirements of being human. Our wishes and desires can be fulfilled only by adjusting to reality. Sometimes these wishes must be abandoned totally in order live a moral, ethical life.

As I suggested earlier, Freud and his followers believe our parents are responsible for this learning and so for our lifelong mental health. If our parents are empathic and sensitive during early childhood, we will develop a strong ego, which enables us to adapt to the crises of life. If they are insensitive, or for some reason their caretaking is poor, ego formation will not be optimal, and we will be vulnerable, prone to the eruption of impulses from the id, and likely to develop problems when encountering the stresses adulthood is certain to bring.

So for Freudian psychoanalysts the way we behave during adulthood is stable, determined by a personality that is set in stone from our early years. Stressful events during adult life, such as becoming ill, being widowed, retiring, or even getting married or becoming parents, are tests of psychological functioning. These changes strain the capacity of the ego, the executive in charge of mental health, to remain firmly in control. If our childhood experiences have not been ideal, it is during these life crises that we break down and develop psychological symptoms. To understand behavior, it is crucial to look beneath the surface. What unconscious needs, fantasies, and wishes are motivating the person's actions? Let's highlight this approach by examining how a psychologist who adopts the traditional psychoanalytic perspective might view the 85-year-old widow and the 50-year-old returning college student described in the section on behaviorism.

For the elderly widow, the psychologist might see the need to be taken care of as a childhood desire that is activated in situations of stress. In this case, being widowed and alone might have provoked the eruption of this basic need. Furthermore, believing that personality basically does not change, this person would feel similar episodes probably punctuated the woman's life. In any difficult situation, the widow would develop psychological problems. In fact, previous life crises probably produced the same symptoms as we observe today. Moreover, in this individual's view, the cure for this pathological behavior would be to fully explore the past. Only in examining and emotionally coming to terms with what happened in the distant years of early childhood, would the widow find answers and an antidote to why she has this inappropriate way of dealing with life.

The psychologist would bring the same approach to the middle-aged student, seeing her pattern of behavior as determined by unconscious childhood needs. However,

psychoanalytic theory
Theory developed by Freud that stresses the primacy of unconscious motivations and early childhood experiences in determining adult personality.

because the student's behavior seems more appropriate and healthy, the psychologist might put her in a different category: "Although we could only know for certain by investigating her childhood, the student's actions imply an ego in control, the psychoanalytic criterion of mental health."

Psychoanalytic theory has made interesting contributions to research in adult development. The concept of unconscious motivations has added a dimension to our understanding of the way personality is measured and changes as we age. The idea that there is more to emotions than what people report has enriched our knowledge of how adults feel about death. By drawing on psychoanalytic ideas about the importance of good parent/child attachments, researchers have developed new approaches to understanding adult love.

However, just from this simple description, we can see why *traditional* psychoanalytic ideas have not been very popular in adult development. Any theory that assumes that nothing important occurs after childhood is bound to seem less than appealing to people committed to exploring the adult years! With its exclusive focus on personality and emotional problems and on the proposition that who we are is set in stone, psychoanalytic theory lacks the breadth, optimism, and practicality of behaviorism. In addition, psychoanalytic ideas are vague, hard to measure, and difficult to prove (or disprove). This theory, like behaviorism, has trouble accounting for the strong differences we often find among people in what look like similar environments. Why is it that one child brought up in a loving family may "turn out" so badly, while another is a model of mental health? Isn't more than just parenting responsible for the ways we act? The effort to answer these questions brings us to a third perspective on adult life.

A BEHAVIORAL GENETIC PERSPECTIVE ON ADULTHOOD.   Notice that, while behaviorism and psychoanalytic theory make different assumptions about what motivates people, these theories are similar in one respect. Both stress the importance of our outer-world experiences (or nurture) in determining our mental health and happiness as adults. Now we look at the role that other category of influence, called heredity (or nature), plays in shaping adult life.

The effort to study inherited aspects of behavior has a long history in psychology. However, during the first two-thirds of the twentieth century, environmental explanations took center stage. As we know from Chapter 1, during this period great advances were occurring in the quality of life in the United States. Perhaps it was partly the improvements in life expectancy and society in general that helped promote this faith in the power of the environment to erase human problems, that accounted for the almost total dominance of behaviorism in American psychology, especially during the middle decades of the twentieth century (Kimble, 1993). During the 1950s and early 1960s, psychoanalytic theory was also in its heyday. It was widely believed to be a highly effective cure for emotional problems. After World War II, we might imagine there would be great resistance to research revealing that inborn, hereditary differences have a major impact on behavior. Americans had recently had an object lesson in the costs of this position taken to its extreme in the horrors of the Nazi idea of a master race.

Within a brief period during the 1970s and early 1980s, the pendulum swung the other way. Suddenly it became routine to emphasize inherited predispositions to explain traits as different as the tendency to become phobic, to bite ones nails, or to gravitate to a particular spouse.

There were important reasons for this shift.[1] One force was the development of medications that were proving as effective as psychotherapy in dealing with many

[1]The information in this section is from Bouchard, 1994; McClearn, 1993; Plomin and McClearn, 1993; and Plomin, DeFries, and McClearn, 1980, unless otherwise noted.

behavioral genetics
Field devoted to studying the impact of genetic predispositions on behavior.

twin studies
Behavioral genetic research strategy in which the similarities between identical twins on a particular trait(s) are often compared with the similarities shown by fraternal twins.

correlation
A statistical technique designed to show how closely related two variables are to one another.

emotional problems. Most important, research advances in a field called **behavioral genetics,** which studies the influence genetics has on behavior, made the inherited contribution to personality and psychopathology clear.

The basic strategies that behavioral geneticists use to examine the influence of heredity on behavior are called twin and adoption studies. In **twin studies,** researchers compare identical (monozygotic) twins, who, because they develop from the same zygote, share 100 percent of their genes, with fraternal (dyzygotic) twins. Fraternal twins, like any siblings, have developed from separate zygotes and so on average share 50 percent of their genes. Researchers reason that, if a trait is highly influenced by genetics, identical twins should be much more alike on that dimension compared to fraternal twins.

Specifically, in twin studies, researchers select large groups of identical and fraternal twins and **correlate** or relate how each group scores along scales measuring particular behavioral dimensions or traits. The statistic used to describe the strength of the association between two measures, called a *correlation coefficient,* can range from ±1, showing perfect predictability in either a positive (+) or a negative (−) direction, to 0, showing no relationship. However, because even the score the same person would get on different occasions is apt to change, when studies reveal, as we can see in Figure 2−1, that twin pairs' scores on complex attributes, such as intelligence, typically correlate at .6 or .8, the magnitude of these relationships is considered to be very high.

Next researchers subtract the correlation coefficients for the two groups of twins. Because logically this number automatically omits half of the genetic influence, they double that figure to arrive at a statistic called heritability. *Heritability* refers to the degree to which variations in that trait can be attributed to genetic influences. For instance, as twin studies suggest that the respective correlations in height between identical twins are about .9, while those for fraternal twins are about 4.5, doubling this difference yields a heritability of .9. This does *not* mean that if we are 5'2", our height is 90 percent due to heredity and 10 percent due to the environment. It tells us that on average the differences we observe in height among Americans today are approximately 90 percent genetic in origin.

In *adoption studies,* the strategy is to compare adopted children with their biological and adoptive parents. Once again, researchers estimate the impact of heredity on a trait by looking at how closely adoptees resemble their birth parents (with whom they share only genes) or their adoptive parents (with whom they share only environments).

Figure 2−1 shows the heritabilities calculated for a variety of traits measured in adolescence using the twin method. Notice that, while certain abilities such as memory and processing speed are less influenced by genetics, personality tendencies, such as extraversion, neuroticism, and general intelligence, are quite "hereditary." About 50 percent of the variation in these important dimensions between teenagers can be attributed to genetic sources.

Statistics such as these offer a compelling argument that genetics is important in accounting for human differences. However, there is one criticism we might make about calculating heritability by comparing reared-together identical and fraternal twins. Perhaps one reason why researchers find more similarity among identical twins than fraternals is that they are really measuring the impact of more similar environments as well as genes. Don't parents treat identical twins more alike, dressing them in the same way, responding to them more similarly than to twins who do not look the same? By finding sets of monozygotic and dyzygotic twins adopted into different families, we would have a tool for separating genetics and environment in a pure form. As you might imagine, finding large enough groups of twin pairs in this unusual situation is a Herculean task. However, we do have several studies in which researchers have

Figure 2–1

Monozygotic (MZ) and Dyzygotic (DZ) Twin Correlations and Heritabilities for Some Important Abilities, Traits, and Interests Measured in Adolescence as Calculated from a Variety of Studies

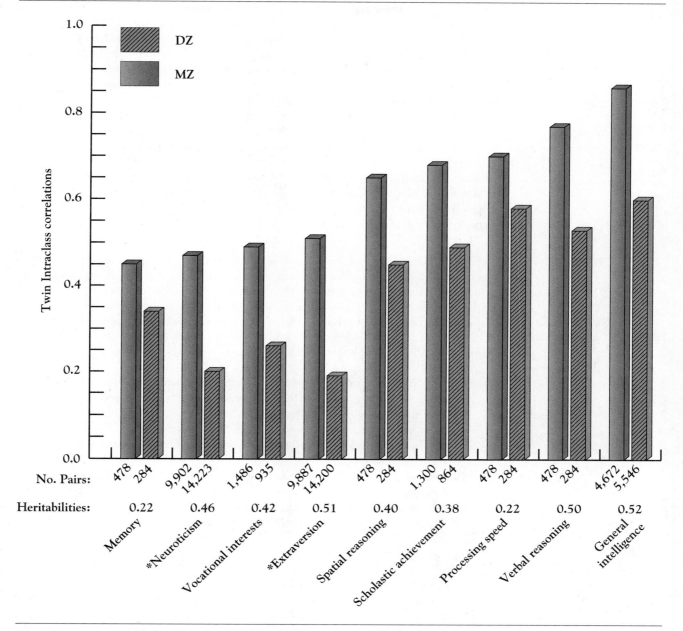

*Neuroticism is a broad personality dimension measuring the tendency to be irritable and emotionally labile, while extraversion refers to the general tendency to be ebullient and outgoing, rather than shy.

Source: Reprinted with Permission from Plomin, R. Owen, M. J., and McGuffin, P., The genetic basis of complex human behaviors, *Science, 264,* copyright 1994, American Association for the Advancement of Science.

Swedish Adoption/Twin
Study of Aging
*Scandinavian behavioral genetic
study in which identical and
fraternal twins adopted into different families were reunited and
compared in late middle-age.*

accomplished this feat. Let's look at the most comprehensive, called the **Swedish Adoption/Twin Study of Aging.**

In Scandinavia, national registries of births make it easier to find that needle in a haystack, twins adopted into different families. During the early 1980s, researchers tracked down 99 identical and 229 fraternal Swedish twin pairs separated and adopted in early childhood. These twins, currently in their fifties and sixties, were then compared to one another as well as to groups of reared-together twins (Plomin and McClearn, 1990).

Once again, the scientists found genetic contributions to a host of temperamental and personality traits. As Feature 2–2 on p. 38 shows, genetics influenced a person's perceptions of his upbringing. It influenced an individual's feelings about current relationships at home and work (Bergeman, Plomin, Pedersen, and McClearn, 1991). There even were significant correlations between the events identical twins had experienced during life, such as being divorced or advancing in a career, that were somewhat under their control (Plomin, Lichtenstein, Pedersen, McClearn, and Nesselroade, 1990). In other words, this study not only confirms that genetic predispositions have a wide influence on behavior, but also illustrates that we cannot really separate what is environmental, or what happens to us in the world, from what is internal, or genetic. As our discussion of the nature of nurture in Feature 2–2 suggests, life experiences are not just "random happenings." Our inherited predispositions to approach life in particular ways shape the experiences or events we encounter, at least to some degree, as we travel through life.

APPLICATIONS AND INTERVENTIONS

Behavioral genetic research has been a welcome antidote to the practice of placing total responsibility on parents for every action and problem in their children. It has offered us a more complex view of personal responsibility, too. Just as the ability of parents to mold their children has limits, a variety of self-destructive behaviors are inherently more difficult for some people to change. Does this mean that life experiences are unimportant or that we are fated by our heredity to behave in certain ways? Behavioral geneticists Robert Plomin and Gerald McClearn (1993) are careful to answer no.

1. *Genetic influence does not imply genetic determinism.* Plomin and McClearn point out that genes are simply reaction tendencies or predispositions. They do not force us to act in a given fashion or take away free will. Not everyone who has a genetic predisposition toward alcoholism will actually be alcoholic. Genes for certain behaviors orient us in a certain direction. They do not mean *we have to behave* in that way.

2. *Behavioral genetic research offers compelling evidence for the power of the environment in shaping behavior.* Plomin and McClearn argue that behavioral genetic research actually offers a strong argument for the importance of the environment in human behavior. Notice that another way of viewing heritabilities of 46 or 51 percent for neuroticism or extraversion and intelligence is that *non-genetic influences* are as influential as heredity in accounting for individual differences in these areas of life. Moreover, as we saw in Figure 2–1, traits vary in the extent to which they are influenced by heredity. Neuroticism and extraversion turn out to be among the most heritable aspects of personality. Traditional masculinity or femininity and tolerance for ambiguity show far less genetic influence. Religiosity and creativity show no heredity component at all.

Interestingly, the degree to which a given attribute is influenced by genetic predispositions varies not just according to the quality we are studying, but also at different times of life. For instance, in the Swedish Adoption/Twin Study, in aspects of personality such as activity level and sociability, the researchers found lower correlations between the scores of the late-middle-aged identical twins than between those typically revealed in studies of younger twins separated at birth. This

During the early decades of the twentieth century, at a time in America when young women of her social class were expected to be homemakers, Margaret Mead, the much loved, first child of a social activist mother and university professor father, received her Ph.D., journeyed alone to Samoa to study this remote culture, and went on to have a distinguished career as America's most renowned anthropologist. In explaining this remarkable adult life, behaviorists would invoke modeling and the direct reinforcement (encouragement) provided by Mead's high achieving parents; psychoanalysts would look to the idyllic quality of Mead's early childhood relationships; behavioral geneticists might see the unfolding of genetic predispositions inherited from both her mother and father's side.

suggests that, at least for these personality traits, genetic influence may wane with age. As we accumulate more and different life experiences, the power of the environment in influencing personality may grow (Brody, 1993).

3. *Genetic influence is very compatible with environmental intervention.* Most important, even when an attribute is influenced by genetics, that does not mean that changing the environment for the better cannot have a crucial impact on that trait. Even though, as we just saw, the variations in height we see among Americans today are largely genetic in origin, perhaps you may be aware that the average American is significantly taller than his counterparts were in previous centuries. The reason is environmental. This change seems due to the fact that health and the general conditions of life have improved so dramatically during the past 100 years. Clearly it was not any change in our DNA that allowed for the 30-year increase in longevity over the twentieth century, but the fact that for the first time Americans lived in an environment that allowed more of us to reach our biological potential.

These arguments illustrate that the quality of the environment is *always* important. As most observers argue, rather than labeling certain abilities mainly genetic or not, we need to explore what gene-environment combinations limit our potential and what conditions bring out our best. In an impoverished environment, no person can fulfill his or her genetic potential. In fact, without adequate nurture, or what researchers call an enabling environment, we can never even know what potential gifts our nature (or heredity) holds.

AN INFORMATION PROCESSING PERSPECTIVE ON ADULTHOOD.
Behaviorism, psychoanalytic theory, and behavioral genetics have long histories in the behavioral sciences. A final influential non-adult-centered approach to behavior only arrived during the mid-1960s with the computer age. This link is not accidental. Computers are the model for psychologists who use the information processing approach.

Your depressed sister complains about your distant, cold family. You believe her emotional state is causing her to forget the warm, loving experiences your family shared. Your brother blames fighting in the family for causing his marital troubles. You have a different idea. Your brother picked arguments with your parents and is acting the same way with his wife. Your mother and father were understanding and sensitive to your needs.

For years, psychologists assumed the family environment was similar for every child. Mothers could be classified as nurturing or rejecting. Families could be categorized as cohesive or conflict-ridden and cold. Moreover, according to psychoanalytic theory, the way adults described their childhood was accurate, and the cause of emotional problems lay in nurture or parenting alone. Behavioral genetic research is revealing how inaccurate these ideas can be.

In the Swedish Adoption/Twin Study, researchers asked adopted-away identical twins to rate the family atmosphere during their childhood along dimensions such as nurturance and acceptance, conflict and cohesion, and the extent of discipline or control.[1] The scientists were astonished to find significant correlations in most ratings, even though the twins were evaluating different families.

We might imagine two interpretations for these results. Perhaps, as in the case of the depressed sister, the twins' adult temperament skewed their memories of family life. Twins with a genetic predisposition to be depressed, for instance, may have seen a full glass as half empty, recalling even loving families as being distant and cold. Another possibility is that the twins' shared temperamental proclivities *created* similar family environments. As in the example of the combative brother, twins with difficult temperaments "produced" more conflict-ridden adoptive families. Rather than nurture molding personality, our nature (or genetic temperament) partly shapes the nurture we get. Notice that both possibilities contradict traditional psychoanalytic theory. Either we cannot trust the accuracy of childhood memories, or parenting is partly a function of the child's inherited personality. Adult problems are not "the fault" of poor parenting alone.

Psychologists have been studying the extent to which our nature (or inherited predispositions) shapes the nurture we receive. We cannot assume children share the same environment just because they grow up in the same family. In fact, argue behavioral geneticists, the family environment can be strikingly different from child to child. To unravel the role genetic influences in particular play in evoking different family environments, researchers measure some aspect of parent behavior, such as warmth and responsiveness or the extent of intellectual stimulation. They then compare the similarities in that behavior for pairs of identical twins, same-sex siblings, and/or step-siblings or adopted children. Once again, if genetics has little impact on these behaviors, the strength of the correlations for each group should be about equal. In other words, there should be little difference in the similarity with which children varying in genetic relatedness to one another are treated.

However, these studies show that differences often *do* appear as a function of genetic closeness. A mother's reading behavior tends to be more similar with identical than fraternal twins. Her warmth and responsiveness scores are apt to differ more greatly for adopted children and step-children than for biologically related siblings. (Be careful. This research does *not* show that adopted children or step-children are treated as "not family." It simply reveals that there is less similarity in the way children who are not genetically related are treated than children who share more similar genetic endowments.)

The fact that nature partly evokes certain kinds of nurture comes as no surprise to any parent. A mother finds herself reading more often to a daughter who loves reading. She admits she mainly plays puzzles with the child with little interest in books. However, one tantalizing outcome of these studies is the suggestion that some parenting behaviors may be more

Continued

responsive to the influence of the partner in this dyad than others. A finding of the Swedish Adoption/Twin Study, replicated in research with adolescents and younger children, is that parental warmth and responsiveness show moderate genetic influence. However, the genetic contribution to the parenting dimension called control (strictness) is minimal.

This finding also makes sense. Parents may philosophically believe in certain kinds of discipline. So the way they approach this aspect of child rearing may be more immune to the personality of a given child. However, emotions such as warmth and responsiveness are inherently more reactive. Affection does not occur in a vacuum. The love we give has to partly depend on the responses we actually receive.

[1] The information this feature is from Plomin (1995).

The **information processing perspective,** unlike the theories above, is devoted to understanding cognition, that is, *how* we think. It makes no assumptions about heredity or environment and draws no inferences about what motivates us to behave in certain ways. The basic assumption underlying this approach is that the mind behaves much like a computer. Just as computers manipulate information, acquiring it and processing it according to rules, human thinking occurs according to similar steps. By proposing models and conducting studies to reveal these steps and expose how they function, information processing researchers attempt to understand the operation of the mind.

Information processing, as is true of the other theories in this section, has been used to understand behavior at every stage of the life span, from the development of memory in childhood to how thinking changes as we grow old. In adult development, the information processing approach is the major model psychologists use in understanding the reasons for age-related cognitive decline. Why is it that older people react more slowly? What is the source of the losses in various abilities we often observe in older adults? By setting up diagrams such as the one in Figure 2–2 and then conducting experiments to localize the problem in one mental processing phase or component, researchers hope ultimately to improve the quality of life in old age.

So an information processing psychologist would have a different interest in looking at the older widow or the middle-aged student described earlier. That person would focus on the mental processes that produced each woman's responses. How did the elderly woman process the information to make that call to her children? What mental steps occurred from the time she got the idea to call to picking up the phone? How exactly does the student manipulate information in memory? Have there been changes in her abilities to process and retrieve the information she needs to excel at school? By conducting research to uncover these answers, an information processing researcher would hope to understand how cognition operates and changes with age.

information processing perspective
Approach to understanding human cognition that uses the operation of computers as an analogy to the functioning of the mind.

APPLICATIONS AND INTERVENTIONS

Emphasis on Age Change in Adult Development

The theories I have been describing are general models of behavior. Now we turn to some theories spelling out specific changes during the adult segment of life. By far the most influential and well known ideas about how we change as adults come from Erik Erikson.

Figure 2–2

A Schematic Model Illustrating the Information Processing Approach to Cognition

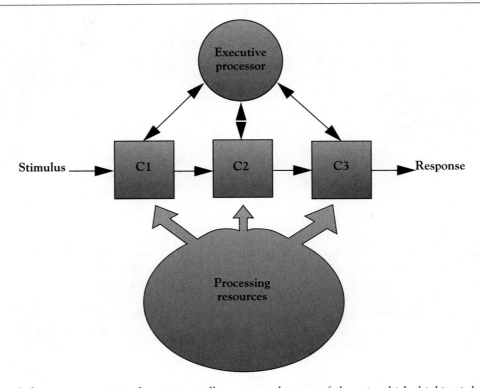

Information processing theorists typically construct this type of chart, in which thinking is broken down into separate processes or steps (C), an executive processor coordinates the activity, and processing resources are the fuel or energy driving cognitive activity.

Source: T. A. Salthouse, The Information-Processing Perspective on Cognitive Aging, in R. J. Sternberg and C. A. Berg (Eds.), *Intellectual Development*, Copyright 1992, reprinted with permission of Cambridge University Press.

ERIKSON'S AGE-LINKED PSYCHOSOCIAL CRISES.   Erikson was a German psychoanalyst who departed from traditional Freudian theory in a few important respects. While Freud focused on sexual and aggressive impulses, Erikson believed that *psychosocial concerns*, or issues relating to identity and relationships, are centrally important in life. Moreover, Erikson did not accept Freud's idea that all growth stops at childhood. He set out to chart the phases through which psychological development occurs throughout life.

According to Erikson (1963), there are eight life tasks, or **psychosocial crises,** we negotiate as we journey from birth to old age, each loosely tied to a particular period of life. These tasks build on each other, in that a person cannot master the issue of a later stage unless the developmental crises of the previous ones have been traversed. Except during early infancy, the crises of childhood center around gradually developing a secure, healthy sense of self. Then, once *identity* is formed in adolescence, we are capable of the process of merging with another, which is the first task of our lives as adults. Here is how

Erikson's age-linked psychosocial crises
Issues that become salient and must be grappled with at particular ages or life phases.

Erikson describes the psychosocial crisis of young adulthood called **intimacy** (1963, p. 263):

> *The young adult, emerging from the search for and the insistence on identity, is eager and willing to fuse his identity with that of others. He is ready for intimacy, that is, to commit himself to concrete affiliations and partnerships and to develop the ethical strength to abide by such commitments, even though they may call for significant sacrifices and compromises.*

In other words, according to Erikson, upon entering the adult world our first challenge is to make a mature adult commitment to another person, whether through long-term, loving friendships or marriage. Once having made this commitment, Erikson feels, we become capable of giving in a larger sense. **Generativity,** or guiding the next generation, is the key to living fully during midlife.

While generativity can mean giving through raising children, Erikson stresses that we do not need to become parents to feel fulfilled in this task. Generativity involves being committed to furthering the development of our fellow human beings in any area of life. The artist who takes pleasure in creating because he knows he will enrich the lives of people who view his paintings, the businesswoman whose joy in work comes from realizing she is producing a helpful product, and the volunteer who serves meals to the homeless experience their middle years differently from the person who focuses only on the self. According to Erikson, without being generative we feel "a pervading sense of stagnation and personal impoverishment" (1963, p. 267) because we have not fulfilled the purpose of our middle years.

Not only do we stagnate in the present, but also we cannot accomplish the final old-age task, called **ego integrity:**

> *the acceptance of one's one and only life cycle as something that had to be and that, by necessity, permitted of no substitutions. . . . a comradeship with the ordering ways of distant times and different pursuits. . . . [but] the possessor of integrity is ready to defend the dignity of his own life style against all physical and economic threats. . . . For he knows that an individual life is the accidental coincidence of but one life-cycle within one segment of history. (1963, p. 268).*

As this quotation suggests, older people who have reached ego integrity feel that their life has meaning. Paradoxically, this sense of personal significance allows them to accept their insignificance in the larger flow of life—that is, the fact that they must soon die. A different fate awaits the older adult who is racked with regret about mistakes made and dreams left unfulfilled. Frustrated and doomed because it is too late to make amends for the years poorly spent, this older person is desperately afraid of dying. In Erikson's words, the emotion that haunts this individual's final years is despair. (Table 2–2 shows the positive and negative outcomes for each task.)

Erikson's ideas have captured the imagination of many social scientists who believe that there is more to growing older than just decline. They have been particularly useful in clinical work with the elderly. For instance, based on Erikson's premise that the task of old age is to come to terms with one's life, one popular activity in senior citizens centers and nursing homes is **reminiscence or life review** sessions, in which older people are encouraged to review their lives in order to ward off depression and enable them to reach the sense of closure that Erikson feels is essential to coming to terms with impending death.

Interestingly, however, despite their enormous popularity, only recently have researchers in adult development begun to test the validity of Erikson's ideas. Are there

intimacy
Psychosocial task of young adulthood (roughly age 21–35) involving forming an adult commitment to another person.

generativity
Psychosocial task of midlife (roughly age 35–65) involving guiding the next generation.

ego integrity
Psychosocial task of later life (65+) involving accepting one's life in order to accept impending death.

APPLICATIONS AND INTERVENTIONS

reminiscence or life review
Intervention to promote ego integrity and mental health by having older adults reminisce about their past.

Table 2-2   Erikson's Tasks: Positive and Negative Outcomes

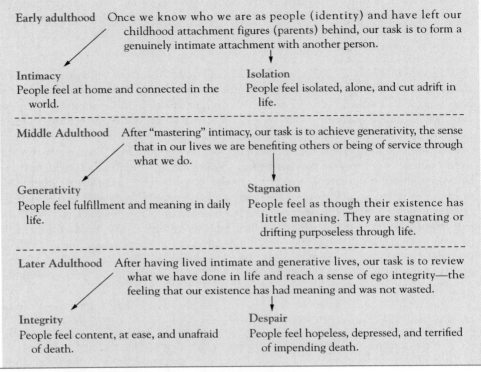

Early adulthood Once we know who we are as people (identity) and have left our childhood attachment figures (parents) behind, our task is to form a genuinely intimate attachment with another person.

Intimacy
People feel at home and connected in the world.

Isolation
People feel isolated, alone, and cut adrift in life.

- -

Middle Adulthood After "mastering" intimacy, our task is to achieve generativity, the sense that in our lives we are benefiting others or being of service through what we do.

Generativity
People feel fulfillment and meaning in daily life.

Stagnation
People feel as though their existence has little meaning. They are stagnating or drifting purposeless through life.

- -

Later Adulthood After having lived intimate and generative lives, our task is to review what we have done in life and reach a sense of ego integrity—the feeling that our existence has had meaning and was not wasted.

Integrity
People feel content, at ease, and unafraid of death.

Despair
People feel hopeless, depressed, and terrified of impending death.

Source: E. Erikson. *Childhood and Society.* New York: Norton, 1963.

really distinct stages of development, central issues such as generativity or ego integrity that appear at certain ages? In view of the variability between cohorts and individuals, is it reasonable to expect that we develop in stages or that certain issues become salient as every human being travels through life? These are some questions we will be discussing when we explore the research on personality in Chapter 8.

One reason why Erickson's ideas may have immediately become so popular is that he did not depart radically from Freudian theory. Erikson accepted the basic principles of psychoanalysis, including the idea that childhood is important, the foundation for what happens in later life. In contrast, Carl Jung does disagree with Freud in a fundamental way. Jung feels our *older years* are the only truly important time of life.

JUNG'S MIDLIFE SHIFT TOWARD MATURITY.   Jung was a protégé of Freud who abandoned the psychoanalytic movement largely because he disagreed with Freud's emphasis on early childhood. Jung believed who we are as adults cannot be reduced to infantile needs. The present and future are centrally important, our goals and life plans, the person we are now and hope to be. As an outgrowth of this prospective (future-oriented) view of human nature, Jung believed that the second half of life is more important than the first (Mattoon, 1981).

Jung divides adult life into two phases, with midlife (age 40 or so) being a turning point. He begins his discussion with the time of life from puberty to about the mid-thirties. During this period, which he calls youth, but which we would call young adulthood, our main goal is to establish ourselves. We are energetic, passionate, self-absorbed, concerned with satisfying our sexuality, and obsessed with carving out our niche in the world. In our late thirties, physical and sexual energy begin to decline. We are settled. We know our capacities, the limits of what we can do. We either are successful or have begun to make peace with the idea of not setting the world on fire. So a turning inward occurs. Introspection and contemplation become primary. Fostering relationships, understanding the meaning of life, and giving to others become our main concerns.

Jung believes that making this **midlife shift toward maturity** is hazardous. Many people are unable to relinquish "the psychology of the youthful phase" and carry this orientation into middle and later life. They stagnate and become vain, unhappy, and rigid. However, if development occurs in an ideal way, we reach a pinnacle. We can be transformed into spiritual beings.

Jung believes that this reorientation completes us psychologically. We can accept and integrate all of the facets of our personality, even those we previously denied. So another consequence of this midlife change is less differentiation between the sexes. Men become more tolerant of the feminine component of their personality. Women give more play to their masculine side.

Jung's ideas about personality change in aging women and men have some interesting research support (see Chapter 8). We also can trace the origins of the familiar concept of a midlife crisis to Jung's theory of personality. However, though they have influenced some psychologists (e.g., Gutmann, 1987), in general Jung's speculations are too arcane, too removed from daily life, and not practical enough to have had a major impact on researchers in adult development.

Jung's midlife shift toward maturity
Theory that in the middle years it is possible to reach an optimally mature state of psychological integration.

BALTES'S SELECTIVE OPTIMIZATION WITH COMPENSATION. Jung was a turn-of-the-century philosopher with a mystical world view that elevated later life. Paul Baltes is a contemporary researcher in adult cognition who has devoted his career to exploring and understanding often negative adult intellectual change. Baltes's theory, called **selective optimization with compensation,** though less inspirational, has the virtues of being clear, applicable to many areas of life, and extremely practical. Baltes spells out strategies we can use to cope adaptively and continue to develop in the face of the losses of advancing age.

As people become aware of their declining capacities, Baltes (1993) believes, they automatically draw on their age-related increases in knowledge to adjust. First, they become selective, focusing on those areas of functioning that are most important personally in their lives. Then they work harder to optimize performance in those critical areas of life. Finally, when losses become extreme, they compensate by using other devices and techniques to make up for the function that has been lost.

Baltes's selective optimization with compensation
Prescription for adapting to age changes by limiting efforts to areas of top priority, working to optimize performance in these areas, and using external aids to compensate for losses.

Let's apply these principles to an athlete to whom running marathons is the most important activity in life. According to Baltes, if she wants to continue functioning at a high level, she must invest more time in that sport and so give up other activities (selection). She will have to work harder to train than before (optimization). Finally, she may need to compensate. She may have to warm up more slowly and perhaps take an aspirin to mask the pain in her joints as she runs.

Here is a real-life example Baltes (1993) describes from the arts: When the concert pianist Arthur Rubinstein was asked in an interview how he managed to be so successful in his old age, he mentioned three strategies: (1) In old age, he concentrated on mastering fewer pieces. (2) He practiced each piece more frequently than before. (3) He introduced more ritardandos in his playing before fast segments so that the playing speed sounded faster than it was in reality. By creatively using selection, optimization, and compensation (masking his loss of dexterity by using a diverting strategy), Rubinstein was able to continue to perform effectively at the activity he loved.

**APPLICATIONS
AND
INTERVENTIONS**

If she creatively uses selection, optimization, and compensation, Baltes believes this woman can continue to excel at her favorite sport.

contextualist life-span developmental perspective
All-inclusive orientation to the life-span that emphasizes the need to adopt a multifaceted, multidimensional, individual-difference-centered orientation when describing, explaining, and improving development.

SYNTHESIZING THE FRAMEWORKS: THE CONTEXTUAL, LIFE-SPAN DEVELOPMENTAL PERSPECTIVE. By now, you may feel overwhelmed by these contradictory points of view. There is the assumption of aging as decline and the belief that we change for the better as we age. There is Erikson's hypothesis that certain issues become salient at different ages and Jung's belief that a single turning point occurs at midlife. There is the idea that our personality is unchanged from childhood (psychoanalytic theory) and the belief that our current environment or perceptions of that environment determine who we are (behaviorism). There are the different speculations about what causes us to act the way we do from reinforcement, to parenting, to heredity. (In Table 2–3 I have summarized the domains of interest of each theory and the kinds of questions it would pose in approaching the middle-aged student and the aged widow.)

The **contextualist, life-span developmental perspective** (Baltes, 1987; Baltes, Reese, and Lipsett, 1980; Baltes and Willis, 1977; Dixon, 1992) includes all of these points of view. This approach to adult life is not a defined theory or assumption about the direction of change, but an overall orientation with a single message: Pluralism (a variety of points of view) is the best policy to follow in understanding human development.

Life-span developmentalists feel pluralism in theories is essential. They believe that there are many different valid ways of looking at behavior. Our actions *do* have multiple causes. Just as we learned something interesting about the student and the older widow by viewing them through each theoretical perspective or lens, pluralism is essential in describing the path by which we develop and change. Change during adulthood is multidirectional. Some abilities improve; some stay the same; others decline. As I stressed in the last chapter, people differ greatly from one another. Their patterns of aging and adapting to life follow different forms.

For instance, wisdom may increase with age, while physical stamina decreases. Reading activities may remain stable, while other interests, such as going to the theater, may rise to a peak and then decline. Along each dimension, people will differ somewhat, depending on their cohort, their ethnic group, their social class, their biological makeup, and their idiosyncratic life experiences. Furthermore, just as we should not always expect consistency between individuals, our personal adult path is determined by many different factors. How we develop over the years is determined by a variety of influences, the total context of who we are and where we are in time.

As you might expect, this all-inclusive perspective is the approach to adult development used in this book. In the following chapters, we will be seeing the value of these theories and others in understanding adulthood, the various interacting influences that affect how we develop and adapt to adult life. We will realize that we do grow better, remain the same, and function less well as the years pass. We will come to appreciate that, despite the important underlying patterns we share, individual variability is also a hallmark of adult life.

The purpose of the life-span approach is to (1) describe, (2) explain, and (3) optimize or improve development. So, in covering each aspect of adulthood, as mentioned in Chapter 1, we first look at what happens and why it may happen; that is, we explore the research describing and explaining development. Then, using this knowledge, we focus on specific strategies designed to improve or optimize the quality of adult life.

RESEARCH METHODS

Does our personality really stay unchanged as we age? Is there any truth to Erikson's or Jung's theory? Which abilities rise in which contexts, and which decline as we advance

The Different Orientations of Each Theory to Adult Development

Table 2-3

	Overall domain of interest	Specific interest in the middle-aged student and the widow
Behaviorism	Any behavior	What are the reinforcers or cognitions accounting for the behavior? How can I change this behavior by modifying the environment?
Psychoanalytic theory	Personality	What childhood experiences have caused adult personality? What unconscious motivations underlie this person's actions?
Behavioral genetics	Any behavior	To what degree is this behavior caused by hereditary predispositions?
Information processing perspective	Cognition	How do each person's thought processes occur?
Erikson's theory	Developmental issues at different stages of life	Is the student manifesting generativity? Is the older woman showing despair?
Jung's theory	Personality growth after midlife	Have these women accomplished the midlife transition? Are they showing the androgeny of the second half of life?
Baltes's theory	Physical and cognitive change	Is each person using selection, optimization, and compensation to adjust to her losses?

in years? To answer these questions, we need techniques specifically designed to examine how people differ at different ages. The strategies that researchers typically use to measure these changes are called cross-sectional and longitudinal studies.

Cross-Sectional Studies

Because cross-sectional research is easier to carry out, this is the approach most often used to measure development. In **cross-sectional studies,** researchers compare *different age groups at the same time* on the trait or ability that they are interested in, be it muscle strength, maximum cardiac output, motor speed, marital happiness, or mental health. Before being tested, the researcher might decide to match or make the different groups comparable on important variables other than age that are likely to affect their scores.

For example, if we are interested in finding out whether people lose faith in government programs as they age, we might use the following approach. We pick equal numbers of young adults, middle-aged people, and elderly people (for instance, 100

cross-sectional studies
Developmental research technique involving testing different age groups at the same time.

Figure 2–3

Hypothetical Cross-Sectional Studies of Attitudes Toward Federal Government Interventions, 1936 and 1996

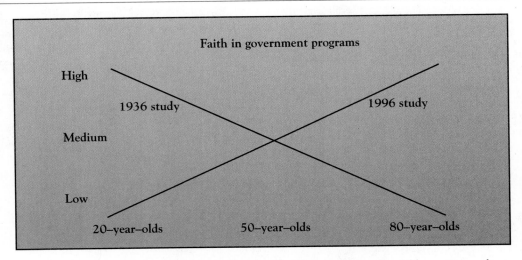

Notice how a cross-sectional study conducted with different cohorts can yield opposite results.

subjects aged 20, 50, and 80), taking care to match our groups for extraneous influences that might affect their scores, such as social class, educational level, or ethnic background. We then administer a scale of "faith in government programs" to each group and compare these scores. If there is a statistically significant trend toward less confidence in successively older groups, we can conclude that, as people grow older, they become more skeptical of government's efforts to help its needy citizens or effect social change.

However, our conclusion would be wrong. Because we are not following people over time, we cannot assume these differences *between* age groups reflect changes that actually occur as people advance in years. For instance, although a study carried out during the Depression might have shown that young people were the most in favor of these interventions, today, as Figure 2–3 shows, the same hypothetical study might reveal the opposite trend. Because of the political climate of the past few decades, young adults might espouse the most anti-government views. The greatest faith in government programs might be held by the old-old subjects, who developed this political philosophy because they grew up during the Roosevelt years.

This points up the crucial problem with cross-sectional studies. They do offer information about **age differences,** but do not reveal **age changes.** In this research strategy, true changes that occur as we advance in years are confounded with differences due to an extraneous factor: being in a different cohort.

As we learned in the last chapter, the time in history during which we journey through adult life (our cohort) shapes that journey in crucial ways. We can see this immediately by looking at photographs of my grandmother and myself taken during the same decade of life. Just as being in one's forties at a given point during the twentieth century obviously influences our external appearance and the way we dress (as well as the quality of the photo itself), it is likely to cause striking differences in other areas of life. So what are called **cohort factors** affect not only the results of cross-sectional studies of political attitudes, but also the outcome of almost any study we might carry out in adult development.

age differences
Differences between groups revealed in cross-sectional studies.

age changes
True changes that occur due to advancing age.

cohort factors
Biasing effect of being in a certain cohort on the results of cross-sectional studies.

These mid-life photos of my grandmother and myself graphically reveal how unalike different cohorts are certain to be at the same stage of life.

1940; age 40   1996; age 48

Cohort factors are an important bias in cross-sectional studies of physical performance. They also tend to affect the results of studies examining how IQ changes with advancing age. In the past, cross-sectional studies gave us excessively gloomy findings in these important areas. For years, researchers falsely concluded that *more loss occurred with age* than really took place.

As we learned in the last chapter, because of the *lifestyle movement* and improved health care, over the twentieth century each cohort has been reaching a given age physically healthier than the previous one. The same had been true of the intellectual environment. Due to regular increases in the number of Americans completing high school and college, particularly during the middle decades of the twentieth century, each younger cohort was arriving at a given age more well educated and so intellectually better off (see Chapter 6). These cohort differences in health and years of schooling gave younger groups a built-in advantage on tests of physical functioning and IQ. Because older cohorts were handicapped by having been born at their particular time, the extent of the physical or mental loss that age brought was seriously exaggerated.

Cross-sectional studies have another important liability. They only tell us how *groups* differ from one another, not about individual patterns of change. This means they cannot offer answers to some of the most important questions we have about development. Even if *on average* sexual activity declines in older age-groups, are there some people who become more interested in sex as they age? If we are very physically fit compared to the typical person our age, are we likely to live longer than our contemporaries? Why is it that some poor women who become pregnant as adolescents are able to construct a successful adult life, while others flounder? If we are emotionally disturbed, or shy, or the valedictorian of the class, what does that predict about our future life? While we can get partial answers to these questions by looking up records or asking people to remember how they used to be, the best strategy is to be on the scene to measure what is going on. This means using the longitudinal approach.

Longitudinal Studies

longitudinal study
Developmental research technique involving selecting one or more cohorts and periodically retesting the same subjects.

In a **longitudinal study,** a researcher selects a cohort (or cohorts) and periodically tests this group, ideally using the same measures, over years. For instance, using the previous example of attitudes toward government programs, a researcher might recruit a large group of 20-year-old college juniors and then give them the "faith in government" questionnaire at regular intervals as they aged. This type of study would provide insights we could never obtain from seeing how different age groups compare. Perhaps even if the cohort as a whole grew less accepting of government programs, we might find that people who had lost their jobs, or had gone back to graduate school at age 35, or had a medical crisis behaved differently. Maybe these people would come to be more in favor of these programs as they aged. Unfortunately, there are problems with this informative research technique.

There are practical problems in conducting this type of research. Longitudinal studies require a huge investment of effort and time. The investigator or research team must remain committed to the study and available to continue it over years or, as in studying adults, decades. Imagine keeping your enthusiasm about a topic for 20 or 40 years. Even if you stay interested, your question might become outmoded. Even the way you choose to measure faith in government programs could become obsolete over the years. Imagine getting subjects willing to make the same demanding commitment. Then think of the time it would take to search them out each time an evaluation is due. All of these impediments become more serious the longer a study goes on. For this reason, longitudinal studies covering decades are not that common. Longitudinal studies spanning all of adult life are very rare.

The difficulty with getting subjects to return over the years is more than just a practical hurdle. It leads to an important bias in itself. Because participating in a longitudinal study requires such a demanding commitment, people who volunteer for this type of research tend to be highly motivated and unusually responsible. Often they are personally involved in the research questions. For instance, Mr. Jones volunteers for a study examining physical aging because he is so interested in his health, while Mrs. Smith, who could not care less or is embarrassed about revealing her couch potato habits, quickly declines. Moreover, once in the study, knowing he will be returning for evaluations helps keep Mr. Jones "on his toes." As the time for each test approaches, he takes care to exercise and watch what he eats. As he gets more comfortable with the procedures, at successive evaluations his blood pressure readings go down, and his visual tracking skills become more efficient. Not only has the researcher selected a high-functioning group to begin with, but also the act of participating in the study has changed its subjects. They react differently, knowing that they are being tested. Through what are called **practice effects,** over time their scores naturally rise.

practice effects
Biasing effect of being familiar with the testing situation on subsequent performance in longitudinal research.

These biases are compounded by a process called **selective attrition,** or *experimental mortality.* In any longitudinal study, people drop out. At each evaluation, fewer volunteers remain. But this attrition is not random. The least capable people are likely to leave. People who stay in the study are often an especially well-off group, almost guaranteed to be unlike the average or typical person their age.

selective attrition
Bias that results when a nonrandom group of the original sample, the least capable or most poorly functioning subjects, tends to drop out as a longitudinal study progresses; also called experimental mortality.

For instance, in research in gerontology, a major reason subjects give for dropping out of longitudinal studies is poor health. People who do not complete the study are often too ill or have died. While health clearly affects how individuals perform on studies examining physical functioning, a moment's thought tells us good health may also influence how people function in almost every area of life. People who are unusually healthy perform better intellectually. They tend to be happier and more involved in life. They may be aging more optimally in almost every way. So the people who remain in a longitudinal study are likely to be high functioning in many areas investigators choose to

In a longitudinal study, this class might be assessed right after graduation, and then recontacted and repeatedly tested over the years. Who do you think would be likely to drop out of this research? How many people would remain in the study after 20 or 40 years?

measure. Findings based on this group will minimize the negative effects of aging and exaggerate the ways the average person changes for the better as he or she grows old.

In sum, these influences combine to give longitudinal studies the opposite bias from much cross-sectional research. Longitudinal research provides too *optimistic* a picture of what normally happens as we grow old.

In addition, our ability to make universal statements about development from longitudinal studies is limited in other ways. First, conclusions based on longitudinal studies should be restricted to the particular cohort(s) being studied. Because each cohort is unique, it is likely to show an idiosyncratic pattern of change as it ages. Moreover, even among this particular cohort, longitudinal studies do not allow age changes to be measured in a pure or an isolated form. Here, too, changes that occur due to the advancing years alone are mixed up with an extraneous influence: societal changes occurring at a certain time.

For example, suppose in our study examining faith in government interventions there was another depression between two of our tests. Imagine how that event might affect our cohort's feelings about the mission of government to provide services, such as jobs or income, to its citizens. Notice what has happened here: An occurrence around the time of measurement has interfered with our ability to measure "true" age changes. This is why this kind of bias is called a **time of measurement effect** (Figure 2–4 illustrates how a time of measurement effect could cause a shift having little to do with age).

time of measurement effects *Biasing effect of societal events occurring around the time of testing on the findings of longitudinal studies.*

Figure 2-4

Time of Measurement Effects in a Study of Attitudes Begun in 1995

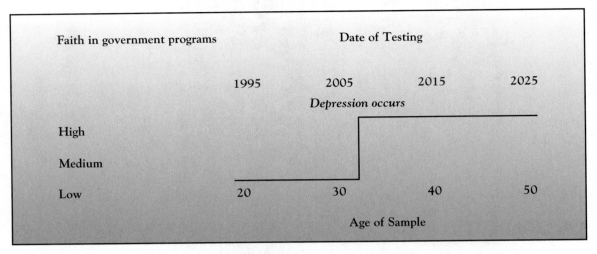

Could we really say this change at age 32 is due to advancing age?

Sequential Studies

sequential strategies
Developmental research technique to uncover true age changes involving conducting several longitudinal and cross-sectional studies and comparing the results.

In 1965, K. Warner Schaie, a prominent researcher in adult development, devised what he called **sequential strategies,** techniques designed to compensate for the biases of cross-sectional and longitudinal studies. Schaie's idea was that by conducting several different longitudinal and cross-sectional studies and comparing their results, it would be possible to disentangle the impact of time of measurement effects and being in a different cohort from "true" changes that occurred with age (as well as control for biases, such as practice effects).

In the longitudinal sequence (Baltes, Reese, and Nesselroade, 1977), researchers begin longitudinal studies in separate years, tracing how different cohorts perform over the same age range. For instance, they might begin a study of 20-year-olds in 1996, start a comparable longitudinal study 10 years later in 2006, and then compare the results. In the cross-sectional sequence, researchers contrast the results of cross-sectional studies carried out in separate years, comparing, for example, how 20-year-olds, 50-year-olds, and 80-year-olds score on the faith in government questionnaire in 1996 and 2006. By seeing if the change patterns in these studies are similar or by exploring in what ways they differ, researchers could estimate the extent of bias due to cohort or time of measurement effects.

Schaie used these contrasting assessments in an influential study to reveal how intelligence test performance really changes as we grow old. However, since sequential strategies are so complicated, studies employing this procedure are rare. This is why throughout this book, when we want to explore development, we will be relying on that precious resource, longitudinal research.

With the caution that they have the problems summarized in Table 2-4, longitudinal studies are invaluable. There is no substitute for the insights we can get by tracing how human beings journey through life. In the following chapters, we will be highlighting the findings of studies covering decades that explore topics as different as

1.	The studies are expensive, are difficult to carry out, and take decades to complete.
2.	The studies offer too optimistic a picture of normal aging.
3.	The studies show how aging occurs in only one cohort.
4.	The studies confuse changes due to external events occurring around the time of measurement with true age changes.

predicting managerial success to examining how poor women who get pregnant as adolescents fare during adult life. Now we look at two comprehensive studies that we will be mentioning again and again in this book: the Baltimore Longitudinal Study of Aging and the Berkeley/Oakland Studies.

Two Important Examples: The Baltimore and Berkeley/Oakland Studies

The National Institute on Aging sponsored the **Baltimore Longitudinal Study of Aging,** begun in 1959, which is our nation's premier effort to examine physical aging. Subjects ranging in age from their twenties to their nineties have been recruited. So far, more than 2,000 men and women have volunteered (women entered the study only in 1978). People who enroll in the study make an intense commitment. Depending on their age, they return either every year or every two years to spend several days at the Gerontology Research Center in Baltimore. At each visit, a medical history is taken. Hundreds of physical capacities are examined, from grip strength, to reaction time, to the amount of body fat, to how deeply a person can breathe. Participants are given tests of memory and learning. Their personalities and methods of coping with stress are probed. The payoff has been worth the investment of effort. As we will see in succeeding chapters, the Baltimore Study has contributed greatly to our understanding not just of normal physical aging, but also of how we develop in many important areas of life (National Institute on Aging, 1993).

The **Berkeley/Oakland Studies** are even more remarkable because in this unique set of studies we have information on people through the *entire* life span. During the late 1920s, two longitudinal studies, the Berkeley Guidance Study and the Oakland Growth Study, were begun by researchers at the University of California at Berkeley. In the Berkeley Guidance Study, subjects were selected from a roster of every third child born in Berkeley during an 18-month period, and these children and their parents were periodically tested through adolescence. In the Oakland Growth Study, boys and girls were followed from preadolescence through high school.

Then the researchers decided to extend these studies to adult life (Clausen, 1991; Eichorn, Clausen, Haan, Honzik, and Mussen, 1981). So they tested each group in their thirties and at regular intervals after that. Other researchers (Maas and Kuypers, 1975) compared the personalities and lifestyles of the parent sample over a 40-year period from young adulthood to later life. Today research on the surviving parents and children is still being carried out. As we will see throughout this book, the Berkeley/Oakland Studies have provided vital data about personality change and consistency. They have helped answer questions as different as what predicts marital happiness, how relationships change after a parent gets ill, how families cope with economic hardship, and what adolescent traits predict success in a career.

Baltimore Longitudinal Study of Aging
Landmark ongoing National Institute on Aging–sponsored study of the aging process, focusing mainly on physical functioning.

Berkeley/Oakland Studies
Only longitudinal study to span a life span, exploring personality and social development in a cohort born in the late 1920s in Berkeley, California.

Evaluating the Research

internal validity
Ability to reach accurate conclusions from a study's findings based on the internal quality of the research design.

external validity
Ability to generalize accurately from the results of a laboratory study to real life.

In evaluating any study in adult development, it is important to look at two considerations. The first, called the **internal validity** of the study, refers to the researcher's ability to conclude what he or she wants to, based on the design. Can we really say that this hypothesis is true from the particular method used in this study, or are there competing, equally logical reasons why this person might have found what he or she did? The second consideration involves what is called **external validity,** our ability to generalize from that study to the wider world. A study might be elegantly designed, with findings that permit no other interpretation, and still have little meaning if it is valid only in the highly controlled laboratory situation or applies only to that particular group a researcher decided to test.

In our critique of longitudinal studies, we saw that practice and time of measurement effects represent significant threats to internal validity. When we see a certain change in our next evaluation, the longitudinal method does not allow us to know if what we are observing is due to the subjects' greater familiarity with the testing situation, or to an external event that occurred between the two testings, or to age. We also saw that, because they involve atypical or **unrepresentative samples,** the external validity of these studies can be severely compromised. How can we claim our study reflects a universal aging process when we are studying only the most interested subjects or when we have only examined how those in the cohort born in 1920 or in 1970 behave as they journey through life?

unrepresentative samples
Subjects selected for study who do not reflect the characteristics of the population that a researcher wants to generalize to.

With these two types of validity in mind, now we turn to several cautions we will be stressing repeatedly in exploring the non-developmental research in this book.

true experiment
Only research method that can truly prove that a specific intervention or prior condition causes a given outcome.

AVOID THE CORRELATION/CAUSATION MISTAKE.   An experiment is the best research technique from the standpoint of internal validity. In a **true experiment,** as illustrated in Table 2–5, a researcher systematically varies some prior condition (called the independent variable) and then randomly assigns subjects to receive either that treatment or another intervention. The strategy of *random assignment* ensures that any preexisting differences between the subjects "wash out." If the study has been planned correctly, the only factor that makes the groups different is the intervention whose impact the researcher wants to assess. If the group exposed to the treatment does differ in the way the person predicts, then she can conclude that her intervention *caused* the particular result. (The hypothesized result is called the dependent variable because this outcome *depends on,* or must be due to manipulating, the independent variable.)

In adult development, our goal is often to make the statement that "this causes that." However, the experimental approach cannot be used to answer the majority of questions we might have about causes.

For example, it would be impossible to do an experiment to test Erikson's idea that reaching integrity causes people not to fear death or to demonstrate that, if the middle-aged student described earlier in this chapter had a pessimistic explanatory style, this attitude might cause her to give up school. We cannot randomly assign subjects to "an integrity group." It would be difficult to experimentally manipulate how people perceive life events. Even questions we are able to examine by conducting an experiment could be criticized as impractical or unethical. For instance, in the study described in Table 2–5, we might legitimately ask how the researcher could really force everyone in the treatment group to exercise four times a week for a year and make sure their behavior did not vary in any other way apart from this specific treatment. Wouldn't you imagine that the less healthy people might drop out of the treatment group or that, once they got interested in exercising, people exposed to this health-inducing intervention might naturally begin to watch their diet, too? Certainly it would be unethical to prevent

Method: 224 male volunteers aged 55–65 were recruited from several large companies at retirement. The men were randomly assigned to a control group (n = 111) and an exercise group (n = 113), with stratification by blue- or white-collar job (*the independent variable*). The exercise group underwent three sessions of training per week for a year and was also encouraged to train one additional session each week on their own. The control group carried on retirement without interference. The training consisted of a 10-minute warm-up, approximately 30 minutes of walking or jogging, and then a 10-minute cool-down.

At the posttest, the performance of the two groups was compared with their base-line performance on various measures of physical functioning: indexes of cardio-respiratory fitness such as heart rate and breathing capacity, blood lipid (fat) levels, grip strength and flexibility, and body weight changes (*the dependent variables*).

Results: There were significant increases in some measures of respiratory capacity among the men in the intervention group compared to those in the control group. There also were significant differences in grip strength favoring the treatment group. However, there were no differences in pre- and posttest body weights or blood lipid levels between the two groups.

Conclusion: Exercise has an impact on some aspects of fitness and little impact on others. In particular, undergoing regular exercise improves respiratory fitness and grip strength.

Source: D. A. Cunningham, P. A. Rechnitzer, J. H. Howard, and A. P. Donner, 1987, Exercise Training of Men at Retirement: A Clinical Trial, *Journal of Gerontology, 42,* 17–23.

people in the control group from deciding to exercise on their own. (In fact, in this study, there were dropouts from the intervention group, and a few of the control group men did begin to regularly exercise. Moreover, the researchers did not check to see whether their treatment may have induced other lifestyle changes that could have produced their findings apart from exercise.)

Because of these difficulties, in most studies in adult development researchers measure some naturally occurring, preexisting difference between people, in integrity, explanatory style, or exercising regularly, and relate this attribute to the other quality of interest, such as low death fear, abandoning school, or health and fitness. This type of strategy involves what is called a *correlational approach* because here, too, we are seeing how one variable relates to another. If a significant correlation exists, then a statement about causality is often made: Reaching integrity makes people fear death less; having a pessimistic explanatory style causes people to abandon their efforts easily; leading an active life promotes health.

This type of conclusion *may* be correct. However, it is equally likely to be wrong. For instance, in the exercise example, the relationship between exercising and health might really be incidental, due to a third underlying cause: genetics. People who are less sickly, or more biologically fit, might have more energy during adulthood and so be prone to exercise more. Or we might be confusing cause and effect. People choose a sedentary lifestyle because their body is giving off signals of the underlying illness to erupt later on. *Poor health causes physical inactivity,* not the reverse.

Earlier in this chapter, we saw a good example of the danger in inferring causality from a correlation. Psychoanalytic therapists listened to patients' reports of poor parenting and then assumed that the emotional difficulties they were observing were caused by deficiencies in the persons' early family life. They did not consider the possibility that a third factor (genetic predispositions) might account in part for both the disturbed family relationships and the persons' current difficulties.

If we could control for every alternate explanation, we could more confidently make statements about causes by using a simple correlational approach. However, as this is not often possible, when viewing this prevalent research strategy in this book, be on guard: Make assumptions about possible causes with care.

LOOK AT THE SAMPLE.   Because they are easier to recruit, the subjects used to examine many questions in adult development tend to be middle-class and white. Moreover, researchers often get these people on a catch-as-catch-can basis, whether from a retirement community or church or by word of mouth. As we saw with longitudinal studies, the *unrepresentativeness* of these samples can severely hinder external validity.

For instance, for years it was believed that many Americans were having extramarital affairs. We also were told that most women reached orgasm every time they had intercourse. The problem was that these "facts about average Americans" were based on sampling some distinctly non-average groups. They came from studies polling the readers of *Playboy* or *Redbook*. Worse yet, they were based on the tiny fraction of people (sometimes only 3 percent) of all readers who chose to respond.

We cannot force people into a study. So even when researchers take care to select a representative sample, they must grapple with the question of who volunteers. This means that before interpreting the findings of *any study*, it is important to consider the subjects. How were they recruited? What characteristics do they have? Ask yourself, Can I generalize from the behavior of this particular group to the wider world?

LOOK AT THE MEASURES.   The overall validity of a study also depends on its measures, that is, how the investigator defines and assesses sexuality or, to take our earlier example, physical fitness and health. Like most concepts in adult development, these vague entities can be conceptualized and **operationalized,** or translated into concrete measures, in different ways. An investigator's findings can depend on the definition and measurement strategy he or she picks. A researcher who defines sexuality by measuring the frequency of orgasm may get a different impression of sexual behavior and how it changes with age than a colleague who measures this quality by asking how often a man has sexual intercourse or feels aroused. An investigator who measures health by asking people to rate their fitness may get a different response than another who rates health from objective measures, such as tests of cardio-respiratory function or blood pressure. (Notice, for instance, in the study in Table 2–5, how the answer to the question "Does exercise benefit people?" differed for each measure of fitness. In other words, the outcome of this research was dependent on *what* the researchers chose to measure.)

In adult development, not only must researchers define and measure their concepts with care, but also they are faced with an additional complication: The defining qualities or critical attributes of what they are measuring may shift with age. The frequency of erection and orgasm might be a reasonable measure of sexuality at age 20, but a poor indicator at 85. For instance, even though by their sixties many men do have trouble performing sexually on occasion, this does not mean they give up intercourse or lose desire. In fact, in one poll, even some elderly men who were totally incapable of having erections reported having a frequent, satisfying sex life (Brecher and the Consumer Reports Book Editors, 1985). The blood pressure or blood cholesterol reading that would signal health does differ for someone who is 80 versus someone who is 35. Moreover, in their later years, people often report being healthy even when they have some disease. Because their assessments are based on how they function, they tend to be more positive than their physicians, who are relying on medical tests (Idler, 1993). Who is correct, the older person or the "objective assessment"? What really is the best measure of health or sexuality in later life?

operationalize a concept
To translate an abstract entity or quality into concrete measures.

At minimum, a researcher's measures must be **reliable.** This means that people must receive the same score if *immediately* administered the test or procedure again. For instance, in the study of fitness, even though we expect long-term changes, we are in trouble if subjects' rankings on the measures fluctuate widely from minute to minute. In fact, without this short-term consistency, the concept of change would be meaningless, as there would be no way to define fitness at all. The researcher's measures should be **valid.** This means that they should accurately measure the entity or quality they are supposed to. Using the example of the study of faith in government interventions, suppose what a person reports on the questionnaire does not reflect his or her behavior in the wider world? If many people who report that they have little faith in government programs support candidates who favor these interventions, we can conclude little from our research.

Not only are questions of measurement reliability and validity important in evaluating any particular study, but also they loom large in controversies in adult development, such as how to define and measure intelligence or emotional problems, such as depression, at different times of life. In the following chapters, we will be seeing these issues in operation. They are the challenges social scientists face in finding out the truth about how we develop and why we behave as we do.

measurement reliability
Minimum condition for a measure's adequacy, when subjects get roughly the same score if they are immediately retested using that measure.

measurement validity
When a scale or measure is really measuring the entity or quality that it is supposed to be measuring.

KEY TERMS & CONCEPTS

theories
traditional behaviorism
classical conditioning
operant conditioning
reinforce
extinguish
modeling
Bandura's social learning theory
cognitive behaviorism
self-efficacy
explanatory style
psychoanalytic theory
behavioral genetics
twin studies
correlation
Swedish Adoption/Twin Study of Aging
information processing perspective
Erikson's age-linked psychosocial crises
intimacy
generativity
ego integrity
reminiscence or life review

Jung's midlife shift toward maturity
Baltes's selective optimization with compensation
contextualist, life-span developmental perspective
cross-sectional studies
age differences
age changes
cohort factors
longitudinal studies
practice effects
selective attrition
time of measurement effects
sequential strategies
Baltimore Longitudinal Study of Aging
Berkeley/Oakland Studies
internal validity
external validity
unrepresentative sample
true experiment
operationalize a concept
measurement reliability
measurement validity

RECOMMENDED READINGS

Theories and Theoretical Perspectives on Development

Baltes, P. B. (1993). The aging mind: Potential and limits. *Gerontologist, 33,* 580–594.
  Baltes spells out his theory of selective optimization with compensation.

Baltes, P. B. (1987). Theoretical propositions of life-span developmental psychology:
On the dynamics between growth and decline. *Developmental Psychology, 23,* 611–626.
  This article describes the contextual life-span developmental approach.

Bandura, A. (1989). Human agency in social cognitive theory. *American Psychologist,*
44, 1175–1184.
  Bandura describes self-efficacy.

Erikson, E. H. (1963). *Childhood and society.* New York: Norton.
  Erikson describes his eight stages of life.

Plomin, R., DeFries, J. C., and McClearn, G. E. (1980). *Behavioral genetics: A primer.*
San Francisco: W. H. Freeman.
Plomin, R., and McClearn, G. E. (1993). *Nature, nurture, and psychology.* Washington,
D.C.: American Psychological Association.
  These two books describe the findings and the basic approach of behavioral geneticists.
  The former book is written for the student without much background in the field; the
  latter book will appeal to more advanced students and researchers.

Research Methods and Research Studies

Baltes, P. B., Reese, H. W., and Nesselroade, J. R. (1977). *Life-span developmental*
psychology: Introduction to research methods. Monterey, CA: Brooks-Cole.
  The authors describe research methods in life-span development as well as the
  contextualist approach.

Eichorn, D. H., Clausen, J. A., Haan, N., Honzik, M. P., and Mussen, P. H. (1981).
Present and past in middle life. New York: Academic Press.
  This book summarizes the Berkeley Studies as of 1981.

Schaie, K. W. (Ed.). (1983). *Longitudinal studies of adult psychological development.* New
York: Guilford Press.
  The authors of chapters in this edited book describe a variety of longitudinal studies that
  have been conducted in adult development.

Shock, N. W., Greulich, R. C., Andres, R., Arenberg, D., Costa, P. T., Lakatta, E. G.,
and Tobin, J. D. (Eds.). (1984). *Normal human aging: The Baltimore Longitudinal Study*
of Aging (NIH Publication No. 84-2450). Washington, DC: U.S. Public Health
Service.
  This book summarizes the Baltimore Study findings as of 1984.

PART II

THE PHYSICAL DIMENSION

Normal Aging and Disease Prevention

Chapter Outline

At age 47, Joe feels at his peak: "At my age, a person is old enough to be wise and young enough to do something about that wisdom." He does not worry about the external signs that reveal he is his age or older: his thinning hair, white beard, and weathered skin. Joe is concerned about internals. Joe is committed to rock climbing. The key to enjoying his passion is defying the physical losses of time.

With rock climbing, the thrill comes from continually improving, from completing gradually more difficult climbs. Every November on his visit to see family in New Mexico, Joe sets his sights on a higher-rated mountain and then practices daily to master that climb. Planning is crucial. One must know the mountain and rehearse the set of moves it requires. Some climbs require upper arm strength; toes must balance on the ledge. The body must be positioned just right to avoid a fall. The steepness of the cliff is important and how far its ledges reach out. While physical stamina and agility are necessary, equally important is knowing oneself. The climber strives for a crucial balance: Push to the limit; do not venture beyond . Courage plus restraint; avoid fear or being foolhardy; know when to stretch and when to rest. Joe feels that for a time his better mental balance may outweigh the physical losses of age. But because at some point nature will take over, Joe is preparing, taking role models for his future life. There is the 65-year-old who is still scaling high-rated mountains, the water skier of 80 he knows. There is also the 40-year-old who says he feels too old to run. Joe is comfortable with aging, provided he can remain vigorous. What terrifies him is the idea of incapacity, the thought that someday he may be forced to give in to bodily decline.

AN OVERVIEW OF THE AGING PROCESS

When we think of personality or intelligence, we are likely to see time as a friend. We imagine we will grow, change for the better, mature over the years. In contrast, a biological perspective on aging involves negatives. As we saw in our interview, loss in functioning is what many people fear. Early cross-sectional studies of physical aging confirmed these gloomy expectations (Birren and Birren, 1990). Researchers catalogued a depressing array of physical processes that universally declined. These losses set in early, soon after physical maturity. Sometimes they went back earlier, to the beginning of life.

atherosclerosis
Accumulation of fatty deposits on the walls of arteries.

For instance, **atherosclerosis,** the gradual accumulation of fatty deposits on artery walls, is a predictable physical change that occurs as Americans advance in years. However, beginning atherosclerosis has been found in infants (Moon, 1955). Advanced signs of this process were found during autopsies of Korean War casualties as young as their early twenties (Enos, Holmes, and Beyer, 1955).

normal aging change
Physical change that is deleterious, is progressive, and normally occurs as people age.

Atherosclerosis exemplifies what is called a **normal aging change** (Elias, Elias, and Elias, 1990). The change is deleterious, making our functioning worse. It is progressive, growing more pronounced over time. While occurring to some degree in almost everyone, the extent to which the change develops varies from person to person due to biological predispositions and the lifestyle we lead. Atherosclerosis exhibits another property typical of many normal aging changes: We do not know whether this change is totally preventable or built into the aging process itself.

primary aging
Physical changes that are absolutely inevitable in the aging process.

secondary aging
Non-inevitable, age-related deterioration caused by environmental damage.

Primary aging changes are universal and inevitable. They are basic to the aging process, intrinsic to our makeup as human beings. **Secondary aging** is bodily deterioration caused by non-inevitable external damaging forces, such as not taking care of our health. Because studies of aging usually explore what *typically* occurs to people, in most research, the two types of aging are intertwined. For this reason, as John Rowe and Robert Kahn (1987) point out, these studies provide an unrealistically gloomy picture of the "true" aging process. Much physical deterioration that normally happens may not *have* to occur. We must be careful about equating what *typically* happens with what *ideally* can take place.

Top Ten Chronic Conditions by Age, 1989[*]

Table 3-1

Condition	Age 45 to 64	65 to 74	75+
Arthritis	253.8	437.3	554.5
Hypertension	229.1	383.8	375.6
Hearing impairment	127.7	239.4	360.3
Heart disease	118.9	231.6	353.0
Cataracts	16.1	107.4	234.3
Deformity or orthopedic impairment	155.5	141.4	177.0
Chronic sinusitis	173.5	151.8	155.8
Diabetes	58.2	89.7	85.7
Visual impairment	45.1	69.3	101.7
Varicose veins	57.8	72.6	86.6

The rates of almost every chronic condition increase, often dramatically, at older ages.

[*]Occurences per 1,000 people

Source: U.S. Senate Special Committee on Aging, 1991, *Aging America: Trends and Projections*, Washington, DC: Author.

Making the distinction between typical and ideal aging, that is, between what is inevitable and what is preventable, is crucial. A second basic characteristic of the aging process is that it is intimately linked to disease. Many physical changes we experience as we advance in years, when they occur to a moderate degree, are called normal. When these changes become extreme, they have a different label: chronic disease (Elias, Elias, and Elias, 1990). Moreover, even when a physiological change does not shade directly into chronic illness, it weakens us and so makes us susceptible to a variety of diseases (Hayflick, 1987). So the chance of developing illnesses increases with age. In addition, older people are more likely to get certain diseases, the chronic conditions that are part and parcel of normal aging. Once again, atherosclerosis is a perfect example. These fatty deposits, when they block or severely narrow arteries, are what produce the top-ranking age-related chronic illnesses, heart disease and stroke.

Chronic diseases, in contrast to infectious diseases such as the flu or a cold, have certain characteristics. They are long-term, progressive, and typically not curable. While a few chronic illnesses are caused by outside agents, such as viruses (AIDS is a perfect recent example), most have no clear-cut external cause. They seem internally generated, produced by a breakdown of the body itself. The emphasis in dealing with these illnesses is on prevention and long-term management, not on an intervention that will produce a dramatic cure (Kart, Metress, and Metress, 1992).

Although children and young adults also suffer from them, because they are linked to normal aging, as we learned in Chapter 1, chronic diseases are typically illnesses of middle and later life. Eighty-five percent of people over age 65 have at least one chronic illness (U.S. Senate Special Committee on Aging, 1991a). As Table 3-1 shows, as we advance in years, chronic disease is a more frequent accompaniment of life.

In fact, heart disease and that other feared illness, cancer, are so closely tied to age that at least one of these diseases has a good chance of being present in the very old person who dies, no matter what the actual cause of death (Manton, Wrigley, Cohen, and Woodbury, 1991). In autopsies performed on the very old, it is typical to find many changes, illnesses that, even though not the immediate cause of death, would have ended the person's life within a matter of months (Comfort, 1979; Hayflick, 1987).

Our discussion shows that, despite the life-expectancy progress we have made, we are not fulfilling our biological potential. Only a small percentage of people live to age 90, much less 115. Many of us spend our final years of life coping with disabilities, our lives restricted by chronic disease. This is why the discovery of long-lived people is so exciting. If there really are locations where people live past 100 and enjoy full, active lives until they die, we would be able to enhance our life span by natural means, without searching for an aging clock.

Three remote areas are supposed to have unusually high proportions of healthy, active centenarians: villages in Ecuador, Pakistan, and the highlands of the Republic of Georgia in Russia. To ascertain why these people live so long, some scientists have looked to culture and environment.

After studying people in Georgia, one group of researchers (Kipshidze, Pivovarova, Dzorbenadze, Agadzanoy, and Shavgulidze, 1987) concluded that their lifestyle explained the longevity among these mountain people. The Georgians ate a low-fat, low-calorie diet of fruits and grains. They were expected to do outdoor work until an advanced age; and, rather than being devalued, in Georgia age brought respect. In fact, in this remote part of the world, living beyond a century was the badge of highest merit, a cause for great acclaim.

Keeping physically active, not eating fats, and being respected for being old may be life-enhancing. However, a more objective look at the older residents in these communities uncovers a disappointing fact: There is no evidence they outlive the rest of us!

When other researchers (Mazess and Forman, 1979) examined birth and census records in Ecuador, information that was difficult to obtain, they found that the long-lived people they interviewed had typically inflated their ages by at least a decade. The records showed *none* of the supposed centenarians in the village had really reached this age.

In these villages, the publicity and status attached to being long-lived plus the lack of birth records may make inflating one's age an overwhelming temptation. Adding those extra years may not even be a fully conscious act because as adults our age becomes unimportant and so we do "forget" how old we really are from time to time.

The practice of adding years to life is not confined to remote villages. In nursing homes, I have noticed residents embellishing on an advanced age to impress listeners, just as a 15-year-old insists he is 18 or a 5-year-old brags that he is really 8. It seems as if our age is a liability only when we leave youth and approach our normal life expectancy. Once we reach our late eighties, age again becomes an achievement. It is transformed into a badge of a life well lived.

A third basic fact about the aging process is that it has a fixed end. Though reports of long-lived people continue to tantalize us, as Feature 3-1 suggests, they are myths. None of us survives beyond about age 115. While scientists argue whether this fixed limit beyond which none of us can live is totally rigid (Fries, 1990) or shifting upward (Manton, 1990), everyone agrees that our **maximum life span** has not changed much since we evolved as human beings (Hayflick, 1987). As we know, what has changed dramatically is our *average life expectancy*, the time on average we can expect to live.

maximum life span
Maximum age to which the members of a species can live.

Our maximum life span is long in comparison with other animals. Although rare species, such as the Galapagos tortoise, do outlive us, human beings survive much longer than any other mammal. The horse lives about 46 years; the goat 20; the mouse slightly more than 3.

While other physical indexes, such as basal metabolic rate, body temperature, and body size, are correlated with mammalian longevity, one theory is that our comparatively large brain is responsible for our long life because a mammal's *index of cephalization*, or ratio of brain weight to body weight, is related to its life span. The survival advantage our

A Hypothetical Look at the Human Survival Curve at Three Different Times in American History and at a Time When We Have Cured All Diseases

Figure 3-1

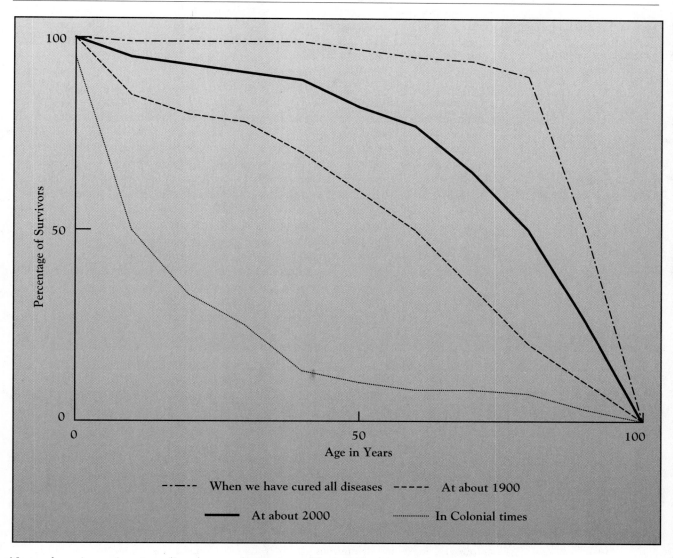

Notice that as more Americans live closer to the maximum life span, the lines appear increasingly rectangular.

large brain may offer is that more neurons can function as reserves to replace those lost in the wear and tear of daily life (Birren and Birren, 1990).

Figure 3-1 illustrates how average life expectancy may have varied in different times in America. As more of us survive to the upper reaches of the possible life span, the life-expectancy curve looks increasingly rectangular. The ideal is shown in the figure. It represents a time when we have cured all illnesses, when all of us fulfill our maximum biological potential, living out the number of years human beings theoretically can (Hayflick, 1987).

BIOLOGICAL THEORIES OF AGING

biological theories of aging
Theories that explain the underlying biological mechanisms involved in aging and death.

Scientists want to understand the reason for these patterns: the association of advancing age with characteristic physical changes and certain diseases, and our maximum life span and its relationship to that of other species (Cristofalo, 1988). They have devised a variety of hypotheses, or **biological theories of aging,** to account for these mysterious phenomena. One important class of theories centers around what is damaging the basic units of our body, our cells.

The body is composed of two basic constituents: cells, either having the ability to divide or non-dividing, and intercellular connective tissue, whose main components are proteins called collagen and elastin. Most biologists assume that problems and processes within our cells are the cause of aging and death. However, some argue that changes in the collagen-rich substance surrounding our cells make a contribution. As we grow old, the normally pliable collagen and elastin molecules link with one another and stiffen. This loss of elasticity is partly responsible for benign signs of aging, such as wrinkled skin. It also causes life-threatening changes, such as **arteriosclerosis,** the loss of elasticity of our artery walls. Biologist Robert Kohn (1978) suggests that stiffened collagen and elastin may in itself be a cause of aging and death because by making our tissues more rigid, it impairs the passage of materials throughout our body and so prevents nutrients from getting to our cells.

arteriosclerosis
Age-related loss of elasticity of artery walls.

The different cellular hypotheses about why we age are often grouped into two categories: theories that view aging and death as occurring because of random damage and theories that suggest a preset biological program oversees the process (Smith, 1990). In reading the following explanations, just a few examples of many biological theories of aging that have been proposed, understand that one account does not rule out the others. It is just as likely that aging has multiple causes as that a single process is responsible for aging's varied signs.

Random Damage Theories of Aging

DNA DAMAGE. According to one random damage perspective, accumulating faults in our cells' ability to produce proteins are the cause of aging and death. Proteins are vital because they are the basis of all cellular reactions and functions. Deoxyribonucleic acid (DNA), the genetic material in the nucleus of each cell, programs how our bodies develop and work by serving as the blueprint from which these molecules are produced. The DNA molecule uncoils to synthesize ribonucleic acid (RNA), which, in a series of steps, serves as the mold from which the appropriate proteins are formed.

However, in the process of repeatedly uncoiling, the DNA molecule develops changes in its structure. These changes, called mutations, probably occur continuously in the course of our being exposed to environmental insults and the cells' work. Being responsible for our evolution from one-celled organisms, mutations are not all bad. However, most are deleterious. If their harmful effects are important or widespread enough, they will cause so many defective proteins to be produced that the cell will die.

Our cells have repair mechanisms to correct these spontaneous DNA mistakes; but as we age, the changes may become more frequent, and the repair system may not work as efficiently. So over time unrepaired damage accelerates.

According to this scenario, the physical changes of aging are the visible signs of DNA damage. As more DNA mistakes accumulate, more faulty proteins are produced, and more cells malfunction and die. Eventually, enough cells, or enough critical cells, are lost from our body to cause our death (Orgel, 1973).

FREE RADICAL DAMAGE. A second type of random damage theory pinpoints the by-products of cellular metabolism as the culprits producing cellular damage and death. In the course of their work, cells produce waste products, which are excreted

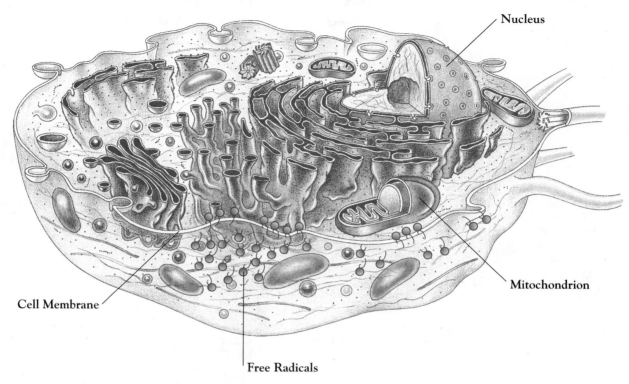

Free radicals, as well as other metabolic waste products, released into the body may contribute
to aging and death.

from the cell. As Figure 3-2 shows, these damaging substances may permeate and coat the
membranes of other cells, impairing their function and causing their death. They also may
do their damage internally, affecting the cells' DNA. One popular candidate for the
production of this destruction are molecular fragments called **free radicals,** released by the
billions into the body by our cells. Considerable evidence supports the idea that free
radicals do play an important role in aging. For instance, by providing dietary supplements
of antioxidants, such as vitamin C, beta carotene, and vitamin E, known to neutralize
these destructive substances, researchers can prolong animals' lives (Kart et al., 1992).

free radicals
Molecules excreted during cellular metabolism that damage the functioning of cells and may contribute to aging and death.

Programmed Aging Theories

Random damage theories assume that no master plan is responsible for aging and death.
There is another, equally reasonable idea: Aging, like growth, is programmed and timed.
Advocates of **programmed aging theories** differ as to where the aging timer is located,
what sets it off, and what operates it. However, they agree that the orderly, predictable
quality of the changes we undergo as we advance in years suggests that aging occurs by
a coordinated plan. Furthermore, the fact that every species has a fixed life span strongly
implies that aging and death are genetically programmed (Hayflick, 1987).

programmed aging theories
Theories that view aging and death as programmed by a timer or clock.

An aging and death clock may be located in each cell. At a certain time, cells are programmed to produce a protein that inhibits DNA synthesis, causing them to self-destruct. Or the clock might be centralized, placed in a system responsible for coordinating many bodily functions. If a central clock exists, two places with a widespread influence on our body seem likely places for it to reside: our hypothalamus and our immune system.

hypothalamus

Brain structure responsible for orchestrating many motivational states as well as helping to program physical and sexual development.

THE HYPOTHALAMUS AS AN AGING CLOCK.   The **hypothalamus** is a tiny structure in the brain responsible for coordinating an amazing list of functions, such as eating, sexual behavior, temperature regulation, and emotional expression. It has a key role in regulating physical growth, sexual development, and reproduction because it is involved in producing hormones. The hypothalamus is definitely responsible for the aging of one body system. By shutting off the production of the hormone estrogen at about age 50, it ushers in menopause and so ends a woman's capacity to conceive a child. Its far-ranging effects make it a good candidate for the regulation of other manifestations of aging, harboring the clock or clocks that time death (Comfort, 1979).

immune system

System whose function is to destroy foreign substances, either microorganisms or incipient cancer.

THE IMMUNE SYSTEM AS AN AGING CLOCK.   Our **immune system** protects us against foreign invaders, such as viruses or bacteria. In response to alien substances, whether microorganisms or cancer cells, (cancer cells are also foreign to our body's tissues), the immune system responds, producing "killer cells" and molecules called antibodies to kill the invaders. The thymus, a gland involved in the intricate immune response, slowly disappears during adulthood. Biologist Roy Walford (1969, 1983) has suggested that this gland may be an aging pacemaker because its disappearance signals a weakening of the immune system that has far-ranging effects.

A well-tuned immune system must make a delicate distinction, recognizing foreign substances and sparing our own cells. As our immune system weakens, Walford reasons, deficiencies develop in both functions. The immune system's weakened ability to fight off foreign attack partly explains why older people recover less easily from infectious illnesses and are more prone to cancer, as it is now believed that our body continuously produces cancer cells, which a strong immune system searches out and destroys. Deficiencies in the immune system's ability to recognize our own cells may cause it to attack our own tissues, accelerating cell loss. This assault on our cells, called an *autoimmune response*, may be partially to blame for illnesses as different as diabetes and dementia. So, because it can account for so many of the problems that befall older people, a failing immune system seems an especially good candidate for the timer causing us to age.

Extending the Maximum Life Span

If the immune system is responsible for aging, we might be able to slow our aging rate by stimulating immune function. If old age is programmed by the hypothalamus, ways of setting this timer back might be found. If the damaging effect of free radicals causes aging, we might be able to slow aging and death by taking vitamin supplements containing antioxidants. This means that these abstract speculations have profound practical impact. Instead of prolonging our lives a bit by pushing up our average life span a few years (the most we can hope for by curing any *specific* disease), the search for why we age has a larger payoff. It might allow us to retard old age for everyone and lengthen our maximum life span.

One method of extending the maximum life span, systematic calorie restriction, has been known for over a half century. In a remarkable series of experiments begun in the late 1930s, researchers have demonstrated that underfeeding rats can increase their maximum life span by as much as 60 percent. The key is an unusual type of underfeeding, what Walford (1983) calls "undernutrition without malnutrition." The animals are restricted to less food, but given an unusually nutritionally rich diet. They are allowed few empty calories.

It had been thought that to be effective undernutrition had to be started when an animal was weaned. The price of extending the life span was delayed puberty. The rats lived longer, but the diet primarily lengthened the period of life before adult fertility. However, more recent studies suggest that mild caloric restriction begun in adulthood extends longevity, too, though its impact is more modest than when this life-extension strategy is begun early on.

Biologists have been feverishly exploring the resilience that underfeeding produces. Dietary restriction postpones chronic diseases, especially cancer, that lead to death (Higami et al., 1995; Snyder, Pollard, Wostmann, and Luckert, 1990). It increases resistance to infection by retarding the loss in immune function that normally occurs with age (Effros, Walford, Weindruch, and Mitcheltree, 1991). It slows age-related biochemical changes in organs, such as the small intestine (Holt, Heller, and Richardson, 1991) and the liver (Mote, Grizzle, Walford, and Spindler, 1991). In other words, underfeeding has widespread anti-aging effects.

There is a qualification. Because of their short lives, this life-extension research has been conducted primarily with rats. In fact, as Richard Weindruch and Edward Masoro (1991) point out, most research on the biology of aging has been done with a single rat strain. While researchers have begun a study of underfeeding in our primate cousins, monkeys, because these subjects have a life span of about 40 years, it will be decades before we have results (Kemnitz et al., 1993; Ingram et al., 1990). So be cautious: There is no proof that calorie restriction works for humans. By following this stringent diet, we may be purchasing a protracted, but painfully deprived, life.

These efforts may be a mixed blessing for humanity as a whole. Imagine the overpopulation problem if we were to push up the maximum life span to 130 or extend a woman's childbearing years by a decade or more. It may be just as likely that this "advance" would be a double-edged sword, extending our time on earth at the price of limiting the quality of all of our years.

NORMAL AGING

While modifying the aging process is not within our grasp yet, we know more about that process than ever. What is physical aging really like? A landmark longitudinal study is unlocking the mystery.

As I described at the beginning of this chapter, traditional cross-sectional studies of physical aging showed that starting right after adolescence the pattern is decline. However, as we know from the last chapter, because each succeeding cohort arrives at a given age healthier, these studies exaggerated the true physical losses that occurred over the years. In addition, because they deal with group averages, cross-sectional studies tell us nothing about individual patterns of aging, the very differences *between people* in aging rates that might allow us to shed light on primary aging, the aging process as it can optimally take place (see Feature 3-2).

The National Institute on Aging–sponsored *Baltimore Longitudinal Study of Aging*, begun in 1959, is our nation's number one effort to probe physical aging in the flesh. As we learned in the last chapter, in this ambitious study volunteers spend several days at the Gerontology Research Center in Baltimore each year or two, having every possible physical function tested and probed. Let's look at some highlights of the research.

Nowhere are the first person stories more encouraging than among people who remain vital and athletic in old age. What is optimal physical aging really like? Listen to these participants in the Senior Activity and Rejuvenation Project directed by Frank Powell at Furman University:

Eighty-three-year-old Ray Wylie celebrates each birthday by peddling 100 miles on his bike. In addition to holding the national championship in bicycle racing in his age group, Ray was a table tennis champion in his younger years. Ray is committed to being a role model, to showing the power fitness has in changing life. However, he is not unidimensional. Before retirement; Ray was the chair of two university math departments. He directed hundreds of graduate theses and wrote a dozen books. He was very involved in raising two boys. Ray's motto is: "You can be physically active and still enjoy a full life. Do it when you can. If I can't exercise for a while, the world won't come to an end." How has Ray changed during his old-old years? In Director Powell's words, "I keep waiting to beat him at table tennis, waiting for him to decline. I keep improving, but so does he. His musculature is better today than at age 75."

At age 85, Helen Yockey also belies every stereotype about the old-old. Helen, who began swimming in competitions about a decade ago, consistently wins national meets. Helen, too, lives a balanced life. In addition to training regularly, Helen works at a soup kitchen and volunteers at Meals on Wheels.

Helen's interest in swimming dates back to her childhood in Akron, Ohio, a city surrounded by lakes. During summer vacation she used to disguise herself as a boy and hitchhike to a local lake with her three brothers. She remembers how upset she was the summer her disguise was finally penetrated and she could no longer swim! During her adult life, Helen continued to swim regularly, but for pleasure. Swimming remained her outlet for troubled times. In 1982, she was in a senior center class when she overheard two men discussing a swim meet. Helen decided to attend, won first place, and was hooked.

Helen's advice is to keep going. A year ago she gave up swimming for a few months, and it was hard getting back. Now she makes sure to lift weights every Monday, Wednesday, and Friday and to swim several miles every day. Helen has had two knee replacements. She wore out the first one and then used the other up. She is a shoo-in to take the gold in the nationals among the age group over 85.

Two Basic Principles of Normal Aging

VARIABILITY AS THE HALLMARK OF NORMAL AGING. The first major finding of the Baltimore Study and many others we already know from just observing friends and relatives. There are tremendous individual differences in aging rates. Some 60-year-olds are physically like 40; some 40-year-olds are more like 65. These differences in appearance are mirrored on physiological tests. Abilities as different as lung function, grip strength, and sugar metabolism all vary widely among people the same age. So individual variability is the first principle of normal aging (Maddox, 1991). In fact, this variability between people in aging rates becomes *more* dramatic as we travel through life (Harris, Pedersen, McClearn, Plomin, and Nesselroade, 1992).

Even within the person, making generalizations is unwise. Different body systems also vary greatly in their aging rate. Our opening interview offers a good example. While to an outside observer Joe looks his age or older, if we looked internally at muscle strength, lung capacity, and other functions, he may be much younger physiologically than the typical middle-aged adult.

At age 70, Jean Sullivan is the baby in the group. Her sports are the long jump and sprinting. Jean is a newcomer to competitive sports, too, although physical activity remains a continual theme in her life. Jean was a physical handful from infancy. Once her parents looked on in horror as she climbed to the top of the high water tower in town. Jean grew up in China, where there were no organized sports. However, she climbed trees, and she loved to run. In eighth grade, she went to boarding school in Shanghai. This marked a turning point. The progressive policy of the school was to allow girls to compete in sports. Jean recalls playing hockey during a war while all around the bombs were falling. It taught her that "sports gave a sense of control. In the midst of disaster, life goes on." Jean came to the United States a year before Pearl Harbor and continued to enjoy women's sports at college. Then she became absorbed in family and work. She became a physician and raised four children. Still, she loved keeping active and enjoyed just running across the yard because it felt good. In 1987, she heard about a track meet and thought: "Well, I'll give that a try." A few years ago Jean won the world and national championships in track and field in the 65–69 age group.

Jean says that "entering competitions is great fun. Life is more stimulating. I travel the country and meet new friends." According to Jean's husband, Frank, also an athlete in the program: "A lot of the credit for Jean's success belongs to me. I keep her in shape because I chase her around the house!"

These "life stories" are a perfect introduction to two themes in this book: (1) There is continuity during adult life. Our interests tend to stay somewhat the same as we age. (2) People who are active physically are often successfully aging in a variety of areas in life.

On the other hand, we must be careful not to equate optimal *physical aging* with aging success. When I worked in a nursing home, I saw people who were just as fulfilled as these senior athletes, who were equally successfully aging even though they were confined to a wheelchair. Think how Jung or Erikson would react to the contemporary idea that the key to aging successfully means winning the war against physical decline!

Source: Adapted from Furman E. and Hawkins, M. E. Positive Models of Aging: Presentations by Members of the Senior Activity and Rejuvenation Project, Symposium at the Annual Meeting of the Southern Gerontological Society, Charlotte, NC, April 1994.

So, even in looking at physical change, we need to adopt the *contextual life-span approach*. Aging rates differ greatly, both from person to person and within ourselves. But even though aging advances differently, there are generalizations we can make. The *process* occurs in predictable ways.

VERY DIFFERENT AGING PATTERNS.   The Baltimore Study shows that there are actually several aging trajectories. One is the pattern found in the cross-sectional studies. Some functions do decline in a regular way over time. However, others are stable, either staying unchanged or declining only in the terminal phase of life. Some may actually improve with age (Shock et al., 1984; National Institute on Aging, 1989, 1993).

In a common pattern, physiological loss occurs, but only when a person develops an age-related illness. For instance, among the high percentage of Baltimore volunteers who showed signs of heart disease, the pumping capacity of the heart declined with age. If a volunteer had no signs of heart disease, his heart pumped as well at age 70 as at age 30 (Shock et al., 1984). While it had been thought that in his middle and later years a man's body generally produces less testosterone (the male sex hormone), the Baltimore researchers found declining testosterone only in their older subjects who were ill.

Interestingly, the Baltimore researchers found that a loss in a normally stable function may be a sign of approaching death. Once again, the immune system offers a

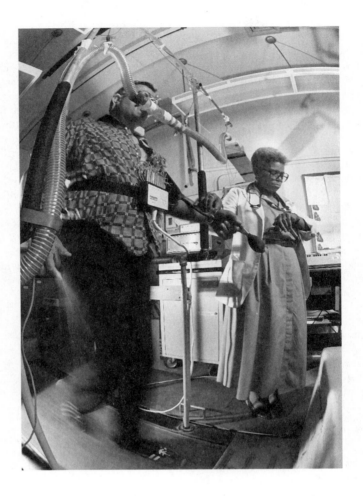

A participant in the Baltimore Study undergoes a test of cardio-respiratory function.

fascinating example. In analyzing blood samples at each test, the Baltimore researchers found that normally the number of lymphocytes (white blood cells) did not drop as volunteers returned over the years. However, among a minority of people, a definite decline in the lymphocyte count did occur. While at the time these people reported feeling healthy and physical examinations revealed no disease, at the next follow-up members of this group were more likely to have died. These deaths were non-specific, occurring due to a variety of causes. Either because it is a marker of existing illness or because it makes people more prone to disease, declining immune function does seem to be implicated in aging and death in a fundamental way (National Institute on Aging, 1993).

In another pattern, while loss occurs, our body compensates physiologically for the change. The most compelling example occurs in the brain. As the years pass, we do lose neurons. However, as we will see in Chapter 6, in response some cells grow more robust, adding new dendrites and establishing new connections, helping preserve thinking and memory (National Institute on Aging, 1993).

So the Baltimore Study reveals that we cannot think of physical aging as *just* loss. Stability exists in this important area of life. And, even when the years do take a physical toll, our body is resilient. We have the capacity to grow and adapt, even in areas such as our brain, where scientists never believed growth after maturity could occur.

Impact of Normal Aging on Daily Life

Despite this upbeat information, the dominant theme of physical aging remains decline. The losses that do take place—in how deeply we can breathe, in the ability of our

Olympic athletes such as Jackie Joyner-Kersee are likely to notice the gradual decline in reserve capacity early on.

kidneys to filter wastes, in our muscle mass—affect how we function in a specific way. Over time, our ability to perform at top-capacity physically will decline. Luckily most systems have substantial **reserve capacity,** or excess beyond what is normally needed, so these changes are only noticeable when we must stretch ourselves to our limit or when they have progressed so far that they interfere with daily life.

reserve capacity
Built-in extra capacity of organs and systems used only under conditions when maximum physical performance is required.

To a world-class athlete, the physical losses that occur early on are painfully apparent. In his or her twenties, a runner or gymnast worries about being "over the hill." Most of us only think "My body isn't working as well" years later. In our forties, it is harder to play a strenuous game of tennis. We do not bounce back as fast from surgery.

The physiological losses of aging become a daily fact of life only when they have progressed further. In our eighties, we may have to take our body into account in planning every day. Normal aging has permeated normal life.

Declining reserve capacity explains why elderly people are vulnerable to any stressful situation, be it running for the bus, undergoing surgery, or functioning in the sweltering summer heat. Age-related physiological losses are especially likely to cause problems when a high level of physical performance is needed, when coping depends on having the reserves to meet the challenge.

Some Important Specifics

Until now, we have been discussing normal aging in general terms. Now we turn to examine specific external and internal aging changes. Because of the behavioral science focus of this text, our tour is selective. I have chosen to briefly describe the most striking external aging signs, hair and skin changes, and to explore aging in two systems especially central to life. Heart attack, stroke, and related disorders, the end result of age changes in the cardiovascular system, cause almost as many deaths as all other illnesses combined. Age-related disorders of the skeletal system, while they are not immediate threats to life, are among the top-ranking chronic diseases and the main cause of disability in our older years (Jette, Branch, and Berlin, 1990; see Table 3-1). In subsequent chapters, we will be exploring aging in two other important systems, our nervous and sensory systems.

Facial wrinkles, that classic tip-off of advancing age, become very extensive in later life. However, notice in this elderly woman that in areas of the face that are used a good deal, such as the forehead, the wrinkling is particularly pronounced.

THE EXTERNALS: HAIR AND SKIN

Hair. Changes in hair color are perhaps our most obvious sign of advancing age. When you are in your twenties, you may look in the mirror, see a few white hairs, and suddenly realize, "I am getting older." Now that I am in my forties, my greying image localizes me in time the way no other marker can. It is an immediate banner telling outsiders that "Dr. Belsky is not a young adult." While each of us has our own genetic timetable for this gradual process, eventually everyone undergoes the loss of pigmentation that causes hair to change.

Hair loses pigment when the cells at the base of the hair follicle that produce the color for each hair die. Interestingly, grey hair is an illusion. Our hair looks grey during those transitional years when hairs that have not lost their pigmentation and non-pigmented hairs are interspersed. As more hairs lose pigment, grey hair lightens and eventually appears white. Notice that people with grey hair tend to be in their forties and fifties and that people have totally white hair in their later years. What accompanies this change is the gradual loss of the hair follicles. This leads to the second impression that strikes us about hair in *both* men and women in their older years. The older person's hair seems more sparse and patchy. Hair grows thinner with advancing age.

Skin. Skin wrinkling, the creases, furrows, and sagging we also ruefully expect over the years, is another obvious "tip-off" of age. We may first notice this wrinkling at about the same time that we find our first white hairs, in our late twenties. However, skin changes are a more variable, less reliable marker of chronological age. The reason is that, rather than just being a function of the passing years, wrinkling has an important environmental cause, exposure to the sun.

Wrinkling begins in the areas that we use the most. People who are used to laughing may find their personality fixed in little lines around their face. Those used to frowning suffer

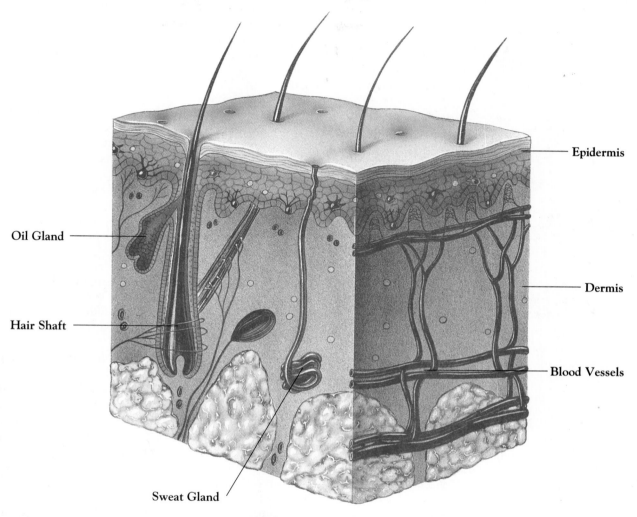

Oil Gland

Hair Shaft

Sweat Gland

Epidermis

Dermis

Blood Vessels

Age-related losses in the functioning of the oil and sweat glands and the blood vessel network in the dermis cause older people to become more vulnerable to extremes of heat and cold.

the same fate; their mood may be imprinted on their face. So our skin is more than an envelope covering our body. It can also be the visible reflection of who we are inside.

Wrinkling is the result of several changes. In the outer, epidermal layer of the skin, cells are continuously formed and migrate to the surface, where they die and are sloughed off (see Figure 3-3). As we age, the rate of new cell production slows, the epidermal turnover rate declines, and so our skin appears more furrowed and rough. More important, the constituents of the skin's thick middle or dermal layer, collagen and elastin, form cross-links and so lose their elasticity. As these molecules stiffen, our skin develops creases. A reduction in the activity of the dermal oil glands compounds the problem, drying out our skin and making it rougher and more easily damaged by the wind and sun.

Changes in our skin are more than cosmetic. This resilient envelope is what insulates us from insults in the external world. As Figure 3-3 shows, the skin consists of the rapidly replenishing epidermis and a thick dermal layer containing a network of blood vessels and sweat glands. An age-related loss in this blood vessel network, which provides nutrients to the skin, combined with the slower rate of new epidermal cell production, slows wound healing. This blood vessel loss, in addition to reducing the activity of the sweat glands, makes older people more vulnerable to extremes of heat and cold. Sweat and blood flow work together to keep our body at a constant internal temperature. In response to a rise in body temperature caused by being in the heat or exercising vigorously, the brain signals the blood vessels of the dermis to dilate and activates sweat production. As the sweat evaporates, it cools the skin's surface and the dermal blood supply, which then flows inward to cool the body. In cold environments, when body temperature begins to decline, the dermal blood vessels constrict, reducing blood flow to the skin and thus conserving body heat. Losses in this regulatory system explain why older people are more susceptible to *hyperthermia* (heat exhaustion) and *hypothermia* (reduced body temperature due to being in the cold).

Hyperthermia and hypothermia can be life-threatening because our internal temperature must be maintained at a fairly constant level for our physiological processes to function. However, the threat to life posed by aging in the skin is minor compared to that caused by age changes in the cardiovascular system, the network of heart and blood vessels literally at the heart of human life.

cardiovascular system
Circulatory system comprised of of the heart and blood vessels.

THE CARDIOVASCULAR SYSTEM.   The heart is the pump for the **cardio-vascular system,** the network of blood vessels bringing vital nutrients to the cells. This four-chambered wonder is remarkably resilient, beating roughly 3 billion times in the average life span, pumping the equivalent of about 900 million gallons of blood throughout its miles of arteries and veins.

Heart weight increases with age (Kitzman and Edwards, 1990). For women, the change is especially pronounced after menopause. The heart walls thicken and constrict to some degree. The valves that regulate blood flow through the chambers of the heart undergo thickening, calcification (hardening), and stenosis (narrowing). These same changes occur in the blood vessels directly feeding the heart, called the *coronary arteries,* as well as in the vascular system as a whole.

As I mentioned earlier, this stiffening and hardening of the arteries, called *arteriosclerosis,* is caused by the loss of elasticity in the connective tissue, collagen and elastin, that occurs with age. The narrowing has a different cause. It is due to *atherosclerosis,* the gradual accumulation of fatty deposits in the heart and blood vessel walls.

The effect of these changes is to impair circulation. The heart pumps less blood at its maximum. The narrower, more rigid blood vessels do not permit as much blood to circulate; so less oxygen and other vital nutrients reach our tissues when "top capacity" is needed. We grow winded more easily. We are less resilient physically to stress (Lakatta, 1987). This circulatory loss, when extreme, affects thinking capacity, too. As we will see in subsequent chapters, heart disease is the major chronic illness linked to losses in thinking speed in middle and later life (Earles and Salthouse, 1995).

Figure 3-4 shows snapshots of the developing process that ends in death. As plaque formation progresses in the artery, damage occurs to its inner wall, causing swelling and deterioration. Platelets, carried in the blood, adhere to the wall and stimulate its muscle to grow, further narrowing the passageway. While these arterial debris sometimes clog the passageway, what happens most often is that a blood clot (thrombosis) forms, blocking the artery. If this blockage occurs in a coronary artery, the blood supply to that area of the heart is severely compromised or cut off, and the heart muscle is damaged or dies. This causes the familiar *myocardial infarction,* or heart attack. If this blockage occurs in a blood

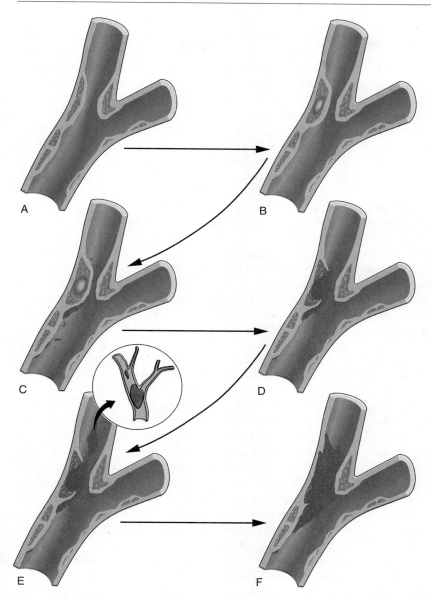

(A) Atherosclerotic plaque collects at an arterial branch; (B) an ulcer forms in the wall; (C) platelets and other products aggregate on the roughened surface; (D) a thrombus (blood clot) forms; (E) emboli form, blocking blood vessels throughout the artery; (F) the thrombus causes total blockage, resulting in a heart attack.

Source: C. S. Kart, E. K. Metress, and S. P. Metress, *Human Aging and Chronic Disease* © 1992, Boston: Jones and Bartlett Publishers. Reprinted with Permission.

vessel supplying the brain (a cerebral artery), the brain cells nourished by that vessel also malfunction and die. This produces that other top-ranking cause of death, a *cerebrovascular accident*, or stroke.

In both cases, depending on the degree of damage, either death or varying degrees of disability may occur. However, even in the absence of the dramatic event called a heart attack or stroke, atherosclerosis causes disease. When the coronary arteries become partially obstructed, a condition called *angina*, a dull pain that limits physical exertion, may develop. When the heart's pumping capacity is diminished by atherosclerosis and other causes, the heart enlarges, and its muscle fibers weaken. The symptoms of this condition, called *congestive heart failure*, include shortness of breath and swelling of the ankles and legs as fluid pools in the person's lungs and lower extremities.

Is this life-threatening progression absolutely inevitable? In the United States, systolic blood pressure, a sign of both atherosclerosis and arteriosclerosis, rises regularly as people age. In Japan, where the diet contains much less fat, blood pressure normally rises with age to only a minor degree, and people tend to develop heart disease much later in life (Fries, 1990). However, even if atherosclerosis is to some extent primary to aging, the *degree* to which it develops is partly under our control. For this reason, as we saw in Chapter 1, heart disease and stroke (along with lung cancer and accidents) are called our top-ranking preventable causes of death.

Prospective studies, a type of longitudinal research tracing illness rates in thousands of people, consistently show that certain prior conditions raise the chance of developing heart disease and stroke. These familiar **risk factors**—smoking, high blood pressure, elevated serum (blood) cholesterol, and diabetes—can be modified by diet, exercise, weight control, and medical interventions. Two other risk factors for heart attack and stroke are not under our control—gender and ethnicity.

Gender, Ethnicity, and Arterial Change.   Heart disease is the top-ranking killer for men and women. However, women tend to develop this illness at an older age, and their death rates never equal those of men. Figure 3-5 illustrates the dramatic gender gap in mortality and how it changes with age. Why are men so much more prone to this killer? While environmental factors may have some impact (men more often engage in high-risk behaviors, such as eating and drinking to excess), compelling evidence suggests that the real cause lurks in biological differences (Hazzard, 1990).

The female hormone estrogen protects women against heart disease. At menopause, which typically occurs at about age 50, the level of estrogen drops dramatically, mirroring the fact that, as Figure 3-5 shows, soon after this age the gender gap in heart disease mortality begins to decline. Another indirect sign implicating estrogen is the fact that postmenopausal women have higher heart disease rates than premenopausal women of the same age. Most telling is the research directly showing that atherosclerosis formation is related to estrogen and menopause. To understand these studies, it is important to know that the extent to which we develop atherosclerosis is related to our relative ratios of two kinds of blood lipids (fats). High risk of heart disease is associated with high levels of low-density lipoproteins (LDLs); low risk is associated with high-density lipoproteins (HDLs). While the HDL/LDL ratio, or proportion of "good" to "bad" cholesterol, favors women before menopause, after menopause the gender ratio becomes more alike. Moreover, giving estrogen to postmenopausal women raises the HDL level and lowers the LDL level, directly demonstrating that this hormone plays a central role in making women naturally more resistant to heart disease (Hazzard, 1990).

While biological predispositions may also play a role in ethnic differences in heart disease and stroke, here the impact of genetics versus that of lifestyle on illness rates is not as clear. As I mentioned, Japanese men have less atherosclerosis and lower rates of

prospective studies
Type of longitudinal study following a large population to see what prior conditions predict premature illness.

risk factors
Prior conditions that raise the probability of premature disease.

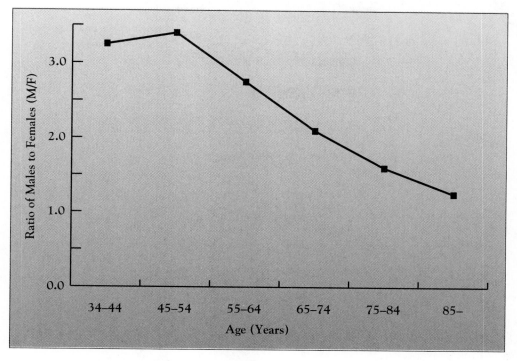

In the United States, males die more frequently than women from heart disease at every age, though after menopause the differences grow steadily less pronounced.

Source: D. L. Wingard, and B. A. Cohn, Variations in Disease-Specific Sex Morbidity and Mortality Ratios in the United States, in M. G. Ory and H. R. Warner (Eds.), *Gender, Health, and Longevity,* © 1990, Springer Publishing Company Inc., New York 10012, used by permission.

heart disease than American men. Japanese and Chinese men living in Hawaii have the same advantage, which may account in large part for why, with a life expectancy at birth of age 78, they are among the longest-living men in the United States (Curb, Reed, Miller, and Yano, 1990). Interestingly, some studies show Mexican-American *men* may be at an advantage, too. When researchers compared Hispanic/Caucasian death rates from heart disease in Texas and New Mexico, they found that Spanish surname men were less likely to die from heart disease, a lower vulnerability that was difficult to explain, as both groups of men were more likely to be diabetic and overweight, each a major risk factor for a heart attack (Markides, Coreil, and Rogers, 1989).

Unfortunately, these advantages do not apply to African Americans. As Figure 3-6 shows, while deaths from heart disease and stroke have declined for both races since 1960, they are still significantly higher among African-American women and men (see Chapter 1). This **excess mortality,** or higher-than-average risk of death, is most dramatic for stroke. African Americans have 1.8 times the chance of developing this terrifying illness as whites (Andersen, Mullner, and Cornelius, 1989; Braithwaite and Taylor, 1992).

excess mortality
Higher-than-average rate of death compared to the general population.

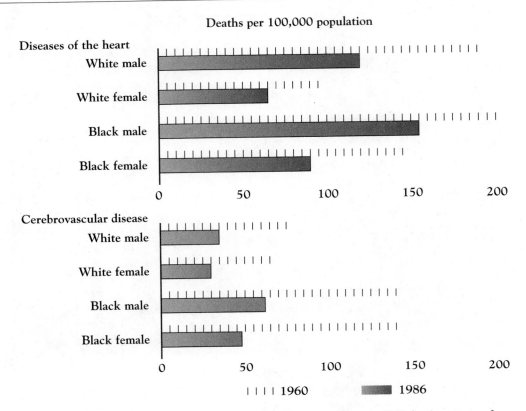

Deaths from heart disease and stroke have declined dramatically since 1960 for Americans of both races. However, African Americans continue to have higher rates of mortality than whites.

Source: U.S. Department of Health and Human Services (1990b). *Health Status of the Disadvantaged, Chartbook 1990.* Rockville, MD: Author.

The main reason is the high rate of hypertension (high blood pressure) among African Americans. Not only are African-American men and women greatly overrepresented among the 58 million Americans suffering from high blood pressure, but also they are more likely to develop this problem at a younger age and to have their problem go untreated (Hildreth and Saunders, 1992). Another contributing factor is diabetes. While, as is true of high blood pressure, diabetes rates normally rise with age, this illness tends to appear earlier in African Americans. African-American women in particular are much more prone to diabetes than are white women (Hildreth and Saunders, 1992; Murphy and Elders, 1992).

Hypertension and diabetes are extremely dangerous conditions. Not only do both greatly increase the risk of heart attack and stroke, but also they affect the kidneys, the eyes, and arteries throughout the body. Because each disease "runs in families," Baltimore Study investigators are currently looking at atherosclerosis formation at the cellular level to see if this stiffening process occurs differently for African Americans. However, even if genetic predispositions make some contribution, lifestyle conditions that promote atherosclerosis formation are more prevalent among African Americans. Being more likely to live in poverty, African Americans often do not have the luxury of buying higher-priced, low-fat foods or taking time to exercise or to generally follow the health-promoting strategies that might prevent cardiovascular disease. As we will describe in Chapter 5, being poorer, they have less access to good medical care (see also Feature 3-3). The most dramatic example of the impact of this lack of access involves hypertension because this problem, when detected, can be medically treated and controlled. Yet there is an alarming rate of untreated hypertension in the African-American community (Hildreth and Saunders, 1992), a problem that is causing great public health concern (Savage, McGee, and Oster, 1989; see Figure 3-7).

THE SKELETAL SYSTEM.   While aging in the heart and arteries tends to affect men and African Americans, age-related problems in the **skeletal system,** the network of joints and bones giving structure to our bodies, have the opposite pattern. They tend to affect women, typically white women. The changes described below are also universal, progressive, and inevitable. However, they develop later than atherosclerosis and take their greatest toll in the old-old.

skeletal system
Network of joints and bones giving structure to the body.

The Bones.   Beginning at about age 40, the density of our bones begins to decrease. The bones become more porous, brittle, and fragile. The degree to which people are prone to this bone loss, called **osteoporosis,** is influenced by genetics as well as lifestyle, the amount we exercise as well as calcium and vitamin intake in our earlier years. Here, too, gender and ethnicity are risk factors. Because white women have smaller bones and the estrogen depletion that occurs at menopause accelerates this skeletal change, the rate of bone loss is much greater for women than for men.

osteoporosis
Age-related skeletal disorder in which the bones become porous, brittle, and fragile.

Osteoporosis is a major indirect cause of disability and death. When bones are porous, they tend to be broken by the slightest fall. Unlike the many cracks that occur in young-adult fractures, the brittle osteoporotic bone tends to break completely. (A good analogy is the difference between what happens when we bend a green stem and a dry twig. The more pliable stem tends to develop fissures, but does not completely crack, while the twig easily snaps in two.) This means that broken bones heal much less easily in the elderly, so they have more serious consequences. Because many older people never totally recover from a fracture (Magaziner, Simonsick, Kashner, Hebel, and Kenzora, 1990), a broken bone may cause a permanent loss of independence. If the person is unable to care for herself, she may even have to enter a nursing home.

Falling in itself is more apt to be life-threatening in old age. (Dunn, Rudberg, Furner, and Cassel, 1992). Being more fragile physically, older people who fall are more apt to suffer serious physical damage. For example, falling may rupture an internal organ or cause trauma to the brain (Simoneau and Leibowitz, 1996). This is why preventing this "female" disorder of aging is a priority for research (Verbrugge, 1990).

The Joints.   A second change that takes place in the skeletal system, called **osteoarthritis,** is a wearing away of the protective cushion that insulates the joints. Throughout life, our joints are subjected to pressure when we move, run, or stretch. This wear and tear causes the protective covering over the ends of our bones to erode. As this protective cartilage is destroyed, bony growths develop at the bone ends, inflammation occurs, and movement is impaired. The exposure of bone to bone causes pain and stiffness. Occasionally the joints may fuse together, making movement impossible. Not every older person has painful osteoarthritis. However, as we saw in Table 3-1, enough do to make this illness the top-ranking chronic condition of later life (U.S. Senate Special Committee on Aging, 1991a).

osteoarthritis
Age-related skeletal disorder in which the cushion insulating the joints wears away.

Stanley Spencer had a stroke. It came from high blood pressure. If only he had listened to his doctor. Now he can't even talk to him.

Stanley Spencer's stroke didn't have to happen. He should have taken his medicine, and stayed on his diet. If *you* have high blood pressure, listen to the doctor.

It's your health. It's your life. It's your move.

The National High Blood Pressure Education Program

The National Heart, Lung, and Blood Institute, National Institutes of Health; Public Health Service, U.S. Department of Health and Human Services.

Public service announcements such as this reflect the priority put on blood pressure control for African-American men.

Source: National Institutes on Health, Bethesda, MD.

More than just wear and tear is involved. Contrary to popular opinion, despite putting punishing pressure on their joints, long-distance runners do not seem more prone to osteoarthritis than the average adult (Lane et al., 1986). Furthermore, movement—that is, exercise—helps increase joint flexibility and reduce pain once a person actually suffers from this disease. Exercise strengthens the muscles that support the joints, which results in less stress on the tendons and ligaments. It may indirectly stimulate joint repair by improving cardiovascular function and thus enabling more blood to get to the joints. Aspirin, which reduces the inflammation as well as the chronic pain, is also an important treatment for this common ailment.

The changes we have been discussing show just how intimately linked physical changes called normal are to chronic disease. Keep in mind the first principle of aging, individual variability. The differences from one person to another in aging rates are dramatic; they grow more pronounced as the years advance. These tremendous individual differences, *no matter what our gender or ethnic group,* are the real message of every study. They are a function of those twin factors: what we inherit (our genetics) and what we expose ourselves to in life.

We cannot change our inherited predispositions. Aging and death are inevitable and built into our species. Our own longevity is determined by our genetic makeup to a moderate degree (McGue, Vaupel, Holm, and Harvald, 1993). While behavioral genetic research suggests that our tendency to expose ourselves to these hazards may also be partly inherited, what we do in the course of living is more capable of being rearranged. This is why in the rest of chapter we focus on secondary aging, specifically, the impact of our lifestyle on aging and disease.

The skeletal disorders, osteoporosis and osteoarthritis, may be largely responsible for why elderly women such as this one walk in a characteristic, hunched over way as they negotiate steps. However, this woman also may be taking special care in this situation because she is well aware of the serious consequences of falling at her age.

LIFESTYLE, AGING, AND DISEASE

How often have you vowed to watch your diet, drink less, or exercise? When you last got sick, did you question your behavior: "Was I working too hard?" "Was I under too much stress?" These feelings are predictable, automatic, and frequent. They are surprisingly contemporary thoughts.

Americans never believed that taking care of one's health was unimportant. What has changed, as suggested in Chapter 1, is the *salience* we give to health practices today. Once again, this change occurred in the 1960s and 1970s as during these remarkable decades the social climate shifted as much in the area of health as family life. Along with questioning the authority of other social norms, we began to lose complete faith in traditional medicine to cure our ills. We shifted to a faith in ourselves (Alonzo, 1993). Exercising, eating right, and taking care of our bodies became the key to winning the race with disease and death. People who took their health seriously, those who jogged daily or watched what they ate for health reasons, had been the exception. They were seen as "health nuts," perhaps this obsessed with their physical state because they suffered from some disease. Today we have become converts to their way of thinking. What evidence supports our new found faith?

Health Practices, Social Relationships, and Longevity

The most powerful study showing that lifestyle does affect longevity was a huge prospective investigation begun in Alameda County, California, in 1965. In contrast to studies that focused on risk factors for single illnesses, such as heart disease, the Alameda Study was unique—the only investigation to focus on how lifestyle *generally* affects disease and death. Thousands of residents of this suburban San Francisco county were questioned about their illnesses, health conditions, and mental health (Berkman and Breslow, 1983). The sample was followed up in 1974 and in 1983. While the researchers

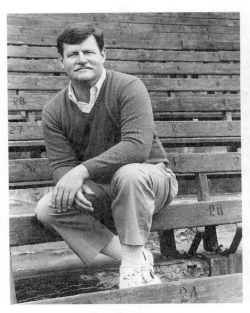

These photos of two men of about the same age illustrate the striking differences in aging-rates that become apparent as people enter their middle years. To what extent are these differences due to genetic factors or to the lifestyles these men are leading?

were also interested in how gender, social class, and race might affect illness rates, their main target was two "ways of living," health practices and social relationships.

The researchers probed seven health behaviors. As we might expect, keeping physically active, not smoking, not being overweight, and not drinking excessively were positively related to life expectancy. In addition, people who slept eight hours a night, ate breakfast, did not snack, and drank moderate amounts of alcohol were more likely to be healthy and had lower mortality rates.

Following these good health practices predicted longevity even at older ages (Guralnik and Kaplan, 1989). The life expectancy at age 60 of the men in the study who followed all of these health behaviors was 82, seven years longer than the men who followed none. Even at age 80, there was a difference between the two groups of one and a half years (Kaplan, 1986).

Following these good health practices also increased the chance of living free from disabling chronic disease (Strawbridge, Camancho, Cohen, and Kaplan, 1993). Most encouraging, the researchers found the motto was "It's never too late." Even over age 50 or 70, people who quit smoking and began to exercise increased their odds of living a longer life (Kaplan, Seeman, Cohen, Knudsen, and Guralik, 1987; Kaplan, 1992).

The fact that good health practices affect longevity comes as no surprise. The shock was the powerful relationship that social isolation had to living a long life. Based on criteria such as being married, having contacts with friends and relatives, and attending church, the researchers constructed a social network index, a measure of how involved the men and women were in close relationships. This index was as highly correlated to life expectancy as health practices! People who were the most socially isolated had a mortality rate over two times as great as those who were most involved (Berkman and Breslow, 1983). Even among people over age 70, being socially isolated significantly increased the risk of death (Kaplan, 1992).

Because these are correlations, we cannot be sure that having close social relationships or even following good health practices protects us from becoming ill. As I implied in our discussion of cardiovascular change, people who engage in activities such as exercising for pleasure or who do not smoke are not a random group. They tend to be middle-class and health conscious, the very people who receive the highest-quality medical care. They may be biologically advantaged. Who would be a more committed jogger, your friend in robust good health or another person made lethargic by disease? A perfect example of the danger of inferring causality from correlations concerns the finding that drinking moderately is associated with longevity. While more recent research does suggest that having one or two glasses of wine with dinner may be good for our health, in the Alameda Study the researchers found out that the increased risk among abstainers was really due to the fact that many people in this group had been drinkers but *due to becoming ill* had given alcohol up (Kaplan, 1992).

We could make the same argument for social isolation: Mrs. Jones withdraws from people *because she is ill*. However, in the Alameda Study, the relationship between social isolation and longevity held independent of disease. In other words, even when the researchers took initial illness into account, being socially isolated still predicted subsequent death.

If close relationships protect us against illness, why do they have this effect? Many experts accept some variation of the *stress buffering hypothesis* (Krause, 1989; Markides and Cooper, 1989). Caring relationships offer us emotional insulation, lessening the impact of emotional stress.

Emotional Stress and Illness

The belief that emotional stress causes illness and death has been popular since ancient times. However, it is only recently that this idea became scientifically respectable, as enthusiastically embraced by our family doctor as the neighbor next door. One set of studies was influential in convincing a highly skeptical medical community that our psyche can affect our physical state.

LIFE EVENTS AND ILLNESS.   In the mid 1960s, Thomas Holmes and Robert Rahe decided to test the "old wives' tale" that stressful life events make people ill. They developed a life-events scale by having a large group of people rank a list of changes according to how great an upheaval each might represent. The scale included both positive and negative events because Holmes and Rahe believed *any* dramatic change compromised health. When the researchers correlated illness rates with scores on their scale, they found that people who reported unusually high change ratings within the past six months were more likely to get sick; that is, they were more prone to illnesses as varied as cancer and colds (Rahe, 1974).

Holmes and Rahe's research was followed by a flood of other studies discovering a link between illness and life change. In one interesting example, researchers infected undergraduate volunteers with the virus producing the common cold. As Holmes and Rahe would predict, the students who came down with actual symptoms were more likely to have experienced more major life events within the past six months (Stone et al., 1993).

Dramatic life change or stress of any kind may provoke illness through several possible physiological routes. In situations where we feel threatened, our body is flooded with the stress hormones adrenaline and noradrenaline, neurochemical substances that produce a burst of energy, a state of heightened arousal that allows us to fight or flee from the source of the threat. This sympathetic nervous system "fight or flight" response, if prolonged, eventually wears the body down. When the situation is hopeless, the pituitary gland produces cortisol, a hormone known to suppress immune function. Changes in immune function, also measured after people undergo uncontrollable stress (Endresen et al., 1991–1992), may increase our vulnerability to a host of diseases (Vogt, 1992).

The most detailed portrayal of the stress/illness connection was first proposed by biologist Hans Selye during the 1950s. According to Selye's **general adaptation syndrome,** any organism's response to a stressor occurs in three phases. During the *alarm*

general adaptation syndrome *Selye's portrayal of the physiological response to stressors involving an alarm phase, a phase of resistance, and an exhaustion phase.*

phase, the adrenal cortex floods the body with hormones, energizing us to respond. Then we enter the *phase of resistance,* in which output remains high and we are capable of superhuman feats. Finally, in the *exhaustion phase,* our capacities give out, and we become ill (Selye, 1976). After the avalanche, a hiker runs miles without feeling the cold and subsists on roots and berries for days. However, unless he is rescued fairly quickly, his resistance dips way down, and he falls prey to disease. In the week before our wedding, we find to our amazement that we can finish a full semester's worth of schoolwork and make sure every detail of the ceremony is right. On our honeymoon, we develop a 103° fever, unable to enjoy the vacation we planned.

Unfortunately, however, the exact physiological path by which stress causes illness is unknown, and the correlations between life events and illness are small. So you must be wary about using major life changes to predict your chances of becoming ill. For one thing, the concept of fixed stress ratings ignores the dramatic differences among people in the stress value of each life event. While getting fired might be a terrible catastrophe to you, to your friend this event might have a very different meaning, perhaps coming as a relief (Costa and McCrae, 1989).

The *internal validity* of much of the research can be criticized. In demonstrating that life change raises the risk of illness, researchers typically ask people to report on their health and then say what happened to them within the past six months. However, because memory fades, fewer events are recalled over time (Glickman, Hubbard, Liveright, and Valciukas, 1990; Gorman, 1993). Furthermore, this forgetting seems selective, skewed by a person's current emotional state. While most of us may forget less desirable events, wouldn't depressed people be likely to both recall more negative life events and report more disease? In other words, rather than being "real," the link between life change and illness may be incidental, a function of the *general* world view of the reporter.

Major personal events are not the only type of stress that can affect health. Today researchers argue for a much broader conception. Stressful events include a range of experiences from disasters, such as being in that avalanche, to minor everyday hassles, to the strains that we chronically endure. In fact, because their impact does not go away, psychologist Leonard Pearlin (1980) argues that chronic strains, such as continually worrying about money or living with and *not* divorcing an abusive spouse, may even be more prone to be life-shortening than major life events. The same applies to little hassles, such as losing our keys or forgetting our notebook when we come to class. When Richard Lazarus and his colleagues devised a scale examining the number of these little hassles, they found that the frequency of these events was more related to subsequent illness than were scores on Holmes and Rahe's scale (Kanner, Coyne, Schaefer, and Lazarus, 1981).

Most important, focusing just on outer-world happenings ignores the dramatic variations in how people perceive and cope with stress. Some of us fall apart under the smallest setback; others are remarkably resilient in the face of the worst tragedy. Some people approach terrible strains, such as living with a chronic illness, by finding joy in every moment. Others create strain when it is not there. Perhaps, argued thoughtful observers, the real reason why the correlations between life events and illness are so small is that what really causes illness resides within us and not outside, that is, in our personality.

PERSONALITY AND ILLNESS

Type A behavior, past and present. The personality dimension that was first linked to illness has become a household word. In a large-scale prospective study that even predated Holmes and Rahe's work, cardiologists Meyer Friedman and Ray

As Pearlin points out, enduring chronic life stresses such as living day to day in this unhappy marriage may be just as illness-promoting as making a major life change such as divorce.

Rosenman (1974) made behavioral science history by finding that men with what they called the **Type A behavior pattern**—those with highly competitive, overachieving, hard-driving, and hostile personalities—were more prone to get heart attacks in midlife. Moreover, because Type A was an *independent* risk factor for coronary disease, predicting illness even when behaviors such as smoking or exercise were controlled, this research was especially influential in winning over the skeptical medical community to the idea that emotions can cause disease.

Type A behavior pattern *Competitive, hard-driving, hostile approach to living that may put an individual at risk of premature heart disease.*

In the years that have followed, the research on Type A has been intense. Books have been published and conferences convened. Researchers have examined the Type A behavior pattern in children and adolescents (Thoresen and Pattillo, 1988), in women, and in different ethnic groups. They have searched for the roots of this behavior in everything from biological predispositions to child-rearing practices that foster excessive self-involvement and lack of self-esteem (Scherwitz and Canick, 1988).

They have speculated about the physiological mechanisms that might link Type A and heart disease. When Type A's enter competitive situations or when their self-esteem is threatened, they seem to respond with exaggerated sympathetic arousal, an intense "fight or flight" response (Contrada, Krantz, and Hill, 1988; Houston, 1988). This excessive reactivity raises blood pressure (Scherwitz and Canick, 1988), increases heart rate (Burns, Friedman, and Katkin, 1992; Lyness, 1993), and has been shown to facilitate atherosclerosis formation in experimental animals (Manuck, Muldoon, Kaplan, Adams, and Polefrone, 1989; Williams, 1989). Type A behavior also may increase the risk of heart disease in an indirect way. One study showed Type A men are more prone to smoke. Women with this trait eat a higher-fat diet than their more relaxed counterparts (Musante, Treiber, Davis, Strong, and Levy, 1992). Because they are so competitive and hostile, Type A's may have poorer relationships (Watkins, Ward, Southard, and Fisher, 1992) and feel more socially isolated (Malcolm and Janisse, 1991), which in itself may heighten their vulnerability to disease.

Unfortunately, however, the seemingly solid evidence that Type A personalities have more heart attacks soon began to evaporate. During the 1970s, negative reports began to accumulate, suggesting that the global concept of Type A had to be rethought (Chesney, Hecker, and Black, 1988). Working too hard did not seem to have health consequences. Only certain dimensions of this personality, excessive hostility accompanied by suspicion, predicted future heart attacks (Haynes and Matthews, 1988; Williams and Barefoot, 1988). At the root of the problem, some experts believe, is a world view that is cynical and untrusting, one that leads the "coronary-prone person" to feel on guard and respond with anger to imagined threats. It is this distrustful state of angry vigilance that puts the unfortunate person at higher risk of heart disease.

Optimism, Control, and Illness.   Another set of traits thought to produce illness is related to feelings of hopelessness and helplessness. These emotions seem to be a logical candidate to make us sick through the second possible physiological mechanism mentioned earlier. If feelings of helplessness and hopelessness are prolonged and intense, the body may secrete the stress hormone cortisol, which impairs immune function.

In a remarkable set of studies, Martin Seligman and his colleagues set out to show that a *pessimistic explanatory style* may make us ill. Remember from the previous chapter that people who have this hopeless and helpless world view see positive life events as extrinsic and random, while negative life events are viewed as global, internal, and permanent: "That failure will always happen. It shows that I'm incompetent and incapable of success."

In one longitudinal study, Christopher Peterson and Seligman (1987) found that college students with a pessimistic explanatory style reported getting more infections. They visited their doctor more often during the next semester of school. In another study, explanatory style measured in youth predicted higher illness rates 30 years later (Peterson, Seligman, and Vaillant, 1994).

Drawing on a longitudinal study of the personalities of Harvard men, Seligman and his coworkers measured explanatory style from interviews recorded in college and then related these ratings to participants' health in their mid-fifties. A pessimistic explanatory style in this one interview was associated with poorer health and even premature death in middle age (Peterson, Seligman, and Vaillant, 1994)!

Seligman's research complements studies suggesting that experimentally modifying control can affect longevity. In their first study, Judith Rodin and Ellen Langer (1977) randomly assigned nursing home residents to two groups. The experimental group was lectured about the choices and opportunities for decision making that existed in the home. They were encouraged to take on responsibilities, such as planning their meals or caring for a plant in their room. The control group listened to a "benign and caring" lecture, which, while just as positive, had a different message: "Let the staff take over your care." The simple control-enhancing communication affected longevity. Over the 18-month period of the study, the death rate for the control group was about 25 percent; during this time, only 15 percent of the residents in the experimental group died.

In subsequent studies, Rodin (1986a) investigated in depth the health consequences of feeling in control. She taught nursing home residents strategies to cope with their environment. Not only did the older people report less stress, but also once again the interventions had physiological effects. The residents taught to take more control had improved health. They were more likely to be discharged from the nursing home.

In a review, Rodin and Judith Timko (1992) have summarized the growing body of evidence that providing people with a sense of *self-efficacy* enhances longevity. They urge caution, however. The research has been done with disabled elderly people. There is no evidence that enhancing efficacy feelings affects longevity in younger people or older

Chauncy, age 62, was one of the youngest residents at the nursing home where I worked. As a gifted mechanic and an avid fisherman who, after suffering a stroke, needed help even to eat and get to the toilet, Chauncy's life was a lesson in the costs of this devastating disease. Like a number of African Americans, Chauncy had untreated high blood pressure. He ate a diet high in fat. He gave up taking his blood pressure medication because of the expense. He disliked the side effects, and, besides, without health insurance, visits for a condition that produced no symptoms were a luxury he could not afford. In a casual conversation, Chauncy's doctor remarked that, while tragic, this man's illness was his own fault: Chauncy would not be in this situation if he had taken better care of his health.

The message of the lifestyle revolution is that illness is preventable and that the key to prevention lies in ourselves. Philosopher Angelo Alonzo (1993) warns against this stance. As we will see, this emphasis on personal responsibility can shade into a blame-the-victim mentality, in which people who develop "preventable" illnesses are held responsible for their disease. The truth is that all diseases have genetic contributions. We are never totally in control of our physical fate.

Blaming the victim ignores the role that the wider social environment plays in disease. As we will see in Chapter 5, the poor and disadvantaged are more prone to developing age-related illnesses early on (Abeles, 1992). In addition to not having ready access to medical care, men such as Chauncy who work 80-hour weeks do not have the time to exercise for leisure. The conditions of their life make it more difficult to avoid the poor health practices that contribute to disease. When we add in the fact that the alcohol and tobacco industries may target the poor, this suggests that by focusing exclusively on personal responsibility we may be getting society off the hook. How free is the "choice" to live a healthy lifestyle in order to protect one's future when staying alive day by day must be a first priority?

adults not made dependent by disease. Even though this caution does not apply to Seligman's research, as his subjects were healthy and young and middle-aged, we should be equally careful about the findings relating to explanatory style. When National Institute on Aging researchers examined a similar personality dimension, neuroticism, they found *no* relationship between this trait and illness (Costa and McCrae, 1987). Another study suggests the idea that pessimism causes illness warrants a *very close* second look. When researchers looked at personality traits measured in childhood in a classic study of gifted children and related them to deaths in middle and later life, they were astonished to find that optimism and cheerfulness were negatively related to longevity. Perhaps because they were less likely to take health risks, dour, conservative, cautious people lived longer than anyone else (Friedman et al., 1993)!

SUMMARY AND CRITIQUE.   By now, it should be apparent that the effort to demonstrate the "obvious" link between emotional stress and health has been more elusive than we might think. Let's summarize what these years of research twists and turns have revealed:

1.   Many studies do suggest that there is a connection between stressful life experiences and illness. However, the correlations between life events and disease are small, and there is little consensus as to what events are especially illness-producing. An even greater sense of confusion exists in the area of personality. With the possible exception of hostility, there is no evidence that *any* personality trait makes us more vulnerable to getting ill.

2. While hypotheses center around sympathetic arousal and impaired immune function, researchers have not pinpointed the exact physiological mechanisms by which stress or personality might affect health.

3. The route by which emotions cause disease is certain to be complex. Do stressful life events directly cause illness, or do they indirectly affect our health by causing us to eat poorly and neglect our body? How does our enduring personality influence the impact of life events? How important a role does social support play in buffering us from life's blows?

This ambiguity suggests that we should pause before labeling a friend's heart attack as due to his driven personality. We should be careful of making statements such as "She got cancer because she was depressed" or "His illness was caused by the death of his wife." Not only is the supporting evidence for these statements more shaky than we might imagine, but also these assumptions may be hurtful. They add insult to injury because they blame the victim for becoming ill (see Feature 3-3).

APPLICATIONS AND INTERVENTIONS

As the link between health practices and illness became common knowledge, a tremendous effort was centered on prevention as the cure for disease. From the fitness centers that are now a fixture in most large companies (see Figure 3-8), in hotels, at universities, and in private homes, to the blood pressure machines at your local supermarket, to runs for the heart, to health fairs, to public service announcements on television or the local bus, the message is out. Living a healthy life is the key to winning the race with premature death.

primary prevention
Efforts to control illness by preventing the development of risk factors for disease.

secondary prevention
Efforts to control illness by eradicating existing risk factors for disease.

These efforts involve **primary prevention,** preventing risk factors for illness from developing, and **secondary prevention,** changing existing risk factors before they result in life-threatening disease. They are having an effect. Starting in about 1970, atherosclerosis-related mortality, responsible for most of the deaths in the United States, began to decline at an average rate of 3 percent a year (Fries, 1990). While no one denies that better medical care is partly responsible, much of this decline is thought to be due to lifestyle changes (Fries, 1990). Since a vigorous public health campaign transformed smoking from a sign of sophistication into a cause for shame, per capita (per person) cigarette consumption has dropped by 40 percent (Fries, 1990; Warner, 1989). During the past decade, the number of cases of lung cancer began to steadily decline.

Large-scale interventions, such as the stop-smoking campaign, can only be evaluated by looking at societywide changes in illness rates. Interventions centered on secondary prevention, changing the behavior of people known to be at high risk for illness, offer direct proof that changing one's lifestyle does have an impact on longevity. This is why I am ending this chapter with two interventions in this category. Because heart disease is the number one cause of death and partly preventable, both involve that important illness.

The Multiple Risk Factor Intervention Trial (Multiple Risk Factor Intervention Trial Research Group, 1982) was our nation's most ambitious effort to make an impact on heart disease rates. Over 100,000 men aged 35–57 who smoked, had high blood pressure, and ate a high-fat diet were assigned to either a special intervention group or regular health care at different centers nationwide. Men in the intervention group received vigorous drug treatment for their hypertension. They participated in group sessions designed to get them to quit smoking and change their diet. They were

U.S. Work Sites Offering Employer-Sponsored Physical Activity and Fitness Programs, 1985 and 1992

Figure 3-8

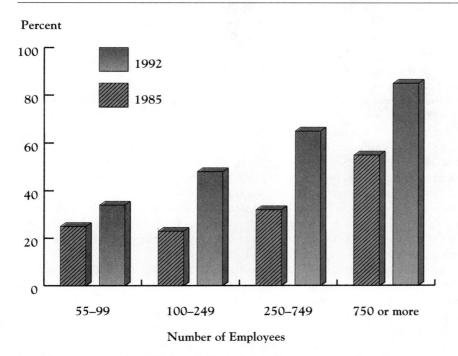

Percent

Over the seven years from 1985 to 1992, workplace fitness programs have become increasingly common in the United States. Today most companies employing over 100 workers offer this service to their employees.

Source: National Center for Health Statistics, 1995, *Healthy People 2000 Review,* Hyattsville, MD: Public Health Service.

counseled individually to reduce these risk factors for disease. The participants were followed for seven years.

The treatment was successful at reducing the risk factors. Blood pressure and cholesterol dropped significantly in the treated men. However, there was no difference in mortality between the groups. Was this because the treatment did not work or because seven years is too short a time to see the benefits of changing behaviors that may have been damaging arteries for many years? Might the drug therapy to reduce hypertension have had an unintended negative effect? Perhaps there simply was not enough difference between the two groups. Over the course of the study, as the link between heart disease and lifestyle became common knowledge, many men in the control group also stopped smoking and reduced their other risk factors for disease. Whatever the reason, this ambitious "failure" illustrates that interventions to reduce illness do not always have a demonstrable effect.

Another study to prevent heart attack had a different outcome. In the Recurrent Coronary Prevention Project, the goal was to modify Type A behavior, specifically, the chronic hostility thought to increase the risk of disease. Men who had had a first heart attack were taught psychological strategies to reduce Type A behavior. They were instructed to change their environment and reduce their tendencies to read personal threats into innocent acts. In situations that had been seen as "threats to my ego," participants learned to substitute more realistic responses. Strategies included direct teaching and modeling the new, more relaxed behavior. The men were told to practice leaving their watch off, smiling, walking slowly. The 50 hours of treatment had an impact. Not only did the men show reductions in Type A behavior, but also the treatment group had significantly fewer second heart attacks over the next four years (Price, 1988).

These two interventions exemplify both the promise of and the problems with conducting genuine trials to show that prevention works. While the correlational evidence that lifestyle affects longevity is overwhelming, ethical and practical problems prevent researchers from *experimentally proving* that changing behavior affects health. The researcher must ask a good deal of the experimental group: modify behaviors, such as not exercising or eating an unhealthy diet for years, and then wait an unknown length of time to see the effects. Not only is it difficult to prevent people in the experimental group from relapsing or dropping out, but also it is impossible and unethical to keep members of the control group from modifying their lifestyle on their own. When we add in the facts that *every* illness has multiple interacting causes and that these risk factors may vary in surprising ways from group to group (recall our discussion of Hispanic men and heart disease rates), it becomes understandable why even the most well thought out program can have negative results (Rakowski, 1992, 1994).

In the next two chapters, as we continue to explore the physical dimension of adult development, we take the same critical look at the research. In Chapter 4, we consider two broad facets of behavior, sexuality and sensory-motor functioning, and how they change with age. Once again, we examine what normally happens, probe individual variations, and spell out strategies to reduce the impact of age changes. In Chapter 5, we focus on what happens after illness has struck, looking carefully at the health care system and chronic disease.

KEY TERMS & CONCEPTS

atherosclerosis
normal aging change
primary aging
secondary aging
maximum life span
biological theories of aging
arteriosclerosis
random damage theories of aging
free radicals
programmed aging theories
hypothalamus
immune system
reserve capacity
cardiovascular system
prospective studies
risk factors
excess mortality
skeletal system
osteoporosis

osteoarthritis
general adaptation syndrome
Type A behavior pattern
primary prevention
secondary prevention

RECOMMENDED READINGS

Berkman, L., and Breslow, L. (1983). *Health and ways of living: The Alameda County Study*. New York: Oxford University Press.
Kaplan, G. A. (1992). Health and aging in the Alameda Study. In K. W. Schaie, D. Blazer, and J. S. House (Eds.), *Aging, health behaviors, and health outcomes* (pp. 69–95). Hillsdale, NJ: Erlbaum.
> These works offer comprehensive summaries of the Alameda Study.

Cristofalo, V. (1988). An overview of the theories of biological aging. In J. E. Birren and V. L. Bengtson (Eds.), *Emergent theories of aging* (pp. 118–127). New York: Springer.
> The author provides an overview of biological theories of aging.

The Biology of Aging. (Fall/Winter 1992). *Generations, 16*.
> The whole issue of this journal, published by the American Society on Aging, is devoted to the biology of aging. Articles review biological theories of aging, cancer in the elderly, and health care, among other topics.

Hazzard, W. (1990). A central role of sex hormones in the sex differential in lipoprotein metabolism, atherosclerosis, and longevity. In M. G. Ory and H. R. Warner (Eds.), *Gender, health, and longevity: Multidisciplinary perspectives*. New York: Springer
> The author reviews research implicating estrogen in the gender difference in heart disease.

Kart, C. S., Metress, E. K., and Metress, S. P. (1992). *Human aging and chronic disease*. Boston: Jones and Bartlett.
> The authors provide an excellent overview of the aging process in each system.

Nuland, S. (1995). *How we die*. New York: Vintage.
> A physician describes the paths to death, focusing on each major killer and describing how it progresses and what exactly causes our demise.

Shock, N. W., Greulich, R. C., Andres, R., Arenberg, D., Costa, P. T., Lakatta, E. G., and Tobin, J. D. (1984). *Normal human aging: The Baltimore Longitudinal Study of Aging* (NIH Publication No. 84-2450). Washington, D.C.: U.S. Public Health Service.
> This book offers a scholarly, comprehensive report of the Baltimore findings. (Also consult NIA publications for the layperson reporting on the Baltimore findings.)

Markides, K. S., and Cooper, C. L. (Eds.). (1989). *Aging, stress and health*. Chichester, England: Wiley.
> This edited book reviews the literature on health and stress.

épreuve d'artiste V/XXX   Marc Chagall

Specifics: Sexuality and Sensory-Motor Functioning

Chapter Outline

Joan was 21 when she married David. She fondly recalls her romance with this dashing officer just back from World War II. After 45 years of marriage, David still brought flowers and told Joan she was beautiful. While their sexual relations had become less frequent over the years, they still had intercourse at least once a month. Then suddenly her husband, to whom this aspect of life was so important, had no interest in sex. He seemed to be tired and depressed, to quickly turn into an old man. A few weeks later David was diagnosed with the liver cancer that would end his life within months.

When Joan became a widow, she was convinced her sexual life was over. Not many men wanted to date an elderly woman. She felt uncomfortable with the few men who did ask her out. Joan had been a virgin at marriage. Being with another man was awkward. There were embarrassing encounters. Anyway, she was too old to be interested in that aspect of life. Then she met John. He physically resembled David. They even had the same last name. He gave her flowers and told her she was beautiful. The relationship was easy and comfortable. Joan found herself involved in a passionate sexual relationship again. Joan feels that she must be exceptional. Her mother gave up sexuality when she became a widow at age 55. She never imagined a woman of 70 could be behaving in this way.

Nowhere are stereotypes about aging more powerful than with sexuality. As we just saw in our interview, we link youth with sexuality and age with automatic sexual decline. That this loss can be anxiety-provoking is clear when we look at a good index of our overall attitudes and fears, the jokes we tell. Erdman Palmore (1971) copied jokes about aging from anthologies and sorted them according to subject. He found that jokes about old age most frequently concerned sexuality. Most centered around the waning physical potency of older men. A tour of the birthday card rack at your local store will suggest that the situation has not changed. It will reveal that anxieties about sexuality, especially male incapacity, are as important an issue for Americans today as when Palmore conducted his survey more than a quarter century ago.

These fears have their parallel in anxieties about how age will affect our ability to sense and respond to the physical world. From the birthday card images relating to failing vision or hearing, to our assumption about "an older person" when we see a driver cautiously inching up the turnpike, sensory losses and slow responses are also central fears we have about growing old.

Sexual and sensory-motor changes may be especially anxiety-provoking because they affect so many areas of life. Sexuality involves more than having sexual intercourse. It can involve our whole world view of ourselves as attractive, desirable human beings. Poor vision and hearing and the slowness we associate with age also strike at the heart of who we are as people in a basic way. This is why in this chapter focusing on specifics, I have chosen to spotlight these far-reaching aspects of life.

SEXUALITY

How does sexuality really change as we grow old? Answering this question is more complicated than might appear. Sexuality includes different components from sexual desire, to the frequency with which we have sex, to the physiological capacity to respond, each of which may change in a different way as we age. Unlike the more biologically based changes discussed in Chapter 3, these complex feelings and activities are extremely dependent on the psychological and social side of life. Age-related physiological changes do affect sexuality. However, sexual feelings and behavior *at any age* depend on how we feel about ourselves, our self-concept as attractive, desirable human beings. As we saw in the interview, these feelings are affected by having an available partner, that is, a person who responds to us sexually. They are affected by the environment in a more basic sense. Society's ideas about what is appropriate sexual behavior shape sexual feelings and behavior not only in our older years, but also at every stage of life.

Setting the Framework

THE HISTORICAL CONTEXT. Because the larger social context is so influential, the historic change called the **sexual revolution** must be our framework for discussing age changes in sexuality. While according to historians there was a mini–sexual revolution during the first third of the twentieth century, during the 1950s the conditions under which "respectable" Americans were supposed to act sexual were once again more restricted and defined (Coonts, 1992). Sexual intercourse outside of marriage was prohibited. Campaigns were undertaken against various forms of "abnormal sex," such as homosexuality. While men were given more freedom, sexual expression in women was especially limited. According to the **sexual double standard,** women were not supposed to initiate sex; they were expected to be virgins until marriage; they were not supposed to feel sexual once they reached a "grandmotherly" stage of life.

> **sexual revolution**
> *Change in mores occurring during the 1960s involving a much more permissive approach to sexuality.*

Then came the decade of the 1960s. Suddenly sexuality before marriage became acceptable. A vigorous gay rights movement questioned the idea that sexual expression had to be confined to heterosexual love. People rebelled against the idea that sexuality should be more rigidly restricted for women or confined to a particular stage of life (Smith, 1994).

> **sexual double standard**
> *Different norms of appropriate sexual behavior for men and women that traditionally allow much more sexual freedom to men.*

Perhaps the most controversial results were an increase in premarital sexual activity and a decline in the age of first intercourse. While occurring for both sexes, the change was most dramatic for women because the double standard had always prohibited women from having premarital sex (see Table 4-1). During the 1940s, the vast majority of unmarried adolescent women reported being virgins (Kinsey and Associates, 1953). By 1990, the situation was reversed. Now, by age 19, the vast majority of U.S. girls report having already had sexual intercourse at least once. (Ehrhardt, 1992).

Several forces were responsible for this change: The baby boomers reached adolescence, so there were millions of unmarried teenagers. The pill was developed. The growing women's movement stressed sexual freedom and equality as a basic right. The result of this quarter century of sexual liberation is the situation we have today: an *anti-Victorian* society in which sexuality is openly discussed in graphic terms, a culture in which talk-show guests parade intimate details of their sexual lives.

Do the media reflect reality? The answer is no. The picture beamed out from our television sets could not be more different from the behavior of most American adults.

SEXUALITY IN THE UNITED STATES TODAY. Until quite recently, well-publicized polls, such as the *Hite Report* and the *Redbook* and *Playboy* surveys, led us to believe that the images on television did reflect American life. We were a nation of swinging singles. A high percentage of husbands and wives engaged in extramarital affairs. The problem is that, while these surveys were billed as "definitive surveys of Americans," the sampling techniques these researchers used were questionable. They surveyed special groups, such as readers of these magazines or subjects gathered from university women's centers. Worse yet, the authors based their conclusions on the tiny fraction of people interested enough to mail back questionnaires. So these studies had little *external validity*. As we saw in Chapter 2, rather than revealing the practices of typical Americans, they only revealed the sexual attitudes and behaviors of Americans unusually interested in sex.

In the early 1990s, researchers at the National Opinion Research Center (NORC) carried out the first representative poll of sexuality in the United States. They carefully

Table 4-1

Percentage of College Students at a Large Southern University Reporting Premarital Intercourse in Surveys Spanning 1965 to 1985

Date	Males (%)	Females (%)	% difference between males and females
1965	65.1	28.7	36.4
1970	65.0	37.3	27.7
1975	73.9	57.1	16.8
1980	77.4	63.5	13.9
1985	79.3	63.0	16.3

Change by 5-Year Intervals: Males

1965–70,		65.1%–65.0%	.1
1970–75,		65.0%–73.9%	−8.9
1975–80,		73.9%–77.4%	−3.4
1980–85,		77.4%–79.3%	−1.9

Change by 5-Year Intervals: Females

1965–70,		28.7%–37.3%	−8.6
1970–75,		37.3%–57.1%	−19.8
1975–80,		57.1%–63.5%	−6.4
1980–85,		63.5%–63.0%	.5

The trends that the researchers found in this survey are typical: (1) Men are much more likely to report premarital intercourse than women. (2) The change in women's sexual behavior has been especially dramatic since the sexual revolution. (3) The greatest shift for both sexes occurred during the late 1960s and early 1970s, when the sexual revolution was at its peak.

Source: I. Robinson, B. Ganza, S. Katz, and E. Robinson, Twenty Years of Sexual Revolution, 1965–1985: An Update, *Journal of Marriage and the Family, 53.* Copyrighted 1991 by the National Council on Family Relations, 3989 Central Ave N.E., Suite 550, Minneapolis MN 55421.

selected a national sample of thousands of men and women from age 18 to 59 in all walks of life to interview (Michael, Gagnon, Laumann, and Kolata, 1994). While, as is true of all surveys, the NORC results depended on volunteers willing to honestly answer questions, in this study we can take confidence in the fact that four out of five people the research team contacted agreed to participate. Let's look at the surprising findings:

1. ***Sexual fidelity and monogamy are the norm.*** In contrast to our myths, most Americans are monogamous. The vast majority of Americans had only one sexual partner within the past year. Only 3 percent of adults had more than five. The vast majority of married people are sexually faithful. In fact, people not in a committed relationship are more likely to have *no* sexual partners than to fit the image of the swinging single on television. When the researchers looked at lifetime sexual experiences, they found the same results. Most Americans have not had a varied, colorful sexual past. The average respondent reported having only about five sexual partners during his or her life.

2. ***Sexual attitudes and activities are much more traditional than we might think.*** The researchers got the same message when they looked generally at sexual practices and attitudes. Although about 6 percent of those surveyed reported having a homosexual experience or desiring someone of the same sex at some point in life,

While the 1950s lovers are clearly no less passionate than the 1990s couple in Photo B, due to the sexual revolution, passionate kissing is much more likely to be the first step to intercourse for the contemporary couple.

only 1.4 percent of the women and 2.8 percent of the men identified themselves as bisexual or homosexual. While most people had tried oral sex, standard intercourse is the preferred form of sexuality. Eight out of 10 people said they *only* had vaginal intercourse in the last year. In addition, in spite of the popular idea that having orgasms is essential to a satisfying sex life, only 29 percent of the women said they always have orgasms (compared to 75 percent of the men). Still, half of the sample said they are very pleased with their sexual relationships. By far the most content are married couples. Dissatisfaction is highest among unattached men and women, the very group that we tend to believe has the most exciting sex life.

As the researchers conclude, "America is not the golden land of eroticism where everybody who is young and beautiful has a hot sex life. Nor is it a land where vast hordes of miserable people, kicked out of the sexual banquet, lick their wounds in silence and resentment. . . . It is a nation of people who are, for the most part content . . . with the sexual lots they have drawn" (Michael et al., 1994, p. 256).

The study did support some stereotypes. Men fantasized about sex more often than women. They were more prone to masturbate, to buy erotic materials, and to be interested in sex apart from love. And, though the study was limited to people under age 60, the researchers did find a reduction in sexual activity with age. Especially among people in their fifties, sexual intercourse rates dropped off (more dramatically for women). The fraction of people who reported very few sexual experiences within the past year rose dramatically during this decade.

We have contradictory ideas about sexuality in our older years. On the one hand, we celebrate signs that older people are sexual. At least in theory, we are happy with the idea that sexuality can occur at any age. On the other hand, we have strong stereotypes that older people are sexually unattractive and that sexual decline is normal after youth (Walz and Blum, 1987). The problem with these ideas is that they may operate as self-fulfilling prophecies, producing the behavior they predict. Having sexual desires, acting on those feelings, and being able to perform physically in a sexual situation are dependent on our attitudes about ourselves. If older people accept the idea that they are unattractive and asexual, their interest, activity, and performance will be affected in a negative way. To what extent are reductions in sexuality due to these stereotypes? What exactly are the physiological changes in sexual performance that occur with age? To

Table 4-2	Changes in Male Sexuality with Age: A Summary Table

1. Erections take longer to develop.
2. Erections, once achieved, are more apt to be lost.
3. Orgasms are less explosive. Older men experience a seepage of fluid during ejaculation.
4. Penile deflation after orgasm is more rapid.
5. A longer interval is required to resume sexual activity after having had intercourse. By their fifties, after ejaculation men typically cannot achieve another erection and reach orgasm for 12 to 24 hours.

answer these questions, we begin our exploration of age changes in sexuality with William Masters and Virginia Johnson's research.

Age Changes in Sexual Responsiveness

In the early 1960s, Masters and Johnson took the unheard-of step of measuring the actual sexual response. Seven hundred volunteers, ranging in age from their twenties to their fifties, agreed to have sexual intercourse in the laboratory and so provide data for the researchers' landmark studies of the physiology of arousal and orgasm.

Masters and Johnson (1966) found several negative changes in their older male volunteers. Erections occurred less spontaneously and required more time and effort to develop. They were more fragile and likely to be lost before ejaculation occurred. There were changes in orgasmic intensity. The older men had less-explosive ejaculations. If a man maintained an erection over a long period, ejaculation resulted in a seepage of seminal fluid, rather than an expulsion. Penile detumescence (deflation) after orgasm was more rapid. Rather than occurring in two stages as it did among the young, it happened all at once. There was a lengthening of the *refractory period,* the time after reaching orgasm before another erection (or orgasm) can occur. Unlike the younger men, Masters and Johnson's subjects in their fifties could not develop an erection for 12 to 24 hours after a previous ejaculation.

These findings, summarized in Table 4-2, confirm that there *are* distinct physiological changes in male sexuality with age. However, they do not mean that middle-aged and elderly men are sexually incapable. Because erections can be maintained longer before the pressure to ejaculate becomes overwhelming, some experts suggest that from a woman's point of view older men are *better* sexual partners than young men (Corby and Solnick, 1980). And, when Masters and Johnson looked at the opposite sex, a different pattern emerged.

Among the older women, the researchers did find minor changes in sexual responsiveness. Breast size did not increase during sexual arousal as it does in young adults. The sex flush, a pinkish rash that occurs during sexual excitement, was not as intense. Contraction of the rectal sphincter during orgasm, an indication of an intense sexual experience, rarely occurred.

In all women, there are changes in the reproductive system after menopause that indirectly affect sexuality (Leiblum, 1990). **Menopause** occurs when the body's production of the hormone estrogen, which regulates the menstrual cycle, falls off dramatically. While its most crucial effect is to end a woman's ability to have children, this estrogen depletion also produces the symptoms described in Feature 4-1 as well as changing the vagina and its surrounding tissues.

During a woman's childbearing years, the walls of the vagina have thick folds, which expand easily to admit a penis or accommodate to childbirth. After menopause,

menopause
Time in life when estrogen production wanes dramatically and a woman is unable to conceive a child.

4-1 The Adult Experience: Menopause, Minimal Event or a Major Change?

When Barbara was growing up, menopause was something that people did not talk about. She remembers thinking it would be horrible. At about age 50, Barbara noticed that her periods were growing scanty. She did have hot flashes, but not often. She said she was too busy to pay attention to them. While she jokes about having one foot in the grave, today, at age 56, Barbara says she really feels young.

Monica's symptoms started at about age 48. It was hard to pinpoint the time because during those years she was grappling with her husband's fatal illness. She recalls flooding up with infrequent periods and having headaches and feeling edgy, but says those symptoms had accompanied her menstrual periods, too. Being so concerned with her husband, she did not have much time to think about her body during those years. (These vignettes are adapted from Thompson, 1995.)

The Victorians felt menopause was a wrenching event, "a change that unhinged the female nervous system and deprives a woman of her personal charm" (Sheehy, 1993, p. 44). We can see echoes of this view in the contemporary biomedical approach, which focuses on menopause as a set of unwelcome symptoms or a "deficiency disease." Most women do have unpleasant sensations. About 90 percent experience the infamous "hot flashes," a sensation of heat in the face and chest. Many report feeling out of sorts or are easily triggered to anger and tears. About 10 percent report symptoms that are very severe (Thompson, 1995). On the other hand, for most women, menopause cannot be that dramatic an emotional upheaval. As we will see in Chapter 9, rates of depression and anxiety do not skyrocket around age 50. In fact, in one survey, middle-class women were most likely to report feeling their lives were "first- rate" during these years (Mitchell and Helson, 1990). According to feminist writers, the symptoms of menopause have been exaggerated, the result of societal attitudes that equate the end of fertility with the end of a woman's productive life (Carolan, 1994). While we might take issue with this position, notice in our interviews that what overshadowed menopause in importance were the events of living that Barbara and Monica were grappling with during their "change of life."

the vaginal walls thin out and become smooth and more fragile. The vagina shortens and its opening narrows. The size of the clitoris and labia decreases. There is a decrease in sexual lubrication. Masters and Johnson found that it takes longer after arousal for lubrication to begin, and not as much fluid is produced. These changes often make intercourse more uncomfortable and so may limit sexual enjoyment or may force some women to stop having sex.

However, estrogen loss has few effects on sexual desire. The male hormone testosterone, present in the female body, too, regulates the sex drive in both men and women (Campbell and Udry, 1994). Masters and Johnson found the clitoral response to sexual stimulation was identical among their older and younger women. This is important because the clitoris is thought to be the seat of sexual arousal. Also, the older women were just as capable of reaching orgasm as the younger group. On average, though, they did have fewer orgasmic contractions and less-prolonged orgasms than the young volunteers.

On the whole, however, Masters and Johnson's findings for women were very upbeat. The researchers concluded with an important statement: "There is no time limit drawn by advancing years to female sexuality" (Masters and Johnson, 1966, p. 247).

Masters and Johnson's studies give us a baseline for looking at changes in sexual interest and activity throughout life. However, because neither these researchers nor the NORC investigators studied people over age 59, to get a full picture of how sexuality changes as we age we turn to research focusing on the latter part of adult life.

Age Changes in Sexual Interest and Activity

The only comprehensive national survey of sexuality after age 50 was sponsored by *Consumer Reports*. In the late 1970s, every *Consumer Reports* subscriber over age 50 was sent a questionnaire covering sexual practices, feelings, and capacities. Because people were encouraged to write about their personal experiences, the book describing this survey is the opposite of a dry statistical report. It is a compelling account of the sexual potential that exists in later life (Brecher and Consumer Reports Book Editors, 1985).

The *Consumer Reports* survey exploded the idea that older people are asexual. Many people, including men and women in their eighties and nineties, golden anniversary couples, and even some people with serious diseases, were enjoying passionate sex lives. However, as a study of the practices of "average Americans," it has the same shortcomings as the sexual reports we described earlier. Not only are *Consumer Reports* subscribers generally upper-middle-class and liberal, but also those who spent hours filling out the questionnaires are probably an especially sexually interested group. So, to supplement the results of this study, we need research examining somewhat more typical older adults. Ideally these studies should be longitudinal so that we can really trace how sexual feelings and behavior change over time. Luckily we have such studies: two longitudinal investigations of aging conducted at Duke University during the 1960s and 1970s and the Baltimore Longitudinal Study of Aging.

As part of a psychiatric interview, the Duke volunteers, who ranged in age from their late forties to their nineties, were asked to estimate how often they had intercourse or, if they had stopped having sexual relations, to say when and explain why. They were told to rate the intensity of their interest in sex and compare it with the strength of their feelings in the past (Verwoerdt, Pfeiffer, and Wang, 1969). Since 1967, the Baltimore men have also been questioned about their sexual feelings and activities as they return over the years. Combining these studies with the *Consumer Reports* and NORC research offers a full picture of sexual change.

The first way sexual interest and activity change as people grow old is predictable. For men and woman, both decline. Interestingly the Duke study shows that the decade of the seventies may be a sexual watershed for men. About three-fourths of the Duke men in their late sixties reported having sexual intercourse, and an even higher proportion said they still had sexual feelings. During their seventies, most reported giving up intercourse. The number who reported a high or moderate sex drive also declined dramatically over these 10 years. By their eighties, about four-fifths of the men no longer had intercourse. However, even at this age, half reported they still had sexual feelings to some extent.

Because their study was longitudinal, the Duke researchers could measure how universal this decline is. Do all men become less sexual over time? Looking at individual subjects over a three-year period, they discovered that sexual loss is not inevitable. Twenty percent of the elderly men reported *more* interest in sex and more frequent activity, at least over this short period.

Is the loss men normally experience a terrible psychological blow? According to the Baltimore Study, the answer is no. When the researchers asked the older male volunteers if they would prefer having their youthful sexuality restored, only 33 percent said yes. Among the 88 men aged 65–79 who reported being less than fully potent, only 10 percent were bothered enough by their problem to seek medical advice (Martin, 1981). So, if we can generalize from this study, age-related sexual loss is not the emotional tragedy we often expect when we are young.

The studies reveal a second striking fact: At every age, women report much less sexual interest and activity than men. In the Duke Study, the difference was especially great in women in their sixties, when the majority of men were still reporting an active sex life. While, as I described earlier, three out of four men aged 65–70 reported sexual feelings; only one in five women this age did. Why in spite of their more steady biological potential do women decline dramatically in sexuality in middle and later life? For answers, let's look at the predictors of staying sexually active in our older years.

Factors Affecting Sexuality in Middle and Later Life

We all have heard about people, such as Picasso, whose sexual exploits in advanced old age were renowned. In order to shed light on what forces make for a Picasso or at least predict lifelong sexuality, the Duke and Baltimore researchers explored how a variety of factors might relate to sexual interest and activity among the volunteers. For both men and women, one force stood out: People who reported being highly sexually active in the present said they were very sexually active in their youth. So, provided we can accept the accuracy of these memories, one key to predicting our sexual future lies in looking at our sexual present and past. People who are extremely interested in sex in youth are likely to remain interested in later life.

Unfortunately, for women, an external force looms large. Will there be a partner? The Duke researchers found that the only factor predicting continued sexual activity for women, other than age and past sexual enjoyment, was marital status. More than 40 percent of the married Duke women over age 65 were sexually active. Only 4 percent of the large group of single and widowed Duke women were. In contrast, 82 percent of the elderly Duke men without a wife said they were still having intercourse, a fraction that was even higher than for the married volunteers!

So one outer-world constraint, that is, having a partner, still plays an important role in female sexuality, even in our more liberated age. As we learned in Chapter 1 and saw in the beginning interview, at older ages widowhood and, increasingly, divorce take their toll. Many women *are* single in their later years. However, women are prevented from finding a new partner not just because the field of men their own age shrinks. Men still prefer younger women. They often do not find aging women attractive mates. As this New York cab driver describes to his female passenger, the sexual odds men face are much different in their later years:

> I asked him if he ever went out with women his own age. . . . The driver . . . replied, "Never. You think that's unfair, right? Well, it's unfair, I don't want to go out with women in their sixties. I'll tell you why—their bodies are just as flabby as mine. And, see, I don't have to settle for that. I've got a good pension . . . on top of what I make driving a cab. Gives me something to offer a younger woman. . . . A woman my age is in a tougher spot. See, she looks just as old as I look but most of the time she's got no money and no job. (as reported in Michael et al., 1994, p. 84)

Aging women do compensate for not having a partner by increasing the frequency of masturbation (Brecher and Consumer Reports Book Editors, 1985; Walz and Blum, 1987). Another adaptation many may make is to lose interest in sex. So, as with any behavior that is not reinforced, sexual desire fades more rapidly as women age.

While for older women the limiting factor is external, for older men the barrier to late-life sexuality tends to be internal: health. In the Duke Study, for men, but not women, both self-reports of health and objective measures were correlated with continued sexual activity. This explains the puzzle of why the seventies were such an important decade sexually for the Duke men. As we saw in Chapter 1, during these years when people become old-old, rates of chronic illness accelerate. When we look at the reasons for male sexual difficulties, we can see why illness has an important effect on aging men.

ILLNESS AND SEXUAL FUNCTION. It is normal for a man to slow down sexuality as he ages, but still be able to have intercourse. However, there also is some truth to the stereotype. **Erectile dysfunction,** the *chronic* inability to have an erection

erectile dysfunction
Chronic inability to have an erection firm enough to complete intercourse.

full enough for intercourse, does become a more common problem as men age. While psychological factors may be important, physical reasons are often responsible. The normal age-related slowing down discussed earlier is compounded by medical problems that inhibit the delicate erection mechanism.

An erection occurs when the web of blood vessels and blood-containing chambers in the penis becomes engorged. The blood flow into and out of the penis is regulated by hormones, nerves, and valves. A variety of age-related conditions may impair this process and so contribute to impotence: disorders affecting the blood vessels, such as arteriosclerosis, high blood pressure, and diabetes; operations done in the pelvic area, such as bladder, prostate, and rectal surgery; injuries to the pelvic region and spine; and diseases, such as kidney ailments and multiple sclerosis.

Being ill may affect a man's sexual performance in a more indirect way: Medications given for chronic illness may have sexual side effects. Drugs taken for common late-life problems, such as high blood pressure, heart conditions, and depression, often either affect a man's capacity to have an erection or inhibit desire.

Feeling sick can have an indirect impact on sexuality, making any older person too tired or depressed to be interested in sex. There can be an element of fear, the idea that sexual excitement is "too taxing" and can lead to sudden death. This anxiety is especially common when a man has the top-ranking chronic illness, heart disease.

When researchers questioned a group of people 11 months after having a heart attack, most reported cutting down the frequency of intercourse dramatically (Bloch, Maeder, and Haissly, 1975). The major cause was emotional, not physical. The person was depressed, frightened of a relapse, or terrified of having another heart attack during sex.

The fear that intercourse can cause a heart attack prevents both people with a heart condition themselves and their partners from fully enjoying sex (Corby and Solnick, 1980). However, though examples of this experience have captured our imagination, actual cases of people having heart attacks during intercourse are rare (Butler and Lewis, 1973). A general rule is that, if a person with heart disease can comfortably climb a few flights of stairs or take a brisk walk around the block, he or she can safely resume having normal sex (Corby and Solnick, 1980).

APPLICATIONS AND INTERVENTIONS

As the Baltimore Study suggests, not all older people care about sexual loss or have any interest in having a more active sex life. To decide that every older person should be interested in sex is just as limiting as assuming the opposite, that the elderly are asexual. However, because the barriers to being sexual in later life are still powerful, strategies to promote sexual fulfillment among older people have special appeal. Since these barriers are physical (mainly for men) and social (mainly for women), we now describe efforts to increase sexuality in each category.

ENHANCING PHYSIOLOGICAL RESPONSIVENESS. While there are emotional reasons why older men are unable to get erections, as we know, physical causes often loom large among people this age. Luckily tremendous advances have been made in treating even impotence that has a medical cause. There are erection-improving medications. If the problem has to do with the blood vessels regulating blood flow into the penis, surgery may keep the penis engorged. Even when the person's condition cannot be cured, there are solutions. Prosthetic devices can be surgically inserted on the penis, artificially producing an erection. These devices, called *penile implants*, allow people to still engage in intercourse. None of these treatments is a panacea. The treatments vary in effectiveness, and they may produce complications. Still, depending on the problem, they may be a great help.

To offset normal age-related losses in libido and performance (and losses in muscle mass), one controversial strategy is to provide testosterone to older men. Behavioral techniques, however, offer an alternate, less invasive route to increasing responsiveness. In one study, middle-aged men were given training in fantasizing to erotic stimuli. Half of the subjects got feedback about their erectile responses during the training sessions through a device attached to the penis. The other half did not get this feedback.

At the end of the study, both groups of men showed significant gains in the rapidity with which they had erections. They reported increasing the amount of time they spent having erotic daydreams and their frequency of intercourse. The changes were most pronounced for the men in the direct feedback group (Solnick, 1978). This suggests that even with male sexuality much decline that normally occurs may not be inevitable or *primary* to advancing age.

CHANGING SOCIETY. For older women, the main barrier to sexuality, finding a partner, would be difficult to erase without changing the ratio of men to women and the higher premium men put on physical beauty and youth (see Chapter 10). However, even when an elderly woman (or man) does have a partner, external barriers can make it difficult to have sex. This is often the case in nursing homes. As we will see in Chapter 5, nursing home residents typically share a room. Staff members can walk in day or night. It can be impossible to have time to be alone. Another barrier is the attitudes of the staff. In one study at a nursing home, researchers noticed that, while the staff expressed very positive feelings about the right of older people to sexual expression, their actions spoke differently. When an elderly couple living at the home escaped and got a room at a motel, the nurses, agitated, immediately wanted to call the police to get them back (Wasow and Loeb, 1978)!

To change this reaction, one nurse uses an experiential teaching technique. She tells her students to close their eyes and imagine themselves as a disabled older person, asking them to think about how their illness affects their sexuality and how caretakers respond. Then the students are given clay and told to sculpt it into an image reflecting their feelings. Next they open their eyes, write down a description of the sculpture, and choose partners for a discussion of the experience. Then they meet to explore the feelings the exercise has provoked. The goal of this experience is to change the ingrained attitudes shared not just by health care workers, but also by many of us that sexuality in old age is unnatural and wrong (Monea, 1978).

SENSORY-MOTOR FUNCTIONING

Basic to living is the ability to receive information about the environment. Just as crucial is the capacity to respond quickly to the information we receive. So, limitations in sensory-motor functioning can have widespread effects. If severe, they may make people less independent, less able to handle life. They may make the elderly feel vulnerable, out of control, less sure of themselves. They may make relationships more difficult and cut off pleasures as simple as enjoying a fragrant rose or a beautiful sunset. This is why, in addition to being the object of gallows humor, sensory-motor losses rank among our top two or three serious anxieties about old age.

Is it true that age brings dramatic losses in our senses or ability to respond? Answering this question is hampered by measurement problems similar to those encountered in exploring sexual decline. People may be reluctant to have their hearing or vision tested, making it difficult to get exact estimates of how prevalent these problems really are. Even in these areas of life, how well people function is surprisingly

In undergoing this hearing evaluation, this elderly woman is apt to be reluctant to report she hears a sound until she is absolutely certain. To what extent will her cautious attitude exaggerate the hearing problems this test may reveal?

dependent on the outer world. Because environmental conditions, such as lighting and noise levels, affect sensory functioning, a small loss under ideal laboratory conditions may cause a genuine handicap in daily life. Or tests measuring sensory-motor abilities may reveal problems that do not really exist.

A person taking a hearing test is presented with a series of low-intensity tones and asked to raise his or her hand when a sound is heard. The vision test involves identifying the letters or numbers on the familiar eye chart. Sensitivity or acuity on these measures is judged by the faintest stimulus that the person can perceive. But older people tend to be more cautious than the young (Botwinick, 1966; Welford, 1977). When a 70-year-old man is unsure whether he really heard a tone, his impulse is to be cautious, deciding "I'd better not guess." When a psychologist measuring age differences in response speed tells an elderly woman to "push lever A as fast as possible when the green light comes on," she is likely to have a similar mind set. Younger subjects, being more likely to guess, are at an advantage. They may be judged as more capable in comparison with the elderly than they really are because their strategy maximizes the chance of doing well.

In addition, in reading about the following losses, keep these optimistic thoughts in mind. It is one thing to measure a loss in the laboratory and another to say it presents problems functioning in the real world (Kline et al., 1992). *Impairing problems* in seeing or hearing or responding are never typical at any age. People probably naturally adjust to the changes they experience and continue to function as fully as before. As with any other physical function, making the distinction between what is inevitable and what is preventable is important with sensory-motor change. Studies strongly imply that our lifestyle, such as being exposed to high levels of noise or leading a sedentary life, can accelerate sensory decline or contribute to a slowing in our responding that is clearly to some extent primary to age. So the problems older adults have today might be escaped in part by future elderly by using a simple strategy: being more health conscious and taking better care of their health.

The sensory information we get from the world arrives from a variety of sources, from sensors found deep within our bodies that give us information about the internal workings of our organs to nerve endings sensitive to pressure, temperature, and pain located directly in our skin. However, vision and hearing are our senses of first rank, those we worry most about losing, those most crucial to daily life. As we might expect, researchers have more information about age changes in these primary senses. For these reasons, while we will briefly consider taste and smell, our main focus will be on vision, hearing, and age.

Vision

Some of the ways age affects our sight are obvious. We notice that we are having more trouble reading the newspaper or realize we need stronger glasses in order to make out the time on the clock across the street. However, our vision also changes in subtle, surprising, and unexpected ways as we grow old.

The most basic seeing problem that increases with age is poor **visual acuity,** the inability to see distinctly at distances measured by the eye chart. Impaired acuity becomes a problem only when it cannot be corrected by glasses or contact lenses. While acuity does gradually decline as people age, uncorrectable poor acuity is never a problem for a majority of older adults. But the number of people who have this problem is dramatically higher in later life. Of the estimated 1.4 million people in the United States unable to read newspaper print with glasses in 1977, almost two out of three were over age 65. Of the more than half million Americans suffering a more serious problem, legal blindness, almost half were elderly (Botwinick, 1978).

Impaired acuity affects all of our activities. A second type of vision problem that occurs as we grow old has a limited impact, though it is a more universal change. This is the familiar problem of not being able to see objects close up, a difficulty whose well-known link to age is shown in its name, **presbyopia** (old eyes). Interestingly this classic sign of age does not appear suddenly when it is likely to be noticed in our forties. Losses in near vision occur gradually from childhood, growing serious during middle age.

Presbyopia and poor visual acuity are obvious problems. The following changes are less apparent. Older people have special trouble seeing in dim light. They have problems distinguishing colors—in particular, blues from greens. They are more bothered by *glare*, that is, being blinded by a direct beam of light. They are not as able to see objects at the corner of their gaze. Figure 4-1 illustrates the impact some of these difficulties can have on the older person's ability to perceive the world.

To understand why these specific problems occur, we turn to the visual system and the way it changes with age.

THE VISUAL SYSTEM AND AGE-RELATED DECLINE. As Figure 4-2 on p. 107 reveals, a variety of specialized structures make up that marvelous organ, the eye: the cornea, the eye's tough outer cover; a viscous fluid called the aqueous humor; the pupil, an opening in the iris; the lens, a circular structure in the middle of the eye; and the vitreous humor, a gel-like substance that cushions and insulates the eye's back rim. This insulation is essential, as on this rim, called the retina, the delicate visual receptors reside.

The major purpose of these outer structures is to filter and focus light so the clearest image appears on the receptors: the rods, which are sensitive to darkness, and the cones, which allow us to see detail and color. The receptors are the crucial link by which we make contact with the visual environment. Here light waves are transformed into the nervous impulses that are carried to the brain. Impulses originating in the rods and cones travel to the brain through the bundle of neurons making up the optic nerve. They arrive at the part of the brain called the visual cortex.

Anywhere along this pathway deterioration can take place that affects our ability to see. Since the visual system does not function in a vacuum, aging in other parts of the brain also affects how well older people perceive visual stimuli (Kline and Scialfa, 1996;

visual acuity
Ability to see clearly at distances measured by the eye chart.

presbyopia
Age-related impairment in the ability to see close objects distinctly.

Figure 4-1

Pictures Simulating the Vision of Typical People in Their Twenties (left) and Late Seventies or Eighties (right).

The upper images illustrate the impact of increased susceptibility to glare; the lower, problems of acuity associated with poor contrast.

Source: Handbook of the Psychology of Aging (1st edition), by J. E. Birren and K. W. Schaie. Copyright 1977 by Van Nostrand Reinhold Company.

Madden, 1990). However, two structures, the iris/pupil and especially the lens, are especially important in explaining the vision difficulties older people have (Fozard, 1990; Kline and Scialfa, 1996).

Iris/pupil changes have a crucial impact on a person's ability to see well in the dark. The iris is a pigmented, circular structure (our iris color is our eye color) with a hole called the pupil in its center. In bright light, the iris reflexively widens, causing the pupil to constrict. This reduces the amount of light reaching the receptors. In dim light, the iris narrows, and the pupil dilates, allowing as much light as possible to get to the back

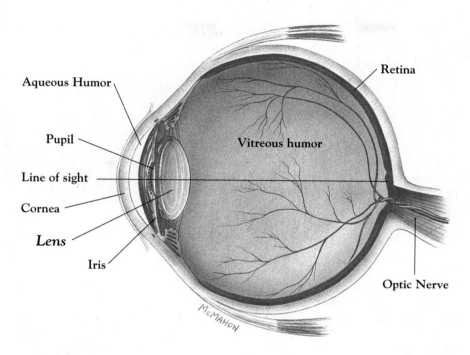

Aqueous Humor

Retina

Pupil

Vitreous humor

Line of sight

Cornea

Lens

Iris

Optic Nerve

McMAHON

Although all structures can contribute, changes in the iris/pupil and especially the lens are crucial in explaining age losses in vision.

of the eye. This rapid change, combined with an increase in the sensitivity of the rods, allows us to see in dim light.

In later life, the iris is less able to constrict. This means that, while in both dim and bright light older people have smaller pupils than the young, the difference is especially great in darkness, when the pupil needs to be as large as possible to permit optimal vision. Having a smaller pupil means having a fixed internal dimmer. In bright light, the dimming effect does not present many problems because not much illumination needs to get in. In dim light, the impact can be dramatic, explaining why older people have more trouble when walking into a movie theater and driving at night.

The degree of dimming is not minor. Changes in the pupil and iris plus in the next structure, the lens, permit only about 30 percent as much light to reach the retina at age 60 as penetrated at age 20 (Saxon and Etten, 1978; Pirkl, 1995).

The **lens,** a clear, circular structure that looks like a contact lens, plays a central role in several age-related vision changes. As we get older, the lens grows cloudier. In the same way that looking through a dirty window makes it more difficult for us to see outside, this internal clouding impairs visual acuity. It also explains why older people are especially sensitive to glare. Notice how, when sunlight hits a dirty window, the rays of light scatter, and it becomes impossible to see out. Because older people have more cloudy lenses, they experience the same effect and so are more likely to be blinded by a

lens
Normally clear, circular structure in the eye that functions to permit close vision and grows more opaque with age.

| Table 4-3 | The Top-Ranking Conditions Producing Blindness in Older People (cataracts are described in the text) |

1. *Glaucoma:*   A build-up of the fluid within the aqueous humor (that results when the normally open passageway that lets the fluid circulate narrows or closes) causes increased pressure within the eye and permanently damages the retinal receptors. With early diagnosis, blindness can be prevented, as medications, laser treatments, and sometimes surgery can reopen the passage. Glaucoma is called the "sneak thief of vision" because it seldom produces early symptoms. As a result, it is important to be regularly tested for this illness in middle and late life.
2. *Senile macular degeneration:*   The neurons in the center of the retina (called the macula) no longer function effectively. Symptoms include blurred vision and loss of central vision. Early detection is important because occasionally laser surgery can improve vision.
3. *Diabetic retinopathy:*   This long-term complication of diabetes, in which the blood vessels that nourish the retina either leak fluid or grow into the eye and rupture, causes serious loss of vision. Laser surgery can sometimes prevent blindness or severe vision loss.
4. *Retinal detachment:*   The inner and outer areas of the retina separate. Detached retinas can often be surgically reattached and sight restored.

cataract

Chronic condition in which the age-related clouding of the lens has progressed to such a degree that vision is seriously impaired.

beam of light shining directly in their eyes. At the extreme of this age-related clouding is a partially or completely opaque lens, a **cataract.**

Because little light can reach the retina when the lens is so cloudy, cataracts, when severe, cause blindness. However, they do not have to have this devastating effect. Unlike many age-related illnesses, vision loss caused by cataracts can be treated. The physician surgically removes the defective lens and either implants an artificial lens in its place or prescribes contact lenses or glasses. Unfortunately, as Table 4-3 shows, the other top-ranking illnesses causing blindness in older adults—glaucoma, macular degeneration, diabetic retinopathy, and retinal detachment—are less easily cured.

A second change in the lens's transparency affects color vision. Because the clouding has a yellowish tinge, it produces a decrease in sensitivity to hues in the blue-green range. This explains why distinguishing between these two colors is so hard for many older adults.

So far, you may have the impression that the lens is merely a non-functioning window. This is not true. This circular structure brings objects at different distances into focus on the retina by changing its shape. When we view near objects, the lens bulges (curves outward). When we view distant objects, it flattens out and becomes elongated.

This near/far focusing deteriorates with age because of a property of the lens itself. Throughout life, the lens grows continuously, adding cells at its periphery without losing old cells. To make way for this growth, the older cells become compacted toward the center of the lens. Over time, this accumulation helps produce this loss of transparency. It also makes the lens too thick at the center to bend well. This reduction in flexibility makes shifting focus from near to far distances more difficult. Because what is lost is the ability to curve, this explains why problems with near vision are a universal age change.

While it had been thought that deterioration in the lens and other parts of the eye explained most normal vision loss, researchers now believe that the neural part of the visual system makes a major contribution to age-related problems in seeing. As we age, the number of rods and cones decreases. We lose neurons in the optic nerve and visual cortex. This neural atrophy (deterioration) seems to explain why vision difficulties accelerate in advanced old age. This loss may also explain why older people process or

Lillian first gave up driving at night. The oncoming headlights were blinding. Sometimes it appeared so dark that she could barely see the road. Then she abandoned highway driving. She had no problem keeping pace with the flow of traffic. Her fear was entering and exiting and being forced to stop quickly or change lanes. For several years, Lillian used her car to get around the neighborhood during daylight to do her shopping and other chores. Then even this became too difficult. She had to sweat and strain to maneuver into a parking space. The freedom of having a car was no longer worth the price. Now Lillian relies on her children to drive her around. She dislikes being dependent, but manages. She stocks up on food and makes appointments the days her daughters are free. According to Lillian, "At my age, 92, any person would be a fool to be on the road."

It makes sense that driving would be especially affected by sensory-motor loss. Driving depends on reacting quickly to signals. To drive, it is essential to see well. Age-related vision changes, such as sensitivity to glare and impaired vision in the dark, should make night driving very difficult for older people. Driving requires good visual acuity and the ability to quickly process visual stimuli, such as road signs or an approaching car. Hearing loss also affects driving because sound provides information about the location of other vehicles. So we would expect, as with Lillian, that driving, especially under difficult conditions, would be a major concern for many older people.

Most elderly people still drive. In one survey, the researchers found many people were still driving in their late seventies or beyond (Jette and Branch, 1992). However, people are aware of their problems and take special care to avoid risks (Kosnik, Sekuler, and Kline, 1990). When another group of researchers compared middle-aged drivers to drivers over age 65, the elderly people reported driving less often at night, on expressways, during rush hour, and during winter (Planek and Fowler, 1971).

Because they drive less often, when we simply compare age groups, elderly licensed drivers have lower accident rates than young adults. However, when we look at crashes per comparable miles driven, the elderly are a high-risk group. According to Karen Ball of Western Kentucky University, the reason is that a small group of impaired older drivers brings the group's average up. The goal is to identify this dangerous group of people, a task that is quite difficult. Requiring driving tests every year after a certain age has been attacked as ageist by senior citizens' groups. The tests themselves are not that informative. Most driving tests measure simple visual acuity. However, the complex array of skills involved in driving depends on much more than seeing well. For older people who live in towns without public transportation, having a car may make the difference between being able to live at home and having to enter a nursing home. How can we balance the individual's right to continue this vital activity with the safety needs of the community at large (Stock, 1995)?

make sense of visual information at a slower rate (Madden, 1990). In other words, vision losses, particularly in our later years, most likely are due to changes in the nervous system as well as the eye.

IMPACT ON DAILY LIFE.   Despite these changes, the typical 70- or 80-year-old does not have *serious* problems seeing. Not only are the losses that occur minor, but also people can compensate for these changes. As Feature 4-2 suggests, a woman gives up night driving. She takes special care when walking into a movie theater or down a gloomy street. She can also increase the lighting in her house or have guests visit her, rather than leaving the house at night. Vision difficulties are associated with disability (Rudberg, Furner, Dunn, and Cassel, 1993). They make it more likely that older people will trip and fall (Simoneau, Cavanagh, Ulbrecht, Leibowitz, and Tyrrell, 1991;

Simoneau and Leibowitz, 1996). However, although poor vision is associated with cognitive deterioration (Lindenberger and Baltes, 1994), even older people with severe vision difficulties do not have more psychological problems than the average adult (Eisdorfer, 1970). Unfortunately this may not be true of losses in that other crucial sense, hearing.

Hearing

While researchers have been unable to link vision losses to emotional problems, hearing problems *may* be more likely to affect well-being (Eisdorfer, 1970). At first glance, this seems puzzling because we tend to think of vision as our most important sense. However, while losing our sight cuts us off from the physical world, poor hearing causes damage in a more important area. It prevents us from using language, the bridge that connects us to other human beings. So it is the human world we are prevented from fully entering when we lose the ability to hear.

We are correct to link poor hearing with being old. About four in five Americans with hearing problems are over age 45, and more than half are over 65 (Fozard, 1990; Kline and Scialfa, 1996). In a 1989 survey of late-life chronic conditions, poor hearing outdistanced poor vision. It was third in frequency, while vision impairments ranked ninth (U.S. Senate Special Committee on Aging, 1991a). To know that poor hearing is more common in older people, we do not need the benefit of statistics; we need only look around. People over 65 are much more likely to wear the visible emblem of this problem, a hearing aid, than any other group.

Hearing begins to decline in our thirties. Losses accelerate in old age. However, with hearing, there is tremendous variability in the extent of decline. Some people begin losing hearing in their twenties; others later on. For most people, the loss is more extensive for high tones. Others do not show this typical age pattern of loss. With hearing, there also is a gender difference. Men tend to lose their hearing earlier than women. They are more likely to develop genuine difficulties at a younger age (Pirkl, 1995).

One reason is that, in addition to being primary to aging, hearing loss has a definite environmental cause, exposure to noise. People in noisy occupations (who are more likely to be male), such as construction workers and rock musicians, lose hearing earlier and may have serious handicaps by midlife. Prolonged exposure to the chronic noise of a city also may contribute to age-related hearing difficulties. So, unfortunately, since noise pollution is still endemic, the outlook seems grimmer for hearing than for other problems of aging. While noise abatement regulations developed in the 1980s require employers to provide workers in factories with hearing protection, people do not think to take the same care of their hearing as of other aspects of health. So, at the same time as we are reducing the rate of other chronic conditions, poor hearing may still be a very common problem in future American adults. (Notice how loud the sound is in your local movie theater to get an indication of the hearing problems "average people" have today.)

Statistics on how many people have hearing losses may err on the low side. People are reluctant to admit they have this difficulty. Poor hearing strikes at our vanity because it is so characteristic of being old. The experience of not being able to hear can easily be rationalized: "Other people are talking too softly. There is too much background noise." Even experts have trouble agreeing on the level of impairment that causes a genuine handicap. The main reason is that a person's hearing varies greatly in different situations, depending on who is speaking and on the level of background noise. In other words, as with vision, age-related hearing losses are not a constant, all-or-none phenomenon. Age-related hearing loss also has a special name—**presbycusis** (old ears).

People with presbycusis have special trouble distinguishing high-pitched tones. They have problems hearing the high-pitched voices of children and greater trouble

presbycusis
Characteristic age-related hearing disorder involving selective difficulties in hearing high-pitched tones.

hearing sounds such as consonants or warning phrases that, even though loud, are shrieked or yelled in a high-pitched voice. They are much more bothered by background noise, such as the hum of traffic on the street and the drone of an air conditioner or fan. Background noise tends to be lower in pitch than speech sounds. So in any noisy environment the background seems amplified, making conversation especially hard to hear.

These selective problems can cause misunderstandings. You notice that your uncle can hear well on one visit and not at all on another. Your natural temptation is to accuse him mentally of pretending, of turning his hearing off deliberately. Everyone is primed to have these suspicions because dealing with hearing problems is so frustrating. It is so exhausting to have to struggle to achieve something we take for granted, a conversation.

THE AUDITORY SYSTEM AND AGE-RELATED DECLINE. As is true of the eye, the ear is a complex structure, with outer parts that concentrate, amplify, and prepare sound vibrations for transmission to the brain by receptors located in the inner ear. As Figure 4-3 shows, these sound-wave-amplifying structures include the pinna, the apricot-shaped structure we call the ear; the ear canal (external auditory meatus); the eardrum (tympanic membrane); and the three bones of the middle ear. Vibrations amplified by these bones travel to the inner ear, where, in the part of the inner ear called the cochlea, the hearing receptors, called hair cells, are located.

Figure 4-4 on p. 113 shows the coil-shaped cochlea with its fluid-filled compartments. Vibrations set up waves in these compartments, which cause the basilar membrane, on which the hair cells sit, to bob up and down. The cells jiggle, shearing against the membrane above. It is this bending that generates the neural firing responsible for our experience of sound. Impulses set off in the hair cells then leave the ear and travel to the auditory cortex.

Our perception of a sound—its pitch (highness or lowness), its volume (loudness or softness), and its timbre (complexity)—depends on the way the basilar membrane moves. Different sounds set up varying patterns of motion in the fluid-filled cochlea, which cause different types of displacements of the basilar membrane. For each sound, a unique pattern of hair cells is stimulated. It is through this complicated mechanism that we experience the jangle of a jackhammer and the stirring tones of a symphony.

Except for very low frequency tones, the location of the hair cells on the basilar membrane that are stimulated is important in discriminating pitch. High-pitched tones cause maximal stimulation of the hair cells at the basal cochlea. Low-frequency tones stimulate the hair cells toward the apex of the cochlea. So our ability to hear high-pitched sounds depends on the stimulation of the hair cells at the base of the cochlea.

In contrast to age changes in vision, where problems in the outer, image-focusing structures often are to blame, presbycusis is due to problems in the inner ear. In fact, one major cause of this difficulty is the loss of the actual hair cells. The hair cells at the base of the cochlea (those coding high tones) are the most fragile, explaining why people selectively lose hearing for higher frequency sounds.

Here, too, changes in the nervous system seem important in explaining hearing problems, especially in advanced old age. In one study, researchers simulated hearing loss in young volunteers, making their impairment on a pure tone hearing test comparable to that of a group of older adults. Then they gave subjects a test of their ability to perceive speech. While the young-old did get scores similar to those of the young, the old-old still performed worse, suggesting that the difficulties very old people have in understanding conversation involve more than just problems with hearing individual sounds (Humes and Christopherson, 1991). They also have trouble comprehending or making sense of the complex array of sounds involved in language, a processing deficit or deficiency in encoding and interpreting incoming information that reflects changes in the brain.

Figure 4-3

Anatomy of the Human Ear, Depicting the Structures of the Outer Ear, Middle Ear, and Inner Ear

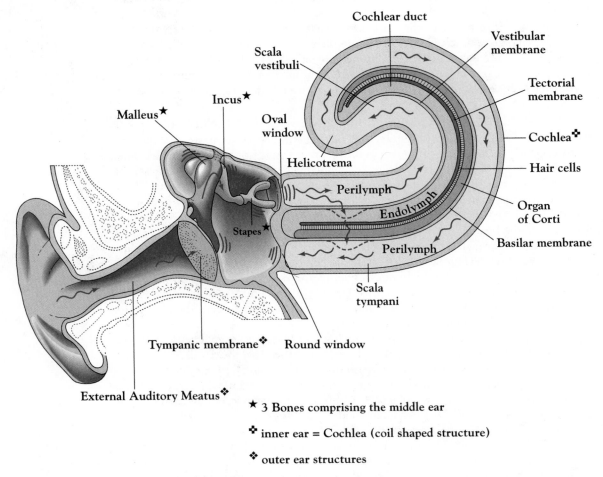

★ 3 Bones comprising the middle ear

✤ inner ear = Cochlea (coil shaped structure)

❖ outer ear structures

The middle ear and outer ear amplify sound waves. The hearing receptors are located in the inner ear or cochlea.

The outer ear and middle ear also can contribute to age-related hearing problems. Excessive wax in the ear canal is a common late-life condition that is often overlooked. The bones of the middle ear may have fused together, which requires an operation to cure. However, when the problem is in these outer parts of the auditory system, the person does not really have presbycusis, that is, selective trouble hearing high-pitched tones. The loss is equal for all tones and so is more like what we imagine a hearing difficulty to be. People with this type of hearing loss are also better off in another way. They are more likely to benefit by a device magnifying all sounds equally, a hearing aid (see Feature 4-3 on p. 114).

IMPACT ON DAILY LIFE.   Not hearing well increases our physical risk. Sound is a crucial way we learn of environmental dangers. However, the main problem this impair-

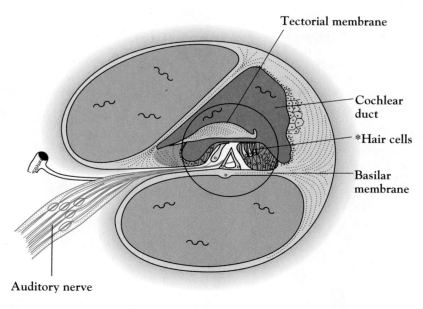

Tectorial membrane

Cochlear duct

*Hair cells

Basilar membrane

Auditory nerve

〰 Fluidfilled compartments
* Hair cells = hearing receptors

The bending of the hair cells against the tectorial membrane generates the neural impulses for sound.

ment causes is social. As we saw earlier, friends and family withdraw, defeated by the struggle to communicate. The older person may turn silent, rather than having to continually say, "Please repeat that." Another reaction might be to grow suspicious, reading betrayal into whispers half-heard. This is why, among *people already predisposed to serious emotional problems,* hearing deficits have been linked to the development of paranoid reactions.

Taste and Smell

Because taste and smell work together to allow us to enjoy food, losses in these senses may make eating less pleasant and so contribute to poor nutrition among the elderly. Smell is an early warning system alerting us to hazards, such as spoiled food or fire. So poor smell can make life less safe as well as limiting our joy in living.

The elderly have less-sensitive taste and smell than younger adults. However, because a variety of illnesses from nasal problems, to Parkinson's disease, to head trauma affect these senses, it is unclear how much of this loss is primary to age. Because sick older people are often being compared with healthy young adults, are the age differences researchers find due to aging itself or illness (Bartoshuk, 1989)? Because, unlike the receptors for vision and hearing, the receptors for taste and smell are located directly on the tongue and nose and are normally replaced every few days, researchers find little fall-off in their number with age. There are clear age differences, however, when elderly people and young people are asked to use these senses where they are most critical, to identify and evaluate foods.

4-3 The Adult Experience: Hearing Aids, Past and Present

In the 1970s, when I worked at a nursing home, I remember a resident who fiddled with his boxlike hearing aid. The sound was always too loud or too soft. Sometimes it must have been unbearable. I could hear the loud whine. The man was always unsatisfied. He would give up in frustration and take his hearing aid off. The device was continually breaking down. Being a person who cared about his appearance, he hated showing this badge of incapacity to the world. One day he threw the hearing aid in the trash, fed up with a device that was an *impediment* to hearing well.

Traditional hearing aids were bulky boxes. Because they magnified all sounds equally, they were not helpful for presbycusis, the characteristic age-related hearing loss. So, even if not bothered by the aesthetics, many older people shunned a hearing aid. Better wear nothing than be victimized by the drone of background noise magnified.

Today technology has transformed the way hearing aids look and sound (Leary, 1988). The newest devices fit into the ear canal and are almost invisible to the eye. The old way of controlling volume through a control box wired to the aid has gone underground. A person can buy a remote-control credit-card-sized apparatus manipulated from the pocket and well out of sight.

More important, progress is being made at differentially magnifying higher-pitched tones. Companies are experimenting with computerized hearing aids that monitor the pitch of sounds, selectively suppressing lower-frequency noise and enhancing conversation sounds. These new hearing aids are not for everyone. They are expensive and most appropriate for people whose impairments are not severe. Their claims to filter out background noise are sometimes not fulfilled. But provided one takes the advice *caveat emptor* (buyer beware) very seriously, for the millions of middle-aged and older adults whose lives are limited by this chronic condition these advances are a welcome step.

In the first of a series of studies on food sensitivity and preferences, Susan Schiffman (1977) blindfolded college students and elderly people and asked them to identify and rate the pleasantness of blended foods after tasting them. Not only were the older people less able to identify the foods, but also they were more likely to rate them as weak-tasting.

In her next study, Schiffman and a colleague demonstrated that these changed perceptions were mainly due to impaired smell. The researchers asked subjects to discriminate between the odors of different foods compared in pairs and to rate what they smelled for pleasantness. Once again, the elderly were poorer at identifying most odors. However, their sensitivity varied from odor to odor. It was best for fruits. So, as we might expect, the older people gave fruit smells the highest marks for pleasantness (Schiffman and Pasternak, 1979).

This research suggests that the reason for the complaint we might hear from an elderly relative, "Food doesn't have as much taste as it used to," is not just nostalgia, or the fact that food was fresher in the good old days, but altered smell. It also offers insights into why the elderly prefer heavily spiced foods and why eating preferences change in apparently strange ways in old age. Older people may grow to prefer those foods, such as candies or fruits, with odors that age impairs the least.

Altered smell sensitivity may partly explain another common complaint older people have: "Food tastes bitter or sour." Foods such as chocolate and some vegetables have a bitter taste that is masked by a highly pleasant odor. When the sense of smell weakens, these foods may come to have an unpleasant taste. So, ironically, smell, not taste, is the true culprit in many age-related problems in the ability to enjoy food.

Response Speed

While sensory change is most apparent to the person, what we tend to notice first about the elderly is their responses. We are struck by their slowness, the fact that they take so much *longer* to respond. This loss of response speed is not only one of the most obvious signs of age, but also one of the most widely studied processes in the psychology of aging.

Responding quickly is essential to performing basic activities, such as crossing a street before the light changes, driving, and avoiding getting hurt by stepping out of the way of environmental obstacles. Slow responding makes older people prone to accidents because they are out of sync with the pace living demands.

Slowness may put older people out of step with others. It can cause conflict because it is so different from the rate at which the rest of us live. As we all have noticed when we find ourselves behind the slow older person at the supermarket checkout counter or the older driver going 40 in the 65 mile per hour zone, irritation wells up. So the slowing that age brings puts a damper on relationships and may be one reason that our fast-paced, time-oriented society has prejudices toward the old.

AGE CHANGES IN RESPONSE SPEED.   When psychologists measure this slowing in the laboratory, they are looking at what is called **reaction time,** the ability to quickly and accurately respond after a signal to take action appears. In a typical *reaction time experiment,* a subject might be instructed: "Push button A as fast as you can when the green light comes on."

A standard finding on these tests is that older groups perform less well. In fact, age differences on these tasks are so universal that "slower responding" is one of the most certain predictions we can make about how our behavior as a young adult will change as the years pass.

However, the extent of the loss depends on the task. Older people perform more poorly on complex tasks than on those demanding simple actions. They perform more poorly when aiming at a target than when striking the table as fast as possible. They do much worse when asked to complete a sequence of steps, rather than making a simple response. The main reason for these exponential declines in performance as task complexity increases is that more complicated tasks require more thinking. And it is "thinking time," not "acting time," that slows most with age.

In reaction-time studies, researchers break down responding into two phases: (1) a thinking phase, during which we mentally process incoming information and figure out how to act; and (2) a phase during which we physically carry the action out. When subjects are told to "press buzzer A when the red light comes on," by measuring the time it takes from when the light appears to when the person begins to lift a hand, researchers can isolate the amount of time the thinking phase takes up in slowed responding. They then can compare this interval with age differences in *movement time,* the time taken to perform the response. While older people also do more poorly in the latter phase (Light and Spirduso, 1990), the most dramatic differences typically occur in the thinking phase.

What happens during this thinking phase, that is, the interval from when the signal to act occurs and the response begins? For hints, we turn to the *information processing* flowchart put forth by Alan Welford in Figure 4-5.

According to Welford (1977), data arriving from the sensory organs is first fed to the brain. There, the information is perceived, an action is decided on, and the response is programmed to be carried out. The end point is the action itself, performed by the effectors, the voluntary muscles and the involuntary reactors of the autonomic nervous system. Furthermore, Welford argues, this sequence probably takes place many times when we take even the simplest actions:

reaction time
Ability to respond quickly and accurately to a stimulus after that signal to act occurs.

Figure 4-5

Hypothetical Flowchart of the Human Sensory-Motor System (stores refer to memory functions)*

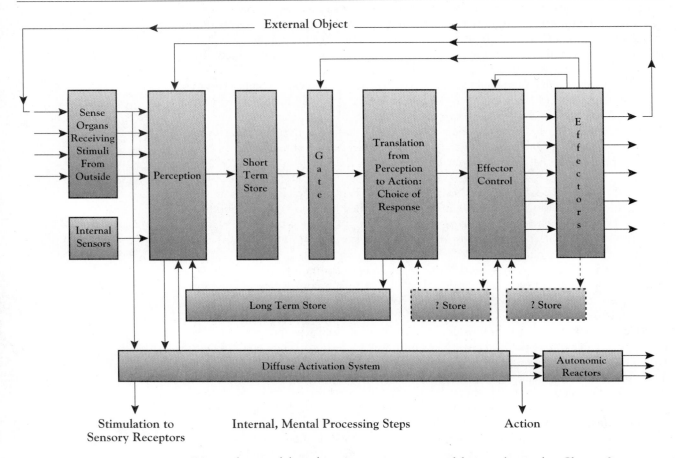

*Notice the use of the information processing type of diagram discussed in Chapter 2.

Source: From *Handbook of the Psychology of Aging* (1st edition), by J. E. Birren and K. W. Schaie. Copyright 1977 by Van Nostrand Reinhold Company.

> *Performance hardly ever consists of a single run through the chain. . . . Even relatively simple actions such as picking up a glass or opening a door involve a . . . process in which an initial action . . . is followed by a series of smaller adjustments each of which depends for its precise form on the outcome of the one before. In other words data from the . . . action and its results on the external world are fed back as part of the sensory input for the next run through the chain. (1977, pp. 450–451)*

So what we think of as "responding," our actual movements, is only the end of a series of internal events. Now we look at where in this chain the older person's problem lies.

This air traffic controller must simultaneously receive audio information from pilots, visually scan the display screen showing the location planes, and react both physically and verbally to this input within a short period of time. So, it is no wonder that in this job requiring such complex information processing skills, that there are age-restrictions in hiring.

THE SOURCE OF THE SLOWING.   Problems in the last step, taking action, may be crucial in explaining slowness in some people, for instance, those who suffer from arthritis or other diseases that greatly limit movement. Problems at the beginning step, sensory input, could account for the slowness of others, people whose hearing or vision difficulties make it a continual struggle to know whether the environment requires taking action. However, since the reaction-time studies involve clear signals to respond and leave out the movement part of the chain, the age differences here suggest that the middle central-nervous-system steps are critical. In other words, the main reason we react more slowly as we age is that our central nervous system is less able to quickly process the information to respond (Cerella, 1990; Salthouse, 1985, 1990, 1991).

IMPACT ON DAILY LIFE.   But if a slower-functioning central nervous system is the problem, then we would not expect the slowing to be limited to physical responses. As we grow older, we should be slower in all our actions, less quick at remembering names or solving puzzles as well as opening doors. Unfortunately, as we will see in our chapters on cognition, this is the case. While performance with verbal responses does not fall off as dramatically as it does with actions that are genuinely physical (Jacewicz and Hartley, 1987b), slower responding is pervasive with advancing age.

There are qualifications. Slowness varies greatly from person to person. Being quick is critical to performance only in some activities. Losses are most apparent on complex tasks. So before assuming an older person is deficient, we need to look carefully at the individual and what he or she is being asked to do.

For instance, in a job such as air traffic controller, where responding quickly to changing stimuli is essential, losses in reaction time may be noticed early on. In this occupation, people cannot be hired for the control tower if they are over age 30. They must retire by age 55 (supervisor of operations, Nashville International Airport, personal communication, 1994). As we will see in Chapter 6, reaction-time losses are much less relevant to most other jobs. But any time work involves a fast physical pace, it can present special problems for older employees.

Workers seem to understand the trouble an older body has with speed. Studies in factories show that older workers want, and are more often found in, jobs involving relatively heavy work, such as lifting or carrying. The reason is that this more strenuous type of work often does not have to be done quickly. Speed-oriented jobs, such as assembly-line worker, present intense hardships for older employees (Welford, 1977).

Even on the assembly line, older laborers do not do as poorly as we might expect on the basis of laboratory tests. Work involves well-practiced activities, and **expertise** compensates for the slowing that occurs with age (see Chapter 6). Attrition also may be involved. Older workers who find their abilities declining may retire early, leaving only the relatively quick on the job. Who are these hardy older people?

INDIVIDUAL VARIABILITY.   Older people who are athletic tend to have quicker reaction times (Toole and Abourezk, 1989). They sometimes have reaction times comparable to those of young adults. Another individual difference that affects reaction time is health. We see slower reaction times in people with heart disease. People with brain diseases, such as strokes, brain tumors, and Alzheimer's disease, have especially slow reaction times (Hicks and Birren, 1970).

The fact that athletic and healthy older people have quicker reaction times highlights the fact that not all slowness is primary to aging. Exercising, keeping physically fit, and taking care of our health may reduce the losses in response speed that are somewhat inevitable to growing old.

The same is true of our senses. While some changes may be inevitable, as we saw in Table 4-3, two of the most common problems producing blindness in the elderly, diabetes and glaucoma, can be controlled or detected by regular checkups. Because hearing losses have an environmental cause, we have a greater ability to prevent them.

According to the Hearing Conservation Amendment passed by Congress in 1982, employers must monitor the noise in a factory and, when it exceeds a certain level, are required to provide employees with hearing protection devices. They must train workers in the need for hearing conservation and must test their hearing at least once a year. They must take steps to externally reduce the levels of noise. In other words, we are now taking steps to reduce or eliminate what had always been a major cause of hearing loss—factory noise.

These efforts involve *primary* and *secondary prevention*. What about the people for whom slowness or sensory problems are *already* a fact of life? Here the key is to rearrange the environment to minimize these disabilities that cannot be cured.

Environmental psychologist Powell Lawton (1975) has spelled out some principles underlying this environment-oriented or **ecological approach** to disabilities. Lawton puts forth the following principle: The more physically impaired the older person, the more crucial the influence of the outside world. People with disabilities are vulnerable to the environment in a way the rest of us are not because we can perform competently in most settings in our society.

A simple example makes Lawton's point. The lighting in your classroom must be adequate to see the board or take notes, or you would vigorously complain. Your local restaurant would go out of business if the noise level made it impossible to hear. In other words, the environments we are exposed to in the course of living are tailored to fit or be congruent with our physical capacities. However, this fit applies to the dominant group in our society, people without disabilities, not those having trouble hearing or seeing or getting around. This brings us to Lawton's second principle: To help people with physical

expertise
Impact of having extensive experience in promoting optimal performance on tasks.

APPLICATIONS AND INTERVENTIONS

ecological approach
Approach to late-life disabilities that explores the impact of the environment on one's functioning.

In addition to specially designed housing, any environmental alteration can enhance full functioning by fostering person/environment congruence. The Golf-Xpress pictured here offers a different type of prosthetic environment, one allowing this disabled golfer to continue to enjoy an activity he has always loved.

impairments function, too, we must redesign the world to fit their capacities. This strategy is referred to as enhancing **person/environment congruence.**

According to Lawton (1975), if the environment offers too much support, it may encourage dependency. If the outside world is too complex or challenging, it may also promote incapacity. So the most appropriate environment is one that fits the person's capacities or, better yet, slightly exceeds them so the individual is pulled to function at his or her best.

These principles underlie an exciting specialty: designing housing to fit the capacities of people with disabilities. Here the idea is that the wider environment can serve the same purpose that glasses or a wheelchair does, as a constant support to compensate for an unchangeable condition. Because devices that compensate for permanent impairments are called prostheses, the specially planned housing and the suggestions for modifying private homes described below are called **prosthetic environments.**

DESIGNING HOUSING FOR THE ELDERLY.   In recent decades, researchers have been exploring how architectural design can help promote person/environment congruence. Workshops have been held, books written, and facilities planned through the collaborative efforts of architects and gerontologists. This housing for the elderly has a special goal: Through its physical design and the services it offers, it attempts to keep the older person with disabilities living as fully as possible for as long as possible. Here is a description of one nursing home planned to increase this congruence:

Set in the rolling landscape of Michigan, Peachwood Inn looks nothing like our image of a nursing home. The front lobby and reception desk resemble a fine hotel. The courtyard offers secure, beautifully landscaped areas for tranquil strolling; intimate spaces with fireplaces give warm, inviting settings for private visiting. Individually decorated bedrooms in the main building are clustered in self-contained neighborhoods, suggesting a community. The nursing stations, located centrally in each wing, resemble hotel concierge desks. The effect is to encourage the idea of ownership and individuality.

person/environment congruence
Adapting of the environment to the older person's capacities in order to enhance independence.

prosthetic environments
Environments that function as permanent supports to compensate for chronic disabilities.

4-4 The Adult Experience: A Conversation with an Architect Who Designs Housing for the Elderly

When she was in college, Sara used to visit her grandmother in a nursing home. She recalls how the staff members passed by without noticing and how the dimly lit rooms and long halls contributed to the neglect she observed. Sara was interested in design and also knew she wanted to help older people. She wanted to use architecture to promote the quality of life in old age.

Sara feels design can have a dramatic effect on people who are suffering from memory problems and sensory-motor decline. However, she is frustrated in her current job at a large architecture firm. Few new nursing homes are being built. The bottom line in constructing any health care setting is cost. The developer controls the shape of the projects. The design that looks the most architecturally appealing to the eye at age 30 or 40 may be detrimental to the person of 85. One developer who hired her firm decided that sliding glass doors should be used to set off two symmetrical wings, one for residents with dementia and one for residents who were physically impaired. While everyone complimented the firm for the beauty of its plan, because everything looked identical the residents bumped into doors or got confused and went in the wrong way. To compound the problem, each wing was painted the same color, which, while aesthetically correct, was psychologically wrong. As we will see in our discussion of dementia, contrasting colors alert people to where they are going. They help orient people to their world. The problem, Sara believes, is that designers and developers do not consider the point of view of the true clients—the older people. Without training in gerontology, they have no idea what changes to vision and hearing occur with advancing age. Sara, with her master's degree in gerontology, sees herself as the advocate in her firm for the elderly. It is a lonely job. Sometimes she can almost hear her coworkers thinking: "There she goes with her obsession again."

The space is planned with residents' physical needs in mind. To enhance vision, bright colors and contrasting hues are used. Rather than subjecting residents to the deafening din in a large dining room, the facility has small eating spaces. These cozy dining rooms are light and airy and offer intimate seating. There is a chance for residents who are physically able to cook on their own. Hallways are short and end in flared areas with seating. Another striking feature is the lack of clutter, which encourages mobility. This institution is planned to promote physical independence and serve residents' psychological and social needs (De Angelo, 1992).

Unfortunately this careful use of design is not typical in housing for the elderly (Rule, Milke, and Allen, 1992). Much housing for the elderly, though built for people with the problems this chapter describes, was designed before gerontologists appreciated the impact design could have in promoting independence (Noell, 1995–1996). As our discussion in Feature 4-4 suggests, there is resistance to building housing that fits older people's needs. So today many facilities have the flaws this observer noticed decades ago (Proppe, 1968): Facilities were poorly lit; they had long corridors without benches where an older person could rest; they were noisy, with floors and walls that amplified sound. If anything, these homes seemed designed to promote person/environment *incongruence*.

ADAPTING PRIVATE HOMES.   Most older people, even those with disabilities, do not live in special housing. They live in their own homes, often in the same place where they have lived for decades. Contrary to popular opinion, older people are the

Suggestions on How to Best Design Home Appliances to Accommodate to "the Older Eye"

Table 4-4

1. Isolate graphic information from its background by using sharply contrasting colors.
2. Combine type with graphic symbols (or pictures) in order to provide the person with several cues.
3. Use consistent color coding to facilitate comprehension.
4. Use non-reflective surfaces to eliminate glare.
5. Cluster information to be read on the appliance within a narrow space to minimize age-related problems with poorer peripheral vision.
6. If the appliance is equipped with lighting, use the gradually adjustable variety so that the person can gradually increase the illumination to an optimal level.

Source: Adapted from J. J. Pirkl, 1995, Transgenerational Design: Prolonging the American Dream, *Generations*, 19, 35.

least mobile segment of society (U.S. Senate Special Committee on Aging, 1991a). In one poll more than one-third of the older people had been living in the same place for 20 years or more (American Association for Retired Persons, 1984).

From the standpoint of physical functioning, a person's home has a major advantage. It is a familiar setting for negotiating life. The emotional advantages can be considerable, that is, the security and link to the past a home lived in for decades provides. However, visits to private homes where disabled people live show they are often deteriorated because of their age (Lawton, 1975). Simple modifications can promote person/environment congruence here, too.

To compensate for vision impairments, the home should be well lit. Overhead fixtures should be avoided, especially those with fluorescent bulbs shining down directly on a bare floor, as they magnify glare. The strategies listed in Table 4-4 will help enhance the visibility of numerals on kitchen appliances, telephones, and other devices around the home (Pirkl, 1995). To prevent accidents caused by poor vision or movement problems, furniture should be sparse, and there should be no raised floor areas. A homeowner should consider installing low-pile wall-to-wall carpet, even in areas such as the kitchen. Not only will carpeting the whole house help cut down on injuries due to falls, but also it can improve both vision and hearing. Recall that bare floors reflect light. Carpeting also absorbs sound and so drastically cuts down on background noise. If the homeowner has a hearing problem, devices can also be bought that amplify the sound of doorbells or telephones. Double-paned windows improve hearing, too, as they reduce the level of background noise.

To minimize losses of speed and strength, doors should open automatically or be light to the touch, shelves and storage places should be made easy to reach, and grab bars should be installed in places like the bathtub where falling is most likely. Faucets should be easy to turn. Controls should be at the front of the stove (Null, 1988). Knobs on appliances should not be too small or too smooth to be easily grasped (Reed, 1995).

With a bit of thought, you could probably add to this list. You also might want to think of ways your neighborhood might be redesigned to make life easier for a disabled older resident. And, drawing on the summary in Table 4-5, it might be helpful to think of some ways you *personally* can take action to increase person/environment congruence with an older relative who has the limitations this chapter describes.

Table 4-5   **Sexuality and Sensory-Motor Change: A Summary**

Function	Change	Intervention
Sexuality	Less resilient erectile system for men Lack of reinforcement, especially for women	1. Allow love-making to occur more slowly; sexual relations need to be paced. 2. Keep healthy and avoid sexually impairing medicines. 3. Work on personal and societal attitudes discouraging sexuality; stay attractive.
Vision	Poor vision in dark; enhanced sensitivity to glare	1. Use strong indirect lighting. 2. Avoid fluorescent lights. 3. Use contrasting colors in the home. 4. Take a flashlight in dimly lit places.
Hearing	High-pitched tone loss	1. Avoid any setting with background noise. 2. Speak distinctly, lower the pitch of your voice, and face the person. 3. Put wall-to-wall carpeting and double-paned windows in the house.
Taste and smell	Loss of sensitivity for non-sweet foods; impaired smell	1. Flavor foods more strongly. 2. Serve older persons fruits. 3. Smoke detectors are imperative in an older person's home.
Reaction time	Overall slowing, especially in cases requiring a series of steps or complex actions	1. Avoid high-risk, speed-oriented situations. 2. Prepare early for situations requiring speed.

KEY TERMS & CONCEPTS

sexual revolution
sexual double standard
menopause
erectile dysfunction
visual acuity
presbyopia
lens
cataract
presbycusis
reaction time
expertise
ecological approach
person/environment congruence
prosthetic environments

RECOMMENDED READINGS

Sexuality

Brecher, E. M., and Consumer Reports Book Editors. (1985). *Love, sex and aging.* Boston: Little, Brown.
> *This survey discussed in the text is enriched by fascinating case histories.*

Masters, W. H., and Johnson, V. E. (1966). *Human sexual response.* Boston: Little, Brown.
> *Masters and Johnson's book on human sexuality is a classic.*

Michael, R. T., Gagnon, J. H., Laumann, E. O., and Kolata, G. (1994). *Sex in America: A definitive survey.* Boston: Little, Brown.
> *This popular report of a national survey describing Americans' sexual practices is highly recommended.*

Compensating for Sensory-Motor Change

Bush-Brown, A., and Davis, D. (1992). *Hospitable design for health care and senior communities.* New York: Van Nostrand Reinhold.
> *This beautifully illustrated book describes examples of architectural design for elderly persons.*

Generations (Spring 1995). Technology and aging: Developing and marketing new products for older people. Vol. *19.*
> *The whole issue of this journal is devoted to promoting person/environment congruence through the use of environmental design*

Disease, Disability, and Health Care

Chapter Outline

Mabel began to feel much older six years ago. She developed painful arthritis. Opening doors was a problem, as was grasping cabinet doors. Her heart was not pumping efficiently. Her ankles were swollen. She gasped and sweated when she exerted herself. Still, she was able to live in her four-bedroom home. Then Mabel fell and hurt her back. Her doctor suggested an operation to remove part of the bone in the spine. Unfortunately the surgery did not help much. Mabel never fully recovered. A year later, on the way to the kitchen, she brushed against a couch and broke another bone. Mabel was frightened. She has no children. Her husband had died of a heart attack several decades before. According to Mabel: "What could I do but enter a nursing home?"

Today, at age 86, Mabel can still get from her bed to the toilet. With effort and creative strategies, she dresses herself. She puts her clothes on the side of her bed so she does not have to walk to the closet. She wears pullovers without buttons instead of dresses. Other problems have developed in recent years. She has needed hip replacement surgery. She wears sunglasses because the light hurts her eyes. Mabel is typical of millions of older people coping with age-related chronic disease.

CHRONIC DISEASE

No matter how much we exercise or watch our diet, unless we die suddenly we will become acquainted with *chronic disease*, the type of enduring illness that often cannot be cured. Sometimes this encounter will last a few weeks; sometimes, as in Mabel's situation, it will last years. Chronic disease accounts for more than three-fourths of all deaths in the United States and other developed countries (U.S. Senate Special Committee on Aging, 1991a). It is our nation's major category of health problem, costing billions of dollars in doctor visits, in days off work, in home and nursing home care. In this chapter, we focus on this age-related enemy in depth.

Disability and Chronic Disease

As Feature 5-1 on p. 128 shows, young adults suffer from chronic illness. However, as we know, the most striking characteristic of this type of disease is its association with advancing age. Recall from Chapter 3 how the frequency of almost every chronic condition increases in older age groups. By their eighties, most people have several chronic diseases.

Figure 5-1, listing the 10 most common chronic illnesses among the elderly, highlights another fact. Many common age-related chronic conditions are not life-threatening. They limit our ability to function in the world. In other words, as we can see in our interview and Feature 5-1, as well as earlier in this book, with chronic illness the enemy is not just death. It is also disability.

Luckily only a minority of people with chronic illnesses are disabled. Of the four out of five Americans over age 65 who said they suffered from a chronic condition in 1989, only about one in six reported that their illness impaired their life to any degree. A much smaller fraction were severely incapacitated, bedridden, or housebound by chronic disease (U.S. Senate Special Committee on Aging, 1991a).

Unfortunately the rate of disabilities does increase in tandem with the age-related rise in disease. Over age 85, more than one in three people reports problems with at least one activity basic to living, such as dressing, bathing, or getting to the toilet without help (U.S. Senate Special Committee on Aging, 1991a).

So, while they are linked, chronic disease is not the same as disability, and it is this behavioral measure of illness that is most important in determining the quality of life. This crucial index of illness is called **functional impairment.**

functional impairment
Gerontological term for disability.

Functional impairment is such an important measure of health in the elderly that various scales have been devised to assess it. These measures, which explore everything

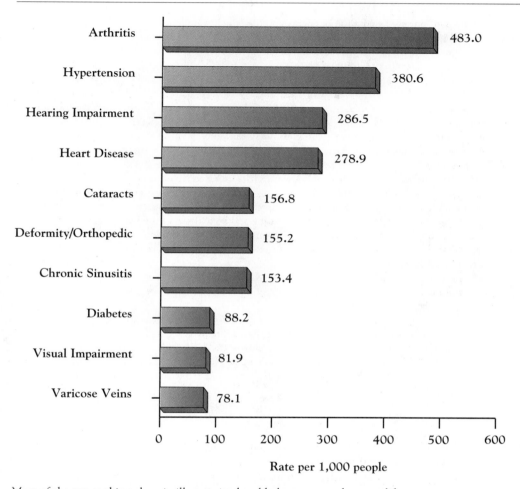

Rate per 1,000 people

Most of the top-ranking chronic illnesses in the elderly are not a threat to life.

Source: U.S. Senate Special Committee on Aging, 1991, *Aging America: Trends and Projections*, Washington, DC: Author.

from walking to working, from communicating with others to caring for oneself, catalog the devastation wreaked by this enemy of our older years (deBruin, deWitte, Stevens, and Diederiks, 1992).

LIVING LONGER SICKER, THE PRICE OF THE LIFE-EXPECTANCY REVOLUTION?   While everyone wants to live to be 80 or 90, far fewer of us would vote to spend these extra years suffering from the disabilities that can make life more a burden than a gift. When we look at the growth of these problems in advanced old age, the clear implication is that our life-expectancy progress may be a double-edged sword. By enabling so many people to live to advanced old age, haven't we been purchasing years suffering from disabilities, not independent life?

5-1 The Adult Experience: Coping with Crohn's Disease

Janice is an intense person, full of energy and life. Having graduated from college with honors and just begun social work school, Janice fits the image of a young adult at the brink of her career. The ill-fitting part of the image is that Janice is 38. Janice has had to take life slowly. She suffers from Crohn's disease.

Crohn's disease is a hereditary illness involving the inflammation and ulceration, or wearing away, of the intestinal wall. To Janice, the symptoms—diarrhea, weakness, and cramping—were known from an early age. Janice's aunt, a cousin, and her mother all have the illness. In the Sulty family, this disease is a shared affair. Janice first noticed the signs at age 15, but was reluctant to worry her mother. A few weeks later, Janice felt ill, ran to the ladies' room at school, vomited blood, and was rushed to the hospital, where she stayed for the next four months.

Crohn's disease often is not fatal. However, it requires constant monitoring and immediate action when a potentially life-threatening event occurs. The patient must avoid high-fiber foods and go on a liquid diet when symptoms begin. The treatment for flare-ups is large doses of steroids, which prevent further swelling and breakdown of the intestinal wall. If the bleeding and diarrhea cannot be controlled, one must resort to surgery to remove part of the large intestine (a colostomy) or, in severe situations, surgery to remove the whole large intestine (an ileostomy).

Janice's case is unusually severe. After months in the hospital on a diet of fluids and high doses of medication, the bleeding never stopped. At age 16 Janice begged for an ileostomy, and it was done.

What followed were years of remissions, complications, and recurrent bouts with disease. After missing her junior year of high school, Janice finally graduated, went to college, and functioned fairly well, but still needed to take medication. Steroids cause the body to retain water. Janice's body was bloated; her face looked like a full moon. She needed different-sized clothes from day to day. These were minor irritants compared to what occurred during finals her sophomore year. Janice woke up and saw two alarm clocks. She had a terrible headache

---

tertiary prevention
Efforts to control illness once an individual suffers from a disease.

morbidity
Medical term for illness.

active life expectancy
Average disease- and disability-free life expectancy.

compression of morbidity hypothesis
Fries's hypothesis that due to the lifestyle movement people are living healthy, close to the maximum life span.

This idea becomes more probable when we consider that medical advances mainly involve **tertiary prevention,** intervening after disease has struck. They postpone death in the face of existing illness, rather than increasing our years of health. Since as we age the *number* of chronic diseases steadily accumulates, it is no wonder many experts feel extended **morbidity** (illness) is the price of inching so many people close to the limit of human life (Manton and Suzman, 1992; Verbrugge, 1989, 1990).

There is a more optimistic view. Because the new emphasis on fitness involves *primary* and *secondary prevention,* it should be pushing back the onset of disease. Therefore, James Fries (1990) argues, the lifestyle revolution has extended **active life expectancy,** our years of healthy life. Furthermore, in Fries's opinion, we are at the brink of witnessing an historic *compression of morbidity:* people living longer healthy, almost until the limit of human life.

The truth lies in between. While the issue is complex (Rogers, Rogers, and Belanger, 1990), researchers calculate that active life expectancy has been increasing along with our total length of life. However, because the ratio of disability-free to illness years is constant, *both* years of morbidity and years of health are increasing as a result of our recent longevity gains (Branch et. al, 1991).

Fries's **compression of morbidity hypothesis** assumes that we are all on the same train headed toward maximum life expectancy. It omits the most important characteristic of physical aging and illness—variability from person to person and group to group.

and could not get out of bed. The doctor rushed her to the hospital, diagnosing a brain tumor. It took weeks to discover that the water-retaining effect of the medicine had extended to the brain. Copious amounts of spinal fluid were being produced, causing intense cerebral pressure. Spinal taps to drain the fluid were not effective. The headaches continued, and Janice's eyes seemed permanently crossed. She had to drop out of college. She was as familiar with the hospital as her home. Today a permanent shunt resides in Janice's neck, draining fluid to the abdomen.

Since then, there have been no more operations. However, periodically, the illness flares up. Sometimes it is a blockage, requiring her to return to a fluid diet and increase her medications. On those days, Janice goes through her closet to pick out "whatever fits." Sometimes it is cramping from something she ate. Sometimes the main symptom is fatigue. As is true of people with chronic illnesses that may be fatal, death haunts her. There is only so much of the small intestine that can be removed. Still, Janice is optimistic and anxious to get on with life. She appreciates her loving family, her close friendships, her new career: "Every day I wake up and feel healthy is a gift."

In this chapter, we will be discussing the chronic conditions related to age, illnesses that tend to disable people gradually as they progress. Not every chronic illness is age-related or fits this picture of steady decline. Chronic illness—at any age—may follow a constant course. A dramatic event, such as a stroke or heart attack or spinal cord injury, may be followed by some improvement and then stability, often with deficits that persist. Crohn's disease follows the "relapsing episodic pattern," one that fits many chronic diseases that affect people earlier in life. People who suffer from young-adult conditions, such as asthma or multiple sclerosis, have periods of normality punctuated by unpredictable flare-ups of disease. They are not always suffering or threatened by death. However, they are always vigilant, wondering when illness might strike again.

Two markers that shape our illness journey are gender and socioeconomic status (Maddox and Clark, 1992).

Gender, Socioeconomic Status, and Chronic Disease

WOMEN, DISEASE, AND DISABILITY.   Our first blow to the compression of morbidity hypothesis comes from looking at the fate of the group likely to travel farthest on the train. While men die sooner from chronic illness, women suffer more years of disability as they approach the upper limits of life (Verbrugge, 1989, 1990).

The main cause is the chronic diseases women are prone to suffer with age. As we saw in Chapter 3, life-threatening fatal illnesses, such as heart disease, enter men's lives earlier. Women are more likely to develop non-fatal conditions that limit functioning, such as osteoporosis and osteoarthritis (Jette, Branch, and Berlin, 1990; Kosorok, Omenn, Diehr, Koepsell, and Patrick, 1992).

Even when they have potentially fatal illnesses, such as heart disease and cancer, women are more likely to live on disabled than to die (Manton, 1990). Women have higher rates of angina, the long-term disabling form of heart disease, than men. When they traced the lives of males and females hospitalized with angina, Jennie Nickel and Thomas Chirikos (1990) found that even here the women were prone to live on suffering impairments in their ability to negotiate life.

It is no surprise that more years of disability are the price women pay for living to their eighties and beyond. However, the phase "living sicker" applies to women *throughout their adult years*. Women visit doctors more often. They report more physical complaints and are more frequently confined by illness to bed. On a variety of measures

This photo of a medical waiting room brings home the fact that women tend to visit doctors more frequently than men. Is the dramatic excess of women pictured here due to the fact that females have more illness, or to the various forces that make it more difficult for men to visit this clinic when they are ill?

of morbidity at every point in adulthood, they do worse (Gijsbers Van Wijk, Kolk, Van den Bosch, and Van den Hoogen, 1992).

While these higher rates are partly due to the reproductive problems and conditions, such as pregnancy and menopausal disorders, that punctuate women's lives, they also seem to be caused by a different orientation to health. Women are more likely to admit illness, to be sensitive to their physical state, to seek professional help early on (Verbrugge, 1989, 1990). In one typical example, while older men were more likely to be hospitalized, elderly women visited the doctor more frequently for preventative visits and minor care (Thomas and Kelman, 1990). Do women's higher illness rates reflect differences in *illness-related behavior* or a truly higher rate of disease? Or perhaps this tendency to be more sensitive to their bodies and take action more quickly in the face of illness contributes to women's life expectancy advantage in itself.

THE DISADVANTAGED, DISEASE, AND DISABILITY.   If the saying that applies to women is "living longer sicker," the phrase that applies to the poor and less educated is "dying sooner, living more ill." Unfortunately another blow to the compression of morbidity hypothesis is that this aging ideal tends to fit a select group, people who are upper-middle-class. Low education and income, the two commonly used indexes of socioeconomic status (SES) described in Chapter 1, were major risk factors for premature illness and death in the Alameda Study. This same connection between social class and mortality and morbidity is not confined to the United States. In every country in the world, the poor have much higher morbidity and mortality rates than people who are affluent (Kaplan, 1992).

The relationship family income in particular has to morbidity and disability is dramatically revealed in Figure 5-2. These statistics are taken from the 1993 National

Percentage of Americans Reporting They Were Either Limited in an Activity Due to Chronic Illness or in Fair or Poor Health, by Family Income, 1993

Figure 5-2

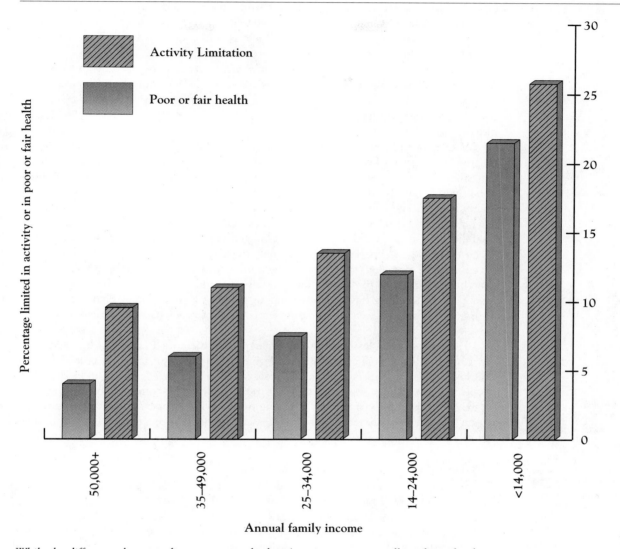

While the differences between the very poor and other Americans are especially striking, family earnings, in general, have a clear relationship to physical health. As we ascend the income rungs, a smaller percentage of Americans report being disabled by illness or in fair or poor health.

Source: National Center for Health Statistics, 1995, *Health, United States, 1994*, Hyattsville, MD, Public Health Service. Information adapted from Tables 62 and 63.

Health Interview Survey, a regular government poll of the health status of U.S. adults. Notice that one-fourth of adults with a family income under $14,000 per year report being disabled by chronic disease; one-fifth are in fair or poor health. For people earning 50,000 a year, the illness rates are much lower—9.7 and 3.9 percent.

Is there a time of life when the social class differences in health are most pronounced? To answer this question, James House and his University of Michigan colleagues decided to break down similar illness/income statistics from an earlier National Health Interview Survey by age. The researchers predicted that social class differences in morbidity should be widest in middle-age and early later life. In youth, age-related illnesses would not have had time to develop. As people reach the upper ends of life and the biological press toward illness affects everyone, the SES variations in disease should converge.

They were correct. The differences in health between the affluent and the poor were especially striking at ages 45–65 (House et al., 1992). Moreover, because such a high percentage of people in the lowest income group reported being disabled by chronic diseases during their middle years, among the poor we might really call old-age illnesses diseases of midlife.

Social class remains a powerful predictor of disability during our older years. When George Maddox and Daniel Clark (1992) traced the lives of Social Security recipients first studied in their sixties, not only were the poor initially more prone to functional impairments, but also during the next decade this group suffered sharper losses in their ability to negotiate life.

House and his colleagues believe that the reason SES is so closely linked to disability is that every risk factor for age-related chronic conditions from having fewer social contacts, to experiencing emotional stress, to being overweight, to drinking to excess is more prevalent in lower socioeconomic groups. The lifestyle revolution may even have heightened the association between SES and disease. Since the most dramatic reductions in smoking have occurred among middle-class people, as Figure 5-3 shows, during the past few decades smoking, especially for women, has become more of a "blue-collar" practice.

However, social class is a summary marker that includes a jumble of biological and environmental factors. The statistics in Figure 5-2 are certain to partly reflect the fact that low SES is the *consequence*, not the cause, of poor health. As we saw in Feature 5-1, people who are sick are less likely to finish their education, are often unable to work, and so are more likely to *become poor*. Focusing on lifestyle neglects another environmental reason why the poor are more prone to disease. Poor people are more likely to suffer from age-related illnesses because they have worse access to medical care.

Medical Care for Chronic Disease

Our first impulse is to imagine that the decision to see a doctor is prompted by need, that is, feeling sick. **Need factors** are only one influence that shapes our choice to get care. According to a widely used framework (Andersen and Newman, 1973), a second category is **predisposing factors,** attitudes we have before illness strikes. As we saw with women, values such as a belief in medicine and a sensitivity to one's physical state influence the decision to seek a doctor's help. The third category of influence is **enabling factors,** real-world barriers to getting care. A person will not visit a clinic if he does not know it exists. He will be less likely to get help for his symptoms if transportation to the doctor is not available, or if the nearest medical facility is many miles away, or if he will lose his job if he takes off from work. In order to visit a doctor, people must be able to financially afford to get the care they need.

The United States is the only advanced industrialized country apart from South Africa without universal paid-for medical care. In our country, health care is financed by personal funds plus private and public insurance. Private insurance is almost exclusively employment-related and not available at many jobs. Public insurance programs include **Medicaid,** the health care system for the poor, and **Medicare,** the universal health care system for the elderly.

need factors
Impact of one's actual physical state on the decision to seek medical help.

predisposing factors
Impact of one's attitude toward medical help-seeking on the decision to seek medical help.

enabling factors
Impact of one's access to medical care on the decision to seek medical help.

Medicaid
Health care system funded jointly by the federal government and the states in which people below a certain income level get free or reduced-cost health care.

Medicare
Universal paid-for-health care for the elderly funded by the federal government.

Prevalence of Cigarette Smoking by Occupation and Gender Among Individuals over Age 20, in 1970, 1978–1980, and 1985

Figure 5-3

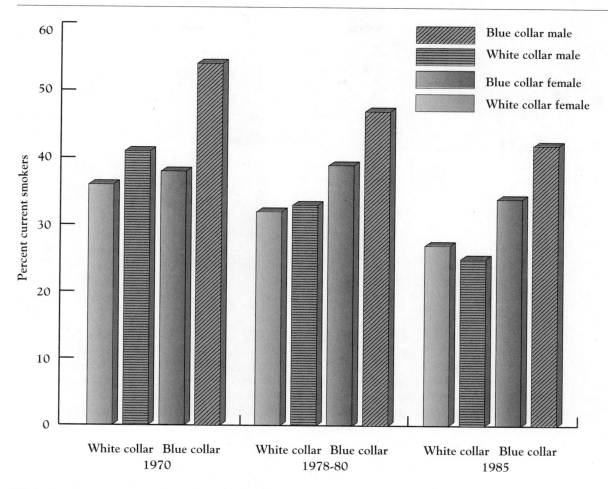

Legend:
- Blue collar male
- White collar male
- Blue collar female
- White collar female

Y-axis: Percent current smokers

White collar Blue collar
1970

White collar Blue collar
1978-80

White collar Blue collar
1985

While overall the number of smokers has declined, the exception is blue-collar (working-class) women, whose smoking rates in 1985 were essentially the same as in 1970.

Source: U.S. Department of Health and Human Services, 1989, Reducing the Health Consequences of Smoking: Twenty-Five Years of Progress: A Report of the Surgeon General: Executive Summary, Rockville, MD: Author.

Each of these public programs contains gaps. As we will see later in the chapter, the problem with Medicare is that it only covers acute conditions, not the ongoing help older people with disabilities need to cope with daily life. Furthermore, its limited coverage and deductibles mean older people must pay out of pocket for a portion of their care. For this reason, most well-off elderly often have private insurance in addition to Medicare. Poor elderly are often on Medicaid.

Medicaid does pay generously for care. However, contrary to popular opinion, this crucial program for the poor does not insure that everyone in need of care receives access to medical services. Because eligibility policies differ from state to state, large groups of

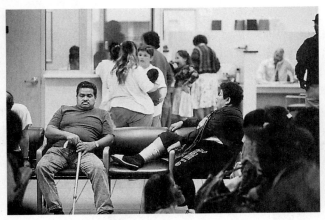

These photos illustrate why poor people may tend to put off visiting a doctor as well as receive more inadequate care when they go for help. Imagine contemplating the thought of waiting for hours at this hectic, unpleasant city hospital clinic when you have symptoms, or are the harried doctor in the background in photo A who has to diagnose and treat far too many patients that day. Contrast this with the inviting quiet of the private pediatric waiting room in photo B where it seems as if the doctor will have the leisure to give each patient the full attention that she needs.

Americans *living under the poverty line* are excluded from Medicaid. These people, often young adults without children, African Americans and Hispanic Americans, and working-class families earning less than $24,000 per year make up the estimated 40 million Americans with no health insurance (National Center for Health Statistics, 1995).

People without health insurance, and those who are underinsured, use less medical care, even though, being poorer, their health is usually worse. They tend to visit a doctor or, more likely, the hospital emergency room in a crisis, when their symptoms have progressed to a more serious, less treatable stage (Schlesinger, 1989). In addition, while the Medicaid program does provide access to a doctor, it does not insure high-quality care. Many physicians do not accept Medicaid. Because some studies suggest that those who do may offer poorer services, this, too, may prevent poor people from receiving the best care (Schlesinger, 1989).

THE POOR, MINORITIES, AND PHYSICIANS. This unequal access may partly explain why the poor and minorities tend to visit doctors later in the course of illness and so have higher mortality rates in the face of chronic disease (Manton, Patrick, and Johnson, 1989; U.S. Department of Health and Human Services, 1990b, 1991). The difference is especially revealing when we look at breast cancer, an illness in which early detection is crucial. When Barbara Wells and John Horn (1992) used census tracts to code for income in metropolitan Atlanta, San Francisco, and Detroit, they found that in each city women of lower SES and African Americans were more likely to visit a doctor when their disease was at a more invasive, less curable stage than were upper-middle-class whites.

In this study, the racial differences in diagnosis were completely accounted for by socioeconomic class. Upper-middle-class women, both white and black, were equally prone to have their cancers diagnosed at the early, "in situ" stage. Another study suggested that, even controlling for income, African Americans may still be less prone to go for medical care. In this national telephone survey, the average annual number of visits to a physician reported by African Americans was 3.4, compared to the 4.4 visits reported by whites, a difference we might expect given the impact income has on access

Concern	White, %	Black %
Did not inquire sufficiently about pain	9.0	23.3
Did not tell how long it takes for medicine to work	31.6	45.0
Did not explain seriousness of illness or injury	27.5	44.2
Did not discuss test or examination findings	14.0	22.7
Hospitalized too short a time	7.2	18.9
Did not discuss prevention	80.6	67.7
Did not spend enough time during last ambulatory visit	5.2	7.0
Treated roughly	1.7	1.4

Patients' Perception of the Care Provided During an Ambulatory Visit for a New Illness, by Race — Table 5-1

In this national telephone survey, in most areas African Americans were significantly more likely to report being dissatisfied with their medical care than were whites.

Source: Blendon, Aiken, Freeman, and Corey, "Access to medical care for black and white Americans", *JAMA*, 261, 278–281, Copyright 1989, American Medical Association.

to medical care. Even after taking income, health insurance, and age into account, however, African Americans still were less likely to have seen a physician within the past year (Blendon, Aiken, Freeman, and Cory, 1989).

A variety of enabling and predisposing factors—from fewer doctors in the neighborhood (medically underserved areas are more often those with large minority populations), to cultural values that accept being sick as a "normal fact of life," to a lack of awareness of the serious consequences of the symptoms of disease—may explain this underuse in the face of what should be greater need (Schlesinger, 1989). However, as Table 5-1 shows, even when the African Americans in this study did get help, they were more dissatisfied with the care they received, more prone both to report that the doctor did not explain their illness fully, and more likely to believe that they had been hospitalized for too short a time.

These answers are not broken down by income. So they might reflect the impact of SES, not race, on feelings about care. They are subjective impressions. Is there objective evidence of racial differences in the quality of medical care?

While no study proves these differences exist, the following survey offers troubling hints: When researchers at the Harvard School of Public Health examined the rates of coronary bypass surgery and coronary angiography and angioplasty (three standard treatments for atherosclerotic heart disease) at Massachusetts hospitals during 1985, even after controlling for age, income, insurance, and other diagnoses, they found that the first two procedures were performed more often on whites (Wennecker and Epstein 1989).

THE ELDERLY AND PHYSICIANS.   We might think that not a hint of bias could apply to that other category of minority, the elderly. As Figure 5-4 shows, people over 65 are the most frequent consumers of medical care. They are more knowledgeable consumers, too. Middle-aged and elderly people engage in more health-oriented strategies, such as watching their diet. They are more health-interested and health-aware. They even report visiting the doctor for checkups more often than younger adults (Leventhal, Leventhal, and Schaefer, 1992).

Figure 5-4

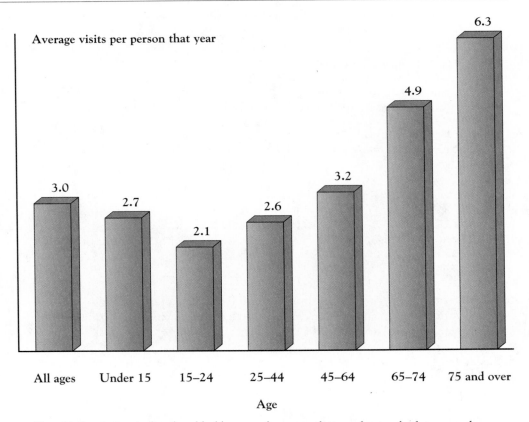

Average visits per person that year

All ages	Under 15	15–24	25–44	45–64	65–74	75 and over
3.0	2.7	2.1	2.6	3.2	4.9	6.3

Age

The elderly—in particular, the old-old—see a doctor much more frequently than any other group.

Source: U.S. Department of Health and Human Services, 1994, *National Health Care Survey, 1994,* Atlanta, Centers for Disease Control and Prevention.

However, older people also complain that doctors give them short shrift. A study conducted by researchers at the Rand Corporation during the 1970s lent these observations scientific weight (Kane, Solomon, Beck, Keeler, and Kane, 1981).

Physicians in private practice were asked to record the amount of time they spent with each of their patients over a number of days. These figures were then looked at as a function of the person's age. The researchers predicted that, because people over 65 were most likely to be seriously ill, they would be given the most attention. Surely doctors would need to devote more effort to examining their elderly patients. They would have to spend more time explaining the complicated treatments needed to manage chronic disease.

Instead, the reverse was true. Comparing people 45–54, 55–64, and over 65, they found relative stability in the average time spent with the two middle-aged groups and significantly lower time spent with the oldest group. This was true of office, hospital, and nursing home visits and of all seven medical specialties the researchers examined.

Our immediate impulse is to assume that these findings show that ageism is rampant among doctors. Before assigning all blame to physicians, let's look at the contribution the partner in this relationship, the patient, makes. Because the elderly have a relatively positive view of their health (Idler, 1993), they may minimize their complaints when they see the doctor. Being brought up in an era when it was inappropriate to question authority, this cohort of old-old people may be less willing to "bother" their physician with questions relating to their health (Haug, 1981). While older people are sensitive to serious symptoms, several studies suggest that they are likely to pass off less serious aches and pains as "normal at my age" (Leventhal et al., 1992). Furthermore, some doctors may avoid treating older patients due to simple lack of knowledge. Their training has not equipped them adequately to deal with the functional disabilities of old age.

As I suggested earlier, medicine has traditionally emphasized lifesaving cures, dramatic procedures used to help people recover from serious disease. The long-term chronic conditions older people have require a different approach. Ongoing management is needed in dealing with these illnesses, regularly monitoring the problem, and increasing functional abilities given an unchangeable diagnosis, an illness that never goes away (Kart, Metress, and Metress, 1992).

Effectively treating the elderly requires doctors to widen their focus from attacking disease to waging war against disability. This means no longer worrying just about life-threatening illnesses, such as cancer and heart disease, but seeing conditions people do not die from as important (Verbrugge, 1989, 1990). Their treatments have to shift. Attacking disability involves using techniques outside the doctor's traditional realm, such as exercise, physical therapy, nutrition, and psychological help. So, to be helpful to their disabled patients, physicians have to work collaboratively, consulting with social workers, dietitians, and physical therapists. They must see these lower-status health care workers as having important contributions to make. In other words, treating older people with multiple chronic illnesses requires a different model of care.

When we pinpoint exactly when older people heavily utilize doctors, the need for this disability-oriented training becomes clear. In one longitudinal national survey of older adults, it was changes in functional status that were most apt to propel a flurry of visits for medical care (Stump, Johnson, and Wolinsky, 1995).

The medical care in the United States is widely viewed as our best hope for defying death in the face of disease. This fact was vividly brought home to the world when in 1980 the Shah of Iran sought treatment for cancer in New York. However, our discussion shows that much needs to be done in assuring high-quality medical care to *all Americans* with chronic disease. The first requirement is a system that will allow everyone access to medical care. In addition to being able to pay for visits to a doctor, enabling factors, such as putting more health care providers in medically underserved communities, are needed, as is offering transportation for ill people who cannot get to a physician's office on their own.

APPLICATIONS AND INTERVENTIONS

Equally important is working with the predisposing factors that make the poor and minorities less likely to seek early care. In one study conducted in an inner-city Chicago neighborhood, while African Americans were more likely to use the hospital emergency room, due to language barriers Mexican Americans often did not seek out *any* medical care when they were ill (Lewin-Epstein, 1991). While not the total answer, one solution is to train more health care providers of different ethnic groups. Minority physicians are more likely to practice in inner-city neighborhoods (Schlesinger, 1989). They can speak the same language and communicate the importance of early detection to the patients in their care. However, as Figure 5-5 shows, while the fraction of minority students in medical school has increased in recent decades, much of the rise has been due to an

Figure 5-5

Minority Students Among Total Enrollment in U.S. Schools of Allopathic Medicine, 1971 through 1988

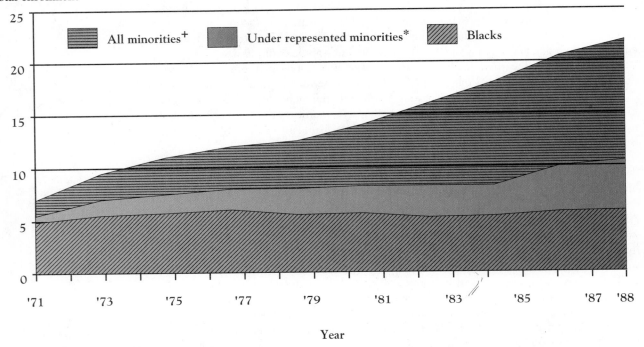

Percent of
total enrollment

Legend: All minorities[+] Under represented minorities[*] Blacks

Year

†Steep increase in total enrollment reflects escalating numbers of Asian-American medical students
*Hispanic Americans and Native Americans

Total minority enrollment in medical schools increased dramatically over this period. However, the fraction of African-American medical students remained constant at about 5 percent. Hispanic-American representation increased slightly to 5.5 percent.

Source: U.S. Department of Health and Human Services, 1990, *Health Status of the Disadvantaged, Chartbook, 1990*, Washington DC: U.S. Government Printing Office.

influx of Asian Americans. The percentage of Hispanic-American medical students has only risen slightly. The number of African Americans has remained stable over the years. Clearly, in erasing this potential barrier to visiting a physician, we have far to go.

More progress has been made in correcting inequities involving older adults. Within the past two decades, the medical profession has developed training programs that address the needs of the population suffering from disabling chronic disease, the elderly. As recently as 1976, only 15 medical schools offered separate courses on aging (Kane et al., 1981). Today almost every medical school offers some training in the special

This young doctor is still very much in the minority. The percentage of African-American physicians has barely increased in the past few decades.

problems of older adults. In 1987, a licensing examination was developed for our nation's youngest medical specialty, **geriatric medicine.**

Specialists in geriatric medicine devote themselves to the medical problems of older adults. They know that in old age disease can present itself differently, that the symptom of a heart attack in an 80-year-old patient may be mental confusion or indigestion, not pain. They understand what is normal physically at 80 and so are careful not to pass off treatable illnesses as normal aging or read pathology into normal age changes. They are committed to treating disability and sharing their authority with other health care professionals. As Feature 5-2 describes, often they work as part of a geriatric team at a hospital or clinic.

geriatric medicine
Branch of medicine specializing in the problems of elderly people.

Do geriatric teams help reduce disabilities? A review of four studies evaluating this new approach suggests yes. While in one study being assigned to a geriatric team made no difference to subsequent health (Kerski, Drinka, Carnes, Golob, and Craig, 1987), in three others it had a positive impact. Compared to groups given standard medical care, elderly patients assigned to geriatric teams had lower mortality, fewer hospitalizations and nursing home placements, or higher morale and functional health at a later point (Rubinstein et al., 1984; Yeo, Ingram, Skurnick, and Crapo, 1987).

Geriatric teams serve only a tiny fraction of older people. Most older adults with functional impairments combine visits to the doctor with the continual emotional and environmental adjustments that need to be made in order to live as fully as possible in the face of disabling chronic disease. As we saw in our interviews in this chapter, they carefully plan around their illness, plotting when to go out and how best to get around. They investigate what devices exist to make their lives easier and how they can fit their home to their new capacities (see Chapter 4). Their main support is family members, who provide most of the care of our nation's ill and infirm. In the rest of this chapter, we focus on the main **formal caregiving supports** available to these millions of disabled Americans and the families struggling with their care.

formal care-giving supports
Community services to help disabled people and care-giving families.

DEALING WITH DISABILITY

As we saw in Chapter 3, functional impairments can be helped by strategies such as exercise (Kiyak and Borson, 1992). Having positive family relationships is important. Enhancing *self-efficacy* is associated with lower mortality in the face of disabling disease (Roberto, 1992; Rodin and McAvay, 1992). Equally crucial is the wider environment. Mrs. Jones's house is at the top of a steep hill and to get to the front door requires

At medical school, James felt uncomfortable. Being a "people person," he was turned off by the emphasis on organs and on the analysis of lab values, and by the neglect of the human being. He disliked the stress on memorizing, on becoming proficient in a narrow speciality. He was interested in social policy and felt more at home with philosophy and history. James considered dropping out and going to law school, but decided to complete his training: "I felt I could always find work with a medical degree." Geriatrics seemed to fit his interests best.

According to James, because geriatrics is so different, it attracts both the best and the worst medical graduates. The dominant trend in medicine is to focus on single pieces of the person, to master a single operation or devote one's life to being an authority on one organ part. Geriatrics is holistic and process-oriented: You treat the total person and pay attention to the relationship. You consider the overall context within which care occurs. The fact that there is no body of knowledge easily measured by multiple-choice tests disturbs many doctors: "There is little support in a reductionist world for what it is we do." Another problem is the lack of a well-defined role for people who specialize in this field. Being a geriatrician might mean working in a nursing home, or doing research, or going out in the community as the head of a geriatric team.

When James took a geriatric fellowship involving community care, he realized another reason why geriatrics will never have broad appeal. The team approach is frustrating. James hated having every medical decision come under scrutiny. He felt threatened when social workers continually questioned what he did. He also understood that he wanted more from his career than doing only patient care. At the same time, this experience convinced him that, in his words, "the way traditional medicine is practiced offers a warped view. Sure, a patient will comply with medicines in the hospital. When you go into the person's home, you see what the obstacles to compliance are. By teaching only what to prescribe, we miss the boat. We lecture about the anatomy of the heart, not the process of care. We teach what is rationally right, not what's good for the patient. The real truth is in ADL (how the person functions), not hematocrit or coronary status. A person is more than a number on a blood pressure machine."

James's next step was to do a research fellowship, training he hoped would prepare him for an academic career. His research, involving analyzing large sets of data, on the surface was the farthest point from direct patient care. However, James's interest remained the same: "This young man sublimating his anger into the world of research wanted to get a window on the doctor/patient relationship, to demonstrate how medicine is failing older adults." When he collected data on sleeping pill prescriptions from pharmacies throughout the state, James found that physicians were overprescribing sleeping pills to their older patients, putting them at risk for toxic reactions and for falls and confusion.

Today James conducts research full-time. He has a job at a prestigious medical school. He makes a decent salary and does some clinical work consulting to the psychiatry staff. He does not feel at home. The institution has no interest in training geriatric physicians. His colleagues are puzzled at what he does: "Geriatrics is not where the money is in medicine. It is not the stuff of winning a Nobel Prize." James wants to teach and to get back to treating people part-time. This is why he is considering an offer at a school that lacks the same status, but where he will be appreciated. The position is for a geriatric physician to do 50 percent research and 50 percent teaching and patient care. James feels excited by the chance to train students because he believes the geriatric approach is right, not just for older people, but also for people of every age. He evens finds some critics beginning to admit that he might be correct. Recently, to his surprise, a surgeon colleague asked James to recommend a geriatric physician for his 90-year-old mother.

Out of the most loving impulses, this devoted son may be producing excess disabilities in his father by taking over this activity that the older man might be able to manage on his own.

climbing steps. So, though she only has some problems walking, she finds herself housebound, unable to go out. Your grandmother is having more trouble cooking and shopping, so your mother takes her in. Soon she is much weaker, unable to leave the house. From the purest motives, your mother has "artificially created" your grandmother's disability by taking over her life.

It is natural for the most loving person to fall into the trap of doing too much. Who doesn't want to make life as easy as possible for an ill loved one? Who wouldn't rush to help when your father is struggling to feed or dress himself? The temptation to take total care is just as strong in nursing homes. Staff members have no idea of residents' real potential. It is easier to dress or feed the disabled elderly in their care than to wait for them to perform these tasks on their own. When, as we saw in our interview with the behaviorist in Chapter 2, crucial reinforcers, such as social contact, occur only when a person is being given help (Baltes and Werner-Wahl, 1992), it is no wonder that artificially induced disabilities are such a risk among the old. Gerontologists have a name for these disabilities that do not need to be there—**excess disabilities.**

As we learned in Chapter 4, excess disabilities tend to occur whenever there is a mismatch between the person's capacities and the environment. So this lack of *person/environment congruence* may happen simply when an older adult is in a setting that offers too much care. When older people have trouble handling life and families cannot care for them, the knee-jerk reaction is to think of a nursing home. But a nursing home may not be needed. As the studies evaluating outpatient geriatric team care show, some nursing home residents do not have to be in an institution. They could live in the community if appropriate alternatives were available or if they took advantage of those that exist. In one project, people at risk of nursing home placement called a special

excess disabilities
Excessive impairment beyond what is necessary on the basis of a person's medical state.

telephone number. Through the use of community resources, the team operating the project was able to keep 25 to 30 percent of these callers at home (Hodgson and Quinn, 1980).

As suggested earlier, disabilities are sometimes reversible. They can improve. When Thomas Chirikos and Gilbert Nestel (1985) followed several thousand middle-aged men over 15 years, while the common pattern was greater loss, the reverse also occurred. More than 9 percent of the men who had problems stooping or kneeling in 1976 did not have the same trouble in 1981. More than 8 percent found their difficulty standing improved. The fear is that putting people in nursing homes when they have these problems may make recovery *less possible* because, as we just saw, the nursing home setting may encourage incapacity, not an independent life.

Nursing home care is expensive, costing thousands of dollars a year. Medicare covers *only 1 percent* of the cost. The Medicare system covers only acute care. Once care is labeled as custodial, or chronic, Medicare will not pay. Although nursing home insurance does exist, it is too expensive for many older adults. Qualifying for this type of insurance can be hard. Companies impose numerous eligibility restrictions. They may weed out anyone with disabilities or even deny coverage if a person answers yes to any health question. Policies have numerous "exceptions" or provide limited coverage for certain types of nursing home care.

This means that older people who are not defined as poor are forced to shoulder the huge economic burden. Often, though not as frequently as had been thought (Liu and Manton, 1991), they begin by paying the nursing home fees privately. When their savings are gone, they become eligible for Medicaid, which does cover custodial care. As Figure 5-6 shows, the surprising statistic is that among the elderly the highest fraction of the out-of-pocket health care dollar goes not to hospitals or doctors, but to nursing homes (U.S. Senate Special Committee on Aging, 1991a). So, once a person is in a nursing home, leaving can be difficult for financial reasons alone (Greene and Ondrich, 1990).

Nursing home care puts a economic burden on us all. The Medicaid bill for nursing homes, paid for by our taxes, was $20.7 billion in 1989 (U.S. Senate Special Committee on Aging, 1991a).

This means that from the perspective of the older person and society we need options that will keep people outside of institutions when they have some functional impairments, but do not need to be in a nursing home. These community services exist. They are links in what is called a **continuum of care,** a range of services tailored to the needs of people at all points on the disability spectrum (see Table 5-2 on p. 144).

Community Options for Disabled Persons

HOME CARE. The most well known alternative to nursing home placement is **home care,** an array of services involving everything from round-the-clock nursing to a few hours per week of help with housekeeping (see Table 5-3 on p. 145). Because of advances in technology, even people who need 24-hour nursing care can get services in their home if they are willing to pay the enormous bill privately. Generally speaking, however, home care, as is true of any community alternative to nursing homes, is most appropriate for people who have minor to moderate disabilities, have an involved family, or need short-term care.

One barrier to utilizing home care or any other community alternative is cost. Because Medicare only covers care defined as "rehabilitative," it will not pay unless the service is defined as cure-oriented and a doctor certifies that a patient needs that type of care. This means that, as we can see in Table 5-3, while the services of a skilled nurse or physical therapist may be covered, Medicare does not pay for the person most responsible

---

continuum of care
Range of services tailored to the needs of people with different degrees of disability.

home care
Service in which a worker comes into the home to provide care.

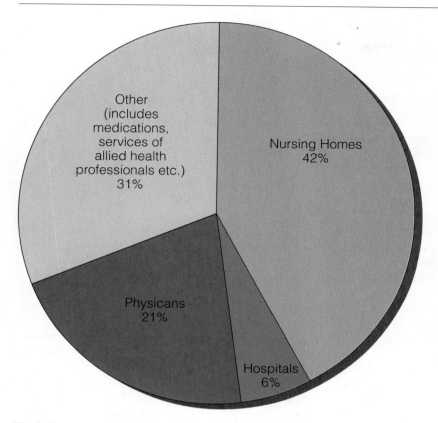

The highest percentage of out-of-pocket health expenses that elderly Americans incur is for nursing homes, even though only a fraction of older Americans ever utilize this type of care. Why? Because the elderly must often pay the nursing home fees privately until they become poor and are eligible for Medicaid.

Source: U.S. Senate Special Committee on Aging, 1991. *Aging America: Trends and Projections*, Washington, DC: Author.

for the disabled person functioning outside of an institution, the attendant or home health aide. While the Medicaid system does cover the services of these workers who provide help with the activities of daily life, how much it pays for varies from state to state. So, though home care was developed to reduce the financial burden of institutionalization, getting ongoing care of this type is expensive, too. It may only be an option when a person needs minor help, is wealthy enough to pay privately for extensive help, or has an income limited enough to qualify for Medicaid.

DAY CARE CENTERS AND PROGRAMS.   In a **day care** program, the person goes to a center offering treatment and social activities. Day centers are usually open five days a week, though registrants may vary in the number of days they attend.

Today a diversity of day care centers exists. Some are for people with Alzheimer's disease; others are for any disabled adult. Some offer a wide array of services; others focus mainly on social enrichment or intensive medical care.

day care
Service in which the disabled person gets care during the day at a center outside of the home.

Table 5-2 **Long-Term Continuum of Care**

Functional impairment level		
Minor: (basically independent, but cannot drive or do heavy work)	*Moderate:* (needs help with activities such as cooking or cleaning; can bathe, dress, and get around on one's own)	*Severe:* (needs help with all activities)
Specialized services, such as transportation, shopping help, and chore help as needed	Home care several hours/day, day care, assisted living situation providing meals and housekeeping	Nursing home

Ideally older people should have services tailored to every level of disability.

Advocates of these centers emphasize their advantages. Day care offers a more stimulating environment than the person might have looking at four walls. It is more cost-effective than one-to-one care. A number of people are getting the services they need in a centralized place. Because the person is not being cared for in an isolated setting, day care may lessen the risk of maltreatment. Home health aides, the primary providers of home care, tend to be older and even more poorly educated than their counterparts in hospitals and nursing homes (Crown, Ahlburg, and MacAdam, 1995). While many provide services above and beyond what they are being paid for (Eustis and Fischer, 1991), there have been alarming reports of abuse with these care providers (Applebaum and Phillip, 1990).

These virtues are offset by disadvantages. Day care does not offer the flexibility of home care. The hours are fixed. Centers are not open at night. They cannot be used during an acute illness. Day programs serve a limited group, people who fit the qualifications for the program. It also may be more difficult to convince older people to attend a day center, rather than having someone come to their home.

These liabilities suggest that day care may never have wide appeal. In one national survey, 85 percent of the day care centers were operating below capacity (reported in Hendrick, Johnson, Inui, and Diehr, 1991). On average, they could have taken a third more people than enrolled.

respite care
Service in which care is given to a disabled person for a limited period when families go on vacation or need time off.

RESPITE CARE. While home care and day care ease the burden on families, their primary function is to help the disabled older person. Helping family care-givers is the goal of **respite care.** The person receiving respite care periodically enters an inpatient setting, such as a nursing home, group home, or hospital or gets home care on an irregular basis so family members can get time off from ministering to the person full-time. Respite care helps prevent care-giver burnout, a risk factor for nursing home placement (Jette, Tennstedt, and Crawford, 1995). It is an ideal alternative for family members who are committed to taking care of a loved one, but need periodic free time (Berry, Zarit, and Rabatin, 1991).

continuing care retirement community
Retirement community providing living arrangements for residents in health and later in disability.

THE CONTINUING CARE RETIREMENT COMMUNITY. While respite care offers peace of mind to relatives, this alternative to a nursing home provides a similar feeling to the older adult. In contrast to traditional retirement housing, a **continuing care retirement community** offers both independent-living apartments and care in disability, allowing people freedom from the fear of being arbitrarily placed in a

Personnel	Services
Social workers	Provide counseling and find, coordinate, and supervise home care services.
Registered dietitians	Plan special diets to speed recovery from illness or to manage conditions such as diabetes.
Physical therapist	Use exercise, heat, light, water, and such to treat problems of movement.
Occupational therapists	Teach people how to function at their best with disabilities—for example, how to do housework from a wheelchair.
Nurses	RNs (registered nurses) provide skilled nursing care; LPNs (licensed practical nurses) offer simpler nursing services. The former are more highly trained and are needed mainly to treat complex medical conditions.
Homemakers/home health aides	Usually are the primary caretakers; may do cleaning, housekeeping, bathing, dressing, and other types of personal care Their job title varies considerably, depending in part on the mix of help provided. For example, "homemaker" or "housekeeper" may be the title when the person mainly does cleaning; "home health aide" or "attendant" may be used when personal care is mainly involved.
Chore workers	Assist with services such as yardwork, home repair, or heavy cleaning.

Home care workers include a variety of professionals. The costs of a home health aide, who takes care of activities of daily living, is not reimbursed by Medicare.

nursing home. All continuing care communities offer some nursing home care as well as more services for people with minor impairments in negotiating life. By the late 1980s, there were approximately 700 continuing care facilities in the United States (Stearns, Netting, Wilson, and Branch, 1990).

Central to the concept of continuing care is freedom from the financial anxieties attached to entering a nursing home. People have banded together to pool their money so they will not be impoverished by needing institutional care. Unfortunately there are drawbacks to this innovative method of insuring for disability.

As is true of nursing home insurance, continuing care communities are expensive and so are only for older people who are relatively well off. They are available only to people who are good health risks. Most communities require applicants to pass a physical examination. Many stipulate that residents be under a certain age to apply.

Even with this screening, living in this type of community does not ensure financial peace of mind. As its residents age and need health care, the community must keep attracting healthy new people to balance out the ill. The cost of health care services may rise, or an unusually high fraction of residents may need long-term care. Statistics are used to compute a community's probable health care needs, leaving residents vulnerable to deviations from the odds. If the health expenses of a community do rise too much, residents face unpleasant alternatives: a steep increase in payments or bankruptcy. As of 1996, there was no federal legislation to protect the life savings of people who invest in continuing care. A 1988 survey showed that only 30 states had passed protective laws

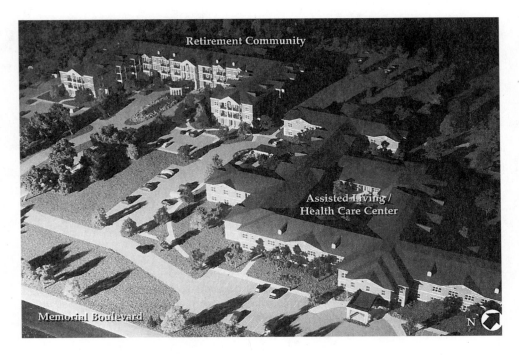

In this continuing care retirement complex (Adams Place in Murfreesboro, Tennessee), elderly residents who enter choose an apartment in the retirement section and are assured that when they have functional impairments, they can move to the assisted living/health care center.

(Stearns et al., 1990). So, despite its advantages, this innovative way of financing for disability is sometimes perilous.

   SPECIALIZED SERVICES.   A variety of services, such as home-delivered meals, transportation, shopping assistance, and home repair, also helps keep people out of nursing homes. One innovative program is the Lifeline Emergency Response System. Subscribers to this hospital-based service pay a monthly fee to have their telephone hooked up to a central switchboard. Someone calls daily to check on each subscriber. If there is no answer, a neighbor is contacted and comes by to check. This system performs an important service. It allows the older person living alone the comfort of knowing help will arrive in a medical emergency when she cannot reach the phone.

   None of these services will make nursing homes obsolete. In fact, in one national survey, physically disabled people who heavily used formal supports were actually *more* at risk of entering a nursing home (Jette et al., 1995). The reason is not that these alternatives are ineffective, but that paid-for care is often used as a last ditch effort by a person poised at the brink of truly needing a nursing home: The older adult is deteriorating physically or cognitively. She cannot function without considerable help. Family members are unavailable, unable to really step in. The explosion of the old-old ensures that this scenario will be familiar. Nursing homes will remain a fixture on the American landscape no matter how available community alternatives become. Now we look at what this fixture on our landscape is really like.

Nursing Home Care

nursing home
Inpatient setting offering care to disabled people over an extended period.

Nursing home is the name for any inpatient setting that provides shelter and services to people in need of medical and personal care over an extended period. While the nursing home population is almost always elderly, occasionally younger people with chronic disabilities are found in these institutions.

   The words *nursing home* strike terror in the hearts of older people. How likely is the average person to suffer this fate? At any given time, only 5 percent of people over 65 are

In The Meals on Wheels Program, volunteers bring home delivered meals to elderly people who are having trouble cooking.

in nursing homes. However, this statistic underestimates the degree to which long-term care touches the lives of older adults.

Because it is cross-sectional, the 5 percent figure does not reveal a person's chance of *ever* being institutionalized, of going to a nursing home at some point in life. This **lifetime risk of placement** is surprisingly high. Experts estimate that almost half of all people who turned 65 in 1990 will enter a nursing home at some time during their remaining years (U.S. Senate Special Committee on Aging, 1991a).

Nursing homes have been described as dumping grounds where people are left to languish unattended as they wait for death. While they may prefer being in an institution to other alternatives, older people often dread the idea of going to a nursing home (Biedenharn and Normoyle, 1991). Are these stereotypes and fears realistic? For answers, let's take a close look at the institutions and people they serve.

THE INSTITUTIONS.   Nursing homes vary tremendously. One may be much like a hospital, offering medical services to seriously ill older people. Another may be similar to a college dormitory, offering room, board, and personal care to less disabled residents. Homes differ in size, staff/patient ratio, and philosophy. Their residents vary, too. Although the law prohibits discrimination in admission, many nursing homes cater to the needs of certain religious or ethnic groups. They serve familiar foods and observe traditional holidays. Some accept people with Alzheimer's disease or the bedridden. Others confine their occupants to people who are not as severely physically or mentally impaired.

Despite this diversity, nursing homes are formally categorized in two ways, by the intensity of care they offer and their type of ownership. The first distinction is crucial. To get reimbursed by Medicaid or Medicare, nursing homes must be classified as offering either skilled or intermediate care.

Skilled nursing care facilities provide the highest level of care, including round-the-clock nursing, physical and occupational therapy, social services, and recreation. **Health-related facilities** are for people who do not need a skilled facility, but do require ongoing assistance in functioning. They offer fewer nursing and personal services. Many

lifetime risk of placement
Risk of going to a nursing home at some point in life.

skilled nursing care facilities
Institutions (or units) offering care tailored to the needs of severely disabled people.

health-related facilities
Institutions (or units) offering care for people who do not require intense services, but need ongoing help functioning.

nursing homes offer both types of care. The advantage of a *multilevel facility* is that, when a resident's physical needs change and a different level of care is needed, that person can get services in the same location.

The different ownership categories of nursing homes are similar to those of hospitals. *Proprietary homes* are owned and run privately for a profit. *Voluntary homes* are operated by non-profit organizations, such as church groups. *Public homes* are owned by the city or state. Then there is the variation that is not formally categorized, the dimension we care so vitally about, quality.

Visit several nursing homes and you will be struck by the differences in quality. Some facilities are beautifully designed, provide excellent services, and have staff members committed to providing humane care. Others richly deserve the label "snake pit."

One influence affecting the quality of a nursing home is its clientele. Nursing homes that serve more affluent elderly look more appealing, have better services, and tend to provide higher-quality care. While well-off older people get better care for obvious economic reasons, there is a more hidden reason why they are often better served.

Staff members at homes catering to well-off residents are more likely to come under scrutiny because affluent older people are more likely to have friends and relatives who visit and complain if they see mistreatment or neglect. The fact that outside visitors keep nursing homes accountable was suggested when researchers compared how much attention the staff at selected homes paid to different residents. Residents who received the most visits were given the most staff time (Gottesman and Bourestom, 1974).

In evaluating nursing home quality, it is important to consider how a facility physically looks, its services, and its staff. Just as crucial is knowing how much autonomy the home offers residents in their daily life. While gerontologists almost universally agree that providing control to disabled older people is important, even the most humane nursing home must restrict people in basic areas of life. Decisions we take for granted, such as where to live, when to get up or eat, or what meals to prepare, are not an option to people living in long-term care. Nursing home residents must wait to be dressed or taken to the bathroom. They often share a room with a person they have never met (Kane, 1995–1996). While many of these restrictions are the unavoidable price of being physically dependent and living in an institution, some go beyond what is necessary. A survey of admission agreements at 200 California nursing homes showed that residents were frequently asked to waive important rights when they entered, such as control over their finances, the chance to get grievances heard, and the ability to make decisions about their medical care (Ambrogli and Lenard, 1988). Many admission contracts were unreadable, omitted essential terms, or contained clauses that were illegal. Residents might be deprived of such critical freedoms as access to their medical records, the right to receive visitors at reasonable times, or the ability to use the pharmacy of their choice.

While one impact of this alarming survey was that in 1987 the California legislature passed a bill with strict guidelines regulating nursing home admission contracts in that state, as of 1996 there has been no federal law discouraging these practices. This study suggests that many nursing homes still tend more to take control away from residents, rather than promoting it.

Research on what goes on behind the walls of long-term care is equally disturbing. When Linda Noelker and Walter Poulshock (1984) explored the relationships among residents and staff members of a nursing home that prided itself on offering "personalized care in a familial atmosphere," they found little intimacy and widespread negative feelings toward the residents on the part of the staff. The same distance, disengagement, and lack of respect characterized the residents' relationships with one another, too, though to a smaller degree. While the average length of time they had lived together was over three years, less than half of these older people reported being close with another

5-3 The Adult Experience: Mabel and Bertha

Bertha Holloway, an LPN in the nursing home where Mabel lives, provided some information for this chapter's beginning interview. Bertha is familiar with Mabel's history because they are close friends. Every day Bertha makes time to visit with Mabel. She comes in after work and on weekends a few times a month. According to Bertha, "When Mabel's fractures healed, she had the chance to go to another setting offering less intense care. She's an independent woman who likes to care for herself. She stayed here because she felt secure and knew there would be a time when she would need this type of care."

Bertha first sought out a relationship with Mabel as a form of therapy. She had lost a favorite aunt and an older sister, and there was a void in her life. One day Mabel mentioned that she had never had a teddy bear. As Christmas was approaching, Bertha bought Mabel the large stuffed animal now proudly displayed in her room, and their friendship began.

Bertha, like Mabel, feels this is her final home. She is almost 60. When she leaves the Health Care Center, it will be to retire. Bertha has been a staff nurse in a variety of hospital settings,. She worked on an intensive care unit for years. Why did she switch to nursing home work? According to Bertha, "I was the baby of 10 children. My parents had me in their forties. I had a sister 22 years older than me. So age never meant anything special. However, for years, I fought against working in a nursing home because I was afraid I would get upset when my patients died. Then my oldest sister needed long-term care. I didn't deal with that well. In order to come to terms with the situation, I decided to try out this work."

Bertha made the right choice: "Each one of these people belongs to me. I know their problems. I have a sense of gratification here that I never had in ICU. There we had young people with hopeless conditions. I went home feeling inadequate, that there was nothing I could do. Now rarely do I leave feeling dissatisfied. When my patients die, I know that it's their time."

There are a few problems. One of Bertha's peeves is how hard it can be to get some doctors to return phone calls. But Bertha rarely has difficulties with the other staff or the five technicians (aides) she currently supervises: In her words, "The patients are my babies. I will not tolerate them being abused."

Mr. Booth, a gentleman in a wheelchair who has been eavesdropping on our conversation, breaks in : "The longer you're in this place, the better you feel about it. I've been here since January and never seen anybody mistreated. When I went to the hospital and came back, the young ladies hugged me because they missed me so much. I am a diabetic, and Mrs. Holloway spends her money to buy me diabetic candy. They baby me. They treat me as good as my mother ever did."

resident. Nursing home residents learn to "live in silence." They keep their complaints to themselves (Kaakinen, 1992). While, as Feature 5-3 shows, many do have supportive relationships with staff members after being institutionalized, most report their primary relationships lie outside the home (Bitzan and Kruzich, 1990).

Another study reinforces the stereotype that incidents of patient abuse within nursing homes are not rare. In this survey of nursing home aides (the main care-givers), 10 percent reported performing a physically abusive act, either using excessive restraint or pushing, hitting, or shoving a resident. Forty-one percent admitted some act of psychological abuse during that year. Nine percent admitted they had sworn at or insulted a person in their care (Pillemer and Bachman-Prehn, 1991).

These studies suggest that every grim idea we have about nursing home workers is right. Other research contradicts the stereotypes, suggesting that these people care vitally about providing good patient care (Burgio, Engle, Hawkins, McCormick, and Scheve, 1990; see Feature 5-3). Furthermore, before blaming nursing home workers, let's look carefully at the conditions of their job. As is true of home health aides, nursing home aides are not well educated. The sad fact is that caring for people on a daily basis is one of the poorest paying, least appreciated occupations society provides. Care recipients can be far from appreciative, too. When I worked as a psychologist in a nursing home, I witnessed patients cursing or becoming physically abusive with no provocation. In fact, in the survey just mentioned, the highest correlate of lashing out at a resident was having been the target of that individual's aggressive act. This suggests that, while not excusable, some of what occurs within nursing homes becomes understandable if we look at the people these institutions serve.

RESIDENTS.   Nursing home residents vary in background, ethnicity, temperament, and almost every other characteristic that can differentiate people. Some enter homes for short-term rehabilitation; others live in long-term care for decades, cognitively intact or comotose and needing 24-hour care (Kane, 1995–1996). Still, the following general statements about this group can be made.

Nursing home residents tend to be very old. Almost half are over age 85. Because of gender differences in longevity and the fact that women are more likely to have disabling illnesses, they are overwhelmingly female. They are mainly white. Minorities have a lower life expectancy, and institutional care is not as available to non-whites. The traditions of maintaining the extended family and caring for one's elders also contribute to the relatively low, but growing, numbers of ethnic minorities in nursing homes. As we know from the fact that their care is mainly financed by Medicaid, most residents are currently poor. Most important, people in nursing homes have functional impairments severe enough to warrant institutional placement (Worobey and Angel, 1990). In order to be admitted to a facility offering skilled or intermediate care, a person must be certified as having a level of disability compatible with care of each type.

Placement in a home is associated with deterioration in cognitive capacities and in the ability to ambulate or move around (Wolinsky, Callahan, Fitzgerald, and Johnson, 1992). It also depends on having "social supports." A relatively high fraction of single, divorced, and widowed elderly people live in institutions, and these residents tend to be healthier than the married. As we will see in our chapter on the older family, a spouse is the first line of defense against institutionalization. If they are physically able, husbands and wives provide the care-giving when a spouse is having trouble functioning. The second line of defense is children, usually daughters. So, people with no immediate family members are at much higher risk of entering long-term care (U.S. Senate Special Committee on Aging, 1991a).

PERSONALITY AND PSYCHOPATHOLOGY.   On almost any measure of mental health, people living in nursing homes rank as disturbed. As we will see in Chapter 7, many suffer from serious cognitive impairments. Apathy, low self-esteem, and depression are also widespread among the residents of long-term care (German, Rovner, Burton, Brant, and Clark, 1992). From our look at what goes on in nursing homes, we might assume these high levels of emotional disturbance are caused by the institution. Surely the living conditions within many nursing homes would demoralize and depress anyone.

A more accurate assumption is that people who have reached the point of applying to nursing homes are already emotionally disturbed. While the institution may not help matters, emotional problems existed before entering long-term care.

In a classic longitudinal study of adaptation to institutional life, Morton Lieberman and Sheldon Tobin (1983) interviewed three groups of equally disabled older people: nursing home residents; elderly who had applied for admission to the home, but were on a waiting list; and elderly who had not sought nursing home care. The waiting list group and those in the home had identical symptoms. Compared to the group not seeking institutional care, they were less emotionally responsive and had lower self-esteem.

Every study reveals high rates of mental disorders among residents of nursing homes. As we saw in Feature 5-3, this does not mean that *every nursing home resident* is emotionally disturbed. Not only do many people live happily for years within nursing homes, but also improvements in mood may occur after entering long-term care (Engle and Graney, 1993). Who is more content after arriving at a nursing home than before?

Researchers find that, if a person's life situation is very difficult, placement results in a rise in morale. For older people who genuinely need an institution—those in poor health who have few financial resources and are living alone—placement is a relief. As we saw with Mabel in Feature 5-3, the nursing home is a haven from the terror of struggling with life outside.

In addition to precarious life circumstances, personality predicts who does well within long-term care. Unfortunately some not very appealing traits predict adjustment to this way of life.

The main purpose of Lieberman and Tobin's study was to follow their waiting list subjects as they entered and adjusted to the nursing home. The researchers found that the residents who declined least mentally and physically or who improved at the end of a year had a set of unpleasant traits. They tended to be aggressive and intrusive. They were likely to blame others, rather than themselves. They were low in empathy and maintained a distrustful distance from other residents.

Given the depressing conditions of institutional life, these findings are no surprise. Aggressive behavior may be an adaptive strategy in a situation where resources are so limited. People who fight are likely to get more of what they need. Keeping emotionally distant from others and unresponsive to their suffering may be helpful in a situation where people have such painful disabilities or are near death.

I hope our discussion has not reinforced more stereotypes than it has erased. In fact, tremendous progress is being made in improving nursing homes. The growth of geriatric medicine, increased attention to the needs of frail older people, studies of the type discussed in this chapter, and media attention to nursing home abuses all have been an impetus to make the 1980s and 1990s an era of exciting change in long-term care.

Today the problems of nursing home residents are not swept out of sight. We focus squarely on improving their daily life. Programs from special services or enriched individual attention, to vigorous rehabilitation, to intensive training to upgrade the skills of the staff are frequently available at the best nursing homes.

Somewhat more attention is being paid to the diversity of needs propelling people to long-term care. For instance, as we will see in Chapter 7, a growing number of facilities now have care units specifically designed for people with Alzheimer's disease (Mor, Banaszak-Holl, and Zinn, 1995–1996).

Special efforts are also being made to promote autonomy and control. Nursing homes have *residents' councils* that meet regularly to discuss residents' complaints and concerns. Nursing home *bills of rights* are clearly available to residents (see Table 5-4). Increasingly, nursing homes have review boards to guard against abuses in terminal care (Miller and Cugliari, 1990; see Chapter 14).

Well-established programs advocate for residents' rights. In the **nursing home ombudsman** program, residents of nursing homes are visited by a volunteer advocate whose job is to listen to and mediate residents' complaints. Watchdog organizations complement these efforts. Nursing home rights groups agitate for residents, guide people through the process of applying to and selecting a nursing home, and spotlight nursing home reform. Today a new type of nursing home also exists—the teaching nursing home.

APPLICATIONS AND INTERVENTIONS:

nursing home ombudsman *Volunteer who acts as an advocate for nursing home residents and mediates their complaints.*

Table 5-4

A Portion of the Nursing Home Patient's Rights Handbook Given to All Residents upon Entering a Facility

Grievance Procedure

Your comfort, safety, health and happiness are our concern and we presume that you will give us the opportunity to assist you should a problem arise. We trust that you will feel free to take any action you choose in resolving any problem. The management will not discriminate nor use any coercion or reprisal against you for taking such steps. You may expect the degree of confidentiality that you request.

If at any time you are not being treated fairly, or if you feel that an employee has mistreated you in any way, please take the following steps:

1. Notify the social worker for assistance in resolving the problem. The social worker serves as the center's in-house "ombudsman." An "ombudsman" investigates complaints on behalf of the administrator and reports findings/resolution to the administrator.
2. If you are not satisfied, notify the director of nursing.
3. Should you remain unsatisfied, please take the concern to the assistant administrator or administrator.

You are welcome to present the problem verbally or in writing. You may expect a response at each level as quickly as possible, certainly within 5 working days.

In the event that you choose to describe the concern in writing, especially if the grievance is one addressed by either federal Civil Rights legislation or Section 504 of the Rehabilitation Act of 1973, you are entitled to a written response within 5 days *at each level*. Section 504 states, in part, that "no otherwise qualified handicapped individual. . . shall, solely by reason of his handicap, be excluded from participation in, be denied the benefits of, or be subjected to discrimination under any program or activity receiving federal financial assistance. . ." The administrator is the designated 504 coordinator for this center and will be happy to address any such issues brought to his/her attention.

In the event that grievances of any sort are not satisfactorily resolved with the center, you may contact an outside representative of your choice:

1. Contact NHC regional or home office staff either directly or through the use of the Patient Care Satisfaction Evaluation provided for your use.
2. File a complaint with the State Survey and Certification agency.
3. Contact your state's ombudsman.
4. File a civil rights or Section 504 grievance.

The names and addresses are available to you upon request to the social worker or administrator and are publicly posted in common areas of the center.

Any of these courses of action is encouraged if you are aware of any patient abuse, either verbal, mental or physical; neglect, misappropriation of property; or discrimination on the basis of race, color, religion, national origin, sex, age or handicap. You, and all other patients are entitled to protection from such behaviors.

Source: National Health Corporation, Murfreesboro, TN.

teaching nursing homes
Nursing homes that serve as training sites for medical and other health care personnel.

At **teaching nursing homes,** affiliated with medical schools, medical residents and nurses in training get experience in providing care to institutionalized older adults and learn about the problems of the frail elderly firsthand. They are trained in the latest techniques for dealing with disability and chronic disease. Teaching nursing homes are also sites for research on interventions to minimize disease and disability in later life (Lipsitz, 1995–1996).

Despite this progress, more needs to be done. We need affordable programs to prevent nursing home placement. It is a tragedy that, once people need chronic care,

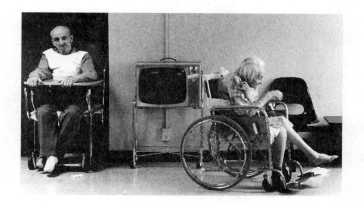

Partly because the staff are over-worked, scenes such as the one here still are likely to confront any visitor to a nursing home.

they must bankrupt themselves in order to receive services or end up going to a nursing home because there is no alternative in between. Much needs to be done to restructure nursing homes themselves. Rules allowing residents little say over their roommates or meals are still standard. The needs of this nation's ethnically diverse resident population are often ignored (Stanford and Schmidt, 1995–1996). It is possible to provide many more chances to exercise free choice (Kane and Caplan, 1990).

Nursing homes need staff members that are better trained and higher paid. *They also need more of them on any given unit or floor.* The life of a nursing home aide can be highly frustrating. Imagine having to get an impossibly large number of people dressed and fed within a given hour. The result must be excess disabilities, offering too much help in the interest of getting things done, or the routine neglect we see exposed on the nightly news. Perhaps as we continue to push life toward our biological maximum, a new health revolution to match the lifestyle revolution of recent decades will occur: one providing high-quality health care to people who suffer from the disabilities that are in part the price of our remarkable life-expectancy progress.

KEY TERMS & CONCEPTS

functional impairment
tertiary prevention
morbidity
active life expectancy
compression of morbidity hypothesis
need factors
predisposing factors
enabling factors
geriatric medicine
formal caregiving supports
Medicare
Medicaid
excess disabilities
continuum of care
home care
day care
respite care
continuing care retirement community

nursing home
lifetime risk of placement
skilled nursing care facilities
health-related facilities
nursing home ombudsman
teaching nursing homes

RECOMMENDED READINGS

Health Care for Minorities

Abraham, L. (1995). *Mama might be better off dead*. Chicago: University of Chicago Press.
   This book presents "a human look at the health care crisis in America." This author, an award-winning reporter, follows the lives of the members of an African-American family in an inner-city Chicago neighborhood as they struggle to cope with chronic disease and negotiate the health care system. It is highly recommended.

Markides, K. S. (Ed.). (1989). *Aging and health: Perspectives on gender, race, ethnicity, and class*. Newbury Park, CA: Sage.
   This edited book offers articles summarizing health issues with regard to different minority groups.

U.S. Department of Health and Human Services. (1990). *Health status of the disadvantaged, Chartbook, 1990*. Washington, DC: U.S. Government Printing Office.
U.S. Department of Health and Human Services. (1991). *Health status of minorities and low income groups*. Washington, DC: U.S. Government Printing Office.
   These publications offer a wealth of statistics on health, illness, life expectancy, and medical care for minorities and the disadvantaged. The former book also offers statistics on minority enrollment in the health professions.

Willis, D. P. (Ed.). (1989). *Health policies and black Americans*. New Brunswick, NJ: Transaction.
   This edited book covers various aspects of health care for African Americans.

Nursing Homes

Generations (Winter 1995–1996). The nursing home revisited, *vol. 19*.
   This issue of Generations takes a critical look at nursing homes, exploring how they are evolving and the problems that continue to exist in providing quality care.

Kane, R. A., and Caplan, A. L. (1990). *Everyday ethics: Resolving dilemmas in nursing home life*. New York: Springer.
   Prominent experts discuss dilemmas relating to daily life in nursing homes. They offer a flavor of the concerns and threats to autonomy that occur in institutional life. This is a great book!

Sheilds, R. R. (1988). *Uneasy endings: Life in an American nursing home*. Ithaca, NY: Cornell University Press.
   This anthropological investigation of life in a nursing home offers an interesting, balanced, and true-to-life picture of nursing home life.

Part III

THE PSYCHOLOGICAL DIMENSION

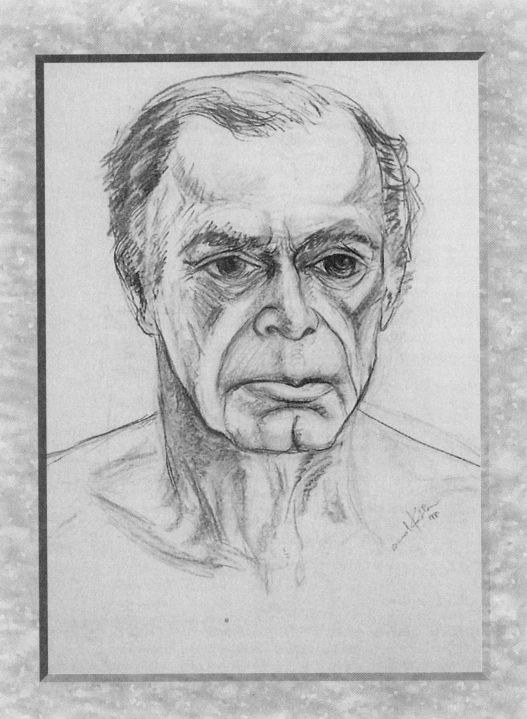

Cognition I: Intelligence

Chapter Outline

According to Jean, "When life presents me with problems, my therapy is to challenge my mind." Jean's master's degree in speech therapy and her doctorate in special education both were received at turning points during her life. After her son died, at age 64, Jean went back to school again to get a Ph.D. in counseling psychology.

Jean finds some differences in her abilities: "I don't switch channels as well as I used to. I can retain at the same rate, but it takes me longer. However, that's no problem because I've always had a bit to spare (I hope that doesn't sound uppity). At the beginning, some students in the program had a patronizing attitude. They seemed reluctant to collaborate on projects because of my age. Now that my 3.8 average is well known, it's no problem. I'm no genius . . . but I always had the feeling that I have had enough intelligence. While I may be poor in some areas—such as statistics—being articulate is a big help. Verbal skills go a long way in school and life. Memory is more difficult, but it's surprising how handy the mental strategies I used to teach my learning disabled kids have come in—if I decide to devote the energy to using them! Being more relaxed is an advantage. At my age, a person enjoys the process, focuses on the moment. I have no interest in getting a job or even a degree. I guess this means in the most important way I'm a better student today than in my younger years.

Think of adults you admire for their intelligence. What qualities do they have? Most likely your list will be somewhat similar to that of the people whose responses are shown in Table 6–1. As is true of Jean, intelligent adults are curious and have an inquiring mind. They have maturity, wisdom, and good sense. They have excellent verbal skills and are fluent, articulate, and able to reason with ease (Berg and Sternberg, 1992a).

The people in this poll disagreed with the idea that intelligence declines as people age. If anything, they believed the reverse is true. Most often, though, they said we cannot generalize. Some aspects of intelligence increase and others decrease over the years. They rejected the concept of intelligence as a fixed or an unchanging trait. Not only are the defining qualities of an intelligent person different at 20 and at 85, but also intelligence can and does change. In fact, intelligence can increase at any age depending on our experiences in the world.

INTELLIGENCE AS MEASURED BY TRADITIONAL PSYCHOMETRIC TESTS

Forty years ago psychologists disagreed with the above ideas. They felt intelligence universally declined after youth. They thought the skills involved in being intelligent did not change. Intelligence was a relatively fixed property of the person, one that could be measured by the same set of skills at every age. Among these qualities curiosity, interest, wisdom, and good sense did not appear. Intelligence at every point during adult life was measured by performance on a set of tasks making up a standardized intelligence test—typically the **Wechsler Intelligence Scale for Adults (WAIS).**

The Wechsler Intelligence Scale for Adults, and now its revised version, the WAIS-R (Weschler, 1981), is an example of a **traditional psychometric intelligence test,** a measure by which people are ranked as having more or less of a fixed quantity called "intelligence" based on their performance compared to their peers. This widely used test has a verbal and a performance scale, each composed of different subtests measuring more specific skills. Notice in Table 6–2 on p. 160 that the verbal part of the test tends to measure factual knowledge—knowledge of historical, literary, or biological facts; of how to function in the world; of mathematics; of the meaning of words.

The performance subtests, which involve copying symbols, arranging or naming pictures, or manipulating puzzles or blocks, measure a different type of skill: the person's

Wechsler Intelligence Scale for Adults
Most widely used intelligence test for adults.

traditional psychometric intelligence test
Intelligence test with a series of items by which people are ranked as having more or less intelligence compared to others.

Factor (general category responses cluster in)

(1) Interest in and Ability to Deal with Novelty
Is able to analyze topics in new and original ways
Is interested in gaining knowledge and learning new things
Is open-minded to new ideas and trends
Is able to learn and reason with new kinds of concepts
Displays curiosity
Discovers new ideas
Is interested in his or her career
Is able to perceive and store new information
Is inquisitive
Thinks quickly
Is able to comprehend new tasks
Thinks about future and sets goals
Is always trying to better himself or herself
Has an active mind

(2) Everyday Competence
Displays good common sense
Acts in a mature manner
Acts responsibly
Is interested in family and home life
Adjusts to life situations
Deals effectively with problems and stress
Has high moral values
Appreciates young and old individuals
Displays wisdom in actions and thoughts
Makes rational decisions

(3) Verbal Competence
Displays the knowledge to speak intelligently
Displays good vocabulary
Is able to draw conclusions from information given
Is verbally fluent
Displays clarity of speech

Do your ideas agree with these traits listed by 140 adults?

Source: Berg, C. A., and Sternberg, R. J. Adults' conceptions of intelligence across the adult life span. *Psychology and Aging, 2,* 221–231. Copyright 1992 by the American Psychological Association, adapted by permission.

ability to solve novel problems. On this part of the test, speed is essential. Not only are the performance subtests timed, but also bonus points are often given for the quickest solution.

A psychologist arrives at the IQ score by adding up the number of items correct and comparing this figure with the scores of other people one's age. In other words, the WAIS, similar to any test graded on a curve, depends on performance compared to a reference group. In this case, the reference group is special, our age group.

Table 6-2

Verbal Scale

Subtest	Measures	Hypothetical item
Information	Fund of knowledge	Who is Bill Clinton?
Comprehension	Social or life knowledge	What do you do when you find an umbrella in your class?
Similarities	Verbal reasoning	Cat is to feline as dog is to ____.
Arithmetic	Mathematical knowledge	Joe had $10 and spent $2.50. How much is left?
Digit span	Memory	Repeat these digits: 8238910.
Vocabulary	Word definitions	What does ebullient mean?

Performance Scale (all tests are timed)

Subtest	Description
Digit symbol	Subject copies symbols.
Picture completion	Subject tells what is missing in a picture.
Block design	Set of blocks with different patterns on each side; subject must arrange them to look like the pattern on a card.
Picture arrangement	Set of pictures; subject must arrange them to tell a story.
Object assembly	Puzzle pieces that, once assembled, look like common objects; subject must arrange them correctly.

The verbal scale measures a person's knowledge base. The performance scale measures a person's ability to quickly solve non-verbal problems.

Source: D. Wechsler 1981, *WAIS-R Manual,* Revised Edition, New York: Harcourt Brace Jovanovich.

During the 1950s, when psychologists tested adults of different ages to establish these reference group standards or *age norms,* they uncovered a depressing fact. Beginning in young adulthood, older groups did worse and worse. The loss was especially dramatic on the performance scale, where, starting in the early twenties, scores steadily declined. The decline in verbal scores started somewhat later and only fell off dramatically among people over age 65. This pattern, less loss on verbal measures requiring knowledge and steady decline beginning very early on timed tests of non-verbal skills, was so consistent a research finding that in the early writings it was given a special name, the **classic aging pattern** (Botwinick, 1967).

No matter how much we emphasize that the verbal losses are small, these findings offer little comfort to anyone past youth. However, being from cross-sectional data, they immediately raised suspicions. Even 40 years ago psychologists knew too much about the difficulties of assuming age changes from *differences* between age groups to take these results as the final word. Would longitudinal studies also reveal this picture of universal decline? Would they show the classic aging pattern, too?

As we might expect, longitudinal studies were more positive. Many showed that people improved on the verbal part of the test through middle age (Labouvie-Vief, 1985). However, even here the classic aging pattern showed up. Even when verbal scores improved, decline, though to a smaller degree, still was typical of the performance tests. Longitudinal studies also revealed the pattern apparent in the early cross-sectional research. At the end of life, the classic aging pattern seemed to break down. Among very old people, verbal scores dropped dramatically, too.

classic aging pattern
Typical age finding on IQ tests of relative stability on verbal measures and steady decline beginning early in adult life on timed, non-verbal scales.

So psychologists were intrigued by these similarities. Both cross-sectional and longitudinal studies revealed the classic aging pattern until old age, followed by universal decline. Then, in 1970, psychologist John Horn made an influential attempt to integrate and make sense of these findings.

Interpreting the Findings: A Two-Factor Theory of Intelligence

Horn (1970) describes two basic types of intelligence. **Crystallized intelligence** reflects the extent to which we have absorbed the knowledge base of our culture. It is the amount of information we have accumulated. This ability is largely measured by the verbal subtests of the WAIS. The second type of intelligence reflects a central nervous system at its physiological peak. **Fluid intelligence** involves quick reasoning, using skills not as dependent on experience. This type of intelligence is what is mainly being measured by the performance subtests.

crystallized intelligence
Category of intelligence reflecting one's knowledge base.

fluid intelligence
Category of intelligence reflecting one's ability to reason well quickly when presented with novel tasks.

Horn believes that fluid intelligence, as is true of many physiological capacities, reaches its peak in early adulthood and then steadily declines. On the other hand, because crystallized intelligence involves experience and learning, it follows a different path as we age. This type of intelligence stays relatively stable or increases as the years pass because the rate at which we acquire new information in the course of life tends to balance out the rate at which we forget. However, in old age, crystallized intelligence also declines. The reason is because at a certain time of life the effect of losses—of work, of relationships, and particularly of health—causes our forgetting to finally exceed the rate at which we acquire knowledge (Horn and Hofer, 1992).

Horn's fluid/crystallized distinction seems appealing. It has stood the test of time. The beauty of his two-factor theory is that not only does it explain test performance, but also it fits so *many* performances in life. As we will see later in this chapter, we can use this framework to explain why people in creative fields dependent on solving totally new problems tend to do their best work earlier in life compared to those in professions in which high-quality work is more dependent on mastering a body of knowledge, such as history or philosophy. The theory explains why age is more of an enemy to the air traffic controller, who must quickly analyze changing information (remember from Chapter 4 the industry ban on hiring people *over age 30* to work in the control tower), than to the CEO of the airline, who by his fifties has accumulated the years of experience to perform at his peak.

More recently another expert in adult intelligence has expanded on the two-factor theory to explain why performance in many life activities remains stable or improves, despite physiological declines. According to Paul Baltes (1993), as we age, the **mechanics,** our fluid abilities or biologically based "hardware," promoting cognition fall off; but that is compensated for by an increase in the **pragmatics** (software) of intelligence, the knowledge we accumulate over the years. This gain in the pragmatics of intelligence not only makes up for fluid losses, but also powerfully determines performance in the real world. Even with worse cognitive mechanics, Baltes believes, if their crystallized knowledge is extensive, older people can outperform the young.

mechanics of intelligence
Biologically based fluid intellectual skills.

pragmatics of intelligence
Experience-based crystallized intellectual skills.

Can experience, or the pragmatics of intelligence, really make up for fluid losses? Marian Perlmutter and her coworkers decided to test Baltes's ideas by focusing on a profession where we might think fast-paced fluid skills would be especially important: food serving. The researchers consulted experts, such as restaurant owners and food critics, about the qualities involved in being an excellent food server, constructed a scale measuring these qualities, and gave this test plus standard intelligence tests to people differing in age and years on the job. Older servers did do less well on the standard intelligence tests. However, with age and years of experience, scores on the test of "food-server intelligence" rose. So did performance. Older workers were better at what they did, serving more people during both busy and quiet times at work (Perlmutter, Kaplan, and Nyquist, 1990). As Baltes predicts, pragmatics can outweigh mechanics in life.

According to Perlmutter, her years on the job (and possibly better social skills), may make this older food server "more intelligent" at what she does than any young adult working in this fast food restaurant.

There is even a neurological basis to the idea that crystallized skills or the pragmatics of intelligence grow until very late in life. As we grow old, we gradually lose neurons. This neural atrophy (or loss) takes place from the dendrite or branching part of the neuron inward (Cotman, 1990; Scheibel, 1996). However, loss is not the whole story. In some parts of the brain, there is an increase in dendrites with age.

In a remarkable set of experiments, Stephen Buell and Paul Coleman (1979) compared the neurons of normal elderly people dying at about age 70 with those of middle-aged adults and elderly people who had died with Alzheimer's disease. They were astonished to find the neurons of the *normal* elderly had more dendrites than those of the middle-aged people. In another study, when Coleman (1986) measured dendrite growth in a part of the brain called the dentate gyrus in young adults, middle-aged people, 70-year-old people, and very old people (aged 90), he found that this growth continued through early later life, though among the very old it stopped. So we do lose this wonderful ability to grow dendrites, but only in advanced old age.

This research offers an example of the principle of physiological *compensation*, discussed in Chapter 3. In reaction to the loss of individual neurons, Coleman believes, the brain automatically "sprouts" new dendrites to preserve thinking, offering a physical parallel to Baltes's and Horn's idea that crystallized intelligence compensates for fluid declines. The analogy becomes more striking when we notice that in Coleman's oldest subjects dendrite growth stopped, reflecting the decline in crystallized abilities that intelligence tests show takes place in advanced old age.

So, by using the fluid/crystallized distinction, many of the findings about intellectual change make sense. Still, we are left with nagging questions relating to the tests. When does performance on IQ tests really begin to decline? Is it in middle age or later, as the longitudinal studies show, or in our twenties, as indicated in the cross-sectional research? Remember that, because people who volunteer for longitudinal studies tend to be a well-off fraction of the cohort and because *selective attrition* occurs, only the most healthy volunteers complete these studies. This means that this research is certain to present an overly positive picture of the "true" loss due to age. Because they confuse *cohort factors*, or influences due to being born at a certain time, with genuine age changes, cross-sectional studies may be biased in the other direction—exaggerating the negative change.

Unraveling the Truth About Change: The Seattle Longitudinal Study

When psychologists carefully thought about what influences, apart from declining ability due to age, might load the test-taking dice against older cohorts, one striking difference

Figure 6–1

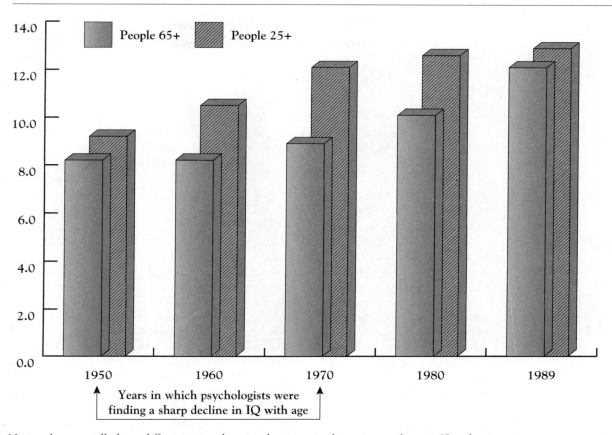

Notice the especially large differences in educational attainment between people over 65 and the general population when psychologists were conducting the early studies on the effects of age changes on IQ. Moreover, the figure shows that the cohort of older people tested during these years had typically left school after the eighth grade. Was it fair for psychologists to conclude based on comparing these old and young people that intelligence declines dramatically at older ages?

Source: U.S. Senate Special Committee on Aging, 1991, *Aging America: Trends and Projections*, Washington, DC: Author.

stood out—years of formal education. On average, older people have many fewer years of schooling than younger adults. Notice from Figure 6–1 how great these educational differences were during the middle third of the twentieth century, when psychologists were routinely finding that beginning in young adulthood intelligence steadily declined.

We might imagine that lack of formal education would greatly affect older cohorts' performance on the verbal part of the WAIS, with its emphasis on school skills, such as mathematics, and vocabulary. A moment's thought suggests that fewer years in the classroom might even affect how well a person scores on the non-verbal scale. Having less experience in school, older cohorts might find any test more strange and anxiety-provoking. In fact, because it involves such stressful and unusual activities, performance anxiety might even be greater for older people on the non-verbal part of the test.

How much of a role do **ability-extraneous influences,** such as differences in education, play in explaining age changes on intelligence tests? To answer this important question, during the late 1950s a research team headed by K. Warner Schaie began a landmark study.

Schaie's **Seattle Longitudinal Study** is *the* central, defining study of intelligence and age. As we learned in Chapter 2, by following cohorts ranging in age from their twenties through their seventies and by conducting a series of simultaneous longitudinal and cross-sectional comparisons between the groups, Schaie believed that he could measure the contrasting biases of each type of research method and so isolate the true impact of age on IQ.

The researchers first selected volunteers, participants in a health organization, seven years apart in age and compared their scores. Then they followed each group longitudinally, testing them at seven-year intervals. At each of these testings, another cross-sectional sample was selected, some of whom were also followed over time (Schaie, 1990, 1996). Instead of using the WAIS to measure intelligence, Schaie decided to use a test called *Thurstone's Primary Mental Abilities Scale (PMA)*. The reason is that this test measures five separate abilities that research suggested were primary or basic to intelligence (see Table 6–3).

In the early 1970s, when most psychologists believed that people lose intelligence beginning in their twenties, the publication describing the first 14 years of this study was a ray of light. "Cohort factors" did turn out to seriously bias cross-sectional studies. The idea that intelligence goes steadily downhill after youth was simply not true!

Schaie's recent analyses, from the fifth wave of this continuing study, offer us a good overall picture of how performance on intelligence tests really changes as we grow old. On average, the Seattle Study shows gains until the early forties and stability until the mid-fifties or until age 60, depending on the test. After age 60, however, seven-year losses are statistically significant for all five PMA scales (Hertzog and Schaie, 1988; Schaie, 1996). In other words, if we have to generalize, intelligence, *as measured by traditional tests*, increases until midlife, then plateaus, and then starts to decline in late middle age.

However, generalizing is hazardous because different abilities show different patterns of change. As we might expect, the crystallized/fluid distinction is very useful in understanding which abilities "stand up" to time. While scores on tests measuring fluid abilities, such as inductive reasoning, begin to decline on average by the early thirties, measures of crystallized skills, such as verbal ability, remain stable until the sixties. In fact, on two non-timed vocabulary tests, Schaie's volunteers performed at their peak at age 67 (Schaie and Willis, 1993).

When Schaie (1990) looked at the fraction of older people at different ages who declined on one or more tests over a previous seven-year period, he found more heartening news. While most volunteers did experience significant losses on at least one facet of intelligence by age 60, even among the oldest group (people aged 81) loss on all five components of intelligence was rare. Three out of four 60-year-olds stayed stable or improved on at least four primary mental abilities. Even at age 81, more than one-half did.

As Schaie's research team began publishing its results, psychologists changed their thinking about intelligence and age. Today most experts are careful to point out that intellectual change is multidirectional. Some abilities rise and some decline. They are apt to emphasize the dramatic differences among people in stability and change. Rather than focusing on what generally happens, many have turned their attention to these individual differences. Why do some people seem to lose intelligence early on, while others stay alert and intellectually active until the limit of human life? What can keep intelligence fine-tuned? How much can intelligence be improved in later life? While, as

1. **Verbal meaning:** Subject is asked to pick the synonym of a word from four choices.
2. **Spatial relations:** Subject is shown an abstract figure and asked to identify which of six other drawings represent the model rotated in space.
3. **Inductive reasoning:** Subject is asked to identify a pattern occurring in a series of numbers or letters by picking the item that should appear next in the series.
4. **Number:** Subject is asked to compute simple arithmetic problems.
5. **Word fluency:** Subject is asked to freely recall as many words as possible according to some rule (i.e. words beginning with the letter "s") within a five minute period.

The Seattle Study shows that performance on crystallized tests, such as verbal meaning, stays stable or rises until the sixties. Scores on tests measuring fluid skills, such as inductive reasoning and spatial relations, begin to decline by early midlife.

Source: K. W. Schaie and S.L. Willis, 1993, Age Difference Patterns of Psychometric Intelligence in Adulthood: Generalizations Within and Across Ability Domains, *Psychology and Aging, 8,* 44–55.

we will see later in this chapter, this multidimensional **contextual perspective on intelligence** has important critics, it dominates how researchers think about age and intelligence today.

Speed, Health, Mental Activity, Stability, and Decline

THE IMPACT OF SPEED.   The first force that comes to mind in explaining the age-related IQ losses we typically observe on the WAIS and the PMA was discussed in the section on motor performance in Chapter 4—thinking speed. Remember that one of the most predictable generalizations we can make about older people is that they are slower. They are not able to mentally process information as quickly as before. How critical is this overall slowing in accounting for age-related changes in IQ?

According to Timothy Salthouse (1991), absolutely critical. Salthouse takes the position that, if we cannot think quickly, by definition we cannot think well. Moreover, he believes, age-related slowness is the root cause of age-related IQ decline. In the following study, Christopher Hertzog tested this *processing rate interpretation* of intellectual change.

Hertzog (1989) measured the rapidity with which people of various ages could copy correctly marked answers in the PMA booklet to an answer sheet within a brief period of time. He then examined how these copying speed scores correlated with his subjects' performance on the various PMA tests. When variations in copying speed were controlled for, the large cross-sectional age declines on each timed PMA test were greatly attenuated. In other words, just as Salthouse predicts, much of the loss researchers find with age on any fluid IQ test seems largely traceable to slower speed.

While some slowness is inevitable or primary to growing old, remember from Chapter 4 that reaction times vary from person to person. Older people who are physically active and especially free from chronic disease tend to be quicker than people who are sedentary and ill. This brings us to another force that looms large in explaining age changes in IQ and their variations from person to person—health.

THE IMPACT OF ILLNESS.   The fact that health might be important in accounting for age-related IQ losses may have entered your mind just by looking at the

contextual perspective on intelligence
Concept that intellectual change is multidirectional and individual-specific and that, rather than making generalizations, we need to explore the conditions and contexts promoting intelligence in the adult years.

information about overall change. Why does Schaie's research show that late middle age is the turning point, the time when clear declines first occur? Why do both this study and the WAIS research pinpoint later life as a period of accelerated loss? Perhaps the enemy is not just advancing years, but illness. By late middle age, chronic illness begins to affect a significant number of people. In the seventies, this aging enemy is extremely common (see Chapter 5).

Our first hint that being in poor health might cause IQ losses actually first came from one of the earliest studies of the aging process. The researchers' original goal in this study was to examine primary aging, that is, the aging process apart from disease. So they tried to recruit a very healthy group of elderly men. During their evaluations, they found by accident that their subjects actually fell into two groups: one totally healthy; the other with minor signs of illness, such as high blood pressure or beginning heart disease. When the groups were given an intelligence test similar to the WAIS, the totally healthy men outperformed the less-than-ideally-healthy group on 10 of 11 subtests (Birren, Butler, Greenhouse, Sokoloff, and Yarrow, 1963).

Older people who report being in poor health and those with a wide range of chronic conditions consistently score comparatively lower on IQ tests (Field, Schaie, and Leino, 1988; Hultsch, Hammer, and Small, 1993; Perlmutter and Nyquist, 1990). However, in order to really demonstrate that being ill causes intelligence to *decline*, we need studies tracing how people perform over time. We have that evidence from the Seattle Longitudinal Study for a very important chronic illness—heart disease.

We might expect heart disease to affect how we function intellectually because, as we saw in Chapter 3, poor *cardiovascular function* affects the blood circulation to the brain. In fact, as we know that heart disease causes slower reaction times, we can be certain that this illness will critically affect performance on any fluid intelligence test (Earles and Salthouse, 1995). Actually Schaie's research team found that men and women with heart disease lost points earlier *on all five PMA abilities* than did the healthy volunteers. Heart disease even predicted which older people would benefit from a training program to improve IQ.

As part of a set of studies demonstrating that coaching can improve performance on IQ tests, discussed at the end of this chapter, the researchers gave elderly people training on inductive reasoning and then examined their medical records for the previous seven years. As they suspected, people who benefited most from the training had better medical histories, having fewer diseases and doctor visits and, in particular, being less likely to suffer from cardiovascular disease (Schaie, 1990).

If illness causes IQ scores to decline, could losses above and beyond what we might normally expect on intelligence tests be a "symptom" of approaching death? This interesting idea, called the **terminal drop hypothesis,** also has a long research history (Berg, 1996).

The fact that intelligence test losses could be a sign of approaching death was discovered almost simultaneously in studies in Germany (Riegel and Riegel, 1972; Riegel, Riegel, and Meyer, 1967) and the United States (Jarvik and Falik, 1963) more than three decades ago. Recently the Seattle Study also shows that—*among certain abilities*—dips in performance can be an ominous sign in middle and later life. Schaie's research team found that in late middle-age the people who subsequently dropped out of the study due to illness had previously scored lowest on tests of crystallized abilities. In old age, unusual losses on these tests were more common among volunteers who died soon after (Cooney, Schaie, and Willis, 1988). In other words, perhaps because crystallized abilities *should* remain relatively stable, changes in this type of intelligence in particular may be one revealing indicator of deteriorating health.

Our discussion of the different aging patterns in Chapter 3 puts this research into a larger framework. Recall that the Baltimore researchers find that a sudden decline in any

terminal drop hypothesis
Theory that age loss on IQ tests above and beyond what is typical is a sign of impending death.

normally stable physical function may be a sign of approaching death. So, just as we saw with the immune system, fading crystallized performance may be another marker of problems, a deviation from a normally steady function signaling that something can be seriously physically wrong. (Terminal drop also may explain why in very old age the classic aging pattern breaks down. As we approach the biological limit of life, crystallized skills have to dramatically slope down because *everyone* is within a few years of death.)

People who are sick and close to death may "lose intelligence" for two reasons: (1) Their physical problems directly affect their thinking, (2) When they take to bed, they lose interest in the world. This brings us to the advice that is regularly dispensed to older people today—keep mentally active.

THE IMPACT OF MENTAL STIMULATION.   Elderly people who participate in mentally stimulating activities score comparatively higher on intelligence tests (Hultsch, Hammer, and Small, 1993). However, as these people may choose to read, or attend classes, or do crossword puzzles because they are *already* more intelligent, to suggest that these mind-stretching activities help us stay intelligent requires at a minimum longitudinal research.

For the past 25 years, Carmi Schooler (1990) has been examining how intellectual flexibility, or our ability to approach problems from different perspectives, changes over the years as a function of having certain jobs. He and his coworkers find that complex work, jobs involving reasoning and thinking, lead to higher intellectual flexibility. Routine work, such as flipping hamburgers, causes intellectual flexibility to decline. The researchers have confirmed these findings for adults of every age in a variety of countries and have even extended them to housewives and children. The more complex our daily life is, the more it requires thinking and reasoning, the more intellectually flexible we tend to become.

Without doubt, the most interesting evidence supporting the advice "keep mentally active" involves experiments in animals. We already know that the brain is able to repair itself and grow by sprouting dendrites. What impact does the environment have in promoting this neural growth? Marian Diamond (1988) has been exploring this question in a series of studies designed to reveal the impact of being in a highly stimulating environment on the brains of laboratory rats. Diamond typically puts animals in either a standard environment or an enriched environment (a large cage with other animals and a variety of "toys," such as mazes wheels and swings) and then compares the width of each group's respective cerebral cortexes after various periods of time.

In her earliest studies, Diamond found that young rats exposed to the enriched condition had markedly thicker cortexes. Would she see the same effect among older rats? The answer is yes. Though the change is less dramatic and requires being in the stimulating environment much longer, older animals put in an enriched environment also have thicker, heavier brains.

CONCLUSIONS, CAUTIONS, AND THE IMPORTANCE OF CONTINUITY.
These studies suggest that intelligence is *plastic*, more changeable *throughout life* than we had believed. However, this does not mean that we should all rush out to become rocket scientists. Recall from Chapter 3 that we must be cautious about generalizing from animal studies. What applies to laboratory rats may not fit human beings. Moreover, as Schooler (1990) points out, exposing ourselves to an environment that is *too* complex may produce anxiety and retreat and so reduce our ability to flexibly deal with life. The concept of *person/environment congruence* (see Chapter 4) seems relevant here. The environment must stretch our capacities, but also fit who we are.

We need to take the same cautious approach to the studies showing that being ill impairs mental functioning. While the saying "a sound mind in a sound body" may be

Ella Fitzgerald and Mother Theresa both continued to enrich lives in their later years, and are just two examples demonstrating that our enduring gifts, who we are as people, are the most important force explaining creative achievement at any age.

accurate to a point, remember that we are describing test score *losses*. Except in extreme cases, such as when a person is seriously ill, our enduring abilities, "who we are as people," are the most important predictors of how we will function intellectually throughout life. As Feature 6–1 shows, when we look at that important example of intelligence in action, creative achievements, continuity is the number one theme. While changes do occur as the years advance, people who are highly accomplished earlier in life tend to be creative and high-functioning in their later years.

NEW CONCEPTIONS AND TESTS OF ADULT INTELLIGENCE

So far, we have been focusing on traditional intelligence tests, exploring their results, the explanations for these results, and the forces affecting these results. Maybe we need to reconsider our basic framework. Are these tests really measuring intelligence in adult life?

The reason for using tests such as the WAIS-R or the PMA is that they are *valid*. How a person performs on these abstract tasks reflects intelligent behavior in the real world. In the past few decades, however, this assumption has been questioned. The argument goes like this:

All intelligence tests are limited, constructed to apply to behaviors, skills, and attributes deemed signs of intelligence at a particular time and place. There can be no absolutely universal intelligence test, as different societies value different behaviors and put a premium on different skills. In a Zulu tribe, being intelligent might include being attuned to nature, able to quickly sense danger, and skilled at throwing a spear. In this place where verbal and mathematical skills are irrelevant, we would be less than intelligent to use the verbal WAIS-R as our standard for intelligence.

Michelangelo and Beethoven produced their most creative work later in life. Tolstoy and Picasso stayed productive and creative until their eighties. On the other hand, many people feel that age is the death knell of creative work. Older artists complain about the premium put on finding young talent, about the fact that few galleries will look at their paintings. In "creative fields," such as advertising, more than other professions, being over 40 is a severe detriment to getting hired. In the Silicon Valley, at age 35, my brother (who started a computer company) was an old man. In the sciences and the arts, the general stereotype is that most creative breakthroughs happen when people are young.

The reason may be that we link creativity with adopting new perspectives or looking at the world in fresh and different ways. In other words, we associate being creative with fluid-type skills. However, in order to produce good work, doesn't a person also have to spend hours practicing, perfecting, and refining his or her knowledge (Abra, 1989; Simonton, 1990a)? Shouldn't the pragmatics of intelligence be important in being creative, especially in certain fields?

Psychologist Dean Simonton (1989, 1990a, 1990b) has systematically studied how creativity among creative geniuses changes with age. In exploring famous writers, Simonton discovered that poets produced their best work when youngest, in their late thirties. The peak age for producing fiction was somewhat older—the early forties. Non-fiction peaked last—at age 50 (Simonton, 1975).

Viewed in terms of fluid and crystallized abilities, these findings make sense. Poets play with language, using words in unexpected ways. In other words, in this type of writing, fluid-type skills seem especially important. Writing a book depends on knowledge, discipline, years spent perfecting a craft. Writing non-fiction especially demands knowledge, talents gained through having studied for years.

Other research confirms that we can estimate the peak creative age based on the mix of "knowledge" versus "newness" required in a given creative field. Wayne Dennis (1966), for instance, discovered that, while dancers tend to reach their peak in the early thirties, historians and scholars do not reach their creative prime until their sixties.

In these studies of famous people, however, the most typical pattern is remarkably similar to Schaie's findings with IQ. Often people reach their creative peak in their forties (Simonton, 1990a, 1990b). In examining more-average scientists, Stephen Cole (1979) discovered the same pattern. Productivity is highest in the early forties, levels off or declines slightly until about age 50, and then drops off slowly after that.

These studies—while interesting—should not fully satisfy any young creative person. That person wants to know, "If I, personally, am unusually accomplished now, how likely am I to change?" Answering this question requires longitudinal research.

In a follow-up to his investigation of scientists, Cole selected mathematicians who had gotten their Ph.D.s between 1947 and 1950 and traced their careers over the next quarter century, classifying his sample as strong publishers, weak publishers, or non-publishers, based on their publications during one five-year period. Then he looked at whether people maintained the same ranking during other periods. Rarely did a person shift significantly; almost half never changed ranks at all. In a similar study of 1,000 academic psychologists, researchers also found that stability was the dominant theme. Though productivity did reach a peak at about age 40, how much a person published was more a function of that individual's enduring characteristics than of being at a certain life stage. People who started out as high publishers continued to be prolific. At 55 to 64, they produced more papers than their less productive contemporaries did at their peak (Horner, Rushton, and Vernon, 1986).

Even Simonton's research on creative geniuses illustrates that *who* we are, not what age we are, is the driving force behind creativity. Simonton (1990a, 1990b, 1991) found that 10 percent of all famous people make a remarkable half of all the important contributions in any field. Why even in dance, that young person's field, Martha Graham still stood head and shoulders above her colleagues until late in life!

Perhaps we are making the same error in our own society. The *criterion situation* intelligence tests were constructed to measure was performance in a particular setting—school. For this reason, while good measures of the most important aspect of intelligence in childhood and adolescence, these measures may not apply as well to adulthood, when being intelligent involves making our way in the real world (Schaie, 1977–1978, 1989).

IQ tests do their job well for children. They are a very good predictor of performance in school. However, beyond the point necessary to get into an occupation, scores on these tests are less effective in predicting real-world success. The best lawyers, or doctors, or race track handicappers (Ceci and Liker, 1986) do not necessarily score higher than other people in their occupation on standard IQ tests, implying that these measures are not measuring the range of skills involved in intelligence in the world (Wagner and Sternberg, 1986).

Another fact that should give us pause becomes evident when we look at age changes on IQ tests in the light of another truth: The most responsible jobs in society are held by men and women in the second half of adult life. It is hard to reconcile even Schaie's positive findings of decline starting in the fifties with the fact that the people who run our country, head our corporations, and hold the most responsible positions in society are often at least that age *and beyond*. While we can explain away the discrepancy between the way middle-aged and older people perform on standard IQ tests and the complexity of the jobs they have by invoking Baltes's assumption that crystallized gains override fluid declines, still what we are saying is that the tests are misleading. They are not really revealing the *mixture of skills* necessary to being intelligent in adult life.

These thoughts have led psychologists to take a new look at what it means to be an intelligent adult. What qualities are involved in real-world or **everyday intelligence?** Can we construct tests that capture the skills crucial to intelligent behavior in adult life?

Sternberg's Tests of Practical Intelligence

One psychologist who has spearheaded this reexamination is Robert Sternberg. Not only have Sternberg's ideas transformed how we generally think of intelligence, but also he has made important contributions to our understanding of creativity, wisdom, competence, and, as we will see in Chapter 10, love. Here we look just at this creative psychologist's efforts to measure **practical intelligence** in adults.

Sternberg and Richard Wagner argue that the items in standard intelligence tests are well defined, are formulated by other people, have little intrinsic interest, and have only one correct response. Real-world challenges, they believe, have little in common with these artificial tasks. Making intelligent decisions at work and in life involves weighing alternatives, reacting to changing situations, and mastering problems that often do not have clear-cut right or wrong answers. It is no wonder that some people who are good at producing the right answers on an IQ test can fail badly at work and life (Wagner and Sternberg, 1986).

Sternberg and Wagner believe that the knowledge needed to function in the real world differs from the skills measured by IQ tests in another important way. Most often it is never directly taught. We are not formally instructed in how to choose the career that best fits our personality or told specifically what we have to do to climb the ladder of success at work. We must figure out this *tacit knowledge* for constructing a successful career and life on our own.

According to Sternberg and Wagner, tacit knowledge at work involves separate domains: knowledge of how to manage oneself, manage coworkers, and manage one's career. People who are skilled at managing themselves know how to maximize their own productivity. They understand what will make it easier to begin and continue working and how to efficiently approach tasks. People who shine in the second area have "people skills." They know how to relate to others, to motivate coworkers to do their best. People

everyday intelligence
In contrast to academic knowledge, being intelligent in daily life.

practical intelligence
Being intelligent at negotiating and managing daily life, especially knowing the optimal way to advance in a career.

Some Items on Sternberg and Wagner's Practical Intelligence in Business Test

Table 6-4

Person is asked to use a scale from 1 (not important) to 7 (extremely important) in rating each alternative.

1. Your company has sent you to a university to recruit potential trainees for management positions. Rate the importance of the following student characteristics as to which lead to later success in business.
   a. Ability to set priorities according to the importance of your task.
   b. Motivation.
   c. Ability to follow through and bring tasks to completion.
   d. Ability to promote your ideas and convince others of the worth of your work.
   e. The need to win at everything, no matter what the cost.

2. A number of factors enter into the establishment of a good reputation in a company as a manager. Consider the following factors and rate their importance.
   a. Critical thinking ability.
   b. Speaking ability.
   c. Extent of college education and prestige of the school attended.
   d. No hesitancy to take extraordinary risky courses of action.
   e. A keen sense of what superiors can be sold on.

3. Rate the following strategies according to how important they are for doing well as a businessperson.
   a. Think in terms of tasks accomplished rather than hours spent working.
   b. Be in charge of all phases of every task or project you are involved with.
   c. Use a daily list of goals arranged according to your priorities.
   d. Carefully consider the optimal strategy before beginning a task.
   e. Reward yourself upon completion of important tasks.

Ans.: 1. a+, b−, c+, d−, e−; 2. a−, b−, c−, d+, e−; 3. a+, b+, c+, d−, e−
(+ means a higher rating, a score of 4 or above given by people more advanced in the field versus less advanced people. − means a relatively lower rating by experts.)

Source: From *The Triarchic Mind* by Robert J. Sternberg, pages 214-215. Copyright © 1988 by Robert J. Sternberg. Used by permission of Viking Penguin, a division of Penguin Books USA Inc.

good at the third domain are attuned to the rules of their profession and sensitive to what exactly is needed in their field to achieve success.

Sternberg and Wagner's next step was to construct tests measuring each domain and show that these measures could identify people less or more successful in particular fields. The first profession they turned to is one they were familiar with—academic psychology. The second is that field that has been the subject of many "how to" books—business management.

They devised scales of tacit knowledge for both professions (see the examples in Table 6–4) and compared the performance of accomplished experts, less successful colleagues, graduate students and total novices (college undergraduates). In each case, they succeeded. Managers of Fortune 500 companies outperformed business school students, who performed much better than undergraduates on the test of tacit knowledge in business. Scores on the tacit knowledge of psychology test were higher for academic psychologists than for graduate students and distinguished people successful in this field. Quality of publications, ranking of scholarly achievement, and employment as a professor in a prestigious psychology department all were related to scoring high on the tacit knowledge in psychology scale. Most important, the tests predicted the criterion *better* than traditional IQ tests. For both professions, performance on these scales was more related to job success than were scores on a standard intelligence test.

You might be thinking, with reason, that this attempt to devise tests of adult intelligence is *too* specific. Certainly it should be possible to make up measures that have wider applicability than to a single career. Moreover, Sternberg and Wagner's studies do not speak to the main issue of adult development, how we change over time. This brings us to Nancy Denney's broader, more developmental approach.

Denney's Optimally Exercised and Unexercised Abilities

Unlike Sternberg, Denney's specialty is adult development, so her main interest is in examining how people change with age. She has constructed tests that measure everyday intelligence in a more general way. Denney's strategy is to devise problems people might find in daily life, ask adults of different ages to provide solutions, and then score these answers for effectiveness. Here is an sample item:

> Let's say that one evening you go to the refrigerator to get something cold to drink. When you open the refrigerator, you notice that it is not cold, but rather warm. What would you do?

In Denney's first study, performance on these problems improved until midlife and then declined. Could she make up a test where younger or older people performed best? To explore this possibility, Denney and her colleagues hit on the idea of devising tests focusing on issues that might crop up at specific ages. They reasoned that young adults should perform best on tests constructed to apply to problems they might encounter. On tests with problems relating to later life, such as retirement, the elderly should perform better than anyone else.

Scores on the young-adult test fulfilled their predictions, reaching a peak in youth and declining at older ages. Unfortunately, on the older-adult test, middle-aged people still outperformed the elderly. *In fact, despite several efforts, on no test Denney has designed have older adults done best* (Denney, 1989).

I must emphasize that other researchers have had better success at making up tests where the pattern is better performance in later life (Cornelius and Caspi, 1987). Still, Denney was not really alarmed by her findings because they fit in perfectly with her **theory of optimally exercised and unexercised abilities.**

Denney's (1989) theory offers a framework for understanding why performance on some activities is best when we are young and other skills are at their peak in midlife, but performance on skills people even work hard on often declines before age 65. Central to Denney's thinking is the distinction between abilities we exercise versus those we do not exercise as well as our biological ceiling, the limit we are capable of when our abilities are "optimally exercised." The bottom curve in Figure 6–2 shows unexercised abilities, how we perform on an activity that we *never* practice at different ages. Optimally exercised potential, the upper curve, shows how well we *could* perform that activity at our maximum, our limit of *reserve capacity*, at various ages. Notice that, while the two curves differ greatly in height, each has the same slope, reaching its peak at about age 30 and then declining.

Exercised abilities, skills we practice, are shown in the middle curve. Denney reasons that performance on these abilities lies somewhere between our biological potential and the lower, unexercised curve. Notice how different the path of this curve is. Because we improve as we practice, performance on continually exercised abilities remains stable or rises over the years, until a certain point. When this curve intersects

theory of optimally exercised and unexercised abilities *Denney's theory charting the age path of abilities that are practiced during adult life versus those that are not.*

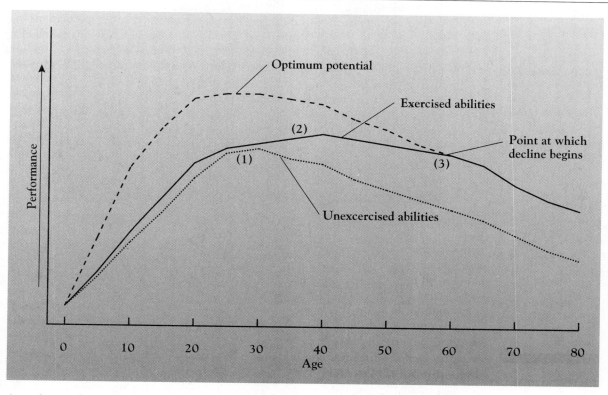

According to this graph, skills we do not exercise reach their peak in the twenties and then decline (1). Performance improves or stays constant on exercised abilities through midlife (2). However, after the point at which exercised abilities meet one's "optimum potential" (3), even performance on these well-practiced activities gradually declines.

Source: Denney, N. A. (1989). Everyday problem solving: Methodological issues, research findings, and a model, in L. W. Poon, D. C. Rubin, and B. A. Wilson (Eds.). *Everyday cognition in adulthood and late life* (pp. 59–73). New York: Cambridge University Press. Reprinted by Permission of Cambridge University Press.

with the curve for optimal potential, even the most highly practiced ability must slowly wend its way down over time.

Let's illustrate with the interview at the beginning of this chapter. When Jean entered college for the first time, her school skills may have been close to the level of unexercised abilities. With her many educational experiences over the years, she may have been pleased to see her performance improve as it floated closer to her biological optimum. However, because at the same time that optimum is falling, at some point she will hit her biological ceiling (the curves will intersect). Then, no matter how much she continues to practice, her performance will decline. We cannot perform *above* the limit of our reserve capacity.

Denney's theory offers an interesting perspective on the impact of practice on performance at different ages. However, notice that she agrees with the traditional idea that youth is *basically* our intellectual peak. The psychologists we turn to now disagree with this assumption. In fact, their whole framework for understanding adult intelligence is different: As we mature, our style, or manner of approaching problems, totally changes.

A Neo-Piagetian Approach to Adult Intelligence

neo-Piagetian perspective on intelligence
Theory that extends Piaget's stage theory of intellectual development to adult life.

The **neo-Piagetian approach to adult intelligence** grew out of the speculations of philosophers, personality psychologists, and creativity researchers as to what really constitutes mature adult thought. These ideas and findings were synthesized by psychologists specializing in adult cognition in order to offer a new alternative to thinking about how intelligence develops.

In contrast to the traditional psychometric approach, in which people are ranked as having either more or less of a fixed quantity called intelligence, the basis of this theory is Jean Piaget's idea that, as the child develops, he or she goes through four different stages of understanding the world. In the same way that Piaget believed the child's thinking in each stage is *different in form,* or qualitatively new, neo-Piagetians believe adult cognition involves a different way of understanding the world. Piaget believed that the pinnacle of intellectual development occurs in adolescence, with the highly abstract scientific thinking called formal operations. Neo-Piagetians believe that there is a stage after formal operations called **postformal thought** (Labouvie-Vief, 1992; Rybash, Hoyer, and Roodin, 1986; Sinnott, 1989, 1991).

postformal thought
Type of adult cognition which transcends the highly logical thinking characteristic of formal operations.

1. **Postformal thinking is relativistic.** Adolescents in formal operations believe that everything has an answer. They think that by logic we can determine absolute rights and wrongs. As we grow older and have more experience with life, we give up these beliefs. We know that many real-world problems have no clear-cut answers. Making intelligent life decisions means understanding the relativity of all decision making. Postformal thinkers accept conflicting opinions and explore the multiple perspectives from which issues can be seen. They embrace the ambiguities of life.

   This awareness of relativity does not mean postformal thinkers avoid making decisions or having strong beliefs. The ability to *integrate* multiple perspectives is the true hallmark of postformal thinking, as wise decisions come from being open to the complexity of life.

2. **Post-formal thinking is interpersonal and feeling-oriented.** Adolescents in formal operations believe that by rational analysis they can understand the world. Postformal thinkers go beyond logic to think in a different mode. With the realization that no objective right answer exists, feelings, intuitions, and personal experiences become the basis for making decisions. Postformal thinkers are skilled at empathizing with others and "in touch" with their inner life.

3. **Postformal thinkers are interested in developing questions and seeing new perspectives, rather than finding solutions.** Formal thinkers want to get the "right" answers, have closure, finish or definitively solve tasks. Postformal thinkers are less focused on solutions. They enjoy the process of developing new questions, exploring new perspectives, seeing new frameworks, coming up with different ways of looking at the world.

As we might imagine, testing for this thinking (so beautifully described in Feature 6–2) requires a new strategy. Rather than using single-answer tests, researchers measure the *way* a person arrives at answers, the process of decision making itself. Everyday dilemmas are the format. However, unlike in Denney's studies, when given these problems people are asked to describe their thinking in writing or aloud. Does the person look at problems from different vantage points and consider the feelings of others in arriving at decisions? Does he understand the subjective nature of his conclusions or refer to his own feelings for guidelines as to what is right? That is how responses to this type of problem are scored:

A wonderful example of postformal thought comes from anthropologist Barbara Myerhoff's description of 93-year-old Jacob, the leader at a senior citizens' center in southern California serving elderly Jewish immigrants. As with most center members, Jacob had immigrated to the United States penniless in the early 1900s. After retiring, Jacob began a new career helping elderly Jews, giving of himself—as he had throughout his life—to his community.

Looking now at Jacob's life to identify some of the specific features that account for his success, it is at once clear that luck contributed a fair share. Jacob was naturally favored with great energy, good health, intelligence and talent. In addition to these fortunate personal endowments, he was lucky in his successful marriage that produced four healthy, intelligent sons. Jacob had his share of bad luck too. He had been a political refugee, was jailed, struggled through the major upheaval of immigration, had had to learn new occupations, to relocate many times, was cheated out of business by his partner, went bankrupt, made and lost money again and again. Through all his reverses and mistakes, he had no regrets, and he rebounded with more perspective and energy from each set-back.

Jacob's autobiographical writings document his active struggle at every stage of his checkered career to integrate conflicting pulls between family obligation and worldly success, and between worldly success and social-political ideals. He struggled also with the contradictions between his internationalist beliefs and his nationalism, in the form of Zionism and American patriotism. And he managed to embrace contradictions generated by his agnostic, even anti-religious attitudes, on one hand, and fervent identification with cultural-ethical Judaism, on the other.

These conflicts, it must be stressed, Jacob integrated. He did not simply resolve and dismiss them—for indeed the contradictions are real. The one who chooses to remain alive to the intrinsic worth of all of these opposing beliefs must continually renegotiate their alliance. Jacob was able to tolerate ambiguity and perhaps this trait was a critical contributor to his successful old age. . . .

Jacob's conceptions about and approach to aging were complex and dynamic. He knew how to intensify the present, how to deepen his satisfaction in small rewards and pleasures, how to bring the past into his life for the continuity that gave it intrinsic meaning; yet he never remained fixed on the past nor used it as a negative standard in terms of which to view the present. He knew how to look at the inevitable destiny the future held and accept it without moving toward it with unnecessary speed. Too, Jacob could provide new standards and desires for himself as the old ones become unattainable, generating from within appropriate measures of accomplishment and worth in a continual process of discarding and creating.

Source: From *Number Our Days* by Barbara Myerhoff pages 218–219. Copyright © 1978 by Barbara Myerhoff. Used by permission of Dutton Signet, a division of Penguin Books USA Inc.

John is known to be a heavy drinker, especially when he goes to parties. Mary, John's wife, warns him that, if he gets drunk one more time, she will leave him. John goes to an office party and comes home drunk. Does Mary leave him? How sure are you of your answer?

According to the theory, adolescents should respond to this dilemma in a logical way. "Mary said she would leave, so, of course, she should. Yes, I am sure I am right." Older people should weigh the consequences of leaving, for Mary, for John, for their children. They should state that there are no absolute answers. They should realize that it is "a judgment call."

How might the mother's reasoning during this discussion differ from that of her adolescent daughter? Would the mid-life adult be more likely to show the relativistic, feeling-oriented thinking typical of post formal thought?

On tests of this type, middle-aged and older people typically use more postformal thinking than adolescents. There even is interesting research suggesting that our sensitivity to feelings grows more intense with age. In exploring age differences in memory for different materials, Laura Carstensen and Susan Turk-Charles (1994) found that older people remembered emotional messages especially well, suggesting that in our later years we may focus more on the interpersonal dimension of life. Does this mean that postformal thought is a genuine *stage of development?* The answer seems to be no.

In order to qualify as a genuine age-linked stage, postformal thinking should satisfy certain criteria. People should progress in sequence, first entering formal operations and then at a certain age leaving this stage and entering postformal thought. Once capable of postformal thought, they should not shift back or "regress." They should think only in this stage. Furthermore, if it is really an age-dependent stage, young people should be incapable of postformal thinking, while most (ideally all) middle-aged and elderly adults should think in this way.

None of these conditions exists. Individuals vary in the extent to which they use postformal thinking at any age. Many young adults can reason in this way; many elderly do not (Labouvie-Vief, Hakim-Larson, and Hobart, 1987). Worse yet, postformal thinkers do not just stay in this stage. With problems that have a correct solution, people use formal reasoning. Only when problems are not well structured, that is, without clear answers, do they adopt a postformal mode (Sinnott, 1989). This suggests that, rather than being a genuine stage of development, postformal thinking might more usefully be seen as a skill that some adults have and can draw on as needed in negotiating life.

Baltes Examines Wisdom-Related Expertise

Paul Baltes and his colleagues take a more focused approach to examining the qualities we expect to grow with age. In a series of studies, these researchers have been exploring wisdom, that core component of postformal thought. As we might imagine, Baltes's research team couches their explorations in terms of his conceptions about the mechanics and pragmatics of intelligence: People who have **wisdom-related expertise** are skilled in the pragmatics of life.

In order to explore age changes in wisdom, the researchers first had to *operationalize* or translate the vague entity called wisdom into concrete characteristics or skills. They came up with five dimensions of wisdom-related expertise: People who are wise have rich factual knowledge about life. They have what the researchers call procedural knowledge; that is, they understand how to implement decisions, for instance, when to take action, to give advice, to evaluate, to monitor, and follow up on plans. People who are wise have "lifespan contextualism." This means that they are attuned to the changing quality of human relationships through life and sensitive to the historical and social environment

wisdom-related expertise
According to Baltes, five dimensions measuring expertise or skill at the pragmatics of living.

Problem with Young Target

Martha, a young woman, decides to have a family and not to have a career. She is married and has children. One day Martha meets a woman friend whom she has not seen for a long time. The friend has decided to have a career and no family. She is about to establish herself in her career.

Problem with Old Target

Martha, an elderly woman, had once decided to have a family and not a career. Her children left home some years ago. One day Martha meets a woman friend whom she has not seen for a long time. The friend had decided to have a career and no family. She had retired some years ago.

This meeting causes Martha to think back over her life.
What might her life review look like?
Which aspects of her life might she remember?
How might she explain her life?
How might she evaluate her life retrospectively?

In this study, a group of older people and young adults were given either the young or the elderly Martha vignette and asked to free associate into a tape recorder. Raters then judged the quality of each subject's responses according to the five wisdom-related criteria.

Source: Staudinger, U. M., Smith, J., and Baltes, P. B. Wisdom-related knowledge in a life-review task: Age differences and the role of professional specialization. *Psychology and Aging, 7,* 271–281, Copyright 1992 by the American Psychological Association. Reprinted by Permission.

within which behavior occurs. Wise people are also attuned to the fact that individuals may have valid competing perspectives and understand the relative nature of values and goals. Finally, wise individuals understand that life is unpredictable and have developed backup plans for coping when the inevitable unexpected event occurs (Smith and Baltes, 1990).

Armed with these criteria, the researchers then needed to devise situations in which older and young adults could demonstrate these five qualities or skills. They decided on the technique used in the research designed to reveal postformal thought: Present people with scenarios describing life problems, have them think aloud, and train raters to score these taped protocols. In this case, subjects' responses were rated along each dimension according to a scale ranging from 1 (poor) to 7 (ideally wise). As the examples in Table 6–5 show, older- and young-adult groups were presented with either a scenario relating to their own life stage or one relating to a similar person at the alternate time of life.

As the researchers expected—under the assumption that wisdom is a rare quality at any age—on average the subjects performed at a low/middle level (about 3) on the tasks. Very few people produced responses that reached the wise end of the scale (5 or above). Interestingly people of each age tended to score somewhat higher if the scenario related to their own time of life. Young adults scored better on the vignette describing the younger person. Older people performed best in the situation where the target person was a 60-year-old. Once again, however, as we saw with postformal thinking, wise responding was more a property of the person than of advancing age. The handful of subjects classified as "wise" were approximately equally distributed between young and old adults (Baltes and Staudinger, 1993).

If chronological age is not sufficient for wisdom, perhaps, reasoned the researchers, experience in activities demanding wisdom-type thinking might produce this expertise. Specifically, if wisdom is a skill involving practice, when a person's occupation or life work involves analyzing human relationships, shouldn't wisdom-related knowledge be comparatively high? To explore this possibility, in their next set of studies the research team compared the performance of a sample of clinical psychologists on their test to that of people in other occupations (Staudinger, Smith, and Baltes, 1992; Smith, Staudinger, and Baltes, 1994).

As they predicted, the clinical psychologists scored significantly higher than people whose work did not involve expertise in human relationships. However, the mean score of the psychologists on the five dimensions was still in the average range. While the numbers spoke in favor of the older clinical psychologists (4 out of 8 older psychologists had total scores qualifying them as wise versus 3 out of 9 young clinicians), even here being older and in an occupation demanding wisdom was no guarantee of showing a high level of competence in this important area of life.

Concluding Questions and Criticisms

By now, you may have noticed that, while these new approaches capture qualities that most of us feel are crucial to intelligence in adult life, no theory or measure of adult intelligence is totally satisfying. Even the effort to develop these new tests is not universally embraced. Some thoughtful critics feel it is a wrong path (Salthouse, 1991).

Psychologists worry that, as we saw with Sternberg's scales, tests based in real life will be too situation-specific to be really useful (Scribner, 1986) or that they will be *more* discriminatory, biased in favor of people with certain types of knowledge (Denney, 1989). As you may have noticed in our discussion of postformal thought or wisdom-related thinking, tests of life intelligence may be subjective, value-laden, and dependent on the evaluator's own personal idea of what constitutes ideal behavior. Furthermore, measures of everyday intelligence (at least of the type Denney or Sternberg proposes) may not even provide information very different from that of traditional psychometric tests. Notice that performance on Denney's tests shows the same pattern as the Seattle research: Scores reach their peak in midlife and then decline. In fact, in one study of older people, scores on a scale of everyday intelligence were highly correlated with performance on a standard measure of fluid IQ (Willis and Schaie, 1986). Should we rush to give up traditional psychometric tests as our main benchmark of intelligence in adult life? Clearly the data are not in.

APPLICATIONS AND INTERVENTIONS

What interventions exist to keep intelligence fine-tuned, especially during the last critical decades of life? How *plastic* is IQ during our older years? First, we look at research specifically designed to answer the second question—studies exploring the extent to which older people can improve their scores on intelligence tests.

Improving Older Adults' Performance on IQ Tests

The Adult Development and Enrichment Project was a systematic research program, begun by Schaie and his colleagues during the late 1970s, designed to demonstrate that age-related IQ losses could be reversed. The researchers specifically targeted fluid abilities, those more biologically based aspects of cognition, to demonstrate that in their words "old dogs can learn new tricks" (Willis, 1989).

Mean Change from Base-Line Score on Figural Relations for Older Adults with a Mean Age of 69 in 1979 after Three Training Sessions Carried Out over a Seven-Year Period

Figure 6–3

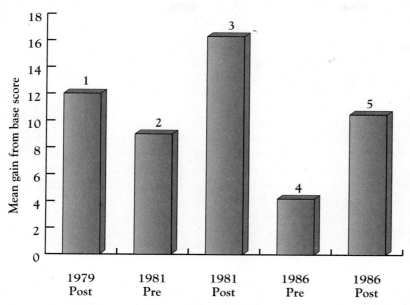

This chart shows that training can dramatically improve performance on this fluid ability and that some gains do persist over time (see 2 and 4). However, as the members of this elderly group advanced to their mid-seventies, the impact of training was clearly not as great (see 5, the 1986 posttest score).

Source: Adapted from Willis, S. L., and Nesselroade, C. S. (1990). Long-term effects of fluid ability training in old-old age, *Developmental Psychology, 26,* 905–910. Copyright 1990 by The American Psychological Association. Reprinted by permission.

These **cognitive remediation** studies have proved their point. Study after study has shown that providing training on inductive reasoning or spatial relations improves performance on these fluid tests. The impact of this training is not just immediate. When a person is reminded to use the strategy, gains can be seen even at a long-term follow-up (Hayslip, Maloy, and Kohl, 1995). There also is some very narrow transfer. After being trained on one measure, a person's scores on other tests of the same fluid ability improve (Schaie, 1996).

Training can even wipe out inroads in performance suffered earlier on. In the Seattle sample, after training most older people who had lost points improved to where they were 14 years before. Those who had been relatively stable performed at a higher level than in middle age (Willis and Schaie, 1986; Willis, 1989).

However, there are qualifications. As I just implied, transfer is narrow, with improvement mainly limited to that specific ability or skill (Baltes and Sowarka, 1989; Baltes, Sowarka, and Kliegl, 1989). Moreover, although, as mentioned, some gains do persist after training, people need periodic booster sessions in order to maintain their skills (Schaie, 1996; see Figure 6–3). This has led critics to question whether these older

cognitive remediation
Intervention showing that with training age-related IQ losses can be ameliorated or reversed.

people really have "become more intelligent" or merely have been taught a set of intelligence-test-taking skills (Salthouse, 1991). There are wide variations in the extent to which people profit from cognitive remediation (Willis, 1989). As we saw earlier in this chapter in discussing heart disease and its impact on IQ, some older people do very well after training. Others do not improve. Moreover, while Schaie and his coworkers have specifically avoided comparing old and young people, other researchers find that young adults benefit as much or more than the elderly from training to improve IQ (Salthouse, 1991).

In other words, there is a limit to plasticity, an upper boundary beyond which people cannot go. Furthermore, the ceiling for optimum performance seems lower in the old. As Denney suggests in her theory and as Diamond's studies of neural growth seem to reinforce, cognitively as well as physically, older people have a lower reserve capacity than the young.

Baltes's research team advocates an approach called *testing the limits* to pinpoint that upper boundary. What is the limit of reserve capacity, the ceiling beyond which people cannot go after being trained? Here individual differences in improvement are crucial. In fact, they can be used in a diagnostic way. In one study, Baltes's colleagues demonstrated that *not* improving after training might be a potential early marker for Alzheimer's disease (Baltes, Kuhl, and Sowarka, 1992).

Since the cognitive remediation studies demonstrate beyond a shadow of a doubt that, with qualifications, older people *can* learn new tricks, they are a good introduction to our second intervention to improve cognition in later life—older-adult education programs.

Education Programs for Older Adults

older-adult education programs
Education programs that cater to people over age 60 or 65.

Based on the idea that mental stimulation is essential to preserving intelligence, lectures, courses, and other learning activities are an integral part of **older-adult education programs** at senior centers, at hospitals, and in nursing homes. As we saw in the interview with Jean at the beginning of this chapter, older people are increasingly returning on their own to college, whether to get undergraduate or advanced degrees or simply to take courses. In fact, today a whole cadre of gerontologists specializes in what is called *lifelong learning*. Their work involves developing and administering education programs specifically for older adults. Let's now sample just three types of educational opportunities set up exclusively for older learners (U.S. Senate Special Committee on Aging, 1991b, 1992).

Elderhostel
Education program in which people over age 60 take short-term courses on college campuses or in educational settings around the world.

The most well known older-adult education program is called **Elderhostel.** In this popular program, open to anyone over age 60, older adults literally go back to college. They enroll in intensive, typically week-long courses "in residence" at universities, museums, and other educational settings. Since its inception in 1975, Elderhostel has grown at an amazing rate and has become widely respected for the quality and diversity of its offerings. As of 1990, 1,500 institutions in the United States, Canada, and 40 countries hosted Elderhostel programs. In that year alone, the 215,000 people who participated in this "adventure of a lifetime" could choose from a dazzling array of options from examining glacier formations in Alaska, to traveling to Australia to study aboriginal culture, to taking courses in art at the Louvre or studying Mozart in New York. Here is one participant's enthusiastic description:

> A week after my program at the University of Notre Dame in Indiana, looking back I have an overwhelming memory: it was simply wonderful. . . . I chose Notre Dame mainly because of three courses offered: "Human Evolution: Prehistory or Poetry", "Pascal on Faith and Reason", and "Wet and Dryland Aerobics." How lucky can you be? Each was better than I had any reason to hope for. . . . Dr. James

This elderly woman taking a course at NASA would no longer be seen as totally out of place on any university campus. Going back to school is widely seen as a vehicle for promoting intellectual and emotional well being in later life.

Ellis was middle aged, bulky, balding, bronzed. . . . He made mankind come alive, showed us how our species is swiftly and not wisely changing the world. His illustrations were stunning: "We Americans are using 75 percent of the world's calories." (And I didn't want to make him a liar as I passed through the cafeteria line). We have imported the sweatshop around the world. . . . Next Sandy Vanslager puts us through our paces in the aerobics class. . . . With my damaged ticker I was concerned, but . . . I felt great, even though part of the class dropped out. Dr. Tom Morris was equally outstanding. . . . The quality of the program was so magnificent that I felt I was in heaven. . . . Notre Dame, I won't forget you! (Mills, 1993, pp. 108–111)

The My Turn Program at Kingsborough Community College in Brooklyn exemplifies another type of avenue for getting higher education, the special program catering to older adults within a traditional college setting. Although, as we saw with Jean, older people can and do return to school without benefit of special services, some may be deterred by the unfamiliar environment. For others, returning to college is not even possible because they are living on a fixed income or because they lack the necessary educational credentials. Remember that many of this cohort of over-65-year-olds left school before getting a high school diploma. My Turn eliminates these barriers by offering *any* New York City or state resident who is over 65 the chance to take courses at this branch of the City University of New York tuition-free, whether or not that person has completed high school. Counseling, tutoring, and peer support while negotiating this new territory are available to the more than 2,000 participants from a variety of backgrounds who take advantage of the program every year.

In contrast, the type of education provided by Operation ABLE occurs outside of the college milieu and has a specific goal: helping older people return to the work force. Begun in 1976 in the Chicago area, Operation ABLE is a non-profit, private organization dedicated to providing workers over age 45 with the skills to successfully find new work. Based on the idea that, if older workers are to compete in today's job market, they must be versed in technology, the Boston chapter of this now national organization recently set up a computer skills training center. IBM has contributed the hardware, software, and related equipment; Digital Equipment Corporation has developed the training modules. Both companies provide staff to help the center develop and teach the courses.

These programs providing learning to the elderly are complemented by hundreds of others that enable the elderly to impart their learning to others. In Los Angeles and other cities, older people are specifically solicited as classroom volunteers. They teach English to immigrants and tutor students in reading and math. If someone is a retired business person, for instance, that individual can join SCORE (Senior Corps of Retired Executives), a government-sponsored program in which retired executives and managers serve as mentors to young people who are setting up their own small businesses (U.S. Senate Special Committee on Aging, 1991b). As Schooler's studies suggest, keeping "mentally stimulated" occurs through being immersed in any type of challenging work, be it teaching or learning or engaging in other personally meaningful activities of life. Moreover, as we will see in our discussion of personality in Chapter 8, this very involvement in meaningful (that is, personally stimulating) activities is crucial—not just to our cognitive functioning, but also to our emotional well-being.

KEY TERMS & CONCEPTS

Wechsler Intelligence Scale for Adults
traditional psychometric intelligence test
classic aging pattern
crystallized intelligence
fluid intelligence
mechanics of intelligence
pragmatics of intelligence
ability-extraneous influences on IQ
Seattle Longitudinal Study
contextual perspective on intelligence
terminal drop hypothesis
everyday intelligence
practical intelligence
theory of optimally exercised and unexercised abilities
neo-Piagetian perspective on intelligence
postformal thought
wisdom-related expertise
cognitive remediation
older-adult education programs
Elderhostel

RECOMMENDED READINGS

U.S. Senate Special Committee on Aging. (1991, 1992). *Lifelong learning for an aging society.* Washington, DC: U.S. Government Printing Office.
> *These government publications review a variety of lifelong learning opportunities available as of the early 1990s. The 1992 edition is annotated.*

Diamond, M. C. (1988). *Enriching heredity.* New York: Free Press.
> *Diamond offers compelling evidence for the importance of a stimulating environment in fostering mental growth.*

Poon, L. W., Rubin, D. C., and Wilson, B. A. (Eds) (1989). *Everyday cognition in adulthood and late life.* New York: Cambridge University Press.
> *This edited book describes a variety of new approaches to measuring memory and intelligence in adult life. In one chapter, Nancy Denney summarizes her studies. In another, Sherry Willis describes the cognitive remediation research.*

Rybash, J. N., Hoyer, W. J., and Roodin, P. (1986). *Adult cognition and aging: Developmental changes in processing, knowing, and thinking.* New York: Pergamon Press.
> *Though this book is somewhat dated, it offers an excellent description of postformal thought.*

Salthouse, T. A. (1991). *Theoretical perspectives on cognitive aging.* Hillsdale, NJ: Erlbaum.
> *This book is only for the aspiring cognitive psychologist, but very interesting. Salthouse punches holes in many of the new approaches to intelligence discussed in this chapter. The message: People do decline dramatically in cognition early on.*

Schaie, K. W. (1996). Intellectual development in adulthood. In J. E. Birren and K. W. Schaie (Eds.), *Handbook of the psychology of aging* (4th ed.) (pp. 266–286). San Diego: Academic Press.
> *Schaie provides the latest description and update of the Seattle Study and others.*

Sternberg, R. J., and Wagner, R. K. (Eds) (1986). *Practical intelligence: Origins of competence in the everyday world.* New York: Cambridge University Press.
> *The contributors to this edited book describe a variety of creative studies examining life intelligence.*

Cognition II: Memory and Dementia

Chapter Outline

Two years before he died we were invited to a Christmas party, and we went. When we got there, I could see that he'd be totally lost and irresponsible in the cocktail crowd preceding dinner. He began drinking wine, and he'd have no memory of having a glass, so he kept drinking glass after glass. It was purely a matter of having no realization beyond the present moment. So I persuaded him to sit down at the table and wait.

I left him at the table, and he proceeded to eat everything in sight, all the salads, drank a lot of wine and wrecked the whole surrounding area of the table. He filled his wine glass with cranberry juice and then put wine in his coffee cup, to which he later added cream and sugar and drank. (Adapted from Aneshensel, Pearlin, Mullan, Zarit, and Whitlatch, 1995, p. 73)

In the last chapter, we explored cognition in a general way. We examined how that global—but elusive—quality we label intelligence changes as we journey through adult life. In this chapter, as in the section on physical development, we focus on two important topics in cognitive aging. First, we look at that crucial aspect of cognition called memory. Not only is memory loss a central stereotype we have about old age, but also memory has consistently been a top-ranking research area for psychologists who study the aging process. Next we take an in-depth look at the top-ranking condition that we fear when we think about growing old, a disease that has generated thousands of research papers and numerous books and academic reports and has captured the attention of the public to an unparalleled degree. This terrible old-age problem, described in our vignette, is called dementia.

MEMORY

While many of us are likely to believe that we will grow more intelligent in important ways with age, our positive feelings do not extend to memory. As I just mentioned, when we think of memory almost all of us are likely to feel our abilities will change for the worse. What exactly are our stereotypes about when these negative changes begin?

When Ellen Ryan (1992) asked visitors to a science museum to evaluate the memory abilities of hypothetical "targets" aged 25, 45, 65, and 85, she found that ratings of every facet of memory from absent-mindedness to the ability to memorize information decreased at each age. In other words, people seem to believe that memory steadily declines as people age, not just in old age. Furthermore, they feel the loss sets in relatively early, by age 45.

However, while middle-aged people (such as myself) may joke about our terrible memory (the wonderful description one radio personality uses is "boomer-brain"), memory is not something we regularly notice in ourselves or our contemporaries as we go about daily life. Memory is a *salient* dimension by which people are judged in their older years.

Judy Rodin and Ellen Langer (1980) vividly demonstrated that this was so when they filmed three actors aged 20, 50, and 70 reading an identical speech. Scattered through the monologue were a few references to lapses in memory, such as "I forgot my keys." People then watched the film of the young, the middle-aged, or the older actor and were asked to write about what the person was like. Those who saw the 70-year-old frequently described him as forgetful. No one who saw the identical words read by the middle-aged person or the young adult mentioned poor memory.

This is just one of several studies showing we are primed to look for memory problems in older people. Once someone is over 60 or 70 or 80, we focus on memory lapses. We interpret forgetting in a more ominous light. Joan Erber and her coworkers suggest that the difference lies in our *explanatory style*. Memory failures in younger people are passed off as situational and external to the person and so irrelevant: "The task was

Thirty elderly and 30 young-adult males memorized lists of paired associates. In the paced conditions, the subject had to respond within a certain time period (1 1/2 or 3 seconds). In the self-paced condition, subjects could control the memory apparatus and learn and answer at their own pace. This results table, showing that self-paced learning leads to comparatively better performance in the elderly, illustrates the dramatic age differences in performance typically found in standard memory studies.

Mean errors until reaching one perfect list recitation for young and elderly subjects

	1 1/2	3 secs.	Self-paced
Young	12.52	7.90	6.27
Old	50.90	25.90	15.30

Source: Adapted From Canestrari, R. E., Paced and Self-Paced Learning in Young and Elderly Adults, *Journal of Gerontology, 18,* p. 166, Copyright @ 1963 The Gerontological Society of America.

too hard"; "He was preoccupied." In older people, forgetting is viewed as internal, intrinsic, and stable—evidence of a basic deficit in the person (Erber, Szuchman, and Rothberg, 1990; Erber and Rothberg, 1991).

This attribution can be costly. If older people avoid mentally stimulating activities based on the idea that their memory is poor and that nothing can be done about this problem, this withdrawal in itself may produce and accelerate decline (Lachman, 1991; Cavanaugh, 1996). If outsiders treat older people as mentally incompetent, which may be likely if the person is old-old and frail and lives in a nursing home, this adds to the problem. As discussed in Chapter 5, due to lack of reinforcement *excess disabilities* can occur. Luckily, because it has been so heavily probed, examined, and researched in the psychological laboratory, we have good information about memory changes and what can be done about them in our later years.

The Tests and the Findings

In traditional laboratory studies of memory and age, older people and young adults are given a list of words, letters, pictures, or nonsense syllables. After a number of presentations, age differences in recall are examined. In the *paired associate technique,* items are presented in pairs, and, given one, the person is asked to remember the other. When the subject is asked to remember the items without hints, the memory test is called *free recall.* When hints are given, such as the first letter of the correct word, the technique is called *cued recall.* Another type of test involves the *recognition approach.* As in multiple-choice tests, the subject must pick out the correct answer from several choices.

Unfortunately, as the sample study in Table 7–1 illustrates, this research shows real cause for our concerns. The elderly almost always perform much more poorly than the young. Moreover, if the task is difficult, age differences in recall do show up by middle age (Crook and Larrabee, 1992). However, as we can also see in the table, when they vary the memory situation, researchers find different degrees of deficiency. Sometimes older people score very poorly. Sometimes their performance is only moderately worse. Understanding the reasons for these variations has been the real purpose of many of these studies: "What is the main source of the problem or difficulty that occurs with advancing age?" (Hultsch and Dixon, 1990).

To understand exactly what may be going wrong, let's look at one popular approach to understanding memory—the **information processing perspective.**

An Information Processing Perspective on Change

As we learned in earlier chapters, psychologists who use an *information processing approach* break up mental activity into hypothetical steps, devise studies designed to isolate these steps and confirm their existence, and, in this way, try to shed light on the mystery of how we think. Researchers believe that, on the way to becoming "a memory," information progresses through three stores, steps, or phases.

First, stimuli arriving from the outside world through the senses are held briefly in a **sensory store** specific to the sense by which it was received. The visual images that impinge on us enter a visual store (or iconic memory); the sounds we hear, an auditory store (or echoic memory). This first memory stage, somewhat like a photocopy, deteriorates rapidly, within ½ to 2 seconds. Features that we notice or attend to enter the second system, called **working memory.**

We can best view this second memory system as serving as a gateway. Working memory is "where the cognitive action is." Here we keep information in awareness for a temporary period while we make the decision to either discard it or act to process it for permanent storage. According to Alan Baddeley (1992), working memory is made up of two limited-capacity holding "bins." As each bin fills to capacity, information is displaced or pushed out. It also consists of an executive function, which controls attention as well as manipulating the material in these holding areas to prepare it for storage.

A real-life example of the fleeting quality of the information in working memory happens when we get a phone number from the operator and immediately make the call. We know by experience that we can dial the seven-digit number without having to write it down and memory will not fail us *if the phone rings*. If we get a busy signal and have to try again, mysteriously memory fades. The information has slipped out of this holding place.

To prevent this from happening, the solution is to process the phone number so that we have "memorized" it. This means that working memory must manipulate or encode the information so it enters a third, more permanent store called **long-term memory.**

When we speak of memory, we are talking about this last system. Long-term memory is the relatively permanent, large-capacity store that is the repository of our past. While researchers find few age differences in tests of sensory memory, the studies clearly show that getting information into and/or out of this permanent warehouse is more difficult as we age. Are age-related memory deficits due mainly to an encoding/acquisition problem or to a retrieval problem? Or, in less technical terms, has the older person inadequately learned the material, or does the problem lie in difficulties with getting information out?

These topics were debated for decades as psychologists designed studies to try to isolate the acquisition and retrieval phases of memory and measure the loss. As it became clear that with age the efficiency of *both* encoding and retrieval seemed to decline, many researchers adopted a different perspective on change.

Timothy Salthouse (1991, 1992) argues that the hundreds of studies of age differences in memory have a similar message: As the task gradually becomes more demanding and complex, older people do worse. This suggests that the critical force affecting memory as we age is not the particular *type* of processing or memory operation (acquisition versus retrieval), but simply *how much* mental processing that task demands. The problem lies in a mechanism powering the system as a whole. Salthouse calls this mechanism **processing resources.**

information processing perspective on memory
Theory that information pro-
ceeds through three stores or
steps on the way to becoming a
memory.

sensory store
Fleeting after-image of a stimu-
lus reaching a sense organ that
rapidly decays.

working memory
Gateway memory system con-
taining the limited amount of
information that can be kept in
consciousness at one time.

long-term memory
Relatively permanent, large-
capacity memory store housing
everything that has been learned.

processing resources
Basic mechanism powering the
memory system.

Tasks such as this one that involve divided attention are particularly difficult for older people. In this case, after talking on the phone and writing down the information her caller had provided, this woman may have considerable trouble remembering where she was in the paper she has been composing on the typewriter.

What exactly is the processing resource deficit, the bottleneck impairing memory with age? As you might imagine from Salthouse's perspective on overall intelligence, he and his colleagues feel the primary candidate is the loss in thinking speed that may underlie so much of the age decline on traditional IQ tests (see Chapter 6). To support this position, Salthouse has conducted studies similar to the one described in the last chapter, in which he controls for age differences in the speed of responding, and has found that the performance of older people is much more similar to that of young adults on standard memory tests.

Other hypotheses center more directly on the capacity of working memory, the gateway for all learning and remembering. There are large age differences in the capacity of working memory. Why does this system grow smaller in our older years? According to Lynn Hasher, the problem lies in a failure of inhibition, specifically, the inability to screen out unwanted stimuli. Manipulating and moving material efficiently though working memory requires good concentration. We must attend to the bits of information we need to process and filter irrelevant information out. In older people, Hasher argues, because of physiological changes in the part of the brain promoting sustained attention, task-irrelevant thoughts tend to intrude, leaving less space or energy in working memory for processing what we want to remember and learn (Hasher and Zacks, 1988).

These hypotheses—each of which has support—suggest that with memory, as with reaction time, we must look to the characteristics of the task in understanding how people perform. Any time the memory task is demanding, older people do particularly poorly. As I just pointed out, and as is illustrated in Table 7–1, one important dimension of difficulty concerns speed. Older people will do much worse on memory tasks in which the information is presented quickly and/or they have to respond or remember fast (Wingfield, Poon, Lombardi, and Lowe, 1985). Older people will perform more poorly on any task that strains attentional capacities. They will do badly, for instance, when performing two tasks concurrently, either keeping one bit of information in mind while carrying out another task or returning to one activity after being interrupted or attending to something else (Smith, 1996). The elderly will be particularly deficient when the task involves an unfamiliar activity, for instance, when remembering and processing totally new information, versus a well-practiced skill.

Now let's look at a different framework on memory that also offers us insights about the kinds of remembering that are most difficult for older adults.

A Memory Systems Perspective on Change

Think of the amazing resilience of some memories and the equally remarkable vulnerability of others. Why can we automatically remember how to hold a tennis racquet, even though we have not been on a court for decades? Why is George Washington, our first president, locked in our consciousness, while it is practically impossible to recall what we had for dinner two days ago? There seems to be a difference between these kinds of memories that goes beyond *how much* mental processing went into embedding them into our mind. These types of remembering seem distinct from one another in a more basic way.

The information processing perspective does not shed light on this question, as in this framework all memory is the same. The only relevant difference is how efficiently the information has been processed, or stored, or retrieved. Endel Tulving's **memory systems theory** offers the answers we need.

Tulving (1985) believes that there are three different types of memory systems. **Implicit or procedural memory** involves information that we learn and remember automatically, without conscious reflection or thought. While this memory system includes several categories of learning, such as classically conditioned emotions, as we just saw, an interesting real-life example involves physical skills. Once we have learned an activity, such as how to hit a tennis ball or ride a bike, we automatically "remember" that activity, without conscious effort, once confronted with that stimulus again.

Tulving's two other memory systems, because they involve conscious recall, are different from the "unreflective," situation-linked memory just described. **Semantic memory** is our fund of knowledge, such as my knowledge of the fact that George Washington is our first president or what a tennis racquet is. **Episodic memory** is our ability to remember specific ongoing events. My memory of getting on the tennis court last Thursday or what I had for dinner last week would be in this memory system. So would any attempt to recall bits of information in laboratory memory tests. (Table 7–2 offers additional everyday illustrations showing the distinctions among the three memory types.)

As these examples suggest, episodic memory is the most fragile system. A month from now we will know who George Washington is (semantic memory). We will remember how to hold the tennis racquet (implicit/procedural memory). However, we are unlikely to remember what we had for dinner two Tuesdays ago. It is recalling the ongoing events of life, from what we ate last Tuesday, to what day last month we decided to play tennis, to the facts you are reading right now that are most vulnerable to time.

Researchers have conducted ingenious studies demonstrating the independence of these memory types (Schacter, 1992). They have evidence that implicit memory is encoded in a different area of the brain than consciously recalled facts (Squire, 1992). Most important for us, there is a good deal of evidence that the memory systems are affected in different ways as we age.

David Mitchell (1989) examined the performance of older and younger adults on tests designed to reveal the three memory types. To measure semantic memory, Mitchell gave subjects vocabulary tests and asked them to name or identify a series of pictures. (In other words, he might show a photo of the White House and ask, "What is pictured here?") During this presentation, Mitchell tested for implicit memory by using a strategy called *repetition priming*. He presented certain pictures in the series once and others twice. By comparing a person's response latency (rapidity of responding) when a picture had been previously presented versus when it had not, Mitchell measured whether this unconscious learning had occurred. Then, in a second phase of the study, Mitchell tested for episodic memory by showing subjects the original set of pictures embedded in a larger series and asking them to recall which photos they had already seen.

memory systems theory
Tulving's framework dividing memory into discrete systems.

implicit or procedural memory
Memory system for information that is learned and/or recalled without conscious effort.

semantic memory
Memory system for one's fund of knowledge.

episodic memory
Memory system for ongoing life events.

Everyday Examples Illustrating the Distinctions Among Implicit/Procedural, Semantic, and Episodic Memory

Implicit—You get into your blue Toyota and automatically know how to drive.
Semantic—You know that you have a blue Toyota.
Episodic—You memorize where you left your blue Toyota in the parking lot of the amusement park.

Implicit—You automatically find yourself singing the words to "Jingle Bells" when the melody comes on the radio.
Semantic—You remember that this is a song.
Episodic—You try to remember when you last heard "Jingle Bells."

Implicit—You begin getting excited as you approach your college campus for the fall semester of your senior year.
Semantic—You know that you are a student at X university and that you are a psychology major.
Episodic—You memorize the locations of classrooms and your professors' names during the first week of the new semester.

Implicit—I unconsciously find the letters I am typing now on my computer.
Semantic—I know that I am writing a book on adult development.
Episodic—I try not to forget that today I must go to the library and photocopy that article on memory that I will need in preparing this chapter.

Implicit memory and semantic memory were as good in the old as the young. The older people did as well on the repetition-priming task. As we might expect, in view of what we know about age changes in crystallized IQ, they could identify or name as many pictures as the young. However, episodic memory was markedly impaired. The older people were much less able to recall exactly which pictures had been previously presented.

Other researchers have found that implicit memory may also decline a bit with age (Hultsch, Masson, and Small, 1991). Age makes inroads in semantic memory, too (Light, 1991). Older people *do* have more trouble recalling familiar facts, such as the names of good friends, or vocabulary words, or photos of well-known places (Salthouse, 1991). However, these lapses are far less frequent or pronounced. Any time the task involves "unconscious" responses or the recall of well-learned material, older people do well. Any time the task involves episodic memory, the more difficult task of remembering the events of daily life, older persons' performance is relatively poor.

How impaired is episodic memory? As we saw in Table 7–1, if we look at traditional memory tests, the answer is a great deal. Young people typically remember more than twice as much material as those over 65. Are older people really as deficient as they seem on these tests? Many researchers answer no.

Measuring Everyday Memory

As I described at the beginning of this section, in standard memory studies young adults and older people are asked to memorize lists of unrelated words, nonsense syllables, letters, or numbers. By now, we may be suspicious of this method: Learning meaningless words or letters has little in common with the memory demands we face in daily life:

"What is that red-haired woman's name?" "How do I get to that person's house?" "I must remember that doctor's appointment at two." So, as was true of IQ tests, researchers began to wonder. Perhaps how a person performs on these tasks may not be a good index of how memory operates in everyday life.

Researchers had always assumed that, by using only meaningless stimuli, they could ensure that the situation was equal for everyone, that memory was being measured in an unbiased way. However, this focus on purity and control has problems: It may be *too* *removed* from real life. As in the old saying, in ridding themselves of the bathwater, were psychologists throwing the baby out?

Moreover, rather than being unbiased, the traditional approach might be especially biased against the old. Imagine that you are an elderly person asked to take a memory test. Not only are you are out of practice in taking tests, but also you probably have entered the experiment with high levels of anxiety. "Perhaps the test might show I have Alzheimer's disease!" While these *ability-extraneous factors* might operate in any memory experiment, some researchers argue that they are intensified when the material that older people are asked to memorize makes no sense (Hulicka, 1967).

Do ability-extraneous influences, such as anxiety, *differentially impair* older people's performance on memory tests? We do not know for sure (Kausler, 1990). What we do know for certain is that older people are often not performing at their best in these studies. To take one example, Robert Hill, Martha Storandt, and Claudia Simeone (1990) found that giving incentives (a lottery ticket for free airline travel) improved performance on memorizing a list of words among older adults. Even if they do not discriminate against the old, the traditional studies do not showcase what older people are truly capable of doing.

everyday memory tasks
Memory tasks similar to the
memory demands people face in
daily life.

One way of making the situation more realistic has been to use **everyday memory tasks,** tests mirroring the memory demands people actually face (Poon, Rubin, and Wilson, 1989). How well can the elderly fit names to faces or remember the locations of objects in space (Crook and Larrabee, 1992; Sharps and Gollin, 1988)? How does our ability to recall a conversation, or a story, or the message of a written passage change with age (Adams, Labouvie-Vief, Hobart, and Dorosz, 1990; Meyer and Rice, 1989; Zelinski and Miura, 1988)? How well can adults of different ages remember telephone numbers (West and Crook, 1990), or television news shows (Stine, Wingfield, and Myers, 1990), or the source of information they have heard (Schacter, Kaszniak, Kihlstrom, and Valdiserri, 1991)?

I wish I could say that using these types of tests erased any age differences. However, as we can see in Feature 7–1 on p. 194, older people perform more poorly on most measures of everyday memory, too, though here the loss is often less dramatic and the results more variable than when memory is measured in the traditional way (Hultsch and Dixon, 1990; West, 1989).

Furthermore, while the material in these tests is more realistic, the overall situation is just as artificial, "a laboratory test." Reading an article in order to remember as much as possible for an experimenter is different than reading that article for pleasure at home. Being tested on how well one matches slides of faces to names is not the same as being introduced to a person at a party and then wanting to memorize his name. As memory expert Robin West (1989) points out, any time the conditions are set by the examiner and the expectation is total recall, the situation changes. Just because a test is labeled everyday memory does not mean it reflects how memory operates in life.

How well does the older person's memory operate in more true-to-life situations? The following study offers heartening clues. Using the Baltimore volunteers, Jan Sinnott (1986) devised a creative naturalistic (real-life) approach to testing differences in everyday memory. She asked participants of different ages to remember different events that occurred while they were being tested at the Gerontology Research Laboratory.

How do you think that this elderly woman's ability to remember these grocery items and their prices might differ from her memory performance on a laboratory memory study? Wouldn't you imagine she would perform at a higher level in this important real life situation than on an artificial test?

Some events were important and needed action: "How do you get from your room to the testing area or the cafeteria?" Or "What are the hours dinner is served?" Others were unimportant: "What materials were on the table while you were solving problems . . . tissues, pencils, etc.?" Or "How many problems were you asked to solve?"

In examining memory for both types of events, Sinnott found the young volunteers outperformed the old only on the items measuring unimportant or irrelevant information. For the relevant material, the information that had to be remembered in order to function, the performance of the older people equaled that of the young.

This study is appealing because it gets to the heart of the problem with making generalizations about life based on laboratory studies. Even if our memory works less well with age, this may not matter so much in the real world. As Sinnott points out, one implication of her study is that older people use *selection* and *optimization* to flexibly compensate for age-related deficits in the ability to recall. They seem to narrow their focus. Rather than remembering "more," they concentrate more on what they really need to remember, and so, when it counts, their memory is relatively unimpaired.

Memory for the Future and Memory of the Past

RECALLING WHAT WE PLAN TO DO. The most interesting studies revealing that memory decline may be compensated for by motivation involve what is called **prospective memory,** remembering to take action in the future (Sinnott, 1989). We must remember to bring our pen and notebook to class, to keep our 10 A.M. appointment, to call and remind our husband to pick up our son from school. At dinner, we cannot forget to get the meat out of the oven on time. These examples show how important prospective memory tasks can be in daily life.

However, in spite of its salience, only recently have researchers explored this type of memory (at least with adults). Studying memory for future actions is more difficult than examining memory for faces, names, or facts. Because it requires such long recall intervals, prospective memory in adults is difficult to study within the laboratory at all.

In most studies of prospective memory, researchers instruct subjects of different ages to remember to mail back postcards on a given day. Possibly because the older people are

prospective memory
Memory for future actions.

7-1 The Adult Experience: Phone Number Recall and Age

Within the past few years, I have noticed that it is more difficult for me to remember a phone number after I call information. I used to be able to dial the number with no problem. Now I have to concentrate carefully. If I have to remember an area code and the number, the last two or three digits frequently slip out of mind. Am I more distracted these days, or has a change occurred in my "working memory" now that I am in my late 40s?

Robin West and Thomas Crook (1990) decided to study this example of everyday memory, systematically examining how the ability to cope with different phone recall tasks changes with age. First, they varied the number of digits to be immediately recalled. Given a 3- digit sequence (as in an area code), a 7-digit sequence (as in a local number), or a 10-digit sequence (as in a long-distance number), would age differences show up in the ability to immediately dial the number? Would there be another pattern of loss when a busy signal occurred?

Under conditions when subjects could "get through right away," there were no age differences with the three-digit sequence, and only the youngest (aged 18–39) and oldest (70+) groups differed significantly in their ability to correctly remember the seven digits (local call). With the 10-digit sequence (long-distance call), age declines emerged earlier, by age 60. Still, the middle-aged subjects continued to perform as well as the young.

This changed when the researchers put in a busy signal and told subjects to dial the 7 and 10 digits again. Then age differences showed up earlier: In every decade after 40, there were significant losses.

So, if I am like the typical person my age, I am probably no worse off, even when calling long distance, provided I get lucky and the phone rings. However, I should not assume my abilities are exactly the same as in my youth. If I get a busy signal, I will need pencil and paper more than ever unless I want to redial information again. Furthermore, I should probably have a pencil by the phone just as practice for what is to come. In my older years, immediately recalling that number will present more problems than before.

more motivated, these studies show a markedly different pattern than other memory tests. Older people are often *better* at remembering than the young (Sinnott, 1989).

So, when we look just at test performance, we neglect to factor in motivation, the heightened attention to memory that may compensate for age loss. The research on prospective memory also clarifies an inconsistency in our thinking about memory and age. In spite of firmly believing memory is poor in the elderly, when it comes to asking an adolescent cousin or our 70-year-old grandmother to remember to feed our cat while we are on vacation, we frequently trust the older person more!

RECALLING OUR PERSONAL PAST.   There is yet a second inconsistent feeling we have about memory in later life. It is not quite true that we believe *all* memory is worse in the elderly. Granted older people may have more trouble recalling what they said or did within the past few hours or days, but don't memories from youth become especially vivid and salient in old age? As with memory for future events, this special type of recall of the more distant personal past also has its own name: **autobiographical memory.**

autobiographical memory
Memory for one's personal past.

Do older people recall their youth especially vividly? To examine the accuracy of this stereotype we have about memory in the elderly, researchers use an interesting technique. They provide older and younger subjects with a cue word and ask them to respond with a specific memory, date this personal event, and rate it for vividness. The idea is that, if older people do indeed "live in the past," in contrast to the typical tendency to remember recent events most readily, older subjects' associations should center more on remote memories (from their younger years).

However, when researchers use this approach, they typically find *no age differences* in the distribution of memories. Recent happenings are equally salient for both the old and the young. The dramatically downward sloping curve as a function of "time since event occurred" apparent in younger people is equally apparent for older adults (Hess and Pullen, 1996).

There are some interesting exceptions. While in general recent events are by far the most salient, older people tend to remember events that occurred when they were teenagers and young adults more frequently than happenings that took place during their middle years (Fromholt and Larsen, 1991; Holland, 1995). One hypothesis is that this interesting *reminiscence peak* may occur because the teens and twenties are an especially turbulent time of life. These are the years when we reach puberty, have our first romantic relationships, leave home, get married, and become parents. As we will see later in this chapter, any event that is emotion-fraught and personally meaningful is apt to be more indelibly etched in our mind. Moreover, provided we look only at *certain* older people, there is more truth to the stereotype that the elderly live in the past.

Carol Holland and Patrick Rabbitt (1991) compared the lifetime distribution of memories of nursing home residents with those of a matched group of normal active elderly. They found that, in contrast to the active elderly, the residents in long-term care *were* most likely to produce memories dating from their earlier years. As Holland (1995) reasons, anyone, young or old, who is immersed in living is highly motivated to remember the present, as recalling events such as just having gone to the grocery store or meeting one's family is critical to negotiating life. However, living in a nursing home removes the requirement to remember the ongoing fabric of daily living, as the institution takes care of the imperative to remember what happened yesterday or what will happen next week. Meals arrive, families visit, life takes place at the whim of others without active effort or control on the older person's part. At the same time as it blots out the motivation to process the present, living in a nursing home heightens the need to recall the distant past. In nursing homes, argues Holland, people may feel compelled to continually rehearse and recall events relating to who they "really are" (mother or daughter or business executive) because these *life review activities* allow them to hang onto a sense of their personal identity as human beings.

This suggests that, by simply exploring age differences in the general tendency to think about the past, we may be missing some interesting information. Even if its frequency may not change as we age, reminiscing might have a different purpose or meaning for younger and older adults. Specifically, we might expect that the elderly, much more than younger adults, engage in the kind of reminiscence that Erik Erikson would label life review.

To explore this possibility, Jeffrey Webster (1995) first spelled out seven distinct types or categories of thinking about the past. According to Webster, people may talk about events in their lives to teach younger people or simply to keep a conversation going. They may think about their lives to reduce boredom, to understand themselves better, to feel close to loved ones they have lost, or to obsess about old hurts, in addition to engaging in the kind of behavior Erikson would define as life review—exploring one's past in preparation for death. Using a scale to measure each type of reminiscence, Webster then charted how frequently subjects ranging in age from their teens to their eighties engaged in these different activities over a certain period of time. As he expected, there were no age differences in the overall quantity of reminiscing that subjects reported (see the first chart in Figure 7–1). However, there were tantalizing differences between the types of reminiscence that were most prevalent at different ages.

It would be natural for this nursing home resident to be ruminating about events in his past rather than his present life. Not only are all of his daily needs being cared for, but thinking about his achievements as a husband or father or worker may allow him to hang on to his sense of self-esteem and identity.

Figure 7–1

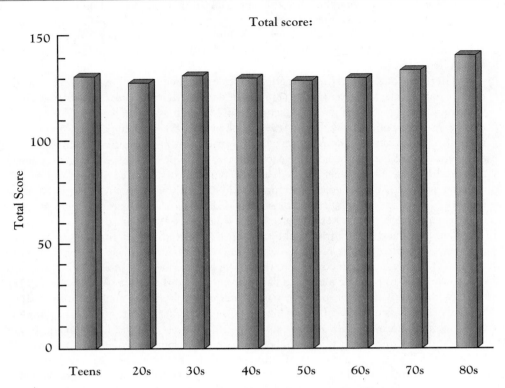

Total score:

In this study, subjects were instructed to rate how often they engaged the seven types of reminiscence on a scale ranging from never to very frequently. Notice that even though there are no overall differences in the total quantity of reminiscing, life-review-type activities become increasingly prevalent at older ages (see next page).

Younger people were more likely to reminisce to reduce boredom, solve problems, or ruminate about unpleasant events. As the chart on p. 197 shows, older people were much more likely to think about their lives in order to prepare for impending death.

APPLICATIONS AND INTERVENTIONS

STIMULATING LIFE REVIEW.   Our discussion suggests that, while it may not be as crucial as long as older adults are healthy and immersed in life, getting people to recall their lives may be helpful psychologically among the institutionalized or very old. This is one reason why, as mentioned in Chapter 2, *reminiscence* or *life review activities* are used to reduce depression and foster a sense of identity in senior centers and especially in nursing homes. In these sessions, a leader may organize group discussions around specific topics, such as favorite holidays or "jobs I have had." Or she may simply ask participants to share memories of important events as children, as adolescents, or as adults. In one group in a nursing home, when 16 residents engaged in this type of reminiscing as well as being taught problem-solving skills, after the 10-session treatment, depression rates were significantly lower among participants than before (Dhooper, Green, Huff, and Austin-Murphy, 1993).

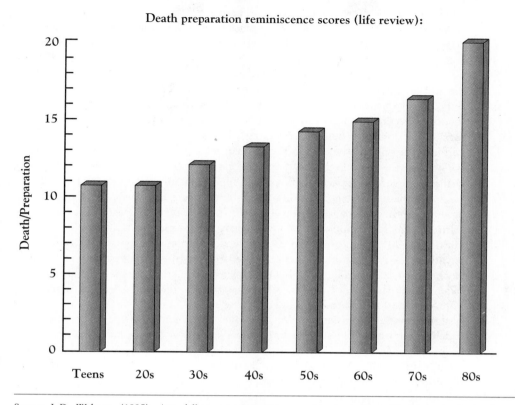

Death preparation reminiscence scores (life review):

Source: J. D. Webster. (1995). Age differences in reminiscence functions. From *The art and science of reminiscing: Theory, research, methods, and applications*, B. K. Haight and J. D. Webster, Taylor and Francis Publishers, Washington D.C., reproduced by permission, all rights reserved.

Reminiscence is a specialized memory-type intervention focused on improving emotional health. In the rest of this section, we focus on a much more central topic relating to cognition and age—specific strategies for helping improve memory in later life.

MEMORY-STIMULATING STRATEGIES.   As with IQ tests, there are great differences in how older people perform on memory tests. This research on individual differences offers lessons for how to minimize age-related memory decline.

1. *Stay in good emotional and physical health.* As we might expect from our discussion of intelligence, people with a wide range of chronic conditions perform particularly poorly on memory tests (Hultsch, Hammer, and Small, 1993). So do people in poor emotional health—in particular, those who are depressed. Not only do older people who are depressed tend to erroneously label their memory as worse (Kahn, Zarit, Hilbert, and Niederehe, 1975), but also one symptom of depression in the elderly is memory impairment, problems remembering that may be so severe they can even be mistaken for Alzheimer's disease. So the first general principle for helping memory in later life is to take care of one's physical and mental health.

2. ***Keep mentally stimulated.*** As is also true of intelligence, older people who are mentally active (Hultsch et al., 1993) and intellectually interested (Arbuckle, Gold, Andres, Schwartzman, and Chaikelman, 1992) do comparatively better on memory tests. This is especially apparent in research examining the type of everyday memory alluded to earlier, remembering the main point of a written passage, such as a newspaper article or page in a book. While most studies show that older people do more poorly on this task, when well-read, intellectual older subjects are compared with younger people the age difference is smaller or disappears (Meyer and Rice, 1989).

   Does being skilled verbally generally inoculate people against memory decline? Answers come from this study in which subjects of different ages were given various tests of everyday memory: Robin West, Thomas Crook, and Kristina Barron (1992) found that scores on a vocabulary test were a more important predictor of memory for a written passage than a person's age. But age alone was the best predictor of performance on the other memory tests. In other words, as we also saw in the chapter on intelligence, being highly accomplished can overpower changes due to the passing years. However, its impact seems specific, limited mainly to that arena of expertise.

   A variety of memory studies show that older people who are expert in an activity, be they pilots asked to read an air traffic control message (Morrow, Leirer, Altiteri, and Fitzsimmons, 1994) or elderly bridge players (Clarkson-Smith and Hartley, 1990), can do as well as or even outperform the young. However, the advantage *expertise* offers is often confined to tests measuring *that type of memory alone*. Though the widespread benefits of keeping active for memory are unclear, older people should not despair. There are specific techniques that can generally improve memory in later life (and at any age).

3. ***Use mnemonic techniques.*** We all have noticed that some experiences are indelibly embedded in our memory (our graduation day or first day at college), while others fade. The main characteristic of the episodic events we remember is their meaningful quality. As I suggested in discussing autobiographical memory, when the details of life are unimportant memory is apt to be poor. Events that are emotionally salient are learned and remembered the best. So one key to remembering any bit of information more easily is to enhance its memorability.

   Mnemonic techniques are strategies to help make information more "memorable." These techniques range from organizing a list of foods into meaningful categories, such as fruits and meats, to facilitate recall at the grocery store to remembering the last four digits of a friend's phone number, XXX-1945, by transforming this sequence from a meaningless array of numbers to the year in which World War II ended. While researchers disagree as to whether older people spontaneously use these special strategies less frequently than the young (Light, 1991), it is clear that teaching these approaches benefits people of any age.

   One technique that enhances meaning is using imagery, imagining a striking visual image of the material to be learned. When asked to memorize the paired associate bat-tree, you might imagine a bat sitting in a tree. In order to recall who wrote this text, you might imagine a large bell on skis wrapped around this book.

   In addition to these internal techniques (examples are listed in Table 7–3) we also, of course, have **external memory aids,** such as calendars or lists. External reminders are really the preferred method for helping us remember, even for memory researchers (see Cavanaugh, 1989). Some experts feel that, rather than focusing on the work of internally encoding information, we might be better off teaching older people to rely more heavily on external aids. (As memory expert Robin West [1989] wisely points out, however, the problem here is that writing down an appointment on a calendar and even checking that calendar require remembering, too!)

   Memory-training studies involving systematic instruction in mnemonic techniques demonstrate that older people can improve their memory (Neely and Back-

mnemonic techniques
Specific techniques to facilitate learning and recall by making information vivid or meaningful.

external memory aids
External reminders to aid memory.

By visualizing these objects, you will more easily remember the name of this textbook's author.

Problem: Remembering names
Solution: Form a vivid visual image involving the word. To remember Belsky, imagine a huge bell on skis wrapped around my head when we are introduced. To remember River Road, imagine a huge river overflowing the street.

Problem: Remembering a list of items*
Solution 1: First, think of several familiar locations around the house. Then form a visual image associating each item on the list with a specific place. Next take a mental walk around your house, "stopping" at each location to retrieve each item (this technique is called the method of loci).
Solution 2: Organize the items to be remembered into meaningful categories— "shoes," "dresses," etc. Then, when packing for a trip, "go category by category" down the list.
*With remembering lists of items, external memory aids—i.e. written lists—are especially useful.

Problem: Remembering where an item was placed
Solution 1: At home or in familiar settings, have a regular place for each item—such as by the front door. Then, when you enter the house, take an extra second to put your keys, your glasses, your purse in that place.
Solution 2: In unfamiliar places, be alert to where you put that item down. Use a visual image linking that item to the place to facilitate recall. (In other words, visualize exactly where your car is when you enter the shopping center.)

man, 1993; West, 1989). Not only are the elderly able to benefit from training, but also they sometimes emerge capable of astonishing memory feats (Hultsch and Dixon, 1990). This research suggests that both intelligence and memory are *plastic,* capable of being improved in later life.

4. ***Enhance memory self-efficacy.*** One problem, however, with telling older people to exercise their memory or even providing instruction in memory techniques is that motivation is involved. In order to have a better memory, people must believe that change is possible, that older dogs really *can* learn new tricks. So it is also important to focus on what is called **memory self-efficacy,** the older person's confidence about being able to improve (Cavanaugh, 1996). As we saw in the research on memory perceptions at the beginning of this chapter, people have a tendency to see loss in this area of life as an intrinsic, irremediable part of growing old. We must educate older adults that they are not suffering from a "hopeless condition." By knowing how memory operates and by using a bit of extra effort, it is possible to have an excellent memory at any time of life.

memory self-efficacy
In the elderly, the faith in one's capacity to have a good memory.

Unfortunately, there is a time when this advice is misguided, when cognitive remediation interventions of the kind discussed in this section and the previous chapter are more likely to fail. This is when people have the condition called dementia.

DEMENTIA

Dementia is a label applying to a variety of chronic diseases characterized by severe memory impairment. However, with dementing illnesses, more than just memory is involved. There is a total breakdown in every function—thinking and reasoning;

dementia
Chronic diseases characterized by serious, often irreversible, deterioration in memory and cognition.

7-2 The Adult Experience: An Insider's Portrait of Alzheimer's

Diana Freil McGowen, diagnosed with Alzheimer's disease at the unusually young age of 53 determined to make the most of her remaining mind. When her illness was in the early stages, she helped found the first network of support groups for *patients* with Alzheimer's disease and wrote a book describing what it is like to experience *Living in the Labyrinth*. Here is the story of the four-hour trek to deliver lunch to her husband that convinced Diana something was seriously wrong:

> As I drove to Jack's office I noticed a shopping center, new to me. It was strange I had not noticed this mall. . . . I traveled this route frequently. . . . Near the driveway leading to [the] office, I observed a fire station which was also new to me. . . . "Jack . . . I'm glad to see that new fire station near your entrance,"[I said.] "Diane, that station has always been here", he chided . . . I started the car and began to pull away. I braked. . . . Where was the exit?
>
> "Jack, I asked shakily, how do I get out of here? . . . Just tell me how to get out of this place." Jack . . . pointed straight ahead . . . I . . . drove from the parking lot.
>
> Suddenly . . ., nothing was familiar. . . . I drove on with tears . . . streaming down my face. Unfamiliar music blared from the radio. I was hopelessly lost and had no idea how to get home. Suddenly, I saw a sign, "Turkey Lake Park" . . . I turned into the entrance . . . and pulled off the road. My body was shaking with . . . uncontrollable sobs. What was happening? . . . I approached the Ranger Station. The guard smiled . . . . "I appear to be lost" . . . "Where do you need to go?" the guard asked politely. A cold chill enveloped me as I realized I did not remember the name of my street.

Source: D.F. McGowen (1993); *Living in the Labyrinth*, New York: Delacourt Press, pp. 5–9.

personality; the ability to walk, dress, or speak. Both older and younger people can develop these terrible illnesses. However, the dementias of old age are almost always progressive. The deficits get progressively worse and end in death.

As the compelling first-person account in Feature 7–2 shows, even in dementia's *early stage* the problems with memory go well beyond the episodic, event-related forgetting of normal aging. A woman may not remember how to get home, even though she has traveled that route for years. She may forget well-established facts, such as the town in which she lives. To qualify for a diagnosis of dementia, the forgetting must be severe enough to genuinely impair the person's ability to function in life.

As the illness reaches its *middle stage*, every aspect of thinking is affected. Abstract reasoning becomes difficult. The person can no longer think through options when making decisions. Language becomes limited. The individual has trouble naming objects. Her speech becomes vague and empty, with excessive use of non-specific words, such as "it" and "thing." She may be unable to recognize familiar objects, such as a chair, or she may forget how to execute well-practiced actions, such as putting on her shoes. Judgment becomes faulty. People may act inappropriately, perhaps undressing in public, running out in traffic, or yelling in the street. They may behave recklessly, unaware they are endangering their lives or health. Agitation, wandering, insomnia, and paranoia are very common among middle-stage demented older adults (Cohen et al., 1993).

As the illness progresses to its *advanced stage*, the person becomes disoriented with respect to time, place, and person. A man may think this is 1943 and he is at sea talking to his commanding officer, rather than understanding that he is a resident of the Four Acres Nursing Home in 1997. The most elementary semantic memories are affected. A woman may forget her name or the fact she has children. At this point, urinary and fecal incontinence is common. The person may need assistance to walk.

In the final or *terminal stage*, the patient is totally dependent. People lose the ability to speak at all. At this point, they are often unable to perform the most basic human activities, such as moving or even swallowing well. Often it is complications at this stage that lead to death.

Though dementia is often characterized by stages, experts caution that not all people deteriorate in a lock-step way. Some individuals may be able to perform basic tasks, such as dressing and going to the toilet, in the presence of the most extreme impairments in memory and reasoning. Others whose thinking is much better may need nursing care for these basic activities of daily living (Zarit, 1980; Zarit, Orr, and Zarit, 1985).

The most heartbreaking variability lies in the time course of these illnesses. While cognition and functional abilities are predestined to worsen over time, often at an accelerating pace, there are marked individual differences in the rate of decline. If the person is more well educated and the illness develops earlier in life, the deterioration tends to progress at a more rapid rate (Teri, McCurry, Edland, Kukull, and Larson, 1995). On average, however, people have the symptoms of dementia for seven or so years (Aneshensel et al., 1995).

The Demography of Dementia

Dementia is less common among people who are over 65 than many of us believe (Gatz and Pearson, 1988). One landmark community study revealed that it affects only about 5 percent of elderly Americans (Folstein, Bassett, Anthony, Romanoski, and Nestadt, 1991). Although this percentage is not high, it translates into several million older Americans living in the community who have problems handling the basics of life. Moreover, this survey polled people living *outside institutions*. Because, as we will see in a later section, dementing illnesses frequently result in nursing home admission as the symptoms progress, the number of older people who suffer from this condition is really higher. It is estimated that at least half or more of all of the residents in long-term care have this most feared disorder of later life (U.S. Senate Special Committee on Aging, 1991a).

On the positive side, compared to other illnesses of aging, dementia strikes quite late in the life span. It is extremely rare before age 50, gradually rises in frequency during the next three decades, and then jumps dramatically in advanced old age. By the mid-eighties, about one in four people living at home suffers from moderate to severe mental loss (Gatz and Smyer, 1992). The fact that dementia does become so much more common at life's uppermost rungs is alarming, however, because of the dramatic growth in the number of the oldest-old. Particularly when the baby boomers enter their eighties and nineties, dementia may be the number one public health problem facing our country.

While a number of rare illnesses can produce these devastating symptoms (see Table 7–4), usually the person with dementia will be suffering from one or a combination of two diseases: vascular dementia and Alzheimer's disease.

Vascular Dementia

Vascular dementia is a disease of the cardiovascular system. In this illness—responsible for an estimated one-fourth of the cases—the cognitive dysfunction is produced by the death of brain tissue as a result of many small strokes. As we know from Chapter 3, a stroke occurs when an artery feeding the brain becomes blocked by atherosclerosis or other causes, the blood supply to that area is disrupted, and the cells nourished by that vessel die. A large stroke produces symptoms that are difficult to miss, such as paralysis, or impaired speech, or death. The person who has vascular dementia has strokes so minor that they may produce few perceptible symptoms. But as their number increases and more brain tissue dies, cognition deteriorates in a stepwise way.

Because strokes are caused by potentially treatable problems, such as high blood pressure, there may be some chance of stemming the progression of this dementing

vascular dementia
Cardiovascular dementing illness of later life.

Table 7-4   Some Rare Dementing Illnesses of Later Life

Creutzfeldt-Jakob disease	This rare dementing disease is caused by a slow-growing virus.
Huntington's chorea	In this tragic genetic illness, the offspring of victims have a 50/50 chance of developing it, yet it manifests itself after the peak childbearing years—in the mid- thirties. The disease causes not only dementia, but also involuntary movements that become more pronounced as the illness progresses.
Normal pressure hydrocephalus	This dementing illness is caused by the buildup of pressure in the ventricles of the brain. Treatment, sometimes effective, consists of surgery to drain the fluid.
Pick's disease	While it produces many of the pathological changes of Alzheimer's, this disease progresses differently—initially affecting different areas of the brain.

Source: J.K. Belsky 1990, *The Psychology of Aging: Theory, Research and Interventions* (2nd ed.), Monterey, CA: Brooks/Cole.

illness by, for example, lowering blood pressure through diet and exercise. Normally, however, the person's deficits get progressively more pronounced because the strokes tend to recur more frequently, affecting larger segments of the brain.

Their greater susceptibility to atherosclerosis and cardiovascular disease means males and African Americans tend to have comparatively higher rates of vascular dementia (Cohen et al., 1993; see Chapter 3). Their longevity, plus the fact that menopause removes estrogen, a hormone that may protect the integrity of neurons, means women are more susceptible to the most common dementing illness—Alzheimer's disease.

Alzheimer's Disease

Alzheimer's disease
Most common dementing illness of later life involving the deterioration of neurons.

About 60 percent of elderly people with dementia have Alzheimer's disease. A smaller percentage have what is called a mixed dementia. They suffer from this condition and vascular dementia combined. **Alzheimer's disease** attacks our humanity at its core. With this illness, which has become an infamous synonym for *any* dementia of old age, the neurons literally wither away.

Normally a neuron looks like a tree. When a person has Alzheimer's disease, it appears as if the tree is slowly being killed by an infection. First, it loses its branches (dendrites), then it swells, and then its trunk (axon and cell body) shrivels to a stump (Zarit et al., 1985). In place of what had been a normal neuron are wavy filaments called **neurofibrillary tangles,** thick bullet-like bodies of protein called **senile plaques,** and other pathological signs of deterioration.

neurofibrillary tangles
Wavy filaments of neural tissue characteristic of Alzheimer's disease.

senile plaques
Thick bodies of protein characteristic of Alzheimer's disease.

At first, the destruction is limited and confined mainly to the area of the brain called the hippocampus. As the illness progresses, it cuts a wider swath. More and more healthy neurons are replaced by these pathological structures. The brain of a person with advanced Alzheimer's disease may be so studded with abnormal fragments that there are few normal neurons left.

In a classic study, British researchers showed that the memory and thinking problems a person manifests are a direct function of the amount of neural destruction that has taken place. After death, the brains of elderly people with memory losses of varying degrees were autopsied. The researchers found a good correlation between the density of senile plaques and the person's intellectual abilities near the time of death (Blessed, Tomlinson, and Roth, 1968; Roth, Tomlinson, and Blessed, 1966).

Unfortunately, *normal* older people also display these changes. They have senile plaques. They have neurofibrillary tangles as well (Scheibel, 1996). But these structures are fewer in number, and they tend to be confined to limited areas of the brain. In dementia, the damage is extensive and widespread.

The presence of these changes in normal older adults provides a physiological underpinning for the losses in memory and thinking that normally occur in later life. And it shows that the link between normal age changes in cognition and their end point—the chronic illness called Alzheimer's disease—is uncomfortably close. The fact that these changes are part and parcel of normal aging highlights another distressing truth. While many people who live to their nineties are sound in mind (as well as body), not infrequently dementia is the price of living to the *ripest* old age.

CAUSES.   What causes the neural decay that results in Alzheimer's disease? Theories center around a handful of agents of destruction. In reading through this list, keep in mind that one lead does not exclude the others. Rather than having a single cause, Alzheimer's disease may be the final result of several different insults to the brain (Gatz, Lowe, Berg, Mortimer, and Pederson, 1994):

1. **Genetics.** Family studies show that the predisposition to *early onset* Alzheimer's disease is inherited. In 1987, researchers identified a specific genetic defect in people with a strong family history of the illness (Barnes, 1987). Interestingly this genetic marker was located on chromosome number 21, the very one people suffering from the birth defect Down's syndrome have an extra copy of. For years, scientists had been intrigued by what they imagined was a connection between these two conditions because victims of Down's syndrome almost universally develop Alzheimer's disease if they live to midlife. This study reveals a reason for the link. Having an extra chromosome 21 may be giving victims of Down's syndrome a double dose of the Alzheimer's-producing genetic program. However, Alzheimer's seems to have several genetic pathways. So far, in addition to chromosome 21, as of this writing chromosomes 14 and 19 have also been implicated in the disease.

2. **A virus.** Because a virus is known to cause the rare type of dementia called Creutzfeldt-Jakob disease, some researchers feel a slow-acting virus, one that may take decades to incubate in the body, might be implicated in Alzheimer's disease. (The HIV virus also can produce a dementia that progresses much like Alzheimer's disease.)

3. **Toxic metals.** Another candidate for an Alzheimer's-instigating substance is aluminum because the brain tissue of Alzheimer's patients contains a high concentration of this metal. Does absorbing too much aluminum over a lifetime play a part in causing the disease? Or are the high levels of aluminum a *result* of the disease process? So far, efforts to definitively link this particular metal to the illness have been inconclusive. In addition to aluminum, speculations also center around the toxic effects of other metals, such as lead and mercury.

4. **A deficit in neurotransmitter production.** Another line of inquiry centers on a prominent feature of the Alzheimer's brain: its striking deficiency of the neurotransmitter acetylcholine. If Alzheimer's disease selectively attacks the acetylcholine-producing (cholinergic) neurons, stimulating the brain's production of this neurotransmitter might be an effective antidote. While so far researchers have not had success, drugs thought to restore acetylcholine continue to undergo clinical trials (Cooper and Mungas, 1993).

5. **Amyloid.** The most important new lead concerns amyloid, an abnormal protein that is a core constituent of both senile plaques and neurofibrillary tangles. Some

Table 7-5

Some Conditions That Can Produce Delirium in the Elderly

Medications—Errors in self-administration; poly-pharmacy (taking different medications simultaneously); abuse of non-prescription drugs; side effects of drugs given appropriately; inappropriate drug dosage for the individual.

Diseases and Physical Conditions—Cardiac problems, including heart attack; neurological conditions, such as stroke, encephalitis, and tumors; metabolic disorders of all types; cancer of the pancreas; pneumonia or any illness causing fever; constipation; heat stroke.

Environmental Changes—Death of a loved one, move, prolonged hospitalization.

Poor Nutrition—Inadequate vitamin or protein intake (older people living alone are at high risk of being malnourished).

Surgery—After-effects of anesthesia; surgical complications.

Accidents or Assaults—Physical and emotional effects.

Source: Belsky, J.K. (1990).

researchers feel that the buildup of this protein plays a central role in the development of these structures. Do the genetic instructions to "produce amyloid" trigger the disease by causing this toxin to accumulate, producing the neural devastation? This hypothesis was given a boost in 1991 when researchers reported producing tangles and plaques in mice after injecting them with human genetic material fostering amyloid synthesis (Marx, 1991). However, the following year these findings were discredited (Marx, 1992). While researchers still are unsure if amyloid is a by-product or a true cause of the disease, the search for agents that might inhibit the formation of this material is occurring at a feverish pace.

Today, while research is intense, the prognosis remains bleak. There is no intervention that can stave off or slow the course of this disease (Pendlebury and Solomon, 1994). This means the diagnosis of Alzheimer's must be made carefully.

Diagnostic Issues

Because no technological advance has enabled physicians to see into the brain to *prove* that the neural deterioration is there, the diagnosis of Alzheimer's is made by exclusion—by taking a careful history, conducting a medical examination, administering psychological tests, and especially ruling out problems that produce mental impairment, but are potentially reversible.

delirium
Any gross disturbance of consciousness that, in contrast to dementia, has a rapid onset and may abate.

As Table 7–5 shows, a long list of conditions from cancer, to medication side effects, to emotional stress can produce **delirium,** a state of confusion that is actually quite different than the slow, progressive deterioration of Alzheimer's disease. Delirium develops rapidly. One hour a rational human being is there; the next a madman appears. Periods of disorientation may fluctuate with lucid periods, that is, times when the person shows no impairment. Still, if people are primed to think of dementia, the danger of misdiagnosis is there.

Another problem that can be erroneously diagnosed as dementia is depression. The reason, as was implied earlier in this chapter, is that this problem also often causes memory impairment. Unfortunately memory deficits are common in older depressed people (Lichtenberg, Ross, Millis, and Manning, 1995; Lyness, Eaton, and Schneider, 1994), sometimes making differentiating between the two conditions difficult.

Diagnostic accuracy has improved dramatically. The use of sophisticated psychological tests, combined with advances in neuroimaging, or pictures of brain functioning and structure, has made the diagnosis of Alzheimer's disease much easier (Tune, 1993).

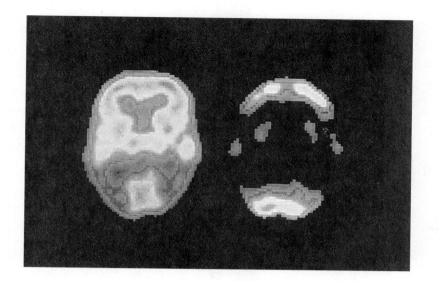

This MRI brain scan is one of the new neuro-imaging techniques that is aiding in the accurate diagnosis of dementing illnesses. Notice the greater activity characteristic of a normal brain (left) compared to that of the brain of a person with dementia (right).

However, until recently, people were sometimes labeled demented when they had other diseases. A 90-year-old man arriving in the emergency room with a heart attack was diagnosed as having Alzheimer's disease. Family members assumed that their 80-year-old mother's confusion was due to dementia, not remembering her symptoms began when the doctor prescribed those heart pills. Because mistakes still occur, if Alzheimer's is suspected, get the diagnosis confirmed by a center specializing in this disease.

Medications can be helpful in reducing the agitation and wandering behavior that so often accompany dementia (Cooper and Mungas, 1994). However, the main interventions for this set of diseases are environmental. They center around making life easier for the person and for family members. With the understanding that any strategy that makes life easier for patients benefits families and helping families equally benefits the victims of these diseases, we now look at each side of the equation separately.

APPLICATIONS AND INTERVENTIONS

HELPING THE VICTIM.   As I mentioned earlier in this chapter, standard memory-enhancing exercises fall flat in dealing with dementia. However, this does not mean one should abandon strategies designed to make the most of the cognitive capacities that exist.

In the same way as for any age-related disability, with dementing illnesses a primary goal is to foster *person/environment congruence*—that is, to modify the living situation to fit the person's new capacities. Any external cue or written aid can heighten orientation from painting the person's room in a bright color, to writing the word "restroom" on the bathroom door, to putting up charts in a prominent place to remind the individual of the day of the week (see Figure 7–2).

A primary concern is safety. People need to be protected from harming themselves, particularly during the highly mobile middle stages of the disease. To prevent the person from wandering off, a common strategy is to double-lock or put buzzers on doors to alert care-givers that the person is about to leave. It is important to keep people with dementing illnesses away from dangerous appliances, such as the stove, and to put toxic substances, such as household cleaners, out of reach. Clothing and shoes that slip on, rather than needing to be buttoned or laced, can help promote functional capacities. There are a variety of other devices on the market, such as tea kettles that whistle when ready and timers that turn the oven off, that can help keep the person functioning fairly independently during the early stages of the disease.

Figure 7–2

The Orientation Board Used For Dementia

TODAY IS <u>FRIDAY</u>

THE DATE IS <u>APRIL 1, 1997</u>

THE WEATHER IS <u>SUNNY</u>

THE NEXT HOLIDAY IS <u>MEMORIAL DAY</u>

THE NEXT MEAL IS <u>DINNER</u>

TOMORROW IS <u>SATURDAY</u>

Another key is to keep the environment as predictable and familiar as possible. As we poignantly saw in the first-person account in Feature 7–2, any challenge to one's cognitive capacities is apt to be utterly overwhelming, especially early in the illness when people are aware of the fact that something is terribly wrong with their mind.

On the other hand, one also must guard against *understimulation*. Remember from Chapter 5 that excess disabilities can occur when the environment is too bland and unchallenging as well as too complex. Based on the principle that people suffering from dementing illnesses need heightened (but non-threatening) input, activities from gardening, to music, to cooking are often used with cognitively impaired older adults. In the following activity, called *sensory stimulation*, even severely demented people can be reconnected with the outside world using the basic senses of touch, sight, and taste:

> Mr. D. . . . was a severely disabled man who apparently recognized none of his loved ones or caregivers. . . . He no longer fed himself and spent most of his day sleeping or staring into space. . . . It was almost Halloween the first time Mr. D. came to sensory stimulation group. Our department had purchased a fine, brilliant orange pumpkin. When his gerichair was wheeled to a place at the table, I gently guided Mr. D.'s hands to the cool, ridged surface of the pumpkin. Contact! His eyes were open, sparkling with life. This man, who hadn't spoken a sentence in weeks, hefted the pumpkin, eyed it approvingly, and said, "Well now isn't that a dandy. Wherever did you get that?" Almost every day thereafter, Mr. D. put in the milk and sugar and stirred his own tea. (Bowlby, 1993, p. 273)

HELPING FAMILIES.   Imagine caring for a loved one with dementia. You know that the illness is permanent. You must helplessly witness your beloved spouse or parent deteriorate. You must deal with a human being turned alien, where the tools used in normal encounters no longer apply. Particularly in the middle stages of the illness, your relative may be physically and verbally abusive. She may be agitated and wake and wander in the night (Cohen et al., 1993). As the person becomes incontinent and needs 24-hour care, you are faced with the difficult decision to institutionalize your loved one. At some point afterward, you must cope with the person's death. As the illness

In this day program for Alzheimer's patients, a staff member encourages a woman to practice the familiar activity of setting the table, and then she and the others will eat together. These simple activities are designed to help people suffering from dementing illnesses preserve a sense of contact with reality.

progresses, it takes its toll on everyone, your children, even your in-laws (Lieberman and Fisher, 1995). Although some people find transforming meanings in this life experience (Farran, et al., 1991), on balance caregiving is a difficult, upsetting task (George and Gwyther, 1986; see Chapter 12).

In a remarkable three-year-long investigation, a team of social scientists set out to intensively trace the lives of 555 care-givers thrust into what they call this "unexpected career" (see Aneshensel et al., 1995). As Figure 7–3 illustrates, the researchers found that care-giving follows a path from *role acquisition* at the beginning of care to *role enactment*, during which care-giving first occurs at home and then usually progresses to nursing home placement. Then there is a phase of institutional care. After the patient dies, there is *role disengagement*, during which the care-giver mourns the loved one and reconstructs a new life. The researchers specify that interventions need to be tailored to the requirements of each given stage.

During the role acquisition stage, people need education, and planning. They need to know what they are dealing with, that is, the symptoms, course, and basic characteristics of the disease. They need to understand how to modify the environment and react to the puzzling behavior as well as understanding what services are available to lighten their load, the *day programs* or *respite services* that exist for demented older adults in their community. Even if they are determined to keep the person at home, they need to consider the possibility that institutionalization may be necessary and look into area nursing homes.

Luckily, this education is readily available. Along with the boom in popular and professional interest, an extensive network has arisen to help families coping with dementing diseases. The *American Association of Retired Persons* and the *National Institute on Aging* are clearinghouses for information and services. The **Alzheimer's Association** is a vigorous national organization devoted just to this disease. This organization sponsors research, lobbies for funding aimed at prevention and cure, operates information hot-lines, and has been the driving force behind the family support groups that have been a lifeline for thousands of care-givers of demented older adults.

Alzheimer's Association
National advocacy, self-help organization addressing concerns related to dementing illnesses.

Figure 7–3

The Progression of the Care-Giving Career

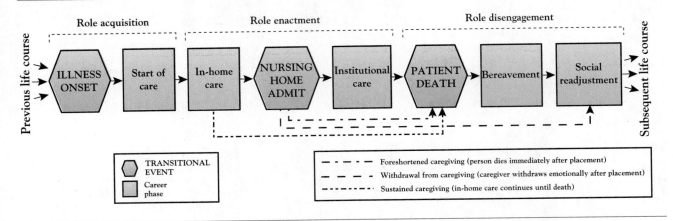

Source: C.S. Aneshensel, L.I. Pearlin, J.T. Mullan, S.H. Zarit, and C.J. Whitlatch, 1995, *Profiles in Caregiving: The Unexpected Career*, San Diego: Academic Press.

family support groups
Self-help groups for family members caring for loved ones with dementing disorders.

Family support groups, in which care-givers meet on a regular basis to share feelings and mutually work to solve problems, come into play during the role enactment period, the long haul spanning home and institutional care. Interestingly the researchers found that one important key to coping best over this protracted period was developing a sense of *self-efficacy*, a feeling of being on top of the day-to-day stresses. Sometimes, as these comments from two participants in the care-giving study reveal, having this sense of mastery was less dependent on controlling the person than on managing one's own attitudes and responses:

> Accept the fact that the patient won't be able to live up to even minimum standards of etiquette. You can waste a lot of good living time and emotion thinking that they have to meet standards they would have earlier. Let it go. That's the way it is. . . . I realized I never knew what would happen but I finally decided that wasn't a reason not to do things. He was happier and I was happier if the ordinary standards of life just didn't apply.

> My approach to the world is more confident. . . . I used to find my mother terribly embarrassing—you overcome that. . . . Laugh at it. It may seem cruel but if you didn't see the humor, it would drive you crazy. Understand that the behavior is not voluntary, that they have no control. (Aneshensel et al., 1995, p. 170)

Here is an intervention aimed at teaching the attitudes these two women report painfully developing over time:

The *Coping with Frustration Class* involves didactic lectures and readings. However, its main purpose is to instruct care-givers in emotion-management skills. Participants are taught relaxation techniques to deal with anxiety (see Chapter 9). A main focus is on changing unproductive cognitions: For instance, rather than getting furious when her husband rakes the yard with a stick, a care-giving wife is trained to think: "He's enjoying himself." Because anger at family members who do not do their fair share can be an important source of stress (see Chapter 12), care-givers learn to be assertive, that is, to calmly say to a brother or sister who has made and then retracted an offer of help: "I'm counting on the time off. I've made plans and I can't change them now." While the effectiveness of this intervention has not been formally evaluated, the preliminary results look encouraging, with most participants giving high marks to the course (Gallagher-Thompson and DeVries, 1994).

When they are contemplating a nursing home, care-givers need to be aware of some new trends in institutional care. One interesting new development is the establishment of **special care dementia units** within some nursing homes, with staff and programs specially devoted to the needs of people with dementing diseases. These units are usually locked or have alarms to prevent patients from wandering. Structured activities, such as those described in the previous section, are prevalent. The environment is designed with the needs of the dementia resident in mind.

special care dementia units *Units in nursing homes catering to the needs of residents suffering from dementing illnesses.*

I must emphasize that many standard nursing homes now have these features (Grant, Kane, and Stark, 1995). It has yet to be proven that a unit provides superior care just because it is labeled as being "for dementia" (Sloane, Lindeman, Phillips, Moritz, and Koch, 1995). Interestingly, in spite of their extreme trepidation, most participants in the care-giving careers study found that, once they had made the difficult decision to institutionalize their loved one, they were relieved and pleasantly surprised with the quality of care their relative received in a nursing home.

Until we find a cure for dementing illnesses, our best hope for minimizing the pain lies in these studies, interventions, and services for both families and patients. We need to make life as easy as possible for the millions of Americans who cope on a daily basis with these difficult diseases.

KEY TERMS & CONCEPTS

information processing perspective on memory
sensory store
working memory
long-term memory
processing resources
Tulving's memory systems theory
implicit or procedural memory
semantic memory
episodic memory
everyday memory tasks
prospective memory
autobiographical memory
mnemonic techniques
external memory aids
memory self-efficacy
dementia
vascular dementia
Alzheimer's disease
neurofibrillary tangles
senile plaques
delerium
Alzheimer's Association
family support groups
special care dementia units

RECOMMENDED READINGS

Memory

Blanchard-Fields, F., and Hess, T. (Eds.). (1996). *Perspectives on cognitive change in adulthood and aging.* New York: McGraw-Hill.
> *While this graduate-level text is devoted to cognition in general, it is particularly strong in its coverage of the latest research on memory.*

Poon, L. W., Rubin, D. C., and Wilson, B. A. (1989). *Everyday cognition in adulthood and late life.* New York: Cambridge University Press.
> *This book, also recommended in the previous chapter, covers memory enhancement techniques and practical memory studies.*

Dementia

Aneshensel, C. S., Pearlin, L. I., Mullan, J. T., Zarit, S. H., and Whitlatch, C. J. (1995). *Profiles in caregiving: The unexpected career.* San Diego: Academic Press.
> *This book is a landmark in research on care-giving for dementia. The authors follow a sample of 555 care-givers over a three-year period, charting their stresses and their lives. (It will be interesting mainly to research-oriented students.)*

Coons, D. (Ed.). (1991). *Specialized dementia care units.* Baltimore: Johns Hopkins University Press.
> *This edited book describes special care dementia units.*

McGowen, D. F. (1993). *Living in the labyrinth.* New York: Delacourt Press.
> *This is a remarkable first-person account of what it is like to have Alzheimer's disease.*

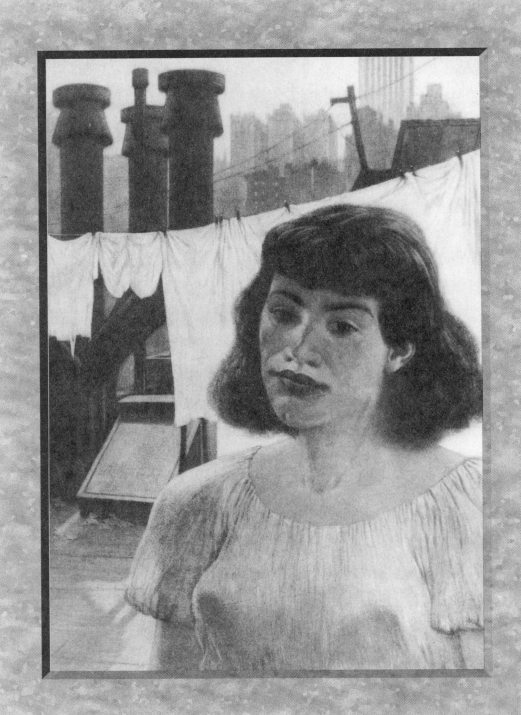

Personality

Chapter Outline

"I feel like I have lived six different lives in my six decades of life," says Jane. "I was born in Indonesia in 1938. My father was from Tennessee, and my mother was British. When I was a young child, my mother became schizophrenic and was sent to an institution—in those days a death sentence, as there were no drugs. Father took me to my mother's sister in England. Then, a few days later, he was gone, buzzed off, out of my life. I was raised by this aunt who impressed on me how nobody wanted me. I knew my salvation was school, but my aunt and uncle refused to pay. At age 16, I contemplated suicide. Then, quite by accident, I got a position as a nanny at the home of the president of a teachers' college. This wonderful man took me under his wing, provided encouragement, and funded my tuition at this school. At age 20, after graduation, life took another dramatic turn. My father's family invited me to Alabama to teach in the Church. At that time, conditions were primitive in the South. Women were expected to get married and become homemakers. I followed that pattern, marrying and moving to an isolated rural community where I spent 12 years as a full-time mom. One day, after driving the kids back from school, I thought: "I am a Taxi Driver." By then, it was the 1970s, and the women's movement was going on. I stopped at a local school and said: "I have a teaching background." I just dumped my kids; my youngest in kindergarten at the time. While working as a teacher, I took my master's in speech and got a job teaching part-time at the University. When you are a professor, people look up to you. In my forties, I was feeling wonderful, very much in control of my life. However, my family was falling apart. My younger child had gotten into drugs and dropped out of college. Tom died of a drug overdose eight years ago. My son was tall and handsome, with a 150 IQ. Another watershed. I couldn't get over his death, past feeling it was my fault. I couldn't stay in our town. I felt people were saying, "What

How have this woman's attitudes, emotions, and approach to life changed from youth to late middle age? Has she really become wiser and more mellow as this photo implies or is she basically the same person as the expectant young girl we see on her wedding day? It is questions such as these that the studies in adult personality development described in this chapter are designed to answer.

a shame about Jane's children being such a mess." You see, a few years earlier my other son told us he was gay.

Last year I turned 60, so I can retire from the system. My son is living in San Francisco with a wonderful partner. They just celebrated their tenth anniversary. Seeing Todd happy has inspired me. I'm going back to get my Ph.D. I think growing older changes us. You don't have the same fears. You get a perspective about what's important. But we also are the same. You see how when life has presented me with problems, my salvation has always been to improve my mind. If I look back over my strange life, despite all the changes, I'm basically the same person today as during my teens."

Think back to the different theories of personality development described in Chapter 2. Do you see evidence in our interview of *Carl Jung's* idea that women become more assertive and self-confident after midlife? Perhaps you are impressed with the role historical events, such as the women's movement, and random life experiences, such as finding a mentor or moving to the United States, played in shaping Jane's interests and goals (the *contextualist, life-span approach*). Or, in reading this vignette, you may be struck with the evidence contradicting *psychoanalytic theory:* People who have a very unhappy childhood may not be doomed to have serious emotional problems. Jane was able to cope productively even with that traumatic life event, the death of a child. On the other hand, notice that Jane herself agrees with the psychoanalytic idea that there is continuity to personality. She believes her basic strategy for handling stressful life events has been consistent from her teens.

Like Jane, you probably have your own implicit theory of personality, your ideas about how you and other people change during adult life. Perhaps you have found yourself describing a family member as "a typical adolescent" or have thought to yourself: "I'm acting middle-aged." Maybe you gravitate to a certain theory, such as Erik Erikson's concept of generativity, to guide your life. How do people such as you and I view personality during adulthood? What issues should we be alert to in evaluating the research on how people really do change? These questions set the stage for the main topic of this chapter, the studies examining personality development during adult life.

SETTING THE STAGE

Personal Conceptions about Change

In order to explore whether people do have defined stereotypes about personality at different stages of life, researchers asked adolescent, middle-aged, and elderly people to rank typical people in their own and the other age groups along specific dimensions: adaptability (how flexible they are), autonomy (how self-sufficient they are), acceptability (how pleasing their personality is), and self-acceptance (how at peace they are with themselves).

On most scales, people ranked adolescence as the most dismal time. Adolescents scored lowest on autonomy, acceptability, and self-acceptance. It was only in adaptability or flexibility that this stage of life ranked especially high. However, while in general middle-aged and older people were rated more positively, subjects thought each age had special strengths. Middle-aged people ranked highest on autonomy. Older people were rated as most integrated and accepting of themselves. Finally, except for a tendency to rate one's own time of life somewhat more positively, people of every age agreed on these rankings, suggesting that we do have shared ideas about what personality traits become salient at different ages (Luszex and Fitzgerald, 1986).

Other psychologists focused on Erikson's and Jung's ideas, asking if young, middle-aged and elderly people believe that they have (or did, or will) become more generative in midlife and that integrity is (or will be) typical of themselves in old age. Do people agree with Jung that they have (or will) become more introspective and less interested in the outside world in later life?

The researchers developed a scale measuring generativity, ego integrity, and introversion; gave their measure to people of various ages; and asked subjects to answer from the perspective of their current, past, and future selves. They found that people generally agreed with Erikson's ideas about generativity and integrity, believing these qualities would characterize them at the appropriate time of life. However, opinions about Jung's theory were mixed. Only older women ranked themselves as more introverted, suggesting that there is less unanimity about the idea that in later life we become more internally focused and withdrawn (Ryff and Heincke, 1983).

These studies have a message similar to that of more comprehensive studies exploring our feelings about adult development. Paul Baltes's research team asked several hundred men and women of different ages to rate the desirability of a long list of adjectives, such as adventurous, stingy, assertive, curious, and cynical. They asked people to decide when these traits began and ended and whether each quality increased, stayed stable, or declined over the years.

These psychologists, too, found that subjects described development as involving losses and gains. Interestingly, while more negative traits were ranked as increasing in the latter part of life, these researchers were also impressed by the shared agreement and the positive views about growing older held by the old and the young. Many desirable qualities were viewed as increasing, even at older ages. In fact, gains outnumbered losses almost until the end of life. Moreover, while people felt their own development generally fit in with these patterns, in this research, too, the fit was not exact. Especially middle-aged and older people painted a more positive picture about themselves and other people at their own stage of life (Heckhausen, Dixon, and Baltes, 1989; Heckhausen and Krueger, 1993).

Are these perceptions and theories accurate? Before turning to this question, let's return to Chapter 2 again—this time to our discussion of research methods.

Problems in Measuring Change

THE ISSUE OF *WHAT* WE TEST.   What do we mean by personality? Under this huge umbrella term lurks an incredible diversity of emotions, attitudes, and activities. Personality includes traits such as shyness and assertiveness. It involves our styles of coping with stress, our likes and dislikes, and our values, preferences, and needs. It includes our self-concept, our feelings about the past, our goals, and our future plans. It involves unconscious motivations as well as actions and intentions of which we are aware.

So the first principle in approaching the research is to look carefully at the way each investigator has chosen to *operationalize* personality. As we saw in our discussion of research methods, we also need to be aware that different ways of defining and measuring this vague entity may produce different conclusions about the extent of change. In other words, the answer to the question "How will I change?" is likely to depend on *what* we test.

THE ISSUE OF *WHO* WE TEST.   In exploring personality development, we want to make general statements, blueprints that will apply to most adults. While it is easier to get the *representative sample* needed to provide that blueprint in a cross-sectional study, this type of research cannot tell us whether the change we are seeing in a particular aspect of personality is due to being in a different cohort or basic to age. A cross-sectional study showing that 70-year-olds were more reserved about expressing emotions might be uncovering a true late-life change or merely be showing that today's

Table 8-1

1. **The Kansas City Studies of Adult Life.** Several hundred middle-class married couples ranging in age from 40 to their nineties living in Kansas City during the middle 1950s are interviewed and given a variety of measures and tests. *Main Personality Measure:* the TAT; subjects are given a series of pictures and asked to tell stories about each. From these story themes, psychologists analyze unconscious motivations.

2. **The Mills College Study.** Members of the 1958 and 1960 graduating classes of Mills College for Women are assessed as seniors and periodically reassessed through their early fifties. *Personality Measure:* the California Psychological Inventory, a self-report scale asking subjects about their attitudes, traits, and coping styles.

3. **The Berkeley/Oakland Studies.** Several studies of child development begun during the late 1920s are merged, and the groups are followed throughout adult life. *Personality Measure:* To make the data comparable, researchers adapt the California Q sort. Based on the personality data, they sort statements on cards referring to personality into three piles as very characteristic, somewhat characteristic, or not characteristic of each person at different ages.

4. **The Baltimore Longitudinal Study of Aging.** Volunteers varying in age take a battery of tests every two years. *Personality Measure:* the NEO-PI, a self-report scale measuring broad personality dispositions or traits.

5. **The Grant Study.** The "best and brightest" men from the Harvard classes of 1939–1940 and 1942–1944 are selected and then intensively interviewed, tested, and assessed periodically over 30 years. *Personality Measure:* defense mechanisms (unconscious styles of coping with life) rated from intensive interviews and open-ended questionnaires.

older people are less likely to be open about their emotions because they grew up before the 1960s when freely discussing personal feelings was more taboo. In addition, because they do not trace the lives of individuals, cross-sectional studies cannot answer some very important questions: "If people are especially reserved as young adults, do they 'grow out' of this tendency?" "How do experiences such as becoming ill or having children change the tendency to be open about one's feelings?" Longitudinal studies, while they can answer these questions relating to individual change patterns and why they may occur, are expensive and take decades to complete. As they involve a long-term commitment, they tend to be carried out with "elite" groups, that is, volunteers who are well educated and upper-middle-class. In addition, even longitudinal studies do not allow us to make universal statements about people because they only trace development in a cohort traveling through time at a given point in history.

So a second principle in considering the studies is to look carefully at *who* is being tested. Because it is more informative, if possible we should focus on longitudinal research. However, we should be aware that this type of study often tells us only about development in a "special" group.

In this chapter, we will follow this strategy. While I will mention other research, we will pay special attention to the five comprehensive studies of personality described in Table 8–1. The first set of studies in the table, the **Kansas City Studies of Adult Life,** does not fully fit our criterion as longitudinal, as the researchers only followed subjects for a few years. However, as the earliest attempt to systematically measure personality change in middle and later life, the Kansas City Studies are a landmark in adult development. Some findings of this research are being debated today. In the other studies, researchers did trace personality over longer periods of adult life. You are already familiar with two of these studies, the *Berkeley/Oakland Studies* and the *Baltimore*

Kansas City Studies of Adult Life
Earliest major study of personality change in middle and later life.

Grant Study
Classic longitudinal study in which a select group of Harvard undergraduates was evaluated while in college and followed through middle life.

Mills College Study
Classic longitudinal study in which Mills College for Women seniors were tested and then followed through midlife.

Longitudinal Study of Aging. In the **Grant Study** and the **Mills College Study,** Harvard men and women at a prestigious women's college, respectively, were first evaluated as undergraduates and then retested several times through middle age.

While they offer our most revealing information about personality change, notice that each of these studies has the limitations I pointed out above. Not one study explores personality development in minorities. Every study involves mainly middle-class adults. With the exception of the Baltimore Study, every study traces the lives of cohorts who came of age or were adults during the middle of the twentieth century, a more traditional time in American life.

Notice from the table that in each study personality was conceptualized and measured in different ways. In the Kansas City and Grant research, the emphasis was on unconscious processes and coping styles. In the Baltimore and Mills College Studies, the focus was on personality traits, such as shyness and assertiveness. Some researchers used scales in which people were asked to rate themselves; others measured personality through interviews or the stories a person told.

As we turn now to explore the findings of these studies and others, keep the crucial issue of *measurement validity* in mind. There is always the nagging question that researchers may not be legitimately measuring a given aspect of personality when using a particular strategy or test. Equally important, these *legitimately* different strategies for viewing and measuring personality are crucial in themselves. As we see now, these very differences in approach to that elusive entity called personality are central in understanding the great consistency/change debate.

THE GREAT CONSISTENCY/CHANGE DEBATE

Phase 1: Focus on Change: The Kansas City Studies of Adult Life

As I just mentioned, research on adult personality change began with the Kansas City Studies of Adult Life. In the early 1950s, a research team headed by University of Chicago psychologist Bernice Neugarten chose a group of "typical" middle-aged and elderly Americans, white, middle-class married couples, living in an average American city (Kansas City, Missouri), and interviewed and tested these people over a period of several years (Neugarten and Associates, 1964).

Because their framework was psychoanalytic, in exploring personality, in addition to their other measures and interviews, the University of Chicago researchers used a test designed to reveal unconscious motivations called the **Thematic Apperception Test** (TAT). In this test, people are shown a series of pictures and asked to tell a story about each scene. The theory is that through these stories people reveal their unconscious concerns, conflicts, and underlying world view. Rather than simply letting themes emerge, the researchers categorized the stories that their subjects produced along dimensions that they labeled "ego energy" and "mastery style."

Ego energy (Rosen and Neugarten, 1964) referred to vigorous, passionate, energetic engagement versus withdrawal. If a person told a story that was rich in detail and full of feelings, one in which the characters were passionately involved in life, the idea was that this same passionate involvement would characterize the person's approach to living. *Mastery style* measured a similar sense of engagement through the story's theme. Was the protagonist confronting and triumphing over a problem or retreating from the world? Once again, if the message of the story was one of personal triumph and success, this style was felt to mirror the person's approach to the world.

Starting in the later-middle-aged group, men and women in their early fifties, ratings of ego energy and active mastery gradually declined, suggesting to the research team that, as people grow old, they tend to become less involved in the world. This

Thematic Apperception Test
Key test used in the Kansas City Studies in which people are thought to reveal their unconscious concerns through telling stories about pictures.

internal withdrawal, complemented by a reduction in the actual number of roles that the researchers found among the men and women in their sixties, caused two members of the team to propose a controversial idea called **disengagement theory.**

According to Elaine Cumming and William Henry (1961), in late middle-age a natural process of disengagement takes place. People begin to emotionally distance themselves from society and withdraw from the world. Furthermore, Cumming and Henry proposed, not only is this withdrawal normal, but also *disengagement is the correct way to age.*

The second change the University of Chicago researchers found was equally provocative. When Neugarten and David Gutmann (1964) gave subjects a TAT card picturing a young man, a young woman, an old man, and an old woman, the younger people (aged 40–54) described the old man and old woman according to standard gender stereotypes. He was dominant, and she was gentle and submissive. The older men and women (aged 55–70) reversed the adjectives: Now the woman was described as powerful and controlling; the man was viewed as passive, submissive, and sweet. So the researchers concluded that in later life the personality differences between the sexes blur or reverse. "Women . . . seem to become more tolerant of their own aggressive egocentric impulses; . . . men . . . of their own nurturant and affilliative impulses" (Neugarten and Gutmann, 1964, p. 89).

Notice that these findings fit in perfectly with Jung's theory. Jung felt that we become more spiritual or "disengaged" and grow more **androgenous,** or less rigidly masculine and feminine, in middle age. They support our stereotypes about how people are supposed to change. In the study of perceptions about change discussed earlier, remember that older adults were seen as less autonomous and self-sufficient than middle-aged people. The elderly were also rated as less open and flexible than younger adults.

However, during the late 1960s and early 1970s, a barrage of criticisms was aimed at the Kansas City results. By that time, a revolution was occurring in women's roles. Could men and women still be described by the gender stereotypes provided by the Kansas City 40-year-olds? Psychologists disputed the theory underlying the TAT, that through telling stories about pictures people reveal their unconscious mental processes. Researchers were becoming more sensitive to the problems of assuming age changes from cross-sectional studies and of inferring universal changes from a sample limited to white, middle-class, married adults. Based on disturbing evidence that tests used to reveal different personality dimensions were often *not* valid measures of those traits (Campbell and Fiske, 1959; Fiske, 1971), psychologists criticized the inferences the University of Chicago researchers made. Perhaps the finding that older people tell less detailed and imaginative TAT stories signifies, not decreasing involvement in life, but simply the fact that, as we learned in previous chapters, the elderly are often more uncomfortable taking *any* test and so naturally would produce more limited responses.

Most important, many gerontologists disputed the idea that disengagement was appropriate in later life. If this idea was allowed to stand, people felt it might justify discriminatory practices, such as mandatory retirement, the idea that older adults should retire to a rocking chair. Wasn't it important as one aged to keep as active as possible, to stay fully engaged in the world (Lemon, Bengtson, and Peterson, 1972)?

As you may have guessed from the previous chapters, this competing advice for ideal aging, called **activity theory,** debated and researched during the late 1960s and 1970s, has won out—with important qualifications. Later Kansas City research showed that whether people were happiest was really more a function of their personality than their level of activity. Among the most well adjusted men and women, the researchers found a mix of active and relatively inactive people, all satisfied with life. Among people who were emotionally disturbed, disengagement combined with low morale was the rule

disengagement theory
Controversial idea that it is normal and appropriate for older people to withdraw from the world.

androgenous
Having balance between masculine and feminine traits.

activity theory
The idea that keeping active is the optimum way to age.

(Neugarten, Havinghurst, and Tobin, 1968). In other words, disengagement could be a satisfying way of life, provided it was actively *chosen* by an emotionally healthy individual.

Moreover, the advice to simply "Be active" is simplistic. Only people who are involved in meaningful activities, ones that are personally relevant and important, rate themselves as happiest in later life (Ogilvie, 1987). On the other hand, as we saw in our chapters on physical and cognitive development, what really distinguishes older people we look up to as ideally aging is *ongoing* involvement in living, a marvelous *lack* of disengagement at even the oldest ages.

CURRENT STATUS AND CURRENT ISSUES. While disengagement theory is no longer debated, the second finding of the Kansas City Studies is still a subject of controversy. Do men and women become more androgenous as they age? Gutmann, as well as a few other researchers in adult development, believe that they do.

Exploring myths, dreams, and anecdotes and pulling together anthropological data from around the world, Gutmann has devoted his career to arguing that a shift toward androgeny is universal during the second half of adult life. However, while he originally felt this change was intrinsic to advancing age, Gutmann now sees this change as due to the different pressures we face as younger versus older adults.

According to Gutmann (1987), personality differences between men and women are needed in the first half of adulthood because of what he calls the **parental imperative.** In order to best raise children, Guttmann feels nature has set up a division of labor that, despite the women's revolution, still usually takes place along traditional lines. The man aggressively provides for the family, and the woman handles the interpersonal sphere, taking care of the day-to-day childcare and offering the female qualities of understanding, patience, and selflessness. Once children have left the nest, women "reclaim" the masculine qualities they had to dampen down to ensure their children's development. Men relax, giving more play to their nurturing, "feminine" side (Cooper and Gutmann, 1987).

Gutmann's ideas are appealing because they fit in with longitudinal research tracing what happens after men and women become parents. As we will see in Chapter 11, there *is* a heightening of sex roles after the birth of the first child. His theory makes sense of studies exploring that very different transition, retirement. As we will discover in Chapter 13, relinquishing work turns out to be painless for many older men, implying that achievement, status, and power may indeed become less important psychologically to males in their later years.

Other cross-sectional studies of personality at different ages support the idea that gender roles and attitudes become less sharply differentiated at older ages (Feldman, Biringen, and Nash, 1981; Lowenthal, Thurnher, Chiriboga, and Associates, 1975). For instance, in exploring conceptions of masculinity and femininity among women ranging in age from their late teens to their forties, Mary Ann Sedney (1985–1986) found that in contrast to the younger subjects 30 percent of the oldest group rejected the idea that there were any differences in personality between the sexes. This suggests that, when we reach midlife, our sense of ourselves as being either stereotypically masculine or stereotypically feminine may break down.

As I mentioned earlier, however, our best clues to whether this change occurs can really only come from examining longitudinal research. In the Mills College Study, described in Table 8–1, Ravinna Helson and Paul Wink (1992) gave an adjective checklist to the women they were following at age 27, during the early parental stage, and again at about age 50, when most were in the empty nest. While as young parents the women rated themselves much lower than their husbands on "masculine traits," such as assertiveness and efficiency, at the empty nest stage the women ranked as *high* on these traits as their spouses.

parental imperative
Gutmann's hypothesis that parenting evokes defined gender roles during the younger, active child-rearing phase of adult life.

There are qualifications. As we will see in the next section, other research does not show that men and women change in *any* systematic way as they age. These changes, if they occur, may not be due to the waning parental imperative. They may be caused by age-related hormonal changes, which may affect personality, or perhaps other experiences life may bring. *Postformal* researchers might even argue that what Gutmann calls androgeny, more acceptance of both masculine and feminine sides of personality, may be a sign of a larger process. People become less rigid, more flexible, and generally more open to complexity in themselves and others as they mature (see Chapter 6).

Gender-role attitudes at specific ages may be less universal than Gutmann believes. In one interesting comparative study, young-adult African-American women ranked themselves as more androgenous on a gender-role scale, although just as child-centered compared to whites (Binion, 1990). In exploring ethnic differences on a general personality test, another group of researchers found traditional masculine/feminine attitudes were especially strong among college-student Asian-American women and men (Dion and Yee, 1987). In other words, instead of being universal to parenthood, defined gender roles in early adulthood may be partly shaped by one's specific cultural group and its norms.

The same social shaping may apply to the shift to androgeny that Guttmann believes automatically occurs after the children are gone. When she first tested the Mills women as they were about to graduate in 1959, Helson (1992) gave an identical checklist to their mothers, who were in their early fifties at the time. These empty-nest mothers showed *no* sign of androgeny!

What accounts for the difference between mothers and their daughters at the same age? Helson believes, once again, that the answer lies in cultural norms, the experiences each cohort had as it traveled adult life. The Mills daughters were young adults during the 1960s, when women entered the work force and being assertive became prized. Their mothers lived during a restricted time in history when middle-class women were supposed to act in defined, "dependent" ways. Helson argues that the Mills mothers could not grow more androgenous because their social circumstances stifled any change toward assertion over time.

Does this mean that our social milieu is the primary force shaping our personality and that who we become as we age is very responsive to our specific experiences in life? A good deal of evidence suggests that the answer is no. In contrast to what Erikson or Jung or, as we saw earlier, most adults believe, personality during adulthood may be surprisingly enduring and stable, immune to cultural change or life experiences. Paul Costa and Robert McCrae have devoted distinguished careers to arguing this point.

Phase 2: Focus on Stability: Costa and McCrae's Big Five Traits

As the researchers who direct the personality studies for the Baltimore Study, Costa and McCrae have been in the position to analyze how a huge group of people of every age scores on paper-and-pencil personality tests over the years. Many psychologists believe their findings have put to rest the idea there are *any* stages of adult development or that people change in predictable ways as they grow old. According to Costa and McCrae, personality stability characterizes adult life. The best prediction about how the years will change us is that they will not (Costa and McCrae, 1980; Costa, McCrae, and Arenberg, 1980; McCrae and Costa, 1990).

The evidence that Costa and McCrae have gathered to show that personality stays remarkably stable during adulthood involves five global dimensions of personality, general predispositions that seem to underlie *all* of the traits, qualities, and attributes by which we describe people (Costa and McCrae, 1988a; McCrae, Costa, and Piedmont, 1993). How is it possible to reduce the thousands of ways we think about personality into just five categories? Costa and McCrae performed this distilling feat using a statistical technique that showed that all of the adjectives used to characterize personality cluster into the following broad categories:

1. *Neuroticism (N)* is a general tendency toward mental health or maladjustment, that is, anxiety, hostility, depression, self-consciousness, and emotional distress. (Is the person stable and well adjusted or psychologically vulnerable and prone to break down?)
2. *Extraversion (E)* reflects outgoing attitudes, such as warmth, gregariousness, activity, and assertion. (Is the person at home and happy with others, or does that individual feel most comfortable being by herself, living a more reflective, solitary life?)
3. *Openness to experience (O)* involves the willingness to take risks, seek out new experiences, and try new things. (Does the person love the unbeaten path, the newest thrill? Or is he cautious and comfortable with the tried and true?
4. *Conscientiousness (C)* relates to how organized, efficient, and dependable the person is. (Is this individual hard-working, self-disciplined, and reliable or erratic, inconsistent, and irresponsible, someone we really cannot trust?)
5. *Agreeableness (A)* incorporates qualities related to love, such as empathy, caring, friendliness, and cooperation. (Is the person caring, sensitive, pleasant, and loving or contentious, scornful, and rude?)

big five traits
Five overarching dimensions of personality encompassing all smaller descriptions and traits.

According to Costa and McCrae, measuring how these **big five traits** change over time allows us to evaluate the truth of most theories and stereotypes about personality development. If people regress, becoming emotionally unstable in later life, neuroticism should peak in the aged. If they grow more generative or mature, scores on agreeableness or conscientiousness should rise. If the idea that age brings rigidity is correct, then, as people grow old, there should be a decline in openness to experience. If we really do pull back from the outer world in our later years, extroversion ratings should decrease. But the Baltimore volunteers' scores on each of these dimensions are quite similar at age 35 and age 85.

The Baltimore men and women are an elite, upper-middle-class group. Can we really expect how they change, or, in this case, do not change, to apply to Americans as a whole? It is one thing to say that among highly educated, relatively healthy people personality remains stable. But what about among less fortunate people, the poor, the uneducated, or ill? To show that the Baltimore findings do apply to the typical American, Costa and McCrae (1986) decided they needed to demonstrate that the Baltimore subjects' scores on neuroticism, extraversion, and openness to experience at each age were similar to those of a more *representative* group.

So the researchers got access to subjects from a national survey involving almost 15,000 respondents and gave these people an abbreviated form of their personality test. They found few differences in the scores of the two samples, suggesting that the Baltimore results can indeed be generalized to most Americans. Furthermore, when they looked at age differences in extroversion, openness, and neuroticism among these thousands of people, here, too, stability was the dominant theme. While older age groups did have slightly lower scores on the three dimensions, the differences were not statistically significant.

CURRENT STATUS AND CURRENT ISSUES. Costa and McCrae's research has had an enormous impact on the field of personality. Once being uncertain as to whether they could capture, quantify, and measure personality, many personality psychologists now agree that the qualities measured by standard personality tests can be distilled to these categories (Ozer and Reise, 1994). These broad dispositions are *valid,* that is, they seem to be accurately measured by Costa and McCrae's self-report test. When a man rates himself as introverted on Costa and McCrae's scale, his spouse and friends are likely to rate him as introverted, too (Costa and McCrae, 1988b). Observers will rate that person as introverted when they meet him in a social situation or watch him at work (McCrae and Costa, 1990). Moreover, other research reveals much consistency to personality, even over longer periods of adult life (Conley, 1984, 1985; West and Graziano, 1989). Even specific pathological ways of viewing the world can be consistent from youth to old age.

Melanie Burns and Martin Seligman (1989) asked elderly men and women to bring in samples of diaries and letters they had written about 50 years earlier, when they were in their late teens and twenties. Then the researchers instructed their subjects to write about specific recent events in their lives. They were looking for similarities in *explanatory style*. Is the tendency to attribute setbacks to temporary, changeable, external causes a stable trend? When people see failures as global, irreversible, and due to the self, is this an enduring way of perceiving the world?

While there was little consistency in interpretations of positive events, Burns and Seligman found there was a statistically significant correlation between attributions for negative life happenings in youth and old age. In other words, a pessimistic explanatory style may indeed be a burden some unfortunate people carry through adult life.

The forces contributing to stability. While many of us might blame our parents, agreeing with Sigmund Freud that our upbringing shapes the way we perceive and react as adults, remember that behavioral genetic studies offer a different view. As described in Chapter 2, studies of identical twins reared apart suggest that extraversion and neuroticism are actually heritable traits (Bouchard and McGue, 1990). Specifically there may even be a hereditary component to perceptions very similar to explanatory style.

When Matt McGue, Betsy Hirsh, and David Lykken (1993) asked reared-apart identical twins to describe how competent and capable they felt in various areas, they found a significant correlation in these assessments. Whether tied to realistic differences in ability or due to inherited predispositions to perceive oneself in certain ways, the twins tended to share *efficacy feelings*, agreeing that they were competent or incompetent in each area of life.

The most interesting behavioral genetic studies are those that turn our ideas about personality and environment upside down. Rather than life experiences determining our personality, who we are as people shapes our "outer world." Genetic predispositions influence our perceptions about the interpersonal world. As we saw in Chapter 2, they affect how giving and generous we recall our parents being during our early years (McCrae and Costa, 1988; Plomin, McClearn, Pedersen, Nesselroade, and Bergeman, 1988). They influence how supportive we perceive family and friends as being today (Bergeman, Plomin, Pedersen, McClearn, and Nesselroade, 1990; Chipuer, Plomin, Pedersen, McClearn, and Nesselroade, 1993). There also are genetic influences on the *objective* experiences we encounter on our journey through adult life.

In the *Swedish Adoption/Twin Study of Aging*, remember that middle-aged twins separated at birth were more likely than chance to report having had similar experiences during adult life (Plomin, Lichtenstein, Pedersen, McClearn, and Nesselroade, 1990). This interesting tendency to report similar life experiences was evident only for happenings over which we potentially have control, such as marital and family conflicts and success or failure at work. It did not appear for uncontrollable events, such as the illness of a spouse and, as in the interview at the beginning of this chapter, the death of a child.

While at first glance the idea that people who share "only genes" might have similar life experiences seems amazing, viewed in the context of our discussion of the

8-1 The Adult Experience: Are Unusually Competent Adolescents High-Achieving Adults?

Esmeralda Santiago was born in Puerto Rico in 1945, the oldest of 11 children. In her autobiography, she vividly describes the dirt floor and the tin walls of the shack where she lived as a child. Her father was abusive, and when Esmeralda was 12, her mother moved out and relocated the family to New York. With her only parent away all day at the factory, Esmeralda had heavy responsibilities. In junior high school, she brought in extra money and took care of her younger siblings. Esmeralda, however, was determined to succeed. At age 15, against her mother's wishes, she applied and won admission to the prestigious High School of Performing Arts in Manhattan. Soon after graduation, she won a scholarship to Harvard, where she met her husband of 25 years.

Today Esmeralda and her husband co-own a film-making company. She has written a book about her experiences and lectures around the country. Her brothers and sisters never graduated from college. She has the only long-lasting, happy marriage among the group. When I asked Esmeralda why she feels she succeeded so brilliantly, she said (a bit tongue in cheek), "Unlike my brothers and sisters, I never felt like a victim. And early on, I knew exactly what I wanted in life: to have a good husband and to be rich."

Can we really see the highly accomplished adult in the competent, self-directed teen? Once again, the Berkeley Study allows us to see if the pattern we observe with Esmeralda is more generally true. By summing adolescent ratings on dependability (measured by such items as "is productive" and "gets things done"), intellectually invested (values intellect and learning), and confident versus victimized (is calm, relaxed, and happy versus is insecure and blames others), John Clausen (1991) got an index of what he labeled planful competence in the Berkeley teens. Then he traced how this quality related to success in adult life.

Planful competence was not correlated with occupational success for girls, perhaps because in this cohort women were not encouraged to have careers. However, this attribute was strongly related to advancing in work for boys. For both genders, competence was associated with other aspects of life success. Competent adolescents were more likely to have more happy, long-lasting marriages. In late middle-age, they were more likely to report being satisfied with how their lives had gone. Not every competent adolescent sailed smoothly through life. Many of the less competent boys and girls did grow in maturity and planful competence over time. But perhaps through the principles of interactional and cumulative consistency discussed on p. 225, early competence was an enduring trait. It also was a harbinger of good things to come.

nature of nurture in childhood in Chapter 2 this phenomenon makes perfect sense. Think of a young adult who scores low on agreeableness and conscientiousness on Costa's scale, someone who is hostile and unreliable. Wouldn't you imagine this person to be more likely to be fired from his job, to fight with friends, to get divorced, to experience more negative events? Now imagine another young person who ranks high on these personality dimensions measuring being able to effectively love and work. While not immune from tragedies, wouldn't this individual's personality set him up for a smoother, more gratifying life? The Swedish Adoption/Twin Study just reinforces the saying: "We make our own luck" (at least the luck that we can control).

As we saw in Chapter 2, behavioral genetic research offers a powerful argument that genetic predispositions do shape personality. A broad range of personality dimensions, from Costa's basic traits to more limited attitudes, such as traditionalism and conservatism, is indeed quite heritable, much more "genetic" than psychologists had ever believed. (For instance, only by invoking genetics can we fully make sense of the fact that, as feature 8–1 shows, some people faced with the worst childhood environments go

This class president seems to be the picture of the planful competence that John Clausen found was correlated with later success in the Berkeley teens (see feature 8-1). However, while our bets are on this commencement speaker for constructing a successful life, an anonymous graduate sitting behind the podium might easily surprise us by surpassing this class president's achievements during adult life.

on to triumph in life.) However, remember that saying a certain trait is *influenced* by inherited predispositions is far different from saying we are *fated* to behave in that way. Nor does it mean that life experiences have little impact on who we are. As I mentioned in Chapter 2, one tantalizing finding of the Swedish Adoption/Twin Study is that the heritabilities for certain important aspects of temperament, such as emotionality and activity level, were lower than those revealed in studies of separated-at-birth twins examined at younger ages. This suggests that, as we age, the power of the environment, or our different life experiences, in shaping personality may increase.

However, inherited predispositions toward neuroticism or agreeableness may also tend to solidify precisely because heredity and environment are not independent entities. The two may work in tandem to accentuate who we are for better or for worse. Let's look at two ways Berkeley researchers Avishom Caspi, Darrell Bem, and Glen Elder (1989) believe that our experiences during life might interact with our temperamental proclivities to make us "more like ourselves" as we age:

Cumulative consistency occurs when the general consequences of having a certain trait operate to reinforce that attribute. Take Joe Smith, who ranks low on agreeableness at age 20. Because Joe is hostile and unpleasant, he tends to repeatedly lose jobs and have trouble with relationships. Each failure reinforces his anger, solidifying and heightening his disagreeable world view. As Joe ages, he grows increasingly more distrustful and angry at the world.

Interactional consistency refers to the immediate interpersonal impact of having a certain personality style. Joe's hostile responses evoke a similar response in others. People react angrily to him. In his next encounter, he is even more prone to lash out. Once again, hostility becomes a more entrenched reaction pattern as the years pass.

With the caution that personal examples such as this can never be used to prove or disprove any concept or idea, let me illustrate the process these researchers describe in the reactions of an acquaintance of mine. This person is abrasive, combative, and unwilling to compromise and so is continually involved in some fight or feud. About two years ago his life seemed to come together as he developed his first long-lasting romantic relationship. When he worked up the courage to propose marriage, his girlfriend, perhaps scared off by the vision of years of conflict, did not return his calls. In response, he has vowed, "Human beings aren't worth it. They just do you in," and resolved to live life alone. Another familiar saying seems to fit this process: "Paranoid people have enemies."

Caspi, Bem, and Elder (1989) use the principles of cumulative and interactional consistency to explain why certain problematic temperaments measured at about age 10 in the Berkeley girls and boys tended to have enduring consequences as adults. Before you assume that *every* child who is labeled as having difficulty in a certain area is destined for a difficult life, let's look at this study in some depth. It tells us that the relationship between temperament and life success is more complicated than we might assume.

The researchers traced the lives of the girls and boys labeled with three difficult temperaments during middle childhood: children subject to severe temper tantrums (explosive children), children ranked as unusually shy, and children judged to be excessively dependent on their parents and other adults.

Children with explosive personalities did indeed do more poorly in their travels through life. They were more likely to experience downward occupational mobility and to report unhappy marriages or be divorced at midlife (Caspi, Elder, and Bem, 1987). In contrast, the impact of being excessively shy or dependent was less detrimental and differed by gender. While shy boys were somewhat worse off, marrying later and entering careers at older ages than those who were not withdrawn, the researchers could find no long-term consequences of shyness for girls.

The findings for dependency were the most interesting. While dependent girls did function somewhat more poorly in midlife, for boys childhood dependency translated into an unusually *happy* adult life. At age 40, boys rated as dependent had an impressive list of qualities. They were calm, giving, insightful, and socially poised. They were more likely to have stable marriages, to be nurturing fathers, and to have satisfied wives (Caspi et al., 1989).

So even if temperament does endure, we cannot be sure how a given style of approaching the world will play out in adult life. While some aspects of personality, such as being explosive, are pure liabilities, the effect of others, such as shyness, is much less negative. The researchers reasoned that being shy may have been more detrimental for the males in the study because men are expected to take a more active or initiative stance in relationships and at work.

But why would the attention-seeking, home-oriented tendencies labeled as excessive dependency in childhood turn out to be positive traits for boys? The key may lie in the impulse to please and be close that defines this trait. It makes sense that this same drive to be attached to one's parents would express itself in having a strong marriage and close father/child relationships. Do we expect too much independence from boys? Does this socialization for autonomy impair some men's ability to be nurturing husbands and fathers? Let's keep these questions in mind for Chapters 10 and 11, when we explore the qualities researchers feel are involved in forming these adult bonds.

This study is one of my favorites because it illustrates the power of longitudinal research. Human beings tend to see the moment and assume forever. We agonize about our son whom we think of as too dependent or not self-reliant enough. What we really are worrying about is his future life. Only the insights offered by following people can tell us whether our worry is warranted and our fears are correct. As this fascinating research reveals, what appears to be a problem at one point in life may sometimes turn out to be a gift.

Cautions about and a critique of stability. While the forces propelling personality consistency seem powerful, does this mean that who we are as adults is set in stone? Costa and McCrae, themselves caution against this conclusion, stressing that their studies only show that *systematic* change is unlikely, not that change does not occur. Moreover, even if our underlying tendencies toward emotional disturbance or openness to experience remain stable, these broad dispositions may translate into different behaviors at particular life stages. A person high in "neuroticism" might be phobic and anxiety-ridden at age 20 and hostile and bitter at 65. People open to experience might even appear to change dramatically from year to year as they shift interests, jobs, and

Pattern of Correlations of the Different Facets of Personality Measured by the Q Sort Over Each Period in the Life Span in the Berkeley/Oakland Studies

Table 8-2

A.	Early to late childhood	Late childhood to early adolescence	Early to late adolescence	Late adolescence to early adulthood	Early to middle adulthood	Middle to late adulthood
1.	.60	.56	.60	.40	.52	.55
2.	94%	83%	78%	22%	56%	56%

B.	Lifespan correlations
1.	.25
2.	0%

Adolescence–young adulthood is the time when personality changes the most. As we might expect, over a life span, personality is far less consistent than during adjacent life phases.

1.= Median of the different correlations for each facet of personality over that life interval
2.= Percentage of correlations for each facet of personality that exceeded 50 percent over that life interval
Source: Haan, N., Millsap, R., and Hartka, E. As time goes by: Change and stability in personality over fifty years. *Psychology and Aging. 1,* 220–232. Copyright © 1986 by The American Psychological Association. Adapted by permission.

friends in pursuit of their drive to search out anything foreign and untried (Costa, McCrae, and Arenberg, 1983). Without denying that we can see seeds of the 70-year-old in the person of 25, let's look at some other reasons why our crystal ball may be fuzzier than these staunch stability advocates assert.

1. Change is more likely over longer time periods and over certain periods of life. Many of Costa and McCrae's analyses have been cross-sectional. Their longitudinal research covers only about a decade. They mainly explored change in people over age 30. Perhaps the evidence for stability would be less impressive if we looked over longer periods of life or explored personality change at different ages.

Once again, the longest running study of development allows us to adopt this life-span view. Norma Haan, Roger Millsap, and Elizabeth Hartka (1986) obtained personality ratings from a core group of the original children in the Berkeley/Oakland Studies at an amazing seven points during their life span: early childhood, late childhood, early adolescence, late adolescence, early adulthood, middle adulthood, and old age.

Interestingly the researchers found that stability and change were *both* dominant themes. Some aspects of personality shifted dramatically over time; others stayed relatively constant. Some periods of life were times of great change; others were more quiescent, producing fewer transformations in the self. Notice from Table 8–2 that the life-span correlations for the different Q sort components of personality are much lower than for adjacent time periods and that these correlations show interesting differences at different points in life.

In fact, the compelling finding of this uniquely long longitudinal study was that childhood and adolescence were the periods of greatest stability. In direct contrast to what Freud predicts, adulthood was a time of greater internal change. The years from late adolescence through young adulthood (about age 17 to 33) were a time of especially intense flux. Perhaps because this period spanned the transition from childhood dependence to full adult maturity, subjects changed more radically over this time period than between any other two points in the study.

To make sense of their finding that early adulthood, not childhood, is when personality is most malleable, the researchers offered this interesting hypothesis: Changes in the outer fabric of life propel internal change. During childhood and adolescence, the external aspects of our life tend to be relatively stable. We are being cared for in a protected environment and insulated from having to prove ourselves by making our way in the world. In our twenties, our lives tend to change radically. Many of us marry, become parents, and establish a career. At this age, we are longer able to rely on our parents. How we cope depends on us. So if bumping up against life's challenges causes change, it makes sense that adulthood might be the time of most internal flux.

2. *Change is more likely if we look beyond traits.* The test used to measure personality in the Berkeley/Oakland Studies, the California Q sort, involves what researchers call an *ipsative approach* to evaluation. Instead of the traditional *normative strategy,* in which people rank themselves according to defined traits or qualities and then their scores are compared to those of others, a person taking this test places statements on cards into piles as either more or less characteristic of himself, and then researchers explore how this internal organization shifts over time.

This holistic, individual-centered measurement strategy may offer different information about change than we would get by seeing how people compare to one another in terms of defined, specific traits (Chaplin and Buckner, 1988; Pelham, 1993). This brings up a question about Costa and McCrae's approach. While knowing about how comparatively neurotic, or agreeable, or open to experience a person is tells us a good deal, is it the final word on who we are?

Psychoanalytically oriented psychologists, such as Gutmann, would argue no. Self-reports and observer ratings of extraversion or agreeableness miss unconscious determinants and motivations, the "core of personality" of which we are not aware. This is why, for psychologists who believe in the psychoanalytic approach, asking people to report on their own or a friend's personality will never be satisfying. Truly measuring personality requires tests of unconscious processes, such as the TAT.

Perhaps the most penetrating critique of what traits tell us and what the big five may leave out has been provided by Northwestern University psychologist Dan McAdams (1992). McAdams views personality as having three parallel levels.

Level one is the dimension Costa is measuring, traits and dispositions, whether we are shy or outgoing, friendly or rude. These are the aspects of the person that we notice when we meet a stranger. We evaluate that person from an external frame of reference. We size up that individual in relation to others we know.

As we get closer and begin to know the person, McAdams believes, our frame of reference shifts. We fill in the details and learn about that individual's specific aspirations and concerns. Now we have entered a new dimension or way of thinking about personality. We are dealing at levels two and three.

Level two refers to the themes and concerns that currently organize a person's life. Is Dr. Belsky's family everything? Is writing this book the passion that shapes my days? Level three refers to the way these plans and goals are integrated into a life plan over the years. McAdams believes that what is most central in personality is what Erikson calls our identity and that we are always in the process of constructing a coherent identity or "life story" as we travel through time.

Level one traits may be stable. McAdams agrees that we probably do not change dramatically in extraversion or openness to experience as the years pass. At the second and third levels, however, personality is more likely to evolve. The actual content of what gives meaning to our days is more likely to change as we have new experiences and enter new phases of life.

Because Costa and McCrae's studies focus only on level one, McAdams believes they are insensitive to level two and three changes. They cannot measure shifts in life orientation and world view that occur as we develop, the very changes Erikson and Jung were trying to address in their theories. So it is no wonder that, despite the fact that people *feel* that they have changed dramatically, often in the ways these theorists predict, traditional studies using personality inventories often show that little change occurs.

Phase 3: Focus on Change: Exploring Life Stories, Goals, Hopes, and Fears

When we look at levels two and three, we do get a different view of change, as we see now in examining the newest trend in adult development personality research—studies exploring our hopes, goals, and fears.

MCADAMS MEASURES GENERATIVITY. In order to test Erikson's idea that generativity is a main theme of adult life, Dan McAdams's research team embarked on a series of steps. First, they pinned down and explicitly spelled out Erikson's elusive concept; then they devised tests tailored to measure these qualities and looked for the predicted differences in people at different ages (McAdams and de St. Aubin, 1992).

McAdams and his colleagues conceptualize generativity as involving the processes, thoughts, and actions illustrated in Figure 8–1. As the diagram shows, in order to be generative, people must be at the right stage of life: According to McAdams (1994): "We do not expect ten-year-old children to provide primary care for the next generation. We generally do not expect them to think about the legacy they will leave after they die. But as people move into young and middle adulthood, we come to expect an increasing awareness of a commitment to their role as providers" (p. 680). These societal expectations must be complemented by inner desire. As shown in the figure, this desire has two facets. It consists of the urge for immortality—that is, to leave something behind of oneself after death—and the yearning to be needed, to be helpful to other human beings. These two conditions evoke generative concern. When the person has a "belief in the species" or a feeling that humans are basically good (Van de Water and McAdams, 1989), concern results in commitment or the motivation to act in a generative way. Commitment provokes concrete actions, such as giving to children or protecting the environment for future generations and, finally, at the third level of personality, produces a life story revolving around generative themes.

Based on this framework, the researchers developed scales to measure the three major dimensions of generativity in the figure: generative concern, generative commitment, and generative action. To measure concern, they constructed the measure shown in Table 8–3 on p. 231. They measured generative commitments by asking people to describe 10 personal goals: "What plans are most important in your life now?" To assess actions, they used a checklist examining how often within the past month people engaged in activities such as serving as a role model or teaching someone a skill. They also looked generally at generativity life-scripts by asking people to describe the high and low points of their lives.

When they administered their tests to young-adult, middle-aged, and elderly people, the researchers found partial support for the idea that generativity reaches a peak in the second half of life. While midlife adults only scored marginally higher on generative concern and action, there were striking differences in generative commitment, with young adults scoring extremely low on this particular facet of generativity. Young people's goals tended to be centered around the self. For instance, a 20-year-old might say, "I want to make my job more interesting" or "I want to figure out what I want

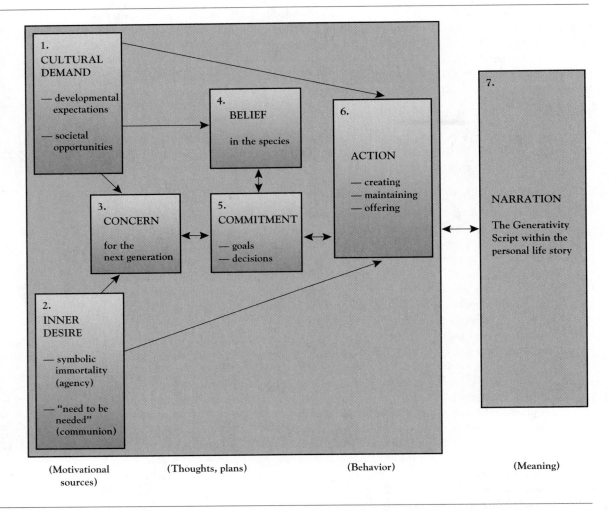

(Motivational sources)   (Thoughts, plans)   (Behavior)   (Meaning)

Source: McAdams, D. P., and de St. Aubin, E. D. S. A theory of generativity and its assessment through self-report, behavioral acts, and narrative themes in autobiography. *Journal of Personality and Social Psychology,* 62, 1003–1015. Copyright © 1992 by The American Psychological Association. Reprinted by permission.

to do with my life." Midlife and older people were more likely to say, "I want to be a positive role model," "I want to help my teenage son," or "I want to agitate for justice and peace in the world."

McAdams finds that the most vivid evidence of generativity and life change may come from the third level of personality, how people describe the transforming events in their lives:

> I was living in a rural North Dakota town in 1977 and was the mother of a 4 year old son. One summer afternoon we had discussed going across the street to visit some friends and I went back to the house for something. Jeff left without me and was hit by a car. When I got there, he was lying in the street unconscious and his breath

Items 1 Through 10 on the Loyola Generativity Scale (A Measure of Generative Concern)   Table 8-3

1. I try to pass along the knowledge I have gained through my experiences.
2. I do not feel that other people need me.
3. I think I would like the work of a teacher.
4. I feel as though I have made a difference to many people.
5. I do not volunteer to work for a charity.
6. I have made and created things that have had an impact on other people.
7. I try to be creative in most things that I do.
8. I think that I will be remembered for a long time after I die.
9. I believe that society cannot be responsible for providing food and shelter to all homeless people.
10. Others would say that I have made unique contributions to society.

Source: McAdams, D. P., and de St. Aubin, E. D. S. A theory of generativity and its assessment through self-report, behavioral acts, and narrative themes in autobiography. *Journal of Personality and Social Psychology, 62,* 1003–1015. Copyright © 1992 by The American Psychological Association. Reprinted by permission.

was gurgly. I felt sure he was dying, and I didn't know of anything I could do to preserve his life. My friend did though and today he is 18 years old and very healthy. That feeling of being helpless and hopeless while I was sure I was watching my son die was a real turning point. I decided I would never feel it again and I became an E.M.T. (McAdams, de St. Aubin, and Logan, 1993, p. 228).

Let's use this interview to illustrate the difference between the trait approach to measuring personality and McAdams's technique. While according to standard personality tests this woman might have always ranked high in conscientiousness and shown no change in this ranking over the years, the *specific path* her life took was responsive to her life experiences. In McAdams's opinion, once we get beyond "decontextualized traits" and fill in the rich, personal details of human experience, we can see stability (see Feature 8–2 and the beginning interview of this chapter). However, we often also see lives being transformed.

MARKUS MEASURES SELF-SCHEMAS.   Hazel Markus reaches the same conclusion using a different approach. Rather than testing a specific theory, Markus's University of Michigan research team has been exploring **self-schemas or possible selves,** our visions of who we will be in the future. Some possible selves are hoped for: For instance, I might imagine this book being lauded as the definitive text in adult development. Others are feared: A person might imagine herself alone for life or fired, out on the street, and not able to support herself.

According to the researchers, self-schemas drive our personal adult development (Markus and Nurius, 1986). They motivate us to put ourselves into certain situations and avoid others. They offer a framework for interpreting life and tell a good deal about how we will react to specific events. While theoretically we are free to construct any possible self, the particular schemas we develop are intimately linked to our past experiences and how we see ourselves behave. A student who has been praised for her abilities in science may develop a hoped-for self as a doctor. Another who remembers being unpopular as a child or feels she does not have friends now may develop a feared self as being alone for life. Each type of person will be sensitive to her own schema-relevant events.

self-schemas or possible selves
Salient images of who we will be that reflect both our idealized hopes and our dreaded fears.

8-2 The Adult Experience: Life Histories Reveal an Enduring Self

Anthropologist Sharon Kaufman, in a minor classic called *The Ageless Self*, uses life interviews with very old people not to demonstrate change, but to show that the self is continuous and enduring. Our identity or the basic themes that organize our life remain constant, despite the changes of old age. Here is an excerpt from the description of Stella, one woman featured in this book.

Whenever I visit Stella in her studio, I am struck by a whirlwind of activity. She is always doing several things at once. I have watched her teach a painting class while at the same time hang a large tapestry on the wall by herself, repair the plumbing under her sink and pay bills. . . . Her energy and determination are remarkable. She happens to be 82 years old.

Stella was born in 1897 on a farm in the Deep South. She looks back on that time, though filled with hard work, as the most peaceful, blissful existence. The independence and self sufficiency her father sought and apparently achieved during her childhood . . . became a pivotal, driving force in her own life. As a child, Stella was a Tomboy. . . . She climbed trees, played with boys, and rode horses. Stella's formal education began at the age of 9 in a "little school house" located about a mile from the family farm. . . . When Stella finished high school, she moved several hundred miles away so she could establish her own life. . . . She was adventurous; she took vacation trips . . . around the country . . . traveling through places where no roads existed, camping along the way. . . . At the age of 24, she moved to Oregon to marry a man she had known for some years. The marriage was brief; her husband left her shortly after her child was born. In the 1930s she was poor, divorced, and had a child to raise on her own. She met the challenge. She got a secretarial job which she held for 35 years. . . . When Stella was 40, her daughter died from injuries sustained in an accident. This tragic event changed the course of her life and turned her into a sculptor and painter.

Now the one central theme in her life is her achievement orientation, especially the need to create art. Stella is future oriented . . . and she is driven by the need to accomplish more and be better. . . . "The only time I look back is when I think, 'I used to do better painting and sculptures'. . . . I have to get back to work so I won't have to say that." Not only does she compete with herself, but she also competes with the other artists and art students who come to the studio she owns and operates. . . . Stella needs to be the best at what she does. She needs to have her work highly regarded by others . . . . But she also needs to meet her own standards of creativity.

Stella's achievement orientation and need for recognition apparently have been part of her identity since her early years, long before she became an artist. When she talks about her childhood and youth she emphasizes her accomplishments, successes, and failures. Achievement provides the framework by which Stella describes her clerical work as well. . . . "I had to be absolutely perfect. I never made an error."

Creativity informs a second theme that emerges from Stella's story: her sense of aesthetics and need for perfection. . . Her role models for perfection are the two most important people in her life, her mother and her daughter. "She [the daughter] was so talented in art. . . In addition, she was a perfectly behaved child. I never had to criticize her for anything she did." The child is frozen in Stella's memory on the brink of . . . promise. There is only perfection to remember. Stella's sense of productivity, beauty, and perfection was first inspired by her mother, later heightened by the way she viewed her child, and finally given supreme value when the child died. (pp. 62–66)

Source: Kaufman, Sharon R. *The ageless self: Sources of meaning in late life* © 1986 Madison, The University of Wisconsin Press. Reprinted by permission of the University of Wisconsin Press.

For instance, students who have psychologist hoped-for selves get extremely upset when it looks as if they might get a B in my course. I can expect them in my office asking for extra credit and agitating for points on the tests. With a friend who has a strong lonely feared self, I am especially solicitous, careful not to break a date. From experience, I know any breach of what looks like caring activates her unloved possible self and can provoke an extreme, often hostile response.

Do schemas change in predictable ways during the adult years? In examining people of different ages, Susan Cross and Markus (1991) found that after adolescence possible selves become more specific and concrete. While an 18-year-old might say, "I want to be rich and famous," a middle-aged man might report, "I want to be a good father, be a better tennis player, and put my children through the college of their choice." In later life, hoped-for selves are more focused on the present. Older people often hope to do more of what they are already doing, such as staying active, useful, and healthy. There also are interesting age differences in the specific schemas people generate. While important for everyone, as we might expect, feared selves related to physical functioning become more salient at older ages (Hooker and Kaus, 1994).

Interestingly, although Cross and Markus found no age differences in life satisfaction, current happiness did relate to the kinds of possible selves people produced. People low in self-esteem generated more personal hoped-for selves, for instance, saying they "wanted to be happy or more content." People high in life satisfaction produced hoped-for selves more centered on occupational and family goals. As the researchers conclude, when we are basically happy with who we are we seem freer to direct our energies outward to focus on external, specific, other-directed hopes and dreams.

DO WE GROW BETTER WITH AGE?

Most of us feel that, as we get older, we will have the ability to handle life in a more mature way. But the studies we have been examining so far offer few hints as to whether this change does occur. While as the years advance our aspirations may become more realistic or our goals more generative, are those really the qualities we are looking for when we imagine growing more mature?

I think many of us hope that age will confer emotional resilience, the ability to cope better with the ups and downs that are the price of being alive. What does the research tell us about this hoped-for future self?

Robert McCrae (1982) questioned the Baltimore men and women about how they had handled recent upsetting events and then looked at differences in the maturity of their coping styles. He found that older volunteers were less likely to report escaping into fantasy or exploding in anger than the younger adults. In a similar cross-sectional study, Jane Irion and Fredda Blanchard-Fields (1987) also found a heartening trend toward fewer immature coping strategies among middle-aged and elderly people, that is, less hostility and self-blame. However, other research on age differences in coping styles is more ambiguous. While older people may differ in the specific techniques they use to handle failures and disappointments, it is hard to classify these different strategies as either more or less mature (Felton and Revenson, 1987; Folkman, Lazarus, Pimley, and Novacek, 1987).

These studies are all cross-sectional. They involve self-reports. People describe how they would cope or have coped when confronted with some unpleasant event. Once again, to truly measure age changes in coping, we should have longitudinal research, preferably studies in which trained observers judge the overall quality of how people handle life. This brings us to the Grant Study.

The Lessons of the Grant Study

Recall from Table 8–1 that in the *Grant Study* an elite group of Harvard undergraduates was first interviewed in college and then tracked through middle age. George Vaillant (1977) reinterviewed these men at about age 50, using the same benchmark of maturity we have been discussing, that is, the strategies people use to cope with stress. Rather than simply rating what the men reported, Vaillant focused on uncovering what are called **defense mechanisms,** unconscious strategies for handling life.

According to psychoanalysts, we all use defense mechanisms to handle upsetting events. However, defenses vary in their maturity, the extent to which they show *ego strength* (see our discussion of psychoanalytic theory in Chapter 2) and so promote adult success. Like most psychoanalysts, Vaillant believed that an important criterion of mental health is the use of mature defense mechanisms. Rather than taking the traditional position that defenses stay the same from childhood, he set out to demonstrate that these coping styles can evolve during our adult years.

Vaillant arranged defense mechanisms into the maturity hierarchy shown in Table 8–4. At level 1 are psychotic coping methods. When confronted with upsetting experiences, the person denies reality. He negates the truth of the actual event. At a slightly higher level, the person might withdraw into fantasy; engage in self-destructive acts, such as drinking to excess; or utilize projection, attributing one's own anger to the outside world. Individuals who use neurotic defense mechanisms, in which they deny the intensity of their feelings or displace their emotions to another arena of life, are operating at yet a higher level. The optimally healthy person uses defense mechanisms that are truly mature. These strategies include turning tragedy into a chance for good, deflecting pain by using humor, and coping with hardship by appreciating what one still has.

Let's take the case of a mother whose daughter has been killed by a drunken driver. One strategy she might use is to deny what has happened and set a place for her child at dinner, totally rejecting the idea that her daughter has died (level 1). Or she could withdraw from loved ones, act out by attempting suicide, or decide that the world is out to do her in (level 2). She might respond by developing a phobia of cars or deny that her pain was really that intense (level 3). Or she might vow to spend her life crusading for stronger controls against drunk driving, vowing that her daughter's death not be in vain (level 4).

While as college students the Grant Study men were twice as likely to use immature as mature defenses, as they grew older the balance tipped. By age 35, the men were more than four times more likely to use the higher-level defenses (neurotic and fully mature coping styles) in handling the stresses of life. Here is how one subject used sublimation and altruism to cope with his upsetting childhood:

> Mr. Goodheart. . . . *was a fearful lonely child whose [lower middle class] parents had created a home life that especially during his adolescence was filled with both covert and overt dissention. Goodheart had been terrified of his [alcoholic] father, and as an adolescent had great difficulty sharing these fears with interviewers . . . but Goodheart had . . . already discovered that writing for the college humor magazine provided an acceptable vent for his angry feelings. Goodheart soon engaged the problem more directly. He had grown up in a family where he was often caught between his embattled prejudiced parents. Many poor whites had migrated to his neighborhood and racial prejudice ran high. He set about mastering this fear provoking situation; hence his life work was spent in the urban ghettos of Detroit and Chicago devising ways to mediate between . . . hard hats and poor blacks. In a very real sense he was protecting his bigoted father from attack, even as he was openly and professionally combating his father's prejudices. (Vaillant, 1977, p. 24)*

defense mechanisms
Unconscious styles of coping with stressful events.

Example: how does Mr. Jones handle getting fired?

1. **Psychotic mechanisms** Denial (It didn't happen. I'll show up for work tomorrow); distortion (It didn't really happen the way it did. I was just told to take a day off); delusional projection (It happened to Mr. Smith, not to me.)

2. **Immature mechanisms** Fantasy (I'll withdraw into my own world); projection (I don't want to kill my boss; he wants to kill me); passive aggressive behavior (I hate myself. I'm going to turn to drugs); acting out (I'll make them pay. I'll make life miserable for them, too.)

3. **Neurotic mechanisms** Intellectualization (It really wasn't so bad); repression (I'm not upset at all); reaction formation (It was actually a good thing. I'm happy about it); displacement (I'm getting anxiety attacks and becoming phobic.)

4. **Mature mechanisms** Sublimation (I'll use this time volunteering at the homeless shelter, or I'll set up a job-finding service for people who are out of work); suppression (I realize it was painful, but I have to get on with life and the search for a new job); use of humor (There goes life again!)

By midlife, Mr. Goodheart had succeeded brilliantly. He was an authority on urban affairs for the Ford Foundation and felt gratified in his professional life. As was typical of Vaillant's subjects who utilized mature defense mechanisms, his success involved both love and work. He had close friends and loving relationships with his family and was at ease and happy with himself.

The Lessons of the Mills Study

Though their strategy for measuring maturity was different, Ravinna Helson and her colleagues found a similar evolution in the Mills women. When Helson and Wink (1992) tested their subjects over a decade from their early forties to their fifties, as Jung would predict the shift toward androgeny described earlier did signal a more mature, more integrated self. The older women were more self-confident, tolerant, and decisive. They showed transformations similar to postformal reasoning. They were more tolerant of ambiguity and more open to varying points of view. They also were happy. In fact, the Mills women reported feeling better about themselves in their early fifties than at any other age.

"It takes a brave poet to claim that [the empty nest] is the prime of life, especially for women," say the researchers (Mitchell and Helson, 1990, p. 452). However, that is exactly what Helson and another colleague found when they surveyed life satisfaction in Mills alumnae of different ages. Notice from Figure 8–2 that at age 26, during a time of life we often think of as a women's best years, subjects are *least* likely to be satisfied. In the fifties, that so-called empty time, twice as many women feel their lives are first-rate.

Do women have to wait until their older years for these transformations? The overall upward trend with a few valleys revealed in this cross-sectional survey of happiness implies that the answer is no. In fact, when Helson and Geraldine Moane (1987) followed the study subjects from their late twenties to their early forties, they found increases in dominance and competence during this earlier adult period, too, mirroring Vaillant's research showing that over the years we gradually grow more mature.

Once again, I must stress that these studies involve the most advantaged Americans. They examined cohorts who lived a large portion of their adult lives during a favored economic time in the United States. They ended in the subjects' early fifties.

Figure 8–2

Percentage of 686 Alumnae of Mills College of Different Ages Reporting Life Is Either "First-Rate" (top curve) or "Fair or Not So Good" (bottom curve)*

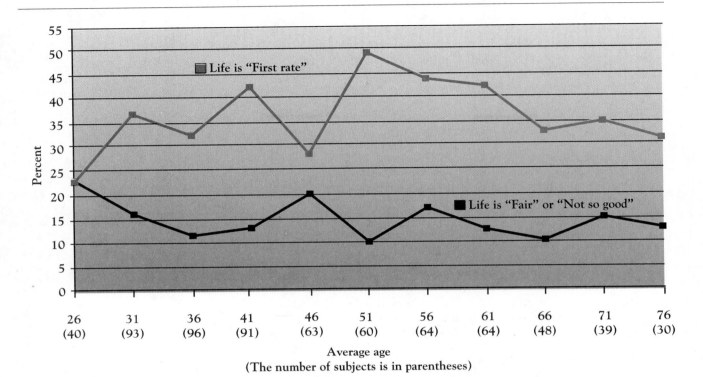

Average age
(The number of subjects is in parentheses)

This chart suggests that the early fifties are the optimum age, the time in life when the highest percentage of women rank their lives as first rate.

Source: Mitchell, V., and Helson, R. Women's prime of life: Is it the 50s? *Psychology of Women Quarterly, 14.* Copyright 1990, reprinted with permission of Cambridge University Press.
*The graphs for each curve do not add up to 100 percent because they do not include responses falling into an intermediate category.

People may grow less mature or regress as they reach old age, become ill, and experience the losses of later life. There was a good deal of variability within even these privileged women and men. Some people did not change for the better, while others declined in maturity and happiness over the years.

Two Keys to Ripening with Age

Who is most likely to improve? The Mills Study and others suggest that one clue comes from examining maturity earlier in life. In addition to using the standard inventory, Helson and Brent Roberts (1994) used a scale measuring ego development to periodically chart subjects' personalities. *Ego development,* scored from a sentence completion test, is another index similar to postformal thought, designed to measure maturity. As is true of the studies probing postformal thinking, people do not advance in ego development in a *systematic* way after about age 30 (Loevinger, 1976; Loevinger and Wessler, 1970). However, Helson and Roberts discovered that, if a woman in her late twenties ranked

This radiant high school teacher exemplifies the Mills Study research showing that in their fifties, middle-class women are especially likely to rate their lives as first rate. To what extent do you think this woman's confident, well-being is a product of living in an era in which women and minorities with talent have been able to fulfill their potential during adult life?

high on this scale compared to her peers, she was most likely to grow in happiness, self-esteem, and competence as she aged.

This suggests that "the good get better" is one defining message relating to who grows with age. As we saw in Feature 8–1, and as was implied in the concepts of interactional and cumulative continuity, people who are initially competent, mature, and psychologically healthy are most likely to grow emotionally during adult life. However, the Mills Study suggests that the environment is also important. Recall that the older Mills mothers could not grow more androgenous because they were living in such a restricted time. Helson and her colleagues found that not only was overall life satisfaction for this cohort lower, but also in their fifties these mothers were more likely to have *declined in maturity* from their young adult years.

So a second conclusion is that in order to grow emotionally with age it is important to have a non-restrictive environment, an external milieu that permits a variety of hoped-for possible selves, a range of interests and capacities to flower. Just as the freedom offered by living in a less gender restricted society benefited the Mills daughters, perhaps we can do more to break down another barrier that confines us during adult life: restrictions based on age.

APPLICATIONS AND INTERVENTIONS

Matilda White Riley and John Riley (1994) agree that we have gone a long way toward replacing the rigid age structure that used to govern adult life. Beginning in the late 1960s, as we saw in Chapter 1, it became possible for older people to express their sexuality, to go back to school, to climb mountains, to continue working or retire. Still,

Figure 8–3

Age-Differentiated Versus Age-Integrated Social Structures

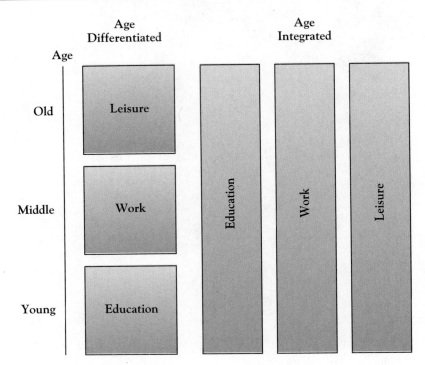

The ideal is to be able to work, retire, and go back to school at any time of life.

Source: Riley, M. W., and Riley, J. W. Age integration and the lives of older people. *Gerontologist, 34,* Copyright © 1994 The Gerontological Society of America.

age-integrated society
Ideal society in which people perform any activity at any time of life.

they argue, we need to take steps to implement a truly **age-integrated society,** a social structure in which people feel free to do what they want at *any point* during adult life. Abandoning the rigid age demarkations for education, work, and leisure shown in Figure 8–3 would offer more options for people of any age. It would allow us more freedom at every phase of life to engineer a lifestyle tailored to our own interests, identities, and possible selves.

Will we be able to achieve this integration? Ironically I think it may be more possible to implement this freedom in our older years. At age 30 or 40, going back to school or retiring or leaving an unfulfilling job collides with the pressures to support a family and to have the money to live. Can it be that older people have more freedom to engineer the lives they want and so are less likely to suffer from emotional problems than the young? How common are the debilitating emotional problems that work to limit us internally from growing more mature at any age? What specific kinds of emotional problems do people have at certain times of life? These are a few of the topics we will be exploring in the next chapter.

KEY TERMS & CONCEPTS

Kansas City Studies of Adult Life
Grant Study
Mills College Study
Thematic Apperception Test
disengagement theory
androgenous
activity theory
parental imperative
big five traits
self-schemas or possible selves
defense mechanisms
age-integrated society

RECOMMENDED READINGS

Caspi, A., Bem, D., and Elder, G. H. (1989). Continuities and consequences of interactional styles across the life course. *Journal of Personality, 57,* 375–406.
> *Caspi, Bem, and Elder report on the midlife consequences of childhood temperaments in the Berkeley/Oakland Studies.*

Gutmann, D. (1987). *Reclaimed powers: Men and women in later life.* Evanston, IL: Northwestern University Press.
> *Gutmann makes his case for androgeny being a universal change of older years.*

Kaufman, S. R. (1986). *The ageless self: Sources of meaning in late life.* Madison, University of Wisconsin Press.
> *This beautifully written book is based on interviews illustrating the author's argument that the self is ageless and enduring.*

McCrae, R. R., and Costa, P. T., Jr.(1990). *Personality in adulthood.* New York: Guilford Press.
> *Costa and McCrae make their case for personality consistency.*

Vaillant, G. (1977). *Adaptation to life.* Boston: Little, Brown.
> *This is Vaillant's classic follow-up of the Grant men.*

Psychopathology

Chapter Outline

"I graduated from college in 1960 and was forced into a family business that was a source of continual fights," says John. "One day I was eating in a cafeteria and my heart began to race. The same thing happened two or three times, and I went to a doctor, who gave me Valium, which was a new drug at that time. By then, the anxiety attacks would occur several times a day. I was sensitized to them. I could feel them coming. It was complete dread. Very often it was in public places and, of course, you were humiliated. It's happened to me in a commuter train going 50 miles an hour. So I would jump off at the next stop and take a taxi for miles to get to my destination. The thing has a pattern where you are so worried about it that you begin to avoid everything. I stopped going to the theater or restaurants because I was afraid an attack might occur and I'd have to rush out. The same thing would happen on dates. I'd be heading for a girl's house and I'd have to turn around. I was taking Valium three times a day and going to see a therapist five times a week at a cost of $12,000 a year, which would be $30,000 today. Time dragged on. I was 40. Years of life had gone by, and nothing had happened. I was confined to my parent's home or to my own apartment. Eventually the only people I trusted were doctors. My friends were getting older and having children, and I was transfixed as a recent college graduate—and the only thing that cured me was the drugs. Now I take Prozac 20 mg a day. I'm pretty much fine now, but it leaves its imprint on you. You don't go out the way you've gone in. Your relationships change because friends and family think you are a crazy person. You are so exhausted fighting it that there is no energy left for anything. It's life played defensively. Everything is your enemy. With my disease, agoraphobia, you're lucky to hang on to where you are."

What is your chance of developing agoraphobia or another mental disorder during adult life? Do emotional problems often appear, as our interview indicates, in the early twenties and then persist to wreak their damage for years? For answers, we turn to a type of illness survey called an epidemiologic study.

THE CONTEXT

epidemiologic studies
Population surveys designed to reveal the prevalence and incidence of diseases within a population.

Epidemiologic studies examine the *prevalence*, or overall frequency, and *incidence*, or rate of new cases, of diseases within a population during a certain time period. How prevalent (or common) was heart disease among Americans during 1996? Did the incidence (or number of new cases) of this illness increase during this year? Is heart disease spreading faster among certain groups? Are there gender, racial, or geographic differences in heart disease rates?

Perhaps you noticed that our starting point in the chapters on physical aging often were epidemiologic studies. Regular surveys, often conducted by government agencies, offered us information about rates of chronic illnesses and disabilities at different ages and among certain groups. By examining these statistics, we knew which problems to "target" as a cause for concern. Epidemiologic studies also offer vital clues about what causes diseases. Recall from Chapter 3 that one hint that estrogen might protect women against heart disease came from the epidemiologic finding that before age 50 heart attacks among women were so rare.

Epidemiologic studies of mental illness offer the same essential information. However, in *psychiatric epidemiology*, the field devoted to exploring mental disorder rates, collecting accurate information on incidence and prevalence presents special challenges.

One hurdle psychiatric epidemiologists face (once again) relates to *who* they test. In epidemiologic surveys, it is crucial to have a *representative sample*. Researchers must ensure that a cross-section of the population agrees to be interviewed and honestly respond. But wouldn't people with a substance abuse problem be reluctant to admit engaging in this socially unacceptable and illegal behavior? Who would be less happy to welcome an interviewer than the paranoid individual, the woman phobic about strangers, or the older adult terrified she has Alzheimer's disease? In other words, because in psychiatric epidemiology some of the very people most likely to have emotional problems might be least likely to volunteer, *minimizing* the true extent of problems is a genuine risk.

A second difficulty psychiatric epidemiologists face (once again) relates to what they test. In this case, the concern is fundamental—the *reliability* and *validity* of mental health diagnoses. Mental health workers must agree on the way they diagnose given people in order for their labels to have any meaning (reliability). Their system for categorizing people must be measuring real disorders or "diseases" (validity). However, psychological symptoms do not cluster into clear-cut categories. They often occur on a continuum. They cannot be measured and quantified in the same way as readings on a blood pressure machine. What complicates the search for reliable and valid diagnoses is that mental disorders may express themselves through atypical symptoms in certain groups. Among the elderly or Hispanic Americans, for instance, critics argue, depression is being underdiagnosed because this problem tends to manifest itself only in memory problems or exaggerated physical complaints (Blazer, Hughes, and George, 1987; Ruiz, 1985).

In struggling to improve reliability and validity, the American Psychiatric Association has repeatedly revised the **Diagnostic and Statistical Manual of Mental Disorders** or **DSM.** The *DSM* is the labeling system mental health workers use to put people into diagnostic categories. A landmark occurred in 1980 with the publication of *DSM-III,* which provided lists of *specific* symptoms that qualified for each diagnostic label (American Psychiatric Association, 1980). This more reliable, symptom-oriented system allowed epidemiologists to feel confident to conduct the first large-scale studies of the prevalence and incidence of emotional problems in the United States.

Diagnostic and Statistical Manual of Mental Disorders (DSM)
Manual used by mental health workers for categorizing mental disorders.

The Scope of the Affected

In the early 1980s, researchers at the National Institute of Mental Health sponsored the **Epidemiologic Catchment Area Survey** (ECA), the first comprehensive survey of mental disorders in the United States. Teams of interviewers examined 20,000 people living in Baltimore, Los Angeles, New Haven, St. Louis, and Durham, North Carolina. These five locations were carefully selected to provide a racial and socioeconomic mix typical of the nation as a whole (Myers et al., 1984). A decade later, from 1990 to 1992, epidemiologists at the University of Michigan conducted similar interviews with more than 8,000 people throughout the United States (Kessler et al., 1994). Though it involves fewer subjects, the **National Comorbidity Survey** (NCS) expands on the earlier survey in several ways: It covers 34 states and includes adolescents (the age group from 15 to 18). It explores **comorbidity,** or the frequency with which people report more than one problem. It examines where Americans get help for the problems they have. Its disadvantage for adult developmentalists is that it does not include people over age 54. For this reason, we look at some highlights of both studies combined.

Epidemiologic Catchment Area Survey
First comprehensive epidemiologic survey of the prevalence of U.S. mental disorders.

National Comorbidity Survey
Most recent comprehensive epidemiologic survey of the prevalence of U.S. mental disorders.

comorbidity
Coexisting presence of two or more disorders.

1. **Mental disorders are surprisingly common.** The ECA researchers found that, depending on the location, within any given six-month period, anywhere from one in five to one in four adults suffers from a mental disorder (Myers et al., 1984). This suggests that the **lifetime prevalence,** or risk of *ever* developing this type of problem, is much higher. It is about one in three. When the NCS interviewers asked directly about lifetime prevalence, with the question "Have you ever had this set of symptoms before?" they found more alarming statistics: One in two Americans will suffer from a mental disorder at some point in life (Kessler et al., 1994).

   On the other hand, problems are concentrated. In the NCS, half of the people who reported one type of disorder also reported two or three. For these vulnerable

lifetime prevalence
Risk of developing a particular disorder at any point in life.

people, about one in six Americans, symptoms tend to be more serious. Periodic struggles with more than one type of mental disorder tend to occur throughout life.

2. ***Mental disorders are surprisingly youth-oriented.*** The ECA and NCS research teams found equally interesting statistics with regard to age. Both studies showed that mental disorder rates are highest among young people and then steadily drop off. In the ECA study, the difference between the youngest and the oldest groups was huge. People aged 18–24 had almost twice the rate of emotional problems as people over age 65 (Weissman et al., 1985).

As we will see later in this chapter, some problems are especially youth-oriented. Others are more stable or bi-modal; that is, they reach a peak in youth and at another age. The risk of having specific problems at certain ages varies in interesting ways for different ethnic groups. Cognitive impairment is one serious condition that makes a dramatic entry in old age. However, the clear message of the research is that mental disorders tend to be youth-oriented diseases. In fact, the reason that the NCS researchers speculated that their overall statistics on illness were so much higher than in the earlier study was because they had included adolescents and ended their survey at middle age (Kessler et al., 1994).

These findings may be partly due to a process called *selective mortality*. Because people who are emotionally disturbed may die earlier, individuals who live to their later years could be an inherently mentally healthier fraction of the cohort. Or this elderly cohort, having grown up at a time in the United States when it was shameful to admit mental problems, may be less likely to freely admit having symptoms in interviews than younger adults. The true prevalence of mentally disturbed older people may have been underestimated in these community surveys because, as we saw in Chapters 5 and 7, older people with serious psychological problems are more likely to be placed in inpatient settings, such as nursing homes. More ominous, changes in society may have increased the pressures on today's young people, making them more susceptible to emotional problems than their parents or grandparents were at the same age (Gatz and Smyer, 1992). However, because these findings seem consistent with some research presented in the previous chapter, I think we can conclude that we may be seeing genuine developmental changes. Youth, the so-called happiest time of life, is really the period of most emotional turmoil. Old age, that supposed era of unhappiness, is the most "problem-free" life stage.

3. ***Mental disorder rates vary in surprising ways by ethnicity and gender.*** The socioeconomic status/illness gradient described in Chapter 5 applies to mental as well as physical health. As education and income levels rise, both research teams found the frequency of almost every mental disorder declines. *However, the NCS researchers discovered that African Americans are less likely to suffer from almost every mental disorder than whites* (Kessler et al., 1994). This is astonishing, as we would expect higher illness rates in view of the poverty, stress, and discrimination African Americans face. While it is possible that they may have been somewhat less open about admitting symptoms in the interviews, African Americans seem remarkably resilient emotionally as they travel through life.

The gender differences in illness-patterns are also tantalizing. While the overall risk of developing mental disorders does not differ much for males and females, men are much more prone to disorders involving alcohol and drugs. Women have strikingly higher rates of depression and anxiety-related disorders as they travel through adult life.

4. ***Mental disorder treatment rates are surprisingly low.*** When they do have emotional problems, what do Americans do? As Table 9–1 shows, the NCS researchers found that even when they have three or more problems, less than

Table 9-1

Utilization of Professional Services by People Reporting No, One, or Three or More Disorders Within the Past Year in the NCS

	No disorder	Any disorder	3 or more disorders
Any professional	7.0%	20.9%	34.2%
Mental health specialist*	2.7%	11.5%	22.5%
Substance abuse facility	.1%	4.0%	8.6%

This chart shows that, when people have mental disorders, they tend to see any health care professional (probably their family doctor), rather than visiting a mental health specialist. However, notice that even among people who have several mental disorders only a minority receive any professional help.

*Treatment by a psychologist or psychiatrist or as an outpatient in a substance abuse facility.
Source: Kessler, R. C., McGonagle, K. A., Zhao, S., Nelson, C. B., Hughes, R., Eshleman, S., Wittchen, H., and Kendler, K. S. Lifetime and 12 months prevalence of DSM III-R psychiatric disorders in the United States, *Archives of General Psychiatry, 51*, 8–19. Copyright 1994 American Medical Association.

one-half of adults get professional help. When they do seek help, less than one in four of these seriously ill people sees a psychologist or psychiatrist. As the researchers conclude, there is a serious gap between the problems Americans are suffering from and the services they receive. This is unfortunate, since tremendous advances in treatment have occurred in recent years.

The Scope of the Treatments

Beginning in the 1960s, major changes took place in the way we approach mental disorders. For much of this century, treatments for psychological problems fell into a single category. As we saw in Chapter 2, mental disorders were believed to be caused by life experiences. Therefore, the main treatment was **psychotherapy,** examining those life experiences in order to eradicate the pathological attitudes and responses. A *traditional behaviorist* would focus on changing the reinforcers maintaining the behaviors. A *cognitive behaviorist* would concentrate on understanding and changing the person's cognitions or thoughts. A *psychoanalytically oriented therapist* would help the person get insights into childhood experiences and how they affect current life.

Today these psychotherapies are still used. However, they have been supplemented by a revolution in biological approaches. At the same time as behavioral genetic studies were convincing social scientists about the role inherited predispositions played in determining personality, great strides in chemotherapy, or drug treatment, for mental illness were occurring. Not only are medications a treatment of first choice for the most serious mental disorders, but also today **psychotropic** (changing the psyche) **medications** play a central role in the treatment of emotional disorders of almost all kinds.

During the late 1960s, these advances in chemotherapy provided the impetus for a large-scale emptying of the large psychiatric hospitals that had housed the seriously mentally ill (see Figure 9–1). This push toward "deinstitutionalizing" mental patients was designed to prevent the fate that Jane describes her mother experiencing in the introductory vignette of the previous chapter, the practice of "warehousing" seriously mentally ill people for life.

While the humanitarian impulse to offer outpatient care for these people had unforeseen consequences, as many mentally disturbed adults we see living on the streets

psychotherapy
Any treatment for emotional disorders involving exploring life experiences and unrealistic pathological perceptions about life.

psychotropic medications
Medications used to treat mental disorders.

Figure 9–1

Patient Care Episodes (Visits) in Different Types of Mental Health Settings in 1955 and 1990

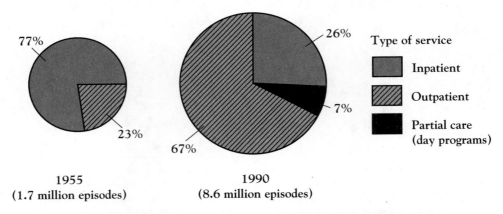

77%

23%

1955
(1.7 million episodes)

26%

7%

67%

1990
(8.6 million episodes)

Type of service

Inpatient

Outpatient

Partial care
(day programs)

This figure reveals how the focus of mental health care in the United States has shifted from inpatient to outpatient services. In 1955, more than three-fourths of all patient visits for treatment occurred within inpatient settings or mental hospitals. Today almost three-fourths of these visits occur in outpatient settings or in what are called partial hospitalization programs, day services for the mentally ill.

Source: U.S. Department of Health and Human Services, 1994, *Mental Health, United States, 1994,* Rockville, MD: Author.

biological revolution in psychiatry
Advances in medication therapy occurring in the 1970s and 1980s that led to the use of psychotropic drugs as a central treatment for mental disorders.

in the United States would have been residents in mental institutions about 40 years ago, the **biological revolution in psychiatry** (alluded to in Feature 9–1 on p. 248) has allowed millions of people whose lives would have been ruined by mental disorders to live a relatively normal life. In addition, the focus on alternate treatments, such as medications, helped bring about another change in the context of mental health care—the effort to extend psychological services to everyone.

The Scope of the Clients: More Attention to Underserved Groups

When psychoanalytic therapy was widely thought to be the most effective form of treatment, outpatient mental health interventions were confined to certain groups. People who were young, affluent, verbal, intelligent, and successful were the preferred clients, as they gravitated to and could afford the years of self-reflection believed necessary for this treatment to work. (This was called the YAVIS syndrome.) Sigmund Freud (1924) himself warned that older people were too rigid to profit from psychotherapy. Minorities did not fit the YAVIS profile. Even when an African American or Asian American could afford treatment, that person's different cultural background might interfere with the therapeutic relationship. It might make it more difficult to develop the collaboration and sense of empathy between patient and therapist that were important for treatment to succeed (Sue, 1992). *Predisposing factors* related to cultural norms and practices deterred prospective patients from getting services, too. Among certain ethnic groups, it is shameful to admit that one has emotional problems or to seek psychological help.

In the 1970s, faced with an increasingly multicultural and elderly United States, therapists realized they needed to reach out to a wider group. Some ethnic-specific

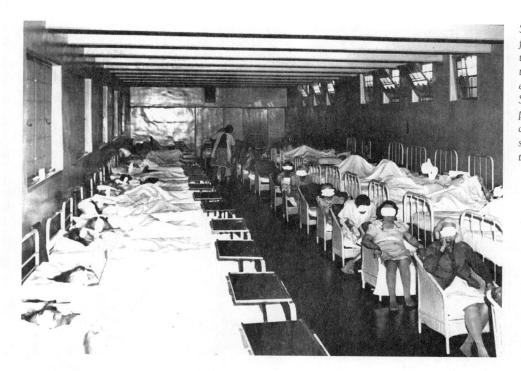

Scenes such as this used to be frequent during the first two thirds of the twentieth century in the large mental hospitals that existed throughout the United States. Today, most of these patients would be living in the community, hopefully with their symptoms controlled by psychotropic drugs.

mental health services were developed. Organizations such as the American Psychological Association sponsored efforts to train more bilingual therapists and develop guidelines for treating minority groups (Ruiz, 1985; Sue, 1992).

At the same time, more attention was being paid to the mental health needs of the old. Starting in the middle 1970s, clinical psychologists could get special training in assessing and treating the elderly. Today nearly half of all departments of psychiatry offer programs in geriatrics. Psychiatrists can be certified in this new field. Textbooks and professional journals are specifically devoted to elderly mental health (Leibowitz, 1993).

In part, this new interest in geriatric mental health grew out of the boom in awareness about Alzheimer's disease (Lebowitz, 1993; see Chapter 7). It was helped along by pioneering psychiatrists who argued that psychotherapy could be effective in people over 65 and by growing concerns that mental disorders in the elderly were being neglected or that psychotropic drugs were being overprescribed. Because the older person metabolizes medicines less effectively, the dose of a drug that is appropriate at age 20 can have toxic effects at age 85. The risk of unwanted side effects in the elderly is also high because older people are more prone to make medication errors and are likely to be taking several different medications at the same time. Not only may drugs interact to produce symptoms ranging from dizziness to sudden death, as highlighted in our discussion of dementia, but also toxic reactions may go unrecognized in the elderly because they mimic the "typical signs" of old age. Today doctors are more aware that drugs need to be prescribed and monitored more carefully in older people and have specific guidelines for their use (Shorr and Robin, 1994).

Barriers still exist. As mentioned earlier, this cohort of elderly did not grow up during the 1960s, the age of self-disclosure. Many older people today still believe it is shameful to go for mental health help (Belsky, 1990). One study suggests that even well-educated, non-immigrant, young-adult Japanese Americans today are reluctant to admit to having emotional problems. They rarely visit professionals, even when they are having serious trouble coping with life (Narikiyo and Kameoka, 1992). If a person does

9-1 The Adult Experience: A Psychoanalyst Reflects on a Changing Field

Tom, a psychiatrist in private practice for 30 years, is an advocate of the analytic approach. Here are his personal views of the field and how it has changed:

When I graduated from medical school in the 1960s, I chose psychiatry because I was fascinated by mental illness. I decided to become a psychoanalyst because I believed it offered the best framework for understanding what makes people act the way they do. It took 12 years to finish my analytic training, which involves course work, a personal analysis, and successfully concluding several training cases. Now, I teach part-time at my analytic institute, supervise students, and have a private practice.

I would like to be doing more psychoanalysis, but we don't get these patients. People can't afford therapy five times a week. They don't want to spend years in treatment. I still feel the training is worth it. Behaviorism and cognitive therapy don't have the nuances you need, the larger perspective on human behavior. Today I work with a variety of patients, including some schizophrenics. I look forward to it all, all kinds of therapy, including medications. I think the biological revolution of the past 20 years is very exciting. It will help us refine our psychoanalytic concepts. It tells you at a molecular level what is going on. The biggest advance is the range of conditions we used to work with only psychologically that we now can treat biologically. The medications make a person who is too anxious reasonably anxious. The medications don't replace psychotherapy. I hope even the biological psychiatrists understand it is important to put into perspective what has been going on in people's lives.

The most threatening change in my professional life involves managed care, the new reimbursement system that has sprung up in recent years to control costs. With managed care, companies contract with individual providers—usually on the basis of who will do the least expensive job. After a certain number of sessions, you must apply to justify more treatment. Suppose your patient is suicidal and the claim is rejected and the person can't afford to pay? Managed care ignores the fact that you cannot quantify how long it takes to recover from mental illness. It pushes us psychiatrists into doing only medication because, of course, we are the most expensive providers. There still will be some private insurance. Some people can afford to pay on their own. Still, for the first time, I'm discouraged at what the future holds for my profession.

not speak English, it can still be difficult to find a bilingual therapist. It can be equally difficult to find a geriatric mental health specialist when one is old (Lebowitz, 1993). Despite more awareness of their detrimental impact, psychotropic drugs continue to be used excessively within and outside of nursing homes (Shorr and Bauwens, 1992; Shorr, Bauwens, and Landefeld, 1990; Shorr, Fought, and Ray, 1994). Still, the climate has changed. For older people and minorities with emotional problems, more help is available than before.

The Scope of the Disorders

What problems are we most likely to suffer from as we journey through adult life? Before exploring this question, let's scan the types of problems we *can* develop—the major categories of disorders spelled out in the most recent *Diagnostic and Statistical Manual,* **DSM-IV.**

In DSM-IV, adult mental disorders are grouped into categories based on their defining symptoms and origins. There are the *organic mental disorders,* a range of conditions that have a clear-cut physiological source and affect either cognition or personality. There are the *mood disorders,* syndromes characterized by disturbances in affect (or mood), and the *anxiety disorders,* whose hallmark is intense anxiety.

DSM-IV

Most current Diagnostic and Statistical Manual of mental disorders.

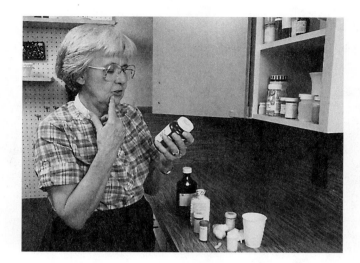

People such as this elderly woman who take a confusing array of different medications are particularly at risk for developing toxic reactions that mimic mental disorders or the physical symptoms of old age.

Schizophrenic and other psychotic illnesses are serious conditions involving a total break with reality. *Substance abuse disorders* involve the excessive use of alcohol or other social drugs. There are disorders limited to specific areas of living (sexual and gender identity disorders, eating and sleep disorders, conditions involving the inability to control anger or inhibit the urge to engage in certain destructive activities) and the *personality disorders,* which involve one's whole mode of approaching the world. There are conditions in which the person develops an imaginary physical illness, either fabricating a medical problem or involuntarily developing symptoms that have no organic cause. There are the *adjustment disorders,* which do not really qualify as full-blown mental disorders, because they involve time-limited symptoms that occur in reaction to life stress.

If we omit this last large category, three types of disorders outshadow all others in prevalence. Approximately one in five people will develop a substance abuse disorder involving alcohol during adult life. One in four people will develop an anxiety disorder, most likely a phobia. About one in five people will suffer from the mood disorder called depression at some point during life (Kessler et al., 1994; Myers et al., 1984).

Because they are the disorders we are most likely to encounter on our "adult journey," in the rest of this chapter we focus on these problems. First, we look at alcoholism. Next we explore phobias, especially the most serious phobic condition called agoraphobia. Then we turn to depression, examining its treatments and causes. (Table 9–2 offers a preview of these problems and the treatments discussed in the next sections.)

ALCOHOLISM

As we know, alcoholic beverages alter our mental state. In the stomach and small intestine, alcohol is absorbed into the bloodstream and carried to the brain. First, there are pleasurable sensations, such as a sense of warmth and well-being. Inhibitions are lowered, and anxiety is relieved. Then negative changes occur. Alcohol causes problems in coordination, balance, judgment, memory, and perception. It makes us irritable, drowsy, and unable to think. At extremely high doses, alcohol causes unconsciousness and, by interfering with breathing, in rare instances, death.

These short-term effects can be life-threatening. Alcohol is implicated in one-half of all fatal traffic accidents. It is a major contributor to deaths by falls and drowning and

Table 9-2   **A Preview of the Mental Disorders and Treatments Discussed in This Chapter**

The Problems
1. **Alcohol disorders.** Obsessive, destructive use of alcoholic substances. The person must be unable to stop using alcohol, even though it impairs social, occupational, or physical functioning
2. **Phobias.** Intense, inappropriate, debilitating anxiety that occurs in certain situations. The anxiety may be connected to a single object (simple phobia) or social situations (social phobia), or it may be more general (agoraphobia).
3. **Depression.** Conditions involving dramatic, long-lasting alterations in mood combined with a range of other physical and psychological symptoms. People who are clinically depressed often have trouble sleeping and eating. They feel apathetic and hopeless, unable to take pleasure in life. They may have trouble concentrating and thinking clearly and may move slowly or be highly agitated.

The Treatments
Psychological treatments
1. **Traditional behavioral approaches.** Therapist manipulates reinforcements to change behavior. *Examples in the chapter:* *Exposure therapy for agoraphobia; Lewinsohn's therapy for depression.
2. **Cognitive approaches.** Therapist identifies and changes illness-producing cognitions or thought patterns. *Examples in the chapter:* *Marlatt's response prevention; Beck's cognitive therapy for depression.
3. **Psychodynamic approaches.** Therapist explores childhood experiences in order to help the patient gain insight into his or her problems. Examples throughout the chapter.

Biological treatments
1. **Antibuse.** Medication causing violent reaction with alcohol. Adjunct treatment for alcoholism.
2. **Anti-anxiety medications.** Medications used to calm anxiety. Treatment for phobias.
3. **Anti-depressant drugs.** Medications used to eradicate depressive symptoms. Treatment for depression and panic attacks.
4. **Electroconvulsive therapy (ECT).** Electric current put through the brain. Treatment of last resort for severe depression.

*Even though these treatments are labeled "traditional behavioral" or "cognitive," they often incorporate both types of approaches.

from fires and burns. The long-term consequences are equally dangerous. Chronic alcohol abuse can cause permanent changes in brain function. Alcohol affects other organs, such as the heart and kidneys. Alcohol's impact on the liver is well known. Cirrhosis, a condition involving the degeneration of this organ, is most often due to chronic alcohol abuse (U.S. Department of Health and Human Services, 1990a; Gallant, 1987).

Uncontrolled drinking wreaks havoc on every aspect of life. It interferes with relationships. It impairs the ability to work. These difficulties in functioning are an important criterion used for labeling people as having a genuine mental disorder related to alcohol.

In DSM-IV, disorders involving alcohol are divided into two main categories. Individuals are classified as having **alcohol dependence** when they meet criteria indicating serious signs of addiction, such as experiencing blackouts and withdrawal symptoms, and their pattern of chronic use impairs their ability to function in life. People who do not meet these conditions, but who have used alcohol repeatedly even though it causes problems in relationships or at work or have used alcohol in hazardous situations, such as driving, are labeled as having a less severe syndrome called **alcohol abuse.**

alcohol dependence and alcohol abuse
Mental disorders characterized by the excessive and/or chronic impairing use of alcoholic beverages.

Epidemiology

Alcoholism is predominantly a "male" disease. An alarming one in five men will develop alcohol dependence; one in six will suffer from alcohol abuse at some point in life. For women, the risk of having each problem is less than half as great (Kessler et al., 1994). Among white males, alcohol dependence and abuse are youth-oriented disorders. Rates peak in adolescence and the early twenties and then rapidly fall off. While as teenagers African-American and Hispanic-American men are far less likely than whites to abuse alcohol, their disorder rates rise during early adulthood and continue to be high (Bucholtz, 1992). This more chronic use pattern may explain the *excess mortality* from liver disease among African Americans compared to whites revealed in Table 1–2 in Chapter One.

The prevalence of alcohol-related disorders varies by ethnicity in other provocative ways. Asian Americans have very low rates of abuse and dependence. Among Native Americans, these rates are several times higher than in the population at large (U.S. Department of Health and Human Services, 1990a). What accounts for these different patterns? Hints come from looking at the reasons why people abuse alcohol.

Perspectives on Causes

While it has been noticed for centuries that alcoholism "runs in families," this observation offers no clues about whether shared heredity or environment is to blame. Behavioral genetic studies allow us to examine the role that inherited predispositions play in these common disorders of adult life.

Figure 9–2 summarizes the findings of studies in which researchers used the *adoption method* to examine the genetic basis of alcoholism, that is, investigations in which scientists compared the alcoholism rates of adoptees with a biological family history of this problem to those without a genetic history of the disease (McGue, 1993).

Notice that the charts show an interesting gender difference. While adopted males with biological relatives who are alcoholic consistently have higher illness rates, only one group of researchers found that females with this family history have an elevated risk. In other words, the evidence for an inherited component to alcoholism is compelling—but, for some strange reason, mainly for men.

Robert Cloninger believes that there are two forms of alcoholism in men, one more clearly "genetic" than the other. In the non-hereditary type of alcoholism, a man tends to begin drinking after age 25 and is likely to first manifest genuine problems in middle age. This type of alcoholic can abstain from drinking, but tends to lose control once having begun. After remaining sober for months, he periodically goes on a binge. This person tends to be guilty, fearful, and upset by his problem. He is not prone to act out under the influence of alcohol and has comparatively good social adjustment, experiencing fewer chronic problems at home and work.

In another more virulent, biologically based form of alcoholism, the onset is earlier, and the difficulty is the inability to inhibit the urge to seek out alcohol. This type of alcoholic tends not to be upset by his condition. He is more likely to be impulsive and hyperactive and to have chronic difficulties with relationships and work. This man is more likely to become abusive when drinking, to regularly drive while intoxicated, to commit crimes and end up in jail (Cloninger, 1987; Cloninger, Bohman, and Sigvardsson, 1981).

Figure 9–2

Risk of Developing an Alcohol Disorder if an Adoptee Has No History or a
Positive History of Alcohol Problems in the Biological Family, Males and Females

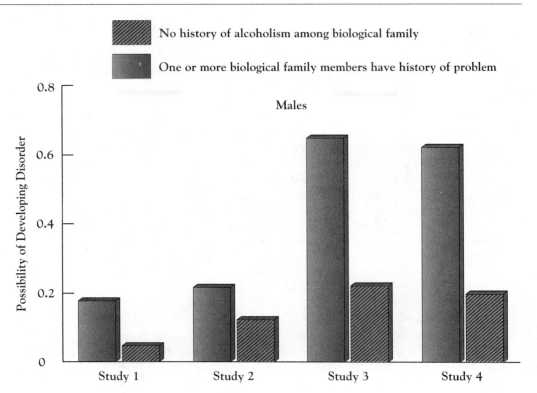

In these studies, researchers compared the rates of alcoholism among male (this chart) and female (next chart) adoptees with a positive or negative biological background of alcoholism. Every study shows that men with this positive history face a greater risk of the disorder. However,
only one group of researchers found that women with a comparable genetic background have
elevated problem rates (see p. 253).

According to Cloninger, people who suffer from the more biologically based form of
alcoholism have a defect in a specific system of the brain. Therefore, it is important to
search for physiological markers or mechanisms that either protect individuals from or
put them at risk for this disease. Interestingly mechanisms of this type clearly do exist.
After ingesting alcohol, many Asians have a skin-flushing reaction accompanied by
unpleasant sensations. This allergic reaction may partly explain the low rate of alcohol
disorders in this ethnic group (Thomasson and Li, 1993).

Even when biological predispositions set the stage, the environment seems intuitively to play a role. Don't most of us automatically link drinking to excess to
outer-world frustrations, stresses, and losses? We speak of the widower who "turns to
alcohol" to cope with bereavement. Another familiar figure is the laid-off worker or
rejected lover who blots out his troubles by spending his days at the local bar.

These observations gain research support from surveys showing that among people
who suffer these life stresses, such as widowers, alcoholism rates are unusually high
(Williams, Takeuchi, and Adair, 1992). The *comorbidity* of alcoholism with depression

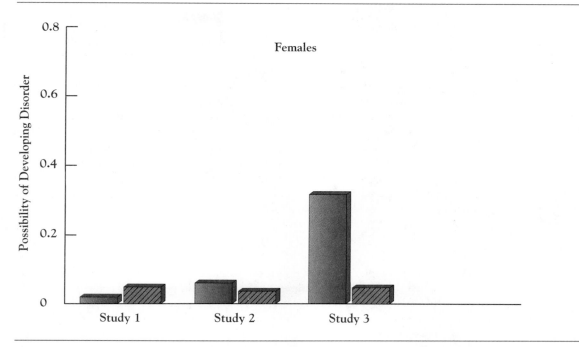

Source: McGue, M., From Proteins to Cognitions: The Behavioral Genetics of Alcoholism. In R. Plomin and G. E. McClearn (Eds.), *Nature, Nurture, and Psychology.* Copyright © 1993 by the American Psychological Association. Adapted by Permission.

and anxiety disorders suggests that people may turn to drink to reduce the pain of internal stress. *Twin studies* suggest that common genetic predispositions play a role in why these diseases cluster together (Kendler, Heath, Neale, Kessler, and Eaves, 1993). Still, people who have these other mental disorders often report turning to alcohol as a "medication" to cope with their painful emotions (Kessler and Price, 1993).

The impact of stressful life experiences on alcohol abuse is also implied by studies linking this disorder to earlier life problems. Some childhood *risk factors* for adult problem drinking include difficulty in school and hyperactivity. Adolescents who become alcoholic are more likely to be delinquent, to have poor relationships with their parents, and to have disorganized family lives (U.S. Department of Health and Human Services, 1990a).

The pull to drink is related to positive expectations. As we might expect, people who drink to excess tend to believe that alcohol lowers anxiety and increases well-being. These expectations may initially be learned at home. The young person may absorb the sense that alcohol is a "magic potion" by observing the lure that drinking exerts on family members or by choosing to *model* a powerful parent who drinks (Ullman and Orenstein, 1994). Another route may be the wider social setting. Alcohol may help ease the fears associated with becoming an adult. Drinking can bring status or acceptance. It can signify being one of the crowd, having fun, and being truly grown up. The fact that alcoholism rates peak in youth for white males strongly suggests that our society's emphasis on drinking as a masculine rite of passage can promote this problem. Moreover, the norm associating drinking with manliness may be especially prevalent among white males, which may help explain why African-American and Hispanic-American teenagers have low rates of alcoholism (Barnes, Farrell, and Banerjee, 1994). The same social forces may account for why abuse and dependence rates decline so sharply after youth among white males. Once men successfully negotiate the challenges of finding a wife and beginning a career, they may feel more secure. When they settle down to a job and family, they have to give up drinking to excess or risk causing havoc in their lives.

This brings us to one possible environmental reason for the later onset and longer duration of problem drinking among African-American men. As we will see in Chapters 11 and 13, not only are African-American males less likely to marry, but also they are more apt to be unemployed or to be laid off repeatedly during their working years and so have fewer controls to counter the lure of alcohol as they travel through life.

In addition to the inhibiting forces of having a family and holding down a job, there is the braking influence exerted by one's cultural group. One epidemiologic study of Mexican Americans in Texas found alcoholism rates were much higher among native-born men than first-generation immigrants (U.S. Department of Health and Human Services, 1991). This study suggests that, in addition to genetic predispositions, the way given cultures react to drinking may account for the interesting ethnic variations in alcoholism.

APPLICATIONS AND INTERVENTIONS

Alcoholics Anonymous
Popular self-help intervention for alcohol disorders emphasizing confession of one's faults in group sessions.

Our look at the complex array of influences in alcohol dependence and abuse implies that treatments should be varied, aimed at the individual person and society as a whole. Actually alcoholism interventions are unusual because with this disorder *primary prevention* plays an important role. There are school programs focused on the danger of drinking, laws against underage purchase, and legal penalties for drinking while driving. Another intervention based more on ritual than research also takes center stage—Alcoholics Anonymous.

Alcoholics Anonymous, or AA, was developed in the 1930s by a surgeon and a stockbroker who found the only cure for their alcoholism in mutual support. The purpose of AA is to offer this support to everyone through attending weekly group meetings plus following the steps to recovery that form the basis of this movement. AA emphasizes spirituality, trust in God, and open confession of one's faults. A central principle is that

To explain this man's addiction to alcohol, genetic predispositions, the association of wine with previous pleasurable experiences, and living in a cultural milieu that condones drinking and offers the easy availability of alcohol may be important. We also would look to the presence of other mental disorders, and to the fact that this individual seems socially isolated and to be experiencing considerable work-related stress. In other words, for each person, there are likely to be multiple reasons provoking alcohol dependence and abuse.

alcoholics suffer from a *lifelong chronic disease*. This means that moderate drinking is impossible. The requirement is total abstinence, "one day at a time."

AA advocates claim remarkable success. Though they may not be permanently sober, everyone who stays with the program gets some gain. Notice that we have no information on who leaves! In fact, without what are called **outcome studies,** in which people in the program are compared with dropouts, those who never enroll, or those receiving other treatments, we have no way of evaluating the effectiveness of *any* intervention. However, AA's appeal is not in dispute. Not only is this treatment the most popular intervention for alcoholism throughout the world, but also it is widely perceived as the most effective treatment. In one survey, emergency room physicians gave higher ratings of effectiveness to AA than to professional mental health help (Chang, Astrachan, and Bryant, 1994).

In addition to having this non-scientific competitor, alcoholism treatment is unusual because with this type of problem *psychotropic medications* do not play a major role. There is no pill that squelches the urge to drink. However, when the person is using alcohol to self-medicate for another problem, treating that condition through drug therapy may help. Psychotropic drugs may ease the painful symptoms of withdrawal (Bohn, 1993). A medication called antibuse, which causes unpleasant symptoms when taken with alcohol, is also sometimes used as a deterrent (Liebowitz, Kranzler, and Meyer, 1990). Some experts swear by antibuse, which produces nausea, headache, sweating, and heart palpitations by interfering with alcohol metabolism. Others call antibuse too dangerous or a crutch that does not teach self-control. Typically antibuse is used as an adjunct to other approaches.

The major mental health treatment for alcoholism is psychotherapy combined with education about alcohol or referral to AA. Group psychotherapy is popular. Particularly when disturbed family relationships are involved, family and marital therapy is used. The most sophisticated new treatments are cognitive behavioral approaches.

Cognitive behaviorists believe that there are many paths to problem drinking. The addiction to alcohol can be influenced by genetic predispositions, by modeling, and by cognitions about alcohol's power, as well as by direct reinforcement based on drinking's physiological effects. Unlearning this addiction depends on diagnosing a given person's pull and then providing tools that offer control (Abrams and Niaura, 1987; Goldman, Brown, and Christiansen, 1987).

This is the goal of **relapse prevention,** a widely used treatment developed by psychologist Alan Marlatt for any form of substance abuse (Marlatt and Gordon, 1985; Rawson, Obert, McCann, and Marinelli-Casey, 1993). In analyzing relapses in recovering alcoholics, Marlatt discovered that people typically "fell off the wagon" in specific situations: when feeling negative emotions; when having arguments; and when finding themselves in social environments, such as at a party, that evoke the craving for alcohol. Labeling these "high risk for relapse situations," Marlatt trains alcoholics to be attuned to these events and arms them with strategies to confront them head on.

Marlatt believes that people revert to drinking when they lack *self-efficacy*. They drink because they feel powerless to control their intake. If they are provided with tools to succeed at not drinking in these high-risk situations, efficacy feelings such as "I know I can handle it" are increased. Self-efficacy then becomes more solid, growing as a function of the number of tempting situations the person masters.

Marlatt first has his clients monitor their urges. They are asked to note when the pull to drink is most intense and their feelings when these triggering situations arise. Then they learn to substitute behaviors for drinking in these enticing situations. Bill, whose path to falling off the wagon is charted in Figure 9–3, might be taught to go down another street on his way home or train his mind on how angry his wife would be if he missed dinner. He would be told to focus on the terrible consequences for his self-esteem of stopping as he drives by the bar. He might be taught to stand up to his unpleasant boss

outcome studies
Research method designed to demonstrate the efficacy of treatments for mental and physical disorders.

relapse prevention
Cognitive behavioral treatment for substance abuse involving enhancing feelings of self-efficacy.

Figure 9–3

Bill's Behavioral Chain for Drinking

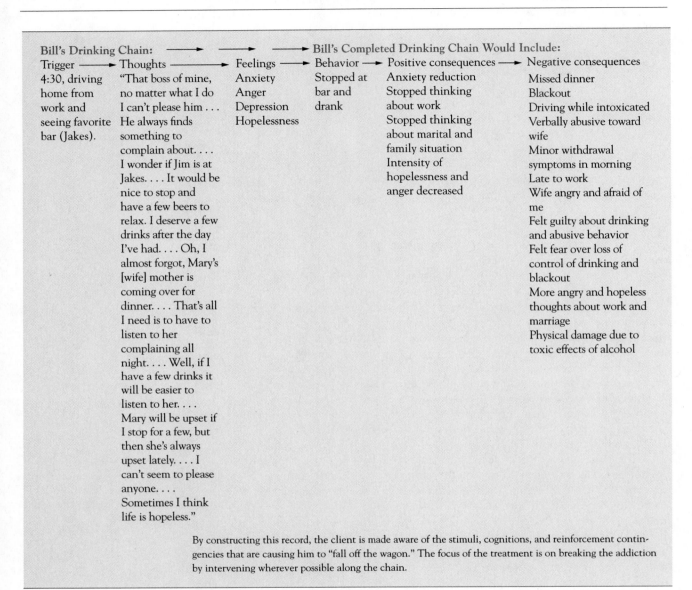

Bill's Drinking Chain:

Trigger	Thoughts	Feelings	Behavior	Positive consequences	Negative consequences
4:30, driving home from work and seeing favorite bar (Jakes).	"That boss of mine, no matter what I do I can't please him . . . He always finds something to complain about. . . . I wonder if Jim is at Jakes. . . . It would be nice to stop and have a few beers to relax. I deserve a few drinks after the day I've had. . . . Oh, I almost forgot, Mary's [wife] mother is coming over for dinner. . . . That's all I need is to have to listen to her complaining all night. . . . Well, if I have a few drinks it will be easier to listen to her. . . . Mary will be upset if I stop for a few, but then she's always upset lately. . . . I can't seem to please anyone. . . . Sometimes I think life is hopeless."	Anxiety Anger Depression Hopelessness	Stopped at bar and drank	Anxiety reduction Stopped thinking about work Stopped thinking about marital and family situation Intensity of hopelessness and anger decreased	Missed dinner Blackout Driving while intoxicated Verbally abusive toward wife Minor withdrawal symptoms in morning Late to work Wife angry and afraid of me Felt guilty about drinking and abusive behavior Felt fear over loss of control of drinking and blackout More angry and hopeless thoughts about work and marriage Physical damage due to toxic effects of alcohol

Bill's Completed Drinking Chain Would Include:

By constructing this record, the client is made aware of the stimuli, cognitions, and reinforcement contingencies that are causing him to "fall off the wagon." The focus of the treatment is on breaking the addiction by intervening wherever possible along the chain.

Source: G. A. Marlatt and J. R. Gordon, 1985, *Relapse Prevention*, New York: Guilford Press, p. 438.

or tell his wife that lunch, not dinner, is when her equally unpleasant mother should come to the house. A woman who drinks heavily at parties because she feels shy and needs something to occupy her hands might be told to immediately get a soft drink when she arrives. To cope with her social anxieties, she might be trained to relax or taught conversational skills.

Relapse prevention has a different focus than AA. Without denying there are genetic tendencies to drink to excess, it minimizes the victim-of-a-hopeless-disease mentality. The person is suffering, not from an uncontrollable condition, but from a defect in knowledge. He or she is unaware of the techniques that can offer full control. Furthermore, because people are active agents, Marlatt believes controlled drinking is possible. One can limit intake as well as abstain.

While outcome studies show that relapse prevention can be highly effective, experts suggest that the real key is to fit the treatment to the individual (McKay and Maisto, 1993). For some people, the intervention of choice may be AA. For others, the focus might be on treating the underlying mental disorder that is provoking the urge to drink. The biggest hurdle with any intervention is to get the individual to *want to change*, as the lure of the drug is a powerful immediate reinforcer. In other words, because it evokes pleasure, substance abuse of any kind can be very difficult to treat. With the emotional problems we turn to now, the pull to stay ill is not an issue. As we saw in the interview at the beginning of the chapter, phobic disorders cause intense suffering. They can make day-to-day life an endurance test.

PHOBIAS

The unpleasant sensations of anxiety are highly adaptive responses. Anxiety allows us to escape from danger. It propels much of the learning that transforms us from unsocialized infants into competent adults. But sometimes anxiety is so intense, pervasive, and inappropriate that it interferes with life. This is when people are classified as having an *anxiety disorder,* a genuine emotional problem involving anxiety.

Phobias, the most common anxiety disorders, are intense fears connected to a situation or range of situations. Because they cause avoidance, that is, an unwillingness to encounter the phobic object, their impact varies as a function of the importance of the object to daily life. A phobia of cars is more disabling than a phobia of snakes unless we earn our living by farming. A woman's fear of airplanes might be mildly incapacitating, robbing her of an enjoyable trip to Hawaii. To her husband, whose job involves regular flying, that fear might mean the end of a career.

Phobias such as those described above, because they are confined to a single object or situation, are called *simple phobias*. While they can be incapacitating, their specificity limits the impairment they can provoke. Two other types of phobias listed in DSM-IV, social phobia and agoraphobia, because they involve so *many* situations, are more serious.

Social phobics become anxious when they feel evaluated or perceive themselves as "on display." They may be afraid of speaking or eating in public or terrified of talking to authority figures or to the opposite sex. In these situations, the feeling of being judged or watched evokes anxiety. The visible signs of this fear then become a source of embarrassment. Social phobics report that the fear of blushing, stammering, sweating, and twitching solidifies and motivates the avoidance of a variety of social situations (Barlow, 1988).

Social phobics suffer because the object of their fear is salient, pervasive, and very important to human life. Imagine being uneasy in many of your interactions. Imagine being so self-conscious that you fail in the very situations, such as dating or dealing with superiors at work, where you really want to succeed. However, the misery social phobics feel can pale compared to the pain suffered by people with the most malignant phobic condition called agoraphobia.

Agoraphobia is the most devastating phobic disorder because, as we saw in the interview at the beginning of this chapter, it *always* severely restricts life. The agoraphobic person is afraid of a range of situations, such as elevators, planes, bridges, or other public places. Often the person is housebound, terrified of venturing out the door.

Agoraphobia is also distinctive because it involves **panic attacks,** spells of anxiety that come on out of the blue. To imagine what a panic attack is like, think of a recent

phobias
Intense, irrational fears connected to a situation or range of situations.

agoraphobia
Most serious phobic condition in which the individual is frightened of a range of outer-world situations.

panic attacks
Intense storms of anxiety that erupt out of the blue.

This famous painting, The Scream, *by the artist Edvard Munch, conveys some sense of what it feels like to be in the midst of a panic attack.*

situation in which you felt anxious magnified tenfold. There is a sense of terror. You cannot breathe. Your heart is pounding. You are faint and dizzy. You think you are going crazy, having a heart attack, or dying.

Naturally people who have had a panic attack are terrified of having another. Their fear is magnified because this internal hurricane is unpredictable and so might strike again at any moment. As we saw in the introductory vignette, what often happens is retreat. The person vows never to be trapped or stranded in public if a panic attack occurs. Being on a train, sitting in a movie theater, and going on a date become situations to be avoided. At this point, the individual has agoraphobia.

People may have repeated panic attacks without developing agoraphobia. They can have agoraphobia without having any panic attacks or any recent ones. However, while experts argue about how frequently agoraphobia occurs without panic, most agree that in this serious type of phobia panic typically plays a central role (Moras, Craske, and Barlow, 1990).

Epidemiology

Phobias are disproportionately "female diseases." Women have a one in seven chance of developing this type of disorder during adult life. For men, the risk is much lower—1 in 15. Women are also at higher risk of developing agoraphobia than men. According to the NCS, while about 7 percent of American women will develop agoraphobia at some point in life, the lifetime prevalence for males is 3 percent (Kessler et al., 1994).

(Interestingly the male/female lifetime prevalences of social phobia in the study were more comparable, though women still had a higher risk of developing this problem.)

Phobias are also youth-oriented conditions. They often appear in adolescence and the twenties. Illness rates decline after midlife. However, as we saw in the interview at the beginning of this chapter, this type of mental disorder seems to be comparatively persistent or chronic. Alcohol or depressive disorders often tend to remit and then perhaps appear again at another point during life. People who suffer from phobias are more apt to be locked in battle with debilitating anxiety for years (Kessler et al., 1994).

Because it is the type of phobia that most severely affects life, we now turn to why certain people develop that devastating condition called agoraphobia.

Perspectives on Causes

What causes the panic attacks that are so often the trigger provoking agoraphobia? Many experts feel a physiological abnormality is to blame. One candidate is lactate, a chemical in the blood. While infusing sodium lactate into most people produces no reaction, when agoraphobics are injected with this chemical, they often experience a panic attack. This suggests that a lactate intolerance may cause panic. In certain people, a higher-than-normal sensitivity to blood lactate produces a panic attack (Barlow, 1988).

Another theory implicates dysfunctional breathing patterns in panic attacks. According to this hypothesis, illustrated in Figure 9–4, some people naturally tend to hyperventilate, or breathe too deeply in response to even minor stress. This causes CO_2 levels in the blood to decline. In order to compensate, the heart pumps more rapidly. The rapid beating or palpitations cause even deeper breathing. When this happens, individuals decide they are suffocating or dying, and a full blown panic attack ensues.

Even if the initial attack is a physiological event, if the outcome is agoraphobia, as Figure 9–4 shows, learning is involved. Once having had a panic attack, as we saw in our beginning interview, the person becomes hypervigilant, alert to any signs of anxiety. However, being in this heightened state of arousal produces the very symptoms the individual fears. In other words, learned anxiety keeps the panic going because the fear of panic makes it more likely that the person will have another attack. This anxiety then turns outward, becoming connected to situations one has been in when a panic attack occurred or places where escaping is impossible in the middle of an attack. This leads to the final step. The person avoids "unsafe" (public) places (Barlow, 1988).

Clearly agoraphobia is influenced by the environment in the sense that the panic attack occurs in a specific setting, which the person then learns to avoid. What role does the wider environment have in producing this condition? Notice that Figure 9–4 suggests that some external trigger sets off the anxiety that puts the panic chain into motion. The person I interviewed at the beginning of this chapter felt that being in a stressful life situation, that is, being forced into a hated family business, caused his anxiety attacks to erupt. Behaviorists, such as David Barlow (1988), agree that stressful situations often do set the stage for this disease *in people who are biologically predisposed to suffer panic attacks*. Psychoanalytically oriented therapists go further. They speculate that specific kinds of childhood experiences are at the root of this disease.

In the psychoanalytic perspective, agoraphobia is caused by excessive dependency or unacceptable unconscious feelings. The person retreats from the outside world because she is afraid of being an independent adult or wants to avoid situations that evoke unwanted urges. For instance, a student might become agoraphobic and drop out of college because the men in her classes evoke frightening sexual feelings or because she is terrified of growing up (Fishman, 1989).

These speculations about dependency and the reluctance to admit to "unladylike" impulses are appealing because they fit in with the fact that women are much more likely to develop agoraphobia than men. Unfortunately they are unproven. Researchers are unable to pinpoint a clear-cut agoraphobic personality (Edelmann, 1992).

The Cognitive/Physiological Process Provoking a Panic Attack

External trigger

Riding on the rush hour bus to work worrying over my job

Physiological reaction

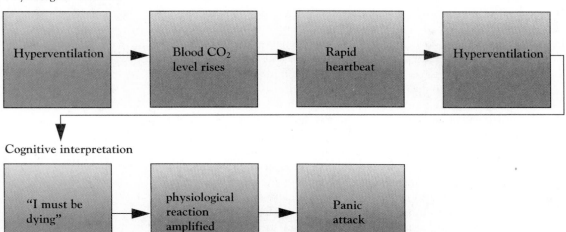

| Hyperventilation | → | Blood CO_2 level rises | → | Rapid heartbeat | → | Hyperventilation |

Cognitive interpretation

| "I must be dying" | → | physiological reaction amplified | → | Panic attack |

The Learning Process Leading to Agoraphobia

1. Bolt from the bus at the next stop, run home, and call in sick.
   → Behavior reinforced (anxiety reduced)

2. Hypervigilant in situations resembling that in which the attack occurred (buses, crowded places) ensuring that the sequence above leading to a panic attack recurs.

3. Further reinforcement for retreating from "unsafe situations" and confining activities to non-panic-producing locations (house).

Once again, multiple causes mean different treatments. Medications that reduce anxiety play a prominent role in treating panic. So do techniques to help people actively cope with their fear.

A few decades ago the sole psychotropic medications used to treat panic were **anti-anxiety agents,** drugs that immediately calm, sedate, and relax. However, most medications of this type, such as Valium, are addictive and so cannot be taken on a long-term basis. Also, as we saw in the beginning case study, these medicines are not effective against the internal hurricane of a panic attack (Barlow, 1988). A few decades ago a surprising medication was discovered to perform this job—anti-depressant drugs.

As we will see in the next section, anti-depressant medications have revolutionized the treatment of depression. They are the first line of attack for this emotional disorder in its most severe form. They are now an important treatment for agoraphobia, too. Anti-depressants act selectively. While they are relatively ineffective with more minor levels of anxiety, they can be very effective at stopping panic attacks (Salzman, 1989).

Anti-depressants are not a complete cure. Even when they do eradicate panic, the anticipatory anxiety plus the learned avoidance response remains. In other words, the person still must master the reluctance to encounter situations involving a panic attack. This is where the following behavioral treatment comes in.

Exposure therapy is designed to get the person in the phobic situations so that the anxiety will extinguish. The treatment involves encountering these situations in graded steps. The therapist first asks the client to construct a hierarchy of panic-related events. The phobic person then gradually progresses through the hierarchy over a period of months. For instance, after constructing the "fear intensity list" illustrated in Table 9–3, the therapist would first have this lawyer practice going to work with a colleague for a few weeks. Then, when he felt comfortable in this situation, he would attempt the next item on the scale. Eventually he should be able to enter the situation evoking the most terror, arguing a case in court. In these encounters, the lawyer would be armed with strategies to follow when fear strikes. He might be taught to use relaxation techniques to counter fear. He may carry a set of cards in his pocket with statements such as "Anxiety is normal. Do not add frightening thoughts." He would be cautioned to expect setbacks. The message is to not give up (Wilson, 1989).

Because company makes this confrontation less daunting, exposure sessions sometimes take place with a therapist, or with fellow sufferers, or with a spouse. Whatever the

anti-anxiety agents
Medications that reduce anxiety.

exposure therapy
Behavioral treatment in which the phobic person confronts the feared situation(s) in graded steps.

A Fear Hierarchy Constructed by a Phobic Lawyer Table 9-3

		Anxiety level (1–10)*
1.	Asking my secretary to take dictation	2
2.	Sharing a ride to work with a colleague	2
3.	Being at a meeting with my colleagues	3
4.	Speaking up at the meeting	5
5.	Going to lunch with a client	6
6.	Speaking with my boss about my work	7
7.	Arguing a case in court	10

In exposure therapy, this person will gradually proceed through this hierarchy until the anxiety is extinguished.

*(1 = very minor; 10 = extremely intense)

strategy, effectiveness depends on regular practice. The person must repeatedly confront the situations that are feared.

Here is an example of this therapy being used with a classic agoraphobic, a woman who is unable to leave the house:

> Mrs. Gerard is married and has no children. Over the last five years she has become more anxious about going out of the house. . . . She remembers her first moment of fear when she was sitting at the back of the bus, short of breath and feeling anxious. After the incident she reported in sick regularly and since then has been declared unfit to work. . . . She hardly even goes out of the house unless her husband accompanies her. After the therapist has explained the rationale to the patient, the next step will be constructing a hierarchy of situations of which the patient is afraid. . . . Before the next session she has to exercise the next assignment which is to walk around the house according to a defined route. . . . Mrs. Gerard devoted 15 sessions to working through the hierarchy. . . . First, she went through the town on her bike, then she went walking. Then, she and her husband went for a spin around the countryside. Currently, Mrs. Gerard is becoming less dependent on her husband. She dares to go out alone and do most of the shopping. For the first time in years they are making plans for the Holidays, though the idea still scares her. (Adapted from Emmelkamp, Bouman, and Scholing, 1992, pp. 92–97)

While outcome studies suggest that exposure is the most effective psychological intervention for agoraphobia and other phobic conditions, it is not a perfect cure. One reviewer found that, while improvement rates hovered around 60–70 percent, the figures declined to 50 percent when dropouts were included (Edelmann, 1992). Even within this group, few people reach the point of being totally anxiety-free (Barlow, 1988). Interestingly exposure seems especially effective when carried out with a spouse, possibly because a loving partner can lessen the person's anxiety and help keep up the pressure to practice. Exposure therapy also works best when it occurs in conjunction with other problem-solving techniques, such as training in being more assertive and coping with interpersonal distress (Edelmann, 1992).

DEPRESSION

depression
Mental disorders involving serious, long-lasting low mood accompanied by other defined symptoms.

The emotional disorder called **depression** is different than just the sadness that is the price of being alive. It is a highly debilitating disorder which seriously erodes the quality of life. As Feature 9–2 shows, depression involves a range of physical and psychological symptoms. In fact, not every person who is depressed may even feel sad or down in the dumps. As I mentioned early in this chapter, among certain individuals depression may only express itself in symptoms such as memory loss or excessive aches and pains.

Depressed people often feel that life has nothing to offer. They have no interest in activities they used to love. Their world view or cognitions about life and themselves change. They feel worthless and helpless. They may be convinced that no one cares for them and be tortured by voices making terrible accusations and whispering warnings of doom. They are usually indifferent to living. Often they have recurrent thoughts of suicide.

Depression involves bodily changes. Depressed people have no energy. They can barely move or get around. There is a disturbance of the sleep cycle. People are often tortured by chronic insomnia. Or sometimes they sleep for 15 hours a day. Appetite changes. Some people eat excessively. Others cannot eat at all. Inability to concentrate and remember and slowed movements or agitated restlessness are also classic signs.

In 1986, while in Paris receiving a coveted literary award, writer William Styron humiliated himself and enraged his hosts by bolting from the luncheon, pleading mental illness. His depression had begun that past summer at his country house on Martha's Vineyard, a lovely island off Cape Cod. Here is his evocative description of how his condition gradually enveloped his life:

> I felt a numbness, an odd fragility—as if my body had become frail, hypersensitive, and disjointed and clumsy. . . . Nothing felt quite right; there were twitches and pains. . . . [The] effect was immensely disturbing, augmenting the anxiety that was never absent from my waking hours and fueling . . . a fidgety restlessness that kept me on the move. . . . By now . . . it was October, and . . . the . . . evening light . . . had none of its familiar loveliness, but ensnared me in a suffocating gloom. . . . I felt an immense . . . solitude. I could no longer concentrate . . . , and . . . writing, becoming . . . exhausting, stalled, then ceased.
>
> The madness of depression is . . . a storm of murk. Soon evident are the slowed . . . responses, paralysis, psychic energy throttled back to zero. . . . The body . . . feels sapped, drained. As the disorder . . . took possession, I began to conceive that my mind was being . . . inundated by floodwaters. [My voice] underwent a strange transformation, becoming . . . faint, wheezy and spasmodic. The libido . . . made an early exit. Most distressing of all the . . . disruptions was that of sleep. Exhaustion combined with sleeplessness is a . . . torture. . . . My few hours of sleep were usually terminated at three or four in the morning, when I stared up into the darkness, . . . writhing. . . . Plainly the possibility [of suicide] was around the corner. . . .

Source: Adapted from W. Styron, 1990, Darkness Visible, New York: Vintage, pp. 42–50.

DSM-IV specifies two main types of depression. In a *major depression*, the symptoms are more serious. The person must have a low mood or be apathetic and have at least five of the other symptoms listed above for at least two weeks. In *dysthymia*, the person must have a depressed mood and two or more of the symptoms most days for at least two years. Partly because of this requirement involving duration, most depressed people are diagnosed with a major depression.

Diagnostic quarrels about depression are intense. Because depressive symptoms occur on a continuum, some experts believe that categorizing people as having either a depressive disorder or no problem is misleading. This strategy misses people who are truly depressed, but whose symptoms are not severe enough to satisfy the criteria specified above (George, 1993). People may have what is called a double depression, one with features of both a major depression and dysthymia (Akiskal, 1989). Another intriguing characteristic of depression is its high comorbidity with agoraphobia (Clark and Watson, 1991; Frances and Hall, 1991). Does the fact that many people with agoraphobia are depressed mean the two problems are a manifestation of the same underlying disease? Or does agoraphobia lead to depression as the person finds herself imprisoned, deprived of the reinforcers that make life worthwhile? One bit of evidence supporting the common underlying illness hypothesis is that anti-depressants are effective with panic. Another is that relatives of agoraphobics have elevated rates of major depression (Munjack and Moss, 1981).

Epidemiology

Depression is the only major mental disorder that is not a youth-oriented problem. Depression rates are fairly uniform at every age through the forties (Kessler et al., 1994).

In this elderly widower, isolated and alone, the presence of suicidal thoughts would be especially ominous, as people in this category are at much higher risk of ending their lives.

However, contrary to the common idea that this mental disorder is endemic among the elderly, the ECA survey showed that people over 65 were *less likely* to suffer from depression than younger adults (Weissman et al., 1985).

There are qualifications. After dipping to a low at about age 60, depressive symptoms rise again dramatically among the old-old (Kessler, Foster, Webster, and House, 1992). Critics believe that the ECA figures are misleading. While many older adults do report signs of depression, these minor symptoms may not qualify for the diagnosis of a genuine psychiatric disorder according to the *DSM* (Blazer et al., 1987). What no one disputes is that depression is a life-threatening disease in the elderly, especially among white men. As Figure 9–5 on p. 266 shows, white males over 65 have the highest suicide rate of any group. As described in Feature 9–3, in assessing the chance of a person taking his life, markers such as advanced age and being male loom large.

No one quarrels about the relationship to gender either. In most cultures, depression is approximately twice as common in women as men. To explain these findings, psychologists have invoked hormonal causes, life stresses, temperament, or other forces (McGrath, Keita, Strickland, and Russo, 1990). There may be no one answer, as there are many pathways to this debilitating disorder of adult life.

Perspectives on Causes

Twin studies show that genetic predispositions are important in the tendency to develop depressive illnesses (Kendler, Heath, Neale, Kessler and Eaves, 1993b). However, early experiences and current stresses also contribute to a person's becoming depressed (Kendler, Kessler, Neale, Heath, and Eaves, 1993; Tsuang and Faraone, 1990). This complexity was revealed in a study in which men and women who reported experiencing childhood family violence had higher rates of depression, but only if they were under current stress (Kessler and Magee, 1994). In other words, as psychoanalysts believe, childhood experiences may be important in triggering this disorder, but mainly when one's current life is not going well.

Depression rates rise after a variety of current stresses: plant firings, divorce, illness. For men, an important depression-promoting stress is losing a spouse. In a reversal of the typical gender difference, in one epidemiologic study researchers found widowed men of any race were more than twice as likely to suffer from a major depression than their female counterparts (Williams et al., 1992; see Feature 9–3). This brings us to the general class of events that looms large in psychological theories about what sets off depression—loss.

One of the most frightening events I faced when working as a clinical psychologist was the possibility that a depressed patient under my care might commit suicide. When a client discussed her feeling that life was not worth living, it was mandatory to directly question that person about whether she had contemplated suicide. If the answer was yes, all antennas went on alert as I carefully explored the extent of planning, motivation, and fantasies about the act. At a minimum, in order to continue treating my patient outside of the hospital I was compelled to extract a promise that this person would not "do anything" before contacting me. Could I really feel confident that, when she was alone and thinking of ending her life, my client would make that call? Had I made a wise decision by sending a possibly suicidal person home after that session today? As you might imagine, these thoughts have caused me, as well as many other mental health workers, many sleepless nights.

What are the major risk factors for suicide? When should you be on the alert to the possibility that a loved one or friend who is depressed or feels indifferent to living might take this drastic step?

As I suggested in the text, two important risk factors relate to gender and age. Suicidal thoughts should be taken seriously in older people, especially if they are male and living alone. (The presence of chronic health problems is an additional risk factor in this group.) As I implied above, in *any adult*, the presence of firm plans involving specific methods is an ominous sign. A history of previous suicide attempts raises the risk that a person will attempt suicide again. Moreover, as you might have gathered from the description in Feature 9–2, the severity of the depressive symptoms is another strong predictor of the strength of the impulse to end one's life. Finally, given two comparably depressed people, those who go on to successfully commit suicide are more likely to be socially isolated and to be experiencing multiple life stresses (Comstock, 1992; McIntosh, 1992; Valente, 1993–1994). In fact, these two risk factors illustrate why—contrary to what we hear in the media—suicide is especially prevalent not among the young, but among the very old.

PSYCHOANALYTIC VIEWPOINTS. Sigmund Freud (1957) was the first person to relate depression to loss, linking this problem to normal mourning. In mourning, Freud reasoned, a person comes to terms with the loss of a loved person by identification. The bereaved person internalizes qualities of the lost loved one; they become part of the mourner's own self. According to Freud, normal mourning turns into depression when the survivor has unconscious negative feelings for the lost person. These negative feelings are also turned inward, resulting in the person's adopting toward the self the unresolved angry feelings once reserved for the other. In Freud's view, then, after the loss of a person who is both loved and hated, anger is turned inward to become self-hate.

Current psychoanalytic views of depression focus on losses of "attachment figures." People are vulnerable to being depressed as adults when the parent/child relationship has been severed in their early years (Bowlby, 1980). The child may have been physically abandoned or separated. She may have been emotionally shut out. According to this theory, any time parents are unavailable, a child is at risk for becoming depressed during adult life.

Psychoanalysts feel childhood losses cause a sense of failure, inadequacy, and distrust that poisons the person's ability to develop satisfying relationships in adult life. Furthermore, current losses re-evoke the early trauma and so produce an exaggerated response (Bemporad, 1990). According to Edward Bibring (1953), in the depression-prone person any loss produces a condition of "ego helplessness." When the person feels

Figure 9–5

Age-Adjusted Death Rates for Suicide: United States, 1987–1992

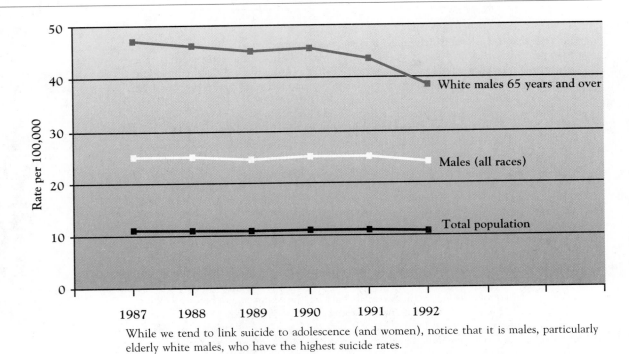

While we tend to link suicide to adolescence (and women), notice that it is males, particularly elderly white males, who have the highest suicide rates.

Source: National Center for Health Statistics, 1995, *Healthy People 2000: Review, 1994,* Hyattsville, MD: *Public Health Service.*

hopeless, and helpless, he or she is depressed. We see the same emphasis on helplessness and hopelessness in the most popular behavioral perspective on depression, too.

BEHAVIORAL VIEWPOINTS.   In the early 1970s, psychologist Martin Seligman noticed that dogs subjected to electrical shocks they could not escape developed strange symptoms. They became apathetic, seemed sad, and were unable to think or move quickly. When in a situation where they could avoid the shocks, they froze. They had learned to be helpless, a lesson in the futility of acting that had spread even to events they could control.

Seligman believed that he had hit on an ideal model for how human depression develops. After a series of inescapable losses, people come to feel that they are helpless or unable to control their destiny. This *learned helplessness* affects their world outlook and the way they behave. They become apathetic, withdrawn, hopeless, depressed (Seligman, 1975).

Seligman and his colleagues then moved beyond focusing on outer-world events. It is their attributions about losses and failures, not the actual experiences themselves, that cause people to become depressed. Depression-prone individuals have a *pessimistic explanatory style.* Rather than seeing negative events as temporary, situational, and extrinsic to the self, they interpret failures in a global, personal, never-changing light (Abramson, Seligman, and Teasdale, 1978).

Seligman's *cognitive behavioral* perspective on depression is not the only behavioral point of view. According to Peter Lewinsohn, the depressive process is set in motion when highly reinforcing "scripted" behavior patterns are disrupted. For instance, this blockage might occur if a person is fired from a job he loves or his fiancée suddenly breaks the engagement off. According to Lewinsohn, the individual then withdraws, further decreasing the frequency of reinforcing events. According to this *traditional behavioral* framework, it is the dearth of adequate reinforcers or lack of pleasurable experiences that produce the depressive symptoms (Hoberman and Lewinsohn, 1989).

BIOLOGICAL TREATMENTS.   The first line of attack against severe depression is **anti-depressant drugs.** These medications are especially effective when, as in the situation described in Feature 9–2, serious symptoms seem to develop "out of the blue." Anti-depressants change the level of neurotransmitters, the chemicals by which neurons communicate with one another. Unlike the anti-anxiety medications, these drugs are not addictive. They cannot be taken to artificially inflate mood. They specifically attack the biochemical problem causing depression so the person suffering from this disorder feels normal again.

However, because of side effects, anti-depressants cannot be used with every individual. They take at least two weeks to have an effect. They must be used more cautiously in older adults. So, in emergencies, such as when the person is suicidal, there is **electroconvulsive therapy** (ECT).

With this intervention, the person is administered an anesthetic and then an electrical current is put through the brain. This causes convulsions, after which the person wakes up. ECT is controversial because it seems barbaric and because there are concerns that it impairs memory and may cause brain damage. However, though its effects are temporary, this treatment can be lifesaving when the person does not respond to medications and immediate intervention is required (Welch, 1989).

These treatments have restored meaningful life to people who had been just existing. However, they are not panaceas. Biological interventions work best with severe depressions. Psychotherapy can be even more effective, especially when there are clear external causes for the person's symptoms (Hollon, DeRubeis, and Seligman, 1992).

PSYCHODYNAMIC/INTERPERSONAL TREATMENTS.   In psychoanalytic therapy, patients are encouraged to look at how their childhood experiences are skewing their perceptions of current events. Can the depth of their despair be understood as emanating from losses in their early years?

Drawing on the idea that depression involves disturbed relationships, a type of psychotherapy called **interpersonal therapy** has an excellent record of success. In this treatment, the emphasis is not on early childhood, but on relationship problems in current life. Patients learn to identify the losses and disturbed interactions that are producing the depression. The goal is to develop new, secure attachments in life (Weissman and Klerman, 1990).

BEHAVIORAL TREATMENTS.   The most popular behavioral treatment for depression, Aaron Beck's **cognitive behavioral approach,** is based on an idea very much like Seligman's: Depression is caused by irrational, unrealistically negative thoughts. According to Beck (1973), these cognitions set off the mood changes, loss of interest in life, slowed thinking and moving, and other symptoms that characterize the disorder. The goal of treatment is to change the depression-generating thoughts.

In the same way as we saw earlier with *relapse prevention,* the client works to identify the content of these cognitions and the triggering situations that set them off. Because the negative thoughts have an automatic quality, this task can be surprisingly difficult. People may know that they feel depressed, but not be able to spell out why. All they feel is symptoms, not the chain of cognitions that is their cause.

APPLICATIONS AND INTERVENTIONS

anti-depressant drugs
Medications that eradicate depressive symptoms.

electroconvulsive therapy
Emergency biological intervention for depression in which an electric current is put through the individual's brain.

interpersonal therapy
Psychoanalytically oriented treatment for depression involving exploring and working to repair relationship disturbances.

cognitive behavioral approach
Cognitive behavioral treatment for depression developed by Aaron Beck involving identifying and changing depression-producing cognitions or thoughts.

Table 9-4

A Partially Completed Dysfunctional Thought Record and the Realistic Responses That Might Be Substituted

Situation: At home, reading—waiting for my son to call.

Emotions: Sad, miserable, abandoned, and lonely.

Automatic Thoughts: Why didn't he call? Why is he rejecting me? I feel so miserable. I don't know what to do. Why does this always happen to me? I just can't go on like this. What did I do wrong?

More Rational Thoughts: (1) Just because he didn't call does not mean that he is rejecting me. I have no proof of rejection. In fact he visited me two weeks ago. (2) It's not true that this always happens to me. Sometimes I don't call him when I say I will and he doesn't think it's the end of the world. (3) Besides, why should I think his not calling is my fault? He may be working late again. (4) Even if he is upset with me for some reason, it does not automatically mean he will not speak to me again. (5) Suppose he is angry with me. I've survived problems with my son before. All relationships have ups and downs. I'll try first to find out if anything is wrong before I give up on myself!

The elderly woman first identifies specific triggering stimuli and then pinpoints the depression-engendering thoughts. Then she substitutes more appropriate, non-depression-generating cognitions.

Source: Adapted from Gallagher, D. and Thompson, L.W. Cognitive therapy for depression in the elderly: A promising model for treatment and research. In L.D. Breslau and M.R. Haug (Eds.) *Depression and Aging: Causes, Care, and Consequences.* Copyright © 1983 Springer Publishing Company, New York, 10012. Used by permission.

According to Beck, depression-generating thoughts magnify the unhappy significance of a single event. They involve overgeneralization. Based on one negative experience, a catastrophic conclusion is reached. They selectively abstract an unwarranted conclusion from what has happened. They arbitrarily infer something negative from a neutral event.

After identifying these thoughts, the person monitors them, becomes aware of their illogic, and substitutes more rational cognitions. A woman may learn to think, "I'm exaggerating," "I'm taking this out of context," "I'm jumping to conclusions" when an idea of gloom and doom arises (see Table 9–4). The therapist encourages this self-monitoring by challenging the logic behind each thought. The hope is that eventually the person will view any unrealistic cognition objectively and replace it with a non-depression-generating idea (Gallagher and Thompson, 1983; Jarrett and Rush, 1989).

Lewinsohn has devised an alternative treatment for depression based on his hypothesis that people become depressed due to a lack of pleasurable experiences. In this therapy, clients try to identify potential reinforcers. For instance, using the example of the older woman sitting by the phone described in Table 9–4, Lewinsohn might have the client think of alternatives to waiting that might give her pleasure, such as going to the movies, or watching a video, or reading a good book. She then would substitute these experiences for just waiting fruitlessly for the call. Moreover, Lewinsohn would work with the woman to develop a richer set of reinforcing experiences: pleasurable events that did not depend on her son, sources of satisfaction she could engineer on her own (Hoberman and Lewinsohn, 1989).

How effective are these strategies? In a National Institute of Mental Health–sponsored study in which cognitive behavior therapy, a widely used anti-depressant, and interpersonal therapy were compared, all treatments were superior to a placebo. At the end of four months, two-thirds of the depressed patients were symptom-free (Klerman, 1989). While the specific interventions that work best vary from person to person, as we saw to some degree with alcoholism and phobias, depression is an eminently treatable disease.

KEY TERMS & CONCEPTS

epidemiologic studies
Diagnostic and Statistical Manual of Mental Disorders (DSM)
Epidemiologic Catchment Area Survey
National Comorbidity Survey
comorbidity
lifetime prevalence
psychotherapy
psychotropic drugs
biological revolution in psychiatry
DSM-IV
alcohol dependence and alcohol abuse
Alcoholics Anonymous
outcome studies
relapse prevention
phobias
agoraphobia
panic attacks
anti-anxiety agents
exposure therapy
depression
anti-depressant drugs
electroconvulsive therapy
interpersonal therapy
cognitive behavioral approach

RECOMMENDED READINGS
General Reference

American Psychiatric Association. (1994). *Diagnostic and statistical manual of mental disorders* (4th ed.). Washington, DC: Author.

> *The current manual for diagnosing mental disorders is required reading for every person in the mental health field.*

Aging and Mental Health

Birren, J. E., and Sloane, R. B. (Eds.). (1989). *Handbook of mental health and aging* (2nd ed.). Englewood Cliffs, NJ: Prentice-Hall.

> *This is a classic textbook on aging and mental health.*

Mental health and aging: Problems and prospects. (1993, Winter/Spring). *Generations, 17.*

> *The whole issue is devoted to aging and mental health.*

Alcoholism

U.S. Department of Health and Human Services. (1990). *Seventh special report to the U.S. Congress on alcohol and health*. Rockville, MD: National Institute on Alcohol Abuse and Alcoholism.

Gallant, D. M. (1987). *Alcoholism: A guide to diagnosis, interventions, and treatment*. New York: W. W. Norton.
> These two books provide comprehensive reviews of alcoholism research and treatment.

Marlatt, G. A., and Gordon, J. R. (1985). *Relapse prevention*. New York: Guilford Press.
> Marlatt describes his therapy for alcoholism.

Anxiety Disorders and Depression

Barlow, D. H. (1988). *Anxiety and its disorders: The nature and treatment of anxiety and panic*. New York: Guilford Press.
> Barlow provides a comprehensive look at anxiety disorders, their causes, and their treatments from a behavioral point of view.

McGrath, E., Keita, G. P., Strickland, B. R., and Russo, N. F. (Eds.). (1990). *Women and depression: Risk factors and treatment issues*. Washington, DC: American Psychological Association.
> This book thoroughly explores depression in women.

Styron, W. (1990). *Darkness visible*. New York: Vintage.
> Styron provides a beautifully written autobiographical account of his depression and eventual cure.

Part IV

THE SOCIAL DIMENSION

Love, Marriage, and Intimate Relationships

John rarely dated during high school. He met Hope during his first semester at college, and they were inseparable for the next four years. A year after graduating they got married. John and Hope have similar values. They are the same religion. John is financially comfortable, with a grandfather willing to help pay for law school. John's mother should be happy. She cannot imagine having a more lovely daughter-in-law. She takes comfort knowing John and Hope have been living together, most recently in "significant other" housing at the graduate dorm. She simply believes that her son, at age 22, is too young to get married. He never had the experience of living on his own. This is why she suggested a prenuptial agreement. It seems shortsighted to enter any marriage today without protection, especially so prematurely in life.

THE CHANGING CONTEXT OF DATING AND MARRIAGE

You might be astonished if you were transported back in time to the 1950s. How strange this mother's worries would seem! A half century ago people were *expected* to date briefly and get married soon after their teens. Young adults went straight from their parents' homes to marriage. The idea that a couple would even mention divorce, much less formalize that possibility at their engagement, would be offensive; the concept of university-sponsored "significant other" housing bizarre.

In the 1950s, marriage was more of an ironclad bond. Most Americans believed that an unhappily married couple had a moral obligation to stay together until their children were adults. Children of divorce were looked down on as products of "a broken home." Even more disapproval was reserved for children called illegitimate, those conceived out of wedlock. If a woman became pregnant, she had to get married or give her baby up for adoption. It was unacceptable to raise a child alone (Council on Families in America, 1995; Furstenberg and Cherlin, 1991).

The Decline of Marriage

Today young adults fan out in all directions, living in a variety of types of housing after they leave home (Thornton, Young-DeMarco, and Goldscheider, 1993). The years of dating have been extended; among *middle-class couples*, the average age of marriage is at an all-time high. Attitudes toward the marital bond have totally changed. Today, rather than staying in an unhappy marriage, couples are often advised to leave if the feelings are

The rituals, expectations, and joyous emotions when couples marry endure. For these 1990s newlyweds, it is the prospects of staying married for life that have drastically declined.

Key Indicators of the Deinstitutionalization of Marriage in the United States, 1960–1990

Table 10-1

	1960	1990
Percentage of childbirths outside of marriage	5	30+
Probability of one's marriage ending in divorce	about14%	66%
Percentage of married adults	72	62
Percentage of children living with one parent	9	40
Percentage of adult life spent with spouse and children	62	43

Source: Council on Families in America, 1995, *Marriage in America: A Report to the Nation,* New York, Institute for American Values.

not there. Two-thirds of young adults will eventually divorce (Weitzman, 1985). As almost one-third of U.S. babies are born to single women, even *getting married* is much less crucial for adult life (Council on Families in America, 1995).

Many experts view this historic **deinstitutionalization of marriage** as an acceleration of a long-term trend (Popenoe, 1988, 1990, 1993). Attitudes toward marriage gradually became more liberal during the first part of the twentieth century. However, after World War II, we once again returned to traditional values and family forms. A booming economy had come on the heels of the deprivation of the Depression and the devastation of war. Life was secure. The American Dream was within reach. For the first time, even working-class couples could have a house, a working husband, and a stay-at-home wife (Coonts, 1992; Popenoe, 1988). This "Leave It to Beaver" time in the United States, which glorified the nuclear family with traditional sex roles, made the changes of the late 1960s look totally new—the women's movement, the *sexual revolution,* the counterculture revolution that stressed freedom from restrictions and rules.

These related revolutions produced the changes in Table 10-1: the decline in marriage and the rise in other family forms. The women's movement, with its emphasis on women as breadwinners and the need to have a career, made living alone a financially possible option for many more women. The sexual revolution, described in Chapter 4, meant men and women no longer needed to get married to satisfy this basic desire. The counterculture movement weakened the strong social pressures against divorce and single motherhood. At the heart of these changes, many experts feel, lay a shift in values from the importance of responsibility and obligation to a glorification of self-expression (Popenoe, 1988, 1993; Rossi, 1987). In a 1960s society bursting with adolescents (the baby boomers), freedom, rebellion, and "doing one's own thing" came to be seen as the key to happiness during adult life. Once marriage became optional and depended on feeling a certain way, it had to become a fragile state (Furstenberg and Cherlin, 1991).

deinstitutionalization of marriage
Phrase describing the fact that marriage is no longer the standard adult life-state in the United States.

The Rise of Cohabitation

People still care about having committed relationships. As Figure 10-1 shows, the decline in marriage has been accompanied by a dramatic increase in **cohabitation,** living together without being married. In 1988, by their early thirties almost half of all Americans reported having lived with someone, a dramatic change since the 1950s, when this lifestyle was condemned as "living in sin." In fact, cohabitation may be a partial substitute for marriage for young adults (Cunningham and Antill, 1994). Most people who live together are under age 35 (Goldscheider and Waite, 1991). If we assume that cohabitation rates count as a kind of marital arrangement among these people, the decline in marriage is dramatically reduced (Popenoe, 1993; Qian and Preston, 1993).

cohabitation
Practice of living together outside of marriage.

Figure 10-1

Unmarried Couples in Selected Years, 1970–1994

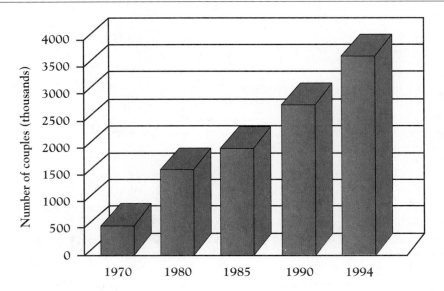

This chart illustrates the dramatic increase in cohabitation that has occurred since 1970. Notice, in particular, that there was a threefold rise in the number of cohabiting couples during the decade of the 1970s.

Source: U.S. Bureau of the Census, 1995, *Statistical Abstract of the United States 1995, The National Data Book,* Washington, DC: U.S. Government Printing Office.

Americans are still a bit uneasy about cohabitation. As late as 1989 only about one-third of adults had *no* reservations about these relationships (Orthner, 1990). Couples who live together tend to have less traditional values. They are more interested in autonomy and independence than the average person their age (Cunningham and Antill, 1994). Choices to live together tend to be made more lightly, as cohabiting couples are more different in terms of religion and ethnicity than those who do wed (Schoen and Weinick, 1993). Whether a young adult cohabits is also influenced by how the older generation feels.

In tracing intergenerational values during the late 1970s and 1980s, William Axinn and Arland Thornton (1993) found that, if a mother had a more accepting attitude toward living together, her child was more likely to cohabit. Interestingly this connection applied to daughters alone. Sons' choices were independent of how mothers' felt. A female child's behavior was highly related to her mother's attitudes. In other words, there is an interesting gender difference in parental influence on our lifestyle choices as young adults. Possibly because girls care more about family approval or because their actions are more carefully monitored and controlled, the impact of what the older generation thinks weighs heavier on daughters than sons.

Parent/child influence is not a one-way street. Because their study was longitudinal, the researchers could examine changes in the older generation's attitudes in the light of their children's choices. Parents' feelings about living together became more positive if their children decided to cohabit.

Percentage of College Students Reporting That These Relationships Are Families

Table 10-2

(Students were asked, "Are these people a family?")

Anna and Anders are a middle-aged couple without children.	84
Bodil and Bertil are a married couple with one child.	100
Cecilia is a divorced mother living with her child.	93
Curt is a divorced father not living with his child.	68
Cecilia and Curt are divorced.	17
Doris and David are grandparents not living with this child.	81
Karl and Krister are living together. They have no children.	39
Jan, Joanna, and Jesper are adult siblings living together.	92
Ingmar and Inger cohabitated and had a child. They now are separated. The child lives with Ingmar.	37

Most people do not consider cohabiting (or divorced) adults to be a family. Notice that "family" involves a sibling, parental, or marital relation alone.

Source: D. Y. Ford, An exploration of perceptions of alternative family structures among university students, *Family Relations*, 43. Copyright 1994. By the National Council on Family Relations, 3989 Central Avenue, N.E., Suite 550, Minneapolis, MN 55421. Reprinted by permission.

So older people seem to have adjusted their values to fit the new ideas. Unfortunately other research contradicts the argument we often hear in favor of living together, that cohabiting improves the chance of making the right marital choice. Couples who live together are *not* more likely to stay together once they do get married. In fact, young adults who live with several different people before marrying have a higher risk of getting divorced (DeMaris and MacDonald, 1993).

No one feels cohabitation is an absolute substitute for marriage, as even couples who live together often say they plan to marry at some point. The Census Bureau does not consider cohabiting couples a family, a view that is shared by your contemporaries. Donna Ford (1994) polled 462 college students, asking which of a variety of relationships they would call a family. Notice from Table 10-2 that, while most people believe that married couples without children and single parents with children are a family, less than half think that couples living together *without being married* deserve that name.

The truth is that Americans have not given up on marriage. We still see it as an important goal. This is apparent when we look at one interesting gauge of society's attitudes toward relationships, the articles in women's magazines. When researchers analyzed magazine articles from 1974 to 1990, the number one theme continued to be relationships leading to marriage (Prusank, Duran, and DeLillo, 1993). Polls show the vast majority of Americans want to be married, the same proportion as 30 years ago (Orthner, 1990). This desire is just as strong among the young. In 1986, the fraction of U.S. high school seniors who said they eventually wanted to get married (97 percent of women and 95 percent of men) had not changed at all in spite of the changing statistics on the single life (Goldscheider and Waite, 1991).

As marriage remains a central life goal, while the number of people who are actually married has dramatically declined, activities centering around selecting a mate loom larger in adult life. What do we know about this selection process?

MATE SELECTION

stimulus-value-role theory
Theory developed by Murstein dividing mate selection and courtship into three distinct phases.

Bernard Murstein (1980), in his **stimulus-value-role theory,** divides mate selection into three phases. During the *stimulus phase*, we see a potential partner and make our first assessment: Could this be a good choice for me? Would this person want me? Since we know nothing about this individual's inner qualities, our judgment is based on superficial signs, such as the person's looks or style of dress. In this screening, we automatically compare our own "reinforcement value" to the other person's along a number of dimensions. (True, I am not as good looking, but she may find me desirable because I am more well educated.) If the person seems of equivalent value, we decide that the individual is a reasonable choice to pursue.

Then we enter the *value comparison* stage. Here we are concerned with our fit with one another in terms of interests, attitudes, and feelings about the world: Does this person share similar beliefs? Does she have the same orientation to life? Do we enjoy doing similar things? If these world views mesh, we enter the *role stage,* in which we actually test out how we function together as a couple.

homogamy
Practice of dating and marrying similar others.

Notice that Murstein feels that **homogamy** (similarity) is the basis on which people select a mate. The idea that opposites attract is not true. The tendency is to gravitiate to someone as similar to us as possible, both in external desirability and in interests, needs, and attitudes. A second assumption Murstein makes is that courtship follows a predictable path. Everyone goes through the same pattern, at each stage jumping closer to marriage and weeding out people who are not an appropriate fit.

Homogamy and Mate Selection

The research on who marries whom clearly supports Murstein's first assumption. From physique to physical attractiveness, from political philosophy to phobic tendencies, couples do tend to be similar. One group of researchers even found husband/wife similarities in how well they could read an eye chart (Byrne and Murnen, 1988)!

This homogamy is especially apparent in long-married elderly people, those wonderful couples who seem able to read each other's thoughts (Atchley and Miller, 1983; Lauer, Lauer, and Kerr, 1990). We also see it early on. Even college student couples are often very much alike in their general attitudes and world views (Hendrick, Hendrick, and Adler, 1988).

The same general trend applies to religion, ethnicity, and social class. Not only, as Murstein implies, does choosing someone similar in these basic areas of life make us more likely to have compatible ideas, but also our social circles are often defined by religion, class, and ethnic group. This means that we have more chance of meeting and falling in love with "our own kind" (Michael et al, 1994).

heterogamy
Practice of dating and marrying dissimilar others.

RELIGION, ETHNICITY, AND INTERMARRIAGE. However, in our increasingly multicultural society, there is more religious and ethnic **heterogamy** (dissimilarity) than in the past. Along with alternatives to marriage becoming more condoned, it has become more acceptable to marry outside of one's religion and, to some degree, outside of one's race. Our chance of marrying heterogamously is higher under certain conditions. If our own parents are of different ethnicities or religions, we are more apt marry outside of our group. If the number of within-group choices is small—for instance, you are one of only a few Jewish families in your town—you may be more likely to select a partner different than yourself (Alba and Golden, 1986). However, again, the most important force lies in your attitudes and especially your social milieu. As Feature 10-1 shows, among groups where intermarriage is severely condemned, the rules are still just as rigid. The whole context of dating is shaped in the service of the need to select a

10-1 The Adult Experience: An Indian/Islamic Perspective on Dating in the United States

To remind us that our "typical" American dating practices do not fit all Americans, here are excerpts of a conversation with Alera, an Indian student in my class:

Dating is not allowed in my religion. That is a very strict rule. If I were to date someone and he was not Muslim, I couldn't marry him. If I met a Muslim, I might be allowed to see him, but it wouldn't be dating in the traditional sense. You can't date for the experience. It's always for the purpose of marriage.

We have loosened up a bit. My parents had a totally arranged marriage. My dad's family came to our village and said they wanted my mother. Then, a few days later, she was married, just like that. Now she says, if she had a choice, she would not have married dad. She and my father argue all the time. But because of religion and because of us, she stays married.

When I was in second grade, we moved from India to Michigan, where there is a big Muslim community. Eight years ago my dad got a better job offer, and we moved to Tennessee. In Michigan, all my friends were Indian, either Hindu or Muslim, and now I don't have one friend who is Muslim. They are all either Hindu or American. They are real cool, but their values are different.

My brother, who is 29 and about to get married, has only dated two girls. In Michigan, we have a Muslim matchmaking bureau. They have an album of girls' photos with biodata sheets in which they describe themselves. When my brother decided he wanted to get married, he went to the bureau and picked out a girl living in Ohio. They corresponded for awhile and then got engaged the first time they met. Then, a few weeks before they were supposed to marry, he called the wedding off. The girl was devastated. He met the woman he is about to marry now at a friend's wedding. She lives in Canada. Every time he visits, her mom chaperones them. The three of them go shopping or to a movie. They don't even act like they are dating. They are not allowed to be alone together, even to kiss. My sister is also engaged, but, once again, when they see each other, it's always with my brother or a friend.

I did have a problem with our practices, but I've accepted them. A few years ago I fell in love with a Hindu guy, but after awhile I realized I had to end the relationship. My mom, it would have broken her heart. I care too much about my family. People would look down on my parents if I married outside of our religion. When I lived at home, I didn't date. Then, when I went to college, I went crazy for about a year. But, let's say that I marry someone who is Hindu or, even worse, Catholic or Jewish, I mean what religion would my children be? Muslims are good people. We are very focused. We have morals. I want to give my children that sense of identity. So I'm comfortable waiting until I meet an acceptable Muslim man.

homogamous mate. As we look more broadly at ethnic intermarriage in the United States, the interesting variations from group to group also make sense when viewed in terms of the importance society places on "selecting among one's own."

While somewhat more tolerated, marriages between whites and racial/ethnic minorities—that is, African Americans, Asian Americans, Hispanic Americans, and Native Americans—are still not widely socially acceptable. They do raise eyebrows. They can cause problems both within one's ethnic group and outside. This partly explains why in the United States it is still relatively unusual to marry "across the color line"—with one exception. Perhaps because they have a history of intermarriage dating back to Colonial times and are our nation's smallest minority, Native Americans are

Though they may feel like they are sharing a private moment on this park bench, this inter-racial couple is apt to evoke, not just considerable attention, but strong emotions from practically every person who passes by.

several times *more likely* to intermarry than not (Alba and Golden, 1986). There also is an interesting gender difference in intermarriage. Among every minority group except African Americans, women are more likely to intermarry than men.

Let's focus on African-American/white intermarriage, still the most rare type of mixed marriage in the United States. In 1989, only 4 percent of U.S. marriages involved African Americans and whites (U.S. Bureau of the Census, 1993). One reason is that the prejudices against interracial marriages are especially strong. As we will see in Chapter 11, a contributing factor may be that for African Americans in particular in recent decades marriage rates in general have dramatically declined. Even the greater residential segregation of African Americans may work against meeting and marrying outside of one's race. Still, some people do overcome these hurdles and take the step.

Belinda Tucker and Claudia Mitchell-Kernan (1990) decided to explore who takes this unusual path. Their focus was Los Angeles, and their source was county census information provided by the African-American males and females who reported being married to someone of a different race in 1980.

For both men and women, the predictors were identical. African Americans who intermarried were younger, more likely to have been married before, and more discrepant in age from their spouses. They also were more likely to have come from somewhere else; often they were either originally from the North or foreign born.

One interpretation is that these are all signs of being more liberal. Younger people have wider interethnic exposure and may have less rigid ideas about marrying within their own race. People who have been divorced, reject the typical practice of marrying someone fairly similar in age, and move to another place may also be more free-spirited than their contemporaries.

Migrating in itself may raise the chance of intermarriage. When we leave home, it may be more easy to shed the circles we are running in, circles more likely to be defined by race. From miles away, the social controls of family and friends that work against marrying someone "not our kind" may weaken. So not only may moving far away broaden our horizons, but also it may broaden our choice of potential partners (Surra, 1990).

In summary, while changing in interesting ways that reflect society's attitudes and prejudices, homogamy is still the number one principle of dating and mating. But, by focusing only on similarity, we are leaving out one well-known difference in mate selection—the different criteria that are important to women and men.

Gender and Mate Selection

Men are supposed to care more about physical beauty and youth in choosing a partner. Intelligence, power, and financial success are supposed to weigh more heavily for women in selecting a man. Traditionally women are supposed to "marry up" in social status. Men "marry down," preferring less well educated, less successful women than themselves.

According to a **socio-evolutionary theory of mate selection,** these preferences are universal, are built into our species, and have evolutionary value (Kenrick, Groth, Trost, and Sadalla, 1993). In order to have viable offspring, males are biologically programmed to select for qualities such as youth, vigor, beauty, and health. Because they need protection when caring for their offspring, females are genetically predisposed to select a partner who is powerful and dominant, the male who has the resources to best protect.

Are looks really more important to men? Alan Feingold (1990) decided to test the truth of this stereotype by looking at four sources: questionnaires in which men and women describe their ideal partners, qualities listed by women and men in personals columns, psychological experiments exploring physical attractiveness and liking, and research relating attractiveness to male/female popularity in life.

For each type of study, the truism was true. In laboratory experiments, males were more likely than females to prefer an attractive stranger. Surveys of high school and college students showed that good looks were especially strongly related to popularity for girls.

In the research examining how people actually act, there was not a huge difference. Good looks were important to both men and women, but a bit more salient for males. The gender difference was much greater in research examining descriptions of one's ideal mate. In one analysis of personals columns, one of every three men mentioned they wanted an attractive woman, while only one in seven women did.

So, as we might expect, men do care more about beauty, with the qualification that this applies more to the kind of woman they *say* they want than to how they actually behave. When we look at the idea that women marry up in age and status and men marry down, we find interesting surprises.

In comparing marriage records in two southern states at the end of the 1960s and a decade later, Robert Schoen and John Wooldredge (1989) found that in both years women did tend to marry older, more well educated men. However, couples who married in the late 1970s were more homogamous in education and age. In analyzing the total U.S. population, other researchers found the same trend: more homogamy during the 1980s than in previous years (Qian and Preston, 1993).

This pattern also reveals how the United States has changed. In the past, the inequalities in schooling and especially in earnings between the sexes ensured that, even if there were no built-in biological preferences, women had to "marry up" and men "marry down." Today, as we will see in Chapter 13, this gender gulf has narrowed. Women are much more equal in status to men. As the baby boomers grow older, men should be forced to choose women closer in age because there is a smaller population of young women from which to select.

However, if socio-evolutionary theory really holds, in spite of these changes, people should attempt to fulfill their biological preferences. Men should want younger, less well educated women. Being highly educated, economically well off, and older should work to a woman's detriment in finding a mate.

This is not the case. In the United States during most of the 1970s, marriage rates declined for everyone. But starting toward the end of the decade, while continuing to fall off for women under age 25, marriage chances for college-educated older women (aged 25–34) rose. Contrary to socio-evolutionary theory and the depressing predictions in the media, college-educated women in their late twenties and early thirties are more likely to get married than any other group! While men still may want attractive women, in this

socio-evolutionary theory of mate selection
Theory that innate predispositions developed in evolution drive gender differences in mate-seeking behavior.

day and age they clearly care about having economically and intellectually desirable partners, too (Lichter, McLaughlin, Kephart, and Landry, 1992; Qian and Preston, 1993).

Socio-evolutionary theory also ignores the fact that criteria for choosing a partner may shift over time. Remember that the principle that men care more about beauty applies more to what people *say* they want than to their actual behavior. When researchers examined how self-ratings of intelligence and personality related to the qualities men reported they wanted in women at various levels of involvement, their subjects reported being more interested in finding a woman similar to themselves in these inner attributes when they imagined a woman they would marry versus a one-night stand (Kenrick et al., 1993).

The idea that our criteria change at different levels of involvement brings us back to the part of Murstein's theory describing how relationships develop. Does Murstein's idea that couples go through stages as they draw closer to marriage fit the way relationships really change?

How Relationships Develop

CHANGES WITHIN THE COUPLE. After asking newlyweds to describe how their relationships developed, one group of researchers identified three patterns: a slow, rocky path; a path that developed quickly at first and then lost momentum; and the gradual rise toward commitment that Murstein spells out (Cate, Huston, and Nessel-roade, 1986). Even though we should be cautious about these findings, as these psychologists did not actually follow these couples as their relationship progressed, this study suggests that the way people get to marriage may be much less patterned than Murstein predicts.

Even if there is a predictable path to marriage, it does not have to be the one Murstein spells out. Timothy Stephen (1984) agrees with Murstein that homogamy guides whom we date and marry and that courtship follows a universal pattern, but believes that couples construct a shared world view. Rather than matching up on unchanging traits, when a relationship is working out a couple *actively* attempts to become more similar in interests and values in order to have a love that endures.

Murstein has responded to these challenges by making his theory less rigid (Surra, 1990). While still using the words *stimulus, value,* and *role phase,* Murstein now describes the stages as less distinct. They meld into one another and are measured in relative terms.

So far, we have focused on what happens *within* the couple. Now we turn to the couple in relation to the outside world.

SOCIAL NETWORK CHANGES. When Robert Milardo, Michael Johnson, and Ted Huston (1983) asked dating couples to report on the time they spent with others, they found that, as the relationship became more serious, subjects interacted with fewer people and spent less time with those they did see. In other words, as couples get more involved, their involvement with others shrinks.

As Catherine Surra (1990) points out, this pulling back is predictable from emotional, cognitive, and behavioral points of view. Putting our emotional eggs in one basket must mean that our feelings for other people have to take second place. Couples intellectually determine to withdraw in order to solidify their sense of separation as a unit apart from the wider world. Finally, in terms of behavior, we simply have less time to be with others when a romance demands more of our time.

However, the idea that couples *just* withdraw from the outside world turns out to be too simplistic. In examining what happened as daters grew more serious, Surra did find that people withdrew from acquaintances and fairly good friends, but not from their closest friends and family. In fact, when a couple was considering marriage, they increased their contacts with these close ties because each person wanted to make the partner's social network one's own.

Another study, exploring how often college students talked about their relationships, also revealed that couples reached out more to close friends and family as they grew very involved (Baxter and Widenmann, 1993). However, some people felt it was important *not* to reveal what was happening to those closest in their lives. Most often the objects of these active efforts at *non-disclosure* were parents, the reason being that these young adults were afraid that their parents might disapprove of their relationship.

So we cannot make general statements. Some people reach out as their relationship grows serious; others hide their love. We need to know the priorities of the couple: How critical is it that a partner get to know and like my friends? How much a part of our lives will family be? What reaction do we anticipate from the people close to us when we tell them about our relationship?

On the other hand, every couple must withdraw from one class of people, alternative possibilities, men or women they might otherwise date. What happens to our feelings about these other fish in the sea when we are in a relationship?

As Jeffrey Simpson, Steven Gangestad, and Margaret Lerma (1990) discovered, we may unconsciously develop defenses against their lures. The researchers (falsely) told undergraduates that they were studying "psychology and advertising." They asked subjects to rate magazine ads for persuasiveness and, as an aside, to rate the attractiveness of the male or female model in the ad. People who reported seriously dating someone rated the opposite sex models as less attractive, suggesting that one way we have of maintaining our commitment in a relationship is to develop perceptual blinders. We guard against the pull of competing possibilities by seeing the competition in a dimmer light.

These studies relate to the more rational aspects of relationships, leaving out the motor that drives the process along, love.

LOVE

Love, the most important human feeling, is one of the vaguest labels in the language. We love ice cream sundaes, friends, children, a trip to the park. Even if limited to partner relationships, love is a mixture of passion, admiration, and caring, an umbrella term for attitudes of different kinds. Here are three efforts by psychologists to intrude on the territory of poets and scientifically pin down love.

Hatfield's Passionate Versus Companionate Love

Drawing on the distinctions among "puppy love," a "crush," "infatuation," and "mature" or "true" love, Elaine Hatfield (1988 p. 191) spells out two different types of love—**passionate love** and **companionate love.** Passionate love is "a state of intense longing for union with another, which (if reciprocated) . . . is associated with fulfillment and ecstasy." Companionate love is "the affection we feel for those with whom our lives are deeply entwined."

passionate and companionate love
Two opposing types of love spelled out by Hatfield.

Passionate love involves thinking about the person continually and engineering every activity around the chance of meeting one's love. However, its essence is emotional; the thrill that its core is intense sexual arousal. Passionate love depends on lows as much as highs. Strong emotions *of any kind* propel this type of love.

While at first we might be skeptical, let's consider how unpleasant feelings can heighten passionate love. This explains why lovemaking can be so arousing after an argument and why going through a terrifying experience with someone suddenly may make that person an object of desire. In fact, researchers have demonstrated that passion can be produced by a range of painful experiences from anxiety, to embarrassment, to jealousy, anger, and even grief.

In one study, undergraduate males were told that the psychological research they had signed up for involved the effect of electric shock on learning. One group was told that the shocks would be minor; the other was warned that they would be intense. Before beginning, the researcher asked how attracted each man felt to his so-called partner in the experiment, a beautiful woman. As expected, the terrified men rated their partners as sexier and more desirable than the calmer men. In a related study, male college students were instructed to cross either an unsteady bridge or a secure bridge to get over a river. At the end was a beautiful woman, who gave them her phone number (supposedly to explain the study's purpose). Nine of the 32 men who navigated the scary suspension bridge called; only two who crossed the solid bridge did (Dutton and Aron, 1974).

These studies demonstrate that passion can be stimulated by intense physiological and visual cues. As the words *crush* and *infatuation* imply, passion does not depend on knowing the person at all. Companionate love involves knowing the person, understanding how he or she thinks, feels, and behaves. According to Hatfield, companionate love involves pure positive feelings. The lover cares deeply about the other's well-being and is relaxed and comfortable. While this type of love does not involve dramatic shifts from elation to despair, it offers warmth, security, and the sense of being loved and accepted for who we are.

Hatfield's dichotomy raises interesting questions. Are the two types of love incompatible because they occur under such different conditions? Must passion, which depends on insecurity and fantasy, erode when we get to know and feel secure with the person we love? These are the topics Robert Sternberg tackles in his **triangular theory of love.**

Sternberg's Triangular Theory of Love

Robert Sternberg (1988b), the psychologist whose research on practical intelligence was discussed in Chapter 6, has also developed a creative theory of love. Sternberg breaks love into three components: **passion, intimacy,** and **decision/commitment.** As Figure 10-2 shows, each component forms the points on a triangle.

Sternberg's passion component is similar to Hatfield's passionate love: an intense desire that has sexual arousal as its basis. Intimacy refers to feelings Hatfield would label companionate love: genuinely knowing the other person, achieving mutual understanding, having concern for the other's welfare, being able to depend on the person. Decision/commitment also relates to companionate love: committing to marriage, deciding that "this person is the one."

Figure 10-2 shows the different relationships that are derived by combining passion, intimacy, and commitment. Six are particularly interesting because they fit the types of relationships often seen in daily life.

Passion without intimacy and commitment describes infatuation, the intense emotion for an idealized person that we do not really know. Most of us have had these fantasies, an obsession with the girl down the street, a movie star, or a handsome professor. At another extreme, intimacy without passion or commitment describes liking, the warm, asexual feelings of closeness we have with a best friend. Decision/commitment without passion or intimacy epitomizes what are called "empty marriages" or "his and her unions." A couple stays together, but they live sterile, emotionally separate lives.

Passion combined with intimacy defines romantic love. A couple is intensely sexually attracted and knows one another well, but has not made a final commitment to get married. On another side of the triangle, we find intimacy and commitment without

triangular theory of love
Sternberg's categorization of love into different types based on combining three qualities forming the poles of a triangle.

passion
Pole of Sternberg's triangle referring to intense sexual arousal.

intimacy
Pole of Sternberg's triangle referring to love based on truly knowing the other person.

decision/commitment
Pole of Sternberg's triangle describing commitment to a partner for life.

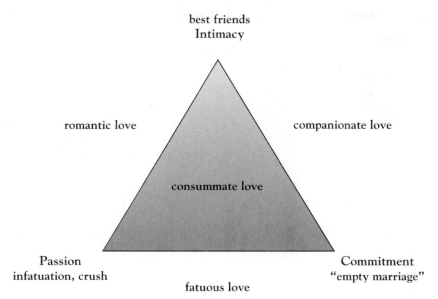

best friends
Intimacy

romantic love   companionate love

consummate love

Passion   Commitment
infatuation, crush   "empty marriage"

fatuous love

By combining the different types of love, we get the relationships seen in life.

Source: R. J. Sternberg, 1988, Triangulating Love, in R. J. Sternberg, and M. L. Barnes (Eds.), *The Psychology of Love*, New Haven, CT: Yale University Press.

passion: companionate love, the deep friendship and loyalty that happy, long-married couples have after passion has left.

At the center of the triangle is the ideal relationship, one combining all three components. This type of love, in which a couple is sexually attracted, feels emotionally close, and is committed to one another, is the kind of relationship we hope for and so rarely can maintain. Sternberg calls this ideal of loving consummate love.

Why is consummate love so rare? Sternberg offers answers by describing the path each component of love follows over time. Sternberg believes that intimacy tends to increase as people get to know one another, then grows at a slower rate, and eventually levels off. Unfortunately, when we know the other person very well, our loved one may become *too* predictable (boring), and so a couple becomes less intimate as the years pass. A husband and wife do not talk the way they used to. Work or children become more absorbing. They find that they are "ships passing in the night."

While it is possible to remain intimate over decades, though it takes effort, passion is inherently ephemeral. According to Sternberg, passion develops rapidly and then declines steeply because the essence of this love is newness. As with any addiction, once the object of our desire becomes familiar, habituation sets in. With predictability, we lose passion because the other person is no longer novel, stimulating, and arousing.

The path commitment follows varies, depending on a couple's success at maintaining intimacy and passion. If a relationship is successful, decision/commitment increases gradually, then speeds up, and plateaus. If the relationship falters and fails, commitment declines and eventually returns to zero as the couple breaks up.

Figure 10-3 **Two Ill-Fitting Pairs of Love Triangles**

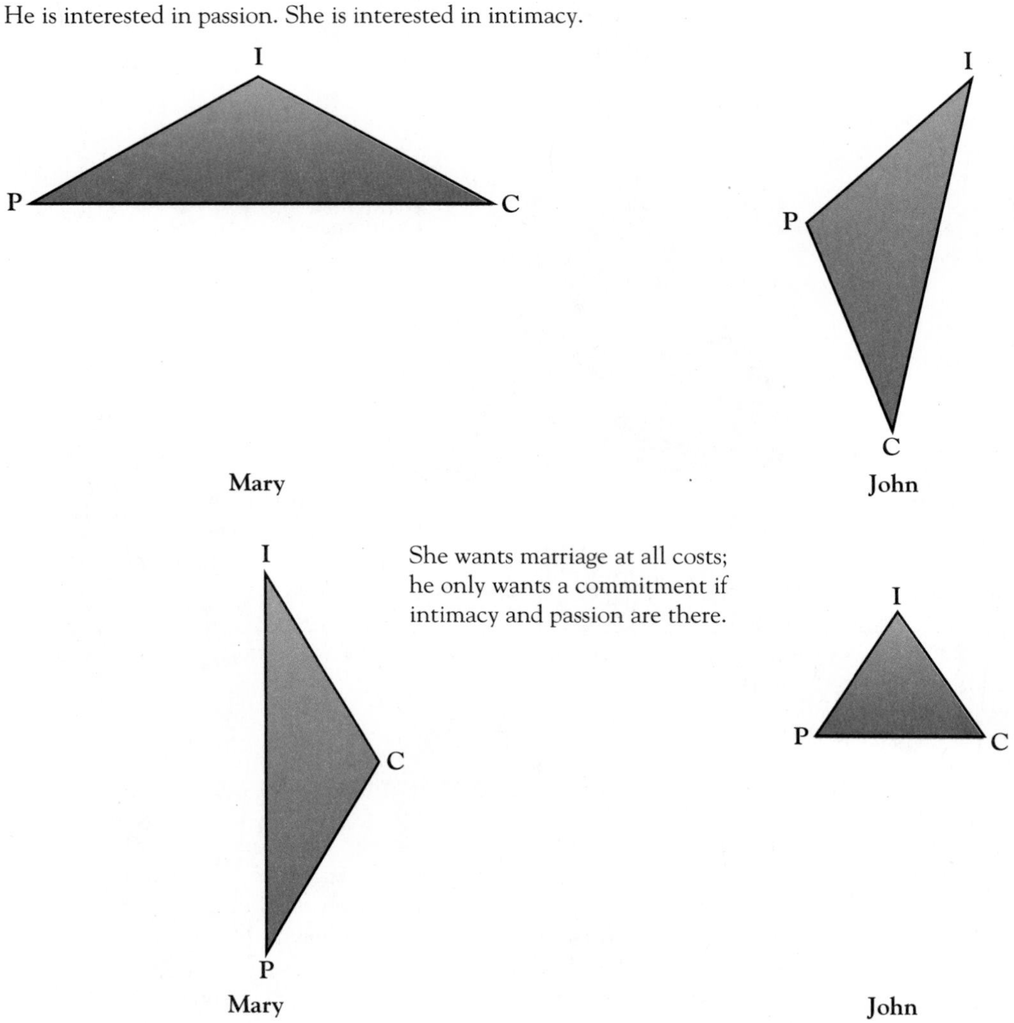

He is interested in passion. She is interested in intimacy.

Mary

John

She wants marriage at all costs;
he only wants a commitment if
intimacy and passion are there.

Mary

John

Notice that this theory emphasizes that relationships are dynamic. So, according to Sternberg, if living happily ever after is to happen, it depends on knowing that love changes over the years. Couples who expect passion to be eternal or intimacy to never end are doomed to disappointment. The more we can pinpoint and understand the facets of love and their time course, the more likely we are to have relationships that last.

Sternberg believes another force, in addition to lack of knowledge, explains why couples break up. Sternberg believes that a major cause of premarital (and marital) misunderstandings is the fact that couples have poorly fitting love triangles (see Figure 10-3).

If a man's feelings about a lover are pure passion, while her love triangle tilts toward intimacy, they will be at odds, as they have different priorities about love:

> *Allen and Wendy knew they loved one another. They also knew they had a problem. For Allen, true love was based on physical passion. . . . [H]e had come to the conclusion that if a couple was good in bed they could get through pretty much everything. For Wendy closeness had to come first. She just couldn't go to bed with Allen if they were having an argument or feeling distant. . . . Wendy's attitude frustrated Allen. . . . At the same time Alan felt frustrated with Wendy. . . . Eventually Wendy and Allen split up, unable to resolve what had become a fundamental difference between them. (Sternberg, 1988b, p. 132)*

This elegant, informative theory helps us make sense of many puzzles about love. Notice that Sternberg also emphasizes that homogamy is important in having enduring relationships. He agrees with the popular idea that "relationships change and take work" (a basic message in the articles in the women's magazines discussed earlier in this chapter). However, as was true of Murstein's theory, Sternberg's ideas have been criticized for being too rigid. Are intimacy, passion, and commitment really *distinct* components? Do they change in the way Sternberg predicts? Is each important for happiness?

Michele Acker and Mark Davis (1992) decided to test these questions by using a scale Sternberg had developed to measure the components, seeing whether items measuring each dimension clustered into separate categories, and relating each component to satisfaction at various relationship stages. Their subjects, adults varying in age and relationship length, were a refreshing contrast to the 20-year-old college undergraduates so often used in studying love.

While commitment and passion were genuinely different, intimacy items were not distinguishable from the other components, suggesting that intimacy may not be a separate aspect of love. Passion did decline in longer-term relationships, and commitment did grow more intense. However, unlike what Sternberg predicts, rather than building gradually and then leveling off and then often declining, scores on intimacy remained stable over time.

High levels of intimacy, passion, and commitment were all related to satisfaction. But the most striking finding of this study was the crucial role commitment played in happiness. Not only was this aspect of love most highly related to happiness for the overall sample, but also its importance increased over time. This led the researchers to conclude that commitment is the most important quality in adult love.

So we come back to commitment as the key to having good relationships, the point sociologists seem to be making when they trace the decline in marriage to an elevation in feelings (or passion) at the expense of commitment (or duty) and the message we hear from an elderly relative when she attributes her 50-year happy marriage to a feeling of commitment that "young people just don't have today." Knowing commitment is important raises questions of its own. Why are some people able to form enduring commitments even in our uncommitted age, while others flit from one relationship to another? For hints, we turn to **attachment theory as applied to adults.**

Love as Attachment

Rather than categorizing love, Cindy Hazan and Philip Shaver (1987) categorize people, so this theory focuses on *individual differences* in the ability to love. Hazan and Shaver believe adult love is similar to the attachment response a child has for a primary care-giver early in life. In the classic studies of attachment conducted by Mary

attachment theory as applied to adults
Theory that draws on infant research describing secure versus insecure attachments to explain individual differences in the ability to love.

Ainsworth and her colleagues, the baby and mother are playing, and the mother leaves the room. Securely attached infants howl with unhappiness and then respond with joy as the mother returns. When infants are insecurely attached, they may either avoid the mother or react with anxiety and ambivalence when she enters the room.

Hazan and Shaver believe that, in the same way as infants can be labeled as having secure or ambivalent/avoidant attachment responses, adults fit into similar categories in their love relationships. Furthermore, our "attachment attitudes" are related to our childhood experiences as well as to our ability to have relationships that endure. People who are securely attached are more likely to report having close relationships with their parents in childhood as well as having more successful love relationships.

Using a scale developed to measure the various attachment styles, researchers have supported many of these ideas. Securely attached couples report higher marital satisfaction (Cohn, Silver, Cowan, Cowan, and Pearson, 1992). They are even happier as newlyweds (Senchak and Leonard, 1992). In one longitudinal study, attachment measured early on predicted which couples broke up or stayed together over the next six months (Simpson, 1990). Moreover, as Hazan and Shaver would predict, securely attached adults report having warmer, more loving early family relationships than people who are insecurely attached (Carnelley and Janoff-Bulman, 1992).

Notice that these studies are correlational. So rather than causing poor relationships, this suspicious style of loving might just as easily be the *consequence* of being in a relationship gone bad. Is there a connection between a person's attachment style and what is happening at the moment in his or her life?

To explore this question, Roger Kobak and Hazan (1991) measured attachment attitudes among married couples and then videotaped their subjects attempting to solve a problem and listening to one another confide feelings. Wives rated as rejecting during the problem-solving task had husbands with a more insecure "working model" of attachment. Husbands rated as less patient when their wives were confiding feelings had spouses with more insecure attachment styles.

Does insecure attachment cause impatient, uncaring behavior, or does impatient, uncaring behavior produce an insecure attachment style? Perhaps we are seeing a cycle that feeds on itself. Insecure attachment may produce rejection, which evokes mistrust and rejection in an escalating chain. In fact, based on the principle of *interactional consistency*, discussed in Chapter 8, we would predict that insecure attachment may solidify partly because a person's behavior provokes the very response that is feared.

Luckily the cycle can go in the opposite direction. When another group of researchers examined the attachment styles of both husbands and wives, they found that high marital distress occurred only when *both partners* were insecurely attached. Couples with one insecure partner were just as happily married as those in which both were securely attached (Cohn et al., 1992). In other words, a securely attached partner may buffer an individual from the detrimental effects of having an insecure attachment style.

These studies suggest that there is no simple association between the feelings we bring to love and our chances of having satisfying, fulfilling relationships. To complicate the situation even more, childhood experiences may not even be the most important type of past experience that influences our attitudes toward love.

Among college students, Katherine Carnelley and Ronnie Janoff-Bulman (1992) distinguished between two kinds of feelings: optimism about marriage and one's faith in being successful in romance. Then they examined how each feeling related to childhood experiences and personal experiences with love. Optimism about marriage was related to what had happened in one's family. Students whose parents had divorced were less hopeful about having a marriage that would last. However, optimism about romantic relationships was much more related to one's personal experiences, whether a person had been successful or had failed in romance before. In other words, rather than what has happened in our childhood, *what has happened to us* is an important force shaping our attachment attitudes. Successful love relationships help breed secure attachment. A failed romance makes us more wary and untrusting in our next encounter with love.

Commitment and Attachment in Action

People who are securely attached (or optimistic about love), we might imagine, enter relationships with a certain mental set. They may pass off criticisms or signs of rejection as temporary or passing and see expressions of love as enduring, permanent, and global. In other words, these people may have an *optimistic explanatory style* in relation to romance.

Frank Fincham and his colleagues asked dating couples to write down their thoughts about their relationships, looking for differences in explanatory style. Does the person describe the reason for being together in external or internal terms? "He only likes me for my money, not for myself." "When my partner tells me he loves me, does he 'want something,' or is he revealing how he truly feels?" Not only did these descriptions relate to current happiness, but also they predicted who was likely to stay involved. People with an optimistic explanatory style were more likely to be with their partners at a three-month follow-up (Fletcher, Fincham, Cramer, and Heron, 1987).

This study is typical of research designed to shed light on how secure attachment is expressed. How do couples who are committed to one another act? Researchers find committed couples use a variety of relationship-maintaining strategies. They discuss problems, compromise, or wait for things to get better when they have conflict (Metts and Cupach, 1990). They agree on rules about handling disagreements, such as remaining rational in public and listening to the other person's point of view (Honeycutt, Woods, and Fontenot, 1993). They take care to demonstrate their affection and to regularly tell the other person about their love (Guerrero, Eloy, and Wabnik, 1993). As we saw earlier, they may also see the competition in a less positive light. These attitudes and behaviors may be important not only in getting to marriage, but also in living happily in any enduring relationship outside of the marital state.

Most of us will get married at some point in life. However, at any given time in the United States, millions of adults are living apart from the marital state. So, before turning our attention to marriage, let's examine some myths about single adults and explore some research relating to people whose life paths as adults do not include marriage.

UNMARRIED PATHWAYS

Single adults are a heterogeneous group. They include people who have been married and are divorced or widowed and an escalating number of never-married mothers. They encompass cohabiting partners, people who have chosen not to get married, and those who are not married by default. Unfortunately these quite different groups are often lumped together in surveys exploring the unmarried state (Fowlkes, 1994; Seccombe and Ishii-Kuntz, 1994).

We have a variety of unflattering stereotypes about single adults. We imagine them as dissatisfied, isolated, and in poorer mental and physical health. Some surveys suggest these anti-single prejudices have a grain of truth. Married people tend to live longer. They are less prone to alcoholism and to accidents and are less likely to enter psychiatric hospitals and to suffer from serious mental illness (Williams, Takeuchi, and Adair, 1992). They report being happier and more contented with life than their single counterparts (Coombs, 1991).

There is a qualification. These findings apply to men! In a reversal of our stereotype of the carefree, joyous bachelor and the bitter spinster, most research shows *unmarried men* (divorced, widowed, and never married) are more at risk of problems. Comparisons between unmarried and married women are very mixed, with some studies showing that married women are more depressed.

Moreover, the differences between married and single adults are evaporating. When Norvall Glenn and Charles Weaver (1988) compared surveys from 1972 through 1986, they found a steady decline in the positive relationship between marital status and reported happiness, especially for men. Let's look at some reasons for this interesting trend.

The studies relating marriage and well-being are correlational, so they tell us little about cause and effect. Our temptation is to assume that being married produces happiness. It provides us with a buffer against disease. However, perhaps emotional and health problems are more common among single men because men who already have these problems are less likely to get married in the first place.

The fact that the male health advantages of marriage have declined in recent decades lends credence to this "selection factor" interpretation. In the past, men who were unmarried may have been a less desirable group. Now that not being married is normal, or much more common, men (and women) who are single are no longer different (deficient). People who are unmarried today are also not as apt to be isolated, as with the rise in alternatives to marriage they are likely to be involved in close, loving relationships, too.

While the previously married are in a different category, two types of single adults are distinctive in that their *whole lifestyle* exists apart from traditional marriage: people who have never married and homosexuals. Who are these individuals, and what are their relationships like?

The Never Married

When marriage was the only acceptable life path, women who never married in particular were painted in the most unfavorable terms and labeled as "spinsters" or "old maids." The demographic statistics offer a far different view. As a group, *older* never-married women are more well educated than their married counterparts. Some studies even show that these women are healthier and happier than any other group. Ironically, though men who remained unmarried traditionally evoked less pity, as we just saw, if anything, it was this group that was disadvantaged emotionally and economically (Fowlkes, 1994).

In interviewing 53 lifelong single elderly women, Barbara Simon (1987) found 76 percent of her sample said they chose this lifestyle because of the freedom and believed that, if they married, they might have to give up a gratifying career. These women were highly involved in their communities and deeply committed to achieving at work. There is another interesting irony here. Now that not marrying has become more socially acceptable, lifelong single women may actually be becoming a less elite, accomplished group. The trend toward having babies without being married, plus the fact that women today can combine marriage with commitment to a career, means that the next cohorts of never-married women are more apt to include more people at the bottom of the socioeconomic totem pole.

Research on lifelong singles is actually very sparse. In the only attempt to probe a national sample, Karen Seccombe and Masako Ishii-Kuntz (1994) focused on the social life of people over age 35 who reported never being married in the National Survey of Families and Households, an ongoing study of American adults. (They used this cutting age because after 35 being single is more apt to be permanent.) As we might expect, never-married men and women on average spent about twice as much time socializing

Katharine Hepburn is just one highly visible example of the high achieving woman who has chosen to live single throughout life.

with friends as did married couples. They were more involved with neighbors, too. Unmarried women in particular were more closely involved with other relatives. However, there was tremendous variability. Some never-married people were very social, spending several or more evenings a week with family and friends; others fit the stereotype of the lifelong isolate. So diversity characterizes the never married, too, a principle that applies to that other important minority group—homosexuals.

Homosexual Couples

Before the late 1960s, many Americans said they had never met a homosexual. Then the gay rights movement exploded on the American scene. While homosexual societies had always existed, the spark that ignited the push to "come out of the closet" (be open about one's sexual orientation) was the 1969 Stonewall rebellion, in which the homosexual community in Greenwich Village rioted for several days after the police raided a gay bar. Energized by the AIDS epidemic, during the 1980s gay men and women banded together even more vigorously to agitate for civil rights (D'Augelli and Garnets, 1995; Michael et al., 1994). Today homosexuals are an obvious presence in the media. Practically every major organizational setting where people congregate—from the Gerontological Society of America to your local college—has its own special interest group for gay and lesbian adults.

This greater visibility has *not* made a major dent on attitudes. Antipathy toward this lifestyle remains intense (Fowlkes, 1994; Smith, 1994). In polls, a substantial number of gay men and women report having been the targets of harassment for their sexual orientation (Herek, 1995). In the NORC survey of sexuality, discussed in Chapter 4, three-fourths of the large cross-section of Americans that the researchers questioned condemned homosexuality as always wrong (Michael et al., 1994).

This prejudice pervades people's lives. While homosexuals are emphatically *not* more psychologically disturbed, particularly the process of coming to terms with one's sexual orientation and telling others is often highly stressful. Gay adolescents and young adults typically experience intense turmoil as they cope with issues relating to their identity and their fears of being ostracized by family and friends (Savin-Williams, 1995). Throughout life, gay women and men must more carefully engineer their social milieu with their sexual orientation in mind. On the most basic level, for instance, they may feel compelled to move to a large city, where it is easier to find a partner and where discrimination may be less pronounced. (In the NORC survey, 9 percent of men in the nation's 12 largest cities reported that they were gay, whereas only 1 percent of men in rural areas did.)

Their minority status and greater invisibility mean gay men and women have more difficulty finding a homogamous mate. Homosexual couples, while united in their sexual orientation, are less well matched in terms of education and other characteristics than their heterosexual counterparts (Patterson and Schwartz, 1994). This lack of fit, plus the ambiguity about the rules for living together, makes relationships of very long duration more difficult to achieve. Homosexual couples have to devise their own norms about sexual monogamy, about who does what around the house; they may have conflicts centering around "how far out of the closet" each member should come. They also may worry about a partner's true sexual orientation (Patterson and Schwartz, 1994). Many people are not exclusively homosexual, but shift in and out of this way of life. For these reasons, while there are many couples who are together for decades, the chance of living outside of a committed relationship is somewhat higher for homosexual adults, especially if they are male (Fowlkes, 1994).

On the other hand, the relationships that these couples do have can be *superior* in important respects. Gay and lesbian couples carefully strive for egalitarian relationships. They are less likely than heterosexual couples to have power struggles relating to income and who does what around the house. Particularly among lesbian couples, researchers find more equal give-and-take and fewer signs of the pathological styles of communicating and relating that we will describe later in this chapter in examining unhappy marriages (Huston and Schwartz, 1995).

Moreover, while sexual orientation cuts across socioeconomic lines, on average those people who identify themselves as homosexuals tend to be an advantaged group. In the NORC survey of sexuality, men and women who reported being gay or bisexual were much more likely than the typical respondent to be college graduates or have graduate degrees (Michael et al., 1994). There is a sad irony here. Even though vilified as being a drain on society, what *really* most distinguishes this stigmatized minority from the rest of the population is this high level of achievement, its exceptional *contributions* to American life.

MARRIAGE

Until now, we have been focusing on the pathways that lead to marriage, or alternative paths to the marital state. Now we look at what happens once we follow the pathway of marital life.

Marital Pathways

continuous decline model of marital happiness
Theory that marital happiness steadily declines over time.

U-shaped curve
Theory that marital happiness declines during the child-rearing years and rises at the empty nest.

According to the early research, the depressing pathway was **continuous decline.** Happiness was at its peak at the honeymoon and decreased over the years. Luckily more recent studies suggest marriages follow a **U-shaped curve** (Glenn, 1990). As we will see in Chapter 11, marital satisfaction does often drop when a couple has children, but the low is followed by an upswing when the nest becomes empty. According to this positive research, couples regain some of what they once had when they are free from the pressures of bringing up children and have the luxury of focusing on one another again.

Almost all of these studies have been cross-sectional. Researchers question people married various lengths of time. So there is no way to tell if marriages do improve after the children leave home or if couples who survive the stresses of child rearing are the cream of the crop, with the more fragile marriages being lost to divorce.

The *Grant Study* (discussed in Chapter 8) and the *Berkeley/Oakland Studies* show that this *selective attrition* applies to longitudinal research, too. When Caroline and George Vaillant (1993) examined the Grant men and their wives who had been married for at least 25 years, they found no signs of either continuous decline or the U-shaped curve. In this study, happiness stayed stable over the decades. When Dorothy Field and Silvia Weishaus (1988) interviewed the Berkeley parents, most of these couples also had marriages classified as stable/positive. Husbands and wives reported being very happy with one another through the years.

PROBLEMS WITH THE RESEARCH. Because following people over such long periods is difficult, the Berkeley and Grant Studies are rare examples of research tracing relationships over decades. We need these studies to show how marriages *really* change. The studies are also difficult to interpret because researchers have *operationalized* the vague concept of satisfaction in different ways (Sabatelli, 1988). If our measure of satisfaction is sexual passion, won't we find much more loss than if we are measuring companionate love? Won't our results be different than those of our colleague who measures happiness by asking about loyalty or friendship?

Critics have questioned the *validity* of some measures of satisfaction. Are statements such as "We do things together" and "We rarely fight" true indexes of how good a marriage is? Do they relate to the intensity of love (Schram, 1979)? As Sternberg would argue, even using *one* measure of happiness across the board may be inappropriate, as the attributes of happy marriages naturally change over time.

The characteristics critical to being happily married may also be culture-bound. When Yoshinori Kamo (1933) analyzed surveys in which Japanese and American couples were asked what qualities were important in marriage, he found that in Japan a husband's financial success loomed larger in relation to satisfaction than in the United States. Perhaps because being well-off financially was more important to feeling happy, in contrast to the typical pattern in the United States, in Japan age was *not* associated with any decline in marital satisfaction.

These studies suggest that, just as we cannot generalize about single adults, it is not a good idea to generalize about married life. Marriages change in different ways, depending on what couples consider important in a relationship and depending on who the couple is. Rather than looking for universal patterns, we might be better off examining the different types of marriages that exist at any age.

Happy and Unhappy Marriages

In a classic study in the early 1960s, researchers found four main types of midlife marriages (Cuber and Harroff, 1965). In the *conflict habituated relationship*, quarreling and nagging were the main forms of communication. In the *passive congenial marriage*, the relationship was less stormy, but equally unfulfilling. Husbands and wives stayed together physically, but remained separate emotionally. The *devitalized couples* started married life close and caring, but lost interest along the way. In Sternberg's framework, all of these midlife couples had empty marriages: commitment bereft of intimacy or love.

The fourth kind of marriage that the researchers found is the one that we wish for or may be lucky enough to have—the **vital marriage.** In this relationship, couples are "intensely bound together psychologically in important life matters. Their sharing and togetherness are genuine. The relationship provides the life essence for both man and woman" (Belsky, 1990, p. 202).

vital marriage
Marriage in which the couple is intensely fulfilled.

In a more recent study, researchers found additional categories. There were couples whose only connection was economic. They were dissatisfied with every area of the relationship except their finances. There were the extremely unhappy couples, the astonishing 40 percent of people who expressed low satisfaction in every area of life. There were couples who collaborated in activities and the children, but shared little of their feelings, and those who had one or two major areas of disagreement within a generally harmonious life. Here, too, a small group of couples (9 percent) reported being very satisfied with all aspects of their relationship, the lucky vital group (Lavee and Olson, 1993).

How can we increase our chances of being in this fortunate group? Based on our earlier discussion, one strategy immediately comes to mind—select a similar mate.

HOMOGAMY AND HAPPINESS. There is a reason why people marry homogamously. We expect that choosing someone who shares our values, interests, and attitudes, as well as being similar in religion and ethnicity, should reduce the risk of disagreements and make it easier to maintain a shared world view. Research confirms this idea. Not only do happily married couples report being more psychologically similar (Acitelli, Douvan, and Veroff, 1993; Lauer et al., 1990), but also marrying a homogamous partner does seem to increase our chance of being happily married as the years pass (Caspi and Herbener, 1990). In addition, marrying someone very much like ourselves has an interesting side consequence. It may help promote personality consistency on our journey through life.

In tracing the lives of the Berkeley/Oakland couples, Avashalom Caspi and Ellen Herbener (1990) found that people who were very similar to one another not only rated

This older couple seems to embody the research showing that homogamous interests are one key to having a happy, enduring marriage. However, we must also remember that other qualities such as mental health and the ability to communicate and compromise are equally important in understanding the quality of their married life.

themselves as more happily married 10 years later, but also changed less internally over the decade. In other words, not only is it a good policy to marry someone who shares our basic interests and values, but also this very selection solidifies a stable sense of self as we travel through time.

Clearly our being just like our mate is not the only important ingredient. Imagine couples who are very much alike in their *pathological traits*, a terrible temper, an inability to listen, difficulty with compromise. As our discussion of attachment styles and their consequences shows, shouldn't an even more basic personality characteristic to look for in a partner be emotional stability, maturity, or mental health?

MENTAL HEALTH AND HAPPINESS.   As we might expect, couples who have low self-esteem or show other signs of emotional disturbance report having less happy marriages (Larson and Holman, 1994). However, because these emotional problems may be the result of being in an unfullfilling relationship, not its cause, for more solid evidence that personality shapes the quality of marriage we need longitudinal research.

In the 1930s, Lowell Kelly recruited 300 engaged couples, gave them a variety of personality tests, and had friends rate their emotional stability. Then his research team followed these couples over a 45-year period ending in 1980 (Kelly and Conley, 1987).

Over the years, 22 couples broke their engagements, and 50 got divorced. Another group stayed unhappily married, together by default. Of the many influences that the

Demographic Indicators

Age. The younger the couple, the less stable the marriage. Teenage couples are at especially high risk of getting divorced.

Education and socioeconomic status. High socioeconomic status is a predictor of marital stability *for men in particular*. Economic insecurity in general is associated with marital unhappiness and divorce.

Race. There is limited evidence that African Americans are more likely to be unhappily married or to divorce than other ethnic groups.

Previous Relationships

Family of origin experiences. There is *limited* support for the idea that people from divorced families are more likely to divorce. However, more important than divorce in a person's family of origin is the overall quality of family life, the general home environment from which the individual comes.

Personal experiences. People who have been divorced are somewhat more likely to divorce. Those who have cohabited, especially people with several of these experiences, are more likely to divorce. People who enter marriage pregnant are more likely to be unhappily married or to divorce.

Sources: J.H. Larson, and T. Holman, 1994, Premarital Predictions of Marital Quality and Stability, *Family Relations, 43,* 228–237; L. A. Kurdek, 1994, Marital Stability and Changes in Marital Quality in Newly Wed Couples: A Test of the Contextual Model, *Journal of Social and Personal Relationships, 8,* 27–48; C. Broman, 1993, Race Differences in Marital Well-Being, *Journal of Marriage and the Family, 55,* 724–732; J.H. Larson, S.M. Wilson, and R. Beley, 1994, The Impact of Job Insecurity on Marital and Family Relationships, *Family Relations,43,* 138–143.

researchers examined—personality traits, early life history, attitudes about marriage, stressful life events during the marriage, sexual history—these failed relationships were distinguished more by the psychopathology of their participants than anything else. If a man's friends rated him as high in neuroticism at his engagement, he was likely to have marital problems. A woman rated as neurotic was set up for an unhappy marriage or future divorce. So, once again, we see that broad personality traits, such as neuroticism, endure and influence the path we follow as adults.

In addition to emotional stability and homogamy, as Table 10-3 illustrates, other factors related to marital distress and divorce range from marrying at an early age, to having had an unhappy childhood, to working at an insecure job, to being pregnant when the marriage takes place. This is why most researchers adopt a **contextual model of marital happiness.** While "couple factors," or forces within the couple, are particularly important, the chance of having a satisfying marriage is affected by many influences, that is, the total context within which the relationship occurs.

contextual model of marital happiness
The principle that marital happiness depends on multiple interacting variables.

MARITAL COMMUNICATION AND MARITAL DISTRESS.   As we saw in the section on dating, the quality of a marriage is revealed in the way a couple "manages" the relationship, that is, in their interactions in daily life. All married people have disagreements. In one survey, the majority of people reported an average of several arguments per month (McGonagle, Kessler, and Schilling, 1992). Unhappy couples disagree more often. Their communications and perceptions are skewed in characteristic ways:

1. *Unhappy couples are less likely to share feelings.* People who report being happily married share their "inner lives" more freely (Hendrick, 1981). However, more than the absolute amount of self-disclosure, the perception of inequity is associated with distress. If you think there is an imbalance, believing that you reveal more (or less) than your spouse, you are more likely to report being unhappily wed.

    On the other hand, revealing feelings is a higher priority from the woman's side. While having a husband who shares feelings is highly related to marital happiness for wives, a wife's revealing her feelings does not have the same importance for the opposite sex. In this case, research confirms the cliché: Sharing feelings in relationships is more important for women than men.

2. *Unhappy couples engage in more negative interactions.* As I mentioned earlier, criticisms, complaints, and sarcastic remarks are more frequent in distressed marriages. Couples who are unhappy command, disagree, and use more put-downs. Happy couples more often approve, agree, and use humor when they relate. Moreover, when unhappy couples fight, the arguing is prone to go on and on, with couples exchanging blow for blow in an escalating chain. One reason is that the participants in these battles are primed to look for hostility in their spouses.

3. *Unhappy couples are less able to sense loving feelings.* Unhappy couples are less sensitive to one another emotionally, especially with respect to picking up on positive responses. While accurately sensing negative feelings, unhappily married husbands in particular miss or pass over expressions of love.

4. *Unhappy couples have a pessimistic explanatory style.* Once again, this suggests the problem may lie in *explanatory style*. Unhappy couples attribute loving actions to external forces: "True, he brought me flowers, but it's only because he wants to look good to his friends." They see negative events in a powerful internal light: "She wouldn't have intercourse with me because she finds me unattractive." Happily married couples adopt the opposite lens, viewing loving behavior as "real" and minimizing insensitivity as situational: "He was short-tempered because he was ill" (Bradbury and Fincham, 1990; Honeycutt, 1993).

Do couples act in these ways because they are unhappy, or do poor communications and pessimistic perceptions really *cause* marital distress? To shed light on this important question, we need longitudinal research.

Building on their study of explanatory style and dating success discussed in the section on love, Frank Fincham and Thomas Bradbury (1993) set out to demonstrate that one's attributional style at the beginning of the marriage could predict later distress. The researchers asked newlyweds to interpret hypothetical negative behaviors, such as "My husband/wife is cool or distant" and "My spouse criticizes something I say," and then followed their sample for a year. As they suspected, people who interpreted these actions as internal (due to the partner's basic personality), permanent, and global (affecting other areas of the relationship) were more likely to report being unhappily married at the follow-up. Most compelling, the relationship between explanatory style and happiness held even when the researchers controlled for depression, self-esteem, and initial satisfaction with the marriage, offering powerful evidence that our world view may play a causal role in why relationships succeed or fail.

APPLICATIONS AND INTERVENTIONS

If poor communications and perceptions are the problem, then changing the way couples relate might save marriages likely to end in divorce. This is the basic idea behind **marital therapy,** the range of treatments in Table 10-4. While all types of marital therapy stress better communication, in behavioral marital therapy teaching communication skills takes center stage.

Major Types of Marital Therapy*

Table 10-4

Psychoanalytic or insight-oriented marital therapy: The therapist focuses on how unconscious influences from childhood are interfering with and shaping the current relationship problems. The therapist makes interpretations designed to reveal these unconscious processes and influences.

Systems-oriented marital therapy: The therapist views the problem as located in the family system, or pattern of interactions, not in each individual. The therapist concentrates on exploring the couple's pathological interaction patterns. Complaints about the other person are viewed as non-pathological, rational responses to a disturbed family system.

Cognitive behavioral marital therapy: The therapist concentrates on the role that negative cognitions, such as a pessimistic explanatory style, have in causing the unhappiness. Partners are trained to monitor their thinking, identify their negative attributions and the situations in which they occur, and substitute more realistic perceptions.

*Many therapists are eclectic, using aspects of different approaches.

Behavioral marital therapy is based on the idea that no matter how attracted people are to one another, love is not enough. In order to have lasting relationships, couples must have concrete skills, such as the ability to negotiate, to deal with conflict, to understand what is important to their spouse (Jacobson and Holtzworth-Monroe, 1986).

As with any behavioral treatment, in this type of therapy the sessions involve homework, the therapist works to educate clients, and specific actions are "targeted" for change. Couples examine their own contributions to problems in the relationship and are given checklists to monitor their negative and positive interactions during the week. The treatment involves pinpointing and changing one's actions and emotions and gaining insights about how to behave from reviewing the partner's forms. Here is a portion of an early therapy session:

marital therapy
Treatment for marital problems in which a couple jointly sees a therapist to improve their communication.

Therapist: *Ok, so we've agreed to spend most of the session reviewing which behaviors . . . increased your partner's satisfaction with the marriage. . . . Would you like to start Bob?*

Bob: *I noticed that a lot of them were under the communication section of her form. . . .*

Therapist: *So you think that . . . communication . . . . might be important to her?*

Bob: *Seems to be. I mean . . . that stuff isn't stuff I normally think about.*

Therapist: *That's important information and very common. . . . What pleases one person may not be what pleases the other person. That's normal. After all, your task is to please your spouse.*

Bob: *Well, I also kept track of her daily marital satisfaction rating . . . and it was higher the days when we talked a lot. . . . On Sunday we had a long talk about my problems at work and her DSR for that day was a six.*

Ann: *That was a good talk. Bob never seems to want to do that anymore.*

Therapist: *Ok, I'm going to ask you to stop. Focus on the positives. . . . Also, focus on yourself and your own behavior. . . .*

Bob: *Yeah, the last couple of days I've been better about talking.*

Ann: *Yeah, it's really true . . . plus I told him I liked it.*

(Adapted from Jacobson and Holtzworth-Monroe, 1986, pp. 41–42)

Is this structured, action-oriented approach effective? To answer this question, we need *outcome studies*, such as those discussed in Chapter 9, in which couples in behavioral marital therapy are compared to couples on a waiting list for treatment or couples receiving a different type of therapy. Many studies show that behavior therapy does improve marital adjustment, at least over a short period. On the other hand, researchers find few differences between this type of therapy and more non-specific, emotion-focused approaches. In one rare long-term follow-up, after four years a *higher* percentage of people in the behavior therapy group had divorced than in a comparison group that had received insight-oriented therapy (Snyder, Wills, and Fletcher-Grady, 1991).

So, as is true of any therapy, behavioral marital therapy may work under some conditions with some couples. The challenge is to understand who benefits more from this approach as well as to demonstrate whether this therapy can produce lasting changes. Unfortunately the dropout rate from every kind of marital therapy is high (Allgood and Crane, 1991). Many unhappily married couples do not seek treatment at all. While in the past these people were more likely to stay locked unhappily in marriage, today the decision they often make is to divorce.

DIVORCE

This change in decision making is highlighted by these statistics: In 1950, only 10 percent of all marriages ended in divorce. Today, as I mentioned early in this chapter, two-thirds of first marriages are estimated to end in this way.

Why So Much Divorce?

divorce revolution
Dramatic escalation in divorce rates during the last third of the twentieth century.

Experts view the **divorce revolution** as having several related causes. The rise in divorce is connected to the women's movement. As women entered the work force and became more self-sufficient, they were freer to leave an unhappy marriage. Men no longer believed they were obligated to stay married to provide for dependent wives (Donovan and Jackson, 1990; Furstenberg and Cherlin, 1991; Popenoe, 1993). Divorce has been linked to changes in the economy. Today, with jobs less likely to pay a living wage to male breadwinners, the need to have two working spouses has increased the pressures on couples.

Divorce is tied to changing attitudes. As different lifestyles became more acceptable, the stigma attached to divorce declined. Today, as we saw at the beginning of this chapter, not only is ending a marriage viewed as more "normal," but also, with the prenuptial agreement, its possibility is even built in at the beginning of married life (Furstenberg and Cherlin, 1991).

Divorce has been linked to confusion based on changing gender roles. Today couples have a harder time agreeing how they should behave with one another and the children because the activities appropriate for wives and husbands are not well defined (Goldscheider and Waite, 1991; see Chapter 11).

Divorce has been blamed on unrealistic expectations about what marriage, and life, can provide. When self-fulfillment is seen as the key to happiness and feelings of romance, or passion, are the basis on which marriage rests, divorce has to become a common life event.

Few people want to go back to a time when men and women were sentenced to living unhappily with one another for life. Many experts vigorously dispute the portrait of today's adults as more narcissistic than in the past. However, no one disagrees that in divorce, issues relating to self-expression often are very important. In the California Divorce Project, a longitudinal study of divorcing couples in the mid-1980s, the most frequent reasons people gave for separating were unmet emotional needs, their growing apart, and boredom/lifestyle differences, highlighting the emphasis we put on personal fulfillment in contemporary life (Gigy and Kelly, 1992; Hopper, 1993).

Gender, social support, economic prospects, whether they have children, who is leaving whom, how well they can communicate afterwards, these are just some of the factors that will interact to influence how this man and woman cope with the trauma of their divorce.

A more neutral *cost/benefit framework* may be most useful in describing these changing forces. Several decades ago the costs of divorcing were prohibitive. No matter how unhappily married a man or woman was, the social, psychological, and economic consequences of leaving the marriage were too appalling to consider change. Today each result is less great, making divorce a much more viable option.

We can use the same cost/benefit framework to make predictions about individual people, that is who makes the decision to divorce or stay together unhappily (White, 1990). In a national survey, people who reported being in stable unhappy marriages tended to be older, felt less in control of their lives, and said they had fewer social contacts. They also were more likely to believe that marriage is a lifelong commitment and that their life would be worse if they divorced (Heaton and Albrecht, 1991). In other words, when outer-world alternatives are few, self-confidence is low, and moral feelings against divorce run high, the decision is more likely to be to stay.

People who divorce, even in our permissive society, face scary consequences. If female, they often must cope with a dramatic reduction in income and the stresses of single parenthood. If male, they face the loss of their children and the need to live life alone. They often deal with feelings of failure. Sometimes they face the scorn of friends and family (Mitchell-Flynn and Hutchinson, 1993). So it is no wonder that in surveys divorced people as a group have lower self-esteem (Kitson and Morgan, 1990).

Patterns of Stress and Adjustment

The best way of viewing divorce is as a process, rather than an event. The decision is often preceded by unhappiness and indecisiveness, a period of ambivalence that many people view as more stressful than the actual parting itself (Hopper, 1993). Then there is the act of leaving, with its high levels of conflict, changes in partners' daily lives, and often ambivalence as to whether the separation should really be permanent (Furstenberg and Cherlin, 1991). The emotional stress does gradually abate as the partners disengage from one another, become adjusted to their new situation, and get farther away in time (Barnat, 1990; Mitchell-Flynn and Hutchinson, 1993). However, people in precarious economic circumstances, those who have been married longer, and especially those with few social supports tend to find it very hard to adjust (Kitson and Morgan, 1990). For women, having young children in the house and having a bitter relationship with one's spouse is also related to feeling chronic strain (Bursik, 1991b). In fact, one influence that makes divorce "a chronic nagging stressor" is the need to have an ongoing relationship with one's ex-husband or ex-wife for the sake of the children (see Feature 11-3, page 328, Chapter 11).

This implies that women should have greater difficulty adjusting to divorce. Women bear most of the objective stress. They have to cope with single parenthood. They may have to radically change their lives by getting a full-time job. Their income often declines dramatically. They may have fewer opportunities to date and remarry. Interestingly, however, while some studies do suggest that men cope more easily, an equal or greater number suggest that women cope better than men (Barnat, 1990; Clark-Stewart and Bailey, 1990).

Men tend to be more bothered by loneliness and isolation afterward (Mitchell-Flynn and Hutchinson, 1993). Women may experience more stress during the predivorce phase, possibly because during this time their husbands may be less attuned to the fault lines in the relationship. While a wife has been agonizing about whether to leave, her spouse may have been oblivious to her distress. In one study of divorcing couples, while the period from thought to action was shorter for men, nearly half of the wives said they had been considering divorce for at least two years (Furstenberg and Cherlin, 1991). Viewed from within a marriage, for women decision making may be particularly painful because life will become so much more difficult afterward. Imagine knowing that you will have to be the main support of your family. You will have to cope with the children alone. Your income will shrink. Your life will become more arduous in so many ways.

But coping with these difficulties can make a person more resilient. A woman (or any person) may learn that she is more capable than she thought. Furthermore, leaving an unhappy marriage removes the stress of living in a conflict-ridden atmosphere. So divorce is a mixed experience, one often greeted with relief and enhanced *self-efficacy* as well as anguish and regrets (Hopper, 1993).

An interesting longitudinal study of separated women by Krisanne Bursik (1991a) hints at these positive effects. Bursik first measured psychological maturity and distress among newly divorced women and then returned to examine her subjects a year later. She found that women who had initially been extremely upset, but were coping well after a year, had grown in maturity. Those who coped well at time one, but were low in adjustment at time two, had regressed, becoming less mature. In other words, turmoil and pain *handled successfully* may ultimately produce emotional growth.

The idea of divorce as a "growth experience" is new. First, researchers documented the negative changes. Now they are turning to the ways that divorce can result in growth (Veevers, 1991). However, the extent to which growth is possible depends not only on a person's psychological resources, but also on the external barriers to making a new life: having few economic resources, an unsupportive social network, little chance to make one's way in the world.

How well people cope is influenced by their ethnic background. Because they are taught from childhood that marriage is for life and also that they should not discuss their emotions, for instance, Asian-American women may be at special risk for unhappiness and social isolation after divorce (Song, 1991). Even more important, however, may be a more fundamental characteristic relating to the marriage: Is the person *choosing* to leave or being abandoned by someone he or she loves? People who are the initiators—those who *want* the divorce—have an easier time afterward (Rossiter, 1991; Veevers, 1991).

APPLICATIONS AND INTERVENTIONS

Our discussion suggests that with divorce, as with marriage, it is important to adopt a contextual approach. Not only does the decision to end a marriage depend on many considerations, but also adjustment depends on a variety of forces. This is why interventions to help divorcing couples include a variety of strategies from help with childcare or a place to live, to counseling, to financial aid. In this section, we focus on two changes involving the legal system that are designed to reduce the turmoil of divorce.

NO-FAULT DIVORCE LAWS. Before the 1970s, in order to end a marriage one person had to prove that the other was guilty of fault. In New York State, the only ground for divorce was adultery. In other states, couples had to demonstrate "mental cruelty," either abuse or some terrible transgression, in order to divorce. This requirement forced even couples who amicably decided to separate to search for evidence of wrongdoing to bring to court. Because establishing the guilt of one's partner was also crucial to the size of the settlement, couples had a strong financial incentive to slander one another, to paint a spouse in the worst possible light. Divorce was always a stressful experience, in part because the legal system added to the humiliation and anger between husband and wife.

Then, in 1970, California passed the nation's first **no-fault divorce law.** The concept underlying no-fault divorce—which quickly spread to every state—was to lessen the trauma by eliminating the need to prove blame. No longer should divorce be dependent on dredging up evidence that one's partner is a terrible person. In order to end a marriage, one party must simply decide to end the marital bond. Furthermore, with no-fault divorce, there is no added incentive to smear one's spouse, as assets are not divided with regard to fault. The basis for a settlement is what is equitable, not who did what to whom.

no-fault divorce law
Law allowing a couple to divorce without having to prove anyone is at fault.

Lenore Weitzman (1985) conducted an influential study of the impact of no-fault divorce, interviewing hundreds of California attorneys, judges, and divorcing couples. She argues that the impact of the law has been mixed. On one hand, no-fault divorce has been praised for making ending a marriage less humiliating. However, by making divorce easier and dependent on "irreconcilable differences," Weitzman argues that the law in itself may have contributed to the number of couples who break up. Now there are few barriers to ending a marriage. Even the law says that "lack of self-fulfillment" is an acceptable reason for dissolving a marital bond.

Weitzman reserves her greatest criticism for the economic consequences of no-fault divorce. Under the old law, women were seen as dependent and so were awarded alimony for life. With the new law, women and men are seen as equal, so wives are only awarded alimony to ease the transition as they get on their feet. The effect is to force women into the labor market immediately, to add to the ranks of single mothers and children who live in poverty today. The idea of equality, while excellent in theory, ignores the fact that a wife who has been out of the labor market taking care of children has lost the ability to be equal in earning power to her spouse. According to Weitzman's calculations, after divorce a woman's income drops an astonishing 75 percent.

Many researchers dispute Weitzman's figures on the economic consequences of divorce. Divorced women, though they typically do lose income, do not often experience this huge change. Interestingly the statistics Weitzman presents are most likely to fit women who were especially well-off financially during their married life (Morgan, 1989, 1991). Other observers argue that, rather than contributing to divorce, the new law only ratified a change in values that had occurred (Bane and Jargowsky, 1988). Still, as is true of so many contemporary family policies, no-fault divorce has positive and negative sides.

DIVORCE MEDIATION. Even with no-fault divorce, the legal system tends to pit couples against each other simply because each person chooses a lawyer to protect his or her rights. In the early 1970s, some attorneys decided that divorcing couples might be better served by a more collaborative approach. They developed **divorce mediation,** in which a single person sits down with husband and wife to settle issues relating to the divorce. Provided by trained professionals, such as lawyers, mediation is practiced in different ways (Nickles and Hedgespeth, 1991). However, in contrast to *divorce therapy,* which deals with emotions relating to the divorce, with mediation the focus is mainly on the equitable division of property and especially custody arrangements between former spouses (see Feature 10-2).

divorce mediation
A trained mediator works collaboratively with a divorcing couple to resolve their issues.

10-2 The Adult Experience: Divorce Mediator

Joanna, a lawyer and certified family mediator, brings an unusual background to her job. While working as a secretary in the police department in a Kentucky city, by chance Joanna and a female police officer witnessed a bank shoot-out. The officer froze. Joanna acted as the hero, and as a result she was recruited as the first female undercover agent for the force. For five years, Joanna participated in drug busts and bought stolen goods. She once had a knife to her throat. Her activities were written up in newspapers and reported on television. Then she moved back to Tennessee and got a job as a paralegal at a law firm. Her boss urged her to go to law school and even helped pay the way. Today, at age 40, she is finishing up a clerkship with Judge Watson and is about to begin a career specializing in mediation and family law.

Joanna feels lucky. Judge Watson believes in mediation and sent Joanna to take the certified mediator course. Mediation fits Joanna's temperament. She prefers being a peacemaker, someone who pulls couples together, not pushes them apart. As a mediator, she is a force for the good in children's lives. Custody arrangements are the main focus of mediation. Joanna's goal is to get couples to step back from their antagonisms and concentrate on the most important issue: "What is best for our child?" Joanna has personal reasons for believing this collaboration works. She and her ex-husband have an amicable, supportive divorce. In fact, her ex-spouse watched their sons during the years Joanna was working full-time and commuting 70 miles three nights a week to get her law degree.

Joanna admits that mediation is not for everyone. In order for mediation to work, couples must be able to compromise. Joanna is about to terminate one case because the man will not give an inch. Mediation depends on amicable lawyers, as each person also retains an attorney who cannot sabotage the arrangement the couple works out. It also depends on having a judge who is willing to go beyond traditional custody arrangements and accept creative new agreements. Equally important, mediation demands more than simple legal expertise. Joanna admits feeling much more comfortable now that she has a psychologist co-mediator to faciliate the emotional end.

Facilitating communication is what mediation is really about. It often takes several sessions of bringing up hurt feelings before couples can begin to reach common ground. Couples enter mediation angry and frightened, terrified of losing their children. Mediation gives them a sense of control over their destiny. The memorandum of understanding that is worked out and sent to the court reflects their decision, not the arbitrary ruling of a judge. This memorandum—once signed and ruled on—while legally binding, is not written in stone. The door is always open to return to mediation if couples want to renegotiate their agreement again.

Divorce mediation has been acclaimed for reducing the overall stress of divorce and for lessening the anger between spouses as well as for being less expensive. Researchers in the California Divorce Project decided to test the truth of these claims by conducting a longitudinal study of couples choosing mediation and those opting for the more traditional route. Interestingly couples deciding on mediation did not differ much in terms of communication skills, anger, or other dimensions of marital quality from those who chose the standard approach. However, mediation users had more faith in their spouses to be fair-minded, which might have allowed them to be more comfortable with this non-traditional choice (Kelly, 1991).

Mediation did not reduce the emotional turmoil associated with divorce. In both groups, changes in feelings were related to the passing of time. Its value lay in its ability to affect future relations with the former spouse. Couples who used mediation were more cooperative after the divorce and more satisfied with the process and its outcome than couples who took the traditional route.

In looking at divorce from the couple's perspective, we have been ignoring the effect that this newly normal transition has on intergenerational life. As we will see in Chapter 11, divorce has made the role of father less central in many men's lives. Divorce multiplies the stress of motherhood because it is difficult for women to be both providers and care-givers. It is the major reason why one-fourth of American children are living in poverty today. As we will see in Chapter 12, divorce has transformed grandparenthood, making it a more hands-on role.

Divorce will change adulthood in the United States in the future in important ways. In the next cohorts of elderly people, there will be fewer married couples and widows and more divorcees. How will having been an absent parent affect men's relationships with their children in old age? Will having survived divorce make future cohorts of elderly women and men hardier emotionally? Or will older people be more fragile, cut off from family when they develop disabilities? We are just beginning to see the impact of the divorce revolution on our journey as adults.

KEY TERMS & CONCEPTS

deinstitutionalization of marriage
cohabitation
stimulus-value-role theory
homogamy
heterogamy
socio-evolutionary theory of mate selection
passionate and companionate love
triangular theory of love
passion
intimacy
decision/commitment
attachment theory as applied to adults
continuous decline
U-shaped curve
vital marriage
contextual model of marital happiness
marital therapy
divorce revolution
no-fault divorce laws
divorce mediation

RECOMMENDED READINGS

The Deinstitutionalization of Marriage

American family decline: 1960–1990: A review and appraisal. (1993). *Journal of Marriage and the Family, 55,* 527–555.

> *In the first section of the August issue of this journal, scholars debate the "family is in decline" thesis from a variety of perspectives, illustrating that social scientists are no less divided about the reasons for family changes in contemporary America than the public.*

Blankenhorn, D. G., Bayme, S., and Elshtain, J. B. (Eds.). (1990). *Rebuilding the nest: A new commitment to the American family*. Milwaukee: Family Service America.
> *Family experts discuss the state of the family from a variety of perspectives. A concluding section offers public policy solutions to improve family life.*

Council on Families in America. (1995, March). *Marriage in America: A report to the nation*. New York: Institute for American Values.
> *This pamphlet documents the deinstitutionalization of marriage and offers varying perspectives on ways to rebuild families.*

Popenoe, D. (1988). *Disturbing the nest: Family change and decline in modern societies*. New York: Aldine de Gruyter.
> *While this book focuses mainly on Sweden, it illustrates this sociologist's idea that family life has changed in dramatic, negative ways in Western nations in recent decades.*

Love, Commitment, and Interventions for Troubled Relationships

(1993, June). *Personal and Social Relationships, 10*.
> *This issue of the journal is devoted to research exploring the strategies couples use to stay committed to one another.*

Jacobson, N. S., and Gurman, A. S. (Eds.). (1986). *Clinical handbook of marital therapy*. New York: Guilford Press.
> *Chapters in this edited book describe the different types of marital therapy, interventions for specific problems, and research on effectiveness.*

Sternberg, R. J., and Barnes, M. L. (Eds.). (1988). *The psychology of love*. New Haven, CT: Yale University Press.
> *The authors provide an overview of various theories of love, including those described in this chapter.*

Homosexual Couples

D'Augelli, A. R., and Patterson, C. J. (Eds.). (1995). *Lesbian, gay, and bi-sexual identities over the lifespan*. New York: Oxford University Press.
> *This book offers a comprehensive look at the issues facing lesbians and gay men at different stages of adult life. It also discusses the social context of homosexuality—gay and lesbian communities, family relationships, and prejudice.*

Divorce

Folberg, J., and Milne, A. (Eds.). (1988). *Divorce mediation: Theory and practice*. New York: Guilford Press.
> *This edited book describes the principles underlying divorce mediation, the ways the technique is practiced, and research evaluating this approach.*

Furstenberg, F. F., Jr., and Cherlin, A. (1991). *Divided families: What happens to children when parents part*. Cambridge: Harvard University Press.
> *This small, research-packed book thoroughly discusses the impact of divorce.*

Weitzman, L. (1985). *The divorce revolution*. New York: Free Press.
> *The author presents an in-depth study of the impact of the no-fault divorce law in California on women, children, and men.*

Parenthood

Mark and Joan Smith just became parents. After five years getting financially established and four years trying to conceive, Lily will be their only child. Mark takes one of the night feedings. He cooks and helps with the baby when he can. However, because his business needs constant attention, Joan is fully responsible for the house and child. Being her one chance at parenthood—an event she has looked forward to for her whole life—Joan would prefer to stay home, especially during Lily's first years. As her income is needed, right now the Smiths' elusive goal is finding good, affordable childcare. Mark and Joan are concerned about the compromises they must make at the beginning of their daughter's life. They worry about Lily's future, about whether they will be able to support her for decades, give her good values, and even spend the time with her that they want. In one sense, their own future is already mapped out: Their daughter is the central focus of their lives.

PARENTHOOD IN CONTEXT

Within the past two centuries, parenthood has changed more than at any time in history. While parents have many fewer children, they lavish unparalleled care and attention on the children they have. The expectations centered around parenthood have risen; the pressures and burdens on parents have increased. Today not only must parents financially support their children for decades, but also they have full responsibility for shaping their emotional development in an uncertain world. At the same time, parenthood is supposed to be the activity that gives ultimate meaning to our lives as adults (Rindfuss, Morgan, and Swicegood, 1988).

A Historical Perspective

Before the late eighteenth century, expectations and attitudes seemed different (see Bowen and Orthner, 1991; Furstenberg, 1988; LeVine and White, 1987; Rossi, 1987; Stearns, 1991; Vinovskis, 1987). Children did not have to find their own occupations. The extended family was the economic unit that they participated in throughout their lives. In these preindustrial families, parental control was absolute. Parents, especially fathers, had the final word over whom a daughter or son married. Children were expected to contribute financially to the family from a young age. In fact, children seemed to exist as much to serve parents' needs as the reverse. Rights were with the older generation, not the young.

Particularly after the Industrial Revolution, the situation changed. Families moved from the farms to the cities. Children had to make their living through unfamiliar jobs. Parents no longer had the knowledge to equip their children for adult life. The philosophies of rebellion, freedom, and self-determination of the American and French Revolutions had swept the land. Children became more assertive, less likely to see their parents as having absolute authority. The job of parenting became more anxiety-provoking: to provide the guidance to prepare children for an independent life.

Compulsory education accelerated these trends. Between 1840 and 1890, attendance at primary school became mandatory. School widened the separation between parents and children, further eroding parental control. It educated a wider audience to the philosophical values of equality, altruism, and child-centeredness put forth by philosophers such as John Locke and Emile Rousseau. Locke believed that children are a "tabula rasa" (blank slate) and emphasized that what happens during the early years shapes adult life. Rousseau stressed that children are born innately good and that childhood should be a special, protected time. Because it removed children from the need to contribute economically to the family, school ensured that childhood became that unique, protected life phase. As dependent children drained family resources and the early years were viewed as a crucial time of life, a change occurred in the act of procreation itself.

Until the late 19th century, scenes such as this were standard in America, revealing a very different feeling about the sanctity of the phase of life called childhood than we have today.

During the nineteenth century, for the first time in history, people deliberately tried to limit the number of children they had. The small, carefully planned nuclear family with distinct sex roles became the ideal. By having fewer children, the growing middle class could put into practice the new child-centered attitudes: the idea that parents give without expecting anything in return, that nurturing children is a woman's most important job. While most historians believe that these attempts to limit family size occurred before the dramatic advances in preventing infant and childhood mortality that began to accelerate toward the end of that century, they were given impetus when parents began to feel confident that each child they gave birth to would survive:

> . . . . All these trends focused more . . . attention on childhood and children than had previously been the case. . . . Children were as never before depicted as valuable, loveable, innocent but intelligent individuals to be cherished, protected, defended and developed . . . Public laws compelling . . . school attendance embodied the assumption that the citizenry bore a collective responsibility for other peoples' children. . . . while romantic sentimentalism promoted an intensification of the parent-offspring bond in the most private and exclusive terms . . . The notion [became] that every child was uniquely valuable to his own parents and the wider society (LeVine and White, 1987, p 286).

Recent Variations and Trends

Today, in developed countries, these trends are in their final stages. With the invention of the pill and the intrauterine device (IUD) in the 1960s, fertility can be totally controlled. The average family size in the United States has dipped below the replacement level for the population, to about 1.8 children. While some experts suggest that the high divorce rates and the rise in alternative lifestyles mean that we are shifting from a child-focused to a self-focused society (Blankenhorn, 1990; Popenoe, 1988; Rossi, 1987), it is difficult to argue that the emotions, hopes, and anxieties revealed in our interview have changed in recent years.

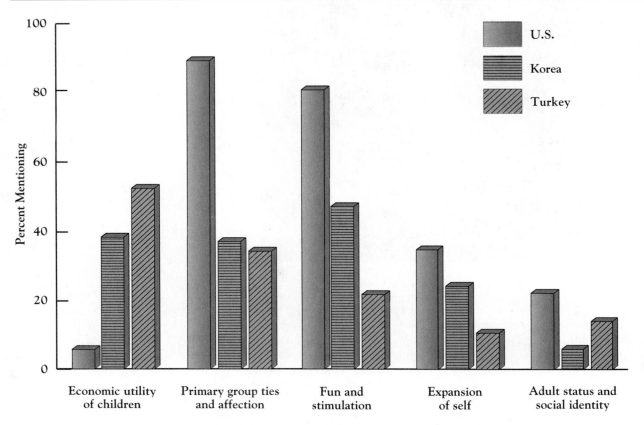

Women in different areas of the world attach different values to having children. Notice the high premium put on emotional gratifications in the United States.

Source: Fawcett, J. T. The value of children and the transition to parenthood. *Marriage and Family Review, 12.* Copyright, 1988, reprinted by Permission of Haworth Press, Binghamton, N.Y.

However, some old attitudes and practices exist in other parts of the world. High rates of fertility are more typical where people are poor and less well educated, where health care services are minimal and conditions of life harsh. In developing countries, especially in rural areas, the average family often has four or more children. In these countries, children still continue to be valued for their economic contribution to the family, as James Fawcett (1988) found when he visited different areas of the world asking people about the advantages and disadvantages children provide.

While, as Figure 11–1 shows, emotional reasons, such as fun, stimulation, and affection, rank highest on the list of gratifications for American wives, for women in Turkey the most important value of children is still to provide economic support. The answers of Korean wives, who live in a country considered midway between the others in level of development, fall between the American stress on emotional gratifications and the Turkish emphasis on the practical, utilitarian value of a child.

Until now, I have been implying that having smaller families has been a steady trend, one that automatically goes along with affluence, an educated population, and a

Percentage of White Women Remaining Childless at Age 25 Born over a 60-Year Period in the United States

Figure 11–2

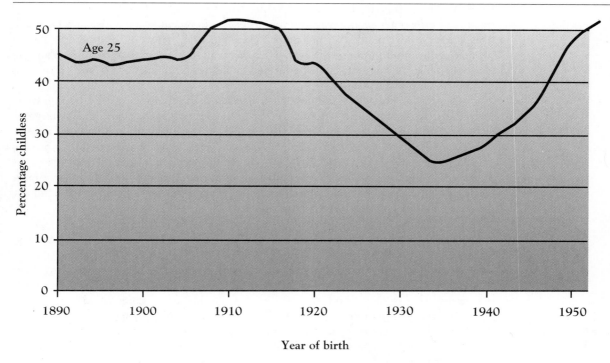

Year of birth

This chart shows the impact of the social context on parenthood in the United States. Notice that more than half of all women born around 1910 were still childless when they reached age 25 (this was during the mid-1930s, at the height of the Depression). Less than a quarter of their daughters, born around 1935, were childless when they reached the same age (this was in the late 1950s, during the boom economy and before women's liberation). Half of their daughters, born in the early 1950s, once again had not given birth by age 25 (this was during the mid-seventies at the height of the women's movement).

Source: Adapted from R. R. Rindfuss, S. P. Morgan, and G. Swicegood, 1988, *First Births in America: Changes in the Timing of Parenthood.* Berkeley: University of California Press.

society's attitude that nurturing children is the most important mission of adult life. A dramatic exception contradicts these ideas. After World War II, when the United States was especially prosperous and the belief in child rearing as a woman's calling was at its peak, the birth rate soared. As we know, this rise in fertility from the late 1940s to early 1960s, which at its highest point produced an average 3.8 children per family, was called the baby boom. In fact, some experts believe that the baby boom was *caused* by the financial boom after World War II. In good economic times, people have larger families and start their families early. In times of economic trouble, people put off having children and limit family size (Rindfuss, Morgan, and Swicegood, 1988).

The idea that prosperity produces large families is also supported if we look only at the twentieth-century United States. During the Depression, women postponed parenthood and had small families. In fact, as Figure 11–2 shows, for the cohort of women reaching their mid-twenties during the Depression (those born around 1910), rates of childlessness were almost as high as those today.

The relationship between finances and fertility becomes more interesting when we look at what is happening in the United States now. As Figure 11–2 implies, starting in the 1970s, U.S. women once again put off having children. While most women still have their first child in their twenties, they no longer typically become mothers in their early twenties, as during the baby boom. While this trend to postpone parenthood seems related to the poorer economy facing young couples in recent years, it also may be due to the women's movement, with its emphasis on career and rejection of motherhood as a woman's only option in life. However, when we focus on the "average trend," we miss an important fact. It is mainly well-educated middle-class women who are putting off motherhood, not the poor.

Actually, in the United States, the *variability* in the timing of motherhood is more extreme than in any other country in the world (Rindfuss, Morgan, and Swicegood, 1988). While on average people are waiting longer, the estimated 1.1 million births to adolescents in 1991 show that early parenthood is another prevalent trend. In fact, in the United States today, it is also true that being poorly educated, living in a more deprived environment, and having poor medical care go along with having more children and becoming a parent early in life (Children's Defense Fund, 1994; Rindfuss, Morgan, and Swicegood, 1988).

These statistics suggest that finances do not affect the timing of parenthood in a single, simple, absolute way. For some couples, such as the one in our interview, economic security is important. They become parents when they feel they can afford a child (Rindfuss, Morgan, and Swicegood, 1988). On the other hand, women with little hope of getting that security are most at risk of having children when they are children themselves. For women who feel they have few options in life, parenthood becomes the only means of self-fulfillment (Children's Defense Fund, 1994). The compelling push for *every* woman to become a parent becomes clear when we look at the gratifications that children are supposed to provide. (See Feature 11–1 on p. 314 for a discussion of women who resist this push.)

Parenthood Values and Expectations

When childless women in the United States and other developed countries are asked why they want children, they list a variety of benefits (see Table 11–1). Having children means a person is an adult. Children offer prestige and a sense of accomplishment; they are the cure for a lonely life. Children bring happiness, excitement, and fun. They are a source of pride, give a person the feeling of being needed, expand horizons, and make the woman more mature. The idea that having children increases closeness with one's husband is also a common idea (Fawcett, 1988; Gormly, Gormly, and Weiss, 1987).

When asked about the disadvantages, people mention economic costs, restrictions on freedom, and worry about the health and well-being of another human being. In addition, not knowing how to care for a child looms high in Western women's concerns. This anxiety does not appear in surveys in developing countries. Most women in developing countries have firsthand experience caring for younger brothers and sisters, cushioning their entry into the parenthood role. They are not subject to the barrage of parenting advice and professional pronouncements that can also heighten feelings of vulnerability, inadequacy, and stress.

These thoughts relate to the first child. The reasons for having more than one child are different. In Fawcett's international surveys, women in developed countries most often say they want a second child as a companion for the first. Gender preferences also become important, such as the wish for a child of the opposite sex, particularly a son. The motivations for having a third, fourth, or fifth child differ from person to person. Moreover, in making this decision, people seem more aware of the costs, such as the increased economic burden and the added amount of work.

Most Frequent Responses Among College Students Who Were Asked Why They Wanted to Be Parents

Table 11-1

Rank	% subjects who gave this response	Motive
1	48.29	To expand myself, have someone to follow me
2	47.91	To achieve adult status or social identity
3	45.25	To provide a family for myself
4	32.70	For the fun and stimulation children bring
5	23.19	To be able to influence or control someone
6	19.39	Because it is the morally correct thing to do
7	8.37	To compete or compare myself with others
8	6.84	For the sense of accomplishment or creativity
9	4.56	For the economic benefit

Notice the emphasis on self-expansion in these responses.

Source: Gormly, A., Gormly, J., and Weiss, H. (1987). Motivations for parenthood among young adult college students. *Sex Roles, 16,* 36. Published by Plenum Press.

While these responses seem well thought out, when we look more deeply we find women and men may not have a realistic view of parenthood. Though especially true of adolescents, this lack of realism also seems to apply to well-educated women past their teenage years. In carefully selecting college graduates to examine motivations for parenthood, Sandra Caron and Ruth Wynn (1992) noticed that the women they polled often gave self-centered answers. Children were wanted "to carry on my name," "to have someone to look after me," and especially "to make my life complete." This last idea in particular is telling because it is promoted, promised, and preached by the parenting experts.

When researchers analyzed the most popular British childcare manuals in bookstores in the late 1980s, they found motherhood described as the pinnacle of a woman's life. Motherhood was pictured as creative and fulfilling, the process by which a woman becomes a complete human being. It was the physical expression of love for one's husband, binding a woman more closely to her man (Woollett and Phoenix, 1991). Let's keep these mental motherhood pictures in mind as we explore the **transition to parenthood,** what *really* happens when women and men become parents.

transition to parenthood
Transition from being a childless couple to being parents.

THE TRANSITION TO PARENTHOOD

Before the 1980s, social scientists knew nothing about what becoming a parent was really like. While there were many studies of parents, the measures of stress or personality that researchers gathered from mothers or fathers were used for a certain purpose: to examine how these attitudes and feelings affected the developing child.

Then Caroline and Philip Cowan (1988, 1992) decided to see how *parenthood* unfolds. In the late 1970s, the researchers started their **Becoming a Family Project,** selecting 72 middle-class San Francisco couples expecting a baby and interviewing the husbands and wives regularly until their children reached kindergarten. At around the same time, a research team headed by Pennsylvania State University psychologist Jay

Becoming a Family Project
Research program conducted by the Cowans, exploring the transition to parenthood among middle-class California couples.

11-1 The Adult Experience: Childless by Choice

Katie and Ken never discussed children while they were dating. When they married soon after high school, there were years before they had to confront that part of life. Neither really wanted children. However, Katie felt a person ought to become a parent as insurance for old age. At age 30, based on the idea that it was "now or never," Katie stopped using contraception; then she became anxious and resumed. For several years, she vacillated, stopping birth control, feeling unhappy, and then rushing back. At Katie's 34th birthday, she and Ken decided to remain childless. Katie's life is her husband. Ken feels children will interfere with their love. Katie admits she may be selfish, lacking in an impulse that in her words "most other women naturally have." Still, since making this decision, she feels better than she has in years.

Married couples are supposed to have children. Those who do not take this step, particularly when they are older, are financially secure, and have been married for some time, are subjected to a chorus of questions, "Why aren't you starting a family?" The idea that a family means children may keep childless couples from participating in family-centered activities at work, at church, and with friends. Relations with parents may deteriorate. Not only do the couple's parents want to be grandparents, but also they wonder where they "went wrong" with their children. Though society may be more tolerant of this lifestyle, couples who do not want children are still viewed as selfish, unloving, and destined for an unhappy old age (Somers, 1993). Women in particular bear the brunt of these stereotypes, as child rearing is widely viewed as a woman's mission in life.

Perhaps this explains why, as was true of Katie and Ken, the decision not to have children is rarely definitive at first. In tracing young adults' attitudes, demographers find that it begins with a series of postponements, which at some point shade into a childless life (Rindfuss, Morgan, and Swicegood, 1988). Who takes this unorthodox path, and what are the consequences?

Mary Joan Gerson, JoAnna Posner, and Anne Morris (1991) examined the truth of traits typically associated with women low in motivation to have a child: high feminism, high narcissism, and unhappiness with their own childhood and parents. On questionnaires measuring these traits, they found few differences among married women motivated to become parents, ambivalent, and disinterested in motherhood. A slight tendency for the unmotivated to rank higher on narcissism only approached significance in comparing these women with the extremely motivated group.

The idea that children are necessary for an emotionally fulfilling old age seems just as untrue. Childless-by-choice couples tend to have especially close marriages (Somers, 1993). When Ingrid Connidis and Julie Ann McMullin (1993) compared life satisfaction among four groups of elderly people—close parents, distant parents, the voluntarily childless, and couples who could not have a child—the childless-by-choice were tied for highest in life satisfaction with the close parent group.

Belsky was conducting similar studies, following rural Pennsylvania couples from pregnancy for the next several years (Belsky, Lang, and Rovine, 1985; Belsky and Rovine, 1990; Belsky, Spanier, and Rovine, 1983). These studies from different sections of the country sketch a remarkably similar portrait of how becoming parents changes a marriage and affects husbands' and wives' well-being. However, both reveal what becoming a parent was like in the United States during the 1980s, a decade of intense changes in women's roles. They also involve two-parent families, mainly white. We have an urgent need for research on how the transition to parenthood is experienced by different ethnic groups and especially single parents.

Does a baby draw couples closer or drive a wedge between husband and wife? We can get hints from recalling the surveys of marital happiness over time (see Chapter 10).

This blissful scene in the first photo is the one that we look forward to when we become parents. The reality of the other photo tends to be minimized or ignored.

With a unanimity rare in psychological research, almost every study reveals that after having a child *on average* marital satisfaction drops (Belsky and Pensky, 1988; Berman and Pederson, 1987; Grossman, 1988; Cowan and Cowan, 1988; McDermid, Huston, and McHale, 1990). The decline varies dramatically from person to person. Some couples become closer after having a child. Still, the clear message is that people should *not* have a baby to save a troubled marriage. If anything, this so-called remedy is more apt to break the marriage apart.

The Becoming a Family Project findings are especially telling because the Cowans compared marital satisfaction in their parent sample with that of a group of couples who had not had a child. While the childless couples grew closer over the same period, the parenthood group reported more distance, more conflict, and a general deterioration in their relationship over time.

Belsky's studies offer deeper insights into exactly how marriages tend to change. His research team found the sharpest losses occurred on "expressions of affection" and "feelings of romance." After becoming parents, couples were more likely to describe their relationship as a friendship, less prone to characterize it as a romance. This interesting study seems to capture the very point in a marriage when the shift from a passionate to a companionate relationship may occur (see Elaine Hatfield's theory in Chapter 10). Rather than being seen as a lover, one's spouse comes to be viewed more as a "partner" and a "fellow worker" after the baby arrives (Belsky et al., 1985; Belsky and Rovine, 1990).

Why might having a baby cause more marital distress? When the Cowans (1988) asked their couples this question, both husbands and wives agreed. Arguments were more frequent because now there were more conflicts over the **division of labor,** or who should do what around the house.

The transition to parenthood affects marriages in a second way: It heightens sex roles. Even in egalitarian marriages, women take over most of the childcare and

division of labor
Manner in which a couple divides the chores of their married life, especially household responsibilities.

Figure 11–3

Changes in Marital Satisfaction for Husbands and Wives After the Transition to Parenthood

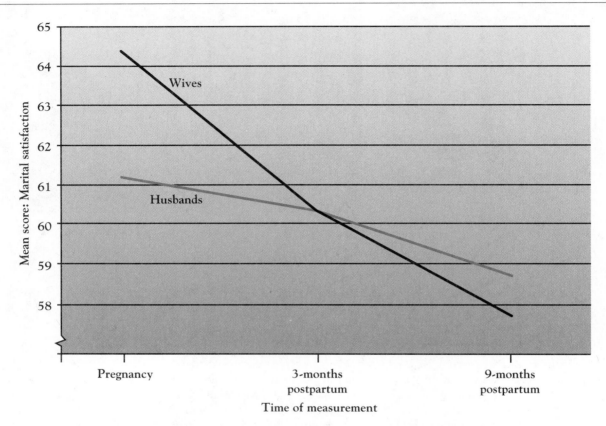

Women experience a more dramatic decline in satisfaction after the birth.

Source: Belsky, J., Lang, M., and Rovine, M. (1985). Stability and change in marriage across the transition to parenthood: A second study. *Journal of Marriage and the Family,* 47, 855–865. Copyrighted 1985 by The National Council on Family Relations, 3989 Central Ave. N.E., Suite 55, Minneapolis, MN 55421.

housework after the baby is born. This change to traditional roles takes some couples by surprise. Before becoming parents, husbands and wives did not expect to be behaving in these ways.

The fact that the woman may feel "stuck" with the childcare may explain another finding. As we can see in Figure 11–3, after the baby's birth marital happiness plummets more for wives. While the Cowans find that the differences even out later, with men having lower satisfaction after six months to one year, wives report higher dissatisfaction and feel generally more let down, especially in the first few months. In other words, men and women may have different time frames for feeling the stress of the transition to parenthood.

The Cowans believe that these divergent emotional paths in themselves can cause poorer relationships. Since the impact of the change hits husbands and wives at different times, couples feel more distant because they are emotionally out of step.

Having a baby may unmask other differences in a couple's world views:

Bill: *I thought we were doing OK. I was pitching in at home. We'd started to make love again. . . . But mostly she's just mad before I go to work in the morning and mad as soon as I get home at night.*

Peggy: *Well, I know we're making love more often, but it still hurts half the time from that terrible episiotomy. And . . . I don't consider changing a diaper or feeding Mindy when you've got nothing else to do much of a pitch. What's really getting to me, though, is that we hardly ever agree on how to handle her. I think you're too rough and you think I'm spoiling her, and neither of us wants to change. (Cowan and Cowan, 1992, p. 112)*

This conversation, from an especially unhappy couple in the Cowans' study, illustrates how after a baby's birth the battle may center around several fronts (Belsky and Pensky, 1988; Grossman, 1988). Not only may the new mother be angry at her husband for not understanding her burden or helping with the baby's care, but also she may be battling about the *kind of care* to provide. The feeling of being embattled can come from outside of the marriage, too. In one study, grandparents, while viewed as helpful, were also sources of anxiety, as likely to be seen as intrusive and critical by new mothers as being a support (Hansen and Jacob, 1992).

Parenthood tends to make couples less *homogamous* in a more basic way. The experience is often more central emotionally for women than men. In order to explore couples' priorities and how they changed after becoming parents, at each evaluation the Cowans (1992) asked both husbands and wives to divide a pie chart expressing how much of their identity was taken up by roles such as parent, worker, spouse, and friend. Women on average devoted far more space to motherhood than any other role, especially during the baby's first year. While the father identity did enlarge over time, at its peak, when the baby was 18 months old, it was still typically less than one-third as wide for husbands as for wives.

So the transition to parenthood may be especially stressful for women because of its enormous emotional salience. Women often have unrealistically rosy expectations of motherhood. They have everything riding on performing well in that job. In a very interesting comparison, the Cowans discovered that men who had the largest fatherhood identities reported the greatest marital happiness. However, because they reported having practically *no other* meaningful identities, women who devoted comparatively high fractions of the chart to motherhood were *most susceptible* to distress.

Which Couples Cope Better or Worse

In spite of these problems, I must emphasize that parenthood is a tremendous source of joy. There are dramatic differences from couple to couple in the extent to which this event changes a marriage for the worse. When Belsky and Michael Rovine (1990) looked more closely, they found that more than 40 percent of their couples reported no change in feelings of love. Thirty percent said that they had fewer arguments after the transition to parenthood. Can we predict who responds badly or well to this life change?

Belsky and Rovine found that, while no single sign predicted poor adjustment, couples whose marriage did greatly deteriorate had a certain constellation of traits: They were younger, were less well educated, and had less money. The husbands ranked low on sensitivity. Both husbands and wives had lower self-esteem.

The complicated role that self-esteem plays in how a person handles having a baby was revealed when researchers decided to test the idea that pregnant women with large discrepancies between their actual self and their ideal self (the person they felt they were in comparison to who they wanted to be) might be at high risk of postpartum depression. Their prediction was correct, but mainly if a woman had a temperamentally difficult baby. Women with low self-esteem may be especially vulnerable when they have a baby who cries excessively or does not eat or sleep well because this can cause feelings of failure, confirming and exaggerating their poor sense of self-worth (Alexander and Higgins, 1993).

Belsky and Rovine also found that the baby's temperament affected the transition from the woman's point of view. In their study, wives with difficult babies were especially likely to report high levels of marital distress. Not only does a difficult baby increase the burden on a new mother and heighten her feelings of insecurity, but also a woman in this stressful situation may expect special help from her husband and so feel more disappointed when he is not doing his share.

However, for the best clues to what will happen, Belsky and the Cowans agree: Look at the relationship. A couple who has a good marriage before the baby tends to be close after the baby is born. A couple who is already having problems with one another finds that their difficulties multiply after having a child. In the Cowans' words, "[T]he transition to parenthood seems to act as an amplifier, tuning couples into the resources they have, and turning up the volume on existing difficulties in managing their . . . relationships" (1992, p. 206).

One interesting warning sign, the Cowans discovered, related to the actual decision to have a child. At their first evaluation, the researchers asked husbands and wives how they felt about becoming parents. As Figure 11–4 shows, there were couples who were ambivalent, those who had carefully planned the child, and a group who welcomed an accidental event. A fourth category of couples disagreed, with only one person genuinely wanting a child. Notice that, while the ambivalent couples had the lowest marital satisfaction during pregnancy, ultimately the couples who disagreed fared much worse. In fact, most of this group had divorced by the time their first child had entered school.

In sum, in predicting how our marriage might change after becoming parents, we need to adopt a modified contextual approach. While influenced by forces such as age, financial resources, and the temperament of our baby, the main key to what will happen lies in our relationship with our spouse now. And yet to predict how we *personally* will feel and react, our gender is critical. The studies clearly imply that being a parent is different for women and men.

MOTHERHOOD

Motherhood and Life Satisfaction

Becoming a parent seems more engrossing and more stressful for women. Are mothers generally more unhappy than other groups? The surprising answer is yes. Large national surveys consistently reveal that mothers, especially when they have young children, rank lower than childless women on overall well-being (McLannahan and Adams, 1987). Mothers report more day-to-day dissatisfactions; they worry more; they are more likely to be depressed. However, let's look closely at what we mean by well-being.

In one survey, Debra Umberson and Walter Gove (1989) found that, while parents ranked lower on *overall* satisfaction, they were more likely to feel that their lives had direction and purpose than people without a child. In other words, if we just measure day-to-day worries, we miss the compensations of being a parent. Children do offer people a sense of meaning and purpose in life.

We miss differences depending on one's parenthood stage. When Umberson and Gove divided their parent sample into an empty-nest group and parents with children in the house, only the second group of parents had lower satisfaction and morale. The empty-nest parents were actually best off, scoring as high on life meaning as the other parents and just as high on day-to-day morale as the childless. In other words, as Feature

Couples' Decision Making About the Birth and Satisfaction with Marriage, from the Becoming a Family Project

Figure 11–4

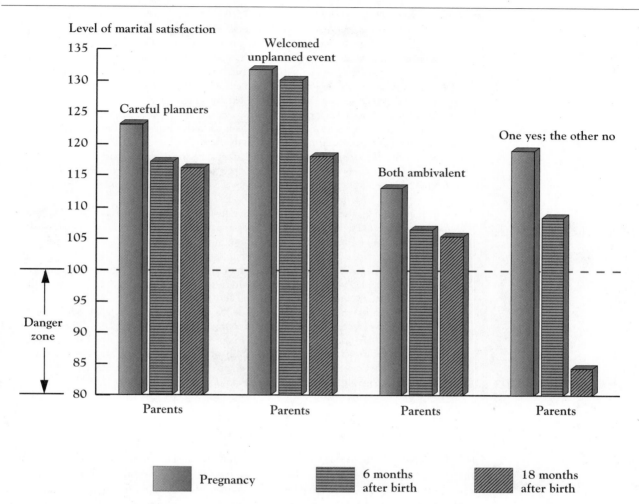

Level of marital satisfaction

- Welcomed unplanned event
- Careful planners
- Both ambivalent
- One yes; the other no

Danger zone

Parents   Parents   Parents   Parents

Pregnancy   6 months after birth   18 months after birth

The Cowans find that disagreement over whether to have a child is a harbinger of marital difficulties later on. Eighteen months after the birth, couples who had differed about whether or not to have a child (the last set of graphs) have extremely low marital satisfaction.

Source: When partners become parents: The big life change for couples, by Caroline Pape Cowan and Phillip Cowan, copyright © 1992 by Basic Books Inc.

11–2 suggests, our image of parenthood as "life's greatest joy" is most likely to be realistic after the children leave home!

Whether a woman finds motherhood very stressful depends on a variety of factors from economic pressures (Pittman, Wright, and Lloyd, 1989), to the quality of her relationship with her husband and children, to whether what she is doing fits her interests or needs (Umberson, 1989a, 1989b). A good example of this complexity comes from summarizing the results of studies exploring whether women with young children who work are happier than those who stay at home.

"I cried all the way home when I left my last child at college," says Jane. "I cried for probably three hours straight. The first few weeks I could cry at the drop of a hat. One night at dinner Ted said, 'Isn't it nice to have things so quiet?' and I burst into tears. Going into their rooms was hard, seeing their things, but this was a fairly short period, and then I got busy with other things. So the bad part was a sense of personal loss and, for me, the guilt: 'What could I have done better? Did I spend too little time with them?' At this time of my life, I am not as rushed as when they were younger and I was working and going to school. But those are bittersweet feelings, so even that was not all negative. The positive side was that it made them appreciate me more. Our relationship improved. The time that you have together is more quality time. Now when they come home, they want to be with family. It's nice not to have their needs always in the back of my mind. There's more time for my husband and me to be together. For instance, we went canoeing three times last week. If the girls had been home, I probably would have gone shopping with one of them. My marriage didn't get much better because it was always really good, but you do get closer, turn inward to one another for support."

In previous eras, the empty nest, like menopause, was seen in purely negative terms. Women were expected to become depressed because they were losing their feminine life role. How does the empty nest affect well-being in our more liberated age?

Using longitudinal data from the National Survey of Families and Households, Lynn White and John Edwards (1990) looked at how personal life satisfaction and marriages changed among couples who first reported having a teenager at home and then being in the empty nest. This study confirmed the U-shaped curve. Launching the children was associated with a rise in marital satisfaction for everyone. However, it was only related to higher *personal* well-being if parents reported frequent contact with their non-resident children. In other words, this study underlines one theme in our interview, a message we now turn to in this chapter and return to in the next: The quality of the parent/child relationship is central at *every* age. People do feel better during the empty nest, provided their launched children still remain caring, involved, and emotionally close.

If a working woman has easy access to childcare and an involved husband and, most important, wants to work, she is likely to be happier than a mother who stays at home full-time (see Chapter 13). However, when working mothers do not like their jobs, have problems arranging childcare, and have husbands who are not involved, they do tend to be more depressed than non-working wives (McLannahan and Adams, 1987; Umberson and Gove, 1989).

The Motherhood Experience

What is the experience of motherhood like? Here we find a huge gap. Even though it is widely viewed as the high point of a woman's life, there is almost no information about what it is like to be a mother from the mothers' point of view. One study examining how women feel about being mothers, *The Motherhood Report,* while based on a national sample of 900 women, cannot qualify as unbiased, as the researchers based their findings on women who were willing to fill out and mail in a detailed motherhood questionnaire. The study involved mainly middle-class women; it had no minorities. Still, let's touch on some highlights of this survey, published as a popular book, because they offer such revealing insights into motherhood from an insider's point of view (Genevie and Margoles, 1987).

In order to explore the most interesting aspects of motherhood, the clinical psychologist researchers asked questions we never find in the large surveys: "What stage of childhood do you like least?" "Do you have a favorite child?" "What makes you feel closer or more distant from one or another child?" "What pushes you to the limit?" "When do you lose control?" In addition to checking off answers, women were asked to describe their experiences in their own words.

Most mothers felt infancy was the most wearing stage. It was a close runner-up to adolescence as the least preferred age. (Toddlerhood and the preschool years got top billing as the favorite years.) Most women expressed dissatisfaction with their husbands' help. The majority said that having a child changed their marriage for the worse. In fact, the authors were surprised by the frustration the women expressed at the quality of their husbands' parenting. Twenty-eight percent ranked their spouse as only a fair father; another 20 percent stated their husband had *no* redeeming qualities as a parent. While, as we might expect from the research on the transition to parenthood, too little attention paid to children was first among their complaints, a close second was lack of patience. Many women felt their husbands were quick to fly off the handle, too rigid and critical. Or, less often, they might criticize their spouse for the opposite problem—too much laxity, an unwillingness to offer any discipline.

Mothers did not spare themselves. More than a third said that they were too impatient. Close to half admitted that they did not control their tempers well. Among the situations that got them most irate, challenges to authority ranked first. Disobedience, disrespect, and even typical "childlike behavior," such as whining and arguing with siblings, might provoke reactions bordering on rage. (One in six admitted feeling so angry at times that she had fantasies of hurting the child.) When confronted with real-life children, even the most committed mothers were shocked to realize that their ideal of being calm, in control, and always empathic came tumbling down.

One influence that affected how closely a woman fit her motherhood ideal lay not in herself, but in her child. Children who were difficult, unruly, and hard to control provoked more irritation, lowered a woman's self-esteem, and changed the emotional experience of motherhood. A "good" child had the opposite effect, evoking loving feelings and making a woman feel competent about herself (Genevie and Margoles, 1987, pp. 220–221):

> Susan is the easiest of my children to love, my favorite. Unlike her brother, she has never given me a problem. . . . Her older brother was such a difficult child—tantrums, not doing his homework, sassing back. . . . Susan has become a caring, generous person. My son often makes me feel I went wrong somewhere. But Susan makes me proud and makes me feel like a success as a mother.

> Lee Ann has been my godsend. My other two have given me so many problems and are rude and disrespectful. Not Lee Ann. . . . I disciplined her in the same way. . . , except that she seemed to require less of it. Usually she just seemed to do the right thing. She is. . . my chance for supreme success after two devastating failures.

These responses destroy another image: the ideal that mothers love all their children exactly alike. Though they said they tried not to let the emotions show, mothers often did admit having favorites, preferences for one or another child. While favorite children were often obedient, easygoing, and loving, achievement in the eyes of the world meant less than a sense of closeness, the feeling of being loved and appreciated by a particular child.

In other words, this study confirms the message of *behavioral genetic* research: The quality of the mother/child relationship does differ from child to child. Moreover, these interviews offer us clues to what exactly may cause the variations in maternal responsiveness from child to child that behavioral genetic researchers find can be so pronounced (see Chapter 2). To borrow from Cindy Hazan and Philip Shaver (1987), "attachment attitudes" in the parent depend on "attachment attitudes" in the child.

This survey also revealed that motherhood produces mixed emotions. While one in four women had totally positive feelings and one in five found motherhood almost all unpleasant, the majority of the women described this experience with ambivalence. While meaningful and not to be missed, it was a job in which the good barely outweighed the bad (Genevie and Margoles, 1987, pp. 410–411):

> Motherhood ties you down, makes you responsible. . . . It makes you do things you'd rather not and miss things you would enjoy. But I have found life much richer because I have a child.

> Motherhood is like the circus; colorful, exciting, scary—you are always looking at different rings and sometimes it stinks like the elephants. But there is always something to grab your attention and keep you going back for more.

I hope these quotations give you a flavor of the complex feelings that cannot be captured when we look at single-answer surveys of parenthood happiness. Motherhood is both painful and joyful; boring and exciting; a mixture of highs and lows. The quality of the experience is shaped both by a woman's marital partner and by the other partner in the motherhood duet, her child. While motherhood often does fulfill a woman's expectations, it also destroys her fantasies about how things are supposed to be. For this reason, let's conclude by returning to our theme of expectations and speculate about the role they play in mothers' stress today.

Expectations and Motherhood Stress

As we saw earlier, before becoming parents women have high expectations of motherhood. These fantasies of motherhood as total joy are encouraged by the experts, by the media, perhaps even by other parents themselves. By portraying motherhood as only bliss, are we doing women a disservice, setting them up for disappointment as they realize that their experience does not live up to this glorified image?

What compounds the stress is unrealistic performance pressures. Notice from *The Motherhood Report* the implication that mothers should be above human faults (that is, be always in control and feel exactly the same way about every child) and especially the emphasis on the child's behavior as validating the quality of a woman's performance as a mother. Good children make a mother feel competent. Disobedient children or, as in the transition to parenthood, temperamentally difficult babies can make a woman feel she failed (Ryff, Lee, Essex, and Schmutte, 1994). As psychologists have grown sensitive to the role genetics plays in shaping personality, it has become clear that mothers do not have anywhere near total control. However, the old *psychoanalytic* and *traditional behavioral* idea that parents mold a passive "product" lives on among the public and some mental health professionals. It is evident in the practice of blaming adult problems on a dysfunctional family and apparent in surveys that show that most Americans point the finger at poor parenting as the number one cause for rising crime and other social ills (Mellman, Lazarus, and Rivlin, 1990). In an age in which parents' control seems especially fragile and we know more about its limits than ever, parents, mainly mothers, still bear the shame of their children's and society's sins (Coonts, 1992).

Finally, motherhood may be especially stressful today because of conflicting ideas relating to changing gender roles. Today most women need to have jobs. Even when they enjoy their work, many women may still feel guilty, thinking they should be at home, especially during their children's early years. Equally important are mismatching expectations centering around fathers' roles (Belsky and Pensky, 1988; Cowan and Cowan, 1992). A man who gets up a few times a week to change a diaper compares his behavior to his father and congratulates himself for being a highly involved man. But his wife is well aware that 98 percent of the job falls on her. Imagine his shock when she accuses him of not pulling his fair share!

The Cowans (1992) argue that childbirth preparation classes can add to unrealistic expectations. By having the father-to-be participate as an equal partner or coach, they set couples up to assume that the man will be equally involved in the actual childcare. In fact, in one interesting survey, women who had the highest expectations of their husbands—believing men should be equal partners in child rearing—were especially likely to report marital distress (Lye and Biblarz, 1993). Are women really the front-line workers at home as the studies of the transition to parenthood suggest? This brings us to the other parenthood partner—fathers.

FATHERHOOD

During the 1970s, as women entered the work force, expectations of fathers changed. Suddenly, being a father meant more than providing financial support for the family or taking a son to basketball games. Fathers were no longer expected to be one step removed from care-giving, second-rate adjuncts to the true parenting figures. It was a badge of honor to change diapers and put children to bed and to admit that children, not one's job, was a first priority. The **new nurturer father** became a middle-class ideal.

new nurturer father
Late twentieth-century idea that fathers should be equal participants in childcare.

The idea that fathers should help out with the children is not new. In studying magazine articles from 1900 to 1989, Maxine Atkinson and Steven Blackwelder (1993) found that at several points over the twentieth century the ideal father was described as being a loving, involved presence in family life. However, the new nurturer father, who *equally shares childcare* with his wife, is different than any previous image of fatherhood. To see how radically new this idea about male parenting really is, let's examine what fathers' roles in America used to be like.

A Brief History of Fatherhood in America

From Colonial times though the early years of the Republic, historians believe fathers were very involved in their children's upbringing (Bowen and Orthner, 1991; Furstenberg, 1988; Lamb, 1986; Stearns, 1991). However, these preindustrial fathers were totally unlike what women expect of the new nurturing man. As suggested at the beginning of this chapter, in those days a father's control over the family was unquestioned. It was the man to whom his wife and children deferred. Because they had control over the land, especially the more affluent fathers could depend on obedience from their offspring, whose economic fate they controlled.

With industrialization, this hands-on-control began to dissipate. Fathers left the house during the day, so they were no longer there to supervise what went on in the home. With the move away from the farm, a father lost his power to determine a child's livelihood and so his absolute power to compel his children to obey. While still the titular boss of the family, fathers became more distant from the core emotional life at home. Mothers took over as primary nurturers. The main job of the father shifted to **provider.** "Being a good breadwinner" was the main criterion by which a father was judged.

provider role
Father's role as the breadwinner.

While this shift in parent power from fathers to mothers is crucial in understanding where we are today, experts caution that at every point in history there were probably a number of different fathering styles. The most compelling sign of this changed balance of power comes from custody laws. Until the 1800s, custody was given to the father at

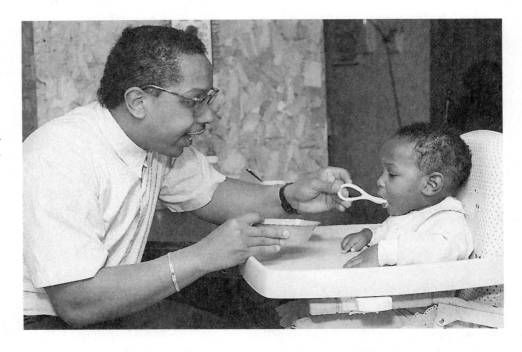

Although this man's father may have spent time with him as he was growing up teaching sports and sharing "masculine" activities, it is far less likely that he showed the kind of nurturing behavior this man is displaying with his infant son. In other words, the new, nurturer father offers a distinctly different blueprint for what contemporary fatherhood is about.

sex-role model
Father's role as the teacher of appropriate gender-role behavior.

divorce. Then, as the nuclear family with defined gender roles became established, increasingly custody was given to the mother. Finally, early in the twentieth century, under the "tender years doctrine" custody was automatically given to the mother, as women were believed to be biologically superior parents (see Feature 11–3 on page 328).

During much of the twentieth century, the idea that mothers were biologically best suited for raising children was unquestioned. However, fathers still played a role in their children's emotional development. As Sigmund Freud's influence increased during the 1950s, attention focused on the father as **sex-role model,** and popular writings during this decade bemoaned the deficiencies of fathers in this area.

According to fatherhood researcher Michael Lamb (1986), each mental image survives, producing a vague mosaic of contradictory roles that contemporary fathers must fulfill. Fathers are supposed to be good sex-role models and sometimes even total authorities. They must be good providers and play a hands-on-role in bringing up their children. What adds to the ambiguity is our increasingly diverse set of cultural norms. Not only do ideas about the ideal father vary from person to person, but also they may differ by ethnic group and social class. So one reason that some women may get angry at their husbands for not fulfilling their responsibilities is that the "right" way to be a father is so poorly defined.

Fathers as Nurturers

How common is the new nurturer father? The studies of father involvement in general echo the research on the transition to parenthood. While fathers are more involved than they used to be, the ideal of father as equal partner in childcare falls far, far short of reality.

Researchers have explored three aspects of involvement: How much time do fathers spend with their children relative to their wives? How often are they available to their daughters and sons? To what extent do they take ultimate responsibility for a child's care? As Lamb and others point out, the last dimension may be especially central. Having responsibility for a child is different than helping out, even helping out for eight hours a day, five days a week. It involves knowing when the child needs to go to the doctor, arranging for babysitting, and being on call when the child is sick. Having responsibility may not translate into many hours spent with the child. However, the worry and weight of concern make this aspect of parenting a 24-hour job.

When wives do not work, fathers spend about one-fifth as much time as mothers do in day-to-day interactions and about one-third as much time being accessible to their school-aged children. The largest discrepancy in involvement is found in responsibility. As Lamb (1986) states, fathers assume essentially no responsibility (in the sense discussed here) for their children's care.

The findings are not much different in families in which the wife works full-time. Here fathers do more, though still on average only about one-third as much as their wives. However, even when mothers work more than 30 hours per week, the ultimate responsibility fathers take is negligible. When we look at the bottom line—where the parenting buck stops—child rearing remains the mothers' job.

Gender-typed behavior occurs in other aspects of child rearing. As we would expect from the fact that their job is to be good sex-role models, fathers spend more time with their sons than their daughters. They tend to be more involved with male children beginning in infancy (Bronstein, 1988; Dickie, 1987; Jones, 1985). There are gender variations in the *way* they interact. Fathers spend most of their time playing with their children; they do little day-to-day care. The work of parenthood—changing diapers and cajoling the child to eat, to get dressed, to do homework, and to get to bed—tends to be the mothers' job (Barnett and Baruch, 1988; Lamb, 1986). There are differences in the style of play. Fathers' play is more arousing, more rough and tumble: They roughhouse; they dangle an infant upside down (Belsky and Volling, 1987). In this way, some observers note, the message that "men and women act differently" gets conveyed to children during the very first months of life (Bronstein, 1988).

There is great variability from the **house husband,** who stays home with the children while his wife works, to the father who fits the older stereotype of the traditional breadwinner. I also must emphasize that the ranks of highly involved fathers are growing. Young fathers in general are more involved with their children than their own fathers used to be. One reason is necessity. When mothers work full-time, men simply have to take on more responsibility at home. Apart from having a working spouse, what else predicts the extent to which a man participates in care-giving?

When Rosalind Barnett and Grace Baruch (1988) explored this question by interviewing middle-class couples with school-age children, they found that one influence is mothers. High participation is unlikely unless there is support from a man's social network, in particular, from his spouse. While women *say* that they want their spouses to be more involved, many get uncomfortable, become jealous, and feel intruded upon when their husbands take over what they see as their territory (Cowan and Bronstein, 1988; Grossman, 1987). Being committed to the role of "kinkeepers" or care-giver/relationship experts, as Barnett and Baruch conclude, wives serve as the gatekeepers, either promoting or putting up barriers to their husbands' entry into their preserve.

Barnett and Baruch found that a woman's attitudes and anxieties about her husband's involvement were particularly important in the **dual-career couples** they studied, those in which both the man and the woman worked. In a family with a non-working mother, the man's feelings about his father's behavior while he was growing up were the most important factor determining the amount of time he devoted to childcare.

In contrast to the idea that men model or mimic their fathers, *less favorable feelings* about one's father's involvement, predicted greater participation in childcare. We can see why this might be true by looking at one highly involved father that the researchers interviewed. In high school, this man vowed never to be like his father, a successful

house husband
Husband who does housework and provides childcare while the wife works.

dual-career couples
Couples in which both husband and wife have careers.

lawyer who had no time for his children and sent them to boarding school. He would be a full-time father and never subject his children to the sense of deprivation he felt.

There were other surprising results. In contrast to the idea that "the more intense the involvement, the better," the consequences of fathers' participation were mixed. As fathers' time with their children became more equal, so did their worry about having enough time for work. Interestingly the highly involved fathers sometimes reported *more* tense marriages than the traditional men. While happier as fathers, they were more critical of their wives as mothers. While the women were proud of their unusual men, they, too, were more likely to stress their deficiencies as mothers and to experience more conflict between family and work.

So the researchers conclude that father participation is not a panacea. It creates stress as well as easing burdens. Because the right way to be a mother or father is still subject to interpretation and is a source of guilt for men and women, equal participation both solves problems and creates tensions in family life.

The Cowans (1988) offer their own insights: While in general their research suggests that having less-stereotyped roles is related to better adjustment, neither a traditional nor an equal division of labor guarantees happiness. It is whether couples agree on who does what that is important. If a husband and wife are both happy with the way the childcare is being handled, that is what really counts (Blair, 1993).

The fact that equal sharing does not always equal a better marriage was underlined in an interesting study illustrating how socioeconomic status might relate to husbands' and wives' satisfaction surrounding who does what around the house. Among a national sample of dual-earner families, Maureen Perry-Jenkins and Karen Folk (1994) categorized couples as to their socioeconomic status (working or middle class) and then explored marital happiness as it related to the division of labor at home. While middle-class wives reported more conflict in their marriage when their sex roles were very traditional, for working-class wives the opposite was true. *Even though they were working full-time, working-class women with the most highly traditional relationships reported the happiest marriages.* This study shows that we should be careful about generalizing from research that has been carried out mainly on middle-class couples. The idea that a husband should pitch in and help at home when a wife shares the breadwinning, though it seems reasonable, is not something every married woman believes.

Fathers as Providers

The idea behind the women's movement was that liberating women would also liberate men. Once fathers no longer had the burden of doing all of the providing, they would become more involved emotionally at home. However, this lifting of the breadwinning burden may have been a double-edged sword. While it has freed *some* men to become more involved with their children, it may have contributed to others' disengagement from family life.

As we learned in Chapter 10, when women are no longer financially dependent on a husband, they have more freedom to leave an unhappy marriage. This is why most experts feel the women's movement is intimately connected to the dramatic rise in divorce. Sociologist Frank Furstenberg and others believe that women's self-sufficency has also made leaving more possible from the men's point of view. Men feel less guilty about getting a divorce knowing their wives and children can get along without their economic support. They no longer feel that they have to marry a woman who is pregnant because she cannot get a job and so needs their protection when she has a child (Cherlin, 1988).

FATHERS AND DIVORCE. The negative consequences of the declining obligation to provide are most poignant in divorce. Today, as we saw in Chapter 10, with

The scenario of this divorced man picking up the children for his non-custodial visit is certain to be fraught with a good deal of anxiety. This woman may be worrying: "Will my ex-spouse bring the children back on time?" "Will he care for them adequately?" While possibly relieved that his daughters were there when he arrived, the man in the photo may have his own concerns. "Can I keep the children entertained this weekend?" "How will my daughters respond to me?"

no-fault divorce laws child support payments are often small. Still, compliance with these orders is dismally low. In 1989, half of all men who were required to pay child support did not fully comply. Only about one in three children living in a single-parent home gets *any* child support (Children's Defense Fund, 1994).

This lack of compliance tends to go along with a general exit from children's lives. Men who are delinquent in child support are more likely to be estranged from their families. A 1981 national survey of children showed some alarming statistics on the amount of contact between non-custodial fathers and their offspring. More than half of the adolescents had not seen their fathers at all within the year (Furstenberg and Cherlin, 1991). Only a sixth saw their fathers as often as once a week (Furstenberg, 1988). What often happens is that men "migrate" to new families, remarrying and becoming stepfathers or having additional children (Furstenberg, 1988), and the cost is poorer relationships. Children report feeling more ambivalent about stepparent relationships (Furstenberg and Cherlin, 1991). In survey after survey, divorced fathers rank as more unhappy than their married counterparts (Umberson and Gove, 1989).

As we can see in Feature 11–3, many divorced fathers fight to be with their children and argue that they are prevented from having the kind of relationship they want. The system tends to load the dice in favor of mothers, causing anguish to thousands of fathers who want to be highly involved in their children's lives. As we will see in Chapter 13, being able to be a good provider is still at the core of many men's identities as adults (Teachman, Call, and Carver, 1994). However, it also is true that among men who *cannot* be good providers marriage rates are especially low (Rindfuss,

11-3 The Adult Experience: Visiting Father

Fatherhood is the critical experience of Henry's life. When Joanna was a preschooler, their destination was the zoo or the playground. As she grew older, Henry took Joanna for lessons and taught her sports. At parent/teacher conferences and school assemblies, Henry stood out as the only man at these female-dominated events. His presence was hard won and, he feels, too rare. Henry had been demoted from father "to person with visitation rights."

Henry and his wife separated when Joanna was almost two. Though according to their agreement the child was supposed to be kept in their former home, one day his ex-wife vanished with the baby. Henry's goal when they next met in court was shared custody, the right to keep Joanna for weekends and every other day. To his astonishment, despite being the wronged party (his wife had violated the law), a psychiatric evaluation was ordered to determine if *he* was emotionally fit. The idea, Henry feels, is that a man who wants to be involved in childcare must have a hidden agenda. One judge asked point blank: "Why would a man want to take care of a two-year-old?" Eventually Henry won standard visitation: one afternoon per week, every other weekend, alternate holidays, the month of July.

Henry has gone to court periodically over the last 10 years to force a greater role in his daughter's life. Once he sued for full custody. (Joint custody requires a mutual decision between ex-spouses.) While no one denied that Henry was a good father, the psychologists testified that a child needed its mother during the early years. Though this tender years doctrine supposedly no longer automatically applies, in Henry's opinion, "the courts would give custody to a murderer if she was the mother of the child."

For years, Henry felt terrible about not being able to see his daughter every day. His work suffered. He was often upset. Now that Joanna is 12, he has adjusted. His daughter has her own room in his apartment. He feels secure that she knows this is her second home. Henry feels he reached an emotional landmark when during "his time" this past summer he was able to let go and allow Joanna to attend sleep-away camp. Still, the heartache of being deprived of one's child never really goes away.

Debra Umberson and Christine Williams (1993) wanted to show that what Henry is feeling is not unusual. In fact, these emotions may be one reason why in surveys divorced men rank comparatively low in happiness. In the first phase of their study, using a national sample, the researchers showed that dissatisfaction with their involvement as parents was an important issue for divorced men. In-depth interviews with a smaller group of fathers revealed that many fought to take an active role in their children's lives. However, as with Henry, these men felt frustrated by a system that seemed to relegate fathers to being financial providers alone. Henry believes this anti-father bias may be producing the lack of involvement described in the text. Why wouldn't some men opt out of the family, rather than confront being peripheral in their children's lives?

Morgan, and Swicegood, 1988). This brings us to the most controversial family trend in the United States and other developed countries—having children without being married.

UNMARRIED MOTHERS

Today the majority of the more than one-third of all children living in a one-parent family *on any given day* are in that situation because their parents were married and then separated or divorced. Births to never married women are more ominous. Divorce rates rose rapidly in the 1970s and are now beginning to level off. The trend of having babies without being married is escalating. As of 1991, almost 30 percent of all children in the United States were born to unmarried mothers (Council on Families in America, 1995).

These statistics need some perspective. If married women were having babies at the same rate as during the baby boom, the fraction of children born to unmarried mothers would only slightly exceed what it used to be (Bane and Jargowsky, 1988). Unmarried motherhood is not just an American concern. Sweden has higher rates of out-of-wedlock births than the United States (Popenoe, 1988). Still, when we look more closely at these children and their mothers, the U.S. pattern becomes especially worrisome.

Unwed mothers cannot always be fit into categories. There are some "Murphy Browns" who are well-off, are highly educated, and plan motherhood alone. However, these women are a minority. While divorce is more equally distributed in the population, it is the poorest and least well educated women who are most likely to have children out of wedlock (Children's Defense Fund, 1994). Unmarried childbearing is the most common pattern for African-American women today.

While the financial situation for mother-headed families in general is bleak—remember from Chapter 1 that they have a median family income *below* the poverty line—never-married mothers are in especially dire straits. Furthermore, while women are often rendered poor by divorce, the situation for never-married women is more chronic. These women were often poor before having children. Motherhood perpetuates the poverty (Kahn and Kamerman, 1988; Kamerman and Kahn, 1988).

The transition to single parenthood may be less stressful when a person has less to lose. In one comparison of single-parent Mexican-American and Anglo women, while the Hispanic women had fewer educational and financial resources and were younger, they coped better emotionally. The Anglo women had to move to a different neighborhood; their economic status declined; their lives were more disrupted by the change (Wagner, 1993). The fact that the mother is unmarried does not mean that there is no father involvement. Some men live with their girlfriends and children and function as true fathers, but do not have a wedding ring. Even fathers who do not live in may be highly involved. In one rare interview study of teenage African-American fathers, 18 months after the child's birth one-quarter of the fathers reported seeing the child daily. Only 2 percent reported that they had no contact at all. During visits, typically lasting for a half day, these fathers took an active role in child care—feeding and diapering the toddler, watching the child while the mother was out (McAdoo, 1988).

Even with strong support, from other family members or the fathers, however, the economic hardship these women and their children face can be overwhelming. While in contrast to our stereotypes, as Table 11–2 shows, most single mothers never used to stay on welfare for more than a short period, mother-headed families have typically made the transition less easily than other groups (Rank, 1986). Teenagers who have babies out of wedlock and drop out of school are much worse off economically at age 25 (Duncan and Hoffman, 1991). Because having a baby without a husband clearly limits a woman's chances in life, why has this choice become so much more common among young, poor women today?

The Conservative and Liberal Positions on Unmarried Motherhood

The common idea has been to blame misdirected government policies, a view first proposed by conservative scholar Charles Murray. In an influential book called *Losing Ground*, Murray (1984) argued that the rate of out-of-wedlock births began to rise at the same time that President Lyndon Johnson instituted the War on Poverty in the 1960s. Johnson's War on Poverty, later called The Great Society, was a massive government effort designed to lift Americans out of poverty. It consisted of the Medicaid Program, established in 1965; expansion of AFDC (Aid to Families with Dependent Children) benefits; housing subsidies; food supplements; job creation programs; and other programs to give poor people a helping hand (some of these *entitlement programs* are described in Table 11–3 on p. 331). Murray believed that these efforts, while well meaning, made long-term poverty more entrenched. Suddenly the reinforcers shifted to favor not

Table 11-2   Myths and Facts About Single Mothers and the Welfare State

Most single mothers on welfare used to have child after child in order to get more benefits.

Fact: The average family size of women on welfare is relatively small. Most women on welfare have one or two children. Moreover, the rise in benefits historically for having additional children has been pitifully small, approximately $50 dollars per month.

All mothers and children living below the poverty line were eligible for welfare.

Fact: In 1994, two-thirds of all people living below the poverty line received no AFDC benefits. Most working-age people living under the poverty line work. (As we will see in Chapter 13, today full-time work at a minimum-wage job still puts a family of three below the poverty line.)

Welfare provided poor mothers with an economic incentive not to work.

Fact: In 1991, there were only three states in which the benefit levels for a family of three reached 75 percent of the poverty line. In 1993, in the median state, benefits put that family at 41 percent of the poverty line. (Even with food stamps, in every state except Alaska welfare benefits fall below the poverty line.)

Sources: Children's Defense Fund, 1994, *The State of America's Children, Yearbook, 1994, Washington, DC:* Author; H. J. Karger and J. Stoetz, 1994, *American Social Welfare Policy: A Pluralist Approach,* New York: Longman.

working, as people could get more money by not being employed than by working at a low-paying job. Furthermore, because welfare benefits were targeted to *single mothers* and their children, they were deterrents to getting married. No longer could two live together as cheaply as one. When a poor woman with children could receive more from the government by not having a husband, it made better sense to raise her children alone.

Liberal scholars do not disagree with the idea that government programs designed to help the poor may have weakened family life. When a woman lost her health care coverage when she married a man who worked at a low-paying job or took that job herself, the reinforcements did seem wrong. Johnson's Great Society programs may have negatively affected the African-American community in particular, as they lessened the need for the strong supportive network of mutual helping, through church, extended family, and neighborly aid, that existed before that time (Jewell, 1988).

However, they point out, Murray's argument has some logical holes. Since the middle 1970s, welfare benefits declined steeply. Yet it was during these very years that the proportion of children born out of wedlock sharply rose. States with relatively generous AFDC benefits did not have more out-of-wedlock births than others who offered less support (Bane and Jargowsky, 1988). As the economic costs of becoming pregnant and not finishing high school became greater during the very decades when non-marital births soared (Duncan and Hoffman, 1991), it is hard to argue that poor women chose to have babies without a husband simply in order to get more money. Perhaps these women did not have the option to have a husband at all.

In his book *The Truly Disadvantaged,* sociologist William Julius Wilson (1987) argues that the real key to out-of-wedlock childbirths, especially among poor African-American women, lies in economic change. During the 1970s, with the decline of manufacturing jobs in the northern cities, the bottom fell out of the labor market for unskilled men (see Chapter 13). This loss hit the African-American community hardest because what jobs were available were in the suburbs, leaving men in the inner cities

Some Government Programs for Poor Mothers and Their Children*   Table 11-3

AFDC (Aid to Families with Dependent Children): This mainstay for unemployed women and their children has been the government's most controversial program. AFDC, or "welfare," provided cash to needy children when parents could not provide for them. In 1996 President Clinton signed an historic bill into law that effectively ended the federal commitment to provide unlimited welfare to the needy. Each state is now given a lump sum of federal money with which it can choose to design its own welfare and work programs.

Food Stamps: Recipients are given an allotment of stamps, based on family size and income, with which to buy food. In 1994, about 9 percent of the American population received food stamps, virtually all with incomes below the poverty line.

WIC (Special Supplemental Nutrition Program for Women, Infants, and Children): This program is specifically for low-income pregnant women, mothers who breastfeed their children, and children up to age five. Qualified beneficiaries receive extra foods each month, which may include items such as milk, cheese, eggs, infant formulas, cereal, fruits, and vegetables.

Housing Programs: The U.S. Department of Housing and Urban Development (HUD) offers low-income families vouchers to help subsidize rentals. Public housing is available to people whose incomes are too low to afford housing on the private market. Unlike the above services, housing aid is not entitlement-based (or available to all families in need) and so serves only about a third of needy families. (The long waiting lists for public housing and rental assistance are one cause of homelessness in the United States.)

*Medicaid, the health care system for the poor, was described in Chapter 5.

without hope of getting work. Poverty became concentrated in these neighborhoods, a process accelerated by the flight of more-affluent African-Americans out of these areas. The **male marriageable pool,** or number of acceptable marital partners, for women living in the inner city dramatically declined (Wilson, 1991).

Most experts agree that a poor pool of marriageable men does partly account for the rise in out-of-wedlock births among minorities. For every three unmarried African-American women in their twenties, there is roughly one man with earnings above the poverty level (Lichter, McLaughlin, Kephart, and Landry, 1992). African-American women, as is true of women in general, are often unwilling to marry men who do not have decent jobs (Bulcroft and Bulcroft, 1993). Men with adequate incomes are more likely to marry than those who are poor (Fossett and Kiecolt, 1993; Mare and Winship, 1991; Rindfuss, Morgan, and Swicegood, 1988). However, the experts also believe that a lack of men cannot really explain the "separation between marriage and childbearing" taking place today. Unwed motherhood was low during the Depression, a time of great poverty and hardship. The two-parent family was typical among African-American families during that time as well as under conditions of worse deprivation than now (Gutman, 1976). Out-of-wedlock births are not just rising in the inner cities, but also becoming common in every sector of society.

The main reason, as we saw in Chapter 10, lies in attitudes. Not only has having a child without being married become more socially acceptable, with more children growing up in single-parent households, fewer Americans of any ethnic group reach adulthood today with firm ideas that marriage is absolutely essential. It is a *myth* that growing up in a single-parent family *makes* a person more likely to have a baby out of wedlock or to divorce. In fact, in a similar way as we saw in the studies of fathers, it may

male marriageable pool
Number of acceptable marital partners for women within a given area.

produce greater determination to have a marriage that endures. The problem is that the *models* of non-marriage that children see are so abundant and pervasive today. As many observers argue, while labor market changes may have an impact, family trends, once set in motion, continue, taking on lives of their own (Jencks, 1992; Mare and Winship, 1991).

A Longitudinal Perspective on Unmarried Motherhood

Does this mean that we should lump all poor women who get pregnant as adolescents into the same category, condemning them and their children to lifelong hardship? So far we know little about the future, how the lives of these women might change. To really understand whether having a child out of wedlock is a permanent detriment, we need long-term longitudinal studies exploring these women's lives. Luckily we do have such a study. It is a remarkable investigation of African-American teenage mothers in Baltimore covering 20 years (Furstenberg, Brooks-Gunn, and Morgan, 1987).

In the 1960s, a hospital in Baltimore began a program for teenagers who had become pregnant out of wedlock and wanted to keep their children. Frank Furstenberg (1976) followed the 400 adolescents getting prenatal care in this program and their parents for the next five years.

Compared to their classmates who had not become pregnant, most of the mothers seemed destined for a life of disadvantage. They were more likely to drop out of school and to be living in precarious economic circumstances. While many did get married before or soon after giving birth (recall that this was the 1960s), after five years most of these marriages had already dissolved. Only a minority regularly practiced birth control. Many had a second or third pregnancy by the five-year point.

Had the study stopped here, we would expect these mothers to keep having children, never return to school, and be pessimistic about their lives changing. However, a chance conversation in the early 1980s led Furstenberg and adolescent specialist Jeanne Brooks-Gunn to ask: Why not recontact the original sample and see if these gloomy stereotypes are correct?

The task of finding these women was difficult, but ultimately the researchers were successful. Eighty-nine percent of the sample were located. The insights gained from exploring what happened to these women were worth the effort.

The bleak prognosis was wrong. By 1984, most of the women had completed high school. Only a third spent any time on public assistance. Half were living on incomes that were fairly secure. Furthermore, contrary to what we might expect from their behavior as they entered their twenties, most had *not* gone on to have more births. After their early twenties, less than 10 percent of the women with two or more children had had an additional child.

This is not to say life was easy for these women now in their early thirties. The idea that being an adolescent mother limits a person's life chances was accurate to some degree. Compared to a national sample of African-American women, the mothers had lower incomes and fewer years of schooling. They were having more trouble socially. Few had stable marriages. Most were continuing to raise and support their families by themselves.

Perhaps the most depressing finding had to do with the children. While at the first follow-up, as preschoolers, the boys and girls were developing normally, at the 1984 evaluation they were doing less well. Half had repeated a grade; 44 percent had been expelled or suspended within the past five years; 23 percent had run away from home; a significant proportion had spent time in jail. Boys in particular seemed to have severe problems. In the researchers' words, the magnitude of their troubles seemed more than just adolescent rebellion. Many seemed destined for a life on the streets.

Although this single mother and her daughter living in a homeless shelter seem destined for a grim life, the Baltimore Study of teen-age mothers suggests that their long term prospects may not be as bleak as we think. What impact will recent changes in the welfare system have on this woman's chances of constructing a decent life for herself and her child?

Was this because in their push to advance the women neglected their children? All signs suggested no. The researchers were impressed with the valiant way that the mothers worked to care for their children while they were struggling at school and work and the love and commitment that shone through. Most expressed the feeling that they did as well as possible in less than ideal circumstances. Despite their children's problems, they were proud of them, but hoped the children would avoid their mistakes.

There was great variability among the Baltimore sample from women who went on to fulfill every prediction about the cycle of poverty and failure to those who confounded the stereotypes. Because their study was longitudinal, the researchers could explore what factors predicted making it educationally and economically after such a poor start.

Forces we might think important, such as the age at which a woman had gotten pregnant, whether she came from a two-parent family, and whether she had married the father of the child, had little impact. Being *currently* married and successfully limiting subsequent births did increase the chance of achieving economic success. The most interesting predictors were related to education. Several school-related factors from whether her parents had completed tenth grade, to whether a girl was at grade level when she got pregnant, to how interested she was in her education affected the odds of being on welfare in 1984. In other words, one clue that tells us whether a woman can overcome the effects of becoming pregnant so early relates to her interest in and aptitude for school.

I hope you agree that this study is an outstanding example of the power of longitudinal research. It teaches us about how wrong it can be to stereotype. It offers lessons in avoiding the natural human impulse to assume that what is happening now sums up a life. While their potential may be more limited, we should not write off mothers that enter adulthood poor, unmarried, and with children. The path of life, even among the most disadvantaged Americans, is more variable and malleable than we might think.

There also are reasons why we might be pessimistic if we look longitudinally to what may come. The lives of women who have babies as teenagers today seem more set in stone because, as suggested earlier, in recent years the economic costs of having a baby as an adolescent have become greater (Duncan and Hoffman, 1991). As we will learn in Chapter 13, because of changes in the economy, upward mobility is less possible for today's poorly educated young adults. The explosion of mother-headed families is an ominous development for children, not because single parents always make worse parents, but because they face greater economic and time hurdles in giving their offspring an optimal start in life. It foreshadows more difficulty for the parent generation in their later years. When fathers leave their families, as we might imagine, they tend to be isolated from their adult children in old age (Booth and Amato, 1994; Webster and Herzog, 1995). Women without husbands, being more likely to move in and out of the labor market, are less likely to have pensions or Social Security to draw on when they are senior citizens (O'Rand, 1988). We must reject the tendency to demonize single mothers. In fact, we should applaud them for doing a heroic job. At the same time, it seems irrational to have a society in which women do the breadwinning and child rearing and men are adrift from family life. While they may quarrel about the details, everyone agrees that the two-parent family is inherently better for both children and adults.

APPLICATIONS AND INTERVENTIONS

How can we strengthen the two-parent family? In addition to cutting welfare benefits to single mothers and their children, many people argue that the key is to promote abstinence and raise more barriers to divorce. Others emphasize a different approach: subsidizing childcare, providing medical care to poor working families, and mandating paid parental leave. They believe that these supports would strengthen two-parent families and lessen the pressures that lead to the formation of poor single ones (Bane and Jargowsky, 1988). Corporations should ease the stress on working women and allow men to be more involved with their children by offering on-site childcare, flex time, and generous leave. Everyone agrees that, after a marriage has broken up, states should vigorously enforce child support laws.

Some of these steps have been taken. In 1993, President Bill Clinton signed the **Family and Medical Leave Act,** requiring that companies with over 50 employees offer 12 weeks of unpaid leave to workers to take care of a newborn or an ill relative. As of 1995, every state has automated systems that track and withhold income from men delinquent in child support. Though surveys show that extensive benefits are rare (Seyler, Monroe, and Garand, 1995), Table 11–4 describes some **family-friendly policies** that some large corporations have implemented to help their parent employees. Now let's look at approaches directly aimed at improving parenting itself:

HANDLING THE TRANSITION TO PARENTHOOD   Because they realized that the transition to parenthood was stressful, the Cowans believed that couples might benefit from help adjusting to this change. If husbands and wives had a place to discuss problems, they reasoned, they might cope better and be less prone to divorce. So early on they added an intervention to the Becoming a Family Project, couples groups.

The Cowans (1992) chose groups because a couple who sees others struggling with the same issues will be less likely to feel their difficulties come from problems in *their* relationship. Groups can offer support as couples confront common problems, such as conflict relating to discipline, problems in juggling work and family, and misunderstandings over the division of labor at home. To evaluate the impact of these groups, the Cowans randomly selected 24 couples from the larger 72-couple sample to participate. The groups met for 24 sessions over a six-month period, three months during pregnancy and three after the baby was born.

Two years after the intervention, while 6 of the 48 non-participant couples had filed for divorce, none of the couples in the intervention group had. This difference, though not large enough to reach significance, seemed encouraging. Unfortunately, soon

Family and Medical Leave Act
Bill signed into law by President Clinton in 1993, requiring companies with over 50 employees to grant employees 12 weeks of unpaid leave to take care of a newborn or an ill family member.

family-friendly policies
Employer-sponsored programs or policies designed to improve the quality of workers' family lives.

Examples of Family-Friendly Policies Offered by Corporations

Table 11-4

1. **Leave for family or child care:** Many companies offer workers leave to care for a newborn or an ill relative—even before mandated to do so by law. However, the vast majority do not offer paid leave. In 1989, 18 percent of private medium-and large-sized companies offered fathers unpaid paternity leave.

2. **Flexible schedules (or flex time):** Companies may offer alternatives to the standard 9–5 work day. Employees may choose their starting and ending times, or they may work a full-time schedule, but do so in less than five days. These arrangements are quite common.

3. **On-site daycare:** In 1989, over 1,000 companies offered on-site or near-site daycare centers for employees. Twenty percent offered free care, and another 40 percent offered care at reduced cost. Some companies help workers make provisions for before- and after-school care. A few offer vouchers to parents to subsidize care found on their own. These programs are fairly rare. *Finding affordable daycare is a major stress for working parents with young children*.

4. **Counseling and resource and referral programs:** Companies may hire people who offer help to their employees in finding child and family care. As part of their employee assistance programs (EAPs), they may also provide counseling for family problems.

5. **Flexible benefits:** Companies may offer "cafeteria programs," in which employees have the freedom to choose a benefits package that suits their needs. For instance, under the Dependent Care Assistance Program, employees can receive assistance covering the costs of caring for dependents.

Source: M. A. Ferber, B. O'Farrell, and L. R. Allen (Eds.), 1991, *Work and Family: Policies for a Changing Workforce*. Washington, DC: National Academy Press.

afterwards, the first intervention couple separated. Six years later the divorce rates among participant and non-participant couples were approximately equal. As the Cowans explain, it may not be reasonable to expect a short-term treatment to survive problems that crop up as couples have second or third children, as life changes, and as new crises emerge.

INCREASING FATHERS' SKILLS. While female roles have evolved to include both providing and nurturing, our chapter suggests that men still have far to go. Many fathers have not become fully involved in nurturing, even while they have moved over to share the provider role. The main approach to getting fathers more involved in their families uses the stick of the legal system to force men to "live up" to their obligation to provide. Fathers groups and courses, such as the one below, focus on the nurturing role.

The Fatherhood Course, developed at Boston University, is part of the Fatherhood Project, devoted to exploring men's changing roles (Levant, 1988). While it also offers information about normal child development and management, the main function of this eight-session course is to teach fathers better communication skills. Men are trained to listen to their children's feelings and express their own emotions through role-playing family situations.

Men who enroll in this course come from all walks of life. They range in age from their twenties through their fifties and have children who are infants and children who are adults. While these men feel satisfied as providers, they take the course because they feel dissatisfied with their relationships with their children and want to have a more nurturing involvement in their lives.

The fact that there is a center at her job where she can visit her infant daughter regularly during the day is a real bonus for the woman in the photo. Worksites that offer this benefit are rare, making it difficult emotionally for the millions of woman who give birth and must quickly return to work.

family support programs
Programs funded by the government and private charities devoted to strengthening families.

OFFERING SUPPORT TO FAMILIES   A variety of programs help parents be better parents indirectly, by generally easing the stress on the family. These **family support programs,** funded by the government and private charities, may operate from schools or hospitals or churches or storefronts. While they often serve poor families, some have a middle-class clientele.

Family Focus Lawndale is an example of a full-service *family resource center.* Located in a low-income Chicago neighborhood, the program was originally set up to serve teenage mothers—offering tutoring, counseling, and other services. However, news about the program spread rapidly, and soon siblings and cousins of the teens wanted a group of their own. In response, the staff, many of whom started out as participants in the program, decided to offer pregnancy prevention programs and counseling for non-pregnant teens. Next they added a group for young men. Today Family Focus Lawndale is the hub for a range of programs—activities for high school students, programs to improve school readiness, and home-based parent education groups. Staff members help families identify services that they may be eligible for, such as housing assistance. They offer emergency housing and food. Evaluations of the parenting program show improvement in skills: Participants talk more to their children and punish them less (Allan, Brown, and Finlay, 1994).

Will these interventions help strengthen families? I think you may agree that more than piecemeal efforts are required. We need to reach out to the parents who, while they may need help coping, do not have these programs available in their communities or will not go for aid. Many experts question the value of *any* government policy intended to change today's high rates of marital disruption and out-of-wedlock births (Bane and Jargowsky, 1988; Furstenberg and Cherlin, 1991). These changes are a function of our different attitudes toward marriage and women's new, less dependent roles.

We cannot put the genie of less-defined gender roles back in the bottle, nor would many people want to, judging from polls. Most Americans support a woman's right to work; they do not want to go back to the time when women were totally dependent. They no longer believe that couples who are unhappy with one another have to stay together, miserable for life. However, the same surveys show that people agree on basic family values, that is, that a sense of commitment and responsibility to our own *and our neighbors'* children is an important benchmark of being adult (Mellman, Lazarus, and Rivlin, 1990). I personally feel that, rather than blaming parents for being deficient, we need to focus more on that commitment to our neighbors' children. In other words, we must appreciate the importance of the wider context within which child rearing occurs. Parents cannot be left to go it alone. The best help for families is a society that supports *all* children and *all* parents. As the African proverb says, "It takes a whole village to raise a child."

KEY TERMS & CONCEPTS

transition to parenthood
Becoming a Family Project
division of labor
new nurturer father
provider role
sex-role model
house husband
dual-career couples
male marriageable pool
Family and Medical Leave Act
family-friendly policies
family support programs

RECOMMENDED READINGS

Fatherhood

Berman, P. W., and Pedersen, F. A. (Eds.). (1987). *Men's transitions to parenthood: Longitudinal studies of early family experience.* Hillsdale, NJ: Erlbaum.

Bronstein, P., and Cowan, C. P. (1988). *Fatherhood today: Men's changing role in the family.* New York: Wiley-Interscience.

Furstenberg, F. F., Jr. (1988). Good dads—bad dads: Two faces of fatherhood. In A. J. Cherlin (Ed.), *The changing American family and public policy* (pp. 93–218). Washington, DC: Urban Institute Press.

The first two books survey the research on fatherhood. Furstenberg's article provides a historical overview of fatherhood and an interesting perspective on how the women's movement has changed fatherhood.

Motherhood

Furstenberg, F. F., Brooks-Gunn, J., and Morgan, S. P. (1987). *Adolescent mothers in later life.* New York: Cambridge University Press.

This is the longitudinal study of adolescent mothers described in the text.

Genevie, L., and Margoles, E. (1987). *The motherhood report: How women feel about being mothers.* New York: Macmillan.

This survey of the inner lives of mothers is also described in the chapter.

Transition to Parenthood

Cowan, C. P., and Cowan, P. A. (1992). *When partners become parents: The big life change for couples.* New York: Basic Books.

Michaels, G. Y., and Goldberg, W. (1988). *The transition to parenthood: Current theory and research.* New York: Cambridge University Press.

The first book describes the Becoming a Family Project. The second book is devoted to research relating to the transition to parenthood.

Poor Families

Murray, C. (1984). *Losing ground: American social policy, 1950–1980.* New York: Basic Books.

Wilson, W. J. (1987). *The truly disadvantaged.* Chicago: University of Chicago Press.

These authors articulate the conservative (Murray) and liberal (Wilson) positions on the growth of unwed motherhood.

Children's Defense Fund. *The state of America's children, Yearbooks.* Washington, DC: Author.

Allan, M., Brown, P., and Finlay, B. (1994). *Helping children by strengthening families: A look at family support programs.* Washington, DC: Children's Defense Fund.

These two publications are from the Children's Defense Fund, a watchdog group devoted to improving children's lives. The first publication—which comes out yearly—offers a comprehensive review of child poverty in the United States and covers topics such as adolescent pregnancy, violence, hunger, and homelessness. The second describes a variety of family support services and programs.

The Older Family

Chapter Outline

The 96-year-old woman in the drawing at the beginning of the chapter is a family pioneer. At age 47, she became a grandparent and has been called Grandma for half of her life. At age 65, she was widowed and has lived as an older widow for 30 years. She has an adolescent great-grandchild. All of her grandchildren are middle-aged. Five years ago she was there to comfort her daughter when she, too, became a widow at age 65. As she approaches her 100th birthday in the year 2000, this woman can survey her family with knowledge no previous generation ever had. My grandmother has participated in a revolution in intergenerational life.

In 1900, many people did not live past their fifties. If both sets of parents were alive at their wedding, a bride and groom felt blessed. Today it is rare not to see grandparents walking down the aisle. Even great-grandparents may be there. Four-generation families are common. Even five generations are no longer unheard of today.

In 1900, parents and children were only adults together for a small fraction of life. The chance of a person in his or her forties having two living parents was only 1 in 10. By 1980, the time the generations shared adulthood had expanded dramatically. Almost half of all Americans in their late fifties still had a mother or father alive. Today even celebrating the 65th birthday of a child is not rare. In that same census, 10 percent of all people over 65 had an "elderly child" (Brody, 1985; Giarrusso, Silverstein, and Bengtson, 1996).

In 1900, widowhood occurred relatively early in life. Being a grandparent meant enjoying young children, if a person was lucky enough to see the third generation born. Today, as we saw with my grandmother, women can be widowed as senior citizens and live for decades. The grandparent role extends well beyond the childhood years. When Gregory Kennedy (1990) polled 704 college students, 9 out of 10 had a living grandparent. The majority had two. Almost a third had a great-grandparent still alive.

These changes are mainly due to the dramatic extension in life expectancy, especially in later life (Rosenwaike and Dolinsky, 1987). Another factor is also involved. In the years immediately after World War II, as we learned in Chapter 11, women began having children earlier, closer to age 20 than during the Depression years. This caused an "acceleration of the generational wheels," a compression in the time generations were formed. Demographers estimate that during the baby boom four generations were conceived in about the same number of years that three had been (Aizenberg and Treas, 1985).

This means that the average age of the family has tilted upward. The decline in fertility among young adults has accentuated this trend, making families older than ever before. As the family has more middle-aged and elderly members, the job of raising children, while still important, is no longer the *only* function of family life. New concerns have emerged: living in a long empty-nest marriage, taking care of a frail old parent for years.

Sociologist Ethel Shanas (1984) describes these new families as "pioneers." Uncharted relationships must be negotiated and new roles carved out. How does a senior citizen daughter relate to her 96-year-old mother? What is it like to be a grandmother to a middle-aged, college professor grandchild? How does the stereotype of the elderly grandmother fit in with a role that often occurs in the vigorous center years of a woman's life?

In this chapter, we concentrate on four of these new relationships: elderly couple, widow, adult child and elderly parent, and grandparent. We examine how these roles have been transformed both by the life-expectancy revolution and by the revolution in family life. Keep in mind that in addition to leaving out siblings and great-grandparents our selective approach cannot fully reflect intergenerational life in another way. The family is a mosaic of relationships. It is more than the sum of its parts.

OLDER COUPLES

In Chapters 10 and 11, we saw that marriage has become a more fleeting state. Paradoxically, the other transformation in marriage involves its extended duration or length. A century ago couples were often widowed before their children grew up. The empty nest lasted on average 1.6 years. Today, if people get married at the typical age (their middle twenties) and do not divorce, two-thirds can expect their marriage to last 40 years. If we combine the first childless years of marriage and the empty nest, one-third of this time together will be spent alone (Aizenberg and Treas, 1985).

Long-Married Couples

Research on long-married older couples offers lessons in the fact that people can indeed live together happily for life. When Robert Atchley and Sheila Miller (1983) interviewed elderly couples married on average 35 years, they found that a high degree of happiness was typical. As we might expect from our discussion of homogamy, these couples were very much alike. On a list of goals and favorite activities, they gave *identical* answers about 80 percent of the time. The researchers concluded: "It was a genuine pleasure to be around these couples. They accepted one another fully, were obviously devoted to one another, and were very much enjoying their lives together" (p. 90).

In another set of studies, researchers compared middle-aged couples married over 15 years with an elderly long-married group, men and women in their sixties married at least 35 years. The elderly couples had fewer arguments, shared more activities, and were less likely to mention children as a cause of distress (Carstensen, Gottman, and Levenson, 1995; Levenson, Carstensen, and Gottman, 1993). Clearly here we are seeing the effects of self-selection; that is, only relatively happy couples tend to "make it" to later life. However, these studies also can be viewed as reinforcing one message of the previous chapters: Children can put distance between a husband and wife. Relationships improve when they are grown and on their own. Marital happiness follows a U-shaped curve.

Some researchers find that the traditional division of labor, often a source of conflict for younger couples, is less distinct in later life. Timothy Brubacker (1985) asked golden anniversary couples about household tasks, such as cooking, cleaning, and yardwork. Would these jobs be broken down according to gender, or do people married this long have a more fluid arrangement for handling these details of their shared life?

Masculine tasks still were done by the husbands. They were responsible for the finances, repairs, and work on the car. In the "feminine" area, the division of labor had broken down. Husbands shared the cooking, cleaning, and shopping. They took over all of the housework if their wives were ill. This blurring fits in with David Gutmann's concept of *psychological androgeny* described in Chapter 8. If older men and women are more psychologically similar, share the housework equally, and are free from the stresses of parenting and work, it makes sense that marriage would be especially happy in later life.

These studies almost all involve select, advantaged couples. When researchers examine larger, more representative groups, they find less upbeat results. Using the National Survey of Families and Households, Maximiliane Szinovacz and Paula Harpster (1994) examined how a couple's retirement status affected the division of labor around the house. As Figure 12-1 illustrates, this study shows that the traditional pattern exists. When both spouses are retired, the woman does most of the housework. Even when the wife is employed and her husband is retired, women still spend more time on female household tasks. Moreover, another study revealed that this inequity upsets retirement-age wives as well as the young. Contemporary women of *any age* often feel unsupported when their husbands never pitch in (Pina and Bengtson, 1995).

Figure 12-1

Hours per Week Spent in Household Work by Men and Women of Different Retirement Statuses

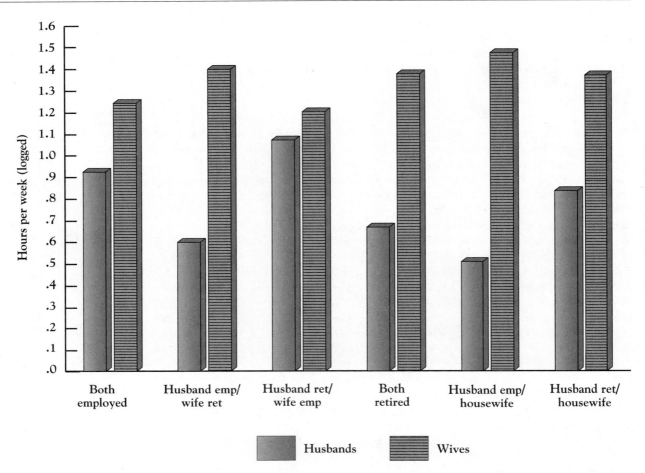

With the caution that there are many exceptions to this "on average data," this survey shows that older husbands tend to share the housework fairly equally only when they are retired and their wives work.

Source: M. Szinovacz and P. Harpster, 1994, Couples' Employment/Retirement Status and the Division of Household Tasks, *Journal of Gerontology, 49,* S125–S136. Copyright © 1994 Gerontological Society of America.

Then there is this survey comparing marital closeness among couples in their late fifties and early sixties, couples aged 65 to 75, and couples over age 75 (Depner and Ingersoll-Dayton, 1985): Here the theme was *less* closeness with advancing age. Especially the old-old couples reported low levels of marital support. This poll suggests that at the end of their lives together husbands and wives emotionally retreat.

So while marital happiness is alive and well among advantaged older couples, those people who have survived physically and emotionally to remain together until their later years, distance, disappointment, and isolation blight long-lasting marriages, too. There may even be a reversal of the U-shaped pattern of satisfaction at the end of life. If this second dip does occur in advanced old age, one logical cause immediately comes to mind: illness.

ILLNESS AND MARRIAGE.   Illness is a good candidate to change a marriage for the worse at any age. It is difficult to reach out to another person when our energy is consumed by aches and pains. It is hard to feel loving when our job shifts from life companion to nurse. When illness hits a couple, the care-giving falls on the well partner's shoulders, even when there are grown children. When a spouse is alive, sons and daughters hold off from really stepping in (Gatz, Bengtson, and Blum, 1990).

In fact, when Atchley and Miller examined the impact of three changes among their older middle-class couples—retirement, moving (being a recent arrival in the town), and being sick—illness was the only stress that had a significant effect. If a husband or wife became ill, the partner's morale declined. While in this study illness had its greatest impact on men, other researchers found that a spouse with health problems is especially likely to affect wives, interfering with life satisfaction and lowering morale (Quirouette and Gold, 1992).

Notice that these researchers have been exploring the individual's morale, not a couple's commitment to one another and the marriage. While illness is more likely to be detrimental in younger adults (Booth and Johnson, 1994) it has surprisingly little impact on that sense of commitment when it is a more "on time" event. Colleen Johnson (1985b) interviewed 76 elderly couples after a spouse had been discharged from the hospital, asking husbands and wives how happy they were with one another and how emotionally satisfying their relationship was. Most couples reported low levels of conflict. Most said that they could rely on their spouses for emotional support. While over time caring for an ill spouse might change these feelings (Johnson and Catalano, 1983), this study is a testament. During this late-life stress, older couples are resilient, able to close ranks and stay committed to one another.

Other research supports Johnson's findings. Even when they are disabled themselves, when spouses need care-giving elderly husbands and wives often shoulder the job alone. They are unlikely to rely on formal sources of help (Penning, 1990). Compared to caregiving by children, spousal care is extensive, likely to occur for a long period before placement in a nursing home (Montgomery and Kosloski, 1994). Spouse care-givers take on the burden with a freer heart, reporting less ambivalence, conflict, and stress than care-giving daughters or sons (Cantor, 1983; Johnson, 1983; Johnson and Catalano, 1983).

Sometimes being thrust into this role can strengthen a marriage. When researchers compared husband and wife care-givers for Alzheimer's patients, one-fourth of the men said nursing their wives intensified their sense of commitment. It increased their feelings of love (Fitting, Rabins, Lucas, and Eastham, 1986). Johnson and Joseph Catalano (1983) use the term "enmeshing" to describe this process. As a spouse needs more care, the couple reduces their outside involvements, withdraws from friends and relatives, and turns inward to the marriage to satisfy all their needs.

This is not to say that caring for an ill spouse is easy. In one of the earliest studies of these care-givers, researchers labeled their subjects "the hidden patients" (Fengler and Goodrich, 1979). However, in spite of the personal pain it may cause, *this cohort* of elderly couples seems to take their vows "in sickness and in health" seriously.

Elderly Lovers and Newlyweds

So far, we have been focusing on people who have been married for decades. However, as we know from Chapter 4, especially now that society has become more tolerant of late-life romance, many people seek out new relationships in their senior citizen years. What are these "autumn love affairs" like?

Performing a wedding ceremony may always be an event this rabbi looks forward to with pleasure. But from the wide grin on his face in the photo, this triumphant testament to the ageless quality of love is likely to have a special place in his heart.

Kristine and Richard Bulcroft (Bulcroft and O'Connor-Rodin, 1986) interviewed a group of elderly lovers, comparing their relationships with those of college students who were romantically involved. Being older did not dim the symptoms of passionate love. The older lovers felt the same heightened sense of reality, awkwardness, heart palpitations, and excitement as the 20-year-olds. It did not weaken the external trappings of romance. Both young and elderly lovers enjoyed candlelit dinners, walks, flowers, and candy. However, among the older lovers, dating was more varied. In addition to going to the movies or out for pizza, older couples might go camping or fly to Hawaii for the weekend. The involvement was faster-paced. People said that at their age there was not much time for playing the field.

There was more ambivalence about sexuality. Because they had grown up before the sexual revolution, the elderly lovers seemed to have more trouble deciding whether having intercourse was right. In spite of their mixed feelings, most decided to go ahead. Sexuality was a vital part of most relationships. Many couples reported that sex was *better* in later life.

There was another interesting difference. Few of the older people wanted the romance to end in a marriage. The woman were especially reluctant. They felt that getting married was not necessary, as they did not want children. They were afraid that remarrying at their age would mean being saddled with the job of nurse. Many had cared for their husbands for months during the final illness. They did not relish the thought of more years spent as care-giver to a sick spouse.

To find out what happens when people marry for a second time after age 65, another group of researchers interviewed elderly couples married between one and six years. While some of these people remarried soon after being divorced or widowed, many had lived for years before finding a new partner. The women were most surprised at the turn their lives had taken. Half said that they were convinced they would never marry again. Among the reasons given for remarrying, companionship stood out. People got married mainly in order to have someone to travel or do things with; falling in love ranked second.

These marriages were working out. The majority of the couples said that they were happier in this marriage than the first. They believed that their marriage was better because at this time of life they were more mature. And marital happiness came easier because the stresses of child rearing and career were no longer there (Pieper, Petkovsek, and East, 1986).

While testing the truth of the old saying that marriage is "better the second time around" requires being on the spot to measure happiness during the first—that is, doing longitudinal research—other studies suggest that older newlyweds are a very happy group. In the Consumer Reports study of sexual behavior over age 50, discussed in Chapter 4, couples married under five years reported the highest levels of happiness. The only group that was almost as content was the golden anniversary couples. So, while it may make a difference in some aspects of romance, the joy of falling in love and marrying seems as intense at 80 as at 25.

WIDOWHOOD

Though the *divorce revolution* has also affected older couples, divorce is a transition that tends to occur relatively early in adult life (Bumpass and Aquilino, 1995). Widowhood remains the number one change in marriage that people can expect in their later years. In contrast to divorce, this transition tends to be a female event. Not only are most older women widowed, but also for women widowhood is often a long stage of life. This is because of women's higher life expectancy, plus their tendency to marry older men.

Being widowed, for both men and women, means mourning the loss of a life companion. As is true with divorce, it means being forced to radically change one's life. Jobs that may have seemed impossible, such as understanding the finances, cooking the meals, or fixing the faucet, fall on the widow or widower. Even waking up takes on new meaning when it is done alone. Relationships with friends may be drastically altered. Many friendships during marriage are based on being part of a couple (Lopata, 1973). Other bonds may weaken, such as relationships with in-laws, the other side of the family. The widowed person must remake an identity whose central focus was often "married person" for all of adult life. British psychiatrist Colin Parkes (1972), whose research on widows is discussed in the next section, beautifully describes how the world tilts: "Even when words remain the same, their meaning changes. The family is no longer the same as it was. Neither is home or a marriage" (p. 93).

Though the distinction is a bit artificial, widowhood research is divided into two categories: studies examining bereavement and those exploring widowhood as a life stage.

Bereavement
The first scientific study of bereavement was begun after the famous Coconut Grove nightclub fire that suddenly killed several hundred people in Boston in 1942. Psychiatrist Erich Lindemann (1944) decided to interview people who had lost a loved one in the tragedy in order to explore the symptoms of **normal mourning.** In addition to crying or having problems eating and sleeping, Lindemann found that mourners were often troubled by guilt, blaming themselves for not doing enough for their loved ones. They felt angry at other people, even those they cared about. They were preoccupied by the image of the dead person, at times so intensely they almost hallucinated his or her presence.

normal mourning
Typical symptoms of bereavement after a loved one has died.

These observations were extended by Colin Parkes (1972) in a study of London widows during the first year of bereavement. Parkes also found that anger, guilt, and a sense of the loved one's presence were common symptoms of bereavement. Some widows showed a total identification with their dead husbands. In one woman's words, "My husband is in me right through and through. I can feel him in me doing everything. . . . I suppose he is guiding me all of the time" (p. 90). We might imagine that these intense emotions are adaptive psychologically, helping the new widow gradually adjust to life alone.

Parkes's widows had other unusual symptoms. They were obsessed with the events surrounding the death, repeatedly going over their husbands' final hours, their last day. Some reported searching for their spouses, even though they knew intellectually that they were being irrational. British psychiatrist and ethologist John Bowlby (1980) believes that this searching behavior is an expression of the attachment response to separation that we can see in infancy when the baby cries and crawls after its mother as she is about to leave the room. According to Bowlby, not only is this impulse for reunion evoked when we lose our most important attachment figure at any time of life, but also it is not specific to human beings. Consider this poignant observation by the ethologist Konrad Lorenz:

> The first response to the disappearance of the partner consists in the anxious attempt to find him again. The goose moves about restlessly by day and night, flying great distances and visiting places where the partner might be found, uttering all the time the penetrating tri-syllabic call. . . . The searching expeditions are extended further and further and quite often the searcher gets lost; or succumbs to an accident. . . . All the objective, observable characteristics of the goose's behavior on losing its mate are roughly identical with human grief. (Quoted in Worden, 1982, p. 9)

Are all these reactions *characteristic* of bereavement? Should we expect them and worry when they do not occur? For answers, we turn to a more scientific study of widows and widowers.

In this investigation, researchers drew on health department records to recruit several hundred men and women over age 55 who had recently lost a spouse. Unlike in the studies described earlier, these psychologists took care to use standard scales of depression and morale and to compare the reactions of the widowed to a control group of married older adults (Breckenridge, Gallagher, Thompson, and Peterson, 1986).

One of the supposedly normal signs of mourning, intense self-blame, while occurring a certain percentage of the time, was *not* a typical response. Only about one-quarter of the widows and widowers reported any feelings of guilt, and most who did said these feelings were mild. Less than 10 percent showed other signs of anger directed against the self, such as the sense of having failed or feelings of being punished. The three most frequent symptoms people did have were typical reactions to any upsetting experience, crying, depressed mood, and insomnia.

The researchers suggest that their findings show self-blame is *not* a normal feature of bereavement. In fact, its presence may indicate that normal mourning is turning into a true emotional problem, depression. One symptom that depressed people may have is irrational guilt, feeling "terrible about myself" (see Chapter 9). These emotions, when intense, suggest that mourning may not be progressing normally, the person is not recovering, and the individual may need professional help. What does progressing normally really mean?

tasks of mourning
Benchmarks that must be negotiated in order to recover from bereavement.

TASK THEORIES OF BEREAVEMENT. Counselors who work with bereaved adults often measure the progress of mourning according to benchmarks or tasks. Here is psychologist William Worden's (1982) version of the **tasks of mourning:**

1. ***Accepting the reality of the death.*** Right after the person dies there is a feeling it has not happened. The new widow may understand the facts intellectually, but still feel that at any moment she will wake up from a dream. The first task of mourning is to gradually accept the fact that the person has died.
2. ***Feeling the pain.*** In order to get over a loved one's death, the widowed person must accept reality emotionally, confronting the painful feelings and mourning deeply and openly.
3. ***Adjusting to a new life.*** The person must learn to function in areas the spouse had taken over. A woman must learn how to do the taxes and take out the garbage. A man must prepare his dinner and take care of the house. Eventually the person must construct a stable, satisfying new life.
4. ***Reinvesting emotionally.*** While it is not necessary to develop a new romantic involvement, it is important to regain the capacity to love in a broader sense. Recovering from mourning means being able to care about life and other people again.

How long should these tasks take? Worden believes that they should be well under way by the end of one year. Another expert, Therese Rando (1984), believes that for widows two or three years is not too long. Still, both *thanatologists* (death specialists) emphasize that recovery is a relative term. According to Worden, asking when mourning is over is a bit like asking "How high is up?"

Does recovering from mourning depend on feeling the pain? The idea that in order to recover a person must do **grief work,** or mourn intensely, is an accepted principle of bereavement (Rando, 1984, 1992–1993; Worden, 1982). On what evidence is this idea based?

grief work
Idea that in order to recover from a loved one's death it is necessary to grieve intensely.

In their early studies, Lindemann (1944) and Parkes (1972) found that people who broke down and experienced the full emotional impact of the death seemed to adjust best to the trauma. People who denied, minimized their feelings, or reacted stoically had more trouble adjusting to their loss. However, in a more recent study of young widows and widowers, Parkes and Robert Weiss (1983) discovered that people with especially severe emotional reactions had the most trouble recovering. Mourning very intensely was a bad sign!

Margaret Stroebe (1993) argues that our emphasis on the need for grief work is misplaced. In some cultures, giving vent to emotions is seen as pathological. The key to recovering from mourning is dampening down grieving and quickly returning to a normal life. There are certain situations, such as when death was highly traumatic, when denial may be the best strategy. There are times when distracting the mourner by "talking about everything else" helps. Counselors need to take a less rigid approach. What works best depends on the situation and the individual.

Bereavement counselors and others may make another error in their efforts to help. Without minimizing the upset, most studies show that older widowed people tend to cope very well (Pellman, 1992; Zisook and Shuchter, 1991). However, this is not the message we hear from people who actually deal with the bereaved. In comparing widows' and professionals' perceptions of bereavement, Shoshanna Conway, Bert Hayslip, and Ruth Tandy (1991) found that doctors, clergymen, funeral directors, and counselors imagined that widowhood caused incapacitating emotional pain, more difficulty than widows themselves described. Are some people doing the widowed a disservice by assuming that they are more devastated and incapable than they really are?

Even the idea that grieving can be fit into defined stages or tasks has been called into question in a longitudinal study of the first two years of bereavement. When researchers interviewed a large sample of elderly widows and widowers at regular times

Table 12-1   **Influences That May Make Mourning More Intense**

Antecedent factors	Concurrent factors	Subsequent factors
Childhood losses	Mode of death (abrupt vs. expected)	Social isolation
Adult losses of significant others	SES	Financial problems
Previous mental illnesses	Immigrant status	Few life opportunities
Never having lived alone before	Age, ethnicity, and gender	
	Character of final illness (e.g., did the person have Alzheimer's disease?)	

during this period, they found that, rather than progressing in an orderly way as task theories imply, bereavement was more chaotic. People experienced conflicting emotions and behaviors simultaneously. An example occurred in the tumultuous first few months. At that time, scores on measures of *both* depression and psychological strength were very high. Rather than just feeling "at their worst," people felt a mixture of emotions, both very distressed and very proud of how they were handling things. Moreover, while there was gradual improvement, there was little truth to the idea that there is a defined time when mourning "is complete." At the end of two years, people were still grieving, still actively reconstructing their new lives. Along with signs of recovery, some even had symptoms supposedly typical of the first weeks, such as shock, disbelief, and avoidance of the fact (Lund, Caserta, and Dimond, 1986).

INFLUENCES AFFECTING RECOVERY.   This is not to say that we should abandon any effort to chart mourning. After some time, the person should get better in the sense of remaking a new life. After a certain time, we should be concerned if our mother is still setting the table for our dead father, or weeping continually, or unable to get any pleasure in living. In this day, it is not appropriate to make mourning a husband a life career.

Table 12-1 suggests that a variety of influences from previous losses of loved ones, to the extent of financial planning, to a history of depression, to whether the death was unexpected may increase the chance that normal mourning will shade into **pathological bereavement** or **chronic grief** (Zisook, Shuchter, and Mulvihill, 1990).

pathological bereavement or chronic grief
When a bereaved person still is actively mourning beyond the time when recovery should have occurred.

One interesting marker is the age of the deceased. As we will see in our chapter on death and dying, when the person is very old it may be easier to come to terms with the loss than when death comes at an "unfair" time, in the prime of life. Now let's examine another basic marker that is supposed to affect mourning, gender.

WOMEN, MEN, AND WIDOWHOOD.   One widely accepted "widowhood principle" is that women adjust better to the death of a spouse than men (Rando, 1984; Worden, 1982). The most compelling example has to do with physical health. When Duke University epidemiologists followed several thousand widowed people, they found that, while widows did not have an elevated death rate, widowers did die more often, both during the first six months of bereavement and afterwards. In fact, a widower's risk of dying only returned to normal if he remarried (Belsky, 1990). In other words, this research confirms one message of Chapter 10: Possibly because women have traditionally watched over their partners' physical well-being, marriage is more health-enhancing for men!

In addition to being the health protectors, another reason why women are supposed to cope better relates to social support. Recall from Chapter 3 that social isolation is a risk factor for disease. When men lose their wives, they often lose their only confidants. Women have close friends and closer relationships with children to cushion the blow. Especially when they are older, women have a built-in support system when they enter widowhood, their widowed friends (see Feature 12-1 on page 352). For older women, the widowhood path is predictable, well staked out, smoothed, and made easier by those who have gone before.

Does widowhood really hit men harder? The longitudinal study of the first two years of bereavement discussed in the last section even casts doubt on this belief. When they looked for gender differences in mourning, the researchers were surprised to find that widowers did not have more intense symptoms than widows. Moreover, both men and women recovered at the same rate. Contrary to the idea that men suffer more, this study suggests that the bereavement responses of elderly widows and widowers are identical (Lund et al., 1986).

Epidemiologist Margery Feinson (1986) makes the same point: The research showing that men suffer more psychologically after a spouse's death is inconsistent. While the evidence that older men suffer more negative physical effects is firmer, this does not hold for a certain group of elderly widowers, men over age 75. In fact, in comparing the bereavement reactions of several hundred elderly men and women, Feinson found *no* gender differences in mourning.

Perhaps, as we saw with divorce, it may be more appropriate to say that women and men have different types of strain. Finances is one area where women fare worse. As is true of divorcees, widows have to cope with less income (Bound, Duncan, Laren, and Oleinick, 1991; Holden and Smock, 1991; Morgan, 1991). For widowers, household management and loneliness may cause more distress (Umberson, Wortman, and Kessler, 1992). However, as Table 12-1 suggests, with widowhood, too, the best policy is to adopt a *contextual* approach. Rather than making generalizations, we need to look at the individual person. How flexible emotionally is the widow? Does she have opportunities to construct a new life? Does her "social support system" foster recovery? The importance of these considerations is revealed when examining research on widowhood as a life stage.

Life as a Widowed Person

Mourning, the first phase of widowhood, tells us little about people who live day to day in "the widowed state." To probe these day-to-day experiences, we have the rich insights of two classic studies by sociologist Helena Lopata (1973, 1979). Lopata studied Chicago women over age 50 who had been widows an average of 11 years. Because Chicago has such a rich ethnic mix, many of her subjects were first-generation immigrants; others were totally Americanized.

Lopata found that most women were living alone in their own homes. Widows complained of being lonely, but often said that they preferred this to moving in with adult children. Not only did they enjoy the freedom of living alone, but also they were afraid conflict would be inevitable if they were to move in with a child. This spirit of self-reliance extended to finances. Although more than half reported that their income had dropped dramatically after their husbands' death, few widows wanted financial help from relatives.

For many of these widows, their identity as wife had been central to their adult lives. One-fifth felt that they had never really gotten over their husbands' death. However, most said that they did not want to remarry, mentioning, among other reasons, their age, their fear that they would have to take care of a sick husband (one out of six had nursed their husbands at home for at least a year before death), and their conviction that they could never find a man as good as their late spouses. This last reason for not

12-1 The Adult Experience: Old Friends

The three widows were close friends for over 60 years. They met as young parents after World War I. After World War II, as empty-nest couples, they sold their homes and moved to the same apartment complex in town. Rose and Ellie comforted Ann when her husband died in 1964. Ann was there to comfort Rose and Ellie when their husbands passed away. They have supported each other through the deaths of middle-aged children and a daughter's divorce. In recent years, they visited, played cards, and, when they felt up to it, entertained one another for dinner. They called every morning, in Ann's words, to "let each other know we are still alive." Last year Ann and Rose were worried about Ellie, at 87 the baby. She had had several heart attacks and was in a wheelchair. A few months ago Ellie died. According to Ann, friends, while never as crucial as family, are important at any age. One of the saddest things about being 94 is that you outlive all your friends.

Gerontologists use the wonderful word *convoy* to describe the network of close relationships that cushion our journey through life. While, as people grow old, family is especially central to this convoy (Levitt, Weber, and Guacci, 1993), friends remain important fellow travelers, even in advanced old age. In studying people ranging in age from 70 to 104, Freider Lang and Laura Carstensen (1994) found that, while the social networks of the very old were only about half the size of those of the younger group, the number of close relationships was the same. Particularly among people without immediate family, friends were a central source of support. In focusing on women over 85, other researchers confirmed that most people still had at least one close friend. However, disability was an impediment, as in this longitudinal survey, when a person became ill, it was difficult to maintain the reciprocal giving necessary for friendships to endure (Johnson and Troll, 1994).

On the other hand, another later-life change may make friends more important sources of this giving in old age. In comparing the two types of women, Sally Gallagher and Naomi Gerstel (1993) found that elderly widows reached out more often than wives to offer help to friends. In the researchers' words, marriage "privatizes help-giving" to family. Once they are widowed, women rely on friends to perform the nurturing, supportive functions that had been confined to the marital bond.

marrying is particularly interesting because it demonstrated a psychological process Lopata called *sanctification*. Many widows put their late husbands on a pedestal, enshrining their memory and idealizing the marriage as total bliss.

Their current relationships were more conflict-ridden. Although children were the most important figures in their lives, relationships with these offspring were rarely totally close. Usually widows felt closest to one child, most often a daughter.

Friends were important for the most well educated widows. Many women reported having problems changing friendships based on being part of a couple. When old friendships could not survive the strain of this life change, the widow had to make new friends. One reason friends were especially important to the better educated women seemed to be that they were able to make these adaptations. They had the skills to transform old relationships and build satisfying new ones.

In fact, education and social class were important predictors of the quality of a woman's widowed life. The least well educated, immigrant widows were most susceptible to depression and social isolation. Lopata suggested that the traditional lifestyle these women had before being widowed was partly to blame, as it stressed being totally dependent on a husband. Traditional women, she argued, could only be happy when their environment remained the same. When being widowed meant having to construct a new life, these women were unprepared to cope.

Unfortunately many women were only barely holding on. Half said that they never went to places such as movie theaters; 4 in 10 never entertained. The same fraction reported that they always ate lunch alone. While lack of money probably played a part in restricting these widows, their answers show that many were living solitary, limited lives.

A rare in-depth study of a small group of widowers suggests that for elderly men life without a spouse can be equally hard. Robert Rubinstein (1986) interviewed men in their seventies who had been widowed for an average of five years, questioning them about activities, relationships, life satisfaction, and loneliness. More than half were floundering, clinging to the past, unable to form new satisfying relationships. These widowers had trouble finding focus for their hours, living "day by day." Rubinstein's case histories suggest that, when they do not get remarried, widowers, too, may have trouble reconstructing new lives.

Luckily many widowed men either marry again or find new female companions to ease their lives (Cleveland and Gianturco, 1976; Treas and VanHilst, 1976). While women are likely to live on without a partner, recent research contradicts the gloomy portrait Lopata paints. Women do get support from other family members to compensate for losing their husbands (Avis, Brambilla, Vass, and McKinlay, 1991; Dean, Matt, and Wood, 1992). While, as was true of Lopata's women, these family relationships, though critically important, can cause strain as well as pleasure (Morgan, 1984), friendships endure and may become more intense after a husband's death (Connidis and Davies, 1992; see Feature 12-1).

National studies show that many women thrust into poverty by widowhood exit this state even without remarrying, implying that widows today *do* have the skills to enter the work world (Bound et al., 1991). Today's non-immigrant widows have been socialized differently than Lopata's traditional women. Especially if they are middle-aged and young-old, contemporary women often do enter widowhood with the resources to construct a new life.

APPLICATIONS AND INTERVENTIONS

The research suggests that the best intervention for widowhood is preparation: Develop a rewarding, multifaceted married life. As was suggested in our chapter on personality, there is continuity between who we are before being widowed and who we will be afterward.

Ironically the *deinstitutionalization of marriage* may pave the way for an easier widowhood. People who have lived alone for years before marrying or who have been divorced are likely to have better survival skills for coping with being single in their later years. In fact, in one study, having already been divorced or widowed did make it easier for a woman to handle the financial hardships of new widowhood (O'Bryant and Straw, 1991).

On a more immediate level, **widowed persons services** ease the transition to this life state. These services, sponsored by churches or human service agencies, may offer seminars for widows and widowers, operate telephone hot-lines, or have widowed volunteers make home visits to the newly bereaved. Almost all of these programs sponsor self-help groups in which people come together to discuss their difficulties and concerns.

widowed persons services *Supportive services to aid widows and widowers.*

Michael Caserta and Dale Lund (1993) conducted an *outcome study* of the effectiveness of these groups. They led sessions for new widows and widowers and examined the mental health of participants before entering and at regular intervals for two years. Interestingly the sessions were only helpful for men and women with the lowest competence, people who entered widowhood with the poorest self-esteem, life satisfaction, and mental health. For people with high emotional resilience, during the first eight weeks the groups actually produced more depression than before! The lesson is that assuming widowhood is an impossible trauma for everyone *can* have negative effects.

In old world, immigrant women widowhood was traditionally a lonely, permanent state. In contemporary older women, as photo B shows, it can be a time of expanded friendships and new interests.

It may only be helpful to "prescribe" widowhood counseling when older people have a good deal of trouble coping with this common late-life event.

ADULT CHILDREN AND PARENTS

Notice that much of the research on older couples and even widows contradicts our stereotype of later life as an unfulfilling, lonely time. We get the same upbeat message when we look at another pioneering relationship, elderly parent and middle-aged child. The idea that today's adult children are alienated from their elderly parents is untrue. The bond between the generations is sturdy. Closeness, caring, and a surprising amount of contact are the norm.

myth of family uninvolvement
Erroneous idea that children are uncaring and uninvolved with elderly parents today.

The first blow to what gerontologists call the **myth of family uninvolvement** was struck by Ethel Shanas in a set of cross-sectional studies conducted decades ago. In 1957, 1963, and 1975, Shanas (1979a, 1979b) examined how many times per week national samples of adult children and their elderly parents visited or called one another. While we would expect the amount of contact to have markedly declined over this age of shifting family roles, there was little change. Children still lived close to their parents, the vast majority within a 30-minute drive. More than a third had seen one another either that day or the one before. About four in five had visited within the past week. Instead of being a nation of isolated nuclear families, the adult child/elderly parent bond was very much intact.

More recent surveys echo this theme. While family mobility is more common than ever, a surprising amount of face-to-face parent/child contact takes place in the United States. In 1984, one out of three adults saw an aged parent daily or every other day. Almost two-thirds reported seeing that person once or twice within the past week

If this elderly mother and her daughter are typical, they live within driving distance of one another, call and visit regularly, and feel very close—perhaps even closer emotionally than during their younger years. However, in contrast to what the mother in the photo may remember when she was young, this intergenerational pair is unlikely to be sharing the same house.

(Crimmins and Ingegneri, 1990). In other polls, more than one-half of children said that they saw an elderly parent at least once a week (Bumpass and Aquilino, 1995). Most said that their relationship with this older person was very close (Lawton, Silverstein, and Bengtson, 1994).

However, one change in the *externals of involvement* has occurred. The older generation used to live with the family. Now they live alone. Shanas's studies captured the years during which this decline in **co-residence** took place. In 1957, a third of the elderly parents and their children shared households. By 1975, the figure was 18 percent (Shanas, 1979a,b).

co-residence
Living as an extended family in a shared household as adults.

This change may partly explain why the myth of family uninvolvement has been so hard to dispel. Older people remember that during *their* childhood their grandmother lived in the house and leap to the conclusion that children are less caring today. This interpretation is wrong. It is the older generation who wants it that way. As we saw in Lopata's studies, older people vigorously reject the idea of moving in with their children (Hamon and Blieszner, 1990). What they want is an arrangement Shanas called **intimacy at a distance,** not living together, but close by. In other words, the young are not barring the door to the old. If anything, the reverse is true.

intimacy at a distance
Phrase reflecting the desire of elderly parents to live near adult children, but not share a residence.

Our "Walton family" vision of the past is unrealistic. There *never* was a rosy time when extended families lived together for decades peacefully. In the past, intergenerational households were always fairly rare simply because the grandparent generation never lived that long. Moreover, when families did share a residence, their arrangement was caused as much by economic necessity as love. Before the Industrial Revolution, the older generation controlled the land. Later on, when parents developed infirmities and could not work, they were too poor to maintain their own house. As we will see in Chapter 13, during the late 1960s and early 1970s Social Security and retirement benefits were greatly expanded. The dramatic decline Shanas found in co-residence over those years was mainly due to the fact that older people finally were financially able to live on their own.

The push to live separately does not apply equally to every ethnic group. Even controlling for socioeconomic status, African-American elderly are more likely to live intergenerationally than whites (Choi, 1991; Taylor and Chatters, 1991; Soldo, Wolf, and Agree, 1990). Italian widows are more likely to live with their children than Jewish widows (Kauser and Wister, 1984). Immigrant status is related to co-residence. In one study, older, unmarried Asian-American women who had migrated to the United States were much more likely to live intergenerationally than their native-born counterparts. Linguistic and economic barriers force many elderly immigrants to be more dependent on their offspring than they want. Living apart from family may be an alien concept for some new Americans, too.

In analyzing data from six Latin American countries, Susan deVos (1990) found that extended family households were the common pattern. Co-residence did vary from country to country, being most prevalent in the Dominican Republic and least common in Mexico. However, these differences mainly showed up among older married people. In each country, it was accepted practice for a parent who was widowed to share a residence with an adult child. Compare this with the fact that in the United States in 1984 almost three out of four widowed people with children lived alone!

In summary, the decision to share households seems propelled by cultural norms and especially by financial need. Furthermore, when they are able to live independently, most adults want to live on their own. This implies that our country may be at the brink of another shift in co-residence. While living together used to be "caused" by problems in the elderly, the balance may be tipping the opposite way. The poor job market for many young adults, combined with the rising number of single-parent families, suggests more pressure to share households, this time emanating from the younger generation's side. In fact, in surveying a national sample of parents and their adult children, Russell Ward and Glenna Spitze (1992) found that markers associated with financial need in a child, such as being young and single or divorced, were the primary correlates of sharing a roof.

What are the consequences for family harmony? Some signs are troubling. In a national poll of African-American families, Robert Taylor and Linda Chatters (1991) found that older people who lived with their children were less satisfied with their family. When University of Chicago researchers interviewed three-generation Chicago families, a young adult grandchild, a middle-aged father and mother, and one aged grandparent, they, too, found that the families in which the generations shared a household were worse off. In this study, particularly young married daughters living with middle-aged mothers tended to be more unhappy and immature (Cohler and Grunebaum, 1981; Hagestad, 1985).

This research does not prove that living together causes problems. Families who share a household are just as likely to choose this arrangement because they are *already* having difficulties with life. Still, rather than symbolizing more closeness, it makes sense that relationships are at risk of deteriorating when parents and adult children share a roof.

In fact, one message of the Chicago study is that a certain amount of distance is good for parents and their adult children as they live together as adults. The researchers wanted to explore what the generations talked about, so they used this technique: They showed a set of cards to each person and asked, "Do you and _____ talk about this?" If the answer was yes, they then asked whether the person had given or gotten advice about the topic from the other family member. The researchers wanted to discover what issues are "hot" topics for families. In what direction does intergenerational advice-giving flow?

While advising flowed in all directions, the most frequent pattern remained the same. Whether a child was 20 or 55, in relation to a parent he got more advice than he gave. The exception was when the parent was widowed or in bad health. Then advice-giving from both sides became more equal or reversed, with the role of advisor shifting to the child.

So the complaint that many of us have about our parents—"They still treat me as a child"—seems to have a grain of truth. Unless they become impaired or needy, parents hold to their role of teacher no matter how old they or their children are.

In this study, the "hot" topics for advising differed by gender. Fathers and grandfathers gave advice about work, education, and money. Mothers and grandmothers concentrated more on interpersonal issues, such as dating and how to relate to family and friends. So, it was in these areas that arguments were most likely to flare up. For grandfathers and fathers, the most sensitive topics for discussion were those in their advising domain. For the women, relationships were a touchy area. It was here that advising had the potential to flow fast and furious among mothers, daughters, and grandmothers, and so here the disagreements were most intense.

Because of this, in order to preserve family harmony, parents and children reported that they had to develop conversational demilitarized zones, to not reveal too much about their anxieties in these central arenas of life. Keeping close meant keeping some separation, knowing when to be silent, and allowing the other generation to make its own mistakes.

The lesson that *more* involvement does not always mean better relationships was forcefully brought home when gerontologists used what they thought would be a good measure of family closeness: the actual amount of contact between parent and child.

Quantity Versus Quality

They found this puzzling result. Often there was *no* relationship between how often parents and children saw one another and how close the generations felt (Mancini, 1984). Some researchers even found an inverse relationship between contact and feelings of intimacy (Talbott, 1990; Walker and Thompson, 1983).

Just as surprising, in spite of the fact that older people say their children are more important than anything else in life, elderly parents who see their daughters and sons very often are no more content than those who see their children more infrequently (Hauser and Berkman, 1984; Lee and Ellithorpe, 1982). Rather than any objective measure of closeness, such as the number of visits or calls, a subjective feeling is related to morale: a parent's satisfaction with what the children are giving; the older person's sense of being cared for and loved.

Why is it that the number of visits is such a poor indicator of intergenerational solidarity, so unrelated to morale? As I implied in the previous section, one reason is that families come together not just out of a positive emotion, the desire to be close, but also out of a negative one, need. As we will see in the section on grandparenthood, a typical example occurs when a child is going through a divorce. In response to this crisis, parent/adult child contact tends to rise dramatically (Aldous, 1995). Grandparents step in, babysitting and offering financial and emotional support.

For the older person, the situation that causes children to flock around tends to be poor health. In fact, poor health in the oldest generation sometimes pulls even parents and children close in the most basic way. Demographers have identified two types of migration among the elderly; the move away from children immediately after retiring, for instance, to a Sun Belt state by middle-class young-old couples in health, and a smaller reverse migration decades later to be near children when, typically in their eighties, disability strikes (Litwak and Longino, 1987). So more contact does not necessarily signify a family good. It can be a sign of a family in trouble.

Joseph Kuypers and Vern Bengtson (1983) believe that family relationships follow a **norm of waning involvement.** As children grow up, they need less time and attention from their parents. When they marry and have their own children, their responsibility to

norm of waning involvement *Unspoken family rule that, as children grow older, they need less care and attention from parents.*

their family of origin takes second place to that of the family they create. Kuypers and Bengtson believe that relationships are most likely to deteriorate when this unspoken rule is breached and either the parent or the child generation needs an excessive amount of help: for example, when a daughter is a single parent or when an elderly parent becomes disabled and needs a child to devote hours to care-giving.

With the younger generation, the norm of waning involvement applies mainly to providing *concrete help*. Listening to problems, exchanging news, offering psychological support, and being a person that a child depends on emotionally enhances parents' self-esteem (Spitze, Logan, Joseph, and Lee, 1994; remember the discussion of motherhood). However, while in one national survey parents who engaged in these activities were likely to report the best relationships with their young adult children, providing "instrumental services," such as financial aid or help with household jobs, was associated with more conflict and distress (Kulis, 1992). The distress is just as great when the cry for help emanates from the older generation's side.

Caring for an Ill Parent

The fact that nursing homes are such obvious features on our landscape masks a hidden reality. At least twice as many severely disabled older people live in the community as live in nursing homes. As we learned in Chapters 5 and 7, families are caring for these frail older people, sometimes at great personal cost (Arling and McAuley, 1984). Nursing home placement is something families work strenuously to avoid. When an older person has living relatives, it is often a last resort when children become unable to manage the care (Brody, 1977).

Care-giving at the end of the life span, as during life's beginning years, is gender-linked (see Figure 12-2). When the disabled older person is a man, sons do take more responsibility (Lee, Dwyer, and Coward, 1993). Almost always, however, the job of caring for an ill parent falls on a daughter or daughter-in-law (Lang and Brody, 1983; Brody, 1985). These **women in the middle** face competing responsibilities. If they are late-middle-aged or young-old when the need arises, they may be caring for grandchildren or an ill husband. If they are in their thirties or forties, they may have children at home.

Today, with most women in the work force (see Chapter 13), they often have full-time jobs. Moreover, it has been argued that today the job of caring for a frail parent has become a "normative event" (Brody, 1985). The increase in the number of people living to advanced old age, combined with the tendency for parents to have fewer children, has made this job one that this cohort of middle-aged daughters can expect to assume, sometimes for years.

Care-giving is far from every contemporary woman's fate (Spitze and Logan, 1990). Even so, the chance of being in this position is higher than ever today. In polling women of different ages, Phylis Moen, Julie Robinson, and Vivian Fields (1994) found that almost two-thirds of their subjects aged 55–65 reported having been care-givers, while less than half of their parents' generation (the cohort born in 1905–1917) had. Despite the growth of services such as home care and day care, paid-for help tends to be used sparingly (Arling and McAuley, 1984). As Figure 12-3 on p. 360 shows, family members, typically daughters, are the main line of defense against a nursing home.

Gerontologist Elaine Brody (1985) argues that women miss the fact that care-giving used to be less intense and feel deficient. No matter how much they are doing for an ill mother or father, they have the nagging sense that they should be doing more. They feel even worse when, unlike their own parents, they have to put a disabled parent in a nursing home. Their feelings are based on a false analogy: The burden of care-giving weighs heavier today.

Brody, who has devoted her career to studying these women in the middle, has examined the heavy burden on care-givers who work. In comparing employed and

women in the middle
Women simultaneously caring for young children or, more often, adult children and grandchildren and ailing elderly parents.

Distribution of Informal Care-Givers by Relationship to Elderly Care Recipient, 1982

Figure 12-2

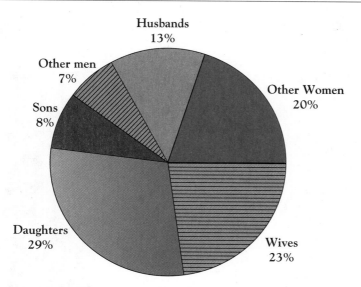

Women provide most of the care for the disabled elderly. Daughters provide the bulk of this care.

Source: U.S. Senate Special Committee on Aging, 1991, *Aging America: Trends and Projections*, Washington, DC: Author.

non-employed care-givers, she found that working daughters provided just as much help with shopping, household tasks, and emotional support as the non-working group, though they did hire home help more often for personal care (Brody and Schoonover, 1986).

This involvement takes a financial toll. In 1982, of the more than 1 million U.S. family care-givers with jobs, 21 percent reported reducing their hours at work. A similar percentage said that they had taken time off without pay. About 9 percent of a total sample of 2.2 million care-givers reported quitting their jobs to provide care (U.S. Senate Special Committee on Aging, 1991a).

Study after study has documented the emotional toll of parent care. As we saw in our in-depth look at families coping with a dementing illness, children caring for disabled parents have high rates of depression and anxiety and low levels of morale (Cantor, 1983; George and Gwyther, 1986; Spitze, Logan, and Lee, 1994). Moreover, rather than producing more closeness, just as Kuypers and Bengtson predict, illness in a parent is related to poorer family relationships. It increases the potential for conflict between parent and child (Walker, Martin, and Jones, 1992). A study of spouse care-givers mentioned earlier in this chapter highlights the different emotional context of parent care. While Colleen Johnson and Joseph Catalano (1983) found that enmeshing, that is, retreating into the relationship, was a common response if the care-giver was a spouse, if the care-giver was a child the main reaction was distancing. The older person's demands caused conflict, the relationship deteriorated, competing demands from family added to the friction, and a child would disengage, either separating herself from a parent emotionally by going into therapy or deciding "I've done all I can" and turning to paid help.

Figure 12-3

Type of Help Received by People Age 70+ with Activity Limitations, 1986

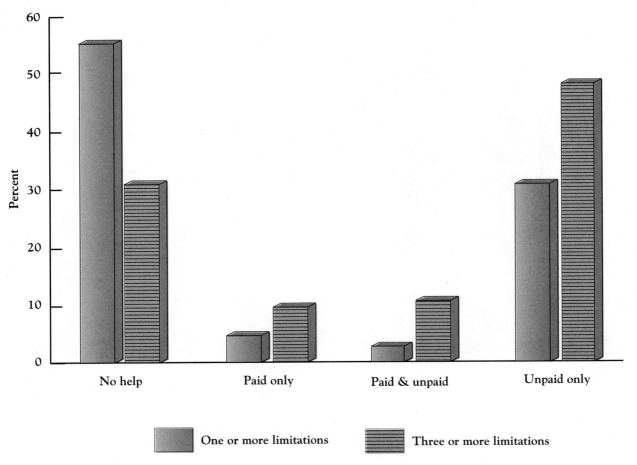

Most help for impaired older people is unpaid help—that is, care from family members.

Source: U.S. Senate Special Committee on Aging, 1991, *Aging America: Trends and Projections,* Washington, DC: Author.

If a parent has emotional problems or Alzheimer's disease, the child is especially likely to put distance between herself and the older person, denying that "my mother is anything like myself" (Albert, Litvin, Kleban, and Brody, 1991). The rejection may be getting through. Dorothy Field and her colleagues (Field, Minkler, Falk, and Leino, 1993) traced how the Berkeley *parent* generation felt about their family during their old-old years. While the researchers found much constancy, one influence associated with a change in feelings was health. Contrary to predictions, older people often reported feeling *more alienated* from their families when they became ill. (Feature 12-2 shows that the impact of a child's ill health on elderly parents is even more devastating.)

FACTORS INFLUENCING THE STRESS. On the other hand, this avalanche of testimony that care-giving is stressful involves self-reports of problems, not

When he was growing up, James seemed to be an ideal boy. He was an excellent student, attractive, a good athlete. He was a "loner," but Martha thought that would pass. It made sense that her only child would prefer to stay close to home. James's father had been abusive. He walked out when James was six.

After college, James began to resemble his father more and more. He was unable to keep a job. He belittled women, went from one failed relationship to the next, and attempted suicide three times. On one occasion, if Martha had not arrived, James would have died. Martha has been trying to show James that he is loved no matter what he does. She helps pay the bills. James stays over at the house. She is there to offer support. However, she is becoming afraid of her 33-year-old son. James has a fascination with guns and the martial arts. He gets into rages. Martha sometimes feels like running away, but she knows she could never abandon her "baby." She blames herself for not realizing there was a problem and getting help for James while he was growing up. Mostly she worries about the future. It has been 15 years of crisis after crisis. Martha is taking anti-depressant drugs. Her son is destroying her life.

In the text, I have been focusing on how parents' problems affect adult children. There is an opposite side. While our interview is an extreme case, anxiety about adult children with problems can be an important stress in parents' lives. A telephone survey underlines how crucial this anxiety can be.

Carl Pillemer and Jill Suitor (1991) asked about four signs of trouble. Did a son or daughter have emotional problems, serious health concerns, problems with alcohol? Had a child been under much stress within the past year? As the researchers expected, the one in four people who answered yes to these questions was likely to be more depressed.

However, this study implies that we cannot equate the anxiety for children with the "burden" that comes from ministering to a parent in need. In contrast to the parent care research, Pillemer and Suitor found that subjects' distress was unrelated to the amount of care-giving, the concrete help provided to the child. In other words, the heartache of a parent for a child is more internal, less tied to *what* is being done. As we saw in our interview and in the previous chapter, adults with children who are "failing" believe that *they* have failed. Their problem is not ambivalence about an unwanted investment of time, but guilt about the past and worry about the future. Where did I go wrong? What will happen to my child?

actual rates of psychiatric disturbance and impaired health (Schulz, Visintainer, and Williamson, 1990). Many studies show that caring for a parent produces mixed emotions. It can increase feelings of closeness even while producing strain (Gatz, Bengtson, and Blum, 1990). Caring for a parent does not weigh equally heavy on everyone. For some people, it is an impossible burden; for others, a labor of love.

Once again, the burden people feel is a function of multiple factors: the intensity of care a parent needs (Miller, McFall, and Montgomery, 1991; Mui, 1995); and the number of additional roles, such as mother, wife, or grandparent, a woman must handle at the same time (Franks and Stephens, 1992). Enduring feelings for the older person play a role. Warm, loving childhood memories make children more willing to say that they will care for ill parents (Whitbeck, Hoyt, and Huck, 1994). The help that they do provide feels less burdensome when it is cushioned by this legacy of love (Walker et al., 1992).

Ethnicity and gender also are relevant. Perhaps because of their strong tradition of multigenerational care-giving, (and their possibly greater emotional resilience described in Chapter 9), African Americans report lower levels of care-giving stress (Fredman, Daly, and Lazur, 1995; Hinrichsen and Ramirez, 1992). Perhaps because they do most of

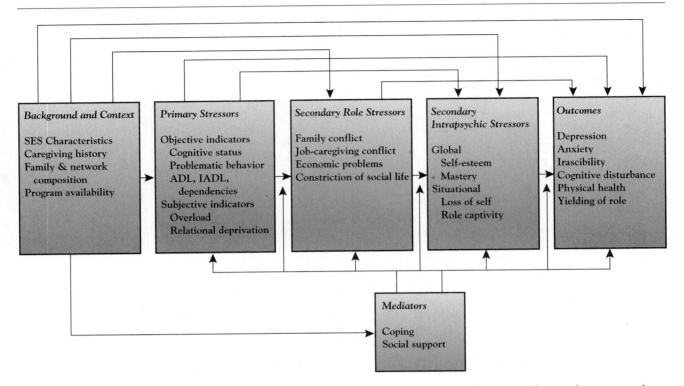

The stress is made up of four domains: the background and context of stress, the stressors, the modulators (mediators) of stress, and the outcomes or manifestations of stress.

Source: L. I. Pearlin, J. T. Mullan, S. J. Semple, and M. M. Skaff, 1990, Caregiving and the Stress Process: An Overview of Concepts and Their Measures, *Gerontologist, 30.* Copyright 1990, The Gerontological Society of America.

the care themselves and they are more susceptible to depression, women feel particularly burdened in the care-giving role (Gatz et al., 1990; Mui, 1995).

The flow chart in Figure 12-4, developed by Leonard Pearlin and his colleagues, highlights the different influences that may interact to produce depression, health problems, and giving up (Pearlin, Mullan, Semple, and Skaff, 1990). Pearlin devised this chart for Alzheimer's disease and used it as a framework to predict and measure family stress in the care-giving careers study discussed in Chapter 7. However, we can apply this same model to any type of parent care.

Pearlin divides stresses into two categories. Primary stressors are directly related to the illness. Is Mrs. Jones's mother incontinent or physically abusive? Does she need 24-hour care? Secondary stressors are the other pressures in the person's life. Does Mrs. Jones have young children? Is she in the middle of a divorce? Background variables, such as socioeconomic status, care-giving history, and family network, affect the intensity of these secondary stressors as well as contributing to the sense of overall burden. The person's vulnerability to problems is determined by her coping skills and the degree of support from family and friends. Does Mrs. Jones's family appreciate what she is doing, or are they jealous and angry? Are her brothers and sisters doing their fair share? When a care-giving child believes that siblings are not equitably sharing the burden, that person tends to feel especially resentful about parent care (Strawbridge and Wallhagen, 1991).

Pearlin's model illustrates that with care-giving once again we need to adopt a *contextual* approach. The impact of this stress varies dramatically. It depends on the total situation within which care-giving occurs. Still, *in general,* care-giving is a stressful experience. To ease the stress, ideally services such as day care, home care, and respite care should be more available. Because, as we know from Chapter 5, these services are costly and not paid for by Medicare, this puts children in the difficult position of having a disabled parent or themselves "run through savings" or doing the care on their own. The Family and Medical Leave Act stipulates that people who take time off from their jobs to care for an older relative can no longer be arbitrarily fired. However, remember that this law allows only 12 weeks of unpaid leave. It would be more helpful to have services that are affordable because a disabled parent often must have ongoing help for many months or even years (U.S. Senate Special Committee on Aging, 1991a).

Once these sources of help are within the average family's economic grasp, we need to educate children to take advantage of them, rather than interpreting the obligation to care for aging parents as "I have to do everything myself." As Susan Selig, Tom Tomlinson, and Tom Hickey (1991) point out, the impulse to care for elderly parents depends on crucial ethical principles: the commandment to "Honor thy father and mother," and a debt from care given one as a child. However, sometimes this moral obligation may be interpreted as absolute, so *every* activity becomes a causality to care-giving.

Even elderly parents do not agree with the idea that children should have absolute responsibility for their care. In one survey, parents, more than children, checked "no" when asked if a daughter should adjust her work schedule to help them (Hamon and Blieszner, 1990). As Elaine Brody suggests, we need to educate this cohort of middle-aged daughters that their situation is different. At no other time in history were people asked to provide care to the older generation for years. We also need to explore ways that are not too expensive to offer the growing numbers of women in the middle help.

GRANDPARENTS

As is true of relationships between adjoining generations, there has been an explosion of interest in grandparenthood in recent years. In part, this is because grandparents today are needed to help keep the more fragile younger family afloat (Aldous, 1985). In part, this may also be because researchers have gone beyond quantity, the frequency of visiting or the number of contacts per day or week, in studying family life.

While the actual amount of contact does matter somewhat, even people who report seeing their grandchildren infrequently still often say that being a grandparent has vital meaning in their lives (Wood and Robertson, 1978). One reason may be that grandparenthood is different than practically any other relationship we have. Normally our value is tied to our achievements, what we do. Grandparents are loved for a quality that transcends the visits or the calls, just "being there."

Lillian Troll (1983) calls grandparents the **family watchdogs.** While they normally wait in the wings, they step in during a crisis to stabilize the family. At these times, their value is illuminated; their hidden importance revealed. Grandparents are the family safety net.

Troll's idea that grandparents are "guardians" or "watchdogs" is supported by looking at what happens during divorce. When comparing the amount of help that a group of midwestern parents gave to their grown-up children, Joan Aldous (1985) found

family watchdogs
Phrase describing the function of grandparents to watch over the younger family and step in when a crisis occurs.

Sally and her husband live in Louisville, about a three-hour drive from her daughter's home. When her daughter and husband were struggling to build up their business, Sally often took the grandchildren. It was her pleasure to help out the struggling couple during those years. During the divorce, it seemed natural for Sally to take the grandchildren for a few weeks during Christmas. Her daughter needed time to get herself together. It was better if the children were not around. Then toward the end of the holiday, Sally's daughter called and asked if she could keep Joe and Sara for a few more months. Sally feels she must help her daughter. She wants to be there to provide a sense of security to the grandchildren during this difficult time. However, she never fully appreciated how exhausting having real responsibility for school-age children would be. From three till bedtime, Sally's time is not her own. She has to help with homework; she drives the children to lessons; there is the nightly nagging to get to bed; she feels anxiety about getting two reluctant children to school on time. Sally no longer has the energy for these battles. Her diabetes has worsened. While she is responsible, she does not feel like the "true parent" in the sense of having authority to set every rule. Most of all she worries: "Will the children really go home to their mother this summer again?"

Because so many more women are being thrust into the position of care-giving grandparent, Margaret Jendrek (1994) decided to examine what prompts people to take on this active watchdog role. Among a sample of 114 white care-giving grandparents, she uncovered three distinct categories. Daycare grandparents watch the child every day while their parents work or are at school. Live-in grandparents have the grandchild residing in their house—most often with the parent, but sometimes, as in Sally's situation, without. Custodial grandparents have full legal custody of the child.

As was true of Sally, the "impulse to make life better for the grandchildren" was the primary reason all of these women gave for providing care. However, there were differences in the reasons for assuming each type of active watchdog role. Custodial grandparents were in this situation because of severe dysfunction in the parent—usually a daughter's mental illness or drug abuse. Live-in grandparents typically were in this arrangement because their daughter could not financially afford to live alone—often because she was unmarried or divorced. Daycare grandparents were helping an intact, functional family. They decided to become care-givers because their daughter worked, they were concerned about the expense of a sitter, and they believed that they could do a better job than paid-for care.

When Jendrek (1993) asked, "Did you feel pressured into providing care?" Two-thirds of the sample answered no. Grandparents genuinely wanted to assume this job. However, they admitted that care-giving had taken a toll. There are signs that live-in grandparents feel under the most stress. They do not have custody of the grandchild and so still operate under the norm of non-interference (see p. 367). They do not have the limited commitment of grandparents living outside of the house. As we saw in the interview, their status is more ambiguous. How much care should they really provide?

that the amount of support provided varied depending on the child's marital status. Was a daughter or son single or married, divorced with children or not? While in general parents gave less help to married children, a dramatic exception occurred when a daughter with children was divorced. Then parents stepped in, providing concrete help, such as babysitting and helping with housework, and offering much more emotional support. In fact, in examining custody cases referred to a Canadian court over a year, Corinne Wilks and Catherine Melville (1990) found that three out of four grandchildren had actually lived in a grandparent's home at some point during this time (see Feature 12-3).

Even during calmer times, the job of family stabilizer is important. Grandparents may help their grandchildren indirectly by helping their children become better parents.

Grandparents can be family mediators, helping adolescent children and their parents resolve their differences (Hagestad, 1985; Kennedy, 1990).

Grandparents are the cement that keeps the extended family close. They are the focal point for family get-togethers, one reason sisters and brothers may fly in to see one another at special times, such as birthdays and holidays. In sociologist Guinhild Hagestad's words:

> Grandparents serve—as symbols of connectedness within and between lives;
> as people who can listen and have the time to do so;
> as reserves of time, help, and attention;
> as links to the unknown past;
> as people who are sufficiently varied, flexible, and complex to defy easy categories and clear-cut roles. (1985, p. 48)

Varied and Flexible Grandparent Roles

Our mental picture of Grandma is a white-haired woman knitting booties, elderly, disengaged, near death. Today this image is more likely to fit great- or even great-great-grandparenthood. In an age when most women become grandmothers in their middle years, Grandma today might just as realistically be portrayed jogging or in a suit coming home from a job.

This may cause confusion if one has trouble reconciling the outmoded mental image with reality (Johnson, 1985a). The fact that grandparenthood today occurs in health and youth may also explain the difference between the latest research and studies done a generation ago. Earlier studies minimized grandparenthood, suggesting that this role had "little significance" to people (Kahana and Coe, 1969). Because today's midlife grandparents have the energy and motivation to be involved in their grandchildren's lives for years, contemporary researchers highlight how crucial this relationship is for both grandparent and grandchild.

Actually, age is one predictor of a person's grandparenting style. Younger grandparents are more likely to be active. Grandparents who are older tend to be more peripherally involved (Cherlin and Furstenberg, 1985; Thomas, 1986). Not only may middle-aged grandparents be "younger in thinking," but also they have the energy to fully participate in a grandchild's life. They can play basketball with an eight-year-old and are *capable* of chasing a toddler around for hours.

In a classic study, Bernice Neugarten and Karol Weinstein (1964) classified this relaxed, non-authoritarian style of relating as "fun seeking." It was one of several ways their middle-class sample of grandparents chose to interpret this free-floating role. "Formal grandparents," who tended to be older, were more stand-offish, more authority figures in their grandchildren's lives. However, they were more involved than the "distant figures," grandparents who rarely saw their grandchildren. At the opposite end of the spectrum were the "surrogate parents," grandparents who assumed day-to-day caretaking responsibilities. While grandmothers predominated among this group, grandfathers were overrepresented among the last grandparent style: the "reservoir of family wisdom," grandparents who functioned as guardians of family history, imparting information about the past.

In more recent studies, researchers have devised other grandparent categories or discovered that some of Neugarten and Weinstein's types are absent (Robertson, 1977). In studying grandparents of a teenaged child, Andrew Cherlin and Frank Furstenberg (1985) found that the "fun seeking" style, a type of relating Neugarten and Weinstein found quite common, did not exist. The reason, the researchers believe, is that grandparents do not act out their role rigidly, but change the way they behave as their grandchildren grow up: "It's easy and natural for grandparents to treat toddlers as sources

Today's vital, active grandparent could not be more different than the mythical grandparent of old. Within just one generation the image of fun-seeking, kite-flying grandma has fully replaced the grandma knitting booties by the fire.

of leisure time fun. But no matter how deep and warm the relationship remains over time, a grandmother doesn't bounce a teenaged grandchild on her knee" (p. 100).

How do grandparents act with their teenage grandchildren? In addition to talking, joking, and advising, Cherlin and Furstenberg's national sample of grandparents exchanged help. Some played a major role in how the teenager was being raised. To see how involved grandparents tend to be when their grandchildren are at this stage of life, the researchers developed scales to measure the amount of advising and disciplining and the flow of services between the grandparent and that particular teenage child.

About one-fourth of the grandparents were classified as "detached," scoring low on the measures of closeness and only seeing a grandchild less than twice a month. A slightly larger fraction were rated as "passive," seeing the grandchild a bit more often. Surprisingly, "active grandparents" made up almost half of the sample. These grandparents not only exchanged help and confidences, but also played a major role in how that grandchild was being raised.

Even at an age when we might expect grandparent activity to be at its lowest ebb, the generations remain involved. Among one national sample of young adult grandchildren, 40 percent reported weekly contact with their closest grandparent. The majority said that they called or visited this person several times a month. Most said that their relationship with this grandparent was important, enduring, and close (Hodgson, 1992).

Grandparent Barriers

These studies examine one-to-one relationships. Wouldn't we find different results if we asked these people about their relationships with a different grandparent or grandchild? In other words, perhaps classifying grandparents and grandchildren as *just* highly involved or distant is not appropriate. Involvement may vary dramatically depending on the particular "grandparenting pair" we select.

When they questioned their respondents about their relationships with other grandchildren, Cherlin and Furstenberg found that classifying a person as "active," "detached," or "passive" was often inaccurate. Involvement did differ from grandchild to grandchild. At least 30 percent of the grandparents reported having favorites, a particular grandchild they felt closest to. Closeness depended on physical proximity. A grandparent was more likely to take an active part in the life of a grandchild who lived around the block than one a six-hour plane ride away. Compatibility was involved, that is, how appealing or responsive a particular grandchild was. Equally important were the needs and desires of the generation in between.

Grandparents report that loving without having the anxiety of bringing up the younger generation is what makes this role particularly satisfying (Robertson, 1977). While certain aspects of closeness relate to mental health, having authority over grandchildren does not (Thomas, 1990b). However, with so many single and full-time working mothers, today's grandparents often must assume a more hands-on role in child rearing than they expect (see Feature 12-3). This not only conflicts with the norm of waning involvement (Hamon and Cobb, 1993), but also goes against another basic grandparenthood principle called the **norm of non-interference:** "Grandparents should not meddle in how the grandchildren are being raised" (Cherlin and Furstenberg, 1985; Johnson, 1985a).

A study by Jeanne Thomas (1990a) comparing grandparent perceptions in single and married mothers illustrates how these rules, combined with a daughter's need, may create an unsatisfying double-bind. In contrast to the married women, the single parents said one of the best things about a grandparent was the help that person offered with childcare. However, both groups vehemently agreed that family harmony was threatened when a grandparent interfered with how a grandchild was being brought up. So, at the same time as daughters welcome their mothers' help, they seem to reject its predictable outcome, having some say in how the grandchildren are raised!

Grandparents are vulnerable. Not only does the norm of non-interference prevent them from being full authorities, but also the parent generation is the gatekeeper who defines how involved they will be. While sometimes the gates open too wide and grandparents are pressured into providing excessive childcare, other times the reverse problem occurs. A grandparent feels shut out, condemned to less involvement with the grandchildren than he or she wants. Most often the person in this outsider position is the mother of a son.

Grandmothers in general tend to be more emotionally involved with their grandchildren than grandfathers (Cherlin and Furstenberg, 1985). Often, however, it is a mother's mother to whom grandchildren report being especially close (Kennedy, 1990). While age may be a bit responsible, since maternal grandmothers are likely to be younger, the main reason is daughters. Women control the family's social relationships. They naturally want closer contact with their own mothers. This **matrifocal orientation to the family** consigns a son's mother to being grandmother of second rank (Hagestad, 1985).

One study shows just how vulnerable mothers of sons are. The researchers found that, while being a highly involved grandparent did not depend on whether a mother's mother got along with her son-in-law, this was not true of the other grandmother. In order to have a close relationship with her grandchildren, this grandmother had to satisfy two requirements: Be close to her son *and* to his wife (Matthews and Sprey, 1985).

The way the matrifocal tilt works against paternal grandparents is most heartbreaking in divorce. When the wife gets custody, a son's parents may be prevented from seeing the grandchildren at all (Wilson and DeShane, 1982).

A study of middle-class grandparents shows how after a divorce mothers of sons work hard to avoid this possibility by trying to preserve their relationships with their

norm of non-interference
Implicit principle that in order to have harmonious relationships with the younger family grandparents must refrain from criticizing how grandchildren are raised.

matrifocal orientation to the family
Fact that extended families are closer knit on the female side.

former daughters-in-law. Colleen Johnson and Barbara Barer (1987) found that, while 36 percent of the paternal grandmothers continued to see their former daughters-in-law at least once a week, only 9 percent of the maternal grandmothers saw their former sons-in-law. In other words, to keep their access to the grandchildren, paternal grandmothers may be unable to just side with their sons after a divorce. They seem to make a special effort to maintain a relationship with the person who controls that access, the custodial parent, their former daughter-in-law.

There is one benefit for these women that occurs as a result of being in this touchy situation. While after the divorce Johnson and Barer found that the family network of maternal grandmothers was likely to shrink because these women often cut off relationships with their former sons-in-law, for a paternal grandmother a child's divorce and remarriage was more likely to mean an enlargement in kin. Not only had many of these women kept close to their former daughters-in-law, but also they added a new set of relatives when their sons married again.

APPLICATIONS AND INTERVENTIONS

Our discussion suggests that, while being a grandparent can be very gratifying, grandparents need help in certain situations. One problem occurs when their children do not have custody after a divorce. Grandparents need safeguards to preserve their relationships with the grandchildren, insurance that they will be able to still visit and call. Until the decade of the 1980s, these safeguards did not exist. Daughters or sons with custody were free to, and sometimes did, shut former in-laws out (Wilson and DeShane, 1982).

Passing laws in this area has pitfalls. Shouldn't parents have final say over their children's welfare? Should the state intrude on a parent's right to determine whom a child sees? However, under pressure from grandparents who had suffered this fate, in 1982 the House of Representatives urged the National Conference of Commissioners on Uniform State Law to develop a model act on grandparent visitation, one that ensured non-custodial grandparents some rights. Today in all 50 states grandparents can petition to see their grandchildren after divorce, although in cases where the children's best interests would not be served by seeing a contentious grandparent, these applications can be denied (Aldous, 1995; Hartfield, 1996).

Grandparents also need help in the opposite situation. They must reconcile their traditional hands-off stance with the reality that they may be called on to take a more active role with grandchildren than their parents did. Because, as we saw throughout this section, grandparents are often compelled to do the parenting, particularly of our nation's most vulnerable children (Minkler and Roe, 1996), the American Association of Retired Persons (AARP) has responded by developing a Grandparent Information Center, offering counseling and legal advice to people in this situation (see Figure 12-5). Grandparents need to understand their vital role as family stabilizer in situations such as divorce. However, as many report feeling partly to blame in this situation (Hamon and Cobb, 1993), this may add to their mixed emotions about taking on this active watchdog role.

We need to educate grandparents that a child's getting divorced or having a baby without being married does not mean that they have personally failed, just as we need to tell them that their responsibilities to the older generation are likely to be more intense. Societywide changes have transformed the middle years into a time of giving to more needy generations on both the bottom and the top (Bumpass and Aquilino, 1995). Strategies to take the pressure off of younger families, such as flex time, family leave time, and affordable childcare, can benefit the grandparent generation, too.

*T*he relationship between grandparents and grandchildren is often a very special one. But for a growing number of grandparents who are the primary caregivers to their grandchildren, this relationship can also be very challenging. Undertaking the full-time responsibility for raising a grandchild means major changes in the lives of these grandparents.

The American Association of Retired Persons (AARP) established the Grandparent Information Center (GIC) to provide information and resources to help grandparents cope with their primary caregiving roles. The Center is working with national and community-based agencies in the child care, aging, legal, and family services fields to address this rapidly emerging phenomenon.

The Center is supported in part by grants from The Brookdale Foundation Group, The Ford Foundation and the Freddie Mac Foundation. AARP's nationwide network of regional and state offices and volunteers, as well as its many programs, are focusing attention on the issue of children at risk and their grandparent caregivers.

It is estimated that 3.7 million children currently live in a household headed by a grandparent. For over one-third of these children (1.4 million) no parent is present and the grandparent assumes the role of primary caregiver to his or her grandchildren or great-grandchildren. This Census Bureau data also indicates that grandparent-headed families represent all socioeconomic levels and ethnic groups.

Grandparents are raising their grandchildren because of: • teenage pregnancy

• substance abuse • death • divorce • parental joblessness • neglect

• incarceration • child abuse • abandonment • AIDS.

Grandparent caregivers may face legal and social problems. They may lack support and respite services, affordable housing, and/or access to medical services and coverage of medical expenses for the grandchildren. They may also have inadequate financial resources to care for their grandchildren. They may find themselves under extreme stress causing physical and mental health problems such as exhaustion or depression.

(over, please)

While the pride the middle aged woman in the photo feels in having three adjoining generations is one blessing of living today, along with the pleasure comes liabilities—being burdened with caring for a more fragile younger and older family.

KEY TERMS & CONCEPTS

normal mourning
tasks of mourning
grief work
pathological bereavement or chronic grief
widowed persons services
myth of family uninvolvement
co-residence
intimacy at a distance
norm of waning involvement
women in the middle
family watchdogs
norm of non-interference
matrifocal orientation to the family

RECOMMENDED READINGS

Aldous, J. (1995). New views of grandparents in intergenerational context. *Journal of Family Issues, 16,* 104–122.

    This review article offers a summary of grandparent research through 1994.

Bengtson, V. L., and Robertson, J. (Eds.). (1985). *Grandparenthood.* Beverly Hills; CA: Sage.

    These editors have collected theoretical and research articles on grandparenthood.

Brubaker, T. (Ed.). (1990). *Family relationships in later life* (2nd ed.). Newbury Park, CA: Sage.

    This edited volume contains articles on families in later life.

Grandparenting at century's end. (1996, Spring). *Generations, 20.*

    This issue of Generations *thoroughly reviews the research on grandparenting. Articles deal with historical conceptions of grandparents, minority grandparents, grandparent visitation, parenting grandparents, and other timely topics.*

Lopata, H. Z. (1973). *Widowhood in an American city.* Cambridge, MA: Schenkman.
Lopata, H. Z. (1979). *Women as widows: Support systems.* Cambridge, MA: Schenkman.

    Lopata's studies of widows' lives are considered classics.

Work and Retirement

Chapter Outline

"I've put in a lot of mileage in my quarter century of work," says Mike. "In 1968, I dropped out of high school, got married, and got a job with Pizza Hut as a delivery boy. Six years later I rose to manager. Then, one night, I was robbed and realized: 'I've got to look for a calmer job!' I went into the steel pipe industry loading trucks. I sold clothes for J. C. Penney. I worked as a dishwasher. I even had a paper route to make ends meet. I got my GED and started at a community college. In 1976, I got a job at Honeywell selling heating and air-conditioning systems. It's like I was in heaven. I had a secretary, profit-sharing, hospitalization. The work was so easy. I could call and within a few months I was being invited for dinner. So I quit college. Then, in 1979, the energy crisis hit, increasing the life expectancy of units already on the market. Sales were down. Honeywell first laid off marginal people. In their next phase, they offered early retirement to people at 55. I was under the impression that, if I did a good job, I would retire with the company. We'd just had a sales contest and out of 169 reps I'd come in second. That Tuesday I went into the office expecting my boss to commend me. I was devastated when he said, 'Mike, there's no easy way to tell you this. I have to lay you off.'"

"My next job was selling medical equipment. Then I worked for another heating and air-conditioning firm. Manufacturing went on strike, and they let go of the sales force. I was desperate. A friend who was a commander at the police department helped me get this job."

"I've been a police officer since 1989 and in college for the past several years. My goal is to have my master's degree in psychology by age 50. There is a real need for someone to develop stress management programs for the officers. There are some walking time bombs with guns out there. Policemen are always on public display. You're emotionally on the job 24 hours. I'm basically a trusting person. Training teaches us not to trust anybody. Being a deputy sheriff in a rural county, I go out on patrol without a partner. Last week I pulled over a car that was driving all over the road. When I asked for the driver's license, the man gets out of the car and starts coming at me. I got lucky. When I pulled my gun, he backed down. I'm basically a non-violent person. I hope until the day I die that I never have to take a life. Much of what we do involves helping people. The other day a man got into my car and said, 'Please put me in jail.' This guy had no place to go, nothing to eat. Sometimes a child will call: 'I've seen Daddy beat Mommy.' I hurt for those people. I've had several women call and say, 'Thank you, officer, for saving my life.' We do a lot of DUI arrests. When I take a drunk off the highway, I feel I've saved somebody's life. It's those times when I know the disappointments had a purpose. I'm finally in the right field."

While Mike's work history, with its ups and downs, changes, and a happy ending only after age 40, is unusual, it illustrates many themes about careers and how they have changed in recent decades.

CHANGES IN AMERICAN CAREERS

A more variable work life. In the 1950s, a man finished school, perhaps had one or two trial jobs, and often settled into his lifework. Once in that job he might stay in the same organization throughout his life. This stability no longer exists. Today the average job tenure for U.S. workers is four and a half years. The typical person has 6 to 10 employers before he or she retires (DeFillippi and Arthur, 1994). In addition, rather than having *a* career, as we saw with Mike some people totally change direction, periodically starting over in new fields. While, as was true with Mike, this freedom to shift careers can have benefits, it has been propelled by a negative cause: Workers are more vulnerable today.

A more vulnerable work life. For a generation after World War II, the United States had what writer Tom Wolfe called a "magic economy." The United States was the producer for the world. In the large corporations, such as U.S. Steel, General Motors,

In the 1950s, the domination of the auto industry by U.S. companies offered millions of working class American men secure jobs, the power to bargain for higher wages, and the chance to construct an economically stable life. The rarity of scenes such as this in America today is one reason for the growing gap between rich and poor.

and IBM, that employed huge numbers of the work force, people could enter feeling confident of having a lifetime job and see their standard of living regularly rise. From 1946 to 1970, the income of U.S. workers doubled. Everyone participated in the success, the factory worker as well as the executive. In fact, the United States was on its way to becoming a genuinely equal society. Due to the many high-paying union jobs, the middle class was expanding. The differences between the rich and everyone else were becoming less extreme.

Then the magic began to dissipate. Beginning in the early 1970s, **real income,** the relative buying power of a salary, increased more slowly; then stalled; and then declined. By 1991, most workers were bringing in lower take-home pay than in 1973. With the rise of global competition and the loss of the high-paying industrial jobs that had allowed so many people to construct a middle-class life, the economic fortunes of Americans began to diverge. During the 1970s and especially the 1980s while the rich continued to do better, the middle class was shrinking, and more people were becoming poor (Peterson, 1993; Reich, 1992).

Figure 13-1 illustrates this **widening income disparity.** The chart shows how the relative slice of the economic pie has been changing to favor the wealthiest 5 percent of the population. In fact, it is the very rich who have reaped the most astonishing windfall in recent years. In 1960, the average CEO's salary was only about 12 times as much as the typical employee's. In 1988, that same executive took home 70 times what that worker did! The high-paying factory jobs have been replaced by others, so people are still employed. However, as these non-unionized service jobs, such as clerk and food server, tend to pay more poorly, today there are many more **working poor,** men and women who have jobs, but cannot earn an adequate wage (Reich, 1992). Unlike their parents, most young adults need two incomes to support a family, solidifying a more dramatic change in work—women as breadwinners.

real income
Actual buying power of a salary.

widening income disparity
Fact that the income gap between rich and poor Americans is growing.

working poor
Full-time workers living in poverty.

Figure 13-1

Percentage of Total U.S. Income Received by Selected Family Income Groupings, 1967–1992

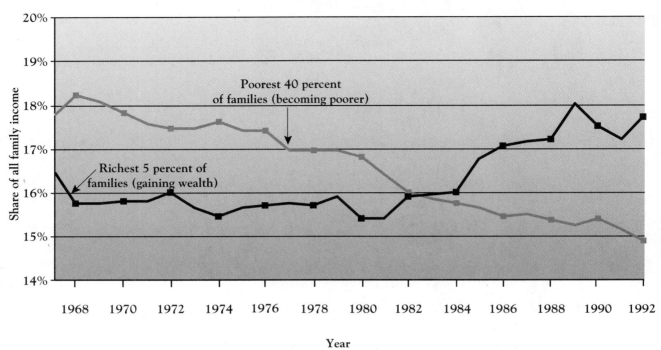

Year

During the 1980s and 1990s, the gap between the haves and have-nots in the United States has widened.

Source: Children's Defense Fund, 1994, *The State of America's Children, Yearbook, 1994,* Washington, DC: Author.

A more universal work force. Women always did more than housework. They might labor in the fields on the family farm. However, during the first half of the twentieth century, paid employment for *middle-class* women was unusual, except for "spinsters" and widows who were forced to have jobs because they had no husbands to provide for them (Betz, 1994). The principle that "middle-class wives should not work" was suspended during World War II as women flooded into male occupations to help the war effort and then reasserted itself in the 1950s as many women retreated to being homemakers again. It was only in the 1960s that *for the first time in history* every woman was encouraged to have a career.

Today this revolutionary idea is an accepted fact of life. Almost three-fourths of all women aged 25–64 are in the labor force. Most married women work. So do 60 percent of mothers with preschool children (Gilbert, 1993). As we will see later in this chapter, women work because they want to. Most women today see having a career as important for a fulfilling life. This feeling is realistic. Remember from Chapter 8 that the Mills Study suggests that working has had a beneficial effect on women's well-being. Women also work because they have to. In addition to the need for two paychecks among married couples, the increase in the number of single mothers has made staying home to raise children a luxury not many women can still afford.

Ironically, at the same time as working has become more essential for both women and men and Americans may be working longer hours than ever (Schor, 1991), the fraction of our lives we devote to our careers has shrunk.

A shorter work life. In 1959, less than half of all Americans aged 35 to 45 were high school graduates. Only 12 percent had college degrees. Today two-thirds of Americans have finished high school. The number of college graduates has more than doubled, to 30 percent (Jencks, 1992). In the past, people did not need to stay in school, as they could make a good living without a college degree. They could even aspire to the most prestigious careers. The fact that our previous governor of Tennessee was only a high school graduate is a relic of the past. Today a college degree is a minimum requirement for most skilled jobs. To enter a profession requires graduate school. In fact, as was true for me (I was in school continuously from kindergarten until age 29), today it is not unusual for people to be preparing for their career until almost midlife. This longer precareer phase has been more than equalled by a dramatic extension in our postwork life.

At the turn of the century, people worked almost until they died. The average person spent 1.2 years being retired. By 1980, the typical man could expect to be retired for 13.8 years, almost one-fifth of his life span (U.S. Senate Special Committee on Aging, 1991a). From a short pause before death, retirement has become a full life phase.

These changes, which have occurred primarily over the past few decades, powerfully shape the way our careers develop. Notice that, while in some ways we have more freedom, there also are more constraints. Today women can work and choose from a wide range of jobs. There is more career flexibility. People can look forward to not working for almost a third of adult life. On the other hand, the educational requirements have tightened, there is more job uncertainty, and realizing the American Dream of doing better than our parents is less possible today. While almost half of the Berkeley/Oakland children had working-class parents, by midlife 90 percent had become middle-class (Jenkins and Maslach, 1994). For today's poor children, upward mobility is more limited (Peterson, 1993). Poverty is more apt to be a chronic state (Duncan and Hoffman, 1991; Zill and Rogers, 1988). Let's keep these changes in the outer framework of work in mind as we focus on the psychological research on careers.

THREE PSYCHOLOGICAL THEORIES OF CAREER CHOICE AND DEVELOPMENT

Mike might never have gone back to school if he had lived during a time when people could not start a new career at age 40 and a master's degree was not a ticket to advancement. However, to understand *why* Mike loves his work and wants to become a police psychologist, we need to look internally, to his personality.

Holland's Personality/Trait Perspective on Career

According to John Holland's **personality/trait perspective,** personality is key to understanding which careers we choose and our happiness at work. People with certain interests gravitate to specific occupations. Specific occupations are suited to people with certain personalities. Most important, career satisfaction depends on *congruence*, matching the occupation we select to our personality (Holland, 1985).

personality/trait perspective on career
Holland's idea that career happiness and success come from matching career to personality.

Holland classifies people into six personality types and then links them to occupations:

1. **Realistic people** enjoy manipulating machinery, tools, and animals. Machinist is a typical realistic job.

2. ***Investigative people*** are analytical, curious, methodical, and precise. A typical investigative career is biologist.
3. ***Artistic people*** are expressive, non-conforming, original, and introspective. Decorator, dancer, and musician are artistic jobs.
4. ***Social people*** like helping others. Bartender, counselor, social worker, and nurse suit this personality type.
5. ***Enterprising people*** enjoy achieving organizational goals. Salesperson and office manager are typical enterprising jobs.
6. ***Conventional people*** like manipulating data and filing. Jobs such as secretary, file clerk, and financial expert fit these types of people.

Career counseling
Professional guidance in choosing or changing a career.

Holland's categories are used in **career counseling,** that is, guidance in choosing the right career. Because we rarely have "pure" interests, counselors use tests that classify people on all six dimensions and then summarize personality in a three-letter code, showing the three main categories in descending order. If a person enjoys working with machinery and organizing data, but also has some interest in the arts, he might be classified as RCA. Mike, whose main passion is helping people, but who also enjoys business and perhaps investigating new things, might be classified as SEI. Notice that this three-letter code offers more information, allowing counselors to pinpoint the exact occupations for which our personality is tailor-made.

Do people whose interests are congruent with their jobs really have greater occupational success? Hundreds of studies suggest the answer is yes (Spokane, 1985). In addition, we do tend to gravitate to careers compatible with our personalities. From counselors to accountants, the people in a particular field tend to cluster in the appropriate personality types. However, some people do *not* have personalities congruent with their careers (Betz, Fitzgerald, and Hill, 1989). What happens to these incongruent individuals?

Holland believes that, when we are in an incongruent job, we will either change careers or shift interests to fit that career. While our discussion of personality continuity in Chapter 8 suggests it should be easier to change jobs than to change our basic interests, sometimes people probably believe that they have to adapt to their career. Who resolves incongruence by changing fields, and who feels compelled to stay? Perhaps we can get some insights by turning to another, quite familiar perspective on what motivates us to act in certain ways.

A Self-Efficacy Perspective on Career

Why do some people with abundant talents and compatible interests shy away from what seems to be an ideal career, while others set their sights on occupations that seem difficult or impossible to attain? Why does one person immediately decide to strike out in a more satisfying direction when disappointed with work, while another, with equal skills, languishes in an unsatisfying job? Nancy Betz and Gail Hackett (1986) realized Albert Bandura's **self-efficacy perspective** offered a framework for understanding these differences in decision making.

self-efficacy perspective on career
Theory that draws on Bandura's concept of self-efficacy to predict career choices, especially for women.

As we know, Bandura (1977) believes that we can predict behavior by exploring efficacy feelings, our confidence in our own competence. Self-efficacy determines which tasks we choose to tackle, how much effort we expend, and how long we persist in the face of obstacles to our goal. Betz and Hackett realized that low self-efficacy could account for why women avoid certain careers.

According to Bandura, we develop efficacy feelings under certain conditions: by performing relevant activities, by modeling, in the presence of low emotional arousal (fear), and by direct instruction. Betz and Hackett argue that each influence works to limit the career choices women make. Women are not encouraged to engage in organized sports in childhood, so they have fewer experiences with the type of competitive team-oriented activities needed in organizations. They are exposed to fewer female role models in a variety of occupations during their early years. Women report higher anxiety (arousal), which inhibits them from trying new things. A final source of lower self-efficacy involves instruction. Women are not often encouraged by parents, school counselors, or teachers to seek out traditionally male careers.

While their research initially involved women, Betz and Hackett (1987) have expanded their focus, demonstrating that efficacy feelings are important in everyone's career choice. Self-efficacy even offers insights into career behavior toward the end of our working years. If older workers have low *occupational self-efficacy,* believing that, when they turn 50 or 60, they are unable to think or learn as well, they might retire early or decide to take a less demanding job (Fletcher, Hansson, and Bailey, 1992). Moreover, since efficacy feelings, at least in theory, are more easy to modify than our basic interests, this approach to understanding careers offers more chance for change. By increasing self-efficacy, it may be possible to broaden our horizons for happiness in a variety of careers.

Notice that, while these theories offer interesting insights into why we choose, or change, or avoid certain careers, they give no hints about how our work life unfolds. Donald Super's theory, developed and tested over decades, provides this life-span view.

Super's Life-Span Perspective on Career

CHARTING CAREER AND LIFE. Super (1957), in his **life-span perspective on career,** divides career motivations and goals into four phases: growth and exploration, establishment, maintenance, and decline. Within this *broad maxi-cycle,* loosely connected to childhood and adolescence, early adulthood, midlife, and later life, are mini-phases of growth and exploration, establishment, maintenance, and decline. Mike, when he took his job at Honeywell, passed through growth and exploration, establishment, maintenance, and finally decline when he was abruptly laid off. Mary Jones, who has just retired, will go through periods of growth and exploration, establishment, and maintenance as she travels through this life stage. In other words, for Super, growth and exploration, establishment, maintenance, and decline comprise both our main career melody and a tune replayed in minor chords throughout our lives.

To test his idea that career motivations progress in this way, Super planned a longitudinal study of 100 men "coming of age" in Middletown, New Jersey, during the late 1950s. When Super's research team tested these men when they were in their early teens, as high school seniors, in their twenties, and in their mid-thirties, they found that most men were exploring as young adults. By their thirties, most had entered the establishment and maintenance stages of their careers (Super, 1985; Phillips, 1982a, 1982b).

Notice that Super carried out his study during a time when people had more stable careers. His subjects were the main workers at the time, white men. To explore whether the theory might apply to women, Suzyn Ornstein and Lynn Isabella (1990) classified female corporate managers into Super's phases and then measured their career satisfaction and commitment. Contrary to what Super predicts, job commitment, desire to relocate for the company, and work satisfaction did not reach their peak during the establishment and/or maintenance phase of a woman's career. In other words, the concept of defined phases and their associated emotions may really mainly fit people who have a more "single-minded" relationship to work (see the section on women and work).

About two decades ago, Super (1980) introduced the **life rainbow,** a way of getting us to focus on the different roles we occupy and their importance during the maxi-cycle of life. I have constructed my own life rainbow to illustrate how this chart is used in

life-span perspective on career
Super's theory focusing on career development throughout life.

life rainbow
Career counseling strategy in which clients use an arc to chart the relative amounts of time they plan to spend in different roles at different times of life.

Figure 13-2

Super's Maxi-Cycle of Life and My Career Rainbow

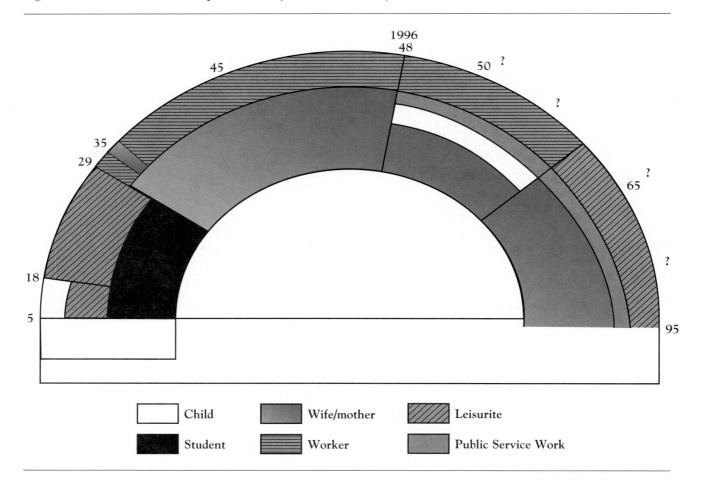

career planning. As Figure 13-2 shows, child was my only role from birth until age five. From elementary school through adolescence, I added two more, student and leisurite. In fact, until I finished graduate school and married at age 29, leisurite and student were still my main roles! Except for a break from work at age 35 to take care of my son, career and family have been my focus in recent years. If I have to care for my aging mother in the future, child may again become a focal role. After I finish this book, I hope to spend more time as a citizen, getting involved in my community. When I retire at about age 65, leisurite and family member should expand again. Do I really want to retire or go on working part-time? How much time do I want to devote to my grandchildren? How involved will I get in my community? Notice how this exercise has forced me to think about where I have come from and where I am going in life.

PREDICTING CAREER SUCCESS.   Super believes that this planning needs to start early. Furthermore, he feels, the more thoroughly we ponder and plan our career future, the better our adjustment to the next stage will be. Super began his Middletown Study while his subjects were still in school in order to test this hypothesis, using a concept he called **career maturity.**

career maturity
According to Super, the maturity with which one contemplates one's future work life.

Career maturity involves attitudes. How committed are you to thinking about your career? It has cognitive aspects. How realistic and knowledgeable are you about your capacities and what is available for someone with your training and skills? These components of what Super calls "readiness," measured through a test, revealed interesting trends when given to the Middletown men. While in 9th grade there was no association, by 12th grade subjects' scores on career maturity were associated with later vocational achievement and happiness. By *late adolescence*, career maturity is one among *several* predictors of doing well early on in our career.

Are there other qualities that we can see in adolescents that predict work success? To answer this question, John Clausen (1991) classified the men in the Berkeley/Oakland Studies into "success categories": those who moved up within the middle class (they had middle-class origins, but had higher-level middle-class jobs than their fathers at age 40); men with working-class origins who moved into the middle class; and men who remained stable or declined in social class.

As we might expect, the upwardly mobile men tended to have higher IQs. As early as junior high school, they also were different in personality. They ranked higher on dependability, productivity, and personal effectiveness. In other words, this study suggests that Super was correct. As in those old high school contests, we can pick out our "most likely to succeed" classmates surprisingly early in life (recall Feature 8-1 in Chapter 8).

Some interesting traits distinguished the especially successful men, those with working-class parents who rose to the middle class. These men had been ranked as nurturing, sympathetic, and giving as adolescents. They also had been rated as more sociable and friendly.

Before concluding that nice guys finish first, I must caution that this unusually successful group was made up of only 32 men. We need larger studies to make generalizations about what traits really are related to high achievement at work. Luckily we have that study—a landmark longitudinal investigation of AT&T managers begun at about the same time as Super started his research with the Middletown men.

CAREER PATTERNS AND PATHS

The Traditional Stable Career

THE AT&T STUDIES. As was true in the large corporations that dominated American industry during the middle of the twentieth century, people who worked for the telephone company were often hired right out of school and then stayed until they retired. Comparing how people in this "constant environment" performed on their trek up the organizational ladder offered an ideal laboratory for studying how a **traditional stable career** unfolds.

Psychologists focused on a group of men who entered the company's management training program during the late 1950s. They examined these trainees, all white men, annually for eight years and then tracked their subjects every three years for the next two decades. In the late 1970s, the researchers decided to compare this group with a second cohort of management trainees. The makeup of these second-generation managers shows how much work had changed over these turbulent decades in the United States. One-third of the new trainees were minorities; almost half were female. Moreover, while the original group had been made up of both high school and college men, in order to enter the training program in the 1970s everyone had to have a college degree (Howard and Bray, 1988).

Among the first cohort of trainees, the researchers found that the men fit into two categories that they labeled "the enlargers" and "the enfolders." Enlargers were

traditional stable career
Career path in which people are employed in a single organizational setting for their working life.

These photos showing a typical managerial conference during the 1950s and a similar meeting today speak volumes about the dramatic change in the work force composition of American corporations that has taken place since researchers began the AT&T studies.

success-oriented, reaching out to job-related activities, such as night school. They were aggressive, competitive, and work-focused. Enfolders put their emotional investment in other areas of life, such as family and church. While both groups were equally satisfied with life, as we might imagine, the enlargers were more successful in their careers. They moved up more rapidly in the company and were much happier at work.

Could success be predicted early on? Here, too, the answer was yes. Predictions from the first assessment related to how far a person advanced not only after 8 years, but also at the 20-year point. However, this does not mean that change did not occur. As we can see in these case histories, as the years passed the enlargers became even more highly motivated. The enfolders grew more disinterested, lagging farther and farther behind.

> *Al was pleased to be promoted to the second level of management before he had completed 2 years with the company. He aggressively made plans for improvement. . . . Al clearly wanted to do the best job possible and his group responded with improved performance and morale. . . . Al was as enthusiastic about higher management as his bosses were about him. . . . He credited the phone company for the way America had advanced the way that it had. In Al's 6th year at Bell . . . he was promoted to the third level, the threshold of middle management. . . . Al was promoted to a division level position in the plant department in year 13 of the study. . . . He now had 2500 people working under him with a 26 million dollar operating budget. . . . He was on call at all times. He loved the responsibility and the fact that the organization was depending on him to such a major extent. In year 19 of the study, he became assistant vice president of customer services and had to relocate to another city. Al thrived on the responsibility and prestige of the position. . . . His now fully developed identification with the company caused him to worry about the young people coming into the business. He viewed them as lacking in the dedication of the older generation, an attitude that was difficult for a fully committed man such as Al to understand. (Howard and Bray, 1988, pp. 181–183)*

> *After high school graduation Charlie primarily looked for a job that offered security. The telephone company seemed ideal to him since it had a reputation in Charlie's words as "a good place with wonderful benefits. The telephone company never lays you off and you get automatic raises." . . . Charlie had thought that he might advance beyond the first level at the beginning of his management*

*career. . . . He had heard there were several jobs open to assistant manag-
ers. . . . On further study, he decided against applying, since, as he put it, "it
wasn't a big enough increase in pay and you'd have to buy white shirts and ties."
During years 10 and 11 of the study, Charlie stated he felt very fortunate not to
have been made part of management and seemed almost expecting to be demoted
to a craft job again. . . . He might even welcome this, since . . . "There's no
reason I shouldn't be a laborer". Charlie . . . was always intensely interested in
his family. . . . "I'll come home on a weekday and play with the kids until supper
and help around, and then after supper I'll play with the kids and take them out
for a walk. Then I bathe them and put them to bed" . At the follow-up he said,
"my children are just great. I try to spend as much time as possible with them".
(Howard and Bray, 1988, pp. 163, 187)*

While Charlie and Al started out with different priorities, notice how, as the study
progressed, the gaps between the men became more extreme. As we would predict from
the stability-promoting force of *interactional consistency*, discussed in Chapter 8, through
the experiences they evoked, traits and interests seen at the first evaluation solidified,
and the men became "more like themselves" and different from one another as they
traveled through life.

Before we assume that Al's drive, joy in his success, and identification with AT&T
were due to a universal achievement-oriented personality type, let's look at some
comparisons with the second cohort of trainees. In this group, success could be predicted
at the first assessment. Here, too, independence, intelligence, and strong work involvement did relate to how far a person rose through the ranks. On the other hand, as Al
suspected, the younger managers were different. As a group, they were less enthusiastic,
less likely to defer to authority, less motivated to excel. Most interesting, they lacked Al's
unwavering commitment and belief in the company. Even during the early 1980s, the
pessimism and distrust in the organization as a reliable employer for life were beginning
to take hold.

Many of the first-generation AT&T managers had also become more disenchanted
and somewhat less enthusiastic during the first eight years. One reason may have been
that, while every trainee started out with high hopes of advancing, many never did rise
the way they expected through the ranks. Is there a standard pattern to promotions in
companies such as AT&T?

THE TOURNAMENT MODEL OF JOB ADVANCEMENT.   To explore this
question, James Rosenbaum (1984) picked a large corporation and analyzed its patterns
of mobility by examining the personnel records of the firm.

Rosenbaum posed two possibilities. The first is the optimistic assumption of equal
opportunity. Even if we don't get promoted initially, we always have a second chance.
Losing out on the first or second promotion is not a permanent barrier to advancement.
Upward mobility is possible at any point. However, Rosenbaum's hunch was that
employees' chances of getting ahead are more limited. Selections made early determine
where people end up. Early in their careers people are categorized and tracked.

Rosenbaum spells out a **tournament model of job advancement.** Work involves a
series of competitions. Winners of each "contest" have a chance to compete for another
promotion, but no guarantee of success. However, if they do not win (get promoted),
they are kept from rising up the ranks. While losers may not be out of the race (fired),
they are doomed to compete in minor contests. Their chance of "reaching the finals" is
gone.

The data confirmed Rosenbaum's gloomy hunch. People promoted early on had a
better chance of being promoted again, a greater probability of reaching management,

**tournament model of ad-
vancement**
*Idea that, if people do not get
promoted early on in a large
organization, they are unlikely to
get promoted in further
"rounds."*

and a higher career ceiling and a lower career floor. The system was more closed than the ideal of equal opportunity would suggest.

Rosenbaum outlines some negative effects of this tracking. It puts a premium on fast starters. It makes late blooming difficult. Because of this, it may make errors of exclusion, keeping talented people who "get it together" late from getting anywhere. Early tracking tends to favor workers (such as men) who have no competing pressures during early adulthood. It stacks the deck against others (such as women) who begin more slowly due to the demands of parenthood. It encourages the frantic need to make it during early adulthood and so may contribute to burnout and job stress in midlife. Even for the organization, it may not be optimal. Early choices may be less informed choices because they are not based on enough data to determine which workers are good. Early tracking encourages workers to think about short-term gains because they need to prove themselves now. It discourages long-term planning, decisions whose wisdom will not show up for years.

Rosenbaum's criticisms apply to a certain type of career, one in which people enter a company and then stay in that organization for years. As we know, this once standard, stable middle-class work pattern has changed in recent years.

The Boundaryless Career

In most studies of career development, researchers focus on a given company and explore how people perform in this stable milieu. This research, while it still applies to some workers, fits fewer careers today. Today, as we saw in our interview with Mike, people cannot enter a company confident of having a lifetime job. Unlike Al, they cannot expect if they work hard to rise through the ranks, to have the luxury of centering their whole identity as a worker around being "an AT&T man." A decade and a half of layoffs have made this identification with any organization, be it a corporation, hospital, law firm, or university, risky. As organizations downsize or restructure (code words for firing people), employees at every level are vulnerable, forced to seek new work. Some become private practitioners. Some get training for other careers. Others move in and out of the smaller, more specialized firms to which the downsized giants contract out their work. In 1990, companies of less than 500 workers employed 56 percent of the work force, a share expected to increase to 70 percent by the beginning of the next century (Bird, 1994). The stable, bounded organizational pattern is being replaced by the **boundaryless career.**

boundaryless career
Career path outside of a stable organizational setting in which individuals must engineer their work lives on their own.

Let's look at how experts describe what is increasingly likely to be your career path (Bird, 1994; DeFillippi and Arthur, 1994; Miner and Robinson, 1994; Mirvis and Hall, 1994):

1. ***The boundaryless career is ill-structured.*** Rather than unfolding in a defined way, as we saw with Mike, boundaryless careers are continually changing shape. There is no set career ladder, no sense of "advancement" in the sense of regularly inching ahead. Progress, success, or advancement comes in fits and spurts as we master new skills, land a new job, or meet a new group with whom to collaborate.

2. ***The boundaryless career is self-directed.*** Without the security of a lifetime job, we as individuals have total responsibility for shaping our fortunes in the world of work. Networking, or who we know, becomes more important as we shift from assignment to assignment and company to company in peddling our skills. Just as important is *what* we know. Having expertise, the right knowledge, and especially being able to reason in innovative ways are keys to getting ahead in the boundaryless career.

3. ***The boundaryless career has psychological benefits and costs.*** The flexibility of this career is appealing. We can spend more time with family. We are not penalized as much for blooming late, or taking time off, or working at odd times. Because they are so self-directed, boundaryless careers are ideal for offering the autonomy,

Right after school, Martha landed a job in a famous architecture firm. For 20 years, she has worked at IMC, never really satisfied. Martha has been in charge of pieces of projects. She spent years doing bathroom fixtures for large buildings. She became the carpet expert, choosing the color of the flooring in a university dorm. Martha sees herself as an artist. Spending her life doing sinks and rugs is not what she expected from a career. She is bothered by the lack of control. You have to deal with contractors who do not deliver and then take the blame when they do the job wrong or do not show up. You have to bend to what your boss, the project manager, says. Recently the manager on Martha's building, a young man who entered the firm well after her, has been making her a scapegoat. This "fair-haired" protégé of a partner is criticizing her, trying to drive her out of the firm. Her friends are making twice her salary. Martha is living in the studio apartment she had after graduate school. How could her career end up so badly when Martha knows that she chose the right field?

Even when we select a profession that fits our interests, that is no guarantee of being content in our work. As Karen Loscocco and Anne Roschelle (1991) argue, a better predictor of happiness comes from looking at the job itself. Jobs that provide challenge, meaning, variety, and complexity are satisfying to every worker. Autonomy is especially important. Having the chance to make or participate in decisions is related to satisfaction across a variety of industries.

Freedom, challenge, control, and autonomy are rewards we get from the actual act of working. While in surveys people rank these *intrinsic benefits* as most important, *extrinsic rewards*, such as pay, are also cited as reasons for liking or disliking a job. In addition, worker satisfaction is related to a "favorable opportunity structure," that is, to the chance to advance. When people are in dead-end jobs or, as with Martha, when they feel that they are at a dead end, work happiness tends to be low (Loscocco, 1990).

Another extrinsic influence is the wider social context, that is where we stand in relation to our reference group. We mentally compare the pay, the status, and the conditions of our job to those of neighbors, friends, and others in our social set. If these comparisons fall short, we feel dissatisfied no matter how gratifying our own situation may be. In sum, we now clearly see why Martha is so miserable. Notice that along every dimension just listed, Martha's job comes out short!

freedom, and creativity that researchers find are crucial in having a satisfying work life (see Feature 13-1).

There are many psychological trade-offs. Can we construct a strong work identity when, as we saw with Mike, we wear so many different "hats" over our lives? What about the network of close relationships, the convoy of friends we develop over years at the same job? Most important is the uncertainty, the insecurity in being cut adrift to sail on our own. This feeling of vulnerability affects people at all socioeconomic levels. However, we might expect the tension to be especially high when loved ones depend on how we are steering our small, one-person boat, that is, among men with families.

GENDER, ETHNICITY, AND WORK

Men and Work

How important emotionally is having a steady source of income to married men? How crucial psychologically is work to men's self-esteem? We already know that men who do not have well-paying jobs are less likely to marry (see Chapter 11). We know that job insecurity relates to marital distress (see Chapter 10). And we have the following interesting study of men's lives:

Realizing that social scientists knew next to nothing about the critical concerns that motivate well-functioning adult men, Robert Weiss (1990) set out to examine uncharted territory, the inner lives of upper-middle-class men. Using lists of heads of households in census tracts, Weiss's research team selected men aged 35 to 55 in upper-middle-income jobs living in suburban Boston to interview. Ultimately they questioned 80 men and their wives in depth from 1983 to 1987.

The researchers were struck with the central importance of work, how critical performing well at a profession was to their subjects' sense of identity. This was not to say that family was unimportant. In fact, having a wife and children was what gave meaning to "the battle to provide." Still, it was in this battle that the real drama of these men's lives lay. Here is how Weiss describes the priorities from the men's perspective:

> [Work is] fundamental to having enough self respect so you feel comfortable with your neighbors. Plus it is truly absorbing. So you give your work whatever it requires. You do as good a job as you can, not worrying about keeping down your hours or whatever. You need self-confidence for your work, because it is challenging and risky. You get the self-confidence by seeing yourself do well and by having others recognize that you do well. . . . You care deeply about marriage and your children. That is far and away the part of your life closest to your heart, though not always the part whose demands you put first. . . . You depend on [your wife] to make a home for you and the children, just as she depends on you to help keep it financed (although she may help). In Weiss's words, "The men of this study want to be men they respect. . . . Being a good man means being able to maintain a respected place among men, being able to serve as the head of one's family" (1990, pp. 252–253).

Even though, as we saw with Al and Charlie, one's work goals may vary, Weiss argues that being able to "serve as the head of a family (support a wife and children)" is critically important to every man. A longitudinal study involving thousands of men supports his claim. When Jay Teachman, Vaughn Call, and Karen Carver (1994) followed this huge, economically diverse sample of young adults for more than a decade, they found that men who were married found new jobs on average twice as quickly after being laid off as the unmarried men, suggesting that the push to be a responsible provider is a powerful impulse for family men.

Women and Work

Helen Astin (1984) argues that the drive to be competent at work is critical emotionally for women, too. A longitudinal survey of American youth suggests that she may be right. When researchers tested a national sample of women in their early twenties, they found that being married was unrelated to a woman's feelings of well-being. Women with young children in the house had lower self-esteem! What was associated with feeling positive and good about oneself was preparing for or having a career.

Notice that these women were too young to believe that at this age they should be married or have children. Perhaps not having attained these other central adult life-goals, marriage and parenthood, may trouble women later on. Still, this study fits in with the research presented on the single life in Chapter 10. Our stereotype that women get their self-esteem from having a husband and children may not be true. Today many women care deeply about achieving in the world of work.

This push to have a career has caused the traditionally large educational differences between women and men to evaporate. Today women are as likely to graduate from

Gender Difference in Weekly Earnings for Full-Time Workers, Selected Years

Figure 13-3

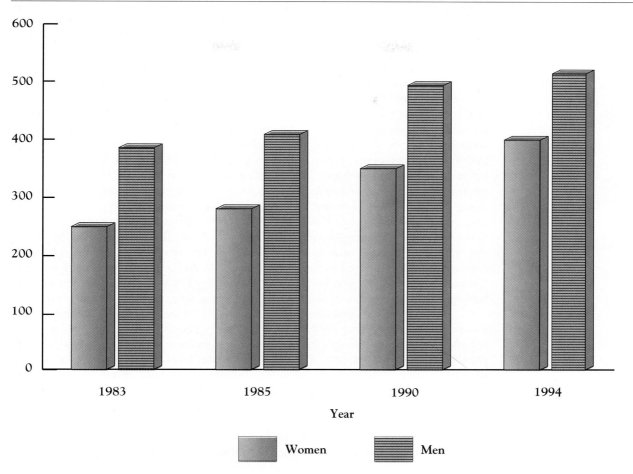

While the pay gap has narrowed slightly, even when women work full-time on average they still earn significantly less than men.

Source: U.S. Bureau of the Census, 1995, *Statistical Abstract of the United States 1995*, Washington, DC: U.S. Government Printing Office.

college as men (Gilbert, 1993). While more men still get professional degrees, women are catching up. Women are entering formerly male professions, such as medicine, law, and higher education, in record numbers. In 1991, a third of all students enrolled in American law and medical schools were women. Women also made up more than one-third of all college teachers in the United States (Gilbert, 1993).

These changes are mirrored in the improving economic status of women. In 1969, the median income of women who worked full-time was only 59 percent of that of men; by the mid-1990s, as Figure 13-3 shows, it had risen to almost 75 percent. Why, even when they work comparable hours, do women on average still earn so much less?

One cause is **occupational segregation.** In the United States and other developed countries, women and men tend to have different jobs (Charles, 1992). More than half of all working women are concentrated in two occupational groups, clerical and service

occupational segregation
Fact that men and women tend to work in different types of jobs.

work (food handling, health service etc.). These jobs typically pay much less than comparable "male" jobs and have few benefits. There is even a relationship between the proportion of women in a field and the salaries in that occupation. Once a high percentage of women enter a given field, that profession tends to pay comparatively less. When men enter a traditionally "female" occupation (physical therapy is a perfect recent example), it is a tip-off that that career is becoming more desirable in terms of salary. (Granovetter and Tilly, 1988).

Even when we look within educational and occupational categories, significant salary gaps remain. Women college graduates earn on average what male high school graduates do. In 1990, the median income of female lawyers and social scientists who worked full-time was still only three-fourths of that of males (Gilbert, 1993). One reason is that in high-status fields, such as law, medicine, and college teaching, women tend to enter lower-paying specialties, choosing family law rather than corporate law, selecting pediatrics instead of surgery, teaching in psychology departments, not in the often better-paying business school. The fact that the women in these traditionally more exclusively male fields on average are younger also may partly account for the differences in pay (Russell, 1994). However, most experts feel discrimination can play an important part. In management, Joyce Russell (1994) reviews studies revealing a widespread bias that women are not aggressive enough to do a good job. Russell argues that women in this "male environment" may feel socially isolated. They do not have as much chance to have mentors, are shunted to lower track positions, and are perhaps sexually harassed. You may have heard the wonderful phrase *glass ceiling* often used to describe this invisible barrier that prevents women managers from rising as far as men.

While complaints about on-the-job discrimination are frequent in surveys, women also seek out lower-paying gender-stereotyped work (Betz, 1994). As our discussion of self-efficacy suggests, from an early age women are socialized into "female-type" jobs. By preschool, the types of jobs that are appropriate for women are learned through modeling, from adults, from television. Children's household chores are defined by gender. The same division applies to adolescents' first real work experiences.

In surveying several thousand working 10th and 11th graders, Ellen Greenberger and Laurence Steinberg (1983) found boys in stereotypically male jobs, such as mowing lawns, delivering newspapers, and coaching baseball teams. Girls often did classically female work, such as being sales clerks and education aides. Even jobs in which boys and girls were represented equally, such as cleaning and food service, still were broken down into women's versus men's work. At restaurants, boys cooked, bussed tables, or washed dishes. Girls were waitresses or hostesses. Boys who cleaned washed cars and equipment. Girls cleaned house. Girls worked fewer hours per week than boys. Particularly in their second jobs, their wages per hour were less. The message seemed to be that work for men was different, more important and highly prized.

Women's divided loyalties also make it unlikely that they will be at the same economic place as men. Even in a boundaryless career, in order to be successful it helps to get off to a good start early, work continuously, and devote oneself single-mindedly to career. This conflicts with the fact that as we saw in Chapter 11, most women want children, are strongly identified with motherhood, and, once they are mothers, do most of the childcare. Unlike Weiss's men, women *do* worry about keeping down their hours at the job. They see family, not work, as their first priority. As long as women are committed to putting family first, they are at a disadvantage in the world of work.

Angela O'Rand (1988) documents the financial consequences of putting family first. When a woman interrupts or delays working during her childbearing years, she pays a price throughout her life. Midlife, "off time" labor force entrants have fewer years to climb the career ladder and a lower economic ceiling at work. Their retirement income is lower because pensions are based on years spent working and salary at work. According

Many women today would identify with the "I give up" expression on this person's face as she struggles to juggle a phone call while coping with a toddler and contemplating cleaning a sink full of dirty dishes before leaving for a long day at her job. Still, in spite of her obvious role overload, if she enjoys her job, the research suggests that this working mother is likely to feel more alive and fulfilled than if she were to stay at home full time.

to O'Rand's calculations, each child means a significant loss in pension income for women, but not for men. In other words, the choices that women make in their earlier years have a direct relationship to how they tend to fare economically in old age.

In spite of these problems, women are right in Sigmund Freud's words to want both "love and work." As I implied at the beginning of this chapter, the research overwhelmingly suggests that working has been good for women's mental health. Working women tend to have greater well-being than full-time housewives (Weitzman and Fitzgerald, 1993). As we saw in the Mills Study in Chapter 8, women who spend their lives as traditional housewives are less likely to grow emotionally or feel fulfilled in their later years. One lesson of the research on motherhood is that it is perilous to define one's self-worth totally through children, to focus everything on succeeding in this one area of life.

Working women complain of **role overload,** the feeling of having too little time and too much to do (Hochschild, 1989). As we saw in Chapter 11, they may feel more dissatisfied with their husbands, especially when they expect them to share the housework equally. Still, having our eggs in a variety of baskets offers a buffer against disappointments in one area of life. Having multiple roles, a complex life, or, in Hazel Markus's words, many different self-schemas is related to having a richer, more fulfilling life (Barnett, Marshall, and Singer, 1992).

Obviously working is not good for every woman. As I mentioned in Chapter 11, the critical issues are whether that person wants to work, how supportive her family is, and

role overload
In working women, having too much to do in negotiating the life roles of homemaker and worker.

especially whether she has a fulfilling job. In comparing husbands and wives in dual-earner families, Diane Hughes and Ellen Galinsky (1994) found, as we might expect from the "role overload" principle, that the women were somewhat more prone to emotional distress. However, when they looked more deeply, the main cause lay in the actual jobs of husbands versus wives. Most of these women worked in clerical jobs. They reported less creativity, less freedom, and so less work satisfaction than their spouses. Working in a boring, routine job is as likely to produce emotional distress in women as men (Barnett, Marshall, Raudenbush, and Brennan, 1993). Conversely, being in an unhappy marriage poisons well-being as much for men as their working wives (Barnett, Brennan, Raudenbush, and Marshall, 1994). We might be tempted to assume that work problems do not matter as much to women and that men are less bothered by an unhappy family life. The reality is that *both* women and men are unhappy when they feel unfulfilled in love or work.

Minorities and Work

Many of the same statistics and concerns apply to minorities—occupational segregation, differences in average income, and widespread feelings of being discriminated against. Recall from Chapter 1 that the median household income of every minority except Asian Americans is well below the American norm. We might argue that, as the minority population has more single mothers with children, this does not tell us much about differences in pay and jobs (Jencks, 1992). However, even when we look just at full-time male workers, African Americans and Hispanic Americans still earn only about two-thirds the pay of whites (Jencks, 1992).

As is true of women, minorities have made huge gains within the past 40 years. In 1950, the average working African-American man earned only 43 percent as much as his Caucasian counterpart. Before the civil rights movement, minorities were invisible in many upper-echelon jobs. In 1964, the doors opened when Title VII of the Civil Rights Act outlawed employment discrimination on the basis of race. In the late 1960s, they opened wider as most firms developed **affirmative action policies** devoted to increasing the percentages of minority and female workers, especially in professional jobs. As we saw in the AT&T study, these policies created a much more diverse work force and an expanded minority middle class. As of 1989, the percentage of African-American professionals was at its highest level ever, 6.1 percent (U.S. Bureau of the Census, 1993).

As with women, these changes have gone hand in hand with educational gains, especially for African Americans. Today African-American young adults are almost as likely to graduate from high school as whites and non-Hispanic minorities (Jencks, 1992). (Partly due to language barriers and the fact that they may be first-generation immigrants, Hispanic Americans are still much less likely to have finished high school.) African-American college graduation rates have also risen dramatically in recent decades.

However, serious problems remain. Despite these educational advances, African-American/white differences in pay for full-time workers have not changed much since 1969 (Hacker, 1992). Moreover, in the same way as for women, substantial differences in income exist even when educational levels and social class differences are controlled. At every comparable educational level, African-American men earn significantly less income than white men. As Figure 13-4 shows, they also are more likely to be unemployed. In the same way as we asked earlier, why, especially when they are upper-middle-class, do African Americans fare more poorly in the job market than whites?

As with women, one explanation lies in job settings. Upper-middle-class African Americans tend to work in public-sector jobs, which tend to pay less than private industry. African-American professionals are more likely to be teachers and school

affirmative action policies *Policies designed to systematically increase minority representation in higher education and in the work force by giving preferential treatment to underrepresented groups.*

Figure 13-4

Unemployment Rates for Whites, Hispanic Americans, and African Americans by Education, 1994

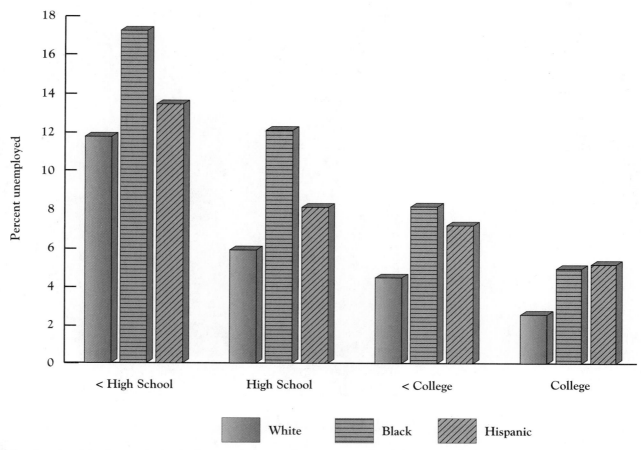

While educational attainment is clearly the most important factor associated with being out of work, at every comparable educational level minorities are more likely to be unemployed than whites.

Source: U.S. Bureau of the Census, 1995, *Statistical Abstract of the United States 1995,* Washington, DC: U.S. Government Printing Office.

administrators than corporate managers of the type Weiss interviewed. African Americans occupying managerial positions in industry have doubled during the past decade (Greenhaus, Parasuraman, and Wormley, 1990). Some have managed to climb close to the top. However, as with women, they are often concentrated in management's lower rungs. Because of this, observers argue that the glass ceiling describing limits to women's advancement also applies to African Americans in corporate settings.

In a self-help book for African-American managers, Floyd and Jackie Dickens (1991) argue that African Americans in corporations have to work especially hard to prove themselves. The perception is that they are there because of affirmative action, are less qualified, and are less capable of doing the job. A study by Jeffrey Greenhaus, Saroj Parasuraman, and Wayne Wormly (1990) exploring the experiences of managers in three

J. Bruce Llewellyn began his business career by mortgaging his house, putting up his worldly goods as collateral, and extracting the reluctant promise of a loan to buy a chain of grocery stores. Today, Llewellyn owns two highly profitable Coca Cola bottling plants and is about to stage his biggest coup: buying the cable T.V. operations for The New York Times. Many of the barriers faced by African Americans in the business world were surely confronted by Llewellyn, explaining why success stories such as this are still inspiring and relatively rare.

companies in the eastern United States suggests that there is a realistic basis for this advice. White supervisors did judge their African-American employees as less competent and less promotable. African-American managers felt less accepted and had lower levels of job satisfaction than their white coworkers.

Unfortunately these difficulties are not confined to private industry. In comparing supervisor-employee relationships among several hundred workers at a university, Sandy Jeanquart-Barone (1993) found that trust levels were especially low, not only when African-Americans reported to white supervisors, but also when whites had African-American bosses.

While every minority group must struggle with these difficulties, the problems that African Americans face are unique. As sociologist Christopher Jencks (1992) points out, unlike other minorities, African Americans did not enter this country as immigrants, assuming that their task was to adapt to a new society they had chosen to make their own. Their history as slaves created a culture in which resistance to authority is more widely tolerated, where it is natural to feel more ambivalent about excelling according to the dominant norm. African-American professionals report these conflicts: the feeling that, if they do what is required to make it, they are abandoning their culture, acting white, or becoming Uncle Toms. These mixed emotions, plus the greater discrimination that they may actually face, make it especially hard for upper-middle-class African Americans to single-mindedly focus on success.

The problems are magnified at the other end of the economic scale. Because blue-collar jobs in industry are so much rarer and the service jobs that have replaced them are less likely to pay an acceptable wage, for every American the value of a high school degree in terms of earnings has decreased in the past few decades. This deterioration cancels out the educational gains that have been so striking at the high school level for African Americans in recent years. While the question of whether there are enough low-paying jobs to go around is hotly debated, as we saw in our discussion of William Wilson's theory in Chapter 11, what jobs exist are more often in the suburbs, not the inner city areas where poor minorities live. Apart from this spatial mismatch, as we might suspect, employers are often more reluctant to give these jobs to poor minority women and men.

Joleen Kirshenman and Katherine Neckerman (1991) conducted interviews with a random sample of 185 employers in Cook County Chicago who hired workers in a range of jobs available to people with minimum skills. Most employers complained of a decline in the work ethic, of how difficult it was to get good, reliable help. When asked directly about ethnic differences, 37 percent rated African Americans as having the poorest work ethic; another 7.6 percent rated African Americans and Hispanic Americans together. No employer rated whites last.

Actually, in this survey, class operated in conjunction with race. Most people reported that they would hire minorities of the "right type." It was men and women living in the inner city that employers felt were shiftless, and it was these applicants that they made efforts to screen out. Employers used various criteria to determine if a job seeker had the "bad work ethic" associated with the ghetto. Some mentioned that they passed over applicants whose resumes showed that they had graduated from the Chicago public schools. Others evaluated job seekers based on the way that they spoke on the phone. Often they looked at an applicant's address. Did the person come from the projects or a poor neighborhood? Job history was important. As we might imagine, people were at a disadvantage if they reported being unemployed for long periods or shifting from job to job. These evaluations were made by *both* minority and non-minority employers. In fact, one African-American jeweler commented that he specifically tried to avoid hiring people who were most in need of a job!

> *I have a great deal of resistance to hire a divorcée that lives by herself and doesn't have a source of income . . . because the type of job I offer doesn't offer enough wages to justify a continuation of that kind of lifestyle. . . . $4 doesn't pay enough to support an apartment and a car and kids in school. So . . . what's going to happen? I mean you've got to have an alternate source or it's going to be my jewelry. (Kirschenman and Neckerman, 1991, p. 214)*

Because of this, minority job seekers had to make a special effort to indicate that the stereotypes did not apply to them, both by taking care to act and dress "middle class" and by using more devious strategies. Some reported that they misrepresented their job history or their financial situation. Others said that they felt compelled to give a false address in order to get hired.

We can understand how a person's motivation to make these adjustments might be lower when the job pays very little, is demeaning and boring, and requires traveling an hour or more by public transportation each way. When a woman loses health benefits and needs to put her children into day care, it may not even make economic sense to work. This is why, when we look at minority status since the civil rights movement, we see both striking gains and striking losses. While some people are doing much better, minorities have suffered from the declining quality of jobs at the lower economic rungs (Winnick, 1988). Ironically, during the same years that their more well educated,

When this plant closed its doors, everyone suffered, the vice president and the minimum wage worker—although because it was universal and not due to their personal shortcomings, the overall impact of this downsizing may have been less traumatic on these workers than being "fired." Ultimately, however, to understand how each individual coped with this event we would have to look at that person's unique life-situation.

advantaged counterparts were making dramatic strides on the professional level, unemployment steadily rose among blue-collar African-American men. More ominous, the main cause was an increase in long-term joblessness, a tripling in the percentage of men who did not work at all within the past year (Gottschalk, 1986; Hacker, 1992).

UNEMPLOYMENT

Today poorly educated workers of every race are especially vulnerable to long-term unemployment as they travel through life. With company downsizing, losing one's job and being unemployed for some period of time is becoming a more common experience at every socioeconomic rung.

As we saw with Mike at the beginning of this chapter, being laid off can cause severe stress. After plant closings, rates of anxiety and depression rise; doctors' visits for physical complaints increase (Dooley and Catalano, 1988; Ezzy, 1993). However, in the same way as with divorce and widowhood, people vary in how well they cope with this life event. Once again, in predicting what makes coping easier or more difficult, let's adopt a *contextual approach,* focusing on just a few of the factors in Table 13-1 that may affect the distress.

Predicting the Strain of Job Loss

One interesting influence centers around the event itself. Was there adequate warning, or is the worker told to pack his bags and leave at the end of the day? Just as important, *why* is the person losing the job? In one study of working-class men, the researchers found that laid-off workers had significantly lower levels of distress than a similar group of men who were fired (Miller and Hoppe, 1994). The reason was that the men who were laid off due to a plant closing tended to blame the economy, while those who were fired personally blamed their employers. As we might expect, losing a job is easier when we can interpret this event as an "act of nature" or nobody's fault, rather than adopting the opposite explanatory style: "My employer (or I) did me in" (see Feature 13-2, p. 396).

Another marker on the table involves our place in the life course. In a series of studies, British researchers have documented that job loss tends to be most devastating

Some Possible Influences Affecting the Stress of Job Loss Table 13-1

Prior factors	Current factors	Subsequent factors
1. Previous job losses	1. Conditions of termination (extent of warning; personal failure vs. nobody's fault; severance pay)	1. Social support
2. Attachment to job	2. Age at termination	2. Duration of unemployment
3. Personality resilience	3. Gender, plus need for income	3. Other economic resources
	4. Reference group (all employed vs. many in same boat)	

for men aged 25–59. Among teenagers and people over age 60, unemployment has a more minor emotional effect. Teenagers have fewer responsibilities. They can live cheaply in their parents' homes. They usually do not have families to support. Unemployed men approaching retirement are less likely to have dependent children (Warr, Jackson, and Banks, 1988). Psychologically they are more able to cope because they can think of themselves as retired (see the next section). As we might predict from Weiss's research, especially for men with families being fired can be a devastating blow.

This suggests that gender should be important. Because they may not need their jobs as much in order to live and have more alternate roles to fall back on, married women with working husbands in particular should be less traumatized by losing their jobs.

When Carrie Leana and Daniel Feldmen (1991) studied people laid off from the Kennedy Space Center after the *Challenger* disaster, they found no immediate gender difference in distress; though over a longer period the men did do worse. While emotional upset was just as intense after six months of unemployment for men, at this point women's scores on a measure of health improved. The researchers reasoned that after some time women were more able to shift to other emotional baskets, such as parenthood or volunteer work. These options are not as available to men.

However, if they have to support themselves, women are worse off in one important respect. In studying layoffs in the auto industry, researchers found that, because they had less seniority, women were less likely to have unemployment insurance. So unmarried women were far more likely to be thrust into poverty by losing their jobs than men (Gordus and Yamakawa, 1988).

This brings up a crucial difference between unemployment and widowhood or divorce: For *any* person, male or female, who has to work, being unemployed is not likely to "get better over time." It can only be cured by finding a new job.

How long does this cure take? While the statistics fluctuate somewhat, on average workers find new jobs within a few months (Wegman, 1991). However, interestingly college men take longer. People with college degrees are more selective. They will not just take any job. Once they are hired, however, they have an advantage in that they are more likely to have a permanent, long-lasting job.

There is another group that has special trouble finding new work: middle-aged people. In contrast to our stereotypes, in the inner city long-term joblessness is highest among older men (Jencks, 1992). This same difficulty can also apply to people at the upper end of the economic scale. As we can see in Feature 13-2, for a variety of reasons middle-aged job seekers take considerably longer on average to find new jobs.

For over two years, David has been searching for work. David would not be counted in the unemployment statistics. He has a part-time job in a small firm. One or two private clients help pay the bills. The problem is that David is *underemployed*, not where he should be in relation to his skills and background, especially at this point in life. A lawyer with David's expertise should be earning at least $150,000 a year, enough to support a family at an upper-middle-class level, especially someone with David's résumé. David was a Phi Beta Kappa. He went to a prestigious law school and then worked at some of the city's best law firms.

The problem, David argues, is that he is a victim of bad breaks. Now, for a person at his level, there are practically no jobs. Firms generally hire people right out of law school. In this profession, the more experienced you are, the less employable you become. David's wife, Anna, believes that the problem is her husband. David's job history is suspicious. He never made partner at his first job. Then he was laid off at his second job when the firm merged and the new partners got rid of David and brought in their own men. Anna admits that the last layoff was not David's fault. His firm folded because not enough clients were coming in. Over time, Anna's nagging has increased. They have been forced to borrow money from relatives. Even though she has a baby, Anna has to work full-time. They may have to sell the house and move to an apartment. Other lawyers with worse credentials are making it. Even when they were laid off at age 40, some of David's colleagues found new full-time jobs. David does not interview well. Anna is angry at her husband for not seeing the signs and searching for work before his last firm closed its doors. Worse yet, David seems unmotivated. He is not really trying to find a new job.

David is in a difficult situation. Older people do have more trouble in the job market. On average, they take twice as long as people in their twenties to find new work (U.S. Senate Special Committee on Aging, 1991a) As we will see in the next section, age discrimination does exist. On the other hand, by blaming her husband, Anna may actually be fostering the behavior she dislikes. In studying out-of-work older professionals, Brent Mallinckrodt and Bruce Fretz (1988) looked at how depression and the intensity of job seeking varied as a function of an individual's length of unemployment, financial concerns, and a variety of types of social support. As we might imagine, social support was particularly important in predicting both emotional distress and how actively a person continued to search for new work. In particular, the researchers found that a dimension of support that they labeled "reassurance of worth" was closely tied to self-efficacy, searching behavior, and self-esteem. In other words, not only may people who feel personally at fault have more trouble coping with job loss, but also their attributions may be partly shaped by the messages that they get from the people closest to them. In order to motivate her husband to more actively search for a job, Anna might be better off by focusing on David's abilities, rather than blaming him for where he went wrong and how he is failing now.

While it is hard to imagine anything positive about losing one's job, even unemployment can sometimes have a silver lining. When Carolyn Perrucci and Dena Targ (1988) examined workers four months after a candy factory closed, the laid-off women and men reported no change in feelings of marital closeness or support. Some reported that their relationships improved as families rallied together to cope. In this study, there were mitigating factors. The workers were warned well in advance. They knew that the problem was not of their own making. They were given a generous benefits package to cushion the blow. Still, the lesson that economic disaster may not always translate into psychological disaster is underlined by the longest-running study of human life.

THE LESSONS FROM THE BERKELEY/OAKLAND STUDIES. Because the *Berkeley/Oakland Studies* were begun in the late 1920s just before the Great Depression, they offered an ideal "natural experiment" in how families cope with financial problems that are ongoing, long-lasting, and severe. The researchers focused on a group that they called the deprived, families who lost more than 35 percent of their income during these years (Elder and Caspi, 1988).

Not unexpectedly this stress *sometimes* took a dramatic toll. Fighting and disorganization did rise precipitously among some families. When this occurred, the primary impetus was the men. The researchers found that often it was erratic behavior in husbands that poisoned the family atmosphere.

Not all of the men reacted poorly. Some remained calm and able to control their frustration. Others deteriorated emotionally, reacting to their problems by becoming abusive toward their children and wives. As we might expect from what we know about personality stability, men who were irritable and explosive before the Depression were often the ones who reacted poorly. Those rated as calm and stable were able to control their inclinations to strike out at their family when they lost their jobs. So once again, we see how enduring dispositions shape the path we follow as adults.

The impact on the children varied in an interesting way. Economic hard times "accelerated the pathway to adulthood" among older children. They had to pitch in to help the family. This took different forms for girls and boys. Adolescent girls took on the housework. Boys tried to find jobs. This earlier-than-normal push to assume adult responsibilities was positive, making for more resilience and self-confidence throughout adult life.

The younger children suffered a different fate. Boys in particular whose families were hard hit by the Depression during their first decade of life suffered emotionally, feeling less adequate and self-assured as adults. Most at risk were boys who were difficult temperamentally, those who had behavior problems, such as temper tantrums, before the Depression. This type of child was liable to be targeted by an out-of-control father and bear the brunt of his anger and frustration. While the risk of these children being mistreated was high, the mother seemed to act as a buffer. If she was affectionate, she could tone down the abuse, and, rather than leading to emotional disturbance, the risk of mental disorders was reduced.

This study once again illustrates how important it is to consider the total context within which lives unfold. While for fathers a single influence—personality—predicted coping, for children we would have to look at their unique situation and place in the life course. In fact, this research beautifully reveals how "being born at a certain time" can affect how we respond to life's blows. When we are at the right place in our development and other conditions are favorable, undergoing a hardship can sometimes produce emotional growth (recall also the discussion of divorce in Chapter 10).

POOR FAMILIES TODAY. In some ways, the Berkeley/Oakland research is extremely relevant to life today. Many of these people did have jobs, but were coping with economic deprivation as a chronic fact of life. The fraction of Americans who are underemployed or working and having trouble making ends meet has increased in recent years. As Figure 13-1 at the beginning of this chapter suggests, the number of families living below the poverty line has risen in recent years (Children's Defense Fund, 1994). Worse yet, the fixed federal poverty line underestimates the true cost of what it takes to live and not just in the more expensive states (Winnick, 1988). In a 1989 Gallup survey, when 3,511 adults were asked what amount of income they would call the poverty line for a four-person family in their community, on average they set the figure as 24 percent higher than the official poverty line (Jencks, 1992)!

However, there are differences between then and now. The Depression was a unique situation in which much of the country was in the same boat. Economic hardship was not seen as due to the person. It was an act of nature that everyone was grappling with. Today, as Feature 13-2 shows, we do make attributions about people who have fallen on economic hard times, seeing their problems as due to their own deficiencies. In addition, the Berkeley/Oakland Study involved two-parent families. Among the single mothers who make up a large fraction of poor families today, there is no other adult in the house to cushion the stress on children. On the other hand, due to the government programs begun by President Franklin Roosevelt during the Depression, today's poor families are somewhat protected against starvation. They can get needed medical care.

Are America's poor children and parents better or worse off today? About the older generation, there is no debate: Older people *on average* are not only healthier, but also better off financially now than at any time in history.

RETIREMENT

The elderly used to be the most vulnerable segment of society. When they developed physical problems and could not work, they had to rely on charity or their families for help. During the Depression, the Social Security Act of 1935 provided universal retirement income at age 65. About three decades ago, Congress raised Social Security benefits, indexed them to increases in the cost of living, and provided older people with free medical care. During this period, pensions proliferated, eventually covering much of the labor force. These changes transformed the economic situation of the elderly and made retiring in comfort possible for the first time. They also transformed retirement into an event that often occurs before age 65.

While we think of 65 as the traditional retirement age, the "true" average retirement age is closer to 60 today (Quinn and Burkhauser, 1990). This trend to retire earlier, illustrated in Figure 13-5, is remarkable considered against the backdrop of our life-expectancy gains. If we were to retire at an "equivalent age" in terms of mortality to what 65 was in 1940, today we should be leaving work at age 70.

The Decision

A variety of influences motivates people to retire (Palmore, Burchett, Fillenbaum, George, and Wallman, 1985). One consideration is financial, whether the person feels he or she has enough income to live. Older workers are pushed to leave work by downturns in the economy, age discrimination, or poor health. Another aspect of the decision is psychological, how much people like their jobs, their commitment to the "work ethic," the extent to which they are looking forward to leisure activities. Let's examine some of these different forces in more depth.

Social Security
Government-sponsored old-age insurance program, which people pay into when working and get benefits from during their retirement years.

FINANCIAL INFLUENCES.   Having money is the reason most people give for retiring (Palmore et al., 1985). As Figure 13-6 on p. 400 shows, **Social Security** provides the highest fraction of retirement income for most older adults. People pay into the Social Security system while they work and then get benefits when they leave the work force at age 65. As we just learned, during the late 1960s and early 1970s there was a marked expansion in Social Security. Benefit levels increased and—very important—rose in tandem with the cost of living. The categories of eligible recipients were increased. The age for collecting partial benefits was extended downward.

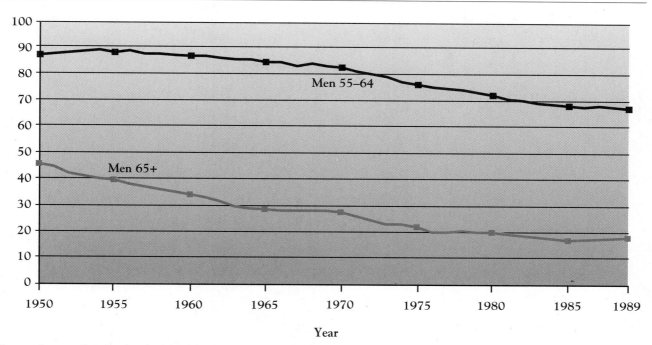

During the very decades that late-life life expectancy increased, early retirement became a more prevalent trend.

Source: U.S. Senate Special Committee on Aging, 1991, *Aging America: Trends and Projections*, Washington, DC: Author.

Today people retiring at age 62 can collect 80 percent of the benefits they would get at age 65. This is one major reason why so many people retire in their early sixties today. In addition, between age 65 and 70, workers who collect Social Security are penalized if they earn over a certain amount. They have to forfeit one dollar of benefits for each three dollars of income that they earn above this ceiling.

The Social Security system also has incentives to discourage retirement. People over age 70 who work can earn an unlimited amount and still collect all their benefits. Workers who retire after age 65 receive a bonus for each year they delay. In an effort to keep the Social Security system solvent, modifications in the Social Security Act were made in 1983. The fraction of benefits awarded at age 62 will be gradually reduced from 80 to 70 percent by 2022. Most important, the age for collecting full Social Security will rise from 65 to 67 by 2027. This change is scheduled to begin gradually going into effect in the year 2000.

Will these efforts really delay retirement? Not much, experts feel (Quinn and Burkhauser, 1990). Today other forces are more important in motivating retirement. While Social Security revved up the retirement engine, that motor now is fueled by other sources.

A primary economic fuel is **pensions.** At least half of all American workers have this additional source of retirement income. In fact, today pension benefits are often used

pensions
Privately sponsored old-age insurance programs in which employers or individuals set aside funds when working to be used during retirement.

Figure 13-6

Percentage of Families with Social Security Benefits as a Major Source of Income, 1992

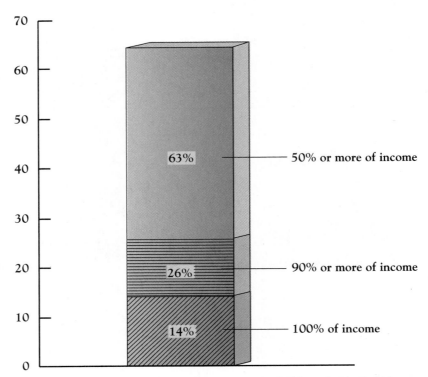

Social Security is the major source of income for 63 percent of all households. For 14 percent of older families, it is the only source of income.

Source: Social Security Administration, 1994, *Fast Facts and Figures About Social Security,* Washington, DC: U.S. Government Printing Office.

as a tool to entice older workers to leave the job. Strategies such as giving credit for five extra years of work if a person retires at 55 or penalizing employees so they get lower benefits if they retire beyond age 60 lure many upper-middle-class workers to retire at an unusually early age (Mehdizadeh and Luzadis, 1994). Still, these lures depend on people willing to take the bait.

THE EMOTIONAL PULL TO RETIRE.   Retirement used to be symbolic of incapacity, the end of productive life. It was the time that a person was put out to pasture because he could no longer perform. As people became able to retire in relative economic comfort, the pasture began to look greener. From a tragedy, retirement was transformed into the time of life people were working *toward*.

For the past quarter century, this new emotion has been the winner. The majority of American workers say they look forward to retiring—even when they say they love their jobs (Glamser, 1976). Looking forward to the idea in some hazy future is different than giving up an activity that, as we know, is often so central to self-esteem. Why is it easy for so many people to take the step?

One reason may be that we begin mentally preparing for retirement long before it occurs. In a longitudinal study of Boston area men, Linda Evans, David Ekerdt, and Raymond Bosse (1985) examined the intensity of retirement-related activities: How often did a man discuss retirement with his wife, relatives, or retired friends? How often did he read articles about retirement? While the amount of these activities increased as retirement age drew near, even men who saw leaving work as 15 years away still did a good deal of informal planning for their retirement life.

Another possibility is that work becomes less compelling after a person has spent decades fighting "the battle to provide." As David Gutmann might predict (see Chapter 8), men are happy to retire because they become less interested in achievement and more concerned with home-oriented values as they age.

One researcher asked men of different ages about the intrinsic satisfaction they got from work and then related their responses to their general morale. While the older men liked their work just as much, for the younger men alone work satisfaction was correlated with satisfaction in life. For the older men the two were disconnected (Cohn, 1979). This suggests that Gutmann may be right. Work may become emotionally less central, less psychologically critical as men age.

In the longitudinal study of Boston area men, David Ekerdt and Stanley DeViney (1993) found that, in the year or two before people expected to leave work, their job satisfaction dipped. This suggests that a process may be occurring similar to what happens when we become romantically involved (see our discussion of courtship in Chapter 10). People also make it psychologically easier to retire by devaluing the alternative: "I don't like my hours. . . . I hate my boss. . . . It's *really* a good idea that I retire."

Not every worker can make these mental transformations. Many people do not want to retire, hate the idea of leaving their jobs, and do equate retirement with emotional death. These sentiments predict actions. Longitudinal studies suggest that people who are reluctant to retire put off the event as long as possible (Sheppard, 1988). The reverse is also true. People who dislike their work are apt to retire as soon as they can (Hanisch and Hulin, 1991).

THE PUSH TO LEAVE WORK.   We already know that employers lure older workers to retire by using the carrot of pensions. To what extent are people pushed out of the labor force? Mandatory retirement is illegal unless a person is a university teacher or working in a profession where age can be a detriment to public safety. Still, as implied in Feature 13-2 describing the underemployed lawyer, **age discrimination** may take a more subtle form.

age discrimination
Any form of discrimination in the workplace on the basis of age.

We have many positive stereotypes about older workers: They are reliable and responsible. However, not only are older workers supposed to cost a company more in salary and benefits, but also they may be viewed as having other liabilities. Older workers are supposed to be absent often for health reasons. They may not have the stamina to complete demanding tasks. They are thought to be prone to accidents, a danger to coworkers as well as themselves. They are supposed to be rigid, less able to learn or adapt (Peterson and Coberly, 1988).

If we think back to our discussion of physical aging and cognition, we immediately realize that these stereotypes must be inaccurate. Only among the old-old do a significant number of people have serious health problems or physical disabilities. While overall intelligence may begin to decline in late midlife, crystallized skills stay stable or grow until the traditional retirement age. Moreover, researchers find that older workers *do* intuitively use *selection, optimization,* and *compensation* to maintain their skills in the face of age-related losses (Abraham and Hansson, 1995). Have these findings made inroads into how we feel?

In one study, managers were asked to read vignettes and make decisions about a hypothetical employee. The stories were identical, but in one condition the protagonist was portrayed as age 30 and in the other, 61. While the managers all *said* how much they valued their older employees, their "recommended solutions" revealed otherwise. If the employee was older, the managers did not believe that he could benefit from retraining and felt he was less adaptable and competent (Peterson and Coberly, 1988).

Once again, the difference may lie in *explanatory style*, a different lens for interpreting older workers' performance on the job. Esther Dedrick and Gregory Dobbins (1991) asked management students to imagine that they were the vice president of a company and their task was to make decisions about the head of accounting, who had just completed a computerized billing system for the firm. One set of scenarios described the accountant as taking longer than expected. The job was done haphazardly. Morale was low. In one version, the accountant was young and in the other, old. In another set (the "success" vignettes), the job was described as having gone well. Here, too, the stories were identical, only differing in the age of the employee.

While good performance in both the young and the old accountants was viewed as a function of the person's basic competence, in the younger accountant failure was passed off as temporary. The person did not have enough experience. With more training, he would get the job right. If the "target" was older, failure was viewed in stable, global, internal terms. The person was not intellectually "up to the job." Most likely training would not be effective. The best solution was to give the accountant simpler, less challenging work.

Do these attributions really operate on the job? Here the research is mixed. While some studies show that employers do view older workers as less competent (Cox and Nkomo, 1992), others do not (Drehmer, Carlucci, Bordieri, and Pincus, 1992; Shore and Bleicken, 1991). However, age discrimination is implied by the figures on **displaced workers,** people who get laid off because of company downsizing. Although making up 13 percent of all workers, in 1989 people over 55 represented 18 percent of people who had suffered this fate (U.S. Senate Special Committee on Aging, 1991a). This raises the suspicion that one strategy companies use to get rid of older workers may be to abolish a job slot (or department) when its occupant becomes too senior—and costly—to keep on the payroll.

According to one engineer at Bell Labs,

> We were all encouraged to retire at 65 even though the law said it should be 70. It was clear that our work was being produced in Korea at lower cost. We were offered a sweetener with the notion that even if we didn't take retirement at that time our chances would be less favorable next year. And, after all they could hire young technicians at half the price they were paying us. (Williamson, Rinehart, and Blank, 1992, p. 41)

A supervisor at Bethlehem Steel reported:

> They said if we didn't leave the company voluntarily (taking the early retirement incentive . . .), they would have to reduce the force at their discretion. I chose not to be one of those. Ordinarily we were a two-man office, but when my boss retired a year before he was not replaced. . . . After vacation you'd have twice as much work because it wasn't being done by anyone else. (Williamson et al., 1992, p. 43).

These vignettes suggest that some of what looks like voluntary early retirement may be more forced than we might think. Moreover, the extent of age discrimination may look more minor because of the legal system. The money awarded for winning this type

displaced workers
Workers who lose their jobs as a result of company downsizing.

of suit is small, the few years of salary a person would earn by working until the normal retirement time. So lawyers tend to be more reluctant to take on age discrimination cases versus more lucrative ones (Peter Strauss, personal communication, 1989). When consulting a lawyer, a victim of even blatant discrimination may be advised to take early retirement. And not wasting years in court can seem a more practical course.

The Consequences

What are the financial effects of not working? Is being retired good or bad for health? How do people adapt psychologically to this life change?

THE FINANCIAL IMPACT.   In 1960, one out of every three older Americans lived below the poverty line, a poverty rate twice that of younger adults. Then our nation became sensitized to the elderly poor. That outcry in a booming economy produced a remarkable change. As I mentioned earlier, Social Security benefits were raised and extended. Medicare was instituted. The impact of these *entitlement programs* has been dramatic. Today, as Figure 13-7 reveals, children, especially the very young, have replaced the elderly as our nation's poorest group.

On the other hand, while fewer older people live in dire poverty, retirees on average still must cope with less income than people under 65 (U.S. Senate Special Committee on Aging, 1991a). However, in a Harris poll conducted in 1980, younger people reported being more upset by not having enough money than older adults (Harris and Associates, 1981).

One reason why retirees may not feel as financially strapped as they should is that they pay a smaller portion of the income they do have in taxes. Older people also tend to have more assets and fewer expenses. One out of four people over age 65 owns a home "free and clear" (U.S. Senate Special Committee on Aging, 1991a). Not only are the furniture and the dishes there, but also the tremendous expense of raising children is gone.

Psychological factors may partly account for the lack of pain. Emotionally retirement is unlike any other economic reversal. The jolt at being unexpectedly forced to belt tighten is not there. People *expect* to live on a more limited budget after they retire. The pinch may hurt less because of another reason. Unlike being fired, retiring does not carry the connotations of having personally failed. As I implied in Features 13-1 and 13-2, when we have the feeling that everyone but us is succeeding, we feel especially resentful and deprived.

THE EMOTIONAL IMPACT.   The same encouraging message relates to retirement's physical and psychological effects. Contrary to our myths, people do not die after they retire; they do not become severely depressed. On average, retirement has no effect on health and morale! The study of Boston area men discussed at several points earlier has an even stronger message. When the researchers compared men who had retired during the past year with a group who continued to work, the retirees reported fewer hassles than those still on the job (Bosse, Aldwin, Levenson, and Workman-Daniels, 1991). Another, more recent investigation confirmed these results: Retirees felt less stress and reported taking better care of their health than a comparable non-retired group (Midanik, Soghikian, Ransom, and Tekawa, 1995).

This is not to say that retiring has no ups and downs. Retirement researcher Robert Atchley (1976) believes that people go through stages in adjusting to this transition. First, there is a honeymoon period when everything is rosy. A man luxuriates in freedom, goes fishing, travels, and packs in activities. A woman makes lunch dates and exercises for hours. Then a letdown sets in. Something is missing. One person may be doing too much and ends up exhausted. Another feels at loose ends without something productive

Figure 13-7

Percentage of Different Age Groups Living Under the Poverty Line, 1992

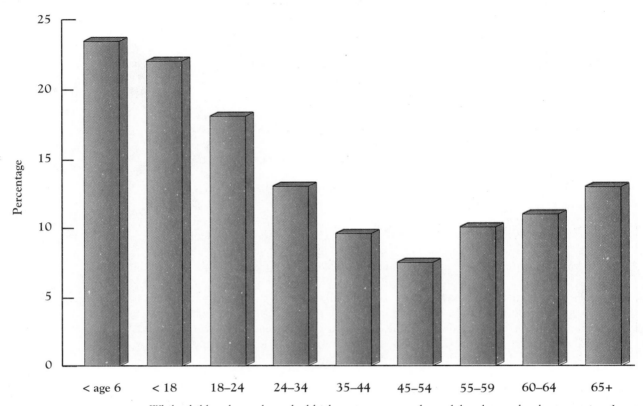

While children have always had higher poverty rates than adults, the gap has been growing. In 1992, young children were almost three times as likely to live in poverty as middle-aged people.

Source: U.S. Bureau of the Census, 1994, *Statistical Abstract of the United States 1994,* Washington, DC: U.S. Government Printing Office.

to do. At this point, the person must re-evaluate: "How do I really want the rest of my life to go?" Finally, retirees find their niche and settle down to a predictable routine.

Interestingly the study of the Boston men tends to support these phases. David Ekerdt, Raymond Bosse, and Sue Levkoff (1985) compared the happiness, activity levels, and optimism of retirees at six-month intervals during their first three years. Compared to the men retired under 6 months, those who had left work 12 to 18 months previously did seem in a slump. They had poorer morale and less optimism. The researchers also found that people emerge from this low. While the optimism of the first months was never totally recaptured, among men approaching the two-year mark morale was higher again.

WHAT DO RETIREES DO?   Until now, I have been discussing retirement as if it were all or nothing, with people either leaving work or remaining full-time on the job. Many retirees want something in between, for instance, to reduce their hours or work at another job part-time (U.S. Senate Special Committee on Aging, 1991a). Some retire to start a new full-time career.

Despite age discrimination, a surprising number of people do get postretirement work. In one national poll, almost half of all private-sector firms said that they hired retirees (Hirshorn and Hoyer, 1994). In another survey, one-fourth of all people who retired from a career job went on to other work (Quinn and Burkhauser, 1990).

As I mentioned in Chapter 6, some retirees go back to school, either participating in programs for "senior learners" or "retired professionals" or returning to get a college or graduate degree. Others find fulfillment in performing community service, or traveling, or engaging in a much loved hobby full-time. These are just a few options to find a sense of meaning in this third stage of life.

APPLICATIONS AND INTERVENTIONS

By now, you may be wondering about an imbalance. With the exception of age discrimination, our retirement section has an upbeat message, while the message about work is more somber. Elderly Americans have done well. Working-age adults, especially if they are single women or minorities, face a more rocky time. This is why, instead of examining programs relating to career development, I end this chapter by exploring **intergenerational equity,** balancing the needs of the old and the young. Let's first hear what economist Peter Peterson (1993) has to say about this controversial topic:

intergenerational equity
Issue of whether government entitlement programs are unfairly benefiting the elderly compared to children.

Proposition 1: Older people have become an overbenefited, favored class.

Peterson argues that today the average retiree can expect to receive Social Security benefits several times in excess of what he or she put in. The elderly receive paid-for medical care (in addition to reduced rates on airlines, at hotels, and at movies and a variety of other perks). These entitlements are not **means-tested,** or dependent on income. They arrive whether a person is a millionaire or not. How fair, Peterson asks, are these benefits when we consider how little help the government provides to the working poor? Today millions of working adults do not have health insurance. Child poverty in the United States is at an all-time high. This cohort of elderly has enjoyed a rising standard of living that their children and grandchildren will never see. Should we continue to subsidize older people, while doing so little to help young people who work, but cannot earn a living wage?

means-tested
Allotted on the basis of need, that is when government entitlements are only provided to people under a certain income level.

Proposition 2: By keeping retirement at its current level, there will be no retirement in future years.

The Social Security and health care benefits enjoyed by retirees are financed by working adults. As the baby boomers retire, the **old-age dependency ratio,** or the ratio of working to retired people, will decline. According to Peterson's calculations, if we were to keep Medicare and Social Security benefits at their current levels one-half of the salary of the working population would go to fund these programs in 2040. How reasonable, Peterson asks, is preserving retirement in health for this cohort for decades at all costs when the price will be robbing young adults of any retirement years?

Peterson believes that in addition to means-testing elderly entitlements and generally redirecting support to the working young, we need to *immediately* increase the age for receiving Social Security and eliminate the Social Security earnings test for retirees who work. Forcefully encouraging people to retire later will not only reduce the

old-age dependency ratio
Ratio of working people to older people collecting Social Security and other benefits.

These contrasting images illustrate the obvious fact that elderly people cannot be stereotyped. The vigorous, married, young old couples play-ing tennis may fit Peterson's portrait of an overbenefited group; the woman scrounging for items in this garbage can brings home the fact that old-old women living alone are very likely to be poor.

burden on young-adult taxpayers, but also be good for society. There is a large, vigorous segment of the population that is not working. We need to capitalize on the wasted talents of retirees (Quinn and Burkhauser, 1990).

Other experts disagree with these dire forecasts. An influx of young-adult immi-grants may raise the dependency ratio, allowing future cohorts of elderly to enjoy their retirement years. Today's baby boomers are living longer healthier and entering retirement with more assets. They are not as likely to overburden the system as Peterson believes. Would we want to push hard to expand and encourage work opportunities for people over age 65 if the price were increasing the unemployment rate for young adults? Would we want to redefine Medicare and Social Security as charity, thereby robbing older recipients of their self-esteem?

Most important, advocates for the elderly vigorously dispute Peterson's portrait of people over 65. It is wrong to paint older people as a stingy, affluent class! The number of elderly near poor, people within striking distance of the poverty line, has barely budged over the past three decades. If we include this group, older adults are much worse off than their counterparts under age 65 (U.S. Senate Special Committee on Aging, 1991a). Some parts of the older population are in very serious economic straits: women, minorities, and the old-old. Because of their job experiences as young and middle-aged adults, as we saw earlier, women and minorities are less likely to have pensions or savings to cushion their retirement years. The old-old may have spent these assets during their sixties and seventies, leaving little left at the end of life. In fact, we get a very different perspective on life-span poverty from breaking down the elderly by age. People over age 85 are poorer than children. Old-old women living alone are in worse economic shape than any other group (Burkhauser, 1994).

The real career issue facing adults in the United States in the twenty-first century, most economists agree, relates to the widening gap between rich and poor at *every age* (Reich, 1992). What can we do about the fact that there is more job uncertainty and especially fewer well-paying jobs for people with less skills?

KEY TERMS & CONCEPTS

real income
widening income disparity
working poor
personality/trait perspective on career
career counseling
self-efficacy perspective on career
life-span perspective on career
life rainbow
career maturity
traditional stable career
tournament model of advancement
boundaryless career
occupational segregation
role overload
affirmative action policies
Social Security
pensions
age discrimination
displaced workers
intergenerational equity
means-tested
old-age dependency ratio

RECOMMENDED READINGS

Career Choice and Paths

Howard, A., and Bray, D. W. (1988). *Managerial lives in transition: Advancing age and changing times*. New York: Guilford Press.
    These authors describe the AT&T studies.

"Special Issue: The Boundaryless Career" *Journal of Organizational Behavior, 15.* (1994, September/October).
    The September/October issue of this journal is devoted to articles exploring and describing the new boundaryless career.

Gender and Work

Walsh, W. B., and Osipow, S. H. (Eds.). (1994). *Career counseling for women*. Hillsdale, NJ: Erlbaum.

Chapters cover various aspects of career counseling as well as reviewing the literature on dual-career families, women in management, the sciences, and other topics.

Weiss, R. (1990). *Staying the course: The emotional and social lives of men who do well at work*. New York: Free Press.
Weiss's research focuses on successful men.

Poor Minorities

Jencks, C. J. (1992). *Rethinking social policy*. Cambridge, MA: Harvard University Press.
This book is required reading for anyone interested in minorities and poverty. Jencks tackles affirmative action, the safety net, welfare, and other topics.

Jencks, C. J., and Peterson, P. J. (1991). *The urban underclass*. Washington, DC: Brookings Institution.
This definitive reference book on the urban poor includes the study of employers' attitudes toward hiring poor minorities described in this chapter.

Unemployment

Voydanoff, P. and Majka, R. C. (Eds.). (1988). *Families and economic distress*. Newbury Park, CA: Sage.
This edited book covers research and theorizing about unemployment.

Morris, R., and Bass, S. (Eds.). (1988). *Retirement reconsidered*. New York: Springer.
Articles in this edited book relate to social policy, politics, older workers, and retirement.

Economics

Peterson, P. (1993). *Facing up: How to preserve the economy from crashing debt and restore the American Dream*. New York: Simon and Schuster.
This compelling, readable book is dedicated to the thesis that we are destroying our children's future by deficit spending, middle-class subsidies, and inflated benefits for the old.

Reich, R. (1992). *The work of nations*. New York: Knopf.
This is another interesting book on economics for the layperson, exploring who will do well and who will do poorly in the global economy of the twenty-first century.

Part V

CONCLUSIONS

Death and Dying

Chapter Outline

Kim, a guest speaker in my Adult Development class, is a nurse who has been HIV positive for six years. At her last checkup, Kim's T cell count was 260. When the count reaches 200, the Centers for Disease Control classify a person as having full-blown AIDS:

"I took care of people who had AIDS as charge nurse on the ward. I was working with this guy and I had a syringe with his blood. I went to recap the needle and accidentally shot the blood in my veins, the first time this has happened at a city hospital. At first I was negative; then, six months later, I tested positive for the disease. They took me off the floor. I felt like they took my life away. People didn't want to be around me because I was so depressed. I worked two more years on and off at other jobs and then was placed on disability for peripheral neuropathy, which is something that the virus causes. I've been on disability and been talking to groups now for three years. It's not just you this disease affects. It affects everybody you love. I come home one day. . . . It took me a year to do this. I come home one day and I know I've got to tell my children. At the time they were 16, 17, and 6. You could hear a pin drop. I'm their mother. I was always there. They don't have grandparents or an involved father. Now they are thinking: 'My mother has HIV. HIV equals AIDS. AIDS equals death.' That was five years ago. Today my children are 21, 22, and 12. I have one granddaughter. I have a lot to live for. Many times early on I was woken up at night by hearing my oldest daughter cry. I would crawl into bed with her. She would say, 'Mom, you are going to die.' When my youngest daughter was 6, she didn't understand. This year, they started studying about AIDS at school. Plus my count was starting to drop. My daughter starts crying in school. She can't function. She's worried. She knows that in my will my youngest sister will get her. She comes to me one day and says, 'Mommy, maybe I should get used to a new house and a new school.' I talked to my sister and she agreed. When my daughter left, I cried myself to sleep for weeks. I get tired of the whole thing; tired of not feeling good, of taking mega-doses of pills, of seeing my T cells go down each time I see the doctor. I get tired of wondering how it will feel to be so sick, the way I've seen others be sick. I wonder about who will be there for me when that happens. But right now I want to be there for my children. What happened was my responsibility. Blaming other people doesn't work. I tell that to teenagers all the time. I wish I had a second chance. I don't, and now all I can do is talk and hope people hear me. I can't take AZT anymore. I've picked out and paid for my plot. I used to be able to give presentations every few days. Now that I'm tired all the time, I'm not coping well. I wake up in the middle of the night crying. I don't regret my life. I'm not afraid of dying. I'm afraid of leaving my children. I want to see my grandchildren. But I'm looking forward to death. I feel like I could talk about this disease forever."

When we think of life's most devastating events, the one Kim is facing ranks first. Who can imagine a more difficult situation than coping for years with the knowledge of certain death? Death and dying are always on Kim's mind, as we might imagine they would be when a person is confronted with a terminal disease. How often do we think of death when we are healthy? What factors affect our fears of death? These questions relate to **death anxiety,** its frequency, its intensity, and its prevalence under different conditions of life.

death anxiety
Fear of death, both conscious and unconscious.

DEATH ANXIETY

To see how often healthy people think about death, researchers interrupted 4,420 people of various ages and asked them what they had been thinking about within the past five minutes (Cameron, Stewart, and Biber, 1973). Then they asked directly about death. Had the thought crossed the person's mind? The researchers approached their subjects at different times of day and in different settings, such as in school and at home, and asked them to rate their current mood. Would people think of death in certain situations or at different times?

Death thoughts did not vary by time and place. They did not even occur mainly when people were feeling sad, being *equally likely* to arise in conjunction with a variety of moods. There were gender and age differences, but only in the percentage of people reporting that the idea of death had fleetingly crossed their minds. Women had these momentary thoughts more often than men; adolescents, young adults, and the elderly more frequently than people of other ages. Finally, although only a tiny fraction (3 percent) of people reported dwelling on death, remarkable percentages (almost 20 percent of the men and 25 percent of the women) said that the idea crossed their minds at least once during this five-minute period.

In asking directly about death, perhaps the researchers prompted people to falsely "remember" having this thought. But what about the puzzling finding that thoughts of death were associated with positive as well as negative moods? Shouldn't we think about death mainly when we are upset or depressed? In fact, when other researchers asked adults to rate a wide range of concepts for pleasantness, death ranked dead last (Kogan and Wallach, 1961).

However, in addition to being the worst imaginable thought, death can be viewed, as in Erik Erikson's theory, as an event that is natural and acceptable after having lived a full life. It can even have uplifting connotations: Death is the moment that we authentically confront life stripped to its essentials. It is the time to meet God, to be reunited with loved ones that have gone before (Ross and Pollio, 1991).

While at first we might be skeptical, research on dreams highlights that fact that joyous feelings can *sometimes* be part and parcel of images of death. Deidre Barrett (1988–1989) catalogued college students' dreams relating to death. While dreams of *dying* ("a stranger is about to shoot me") were often nightmarish, dreams of *being dead* were usually inspirational:

> I begin to float up an arch-like rainbow . . . it was so beautiful. . . . The whole time the dream was going on, I felt better than I ever have in my whole life.

> The clock hands pointed to 12 and suddenly I had a dizzying rush. My mother and I turned into pure energy, pure light. We could go anywhere, free of our bodies. (p. 99)

Barrett's study and our interview suggest that, as with any other life event, we cannot take a simplistic approach to death. Feelings about death are multifaceted. They should be measured by multidimensional approaches. As we just saw, one distinction relates to what happens afterwards versus before (Buhler, 1995; Gesser, Wong, and Reker, 1987–1988). Some people may be terrorized by the thought of *being dead*; others of *dying*, of suffering the pain of terminal disease. Probing death anxiety may require using non-traditional measures, such as dreams, because feelings and attitudes revealed through these unconscious techniques might offer information that we might not get by simply asking: "How fearful are you of death?" The need for this more complex strategy becomes apparent as we explore some logical predictors of death anxiety.

Predicting Death Anxiety

LIFE-THREATENING ILLNESS.   When we think of what seems certain to heighten anxiety, what first comes to mind is serious disease. People with life-threatening illnesses should surely be more anxious about dying than healthy adults.

This obvious assumption has been surprisingly difficult to prove. While some studies do show that people with illnesses such as cancer and AIDS get higher scores on death anxiety scales, often their anxiety ratings are average or even very low (Dougherty, Templer, and Brown, 1986). One reason, as we will see later, is that people coping with terminal illness experience a variety of emotions from fear to peace to depression to hope. Death anxiety varies as a function of overall personality, whether a person is generally anxious or not (Hintze, Templer, Cappelletty, and Frederick, 1993). Or, perhaps measures in which people are directly asked about their feelings may not be adequate to measure the fear.

Bert Hayslip, Debra Luhr, and Michael Beyerlein (1991–1992) explored death anxiety among HIV-positive men using direct questions and a sentence completion test of fear. While the men did not rank high in anxiety on the measure that specifically questioned them about their fear, on the test exploring less-conscious anxiety their scores were elevated compared to a group of healthy men. As the researchers conclude, when faced with death, denial is an important coping mechanism, making self-reports an inadequate, not genuinely *valid* method of assessing fear (Earl, Martindale, and Cohn, 1991–1992).

AGE.   Another marker that logically should influence anxiety is age, although here the exact direction of the relationship is unclear. On one hand, being closer in the life span to death, older people might rank higher in anxiety than younger adults. Or perhaps, as Erikson suggests, in our later years we may view death through a calmer lens. We have tasted what life can offer, experienced the death of loved ones. At this time in life, fear should be especially low because death is natural, appropriate, right. In the words of thanatologist Therese Rando (1984):

> *The dying young adult is filled with rage and anger for the interruption of her life at the moment of its fulfillment. . . . There is frustration, rage, and a sense of unfairness and of being cheated. The patient holds onto life more tenaciously than at any other age. The losses are now especially acute, as the patient will never see the promise for self and significant others (especially children) fulfilled (p. 246).*

Most of us do feel that dying young is more tragic than dying after a full life (Callahan,1994; Jecker and Schneiderman, 1994). When researchers asked a group of students and older people to rank imaginary people for priority to get a life-preserving kidney transplant, this age gradient was revealed (Busschbach, Hessing, and Charro, 1993). Notice from Figure 14-1 that after age 10, when we might imagine the recipient could survive for a long time, the young were first in line. Moreover, the older people and the young adults agreed: Preserving life in a young person far outweighs preserving life in a person of 60, after a full life.

This norm is reflected in what people say about their own deaths. Often, as Erikson would predict, elderly people *report* having very little fear (Gesser, Wong, and Reker, 1987–1988; Kastenbaum and Costa, 1977). In a longitudinal study of older adults, when respondents were asked: "Are you afraid to die?" only 10 percent said yes. Another 55 percent were ambivalent, saying: "No, but I want to live as long as possible," or "No, but I don't want to be sick or dependent for a long time." The remaining group answered a resounding no (Jeffers and Verwoerdt, 1977).

On the other hand, comparing age groups may be misleading. This cohort of elderly grew up before the 1960s, when openly admitting feelings became culturally acceptable. When today's older people were young, disclosing fears was less socially sanctioned; people were supposed to keep "a stiff upper lip," especially in the face of events such as death. The biasing impact that this norm of self-disclosure might have was highlighted in a study comparing the responses of college students in the 1930s and in 1991 to an *identical* death anxiety scale (Lester and Becker, 1992–1993). The Depression-era

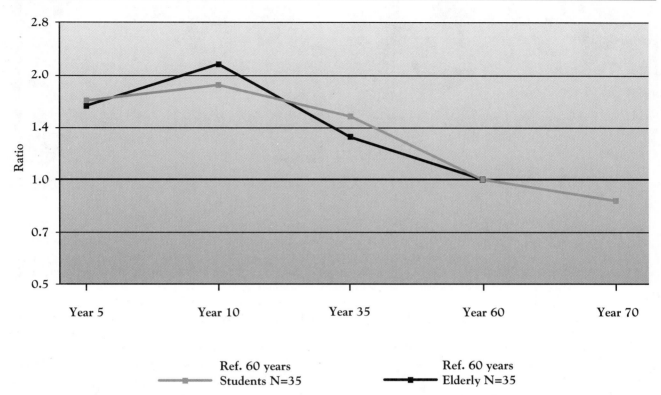

This study shows that there is considerable consensus and a clear age-gradient as to the value we put on having the chance for a healthy life. Both young adults and older people agree, the young should be given priority compared to the old.

Reprinted from *Social Science and Medicine*, 37, Busschbach, J. J., Hessing, D. J., and Charro, F. T. (1993). The utility of health at different stages of life: A quantitative approach. 153–158, 1993, with kind permission from Elsevier Science Ltd., The Boulevard, Langford Lane, Kidlington, OX 5, IGB, U.K.

students' scores were much lower, suggesting that one reason we may find age differences in anxiety today may be that this cohort of elderly was *always* less likely to admit being afraid of death.

Older people may not want to admit fear to themselves. Perhaps, as we saw earlier in the study of death anxiety in HIV-positive men, denial operates at the upper end of the life span, protecting people emotionally when they know their lives are measured in years or months. This implies that to really demonstrate that older people are less fearful we should look at both self-report scales and less-conscious measures of anxiety (Handal, Peal, Napoli, and Austrin, 1984–1985; Hayslip and Stewart-Bussey, 1986–1987).

In an interesting study, researchers gave three tests of death anxiety varying from self-report to progressively less conscious fear to adults of different ages (Feifel and Branscomb, 1973). When asked, most people denied being afraid of death. When instructed to fantasize, their imagery showed mainly ambivalence. On the final scale, a

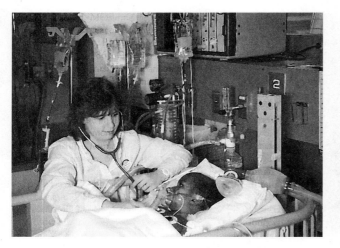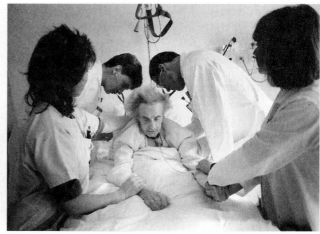

Given equal odds of recovery, most people would feel that ICU nurses should give priority to the patient in the first photo, the little boy, than to the elderly man at the end of his natural life.

word-association test, their answers showed frank fear. Furthermore, while on the tests of more-conscious anxiety, the elderly scored less fearful, at this deepest level older subjects ranked just as afraid as anyone else. So especially the elderly may be much more apprehensive about death than they admit.

In addition, even if having lived a full life reduces our fears about life drawing to a close, it should do little to touch our anxieties about the dying process itself. Thanatologist Therese Rando (1984) hypothesizes that, while the fear of *being dead* is indeed at a low ebb in old age, the fear of dying becomes more intense. The older person's anxiety is "Who will take care of me?" "Will I suffer greatly, and be a burden to those I love?" "Will I die alone?"

RELIGIOUS FAITH.   A third factor that seems tailor-made to influence anxiety is religious faith. Wouldn't religious people have low levels of fear, as isn't the whole idea of an afterlife to transform death from a hated end to a transition to a better state (see Feature 14-1)?

Many studies do show that people who are religious report fearing their own and their loved ones' deaths less (Powell and Thorson, 1991; Smith, Range, and Ulmer, 1991–1992). Religious people are more likely to describe death in positive terms, as a "portal," rather than a "wall" (Ross and Pollio, 1991; Westman and Brackney, 1990). The dramatic protection religion can provide against fear was revealed in a study of people in close proximity to death. Among a group of Israeli soldiers serving in Lebanon during a war, having had a life-threatening experience heightened death anxiety if a soldier was not religious; if the soldier had a strong religious faith, the same event had a minimal impact on fear (Florian and Mikulincer, 1993).

On the other hand, once again, not all studies reveal that people who are religious score lower on death anxiety scales! As my student Lita Buhler (1995) concluded in reviewing this research, to make sense of the contradictions again it is helpful to make the distinction between different components of fear. In Buhler's study, while older people who were religious did report less fear of what happens *after* death, they were no less afraid of the process of dying itself.

Our in-depth look at death anxiety once again illustrates the hurdles researchers face in measuring what appear to be the simplest facets of personality. It shows that even in this area of life it is important to adopt the multifaceted *contextual* point of view. The

Mr. Jones, a 100-year-old African-American man, attributes his long life to his religious faith. He grew up in the church and attended services several times a week. He knows he is going to heaven because he has lived a moral life. While gratified that the Lord has allowed him to reach this age, his real emotion is expectation. He is looking forward to the transition to come.

Religion serves many functions besides easing fear of death. It teaches ethics, offers a sense of community, and gives a moral grounding to life. The religious concept of an afterlife, however, is central to easing the terror of non-being at the core of the fear of death. How prevalent is this belief?

According to a 1978 poll, most Americans believe in life after death. Only about one in five is a non-believer. About 1 in 10 says that he or she does not know. In this survey, as we might expect, belief was highest in the heartland—the South and "West North Central Region" (Minnesota, the Dakotas, Kansas, and Nebraska)—and less prevalent in New England and the Middle Atlantic states. However, in contrast to our stereotypes, African Americans were less prone to be believers than whites (55 percent versus 71 percent). The elderly were *less* likely to accept the idea than people 30 to 59 (Klenow and Bolin, 1989-1990)!

This survey also reveals that we cannot automatically equate being religious with believing in the idea of an afterlife. Because their religion does not stress the concept, Jews are much less likely to believe in life after death than Protestants and Catholics. Interestingly even Protestants and Catholics who describe themselves as very religious do not always accept this central tenet of their faith. In this survey, about 14 percent of self-described religious Protestants reported being non-believers; about one in five Catholics did. So religion means many things to people other than heaven or a path to the world to come. It is possible to be a committed churchgoer and still believe this life is all we have.

need to avoid global generalizations and prescriptions is even more crucial as we turn to the main topic of this chapter—dying.

DYING

At your university, most likely there is a course devoted to death and dying. You would not have been able to take this offering 30 years ago. As was true of that other taboo topic, sexuality, people used to avoid mentioning or studying death. It took the events of the late 1960s to bring dying out of the shadows (Kastenbaum and Costa, 1977). The revolution that emphasized openness and self-determination in so. many areas of life produced an explosion of interest in death.

During the 1970s, not only did death and dying become a hot topic at universities, but also changing the way we treat the terminally ill became an activist cause. We can see the latest expression of the "death with dignity movement" in Dr. Jack Kervorkian and his suicide machine. Let's look at the classic research that produced this movement, where we have come from and what we know about death and dying today.

The Person

KUBLER-ROSS'S STAGES OF DEATH: DESCRIPTION AND CRITIQUE: A watershed in the movement to humanize dying was Elizabeth Kubler-Ross's **stages of death theory** that we progress through defined phases in coming to terms with

stages of death theory *Kubler-Ross's theory that the terminally ill go through five stages in coping with impending death.*

Even if you reject the idea of an afterlife or do not believe in God, as this photo shows, religion can offer a shared sense of community and human connectedness rarely provided in any other area of life.

being terminally ill. While working as a psychiatrist in a general hospital in the 1960s, Kubler-Ross became convinced that the medical staff was neglecting the emotional needs of the terminal patients. As part of a seminar for medical students, she got permission to interview dying patients. While the staff was resistant, the interviewees had a different response. Many were relieved to talk openly. To everyone's surprise, many knew their prognosis, even though an effort had been made to conceal the facts. Kubler-Ross published her discovery that open communication was important to the dying in *On Death and Dying*, a slim best-seller that offered a powerful indictment of terminal care.

Kubler-Ross (1969) believes that people progress through five stages in coming to terms with impending death: *denial, anger, bargaining, depression*, and *acceptance*.

When the person first hears the diagnosis, the response is "There must be a mistake." *Denial* is accompanied by the quest for contradictory evidence, the visit to specialist after specialist searching for a different diagnosis, a new, more positive set of tests. When these efforts fail, denial gives way to *anger*.

In this stage, the person lashes out, bemoaning fate, railing at loved ones. Mr. Jones castigates his doctors as uncaring and insensitive. He gets furious at his father, who is still alive. The idea that "I am dying" is so unfair. Eventually this emotion yields to a more calculating one—*bargaining*.

In this stage, the person pleads for more time, promising to be "good" if death can be put off a bit, striking a deal with God. Kubler-Ross uses this example of a woman who begged God to let her live long enough to attend the marriage of her oldest son:

> *The day preceding the wedding she left the hospital as an elegant lady. Nobody would have believed her real condition. She . . . looked radiant. I wondered what her reaction would be when the time was up for which she had bargained. . . . I will never forget the moment she returned to the hospital. She looked tired and somewhat exhausted and before I could say hello—said, "Now don't forget I have another son".* (p. 83).

When this reaction abates, it is replaced by the fourth stage, *depression*. Then, usually immediately preceding death, this response gives way to *acceptance*. By this time, the person, quite weak, is not upset, angry, or depressed. Mr. Jones calmly awaits death. He looks forward to the end.

Kubler-Ross never envisioned these stages as a straitjacket, a blueprint for the "correct way" to die. Unfortunately, her theory was sometimes uncritically used in this way. Overzealous counselors might label people abnormal if their responses did not fit into the five-stage sequence. Attempts were even made to hurry terminally ill people from stage to stage! By now, we should know that the idea that people react in a rigidly patterned way to *any* life stress is wrong. In this case, it also may be dangerous because it justifies distancing ourselves and negating an ill person's feelings. Rather than understanding that depression in a person facing death is appropriate, seeing it as "a phase" encourages us to view this emotion through a clinical lens, as somehow not real. Legitimate complaints about doctors, family, or friends can be discounted, passed off as "predictable" signs of the anger stage. So most experts view this effort to chart the feelings of the dying with mixed emotions. While it focused attention on a neglected topic, it also encouraged its own rigid, judgmental approach to death (Corr, 1993).

Terminally ill people *do* get angry, deny their illness, or grow depressed. However, these emotions do not fall into distinct *stages*. Steven Antonoff and Bernard Spilka (1984–1985) videotaped terminal patients at random points during the early, middle, and late phases of their disease. Based on Kubler-Ross's thinking, the researchers predicted that facial expressions should show mainly anger, then sadness, and then acceptance as the disease advanced. This was not the case. Expressions of sadness increased in a linear way as death approached. Anger and acceptance (measured by contented expressions) showed no pattern. People were just as likely to look angry in their final days as early on, equally as apt to look contented (accepting) right after their diagnosis as in their final days or weeks.

Another comparison of people who told a loved one that they knew they were dying also showed few differences between those nearer versus those more distant from death. People within days of dying gave no signs of being more "accepting." *Everyone* in this study ranked low on calmness and contentment (Baugher, Burger, Smith, and Wallston, 1989–1990).

In psychologist Edwin Shneidman's words (1976), "a complicated clustering of intellectual and affective states, some fleeting, lasting for a moment, or a day" characterizes the emotional life of people coping with this stress. Furthermore, contrary to what Kubler-Ross implies, even when people know their illness is terminal, the idea that "I am dying" may not penetrate in an all-or-none way. People cycle between awareness and denial. Denial and awareness can be present simultaneously.

Psychiatrist Avery Weisman (1976) uses the phrase **middle knowledge** to illustrate this suspension between knowing and not knowing, a psychological state that he has frequently observed in working with the terminally ill. Weisman believes that middle knowledge tends to manifest itself at transition points, such as when a relapse occurs and the emotional climate shifts. Loved ones turn less optimistic. The doctor averts his eyes when questions about recovery arise:

> *Middle knowledge is marked by unpredictable shifts in the margin between what is observed and inferred. Patients seem to know and want to know, yet they often talk as if they did not know and did not want to be reminded of what they have been told. Many patients rebuke their doctors for not having warned them about complications in treatment or the course of an illness even though the doctors may have been scrupulous about keeping them informed. These instances of seeming denial are usually examples of middle knowledge. (1976, p. 459)*

Any reader acquainted with a person coping with life-threatening illness may have noted that another central emotion until almost the last days of life can be hope. As Daniel Klenow (1991–1992) points out, the hope observed in dying people can have various

middle knowledge
State of being aware on some level, yet not fully realizing, that one is terminally ill.

sources. If an individual is religious, he may believe in divine intervention: "God will provide a miraculous cure." Others may put faith in medical science: "Even though I have AIDS, I may be cured by that new drug now in experimental trials." Someone may pin her hopes on meditation, alternative therapies, or exercise. As Kubler-Ross suggests, another source of hope is medical fallibility: "True, I have that diagnosis, but I know of cases where a person was told she had 6 months and has been living for 10 years."

A fascinating study comparing the dreams of cancer patients and those of healthy adults shows that, even on a less conscious level, people wrestle with ambivalence and hope (Coolidge and Fish, 1983–1984). As we might expect, the dreams of the ill people contained more death imagery than those of the healthy older adults. However, only one person dreamt directly about his or her own death. The ill person would dream that someone else was dead or dying, sometimes trying to search for that person's identity.

From a 27-year-old woman one year before she died:

> I went to an outside all night movie and I was standing in the middle of the street when this car pulled up and dumped out a young pregnant dead woman. . . . I ran over when it was over and I was looking at me on the floor but the girl really didn't look like me (p. 3).

The researchers believe that this type of dream shows both anxiety and uncertainty. The dreamer's own death, while the central concern, is too horrifying to be dreamed about directly. The person is grappling with this crucial question: "Am I really going to die?" Interestingly, as was true in this dream, compared to the control group, the ill people dreamed not only about death more often, but also about its opposite. They dreamed about pregnancy, birth, or babies, as if fashioning these themes to compensate for the terror of their waking hours.

From a woman in her forties one month from death:

> I saw a woman who was very happy. The dream took place in a department store. The woman had a lovely dress and shoes. She was carrying a baby in her arms. She loved the baby very much. When I woke up, I felt very happy and safe. As I was writing down the dream this fear started all over again (p. 6).

COPING AND LONGEVITY.   This is not to say that making any distinctions is unwarranted. People cope in characteristic ways with life-threatening disease. Some, such as Kim in our interview, try to give their illness meaning by helping others or to maximize the time that they have left by becoming closer to loved ones. Others become incapacitated by depression or immobilized by anxiety (Hinton, 1975). Can the way a person copes influence the actual *length* of his remaining time?

In following cancer patients, Avery Weisman and William Worden (1975) discovered that people who lived longer than expected on the basis of the severity of their illness had distinctive traits: They maintained responsive relationships with others, especially in the final phase of their illness. They were more assertive, showing more "fighting spirit" than those who died earlier on. In another study, compared to a group of survivors, people who died early had similar coping styles, expressing little anger, but much self-criticism, guilt, depression, and fear of bodily harm. The non-survivors were less involved in reciprocal social relationships, too (Viney and Westbrook, 1986–1987).

On the other hand, as we might imagine from our review of emotions and health in Chapter 3, other studies show *no* relationship between the course of a fatal illness and any coping style or personality trait (Schultz and Schlarb, 1987–1988). Even if adopting a fighting spirit or having close relationships were correlated with survival, we cannot conclude that this way of responding is *causally* involved in living a longer time. An equally likely possibility is that people with a fighting spirit are healthier, less temporally close to dying to begin with. (Notice from our interview, for instance, that, as Kim has become more debilitated, she is withdrawing from her lecture commitments and has become more depressed.) Or being assertive may promote survival in an *indirect* way. People who "fight" or have involved family and friends tend to get more life-prolonging medical care.

WHAT IS A "GOOD" DEATH? Even if the way we cope has no impact on the length of our life, we do want, in Weisman's words, an **appropriate death,** one as meaningful and free from anxiety as possible. The need to foster an appropriate death becomes especially compelling when we realize that most people, like Kim, who undergo their "final passage" are reasonably certain for some period, whether a week or months, of their fate (Schultz and Schlarbe, 1987–1988). What do we mean by an appropriate death?

appropriate death
When the dying process is as optimal or "correct" psychologically as possible.

Charles Corr (1991–1992) spells out one interpretation in his **task-based approach to terminal care.** Unlike the tasks of bereavement described in Chapter 12 or Kubler-Ross's stages, Corr's four tasks concern what we hope for when we are terminally ill:

task-based approach to terminal care
Corr's criteria for an appropriate death.

1. We want to minimize physical distress, to be as free as possible from debilitating pain.
2. We want to maximize our psychological security, to reduce fear and anxiety and feel in control of how we die.
3. We want to enhance meaningful social relationships, to be as close as possible to the people we care about most.
4. We want to foster spirituality and have the sense that there was integrity and purpose to our lives.

In reaching these goals, the primary care-givers of the dying, health care professionals, can play a pivotal role.

Health Care Providers

How do doctors and nurses treat dying patients? How do they feel about dying and death? These questions have been examined through questionnaires as well as by observing how hospital staff members act with the terminally ill.

QUESTIONNAIRE STUDIES. Do doctors withdraw from their dying patients once they know that their interventions will not stave off death, acting insensitively and so promoting an inappropriate death? An early survey supports the prejudice that they may. When 73 doctors were asked to fill out a questionnaire about how they treated dying patients, only 13 complied. Most refused when the nature of the topic was revealed (Caldwell and Mishara, 1972). Another study suggests the opposite: Doctors are caring, committed, and emotionally involved (Rea, Greenspoon, and Spilka, 1975). Of the 174 physicians solicited for this study, only 11 refused. Most were deeply affected by the topic being addressed. Many elaborated on their answers to a long questionnaire by extensive remarks. The researchers were touched by the deep humanity and concern for the terminally ill that shone through, empathy illustrated by the comments of the pathologist who wrote that he "often felt like crying after a day of doing diagnostic sections in connection with surgery. . . . 'It upsets me to think of the devastating effect my diagnosis will have on patients and families' " (p. 300).

A closer look at these incompatible studies shows a common theme. Doctors are deeply affected by the plight of the fatally ill. Avoidance and its opposite are two ways of handling the intense feelings that this topic evokes. However, the *way* these feelings are expressed does make a difference, as nurses and doctors who are comfortable with their feelings should provide more sensitive, humane terminal care. What affects a health care provider's feelings of comfort with death?

When researchers explored death anxiety among internists, surgeons, and psychiatrists varying in age and years in practice, they found that, irrespective of specialty, doctors just starting out were most terrorized by death (Kane and Hogan, 1985–1986). A study comparing residents and nurses also showed that the older, more experienced nurses were likely to view death in positive terms, as peace or liberation. The young doctors more often saw it as a disaster, a terrible event (Brent, Speece, Gates, and Kaul, 1992–1993; Campbell, Abernathy, and Waterhouse, 1983).

One ingredient common to being older, having experience, even being in nursing, is that each suggests the person will have more *firsthand contact* with people whose death is imminent. This personal exposure to dying patients may be critical in reducing fears.

In examining nursing students' attitudes about terminally ill patients, researchers found that their subjects' feelings became less aversive as a function of their previous experiences with death. Interestingly personal and professional contact with the dying had a different fear-reducing impact. Professional experience with dying people eased anxiety, reducing a nurse's reluctance to touch or treat the terminally ill. Personal experiences with the deaths of loved ones enhanced the positive pull toward working with this group. Students rated caring for the dying as more rewarding when a person they were close to had died (Brockopp, King, and Hamilton, 1991).

This research offers us interesting insights into the emotions that health care providers bring to dying patients. However, to really know how the terminally ill are treated, we need to study actions, not attitudes or self-reports. Physicians' responses to surveys may not be a good gauge of the way they actually act when confronted with dying people. What really happens in hospitals when patients are not expected to live? This brings us to a second landmark study that helped foster the movement to humanize terminal care.

DIRECT OBSERVATIONS.   During the late 1960s, sociologists Bernard Glaser and Anselem Strauss (1968) spent several months unobtrusively watching the behavior of nurses, doctors, and aides who worked on different hospital wards in which dying patients were housed. Their lens for interpreting their observations was unique: Caring for the dying was a job, like any other. It was important to understand the way that job was organized.

The work of treating the dying was structured in a clear, though implicit, fashion: according to the course that the patient's illness was likely to take. Based on the person's diagnosis and physical state at admission, an expectation was set up about how that individual's pattern of dying was likely to proceed. This "dying schedule" governed how the hospital staff acted. Glaser and Strauss used an interesting phrase to refer to this schedule—the **dying trajectory.**

dying trajectory
Illness path that people follow on the way to death.

Glaser and Strauss pinpointed several dying trajectories. One frequently found in emergency rooms was "expected swift death." Someone would arrive whose death was imminent, perhaps from an accident or a heart attack, and who had no chance of surviving. "Expected lingering while dying" was another common trajectory, one typical of progressive, fatal chronic diseases, such as cancer. Or with an illness of this type the trajectory might be "entry–re-entry." The person would return home several times in between hospital stays. Or it might be "suspended sentence," discharge for an unknown length of time before readmission in the final crisis before death.

Trajectories could not always be predicted. "Expected swift death" could turn into "expected lingering while dying" or even "expected to recover" if the patient rallied.

"Expected to recover" might become "expected swift death" if the individual took a turn for the worse. These deviations impaired the functioning of the work. The plan became outmoded. Care had to abruptly change. The paradox was that if "off schedule" *living* might be transformed into a negative event:

> One patient who was expected to die within four hours had no money, but needed a special machine in order to last longer. A private hospital at which he had been a frequent paying patient for thirty years agreed to receive him as a charity patient. He did not die immediately but started to linger indefinitely, even to the point where there was some hope he might live. The money problem, however, created much concern among both family members and the hospital administrators. . . . . [T]he doctor continually had to reassure both parties that the patient (who lived for six weeks) would soon die; that is to try to change their expectations back to "certain to die on time." (pp. 11–12)

Another miscalculation had the same effect, one in which the patient vacillated between "certain to die on time" and "lingering." In this pattern, loved ones would sadly say good-by, only to find that the person began to improve. Family members, nurses, and doctors sometimes went through this cycle repeatedly. The chaplain might also be involved. Here, too, everyone breathed a sigh of relief when the end was really near. (This is not to imply that hospital workers were typically insensitively wishing for death. The opposite error, a patient expected to recover who then died, was even more upsetting.)

Miscalculated trajectories not only upset the staff, but also injured the patient. If someone was "vacillating" or "lingering too long," nurses and doctors might get annoyed. They could become less responsive, give more perfunctory care, and possibly hasten death. Another type of mistake also might speed up death: assigning the individual to a service unfit for his trajectory. Sometimes a patient needing constant care was put on a ward where only periodic checks were provided, and he died between observations.

To Glaser and Strauss, their observations suggested that the hospital's mode of approaching the terminally ill was flawed. The goal was efficient work, providing care with a minimum of steps. This focus, when it clashed with the reality that dying is inherently unpredictable, was tailor-made for producing staff frustration and poor patient care.

This indictment, published at about the same time as Kubler-Ross's book, brought home the fact that patients were not getting care compatible with having an appropriate death. More humane approaches to dying were required.

APPLICATIONS AND INTERVENTIONS

The first step in the movement to humanize terminal care was to uncouple dying from traditional medicine, with its emphasis on high-tech machines aimed at defying death. Just like birth, death is a natural process. When curative interventions are impossible, the focus should shift to providing a good death.

Hospice Care

This philosophy led to that well-known alternative to traditional hospital and nursing-home care called the **hospice.** Hospice care is for people for whom death is certain, but who may have as much as six months to live. The purpose of hospice care is different

hospice
Formal program offering palliative care tailored to the needs of the terminally ill and their families.

The Murfreesboro Hospice operates from a cozy little house across the street from our local hospital. Here are some excerpts from an interview with the hospice team (nurse, social worker, and volunteer coordinator):

"How do you get referrals, who chooses Hospice, and what do you do?" Usually we get referrals from physicians. People may have a wide support system in the community or they may be new to the area. Even when there are many people involved, there is almost always one primary care-giver, typically a spouse or adult child.

We see our role as empowering families, giving them the support to care for their loved ones at home. We go into the home as a team to make our initial assessment: What services does the family need? We provide families training in pain control, in making beds, in bathing. A critical component of our program is respite services. Volunteers come in for part of each day. They may take the children out for pizza, or give the primary care-giver time off, or bathe the person, or just stay there to listen.

Families will say initially, "I don't think I can stand to do this." They are anxious because it's a new experience they have never been through. At the beginning they call a lot. Then you watch them really gain confidence in themselves. We see them at the funeral, and they thank us for helping them give their loved one this experience. Sometimes the primary care-giver can't bear to keep the person at home to the end. We respect that, too. The whole thing about Hospice is choice. Some people want to talk about dying. Others just want you to visit, ask about their garden, or talk about current affairs. We take people to see the autumn leaves, to see Santa Claus. Our main focus is: "What are your priorities?" We try to pick up on that. We had a farmer whose goal was to go to his farm one last time and say good-by to his tractor. We got together egg crates and a big tank of oxygen, and carried him down to his farm. We have one volunteer who takes a client to the mall. We keep in close touch with the families for a year afterwards, providing them counseling or referring them to bereavement groups in the community. Some families keep in contact with notes for years. We run a camp each summer for children who have lost a parent [see Figure 14-2]. We have an unusually good support system among the staff. In addition to being with the families at 3 A.M., we call one another at all times of the night. Most us have been working here for years. We feel we have the most meaningful job in the world.

from that of traditional health care settings: to cure. It is to provide the best care. Hospice personnel are skilled in techniques to minimize physical discomfort and trained in providing a supportive psychological environment, one that assures patients and family members that they will not be abandoned in the face of approaching death (Cohen, 1979; Rossman, 1977).

Initially hospice care was delivered in an inpatient setting called a hospice. The current emphasis of the hospice movement is on providing services and support that allow people to die with dignity at home. As Feature 14-2 shows, a multidisciplinary hospice team goes into the person's home, offering care on a part-time, scheduled, or daily basis. The team members offer 24-hour help in a crisis, giving family care-givers the support that they need to allow their relative to spend his or her final days at home. Their commitment does not end after the person dies. An important component of hospice care is bereavement counseling.

As Corr spells out in his first task, pain control is fundamental to the hospice philosophy, reducing the physical suffering of the dying. The goal is to decrease pain while keeping the patient as alert and independent as possible. Hospice workers are

CAMP
FORGET-ME-NOT

Sponsored by
Hospice of Murfreesboro
a service of Middle Tennessee Medical Center

June 13, 14, and 15, 1995
10:00 a.m. - 2:00 p.m.

For children K - 6th grade, who have
experienced the death of a loved one.

Recreation - Lunch - Discussion

Deadline to register: May 22, 1995

There is no charge.
Transportation provided, if needed.
Camp will be held at Trinity Methodist Church
Murfreesboro, TN

Hospices around the country offer programs of this type to bereaved children.

skilled in using medications. They may employ psychological techniques to reduce pain, such as teaching the person to mentally shift focus from the discomfort, emphasizing pleasurable activities, and training families to avoid expressions of anxiety that intensify the pain:

> One woman, for example, was in great misery because she wanted to live to see a grandchild about to be born, but knew it was impossible. The controlling of her pain, however, made it possible for her to recover enough strength to knit a gift for the child she would never see, thus helping brighten her last days. Another hospice patient had been lying all of the time in a fetal position with a hot water bottle clutched to his chest, staring into space, moaning in his private hell which he said was compounded

by pain that was like fire . . . but when the hospice team showed him they could control his pain he became a different person, able to live rather than vegetate during his last days. (Rossman, 1977, p. 126)

Hospice care is not appropriate for everyone. To utilize this service, a person must agree to abandon curative treatments and be judged by a physician as within six months from death. Almost always, as Feature 14-2 shows, the individual has family members committed to the physically and emotionally draining task of day-to-day care-giving.

Statistics collected by the Centers for Disease Control offer a portrait of who does enroll. In 1993, of the 50,000 patients per day receiving services from the 1,000 hospice agencies in the United States, 71 percent had cancer. These patients tended to be elderly. In that year, more than 70 percent of people utilizing these services were over age 65. However, as Figure 14-3 shows, most hospice patients are young-old. One reason is that, in contrast to the very old, this group of elderly is "richer" in social supports. Hospice patients are typically cared for by a spouse (Bass, Garland, and Otto, 1985–1986). Compared to terminally ill hospitalized older patients, these patients have more people living in the home.

CAUTIONS ABOUT HOME DYING: As Feature 14-2 shows, hospice can offer tremendous solace to the dying person and loved ones, allowing families to offer one last demonstration of love. Without minimizing these benefits, so beautifully described by the hospice team, let's focus on some cautions about this still non-traditional choice.

Even with the backup provided by the hospice, it may be too anxiety provoking for some families to be thrust into being responsible for managing the terrifying crises of impending death (Arras and Dubler, 1994). While polls show that the vast majority of Americans do feel that dying at home is best, even from the ill person's perspective this may not be totally true.

Ironically the person may have less privacy at home than in a hospital. In a hospital, care for bodily functions is routinized and impersonal. At home, people are subject to the humiliation of family members caring for their physical needs. Patients may want to spare their loved ones the vision of themselves incontinent and naked; they may want time alone to cry out, to vent their anger, anguish, and pain. In a hospital, there is the chance to express these emotions in privacy. At home, visiting hours are continuous; patients are apt to feel constrained to act in a certain way.

Just as important, care by strangers can equal care that is free from guilt. Many people do not want to be a burden to their loved ones. Dying at home can strain the financial resources of families (Arno, Bonuck, and Padgug, 1994). It is always draining emotionally, too. At home, there is the risk of feeling like a burden, of feeling shame about being needy that adds to the pain of the illness itself. Recall from Chapter 12 that offering "too much" care can evoke uncomfortable emotions in care-providers too. Family members may feel put upon and then feel guilty. Relationships with the ill person may grow more strained and distant, rather than becoming more close. For these reasons, we should not automatically assume that everyone, even a person with the most supportive family, is better off dying at home.

Hospice programs serve only a small fraction of the terminally ill (Sachs, 1994). Many people do not have family members who can take on this job. Even when loved ones are intent on a home death, as we saw in Feature 14-2 anxiety or the objective demands of care-giving may be overwhelming and the person ends up being admitted to a hospital and/or nursing home in the terminal phase of life. So efforts have also focused on humanizing the primary setting where death still occurs, the hospital or nursing home.

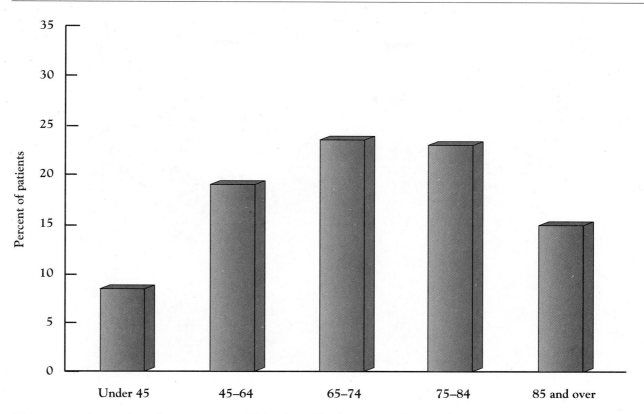

While most patients utilizing hospice care are elderly, about 30 percent are under age 65.

Source: National Center for Health Statistics, 1995, *Health, United States,1994,* Hyattsville, MD: Public Health Service.

Humanizing Hospital Care

CHANGING INSTITUTIONAL PRACTICES: Traditional health care settings have incorporated many hospice strategies. Doctors now are able to give as much medication as necessary to control pain in the terminal phase of life. Patients are sometimes removed from the intensive care unit when they are about to die. They are unhooked from machines and given unlimited time to be with family during their last hours. Hospital administrators routinely bend visiting rules in a person's final days. For instance, a wife may be allowed to sleep in her husband's hospital room and children can visit at any hour (Kastenbaum, 1976–1977; Rando, 1984). Some hospitals have palliative care units similar to inpatient hospices where patients can go during their last few weeks or days of life.

In order to see if these hospital-based units do help promote a more appropriate death, researchers explored whether terminally ill cancer patients in two of these units were better off emotionally than a comparison group of patients who spent their last days on the traditional ward. After conducting open-ended interviews, they coded patients'

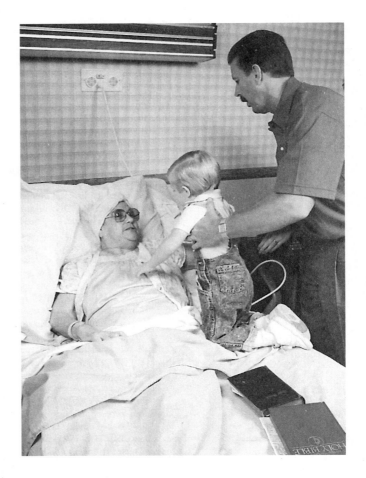

This woman in a hospice-like palliative care unit can have her final days eased by unlimited visits with the people she cares most about in life.

answers according to the amount of positive versus negative responses. Patients in the palliative care units expressed more positive emotions and less anger. They were less anxious about dying and death (Viney, Walker, Robertson, Lilley, and Ewan, 1994).

CHANGING PEOPLE.   Unfortunately, perfunctory care and anxious avoidance still do sometimes characterize traditional terminal care. As we might imagine from our previous discussion, one reason is that health care providers still are uncomfortable and anxious in the face of death. As Greg Sachs (1994), a physician who works with the terminally ill, points out, "It is as if the words dying and death have almost disappeared from the vocabulary of physicians entirely. . . . We have heard patients, even those expected to die in a matter of hours or days described as 'not doing well, having a poor prognosis, or having little chance of making it' " (p. 22). Sachs believes that this reluctance to confront the truth works to the detriment of the terminally ill. To truly humanize hospital care, we must change the emotions and attitudes that health care workers have about dying and death.

This is the goal of *death education courses*, which during the last few decades have become standard offerings at medical, social work, and nursing schools (Dickinson, Sumner, and Frederick, 1992). Death education courses can be didactic, focused on imparting information, or experiential, with students role-playing situations or getting firsthand experience in dealing with the terminally ill. Because doctors set the tone for all other care and, as one of our earlier studies suggests, may have the most trouble dealing emotionally with death, let's look now at one of the earliest experiential courses in death and dying offered at a medical school (Davis and Jessen, 1980–1981):

In addition to attending a regular seminar, students who enrolled in this course spent one night (from 5:30 P.M. to 8:00 A.M.) "on call" with the chaplain at a community hospital. The on-call chaplain visits the emergency room and the intensive care and coronary care units, consulting with the staff and comforting dying patients and their families. When they accompanied the chaplain on these rounds, students were encouraged to discuss the ethical and psychological issues that arose during this experiential introduction to death. They then wrote an essay about what they learned:

> It was perhaps most meaningful that we ended our night with a cesarean section and a live healthy baby! Once again, however, life was taken for granted and really not much attention was given to it. Procedure was high priority. . . . Doctors examine noses, anuses—in essence every projection or hole in the human body—and yet the very thing that holds these examined parts together—life—is not examined seemingly or fully. . . . It seemed ironic to end our "death" call with a birth—maybe we peeked into the meaning of death. (p. 163)

As this essay reveals, the immediate impact of this experience can be profound. Can a single course produce a lasting change in how students think? A one-shot glimpse of death from a personal perspective can be easily forgotten amid the avalanche of technical-care-oriented courses of medical school.

To determine whether psychologically oriented death education has value, researchers have explored whether having taken this course influences attitudes and ways of treating the terminally ill (Dickinson and Pearson 1980–1981). They have examined the impact that training has on reducing participants' own anxieties about death (Hayslip, Galt, and Pinder, 1993–1994). As we might imagine, in part because of the difficulty of changing (and measuring) death anxiety, death education does not reliably affect participants' own anxieties and fears about death. However, when the instruction is experientially focused, death education—whether in universities, in nursing programs, or in medical schools—does make for more sensitivity toward dying patients (Durlak and Riesenberg, 1991).

Current Trends: Controlling the Timing of Death

As we just saw, the original focus of the "death with dignity" movement was to permit a technology-free, natural death. Today this principle has been extended one step: Perhaps we should also give terminally ill people more freedom to control *when they die.* In this section, we look at two types of interventions in this second-wave movement to humanize terminal care. The first offers dying patients and their loved ones a mechanism to make their wishes known about artificial, life-prolonging treatment when they are mentally incapacitated. The second is that step embodied by Dr. Kervorkian and his suicide machine: People should be allowed to get help in ending their lives.

ADVANCE DIRECTIVES.   Any specific instruction in advance about preferences for life-sustaining treatment is called an **advance directive.** The most well known example is the **living will.** In this document—legal in most, but not all, states—a person instructs the doctor about his wishes to be kept alive by artificial means if he becomes permanently comatose (see Figure 14-4). Another document is the **do not resuscitate (DNR) order** frequently found in patients' charts, especially in nursing homes. Here typically the family or a conservator and the physician direct the hospital or nursing home staff that, should a medical crisis occur in a permanently mentally impaired or terminally ill person, CPR should not be performed to save the person's life. Another type of advance directive is called the **durable power of attorney.** In this document, a person designates a specific individual, usually a family member, to make end-of-life

advance directives
Specific instructions given in advance about preferences for life-sustaining treatment, should an individual be unable to make his or her wishes known.

living will
Document in which a person spells out his or her preferences with regard to life-sustaining treatment in the case of incapacity.

do not resuscitate (DNR) order
Document in an impaired person's hospital chart stipulating that CPR not be performed during a medical crisis.

durable power of attorney
Document in which an individual designates a specific person to make health care decisions in the event of incapacity.

We might imagine that during her session with an elderly client this lawyer could be describing the pluses and minuses of drawing up advance directives such as a durable power of attorney or living will.

decisions at such time as that individual is not capable of deciding on his own. While we tend to think of advance directives solely in terms of withholding treatment, these instructions also may stipulate that the person be *given* care.

Advance directives serve a laudable goal. Often end-of-life care decisions occur in a vacuum, as no one knows how the comatose or severely demented person feels about receiving procedures that only artificially prolong death. Under the *Patient Self Determination Act,* which became law in 1991, all health care institutions receiving Medicare and Medicaid funds are required to provide information to patients upon their entering the facility about their right to sign a directive of this type. However, these documents are used less frequently than we might expect. The reason is that advance directives have serious problems, too.

For one thing, only a small fraction of people, even those with life-threatening illnesses, takes the step of filling out a written directive. People are naturally reluctant to confront their own future incompetence and demise (Sachs, 1994). Only about 40 percent of Americans have a will! As implied earlier, physicians tend to be reluctant to initiate these discussions. They miss opportunities to discuss end of life care when the patient is in the first stages of what looks like a terminal disease (Council of Ethical and Judicial Affairs, American Medical Association, 1991). The idea of advance directives flies in the face of some cultural norms. In the traditional Chinese culture, for instance, any talk about death is taboo (Dubler, 1994).

Especially when they have not had good access to health care, people are reluctant to sign documents stipulating withholding treatment. As one patient put it, "I've been fighting to get what I need all my life. I'm not going to make it easy for them to hold back care." People who sign advance directives tend to be well educated and affluent (Sachs, 1994), those most at risk of getting "too much care." Moreover, advance directives were developed as a response to a health care system with strong incentives to overtreat. With the growth of cost-containing measures, such as managed care (see the interview with the psychiatrist in Feature 9-1 in Chapter 9), the climate is shifting away from using expensive technologies to preserve life. When patients perceive that the danger may be in *doing too little,* there is likely to be less interest in signing a document focused on what not to provide (Wetle, 1994; Danis, 1994).

Even when people sign this document, there is no guarantee that their preferences will be followed. Many people do not discuss their decision with their family or doctor (Dresser, 1994). The information in the document is vague. What a person says months or years earlier cannot be seen as utterly binding; it cannot cover all situations and circumstances for all time. In one study, patients at hospitals and nursing homes were asked about their preferences for care, and these documents were placed in their charts.

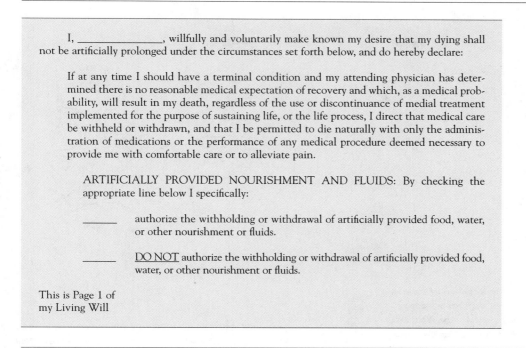

I, _____, willfully and voluntarily make known my desire that my dying shall not be artificially prolonged under the circumstances set forth below, and do hereby declare:

If at any time I should have a terminal condition and my attending physician has determined there is no reasonable medical expectation of recovery and which, as a medical probability, will result in my death, regardless of the use or discontinuance of medial treatment implemented for the purpose of sustaining life, or the life process, I direct that medical care be withheld or withdrawn, and that I be permitted to die naturally with only the administration of medications or the performance of any medical procedure deemed necessary to provide me with comfortable care or to alleviate pain.

ARTIFICIALLY PROVIDED NOURISHMENT AND FLUIDS: By checking the appropriate line below I specifically:

_____ authorize the withholding or withdrawal of artificially provided food, water, or other nourishment or fluids.

_____ DO NOT authorize the withholding or withdrawal of artificially provided food, water, or other nourishment or fluids.

This is Page 1 of my Living Will

Of the life-threatening episodes examined, one-fourth of the time care was deemed inconsistent. Interestingly a patient typically stipulated *more*-aggressive treatment than occurred. For instance, a nursing home resident with end-stage heart failure might request CPR and transfer to a hospital in the case of a cardiac arrest, but after repeated hospitalizations the family and doctor might decide to forgo another hospitalization, feeling that nothing more could be done (Danis, et al., 1991).

In fact, when mentally competent kidney dialysis patients were asked, almost two-thirds felt that their doctors should have leeway in overriding their own advance directives if their physicians saw the need (Sehgal et al., 1992). How binding can advance directives be? *How binding do people really want them to be?*

When surrogates (other people) make decisions for the impaired person, there are different concerns. First, there is the question of when exactly a person is mentally incompetent, an issue that often arises in nursing homes. Since only rarely is the person formally judged incompetent by the courts, responsibility for determining competence often rests with the doctor and other health care professionals. Making this determination is not always clear-cut. People may be lucid sometimes or lucid, but incapable of genuinely understanding the consequences of certain interventions. As Figure 14-5 shows, some elderly who might not be able to make informed choices about life-prolonging procedures, such as tube feeding, can be rendered "competent" by special techniques (Krynski, Tymchuk, and Ouslander, 1994). Because of these difficulties, nursing homes have become sensitive to the need to develop formal guidelines for determining competence. In one survey, in just a two-year period, from 1986 to 1988, the proportion of New York State nursing homes reporting that they had or were developing these guidelines shot up from a small minority to more than half (Miller and Cugliari, 1990).

Figure 14-5

Four Pages from an 11-Page Vignette Designed to Help Elderly People Make Advance Directive Decisions About Enteral Tube Feeding

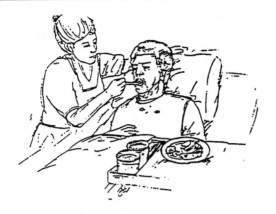

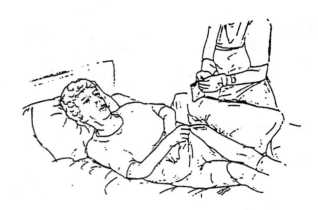

THE PROBLEM:

Let's think for a minute that you can no longer eat all the food your body needs. From now on, you will need someone to feed you—either by hand or through a feeding tube. You can't eat well because you have a serious disease. This disease is making you lose more and more of your mental and physical abilities. Right now you can't even walk anymore. You can still recognize people and talk to them.

If you don't get enough food, you will become very weak. You could get sores on your skin because you are weak. You could also get infections that might make you very sick or even kill you.

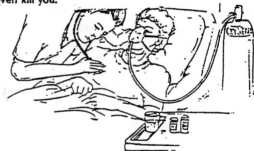

THE GOOD THINGS ABOUT THE FEEDING TUBE:

With a feeding tube, you could probably get all the food and fluids your body needs. You would probably live longer than if you didn't have the tube. This way you might not get sores on your skin or infections.

THE BAD THINGS ABOUT THE FEEDING TUBE:

Some bad things might happen as well. You might get more diarrhea (loose stool) by being fed through the tube. You could also get pneumonia from food getting into your lungs. You could die from pneumonia. You might get pneumonia even <u>without</u> the feeding tube, because of the disease that is making you unable to eat well.

Source: Krynski, M. D., Tymchuk, A. J., and Ouslander, J. G. (1994). How informed can consent be? New light on comprehension among elderly people making decisions about enteral tube feeding. *Gerontologist, 34,* 36–43. Copyright © 1994, The Gerontological Society of America.

Nancy Dubler, director of the Bio-ethics Department of Montefiore Medical Center in New York City, has been a pioneer in the emerging field of hospital-based medical ethics. Dubler argues that the role of the ethicist in a hospital is to "level the playing field." Families are intimidated by hospitals. They enter overwhelmed by "the maelstrom of personnel." If the staff is primarily people of color, whites may feel excluded. If the staff is white, or male, people of different ethnicities may be shut out. The ethicist acts as mediator and interpreter as much as an actual judge of end-of-life concerns. Here is a case of a man in congestive heart failure that offers a flavor of the issues that arise:

> *[An elderly man] . . . was admitted to the intensive care unit (ICU). . . . After a week during which [he] became progressively worse, the physician . . . . and the nursing staff met with the family and suggested that the patient soon be moved to a regular medical floor. They stated that the ICU was no longer an appropriate locus for care because the patient was dying, and they suggested that he should . . . be permitted to die. The family . . . . insisted that the patient remain in the ICU and be treated with all possible interventions. The opposition to the suggested care plan seemed to the staff to pose a bioethical dilemma and they called me to mediate. . . .*
>
> *As is my standard process, I first met with the staff to try to understand the patient's history . . . and prognosis. All of the staff were incensed. Mr. Malling's daughters were screaming at the nurses, had refused to talk to the physician and were generally disrupting the unit. A meeting with the family revealed that . . . [they] felt . . . intimidated by the staff and thought that their lack of education had led to their being ignored. They did not understand the accent of the cardiologist. They had overheard residents saying that medication was "wasted" on Mr. Malling. . . . None of these are bioethical issues. . . . The disagreement seemed to be about whether to transfer the patient. . . . But once the other issues had been uncovered and addressed, that bioethical issue disappeared. Two of the daughters were realistic about their father's chance of recovery. A solution emerged.*

Source: Dubler, N. (1994). Special Issue on Current Ethical Issues on Aging. *Generations*, 18, vol 1, p 7.

There is the problem of who speaks for the person once it is clear that she cannot speak for herself. There are few difficulties when a durable power of attorney has been given to a specific individual in advance. Often, however, there is no clear person in charge, and the doctor either turns to one or another family member or stumbles along making critical decisions about the impaired person's care. There is the temptation to overtreat when a doctor believes that he might be sued. There is the potential for abuse when family members withhold life-saving treatment that the person might want or insist on years of expensive, mainly taxpayer financed, futile care (Callahan, 1987). There is the potential for conflict when the family feels differently than the physician or when different family members feel different ways (Kapp, 1991). Suppose you believe that Mom's suffering should no longer be prolonged, while your brother insists that treatment continue at all costs.? Clearly these clashes can poison family relationships for years. Because of the potential for conflicts, as illustrated in Feature 14-3, most hospitals and nursing homes now have ethics committees to help mediate end-of-life concerns (Mezey, Ramsey, and Mitty, 1994).

DNR directives deserve special mention because these orders are so common in nursing homes. While the American Medical Association (AMA) has emphasized that doctors should discuss this decision with patients when they are competent, most often it is the doctor and the family who make the decision to put this order in the chart. For this reason, the AMA has spelled out guidelines for when these orders should apply:

Today at large hospitals, during clinical conferences such as this one, a medical ethicist is apt to be sitting around the table to offer his or her unique perspective on the proposed plan of care.

Physicians have the ethical obligation to honor the preferences of the patient and his surrogates with regard to resuscitation. They should not permit their own feelings about the person's quality of life to interfere. On the other hand, when the doctor believes that prolonging life is futile, he may decide to put his order in the patient's chart, provided the family knows and is given ample time to respond or change doctors if they wish. Finally, DNR orders only apply to the decision not to conduct CPR during a cardiac arrest, not to other life-prolonging techniques (Council of Ethical and Judicial Affairs, American Medical Association, 1991).

Physician-Assisted Suicide

physician-assisted suicide
When a physician helps a terminally ill person who desires to die commit suicide.

If you think that advance directives pose ethical problems, consider this newest thrust in the "death with dignity" movement. There is a huge leap from letting death proceed naturally when cure is impossible to allowing physicians to hurry that process along. Should *euthanasia* (mercy killing) or **physician-assisted suicide** be legal in the United States as it currently is in Holland? Should it be legal to assist patients who want to kill themselves not only when they are terminally ill, but also at any time?

As we just saw, physicians are required by law to honor a patient's wishes to refuse life-prolonging treatment, even though this refusal might hasten death. However, as of this writing, in most states it is against the law to actively intervene to help a person who has asked to die. As Bernard Gert, James Bernat, and Peter Mogielnicki (1994) point out, the distinction is between complying with a refusal and actively assisting in a request. The patient has the freedom to be allowed to die. The doctor is prohibited from performing the intervention that ends a person's life.

Killing of any type violates the religious principle that only God can give or take a life. This is why, though surveys show widespread public support for legalizing physician-assisted suicide (Morrison and Meier, 1994), people who are highly religious, those who are part of the right-to-life movement, and those who believe strongly in an afterlife are most loathe to accept this step in self-determination of death (Holden, 1993). Apart from religious considerations, there are other arguments against this practice, too.

By agreeing to physician-assisted suicide, critics fear that we may be opening the gates to involuntary euthanasia, allowing doctors to "pull the plug" on people who may not really want to die. Even when the person requests help ending his life, there are problems. He may not really be terminally ill. He may have been misdiagnosed or may have years of productive life left. As psychiatrist Herbert Hendlin (1994) points out, by helping a person die one is performing an irrevocable act based on what can be a temporary feeling. People who are suicidal are often depressed (see Chapter 9). If the depression were treated, the individual might feel very differently about ending his life.

In support of his views, Hendlin cites the case of a young man in his thirties diagnosed with leukemia and given a 25 percent chance of survival. Fearing both experiencing the side effects of the treatment and burdening his family, he begged for assistance in killing himself:

> Once the young man and I could talk about the possibility of his dying—what separation from his family and the destruction of his body meant to him—his desperation subsided. He accepted medical treatment and used the remaining months of his life to become closer to his wife and parents. Two days before he died, he talked about what he would have missed without the opportunity for a loving parting. (1994, p. A19)

There are also excellent arguments on the other side. People who are terminally ill are often in severe pain, suffering that sometimes cannot be fully controlled by medications. Should these patients be forced to unwillingly endure the pain and humiliation of dying when doctors have the tools to mercifully end life? Knowing the agony that terminal disease can cause, is it really humane to stand by and let nature gradually take its course (Morrison and Meier, 1994)? Is legalizing physician-assisted suicide a true advance toward humane self-determination or its opposite, the beginning of a "slippery slope" that might end in sanctioning killing anyone whose quality of life is impaired?

A RELATED ETHICAL ISSUE: AGE-BASED RATIONING OF CARE:

Perhaps you noticed that there is an age component to the "slippery slope" of deciding when not to treat. Many patients with DNR directives in their charts are elderly, at the end of their natural lives. As we saw earlier in this chapter, there is a norm that gives preference in performing heroic measures to preserve life to the young. Should society put limits on the extent to which it marshals the arsenal of life-perpetuating strategies for people who are disabled and at the end of their natural lives?

In a controversial book entitled *Setting Limits*, Daniel Callahan (1987), our nation's most prominent biomedical ethicist, argues that we should not treat the health needs of the disabled elderly as if they were the equal to those of younger adults. There is a time when "the never-to-be-finished fight against death" should stop. According to Callahan, waging total war for everyone might be more acceptable if everyone had equal access to health care. However, when Medicare puts no controls on payments for expensive life-prolonging strategies, we implicitly favor older people, while 35 million younger Americans have no health insurance at all.

Callahan (1994) spells out the following principles in what he calls a **life-cycle approach to medical care:**

1. *After a person has lived out a natural life span, medical care should no longer be oriented to resisting death.* While stressing that no precise age should be set for this determination, Callahan puts this marker at around the late seventies or eighties. In his view, this does not mean that life at this age has less value. It simply means that at a certain age death is inevitable and should not be vigorously defied.

2. *Provision of medical care for those who have lived out a normal life span will be limited to the relief of suffering.* At the end of life, the focus should shift from heroic strategies aimed at preserving life to methods for relieving pain.

3. *The existence of medical technologies capable of extending the lives of elderly who have lived out a natural life span creates no presumption whatever that the technologies must be used for that purpose.* Callahan believes that the proper goal of medicine is to stave off premature death. We should not become slaves to technologies developed to further this goal, blindly using each expensive technological advance on *every person* merely because it exists.

life-cycle approach to medical care
Callahan's controversial idea that heroic, costly life-sustaining treatments should not be performed on people at the end of their natural lives.

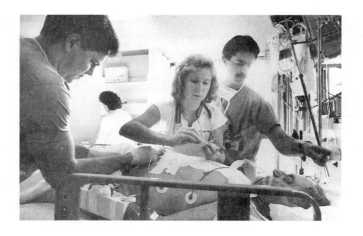

Scenes such as this in which astronomical human and monetary resources are being lavished on this comatose elderly man may have prompted Callahan to develop his life-cycle approach to medical care.

To some extent, doctors follow these prescriptions on an implicit basis today. A physician may decide that an 80-year-old is "too frail" to have a possibly life-saving operation that he would not hesitate to perform on a younger adult. A family and the doctor agree that an older nursing home resident should be given only comfort care. However, some gerontologists vigorously argue that *formally* adopting age-based rationing will put us on a scary, slippery slope. It is true that intervention to cure cancer in a 90-year-old is not only more dangerous, but also more futile because he will soon die of a heart attack (see Chapter 3). As we vividly saw in Chapter 7, life does seem much less worth living to the person suffering from a dementing disease. On the other hand, we need to protect that cognitively impaired person, not to presume that his life is worth nothing or much less (Dresser and Whitehouse, 1994). Once we deny treatment based on age or mental incapacity, we may open the door to refusing treatment based on gender, or race, or ethnic group. Won't taking this step lead to another and ultimately bring us back to the horrific genocidal practices of the societies described in Feature 1-1 on ageism in Chapter 1? As Nancy Jecker and Laurence Schneiderman (1994) argue, health-care decision making should be based on considerations of medical futility, not having lived a full life.

Perhaps you noticed that our discussion brings us full circle back to topics explored earlier in this book: the process of physical aging and disability, the manner in which the health care system treats people of different ages, the way to balance the rights of the young and old, the importance of having a sense of self-efficacy (or control) as we journey through adult life. In dying as adults in America, we see many issues related to living as adults in America, too.

Age-based rationing of health care is just one of several important social challenges that will be facing us in the twenty-first century. In the following pages, I conclude this extensive tour of the adult experience on a brief, subjective note, offering some comments about gaps and future directions for our field and expressing a few personal concerns about what lies ahead in our journey as American adults.

KEY TERMS & CONCEPTS

death anxiety
stages of death theory
middle knowledge

appropriate death
task-based approach to terminal care
dying trajectory
hospice
advance directives
living will
do not resuscitate (DNR) orders
durable power of attorney
physician-assisted suicide
life-cycle approach to medical care

RECOMMENDED READINGS

Dying Process
Glaser, B., and Strauss, A. L. (1968). *A time for dying*. Chicago: Aldine.
> *The study of dying trajectories is explained in this very interesting and well written book.*

Kubler-Ross, E. (1969). *On death and dying*. New York: Macmillan.
> *Kubler-Ross has written the most widely known book on death and dying.*

Ethical issues
Callahan, D. (1987). *Setting limits: Medical care in an aging society*. New York: Simon and Schuster.
> *Callahan spells out the argument for age-based rationing of care. We should "set rational limits" on the medical care that we provide to the infirm aged.*

Current ethical issues in aging. (1994, Winter). *Generations, 18*.
> *This issue of* Generations *is devoted to ethical issues relating to terminal care of the elderly.*

Advance directives (1994, November-December). *Hastings Center Report, 24*, 6.
> *A special supplement to this issue thoroughly discusses advance care planning and the problems with advance directives. The* Hastings Center Report, *which comes out bimonthly, is the best single source for information on ethical issues related to death and dying.*

Endnote

When the children in the Berkeley/Oakland Studies entered adulthood in the middle decades of the twentieth century, their futures were well mapped out. A woman was expected to be a homemaker; it was fairly unusual to go to college or have a career. A man could look forward to working at the same company until he retired. Dramatic advances in the standard of living were occurring at the same time that a revolution in health care was allowing most people for the first time to reach old age. Marriage for life was the only acceptable pattern. The United States was a more uniform, less diverse nation than today.

The adult experience will be different for the multicultural cohort coming of age in the United States in the new century. Young adults have the benefit of more freedom to choose how to live. However, they face the liabilities of living in a more uncertain time. We need new Berkeley/Oakland studies that explore what it is like to develop in our more unstructured age. How do men cope as they move in and out of families and from job to job? How do women negotiate becoming pregnant, giving birth, and raising children on their own? How do non-white and less advantaged Americans develop during adult life?

We know a good deal about what happens physically and cognitively as we grow old. However, much of what we know deals with age-related decline. To complement the mountain of studies on care-giving and coping with disability, we should pay more attention to the ways that we grow better with age. We need to understand why the epidemiologic studies reveal that emotional problems are less prevalent in old age. We need to explore whether the Grant and Mills College research showing that we grow more mature with age is more generally true. We need more efforts to flesh out and examine Erik Erikson's and Carl Jung's provocative ideas about adult life.

When the Berkeley/Oakland children entered adulthood, a vast "social support" network was steadily expanding. Now we are pulling back from the idea that government should be responsible for the poor and the old. How will this change in the outer context of life affect the new American family? How will society deal with the vast numbers of frail older people that we can expect in the next few decades as my cohort, the baby boomers, moves into later life?

These are just a few topics I find compelling in my tour of the research. Now that I have guided you through this exciting, evolving territory, what topics would you like to explore in more depth?

References

A

Abeles, R. P. (1992). Social stratification and aging: Contemporaneous and cumulative effects. In K. W. Schaie, D. G. Blazer, & J. S. House (Eds.), *Aging, health behaviors, and health outcomes* (pp. 33–37). Hillsdale, NJ: Erlbaum.

Abra, J. (1989). Changes in creativity with age: Data, explanations, and further predictions. *International Journal of Aging and Human Development, 28,* 105–126.

Abraham, J. D., & Hansson, R. O. (1995). Successful aging at work: An applied study of selection, organization, optimization, and compensation through impression management. *Journals of Gerontology, 50B,* P94–P103.

Abraham, L. (1995). *Mama might be better off dead.* Chicago: University of Chicago Press.

Abrams, D. B., & Niaura, R. S. (1987). Social learning theory. In H. T. Blane & K. E. Leonard (Eds.), *Psychological theories of drinking and alcoholism* (pp. 131–180). New York: Guilford Press.

Abramson, L. Y., Seligman, M. E., & Teasdale, J. D. (1978). Learned helplessness in humans: Critique and reformulation. *Journal of Abnormal Psychology, 87,* 49–74.

Acitelli, L. K., Douvan, E., & Veroff, J. (1993). Perceptions of conflict in the first year of marriage: How important are similarity and understanding? *Journal of Social and Personal Relationships, 10,* 5–19.

Acker, M., & Davis, M. H. (1992). Intimacy, passion, and commitment in adult romantic relationships: A test of the triangular theory of love. *Journal of Social and Personal Relationships, 9,* 21–50.

Adams, C., Labouvie-Vief, G., Hobart, C. J., & Dorosz, M. (1990). Adult age group differences in story recall style. *Journals of Gerontology, 45,* P17–P27.

Aizenberg, R., & Treas, J. (1985). The family in late life: Psychosocial and demographic considerations. In J. E. Birren & K. W. Schaie (Eds.), *Handbook of the psychology of aging* (2nd ed., pp. 169–189). New York: Van Nostrand Reinhold.

Akiskal, H. S. (1989). The classification of mental disorders. In H. I. Kaplan & B. J. Sadock (Eds.), *Comprehensive textbook of psychiatry* (5th ed., pp. 583–598). Baltimore: Williams & Wilkins.

Alba, R. D., & Golden, R. M. (1986). Patterns of ethnic marriage in the United States. *Social Forces, 65,* 202–223.

Albert, S. M., Litvin, S. J., Kleban, M. H., & Brody, E. M. (1991). Caregiving daughters' perceptions of their own and their mothers' personalities. *Gerontologist, 31,* 476–482.

Aldous, J. (1985). Parent-adult child relations as affected by the grandparent status. In V. L. Bengtson & J. F. Robertson (Eds.), *Grandparenthood* (pp. 117–132). Beverly Hills, CA: Sage.

Aldous, J. (1995). New views of grandparents in intergenerational context. *Journal of Family Issues, 16,* 104–122.

Alexander, M. J., & Higgins, E. T. (1993). Emotional trade-offs of becoming a parent: How social roles influence self-discrepancy effects. *Journal of Personality and Social Psychology, 65,* 1259–1269.

Allan, M., Brown, P., & Finlay, B. (1994). *Helping children by strengthening families: A look at family support programs.* Washington, DC: Children's Defense Fund.

Allgood, S. M., & Crane, D. R. (1991). Predicting marital therapy dropouts. *Journal of Marital and Family Therapy, 17,* 73–79.

Alonzo, A. A. (1993). Health behavior: Issues, contradictions, and dilemmas. *Social Science and Medicine, 37,* 1019–1034.

Ambrogli, D. M., & Lenard, F. (1988). The impact of nursing home admission agreements on resident autonomy. *Gerontologist, 28,* 82–89.

American Association of Retired Persons. (1984). *Data gram: Housing satisfaction in older Americans.* Washington, DC: Author.

American family decline, 1960–1990: A review and appraisal. (1993). *Journal of Marriage and the Family, 55,* 527–555.

American Psychiatric Association. (1980). *Diagnostic and statistical manual of mental disorders* (3rd ed.). Washington, DC: Author.

American Psychiatric Association. (1994). *Diagnostic and statistical manual of mental disorders* (4th ed.). Washington, DC: Author.

Andersen, R., & Newman, F. (1973). Societal and individual determinants of medical care utilization in the United States. *Milbank Memorial Fund Quarterly, 51,* 95.

Andersen, R. M., Mullner, R. M., & Cornelius, L. J. (1989). Black-white differences in health status: Methods or substance? In D. P. Willis (Ed.), *Health policies and black Americans* (pp. 72–99). New Brunswick, NJ: Transaction.

Aneshensel, C. S., Pearlin, L. I., Mullan, J. T., Zarit, S. H., & Whitlatch, C. J. (1995). *Profiles in caregiving: The unexpected career.* San Diego: Academic Press.

Antonoff, S. R., & Spilka, B. (1984–1985). Patterning of facial expressions among terminal care patients. *Omega: Journal of Death and Dying, 15,* 101–108.

Applebaum, R., & Phillip, P. (1990). Assuring the quality of in-home care: The "other" challenge for long-term care. *Gerontologist, 30,* 444–450.

Arbuckle, T. Y., Gold, D. P., Andres, D., Schwartzman, A., & Chaikelman, T. (1992). The role of psychosocial context, age, and intelligence in memory performance of older men. *Psychology and Aging, 7,* 25–36.

Arling, G., & McAuley, W. J. (1984). The family, public policy, and long term care. In W. H. Quinn & G. A. Hughston (Eds.), *Independent aging: Family and social systems perspectives* (pp. 133–148). Rockville, MD: Aspen.

Arno, P. S., Bonuck, K. A., & Padgug, R. (1994). The economic impact of high technology home care. *Hastings Center Report, 24,* S15–S19.

Arras, J. D., & Dubler, N. N. (1994). Bringing the hospital home: Ethical and social implications of high tech home care. *Hastings Center Report, 24,* S19–S28.

Arthur, M. B. (1994). The boundaryless career: A new perspective for organizational inquiry. *Journal of Organizational Behavior, 15,* 295–306.

Astin, H. S. (1984). The meaning of work in women's lives: A sociopsychological model of career choice and work behavior. *Counseling Psychologist, 12,* 117–126.

Atchley, R. C. (1977). *The social forces in later life* (2nd ed.). Belmont, CA: Wadsworth.

Atchley, R. C., & Miller, S. (1983). Types of elderly couples. In T. H. Brubaker (Ed.), *Family relationships in later life* (pp. 77–90). Beverly Hills, CA: Sage.

Atkinson, M. P., & Blackwelder, S. P. (1993). Fathering in the 20th century. *Journal of Marriage and the Family, 55,* 975–986.

Avis, N. E., Brambilla, D. J., Vass, K., & McKinlay, J. B. (1991). The effect of widowhood on health: A prospective analysis from the Massachusetts Women's Health Study. *Social Science and Medicine, 33,* 1063–1070.

Axinn, W. G., & Thornton, A. (1993). Mothers, children, and cohabitation: The intergenerational effects of attitudes and behavior. *American Sociological Review, 58,* 233–246.

B

Baddeley, A. D. (1992). Working memory: The interface between memory and cognition. *Journal of Cognitive Neuroscience, 4,* 281–288.

Baltes, M. M., Kuhl, K. P., & Sowarka, D. (1992). Testing for limits of cognitive reserve capacity: A promising strategy for early diagnosis of dementia? *Journals of Gerontology, 47B,* P165–P167.

Baltes, M. M., & Werner-Wahl, H. (1992). The behavior system of dependency in the elderly: Interaction with the social environment. In M. G. Ory, R. P. Abeles, & P. D. Lipman (Eds.), *Aging, health, and behavior* (pp. 83–108). Newbury Park, CA: Sage.

Baltes, P. B. (1987). Theoretical propositions of life-span development psychology: On the dynamics between growth and decline. *Developmental Psychology, 23,* 611–626.

Baltes, P. B. (1993). The aging mind: Potential and limits. *Gerontologist, 33,* 580–594.

Baltes, P. B., & Baltes, M. M. (1990). Psychological perspectives on successful aging: The model of selective optimization with compensation. In P. B. Baltes & M. M. Baltes (Eds.), *Successful aging: Perspectives from the behavioral sciences* (pp. 1–34). New York: Cambridge University Press.

Baltes, P. B., Reese, H. W., & Lipsett, L. P. (1980). Lifespan developmental psychology. *Annual Review of Psychology, 31,* 65–110.

Baltes, P. B., Reese, H. W., & Nesselroade, J. R. (1977). *Life-span developmental psychology: Introduction to research methods.* Monterey, CA: Brooks/Cole.

Baltes, P. B., Sowarka, D., & Kliegl, R. (1989). Cognitive training research on fluid intelligence in old age: What can older adults achieve by themselves? *Psychology and Aging, 4,* 217–221.

Baltes, P. B., & Staudinger, U. M. (1993). The search for a psychology of wisdom. *Current Directions in Psychological Science, 2,* 75–80.

Baltes, P. B., & Willis, S. L. (1977). Toward psychological theories of aging and development. In J. E. Birren & K. W. Schaie (Eds.), *Handbook of the psychology of aging* (pp. 128–154). New York: Van Nostrand Reinhold.

Bandura, A. (1977). Self-efficacy: Toward a unifying theory of behavioral change. *Psychological Review, 84,* 191–215.

Bandura, A. (1989). Human agency in social cognitive theory. *American Psychologist, 44,* 1175–1184.

Bandura, A. (1992). Exercise of personal agency through the self-efficacy mechanism. In R. Schwarzer (Ed.), *Self-efficacy: Thought control of action* (pp. 3–38). Washington, DC: Hemisphere.

Bane, M. J., & Jargowsky, P. A. (1988). The links between government policy and family structure: What matters and what doesn't. In A. J. Cherlin (Ed.), *The changing American family and public policy* (pp. 219–261). Washington, DC: Urban Institute Press.

Barlow, D. H. (1988). *Anxiety and its disorders: The nature and treatment of anxiety and panic.* New York: Guilford Press.

Barnat, H. S. (1990). Divorce stress and adjustment model: Locus of control and demographic predictors. *Journal of Divorce, 1,* 93–109.

Barnes, D. M. (1987). Defect of Alzheimer's is on chromosome 21. *Science, 235,* 846–847.

Barnes, G. M., Farrell, M. P., & Banerjee, S. (1994). Family influences on alcohol abuse and other problem behaviors among black and white adolescents in a general population sample. *Journal of Research on Adolescence, 4,* 183–201.

Barnett, R. C., & Baruch, G. K. (1988). Correlates of fathers' participation in family work. In P. Bronstein & C. P. Cowan (Eds.), *Fatherhood today: Men's changing role in the family* (pp. 66–78). New York: John Wiley & Sons.

Barnett, R. C., Brennan, R. T., Raudenbush, S. W., & Marshall, N. L. (1994). Gender and the relationship between marital-role quality and psychological distress: A study of women and men in dual-earner couples. *Psychology of Women Quarterly, 18,* 105–127.

Barnett, R. C., Marshall, N. L., Raudenbush, S. W., & Brennan, R. T. (1993). Gender and the relationship between job experiences and psychological distress: A study of dual-earner couples. *Journal of Personality and Social Psychology, 64,* 794–806.

Barnett, R. C., Marshall, N. L., & Singer, J. P. (1992). Job experiences over time, multiple roles, and women's mental health: A longitudinal study. *Journal of Personality and Social Psychology, 62,* 634–644.

Barrett, D. (1988–1989). Dreams of death. *Omega: Journal of Death and Dying, 19,* 95–101.

Bartoshuk, L. M. (1989). Taste: Robust across the age span? In C. Murphy & D. M. Hegted (Eds.), *Nutrition and chemical senses in aging: Recent advances and current research needs* (pp. 65–75). New York: New York Academy of Sciences.

Bass, D. M., Garland, T. N., & Otto, M. E. (1985–1986). Characteristics of hospice patients and their caregivers. *Omega: Journal of Death and Dying, 16,* 51–68.

Baugher, R. J., Burger, C., Smith, R., & Wallston, K. A. (1989–1990). A comparison of terminally ill persons at various time periods to death. *Omega: Journal of Death and Dying, 20,* 103–115.

Baxter, L. A., & Widenmann, S. (1993). Revealing and not revealing the status of romantic relationship to social networks. *Journal of Social and Personal Relationships, 10,* 321–337.

Beck, A. T. (1973). *The diagnosis and management of depression.* Philadelphia: University of Pennsylvania Press.

Belsky, J., Lang, M., & Rovine, M. (1985). Stability and change in marriage across the transition to parenthood: A second study. *Journal of Marriage and the Family, 47,* 855–865.

Belsky, J., & Pensky, E. (1988). Marital change across the transition to parenthood. *Marriage and Family Review, 12,* 133–156.

Belsky, J., & Rovine, M. (1990). Patterns of marital change across the transition to parenthood: Pregnancy to three years post-partum. *Journal of Marriage and the Family, 52,* 5–29.

Belsky, J., Spanier, G. B., & Rovine, M. (1983). Stability and change in marriage across the transition to parenthood. *Journal of Marriage and the Family, 45,* 567–577.

Belsky, J., & Volling, B. L. (1987). Mothering, fathering, and marital interaction in the family triad during infancy: Exploring family systems processes. In P. W. Berman

& F. A. Pederson (Eds.), *Men's transitions to parenthood: Longitudinal studies of early family experience* (pp. 37–63). Hillsdale, NJ: Erlbaum.

Belsky, J. K. (1990). *The psychology of aging: Theory, research and interventions* (2nd ed.). Monterey, CA: Brooks/Cole.

Bemporad, J. R. (1990). Psychoanalytic therapy of depression. In B. B. Wolman & G. Stricker (Eds.), *Depressive disorders: Facts, theories, and treatment methods* (pp. 296–309). New York: John Wiley & Sons.

Bengtson, V. L. (1989). The problem of generations: Age group contrasts, continuities and social change. In V. L. Bengtson & K. W. Schaie (Eds.), *The course of later life: Research and reflections* (pp. 25–54). New York: Springer.

Berg, C. A., & Sternberg, R. J. (1992). Adults' conceptions of intelligence across the adult life span. *Psychology and Aging, 7,* 221–231.

Berg, S. (1996). Aging, behavior, and terminal decline. In J. E. Birren & K. W. Schaie (Eds.), *Handbook of the psychology of aging* (4th ed., pp. 323–337). San Diego: Academic Press.

Bergeman, C. S., Plomin, R., Pedersen, N. L., & McClearn, G. E. (1991). Genetic mediation of the relationship between social support and psychological well-being. *Psychology and Aging, 6,* 640–646.

Bergeman, C. S., Plomin, R., Pedersen, N. L., McClearn, G. E., & Nesselroade, J. R. (1990). Genetic and environmental influences on social support: The Swedish Adoption/Twin Study of Aging. *Journals of Gerontology, 45,* P101–P106.

Berkman, L., & Breslow, L. (1983). *Health and ways of living: The Alameda County Study.* New York: Oxford University Press.

Berman, P. W., & Pederson, F. A. (Eds.). (1987). *Men's transitions to parenthood: Longitudinal studies of early family experience.* Hillsdale, NJ: Erlbaum.

Berry, G. L., Zarit, S. H., & Rabatin, V. X. (1991). Caregiver activity on respite and nonrespite days: A comparison of two service approaches. *Gerontologist, 31,* 830–835.

Betz, N. E. (1994). Career counseling for women in the sciences and engineering. In W. B. Walsh & S. H. Osipow (Eds.), *Career counseling for women* (pp. 237–261). Hillsdale, NJ: Erlbaum.

Betz, N. E., Fitzgerald, L. F., & Hill, R. (1989). Trait-factor theories: Traditional cornerstone of career theory. In M. B. Arthur, D. T. Hall, & B. S. Lawrence (Eds.), *Handbook of career theory* (pp. 26–40). New York: Cambridge University Press.

Betz, N. E., & Hackett, G. (1986). Applications of self-efficacy theory to understanding career choice behavior. *Journal of Social and Clinical Psychology, 4,* 279–289.

Betz, N. E., & Hackett, G. (1987). Concept of agency in educational and career development. *Journal of Counseling Psychology, 34,* 299–308.

Bibring, E. (1953). The mechanism of depression. In P. E. Greenacre (Ed.), *Affective disorders* (pp. 13–48). New York: International Universities Press.

Biedenharn, P. J., & Normoyle, J. B. (1991). Elderly community residents' reactions to the nursing home: An analysis of nursing home-related beliefs. *Gerontologist, 31,* 107–115.

Binion, V. J. (1990). Psychological androgeny: A black female perspective. *Sex Roles, 22,* 487–507.

The biology of aging. (1992, Fall/Winter). *Generations, 16*(4).

Bird, A. (1994). Careers as repositories of knowledge: A new perspective on boundaryless careers. *Journal of Organizational Behavior, 15,* 325–344.

Birren, J. E., & Birren, B. A. (1990). The concepts, models, and history in the psychology of aging. In J. E. Birren & K. W. Schaie (Eds.), *Handbook of the psychology of aging* (3rd ed., pp. 3–20). San Diego: Academic Press.

Birren, J. E., Butler, R. N., Greenhouse, S. W., Sokoloff, L., & Yarrow, M. R. (1963). *Human aging: A biological and behavioral study.* Washington, DC: U.S. Public Health Service.

Birren, J. E., & Schaie, K. W. (Eds.). (1996). *Handbook of the psychology of aging* (4th ed.). San Diego: Academic Press.

Birren, J. E., & Sloane, R. B. (Eds.). (1989). *Handbook of mental health and aging* (2nd ed.). Englewood Cliffs, NJ: Prentice-Hall.

Bitzan, J. E., & Kruzich, J. M. (1990). Interpersonal relationships of nursing home residents. *Gerontologist, 30,* 385–390.

Blair, S. L. (1993). Employment, family, and perceptions of marital quality among husbands and wives. *Journal of Family Issues, 14,* 189–212.

Blanchard-Fields, F., & Hess, T. M. (Eds.). (1996). *Perspectives on cognitive change in adulthood and aging.* New York: McGraw-Hill.

Blankenhorn, D. (1990). American family dilemmas. In D. G. Blankenhorn, S. Bayme, & J. B. Elshtain (Eds.), *Rebuilding the nest: A new commitment to the American family* (pp. 3–25). Milwaukee: Family Service America.

Blankenhorn, D. G., Bayme, S., & Elshtain, J. B. (Eds.). (1990). *Rebuilding the nest: A new commitment to the American family.* Milwaukee: Family Service America.

Blazer, D., Hughes, D. C., & George, L. K. (1987). The epidemiology of depression in an elderly community population. *Gerontologist, 27,* 281–287.

Blendon, R. A., Aiken, L. H., Freeman, H. E., & Corey, C. (1989). Access to medical care for black and white Americans. *Journal of the American Medical Association, 261,* 278–281.

Blessed, G., Tomlinson, B. E., & Roth, M. (1968). The association between quantitative measures of dementia and of senile changes in the cerebral grey matter of elderly subjects. *British Journal of Psychiatry, 114,* 797–811.

Bloch, A., Maeder, J., & Haissly, J. (1975). Sexual problems after myocardial infarction. *American Heart Journal, 90,* 536–537.

Bohn, M. J. (1993). Alcoholism. *Psychiatric Clinics of North America, 16,* 679–692.

Booth, A., & Amato, P. R. (1994). Parental marital quality, parental divorce, and relations with parents. *Journal of Marriage and the Family, 56,* 21–34.

Booth, A., & Johnson, D. R. (1994). Declining health and marital quality. *Journal of Marriage and the Family, 56,* 218–223.

Bosse, R., Aldwin, C. M., Levenson, M. R., & Workman-Daniels, K. (1991). How stressful is retirement? Findings from the Normative Aging Study. *Journals of Gerontology, 46,* P9–P14.

Botwinick, J. (1966). Cautiousness in advanced age. *Journal of Gerontology, 21,* 347–353.

Botwinick, J. (1967). *Cognitive processes in maturity and old age.* New York: Springer.

Botwinick, J. (1978). *Aging and Behavior* (2nd ed.). New York: Springer.

Botwinick, J., & Birren, J. E. (1963). Mental abilities and psychomotor responses in healthy aged men. In J. E. Birren, R. N. Butler, S. W. Greenhouse, L. Sokoloff, & M. R. Yarrow (Eds.), *Human aging: A biological and behavioral study.* Washington, DC: U.S. Public Health Service.

Botwinick, J., & Storandt, M. (1974). Cardiovascular status, depressive affect and other factors in reaction time. *Journal of Gerontology, 29,* 543–548.

Bouchard, T. J. (1994). Genes, environment, and personality. *Science, 264,* 1700–1701.

Bouchard, T. J., & McGue, M. (1990). Genetic and rearing environmental influences on adult personality: An analysis of adopted twins reared apart. *Journal of Personality, 58,* 263–292.

Bound, J., Duncan, G. J., Laren, D. S., & Oleinick, L. (1991). Poverty dynamics in widowhood. *Journals of Gerontology, 46,* S115–S124.

The boundaryless career [Special issue]. (1994, July). *Journal of Organizational Behavior, 15*(4).

Bowen, G. L., & Orthner, D. K. (1991). Effects of organizational culture on fatherhood. In F. W. Bozett & S. M. H. Hanson (Eds.), *Fatherhood and families in cultural context* (pp. 187–217). New York: Springer.

Bowlby, C. (1993). *Therapeutic activities with persons disabled by Alzheimer's disease and related disorders.* Gaithersburg, MD: Aspen.

Bowlby, J. (1980). *Loss.* New York: Basic Books.

Bradbury, T. N., & Fincham, F. D. (1990). Attributions in marriage: Review and critique. *Psychological Bulletin, 107,* 3–33.

Braithwaite, R., & Taylor, S. (1992). African American health: An introduction. In R. Braithwaite & S. E. Taylor (Eds.), *Health issues in the black community* (pp. 3–5). San Francisco: Jossey-Bass.

Branch, L. G., Guralnik, J. M., Foley, D. J., Kohout, F. J., Wetle, T. T., Ostfeld, A., & Katz, S. (1991). Active life expectancy for 10,000 men and women in three communities. *Journals of Gerontology, 46,* M145–M150.

Brecher, E. M., & Consumer Reports Book Editors (1985). *Love, sex, and aging.* Boston: Little, Brown.

Breckenridge, J. N., Gallagher, D., Thompson, L. W., & Peterson, J. (1986). Characteristic depressive symptoms of bereaved elders. *Journal of Gerontology, 41,* 163–168.

Brent, S. B., Speece, M. W., Gates, M. F., & Kaul, M. (1992–1993). The contribution of death-related experiences to health care providers' attitudes toward dying patients: 11 medical and nursing students with no professional experience. *Omega: Journal of Death and Dying, 26,* 181–205.

Brock, D. W. (1994). Good decision making for incompetent patients. *Hastings Center Report, 24,* S8–S11.

Brockopp, D. Y., King, D. B., & Hamilton, J. E. (1991). The dying patient: A comparative study of nurse caregiver characteristics. *Death Studies, 15,* 245–258.

Brody, E. M. (1977). *Long term care of older people.* New York: Human Sciences Press.

Brody, E. M. (1985). Parent care as a normative family stress. *Gerontologist, 25,* 19–29.

Brody, E. M., Kleban, M. H., Johnsen, P. T., Hoffman, C., & Schoonover, C. B. (1987). Work status and parent care: A comparison of four groups of women. *Gerontologist, 27,* 201–208.

Brody, E. M., & Schoonover, C. B. (1986). Patterns of parent care when adult daughters work and when they do not. *Gerontologist, 26,* 372–381.

Brody, N. (1993). Intelligence and the behavioral genetics of personality. In R. Plomin & G. E. McClearn (Eds.), *Nature, nurture, and psychology* (pp. 161–178). Washington, DC: American Psychological Association.

Broman, C. (1993). Race differences in marital well-being. *Journal of Marriage and the Family, 55,* 724–732.

Bronstein, P. (1988). Father-child interaction: Implications for gender role socialization. In P. Bronstein & C. P. Cowan (Eds.), *Fatherhood today: Men's changing role in the family* (pp. 107–126). New York: John Wiley & Sons.

Bronstein, P., & Cowan, C. P. (Eds.). (1988). *Fatherhood today: Men's changing role in the family.* New York: John Wiley & Sons.

Brubaker, T. (1985). Responsibility for household tasks: A look at golden anniversary couples aged 75 years and older. In W. A. Peterson & J. Quadagno (Eds.), *Social bonds in later life: Aging and interdependence* (pp. 27–36). Beverly Hills, CA: Sage.

Brubaker, T. (Ed.). (1990). *Family relationships in later life* (2nd ed). Newbury Park, CA: Sage.

Bucholz, K. K. (1992). Alcohol abuse and dependence from a psychiatric epidemiologic perspective. *Alcohol Health and Research World, 16,* 197–208.

Buell, S. J., & Coleman, P. D. (1979). Dendritic growth in the human aged brain and failure of growth in senile dementia. *Science, 206,* 854–856.

Buhler, L. K. (1995). *The relationship between intrinsic religiosity and death anxiety in the elderly.* Unpublished master's thesis, Middle Tennessee State University, Murfreesboro.

Bulcroft, K., & O'Connor-Rodin, M. (1986). Never too late. *Psychology Today, 20,* 66–69.

Bulcroft, R. A., & Bulcroft, K. A. (1993). Race differences in attitudinal and motivational factors in the decision to marry. *Journal of Marriage and the Family, 55,* 338–355.

Bumpass, L. L., & Aquilino, W. S. (1995, March). *A social map of midlife: Family and work over the middle life course.* (Available from the John D. & Catherine T. MacArthur Foundation Research Network on Successful Midlife Development, Gilbert Brim, Director, 1625 Tenth Ave., Vero Beach, FL 32963.)

Burgio, L. D., Engel, B. T., Hawkins, A., McCormick, K., & Scheve, A. (1990). A descriptive analysis of nursing staff behaviors in a teaching nursing home: Differences among NAs, LPNs, and RNs. *Gerontologist, 30,* 107–112.

Burkhauser, R. V. (1994). Protecting the most vulnerable: A proposal to improve Social Security insurance for older women. *Gerontologist, 34,* 148–149.

Burns, J. W., Friedman, R., & Katkin, E. S. (1992). Anger expression, hostility, anxiety, and patterns of cardiac reactivity to stress. *Behavioral Medicine, 18,* 71–78.

Burns, M. O., & Seligman, M. E. (1989). Explanatory style across the lifespan: Evidence for stability over 52 years. *Journal of Personality and Social Psychology, 56,* 471–477.

Bursik, K. (1991a). Adaptation to divorce and ego development in adult women. *Journal of Personality and Social Psychology, 60,* 300–306.

Bursik, K. (1991b). Correlates of women's adjustment during the separation and divorce process. *Journal of Divorce and Remarriage, 14,* 137–162.

Bush-Brown, A., & Davis, D. (Eds.). (1992). *Hospitable design for health care and senior communities.* New York: Van Nostrand Reinhold.

Busschbach, J. J., Hessing, D. J., & Charro, F. T. (1993). The utility of health at different stages in life: A quantitative approach. *Social Science and Medicine, 37,* 153–158.

Butler, R. N. (1980). Ageism: A foreward. *Journal of Social Issues, 36,* 8–11.

Butler, R. N., & Lewis, M. I. (1973). *Aging and mental health.* St. Louis: Mosby.

Byrne, D., & Murnen, S. K. (1988). Maintaining loving relationships. In R. J. Sternberg & M. L. Barnes (Eds.), *The psychology of love* (pp. 293–310). New Haven, CT: Yale University Press.

C

Caldwell, D., & Mishara, B. L. (1972). Research on attitudes of medical doctors towards the dying patient: A methodological problem. *Omega: Journal of Death and Dying, 3,* 341–346.

Callahan, D. (1987). *Setting limits: Medical care in an aging society.* New York: Simon & Schuster.

Callahan, D. (1994). Aging and the goals of medicine. *Hastings Center Report, 24,* 39–41.

Cameron, P., Stewart, L., & Biber, H. (1973). Consciousness of death across the life-span. *Journal of Gerontology, 28,* 92–95.

Campbell, B. C., & Udry, J. R. (1994). Implications of hormonal influences on sexual behavior for demographic models of reproduction. In K. L. Campbell & J. W. Wood (Eds.), *Human reproductive ecology: Interactions of environment, fertility, and behavior* (pp. 117–127). New York: New York Academy of Sciences.

Campbell, D., & Fiske, D. (1959). Convergent and discriminant validation by the multitrait-multimethod matrix. *Psychological Bulletin, 56,* 81–105.

Campbell, T. W., Abernethy, V., & Waterhouse, G. J. (1983). Do death attitudes of nurses and physicians differ? *Omega: Journal of Death and Dying, 14,* 43–49.

Canestrari, R. E. (1963). Paced and self-paced learning in young and elderly adults. *Journal of Gerontology, 18,* 165–168.

Cantor, M. H. (1983). Strain among caregivers: A study of the experience in the United States. *Gerontologist, 23,* 597–604.

Carnelley, K. B., & Janoff-Bulman, R. (1992). Optimism about love relationships: General vs. specific lessons from one's personal experiences. *Journal of Social and Personal Relationships, 9,* 5–20.

Carolan, M. T. (1994). Beyond deficiency: Broadening the view of menopause. *Journal of Applied Gerontology, 13,* 193–205.

Caron, S. L., & Wynn, R. L. (1992). The intent to parent among young, unmarried college graduates. *Families in Society, 73,* 481–487.

Carstensen, L. L., Gottman, J. M., & Levenson, R. W. (1995). Emotional behavior in long-term marriage. *Psychology and Aging, 10,* 140–149.

Carstensen, L. L., & Turk-Charles, S. (1994). The salience of emotion across the adult life span. *Psychology and Aging, 9,* 259–264.

Caserta, M. S., & Lund, D. A. (1993). Intrapersonal resources and the effectiveness of self-help groups for bereaved older adults. *Gerontologist, 33,* 619–629.

Caspi, A., Bem, D., & Elder, G. H. (1989). Continuities and consequences of interactional styles across the life course. *Journal of Personality, 57,* 375–406.

Caspi, A., Elder, G. H., & Bem, D. J. (1987). Moving against the world: Life course patterns of explosive children. *Developmental Psychology, 23,* 308–313.

Caspi, A., & Herbener, E. S. (1990). Continuity and change: Assortative marriage and the consistency of personality in adulthood. *Journal of Personality and Social Psychology, 58,* 250–258.

Cate, R. M., Huston, T. L., & Nesselroade, J. R. (1986). Premarital relationships: Toward the identification of alternative pathways to marriage. *Journal of Social and Clinical Psychology, 4,* 3–22.

Cavanaugh, J. C. (1989). The importance of awareness in memory and aging. In L. W. Poon, D. C. Rubin, & B. A. Wilson (Eds.), *Everyday cognition in adulthood and late life* (pp. 416–436). New York: Cambridge University Press.

Cavanaugh, J. C. (1996). Memory self-efficacy as a moderator of memory change. In F. Blanchard-Fields & T. M. Hess (Eds.), *Perspectives on cognitive change in adulthood and aging* (pp. 488–507). New York: McGraw-Hill.

Ceci, S. J., & Liker, J. (1986). Academic and non-academic intelligence: An experimental separation. In R. J. Sternberg and R. K. Wagner (Eds.), *Practical intelligence: Origins of competence in the everyday world* (pp. 119–143). New York: Cambridge University Press.

Cerella, J. (1990). Aging and information-processing rate. In J. E. Birren & K. W. Schaie (Eds.), *Handbook of the psychology of aging* (3rd ed., pp. 201–221). San Diego: Academic Press.

Chang, G., Astrachan, B. M., & Bryant, K. J. (1994). Emergency physicians' ratings of alcoholism treaters. *Journal of Substance Abuse Treatment, 11,* 131–135.

Chaplin, W. F., & Buckner, K. E. (1988). Self-ratings of personality: A naturalistic comparison of normative, ipsative, and idiothetic standards. *Journal of Personality, 56,* 509–530.

Charles, M. (1992). Cross-national variation in occupational sex segregation. *American Sociological Review, 57,* 483–502.

Cherlin, A. J. (1988). The changing American family and public policy. In A. J. Cherlin (Ed.), *The changing American family and public policy* (pp. 1–29). Washington, DC: Urban Institute Press.

Cherlin, A. J., & Furstenberg, F. F. (1985). Styles and strategies of grandparenting. In V. L. Bengtson & J. F. Robertson (Eds.), *Grandparenthood* (pp. 97–116). Beverly Hills, CA: Sage.

Chesney, M. A., Hecker, M. H. L., & Black, G. W. (1988). Coronary-prone components of Type A behavior in the WCGS: A new methodology. In B. K. Houston & C. R. Snyder (Eds.), *Type A behavior pattern: Research, theory, and intervention* (pp. 168–188). New York: John Wiley & Sons.

Children's Defense Fund. (1994). *The state of America's children, Yearbook, 1994.* Washington, DC: Author.

Chipuer, H. M., Plomin, R., Pedersen, N. L., McClearn, G. E., & Nesselroade, J. R. (1993). Genetic influence on family environment: The role of personality. *Developmental Psychology, 29,* 110–118.

Chirikos, T. N., & Nestel, G. (1985). Longitudinal analysis of functional disabilities in older men. *Journal of Gerontology, 40,* 426–433.

Choi, G. N. (1991). Racial difference in the determinants of living arrangements of widowed and divorced elderly women. *Gerontologist, 31,* 496–504.

Clark, L. A., & Watson, D. (1991). General affective dispositions in physical and psychological health. In C. R. Snyder & D. R. Forsyth (Eds.), *Handbook of social and clinical psychology: The health perspective* (pp. 221–245). New York: Pergamon Press.

Clarke-Stewart, A., & Bailey, B. L. (1989). Adjusting to divorce: Why do men have it easier? *Journal of Divorce, 13,* 75–93.

Clarkson-Smith, L., & Hartley, A. H. (1990). The game of bridge as a exercise in working memory and reasoning. *Journals of Gerontology, 45,* P233–P238.

Clausen, J. S. (1991). Adolescent competence and the shaping of the life course. *American Journal of Sociology, 96,* 805–842.

Cleveland, W., & Gianturco, D. (1976). Remarriage probability after widowhood: A retrospective method. *Journal of Gerontology, 31,* 99–103.

Cloninger, C. R. (1987). Neurogenetic adaptive mechanisms in alcoholism. *Science, 236,* 410–416.

Cloninger, C. R., Bohman, M., & Sigvardsson, S. (1981). Inheritance of alcohol abuse: Cross-fostering analysis of adopted men. *Archives of General Psychiatry, 38,* 861–868.

Cohen, D., Eisdorfer, C., Gorelick, P., Paveza, G., Luchins, D. J., Frels, S., Ashford, J. W., Smela, T., Levy, P., & Hirschman, R. (1993). Psychopathology associated with Alzheimer's disease and related disorders. *Journals of Gerontology, 48,* M255–M260.

Cohen, E. S., & Kruschwitz, A. L. (1990). Old age in America represented in nineteenth and twentieth century popular sheet music. *Gerontologist, 30,* 345–354.

Cohen, K. P. (1979). *Hospice: Prescription for terminal care.* Germantown, MD: Aspen.

Cohler, B. J., & Grunebaum, H. V. (1981). *Mothers, grandmothers and daughters: Personality and childcare in three-generation families.* New York: Wiley.

Cohn, D. A., Silver, D. H., Cowan, C. P., Cowan, P. A., & Pearson, J. (1992). Working models of childhood attachment and couple relationships. *Journal of Family Issues, 13,* 432–449.

Cohn, R. M. (1979). Age and the satisfactions from work. *Journal of Gerontology, 34,* 264–272.

Cole, S. (1979). Age and scientific performance. *American Journal of Sociology, 84,* 264–272.

Coleman, P. D. (1986, August). *Regulation of dendritic extent: Human aging brain and Alzheimer's disease.* Paper presented at the 94th Annual Meeting of the American Psychological Association, Washington, DC.

Comfort, A. (1979). *The biology of senescence* (3rd ed.). New York: Elsevier/North Holland.

Comstock, B. S. (1992). Decision to hospitalize and alternatives to hospitalization. In B. M. Bongar (Ed.), *Suicide: Guidelines for assessment, management, and treatment* (pp. 204–217). New York: Oxford University Press.

Conley, J. J. (1984). Longitudinal consistency of adult personality: Self-reported psychological characteristics across 45 years. *Journal of Personality and Social Psychology, 47,* 1325–1333.

Conley, J. J. (1985). Longitudinal stability of personality traits: A multitrait-multimethod-multioccasion analysis. *Journal of Personality and Social Psychology, 49,* 1266–1282.

Connidis, I. A., & Davies, L. (1992). Confidants and companions: Choices in later life. *Journals of Gerontology, 47,* S115–S122.

Connidis, I. A., & McMullin, J. A. (1993). To have or have not: Parent status and the subjective well-being of older men and women. *Gerontologist, 33,* 630–636.

Contrada, R. J., Krantz, D. S., & Hill, D. R. (1988). Type A behavior, emotion, and psychophysiologic reactivity: Psychological and biological interactions. In B. K. Houston & C. R. Snyder (Eds.), *Type A behavior pattern: Research, theory, and*

intervention (pp. 254–274). New York: John Wiley & Sons.

Conway, S. W., Hayslip, B., & Tandy, R. E. (1991). Similarity of perceptions of bereavement experiences between widows and professionals. *Omega: Journal of Death and Dying, 23,* 37–51.

Coolidge, F. L., & Fish, C. E. (1983–1984). Dreams of the dying. *Omega: Journal of Death and Dying, 14,* 1–8.

Coombs, R. H. (1991). Marital status and personal well-being: A literature review. *Family Relations, 40,* 97–102.

Cooney, T. M., Schaie, K. W., & Willis, S. L. (1988). The relationship between prior functioning on cognitive and personality dimensions and subject attrition in longitudinal research. *Journals of Gerontology, 43,* P12–P17.

Coons, D. (1992). *Specialized dementia care units.* Baltimore: Johns Hopkins University Press.

Coonts, S. (1992). *The way we never were.* New York: Basic Books.

Cooper, J. K., & Mungas, D. (1993). Alzheimer's disease drug treatment. *Journal of Geriatric Drug Therapy, 8,* 5–18.

Cooper, K. L., & Gutmann, D. L. (1987). Gender identity and ego mastery style in middle aged, pre and post empty nest women. *Gerontologist, 27,* 347–352.

Corby, N., & Solnick, R. L. (1980). Psychosocial and physiological influences on sexuality in the older adult. In J. E. Birren & R. B. Sloane (Eds.), *Handbook of mental health and aging* (pp. 893–921). Englewood Cliffs, NJ: Prentice-Hall.

Cornelius, S. W., & Caspi, A. (1987). Everyday problem solving in adulthood and old age. *Psychology and Aging, 2,* 144–153.

Corr, C. A. (1991–1992). A task-based approach to coping with dying. *Omega: Journal of Death and Dying, 24,* 81–94.

Corr, C. A. (1993). Coping with dying: Lessons that we should and should not learn from the work of Elisabeth Kubler-Ross. *Death Studies, 17,* 69–83.

Costa, P. T., & McCrae, R. R. (1980). Influence of extraversion and neuroticism on subjective well-being: Happy and unhappy people. *Journal of Personality and Social Psychology, 38,* 668–678.

Costa, P. T., & McCrae, R. R. (1986). Cross-sectional studies of personality in a national sample: Development and validation of survey measures. *Psychology and Aging, 1,* 140–143.

Costa, P. T., & McCrae, R. R. (1987). Role of neuroticism in the perception and presentation of chest pain symptoms and

coronary artery disease. In J. W. Elias & P. H. Marshall (Eds.), *Cardiovascular disease and behavior* (pp. 39–66). Washington, DC: Hemisphere.

Costa, P. T., & McCrae, R. R. (1988a). From catalog to classification: Murray's needs and the five-factor model. *Journal of Personality and Social Psychology, 55,* 258–265.

Costa, P. T., & McCrae, R. R. (1988b). Personality in adulthood: A six-year longitudinal study of self-reports and spouse ratings on the NEO Personality Inventory. *Journal of Personality and Social Psychology, 54,* 853–863.

Costa, P. T., & McCrae, R. R. (1989). Personality, stress, and coping: Some lessons from a decade of research. In K. S. Markides & C. L. Cooper (Eds.), *Aging, stress, and health* (pp. 269–285). Chichester, England: John Wiley & Sons.

Costa, P. T., McCrae, R. R., & Arenberg, D. (1980). Enduring dispositions in adult males. *Journal of Personality and Social Psychology, 38,* 793–800.

Costa, P. T., McCrae, R. R., & Arenberg, D. (1983). Recent longitudinal research on personality and aging. In K. W. Schaie (Ed.), *Longitudinal studies of adult psychological development* (pp. 222–225) New York: Guilford Press.

Cotman, C. (1990). Synaptic plasticity, neurotrophic factors, and transplantation in the aged brain. In E. L. Schneider & J. W. Rowe (Eds.), *Handbook of the biology of aging* (3rd ed., pp. 255–265). San Diego: Academic Press.

Council of Ethical and Judicial Affairs, American Medical Association. (1991). Guidelines for the appropriate use of do-not-resuscitate orders. *Journal of the American Medical Association, 265,* 1868–1871.

Council on Families in America. (1995). *Marriage in America: A report to the nation.* New York: Institute for American Values.

Cowan, C. P., & Bronstein, P. (1988). Father's roles in the family: Implications for research, intervention and change. In P. Bronstein & C. P. Cowan (Eds.), *Fatherhood today: Men's changing role in the family* (pp. 341–348). New York: John Wiley & Sons.

Cowan, C. P., & Cowan, P. A. (1988). Who does what when partners become parents: Implications for men, women, and marriage. *Marriage and Family Review, 12,* 105–132.

Cowan, C. P., & Cowan, P. A. (1992). *When partners become parents: The big life change for couples.* New York: Harper & Row.

Cox, T., & Nkomo, S. M. (1992). Candidate age as a factor in promotability ratings. *Public Personnel Management, 21,* 197–210.

Crimmins, E. M., & Ingegneri, D. G. (1990). Interaction and living arrangements of older parents and their children: Past trends, present determinants, future implications. *Research on Aging, 12,* 3–35.

Cristofalo, V. (1988). An overview of the theories of biological aging. In J. E. Birren & V. L. Bengtson (Eds.), *Emergent theories of aging* (pp. 118–127). New York: Springer.

Crook, T. H., & Larrabee, G. J. (1992). Changes in facial recognition memory across the adult life span. *Journals of Gerontology, 47,* P138–P141.

Cross, S., & Markus, H. (1991). Possible selves across the life span. *Human Development, 34,* 230–255.

Crown, W. H., Ahlburg, D. A., & MacAdam, M. (1995). The demographic and employment of characteristics of home care aides: A comparison with nursing home aides, hospital aides, and other workers. *Gerontologist, 35,* 162–170.

Cuber, J., & Harroff, P. (1965). *Sex and significant Americans.* New York: Appleton Century Crofts.

Cumming, E., & Henry, W. (1961). *Growing old.* New York: Basic Books.

Cunningham, D. A., Rechnitzer, P. A., Howard, J. H., & Donner, A. P. (1987). Exercise training of men at retirement: A clinical trial. *Journal of Gerontology, 42,* 17–23.

Cunningham, J. D., & Antill, J. K. (1994). Cohabitation and marriage: Retrospective and predictive comparisons. *Journal of Social and Personal Relationships, 11,* 77–93.

Curb, J. D., Reed, D. M., Miller, F. D., & Yano, K. (1990). Health status and life style in elderly Japanese men with a long life expectancy. *Journals of Gerontology, 45,* S206–S211.

Current ethical issues in aging. (1994, Winter). *Generations, 18*(4).

D

D'Angelo, C. (1992). Cartello. In A. Bush-Brown & D. Davis (Eds.), *Hospitable design for health care and senior communities* (pp. 160–161). New York: Van Nostrand Reinhold.

Danis, M., Southerland, L. I., Garrett, J. M., Smith, J. L., Hielema, F., Pickard, G., Egner, D. M., & Patrick, D. L. (1991). A prospective study of advance directives for

life-sustaining care. *New England Journal of Medicine, 324,* 882–888.

D'Augelli, A. R., & Garnets, L. D. (1995). Lesbian, gay, and bisexual communities. In A. R. D'Augelli & C. J. Patterson (Eds.), *Lesbian, gay, and bisexual identities over the lifespan: Psychological perspectives* (pp. 293–300). New York: Oxford University Press.

D'Augelli, A. R., & Patterson, C. J. (Eds.). (1995). *Lesbian, gay, and bisexual identities over the lifespan: Psychological perspectives.* New York: Oxford University Press.

Davis, G., & Jessen, A. (1980–1981). An experiment in death education in the medical curriculum: Medical students and clergy "on call" together. *Omega: Journal of Death and Dying, 11,* 157–166.

Dean, A., Matt, G. E., & Wood, P. (1992). The effects of widowhood on social support from significant others. *Journal of Community Psychology, 20,* 309–325.

deBruin, A. F., deWitte, L. P., Stevens, F., & Diederiks, J. P. (1992). Sickness Impact Profile: The state of the art of a generic functional status measure. *Social Science and Medicine, 35,* 1003–1014.

Dedrick, E. J., & Dobbins, G. H. (1991). The influence of subordinate age on managerial actions: An attributional analysis. *Journal of Organizational Behavior, 12,* 367–377.

DeFillippi, R. J., & Arthur, M. B. (1994). The boundaryless career: A competency-based perspective. *Journal of Organizational Behavior, 15,* 307–324.

Deimling, G. T., & Bass, D. M. (1986). Symptoms of mental impairment among elderly adults and their effects on family caregivers. *Journal of Gerontology, 41,* 778–784.

DeMaris, A., & MacDonald, W. (1993). Premarital cohabitation and marital instability: A test of the unconventionality hypothesis. *Journal of Marriage and the Family, 55,* 399–407.

Denney, N. A. (1989). Everyday problem solving: Methodological issues, research findings, and a model. In L. W. Poon, D. C. Rubin, & B. A. Wilson (Eds.), *Everyday cognition in adulthood and late life* (pp. 330–351). New York: Cambridge University Press.

Dennis, W. (1966). Creative productivity between the ages of 20 and 80 years. *Journal of Gerontology, 21,* 1–8.

Depner, C. E., & Ingersol-Dayton, B. (1985). Conjugal social support: Patterns in later life. *Journal of Gerontology, 40,* 761–766.

deVos, S. (1990). Extended family living among older people in six Latin American

countries. *Journals of Gerontology, 45,* S87–S94.

Dhooper, S. S., Green, S. M., Huff, M. B., & Austin-Murphy, J. I. (1993). Efficacy of a group approach to reducing depression in nursing home elderly residents. *Journal of Gerontological Social Work, 20,* 87–100.

Diamond, M. C. (1988). *Enriching heredity.* New York: Free Press.

Dickens, F., & Dickens, J. B. (1991). *The black manager: Making it in the corporate world.* New York: American Management Association.

Dickie, J. R. (1987). Interrelationships within the mother-father-infant triad. In P. W. Berman & F. A. Pederson (Eds.), *Men's transitions to parenthood: Longitudinal studies of early family experience* (pp. 113–143). Hillsdale, NJ: Erlbaum.

Dickinson, G. E., & Pearson, A. A. (1980–1981). Death education and physicians' attitudes towards dying patients. *Omega: Journal of Death and Dying, 11,* 167–174.

Dickinson, G. E., Sumner, E. D., & Frederick, L. M. (1992). Death education in selected health professions. *Death Studies, 16,* 281–289.

Dion, K. L., & Yee, P. H. (1987). Ethnicity and personality in a Canadian context. *Journal of Social Psychology, 127,* 175–182.

Dixon, R. A. (1992). Contextual approaches to adult intellectual development. In R. J. Sternberg & C. A. Berg (Eds.), *Intellectual development* (pp. 350–380). New York: Cambridge University Press.

Donovan, R. L., & Jackson, B. L. (1990). Deciding to divorce: A process guided by social exchange, attachment and cognitive dissonance theories. *Journal of Divorce, 13,* 23–35.

Dooley, D., & Catalano, R. (1988). Recent research on the psychological effects of unemployment. *Journal of Social Issues, 44,* 1–12.

Dougherty, K., Templer, D. I., & Brown, R. (1986). Psychological states in terminal cancer patients over time. *Journal of Counseling Psychology, 33,* 357–359.

Drehmer, D. E., Carlucci, C. A., Bordieri, J. E., & Pincus, L. B. (1992). Effects of age on ranking for reduction in work force. *Psychological Reports, 70,* 1203–1209.

Dresser, R. (1994). Advance directives: Implications for policy. *Hastings Center Report, 24,* S2–S5.

Dresser, R., & Whitehouse, P. J. (1994). The incompetent patient on the slippery slope. *Hastings Center Report, 24,* 6–12.

Dubler, N. (1994). Introduction. *Generations, 18,* 2–7.

Duncan, G. J., & Hoffman, S. P. (1991). Teenage underclass behavior and subsequent poverty: Have the rules changed? In C. J. Jencks & P. P. Peterson (Eds.), *The urban underclass* (pp. 155–174). Washington, DC: Brookings Institution.

Dunn, J. E., Rudberg, M. A., Furner, S. E., & Cassel, C. K. (1992). Mortality, disability, and falls in older persons: The role of underlying disease and disability. *American Journal of Public Health, 82,* 395–400.

Durlak, J. A., & Riesenberg, L. A. (1991). The impact of death education. *Death Studies, 15,* 39–58.

Dutton, D. G., & Aron, A. P. (1974). Some evidence for heightened sexual attraction under conditions of high anxiety. *Journal of Personality and Social Psychology, 30,* 510–517.

E

Earl, W. L., Martindale, C. J., & Cohn, D. (1991–1992). Adjustment: Denial in the styles of coping with HIV infection. *Omega: Journal of Death and Dying, 24,* 35–47.

Earles, J. L., & Salthouse, T. A. (1995). Interrelations of age, health, and speed. *Journals of Gerontology, 50B,* P33–P41.

Edelmann, R. J. (1992). *Anxiety: Theory, research, and intervention in clinical and health psychology.* Chichester, England: John Wiley & Sons.

Effros, R. B., Walford, R. L., Weindruch, R., & Mitcheltree, C. (1991). Influences of dietary restriction on immunity to influenza in aged mice. *Journals of Gerontology, 46,* B142–B147.

Ehrhardt, A. A. (1992). Trends in sexual behavior and the HIV pandemic. *American Journal of Public Health, 82,* 1459–1461.

Eichorn, D. (1981). Samples and procedures. In D. H. Eichorn, J. A. Clausen, N. Haan, M. P. Honzik, & P. H. Mussen (Eds.), *Present and past in middle life* (pp. 33–54). New York: Academic Press.

Eichorn, D. H., Clausen, J. A., Haan, N., Honzik, M. P., & Mussen, P. H. (Eds.). (1981). *Present and past in middle life.* New York: Academic Press.

Eisdorfer, C. (1970). Developmental level and sensory impairment in the aged. In E. Palmore (Ed.), *Normal aging* (pp. 238–242). Durham, NC: Duke University Press.

Ekerdt, D. J., Bosse, R., & Levkoff, S. (1985). An empirical test for phases of retirement: Findings from the Normative Aging Study. *Journal of Gerontology, 40,* 95–101.

Ekerdt, D. J., & DeViney, S. (1993). Evidence for a preretirement process among older male workers. *Journals of Gerontology, 48,* S35–S43.

Elder, G. H., & Caspi, A. (1988). Economic stress in lives: Developmental perspectives. *Journal of Social Issues, 44,* 25–45.

Elias, M. F., Elias, J. W., & Elias, P. K. (1990). Biological and health influences on behavior. In J. E. Birren & K. W. Schaie (Eds.), *Handbook of the psychology of aging* (3rd ed., pp. 79–102). San Diego: Academic Press.

Emmelkamp, P. M. G., Bouman, T. K., & Scholing, A. (1992). *Anxiety disorders: A practitioner's guide.* Chichester, England: Wiley.

Endresen, I. M., Relling, G. B., Tonder, O., Myking, O., Walther, B. T., & Ursin, H. (1991–1992). Brief uncontrollable stress and psychological parameters influence human plasma concentrations of IgM and complement component C3. *Behavioral Medicine, 17,* 167–176.

Engle, V. F., & Graney, M. J. (1993). Stability and improvement of health after nursing home admission. *Journals of Gerontology, 48,* S17–S23.

Enos, W., Holmes, R., & Beyer, J. (1955). Pathogenesis of coronary disease in American soldiers killed in Korea. *Journal of the American Medical Association, 158,* 192.

Erber, J. T., & Rothberg, S. T. (1991). Here's looking at you: The relative effect of age and attractiveness on judgments about memory failure. *Journals of Gerontology, 46,* P116–P123.

Erber, J. T., Szuchman, L. T., & Rothberg, S. T. (1990). Age, gender, and individual differences in memory failure appraisal. *Psychology and Aging, 5,* 600–603.

Erikson, E. H. (1963). *Childhood and society.* New York: Norton.

Eustis, N. N., & Fischer, L. R. (1991). Relationships between home care clients and their workers: Implications for quality of care. *Gerontologist, 31,* 447–456.

Evans, L., Ekerdt, D. J., & Bosse, R. (1985). Proximity to retirement and anticipatory involvement: Findings from the Normative Aging Study. *Journal of Gerontology, 40,* 368–374.

Ezzy, D. (1993). Unemployment and mental health: A critical review. *Social Science and Medicine, 37,* 41–52.

F

Farran, C. J., Keane-Hagerty, E., Salloway, S., Kupferer, S., & Wilken, C. (1991). Finding meaning: An alternative paradigm for Alzheimer's disease family caregivers. *Gerontologist, 31,* 483–489.

Fawcett, J. T. (1988). The value of children and the transition to parenthood. *Marriage and Family Review, 12,* 11–34.

Feifel, H., & Branscomb, A. B. (1973). Who's afraid of death? *Journal of Abnormal Psychology, 81,* 282–288.

Feingold, A. (1990). Gender differences in effects of physical attractiveness on romantic attraction: A comparison across five research paradigms. *Journal of Personality and Social Psychology, 59,* 981–993.

Feinson, M. C. (1986). Aging widows and widowers: Are there mental health differences? *International Journal of Aging and Human Development, 23,* 241–255.

Feldman, S. S., Biringen, Z. C., & Nash, S. C. (1981). Fluctuations of sex-related self attributions as a function of stage of family life cycle. *Developmental Psychology, 17,* 24–35.

Felton, B. J., & Revenson, T. A. (1987). Age differences in coping with chronic illness. *Psychology and Aging, 2,* 164–170.

Fengler, A. P., & Goodrich, N. (1979). Wives of elderly disabled men: The hidden patients. *Gerontologist, 19,* 175–183.

Ferber, M. A., O'Farrell, B., & Allen, L. R. (Eds.). (1991). *Work and family: Policies for a changing work force.* Washington, DC: National Academy Press.

Field, D., Minkler, M., Falk, R. F., & Leino, E. V. (1993). The influence of health on family contacts and family feelings in advanced old age: A longitudinal study. *Journals of Gerontology, 48,* P18–P28.

Field, D., Schaie, K. W., & Leino, E. V. (1988). Continuity in intellectual functioning: The role of self-reported health. *Psychology and Aging, 3,* 385–392.

Field, D., & Weishaus, S. (1988). A half century of marriage: Continuity or change? *Journal of Marriage and the Family, 50,* 763–774.

Fincham, F. D., & Bradbury, T. N. (1993). Marital satisfaction, depression, and attributions: A longitudinal analysis. *Journal of Personality and Social Psychology, 64,* 442–452.

Fischer, D. H. (1977). *Growing old in America.* New York: Oxford University Press.

Fishman, G. G. (1989). Psychoanalytic psychotherapy. In American Psychiatric Association (Ed.), *Treatments of psychiatric disorders: A task force report of the American Psychiatric Association* (Vol. 3, pp. 2010–2024). Washington, DC: American Psychiatric Association.

Fiske, D. (1971). *Measuring the concepts of personality*. Chicago: Aldine-Atherton.

Fitting, M., Rabins, P., Lucas, M. J., & Eastham, J. (1986). Caregivers for dementia patients: A comparison of husbands and wives. *Gerontologist, 26*, 248–252.

Fletcher, G. J., Fincham, F. D., Cramer, L., & Heron, N. (1987). The role of attributions in the development of dating relationships. *Journal of Personality and Social Psychology, 53*, 481–489.

Fletcher, W. L., Hansson, R. O., & Bailey, L. (1992). Assessing occupational self-efficacy among middle-aged and older adults. *Journal of Applied Gerontology, 11*, 489–501.

Florian, V., & Mikulincer, M. (1993). The impact of death-risk experiences and religiosity on the fear of personal death: The case of Israeli soldiers in Lebanon. *Omega: Journal of Death and Dying, 26*, 101–111.

Folberg, J., & Milne, A. (1988). *Divorce mediation: Theory and practice*. New York: Guilford Press.

Folkman, S., Lazarus, R. S., Pimley, S., & Novacek, J. (1987). Age differences in stress and coping processes. *Psychology and Aging, 2*, 171–184.

Folstein, M. F., Bassett, S. S., Anthony, J. C., Romanoski, A. J., & Nestadt, G. R. (1991). Dementia: A case ascertainment in a community survey. *Journals of Gerontology, 46*, M132–M138.

Ford, D. Y. (1994). An exploration of perceptions of alternative family structures among university students. *Family Relations, 43*, 68–73.

Fossett, M. A., & Kiecolt, K. J. (1993). Mate availability and family structure among African Americans in U.S. metropolitan areas. *Journal of Marriage and the Family, 55*, 288–302.

Fowlkes, M. R. (1994). Single worlds and homosexual lifestyles: Patterns of sexuality and intimacy. In A. S. Rossi (Ed.), *Sexuality across the life course* (pp. 151–184). Chicago: University of Chicago Press.

Fozard, J. L. (1990). Vision and hearing in aging. In J. E. Birren & K. W. Schaie (Eds.), *Handbook of the psychology of aging* (3rd ed., pp. 150–170). San Diego: Academic Press.

Frances, A., & Hall, W. (1991). Work in progress on the DSM-IV mood disorders. In J. P. Feighner & W. F. Boyer (Eds.), *The diagnosis of depression* (pp. 49–64). New York: Wiley.

Franks, M. M., & Stephens, M. P. (1992). Multiple roles of middle-generation caregivers: Contextual effects and psychological mechanisms. *Journals of Gerontology, 47*, S123–S129.

Fredman, L., Daly, M. P., & Lazur, A. M. (1995). Burden among white and black caregivers to elderly adults. *Journals of Gerontology, 50B*, S110–S118.

Freud, S. (1924). *On psychotherapy: Collected papers* (Vol. I). London: Hogarth.

Freud, S. (1957). *Mourning and melancholia: Standard edition* (Vol. 14). London: Hogarth.

Friedman, H. S., Tucker, J. S., Tomlinson-Keasey, C., Schwartz, J. E., Wingard, D. L., & Crique, M. H. (1993). Does childhood personality predict longevity? *Journal of Personality and Social Psychology, 65*, 176–185.

Friedman, M., & Rosenman, R. (1974). *Type A behavior and your heart*. New York: Knopf.

Fries, J. F. (1990). Medical perspectives upon successful aging. In P. B. Baltes & M. M. Baltes (Eds.), *Successful aging: Perspectives from the behavioral sciences* (pp. 35–49). New York: Cambridge University Press.

Fromholt, P., & Larsen, S. F. (1991). Autobiographical memory in normal aging and primary degenerative dementia (dementia of Alzheimer type). *Journals of Gerontology, 46*, P85–P91.

Furman, F., & Hawkins, M. E. (1994, April). *Positive models of aging: Presentations by members of the senior activity and rejuvenation project*. Presentation at the Annual Meeting of the Southern Gerontological Society, Charlotte, NC.

Furstenberg, F. F. (1976). *Unplanned parenthood: The social consequences of teenaged childbearing*. New York: Free Press.

Furstenberg, F. F., Brooks-Gunn, J., & Morgan, S. P. (1987). *Adolescent mothers in later life*. New York: Cambridge University Press.

Furstenberg, F. F., Jr. (1988). Good dads—bad dads: Two faces of fatherhood. In A. J. Cherlin (Ed.), *The changing American family and public policy* (pp. 93–218). Washington, DC: Urban Institute Press.

Furstenberg, F. F., Jr., & Cherlin, A. J. (1991). *Divided families: What happens to children when parents part*. Cambridge: Harvard University Press.

G

Gallagher, D., & Thompson, L. W. (1983). Cognitive therapy for depression in the elderly: A promising model for treatment and research. In L. D. Breslau & M. R. Haug (Eds.), *Depression and aging: Causes, care, and consequences* (pp. 168–192). New York: Springer.

Gallagher, S. K., & Gerstel, N. (1993). Kinkeeping and friend keeping among older women: The effect of marriage. *Gerontologist, 33*, 675–681.

Gallagher-Thompson, D., & DeVries, H. M. (1994). "Coping with frustration" classes: Development and preliminary outcomes with women who care for relatives with dementia. *Gerontologist, 34*, 548–552.

Gallant, D. M. (1987). *Alcoholism: A guide to diagnosis, intervention, and treatment*. New York: Norton.

Gatz, M., Bengtson, V. L., & Blum, M. J. (1990). Caregiving families. In J. E. Birren & K. W. Schaie (Eds.), *Handbook of the psychology of aging* (3rd ed., pp. 405–427). San Diego: Academic Press.

Gatz, M., Lowe, B., Berg, S., Mortimer, J., & Pederson, N. (1994). Dementia: Not just a search for the gene. *Gerontologist, 34*, 251–255.

Gatz, M., & Pearson, C. G. (1988). Ageism and the provision of psychological services. *American Psychologist, 43*, 184–188.

Gatz, M., & Smyer, M. A. (1992). The mental health system and older adults in the 1990s. *American Psychologist, 47*, 741–751.

Gekoski, W. L., & Knox, V. J. (1990). Ageism or healthism? Perceptions based on age and health status. *Journal of Aging and Health, 2*, 15–27.

Genevie, L., & Margoles, E. (1987). *The motherhood report: How women feel about being mothers*. New York: Macmillan.

George, L., & Gwyther, L. (1986). Caregiver well being: A multidimensional examination of family caregivers of demented adults. *Gerontologist, 26*, 253–259.

George, L. K. (1993). Depressive disorders and symptoms in later life. *Generations, 17*, 35–38.

German, P. S., Rovner, B. W., Burton, L. C., Brant, L. J., & Clark, R. (1992). The role of mental morbidity in the nursing home experience. *Gerontologist, 32*, 152–158.

Gerson, M. J., Posner, J. A., & Morris, A. (1991). The wish for a child in couples eager, disinterested, and conflicted about having children. *American Journal of Family Therapy, 19*, 334–343.

Gert, B., Bernat, J. L., & Mogielnicki, R. P. (1994). Distinguishing between patients' refusals and requests. *Hastings Center Report, 24*(4), 13–15.

Gesser, G., Wong, P. T., & Reker, G. T. (1987–1988). Death attitudes across the lifespan: The development and validation of the death attitude profile (DAP).

Omega: Journal of Death and Dying, 18, 113–128.

Giarrusso, R., Silverstein, M., & Bengtson, V. (1996). Family complexity and the grandparent role. *Generations, 20*(1), 17–23.

Gigy, L., & Kelly, J. B. (1992). Reasons for divorce: Perspectives of divorcing men and women. *Journal of Divorce and Remarriage, 18,* 169–187.

Gijsbers Van Wijk, C. M., Kolk, A. M., Van den Bosch, W. J., & Van den Hoogen, H. J. (1992). Male and female morbidity in general practice: The nature of sex differences. *Social Science and Medicine, 35,* 665–678.

Gilbert, L. A. (1993). *Two careers/one family: The promise of gender equality.* Beverly Hills, CA: Sage.

Glamser, F. D. (1976). Determinants of a positive attitude towards retirement. *Journal of Gerontology, 31,* 104–107.

Glaser, B., & Strauss, A. L. (1968). *Time for dying.* Chicago: Aldine.

Glenn, N. D. (1990). Quantitative research on marital quality in the 1980's: A critical review. *Journal of Marriage and the Family, 52,* 818–831.

Glenn, N. D., & Weaver, C. N. (1988). The changing relationship of marital status to reported happiness. *Journal of Marriage and the Family, 50,* 317–324.

Glickman, L., Hubbard, M., Liveright, T., & Valciukas, J. A. (1990). Fall-off in reporting life events: Effects of life change, desirability, and anticipation. *Behavioral Medicine, 16,* 31–38.

Goldman, S., Brown, S. A., & Christiansen, B. A. (1987). Expectancy theory: Thinking about drinking. In H. T. Blane & K. E. Leonard (Eds.), *Psychological theories of drinking and alcoholism* (pp. 181–226). New York: Guilford Press.

Goldscheider, F., & Waite, L. I. (1991). *New families, no families?* Berkeley: University of California Press.

Gordus, J. P., & Yamakawa, K. (1988). Incomparable losses: Economic and labor market outcomes for unemployed female versus male autoworkers. In P. Voydanoff & L. C. Majka (Eds.), *Families and economic distress: Coping strategies and social policy* (pp. 38–54). Newbury Park, CA: Sage.

Gorman, D. M. (1993). A review of studies comparing checklist and interview methods of data collection in life event research. *Behavioral Medicine, 19,* 66–71.

Gormly, A., Gormly, J., & Weiss, H. (1987). Motivations for parenthood among young adult college students. *Sex Roles, 16,* 31–40.

Gottesman, L. E., & Bourestom, N. C. (1974). Why nursing homes do what they do. *Gerontologist, 14,* 501–506.

Grandparenting at century's end. (1996, Spring). *Generations, 20*(1).

Granovetter, M., & Tilly, C. (1988). Inequality and labor processes. In N. J. Smelser (Ed.), *Handbook of sociology* (pp. 175–221). Newbury Park, CA: Sage.

Grant, L. A., Kane, R. A., & Stark, A. J. (1995). Beyond labels: Nursing home care for Alzheimer's disease in and out of special care units. *Journal of the American Geriatrics Society, 43,* 569–576.

Greenberger, E., & Steinberg, L. D. (1983). Sex differences in early labor force experience: Harbinger of things to come. *Social Forces, 62,* 467–486.

Greenhaus, J. H., Parasuraman, S., & Wormley, W. M. (1990). Effects of race on organizational experiences, job performance evaluations, and career outcomes. *Academy of Management Journal, 33,* 64–86.

Greene, V. L., & Ondrich, J. I. (1990). Risk factors for nursing home admissions and exits: A discrete-time hazard function approach. *Journals of Gerontology, 45,* S250–S258.

Grossman, F. K. (1987). Separate and together: Men's autonomy and affiliation in the transition to parenthood. In P. W. Berman & F. A. Pederson (Eds.), *Men's transitions to parenthood: Longitudinal studies of early family experience* (pp. 89–112). Hillsdale, NJ: Erlbaum.

Grossman, F. K. (1988). Strain in the transition to parenthood. *Marriage and Family Review, 12,* 85–104.

Guerrero, L. K., Eloy, S. V., & Wabnik, A. I. (1993). Linking maintenance strategies to relationship development and disengagement: A reconceptualization. *Journal of Social and Personal Relationships, 10,* 273–283.

Guralnik, J. M., & Kaplan, G. A. (1989). Predictors of healthy aging: Prospective evidence from the Alameda County study. *American Journal of Public Health, 79,* 703–708.

Gutman, H. G. (1976). *The black family in slavery and freedom, 1750–1925.* New York: Pantheon.

Gutmann, D. (1987). *Reclaimed powers: Toward a new psychology of men and women in later life.* New York: Basic Books.

H

Haan, N., Millsap, R., & Hartka, E. (1986). As time goes by: Change and stability in personality over fifty years. *Psychology and Aging, 1,* 220–232.

Hacker, A. (1992). *Two nations.* New York: Scribners.

Hagestad, G. (1985). Continuity and connectedness. In V. L. Bengtson & J. Robertson (Eds.), *Grandparenthood* (pp. 31–48). Beverly Hills, CA: Sage.

Hamel, M., Gold, D. P., Andres, D., Reis, M., Dastoor, D., Grauer, H., & Bergman, H. (1990). Predictors and consequences of aggressive behavior by community-based dementia patients. *Gerontologist, 30,* 206–211.

Hamon, R. R., & Blieszner, R. (1990). Filial responsibility expectations among adult child–older parent pairs. *Journals of Gerontology, 45,* P110–P112.

Hamon, R. R., & Cobb, L. L. (1993). Parents' experience of and adjustment to their adult children's divorce: Applying family stress theory. *Journal of Divorce and Remarriage, 21,* 73–94.

Handal, P. J., Peal, R. L., Napoli, J. G., & Austrin, H. R. (1984–1985). The relationship between direct and indirect measures of death anxiety. *Omega: Journal of Death and Dying, 15,* 245–262.

Hanisch, K. A., & Hulin, C. L. (1991). General attitudes and organizational withdrawal: An evaluation of a causal model. *Journal of Vocational Behavior, 39,* 110–128.

Hansen, L. B., & Jacob, E. (1992). Intergenerational support during the transition to parenthood: Issues for new parents and grandparents. *Families in Society, 73,* 471–479.

Harris, J. R., Pedersen, N. L., McClearn, G. E., Plomin, R., & Nesselroade, J. (1992). Age differences in genetic and environmental influences for health from the Swedish Adoption/Twin Study of Aging. *Journals of Gerontology, 47,* P213–P220.

Harris, L., & Associates. (1981). *Aging in the eighties: America in transition.* Washington, DC: National Council on the Aging.

Hartfield, B. (1996). Legal recognition of the value of intergenerational nurturance: Grandparent visitation statutes in the nineties. *Generations, 20*(1), 53–56.

Hasher, L., & Zacks, R. T. (1988). Working memory comprehension and aging: A review and a new view. In G. H. Bower (Ed.), *The psychology of learning and motivation: Advances in research and theory* (Vol. 22, pp. 193–225). San Diego: Academic Press.

Hatfield, E. (1988). Passionate and companionate love. In R. J. Sternberg & M. L. Barnes (Eds.), *The psychology of love* (pp. 191–217). New Haven, CT: Yale University Press.

Haug, M. (Ed.). (1981). *Elderly patients and their doctors.* New York: Springer.

Hauser, B. B., & Berkman, S. L. (1984). Aging parent/mature child relationships. *Journal of Marriage and the Family, 46,* 294–299.

Hayflick, L. (1987). The human life span. In G. Lesnoff-Caravaglia (Ed.), *Realistic expectations for long life* (pp. 17–34). New York: Human Sciences Press.

Haynes, S. G., & Matthews, K. A. (1988). The association of Type A behavior with cardiovascular disease: Update and critical review. In B. K. Houston & C. R. Snyder (Eds.), *Type A behavior pattern: Research, theory, and intervention* (pp. 51–82). New York: John Wiley & Sons.

Hayslip, B., Galt, C. P., & Pinder, M. M. (1993–1994). Effects of death education on conscious and unconscious death anxiety. *Omega: Journal of Death and Dying, 28,* 101–111.

Hayslip, B., Luhr, D. D., & Beyerlein, M. M. (1992). Levels of death anxiety in terminally ill men: A pilot study. *Omega: Journal of Death and Dying, 24,* 13–19.

Hayslip, B., & Stewart-Bussey, D. (1986–1987). Locus of control-levels of death anxiety relationships. *Omega: Journal of Death and Dying, 17,* 41–48.

Hayslip, B., Jr., Maloy, R. M., & Kohl, R. (1995). Long-term efficacy of fluid ability interventions with older adults. *Journals of Gerontology, 50B,* P141–P149.

Hazan, C., & Shaver, P. (1987). Romantic love conceptualized as an attachment process. *Journal of Personality and Social Psychology, 52,* 511–524.

Hazzard, W. (1990). A central role of sex hormones in the sex differential in lipoprotein metabolism, atherosclerosis, and longevity. In M. G. Ory & H. R. Warner (Eds.), *Gender, health, and longevity: Multidisciplinary perspectives* (pp. 87–108). New York: Springer.

Heaton, T. B., & Albrecht, S. L. (1991). Stable unhappy marriages. *Journal of Marriage and the Family, 53,* 747–758.

Heckhausen, J., Dixon, R. A., & Baltes, P. B. (1989). Gains and losses in development throughout adulthood as perceived by different adult age groups. *Developmental Psychology, 25,* 109–121.

Heckhausen, J., & Krueger, J. (1993). Developmental expectations for the self and most other people: Age grading in three functions of social comparison. *Developmental Psychology, 29,* 539–548.

Helson, R. (1992). Women's difficult times and the rewriting of the life story. *Psychology of Women Quarterly, 16,* 331–347.

Helson, R., & Moane, G. (1987). Personality change in women from college to midlife. *Journal of Personality and Social Psychology, 53,* 176–186.

Helson, R., & Roberts, B. W. (1994). Ego development and personality change in adulthood. *Journal of Personality and Social Psychology, 66,* 911–920.

Helson, R., & Wink, P. (1992). Personality change in women from the early 40's to the early 50's. *Psychology and Aging, 7,* 46–55.

Hendin, H. (1994, December 16). Scared to death of dying. *The New York Times,* p. A19.

Hendrick, S., Johnson, J. R., Inui, T. S., & Diehr, P. (1991). Factors associated with participation in a randomized trial of adult day health care. *Gerontologist, 31,* 607–610.

Hendrick, S. S. (1981). Self-disclosure and marital satisfaction. *Journal of Personality and Social Psychology, 40,* 1150–1159.

Hendrick, S. S., Hendrick, C., & Adler, N. L. (1988). Romantic relationships: Love, satisfaction, and staying together. *Journal of Personality and Social Psychology, 54,* 980–988.

Herek, G. M. (1995). Psychological heterosexism in the United States. In A. R. D'Augelli & C. J. Patterson (Eds.), *Lesbian, gay, and bisexual identities over the lifespan: Psychological perspectives* (pp. 321–346). New York: Oxford University Press.

Hertzog, C. (1989). Influences of cognitive slowing on age differences in intelligence. *Developmental Psychology, 25,* 636–651.

Hertzog, C., & Schaie, K. W. (1988). Stability and change in adult intelligence 11: Simultaneous analysis of longitudinal means and covariance structures. *Psychology and Aging, 2,* 122–130.

Hess, T. M., & Pullen, S. M. (1996). Memory in context. In F. Blanchard-Fields & T. M. Hess (Eds.), *Perspectives on cognitive change in adulthood and aging* (pp. 387–427). New York: McGraw-Hill.

Hicks, L. H., & Birren, J. E. (1970). Aging, brain damage, and psychomotor slowing. *Psychological Bulletin, 74,* 377–396.

Higami, Y., Yu, B. P., Shimokawa, I., Bertrand, H., Hubbard, G. B., & Masoro, E. J. (1995). Anti-tumor action of dietary restriction is lesion-dependent in male Fischer 344 rats. *Journals of Gerontology, 50A,* B72–B77.

Hildreth, C. D., & Saunders, E. (1992). Heart disease, stroke, and hypertension in blacks. In R. Braithwaite & S. E. Taylor (Eds.), *Health issues in the black community* (pp. 90–105). San Francisco: Jossey-Bass.

Hill, R. D., Storandt, M., & Simeone, C. (1990). The effects of memory skills training and incentives on free recall in older learners. *Journals of Gerontology, 45,* P227–P232.

Hinrichsen, G. A., & Ramirez, M. (1992). Black and white dementia caregivers: A comparison of their adaptation, adjustment, and service utilization. *Gerontologist, 32,* 375–381.

Hinton, J. (1975). The influence of previous personality on reactions to having terminal cancer. *Omega: Journal of Death and Dying, 6,* 95–111.

Hintze, J., Templer, D. I., Cappelletty, G. G., & Frederick, W. (1993). Death, depression, and death anxiety in HIV-infected males. *Death Studies, 17,* 333–341.

Hirshorn, B. A., & Hoyer, T. D. (1994). Private sector hiring and use of retirees: The firm's perspective. *Gerontologist, 34,* 50–58.

Hoberman, H., & Lewinsohn, P. (1989). Behavioral approaches to the treatment of unipolar depression. In American Psychiatric Association (Ed.), *Treatments of psychiatric disorders: A task force report of the American Psychiatric Association* (Vol. 3, pp. 1846–1862). Washington, DC: American Psychiatric Association.

Hochschild, A. (1989). *The second shift: Working parents and the revolution at home.* New York: Viking Press.

Hodgson, J. H., & Quinn, J. L. (1980). The impact of the triage health care delivery system on client morale, independent living, and the cost of care. *Gerontologist, 20,* 364–371.

Hodgson, L. G. (1992). Adult grandchildren and their grandparents: Their enduring bond. *International Journal of Aging and Human Development, 34,* 209–225.

Holden, J. (1993). Demographics, attitudes, and afterlife beliefs of right-to-life and right-to-die organization members. *Journal of Social Psychology, 133,* 521–527.

Holden, K. C., & Smock, P. J. (1991). The economic costs of marital dissolution: Why do women bear a disproportionate cost? *Annual Review of Sociology, 17,* 51–78.

Holland, C. (1995). Memory changes in older people. In F. Glendenning & I. Stuart-Hamilton (Eds.), *Learning and cognition in later life* (pp. 74–94). Brookfield, VT: Ashgate.

Holland, C. A., & Rabbitt, P. M. (1991). Ageing memory: Use versus impairment. *British Journal of Psychology, 82,* 29–38.

Holland, J. L. (1985). *Making vocational choices: A theory of careers* (2nd ed.). Englewood Cliffs, NJ: Prentice-Hall.

Hollon, S. D., DeRubeis, R. J., & Seligman, M. E. P. (1992). Cognitive therapy and the prevention of depression. *Applied and Preventive Psychology, 1*, 89–95.

Holt, P. R., Heller, T. D., & Richardson, A. G. (1991). Food restriction retards age-related biochemical changes in rat small intestine. *Journals of Gerontology, 46*, B89–B94.

Honeycutt, J. M. (1993). Marital happiness, divorce status, and partner differences in attributions about communication behaviors. *Journal of Divorce and Remarriage, 21*, 177–201.

Honeycutt, J. M., Woods, B. L., & Fontenot, K. (1993). The endorsement of communication conflict rules as a function of engagement, marriage, and marital ideology. *Journal of Social and Personal Relationships, 10*, 285–304.

Hooker, K., & Kaus, C. R. (1994). Health-related possible selves in young and middle adulthood. *Psychology and Aging, 9*, 126–133.

Hopper, J. (1993). The rhetoric of motives in divorce. *Journal of Marriage and the Family, 55*, 801–813.

Horn, J. L. (1970). Organization of data on life-span development of human abilities. In L. R. Goulet & P. B. Baltes (Eds.), *Life-span development psychology: Research and theory* (pp. 423–466). New York: Academic Press.

Horn, J. L., & Hofer, S. M. (1992). Major abilities and development in the adulthood period. In R. J. Sternberg & C. A. Berg (Eds.), *Intellectual development* (pp. 44–99). New York: Cambridge University Press.

Horner, K. L., Rushton, J. P., & Vernon, P. A. (1986). Relation between aging and research productivity of academic psychologists. *Psychology and Aging, 1*, 319–324.

House, J. S., Kessler, R. C., Herzog, A. R., Mero, R. P., Kinney, A. M., & Breslow, M. J. (1992). Social stratification, age, and health. In K. W. Schaie, D. G. Blazer, & J. S. House (Eds.), *Aging, health behaviors, and health outcomes* (pp. 1–32). Hillsdale, NJ: Erlbaum.

Houston, B. K. (1988). Cardiovascular and neuroendocrine reactivity, global Type A, and components of Type A behavior. In B. K. Houston & C. R. Snyder (Eds.), *Type A behavior pattern: Research, theory, and intervention* (pp. 212–253). New York: John Wiley & Sons.

Houston, B. K., & Snyder, C. R. (Eds.). (1988). *Type A behavior pattern: Research, theory, and intervention*. New York: John Wiley & Sons.

Howard, A., & Bray, D. W. (1988). *Managerial lives in transition: Advancing age and changing times*. New York: Guilford Press.

Hughes, D. L., & Galinsky, E. (1994). Gender, job and family conditions, and psychological symptoms. *Psychology of Women Quarterly, 18*, 251–270.

Hulicka, I. M. (1967). Age differences in retention as a function of interference. *Journal of Gerontology, 22*, 180–184.

Hultsch, D. F., & Dixon, R. A. (1990). Learning and memory in aging. In J. E. Birren & K. W. Schaie (Eds.), *Handbook of the psychology of aging* (3rd ed., pp. 258–274). San Diego: Academic Press.

Hultsch, D. F., Hammer, M., & Small, B. J. (1993). Age differences in cognitive performance in later life: Relationships to self-reported health and activity life style. *Journals of Gerontology, 48*, P1–P11.

Hultsch, D. F., Masson, M. E., & Small, B. J. (1991). Adult age differences in direct and indirect tests of memory. *Journals of Gerontology, 46*, P22–P30.

Humes, L. E., & Christopherson, L. (1991). Speech identification difficulties of hearing-impaired elderly persons: The contributions of auditory processing deficits. *Journal of Speech and Hearing Research, 34*, 686–693.

Huston, M., & Schwartz, P. (1995). The relationships of lesbians and of gay men. In J. T. Wood & S. Duck (Eds.), *Under-studied relationships: Off the beaten track* (pp. 89–121). Thousand Oaks, CA: Sage.

I

Idler, E. L. (1993). Age differences in self-assessments of health: Age changes, cohort differences, or survivorship? *Journals of Gerontology, 48*, S289–S300.

Ingram, D. K., Cutler, R. G., Weindruch, R., Renquist, D. M., Knapka, J. J., April, M., Belcher, C. T., Clark, M. A., Hatcherson, C. D., Marriott, B. M., & Roth, G. S. (1990). Dietary restriction and aging: The initiation of a primate study. *Journals of Gerontology, 45*, B148–B163.

Irion, J. C., & Blanchard-Fields, F. (1987). A cross sectional comparison of adaptive coping in adulthood. *Journal of Gerontology, 42*, 502–504.

J

Jacewicz, M. M., & Hartley, A. A. (1987). Age differences in the speed of cognitive operations: Resolution of inconsistent findings. *Journal of Gerontology, 42*, 86–88.

Jackson, J. S., Antonucci, T. C., & Gibson, R. C. (1990). Cultural, racial, and ethnic minority influences on aging. In J. E. Birren & K. W. Schaie (Eds.), *Handbook of the psychology of aging* (3rd ed., pp. 103–123). San Diego: Academic Press.

Jacobson, N., & Holtzworth-Monroe, A. (1986). Marital therapy: A social learning, cognitive perspective. In N. S. Jacobson & A. S. Gurman (Eds.), *Clinical handbook of marital therapy* (pp. 29–75). New York: Guilford Press.

Jacobson, N. S., & Gurman, A. S. (Eds.). (1986). *Clinical handbook of marital therapy*. New York: Guilford Press.

Jantz, R. K., Seefeldt, C., Galper, A., & Serock, K. (1976). *Children's attitudes towards the elderly: Final report*. College Park: University of Maryland.

Jarrett, R., & Rush, A. (1989). Cognitive-behavioral psychotherapy for depression. In American Psychiatric Association (Eds.), *Treatments of psychiatric disorders: A task force report of the American Psychiatric Association* (Vol. 3, pp. 1834–1845). Washington, DC: American Psychiatric Association.

Jarvik, L. F., & Falik, A. (1963). Intellectual stability and survival in the aged. *Journal of Gerontology, 18*, 173–176.

Jeanquart-Barone, S. (1993). Trust differences between supervisors and subordinates: Examining the role of race and gender. *Sex Roles, 29*, 1–11.

Jecker, N. S., & Schneiderman, L. J. (1994). Is dying young worse than dying old? *Gerontologist, 34*, 66–72.

Jeffers, F. C., & Verwoerdt, A. (1977). How the old face death. In E. W. Busse & E. Pfeiffer (Eds.), *Behavior and adaptation in later life* (pp. 142–157). Boston: Little, Brown.

Jencks, C. (1992). *Rethinking social policy*. Cambridge: Harvard University Press.

Jendrek, M. P. (1993). Grandparents who parent their grandchildren: Effects on lifestyle. *Journal of Marriage and the Family, 55*, 609–621.

Jendrek, M. P. (1994). Grandparents who parent their grandchildren: Circumstances and decisions. *Gerontologist, 34*, 206–216.

Jenkins, S. R., & Maslach, C. (1994). Psychological health and involvement in interpersonally demanding occupations: A longitudinal perspective. *Journal of Organizational Behavior, 15*, 101–127.

Jette, A. M., & Branch, L. G. (1992). A ten-year follow-up of driving patterns among the community-dwelling elderly. *Human Factors, 34*, 25–31.

Jette, A. M., Branch, L. G., & Berlin, J. (1990). Musculoskeletal impairments and physical disablement among the aged. *Journals of Gerontology, 45*, M203–M208.

Jette, A. M., Tennstedt, S., & Crawford, S. (1995). How does formal and informal community care affect nursing home use? *Journals of Gerontology, 50B*, S4–S12.

Jewell, K. S. (1988). *Survival of the black family: The institutional impact of U.S. social policy.* New York: Praeger.

Johnson, C. L. (1983). Dyadic family relationships and social supports. *Gerontologist, 23*, 377–383.

Johnson, C. L. (1985a). Grandparenting options in divorcing families: An anthropological perspective. In V. L. Bengtson & J. Robertson (Eds.), *Grandparenthood* (pp. 81–96), Beverly Hills, CA: Sage.

Johnson, C. L. (1985b). The impact of illness on late-life marriages. *Journal of Marriage and the Family, 47*, 165–173.

Johnson, C. L., & Barer, B. M. (1987). Marital instability and the changing kinship networks of grandparents. *Gerontologist, 27*, 330–335.

Johnson, C. L., & Catalano, D. (1983). A longitudinal study of family supports to impaired elderly. *Gerontologist, 23*, 612–618.

Johnson, C. L., & Troll, L. E. (1994). Constraints and facilitators to friendships in late late life. *Gerontologist, 34*, 79–87.

Jones, L. C. (1985). Father infant relationships in the first year of life. In S. M. Hanson & F. W. Bozett (Eds.), *Dimensions of fatherhood* (pp. 92–114). Newbury Park, CA: Sage.

K

Kaakinen, J. R. (1992). Living with silence. *Gerontologist, 32*, 258–264.

Kahana, E. A., & Coe, R. M. (1969). Perceptions of grandparenthood by community and institutionalized aged. *Proceedings of the 77th Annual Convention of the American Psychological Association, 4*, 736–737.

Kahn, A. J., & Kamerman, S. B. (1988). Child support in the United States: The problem. In A. J. Kahn and S. B. Kamerman (Eds.), *Child support: From debt collection to social policy* (pp. 10–19). Newbury Park, CA: Sage.

Kahn, R. L., Zarit, S. H., Hilbert, N. M., & Niederehe, G. (1975). Memory complaint and impairment in the aged: The effect of depression and altered brain function. *Archives of General Psychiatry, 32*, 1569–1573.

Kamerman, S. B., & Kahn, A. J. (1988). *Mothers alone: Strategies for a time of change.* Dover, MA: Auburn House.

Kamo, Y. (1993). Determinants of marital satisfaction: A comparison of the United States and Japan. *Journal of Social and Personal Relationships, 10*, 551–568.

Kane, A. C., & Hogan, J. D. (1985–1986). Death anxiety in physicians: Defensive style, medical specialty, and exposure to death. *Omega: Journal of Death and Dying, 16*, 11–22.

Kane, R. A. (1995–1996). Transforming care institutions for the frail elderly: Out of one shall be many. *Generations, 19*, 62–68.

Kane, R. A., & Caplan, A. L. (Eds.). (1990). *Everyday ethics: Resolving dilemmas in nursing home life.* New York: Springer.

Kane, R. L., Solomon, D. H., Beck, J. C., Keeler, E., & Kane, R. A. (1981). *Geriatrics in the United States: Manpower projections and training considerations.* Lexington, MA: Heath.

Kanner, A. D., Coyne, J. C., Schaefer, C., & Lazarus, R. S. (1981). Comparison of two modes of stress measurement: Daily hassles and uplifts versus major life events. *Journal of Behavioral Medicine, 4*, 1–39.

Kaplan, G. (1986, August). *Aging, health, and behavior: Evidence from the Alameda County Study.* Paper presented at the 94th Annual Meeting of the American Psychological Association, Washington, DC.

Kaplan, G. A. (1992). Health and aging in the Alameda County Study. In K. W. Schaie, D. G. Blazer, & J. S. House (Eds.), *Aging, health behaviors, and health outcomes* (pp. 69–95). Hillsdale, NJ: Erlbaum.

Kaplan, G. A., Seeman, T. E., Cohen, R. D., Knudsen, L. P., & Guralnik, J. (1987). Mortality among the elderly in the Alameda County Study: Behavioral and demographic risk factors. *American Journal of Public Health, 77*, 307–312.

Kapp, M. B. (1991). Health care decision making by the elderly: I get by with a little help from my family. *Gerontologist, 31*, 619–623.

Karger, H. I., & Stoetz, D. (1994). *American social welfare policy: A pluralist approach.* New York: Longman.

Kart, C. S., Metress, E. K., & Metress, S. P. (1992). *Human aging and chronic disease.* Boston: Jones & Bartlett.

Kastenbaum, R. (1976–1977). Toward standards of care for the terminally ill. III: A few guiding principles. *Omega: Journal of Death and Dying, 7*, 191–193.

Kastenbaum, R., & Costa, P. (1977). Psychological perspectives on death. *Annual Review of Psychology, 28*, 225–249.

Kaufman, S. (1986). *The ageless self: Sources of meaning in late life.* Madison: University of Wisconsin Press.

Kauser, T., & Wister, A. (1984). Living arrangements of older women: The ethnic dimension. *Journal of Marriage and the Family, 46*, 301–311.

Kausler, D. H. (1990). Motivation, human aging, and cognitive performance. In J. E. Birren & K. W. Schaie (Eds.), *Handbook of the psychology of aging* (3rd ed., pp. 171–182). San Diego: Academic Press.

Kelly, E. L., & Conley, J. J. (1987). Personality and compatibility: A prospective analysis of marital stability and marital satisfaction. *Journal of Personality and Social Psychology, 52*, 27–40.

Kelly, J. (1991). Parent interaction after divorce: Comparison of mediated and adversarial divorce processes. *Behavioral Sciences and the Law, 9*, 387–398.

Kemnitz, J. W., Weindruck, R., Roecker, E. B., Crawford, K., Kaufman, P. L., & Ershler, W. B. (1993). Dietary restriction of adult male rhesus monkeys: Design, methodology, and preliminary findings from the first year of study. *Journals of Gerontology, 48*, B17–B26.

Kendler, K. S., Heath, A. C., Neale, M. C., Kessler, R. C., & Eaves, L. J. (1993a). Alcoholism and major depression in women: A twin study of the causes of comorbidity. *Archives of General Psychiatry, 50*, 690–698.

Kendler, K. S., Heath, A. C., Neale, M. C., Kessler, R. C., & Eaves, L. J. (1993b). A longitudinal twin study of 1-year prevalence of major depression in women. *Archives of General Psychiatry, 50*, 843–852.

Kendler, K. S., Kessler, R. C., Neale, M. C., Heath, A. C., & Eaves, L. J. (1993). The prediction of major depression in women: Toward an integrated etiologic model. *American Journal of Psychiatry, 150*, 1139–1148.

Kennedy, G. E. (1990). College students' expectations of grandparent and grandchild role behaviors. *Gerontologist, 30*, 43–48.

Kenrick, D. T., Groth, G. E., Trost, M. R., & Sadalla, E. K. (1993). Integrating evolutionary and social exchange perspectives on relationships: Effects of gender, self-appraisal, and involvement level on mate selection criteria. *Journal of Personality and Social Psychology, 64*, 951–969.

Kerski, D., Drinka, T., Carnes, M., Golob, K., & Craig, W. A. (1987). Postgeriatric evaluation unit follow-up: Team versus nonteam. *Journal of Gerontology, 42,* 191–195.

Kessler, R. C., Foster, C., Webster, P. S., & House, J. S. (1992). The relationship between age and depressive symptoms in two national surveys. *Psychology and Aging, 7,* 119–126.

Kessler, R. C., & Magee, W. (1994). Childhood family violence and adult recurrent depression. *Journal of Health and Social Behavior, 35,* 13–27.

Kessler, R. C., McGonagle, K. A., Zhao, S., Nelson, C. B., Hughes, R., Eshleman, S., Wittchen, H., & Kendler, K. S. (1994). Lifetime and 12 month prevalence of *DSM III-R* psychiatric disorders in the United States: Results from the National Comorbidity Study. *Archives of General Psychiatry, 51,* 8–19.

Kessler, R. C., & Price, R. (1993). Primary prevention of secondary disorders: A proposal and agenda. *American Journal of Community Psychology, 21,* 607–633.

Kimble, G. A. (1993). Evolution of the nature-nurture issue in the history of psychology. In R. Plomin & G. E. McClearn (Eds.), *Nature, nurture, and psychology* (pp. 3–25). Washington, DC: American Psychological Association.

Kimmel, D. (1974). *Adulthood and aging: An interdisciplinary, developmental view.* New York: Wiley.

Kinsey, A., & Associates. (1953). *Sexual behavior in the human female.* Philadelphia: Saunders.

Kipshidze, N. N., Pivovarova, I. P., Dzorbenadze, D. A., Agadzanov, A. S., & Shavgulidez, N. A. (1987). The longevous people of Soviet Georgia. In G. Lesnoff-Caravaglia (Ed.), *Realistic expectations for long life* (pp. 83–110). New York: Human Sciences Press.

Kirschenman, J., & Neckerman, K. M. (1991). "We'd love to hire them, but. . . .": The meaning of race for employers. In C. J. Jencks & P. E. Peterson (Eds.), *The urban underclass* (pp. 203–235). Washington, DC: Brookings Institution.

Kitson, G. C., & Morgan, L. A. (1990). The multiple consequences of divorce: A decade review. *Journal of Marriage and the Family, 52,* 913–924.

Kitzman, D. W., & Edwards, W. D. (1990). Minireview: Age-related changes in the anatomy of the normal heart. *Journals of Gerontology, 45,* M33–M39.

Kiyak, H. A., & Borson, S. (1992). Coping with chronic illness and disability. In M. G. Ory, R. P. Abeles, & P. D. Lipman (Eds.), *Aging, health, and behavior* (pp. 141–173). Newbury Park, CA: Sage.

Klenow, D. J. (1991–1992). Emotion and life threatening illness: A typology of hope sources. *Omega: Journal of Death and Dying, 24,* 49–60.

Klenow, D. J., & Bolin, R. C. (1989–1990). Belief in an afterlife: A national survey. *Omega: Journal of Death and Dying, 20,* 63–74.

Klerman, G. (1989). Mood disorders, In American Psychiatric Association (Ed.), *Treatments of psychiatric disorders: A task force report of the American Psychiatric Association,* (Vol. 3, pp. 1726–1744). Washington, DC: American Psychiatric Association.

Kline, D. W., Kline, T. J., Fozard, J. L., Kosnik, W., Schieber, A., & Seckuler, R. (1992). Vision, aging, and driving: The problems of older drivers. *Journals of Gerontology, 47,* P27–P34.

Kline, D. W., & Scialfa, C. T. (1996). Visual and auditory aging. In J. E. Birren & K. W. Schaie (Eds.), *Handbook of the psychology of aging* (4th ed., pp. 181–203). San Diego: Academic Press.

Kobak, R. R., & Hazan, C. (1991). Attachment in marriage: Effects of security and accuracy of working models. *Journal of Personality and Social Psychology, 60,* 861–869.

Kogan, N., & Wallach, M. A. (1961). Age changes in values and attitudes. *Journal of Gerontology, 16,* 272–280.

Kohn, R. (1978). *Principles of mammalian aging* (2nd ed.). Englewood Cliffs, NJ: Prentice-Hall.

Kosnik, W. D., Sekuler, R., & Kline, D. W. (1990). Self-reported visual problems of older drivers. *Human Factors, 32,* 597–608.

Kosorok, M. R., Omenn, G. S., Diehr, P., Koepsell, T. D., & Patrick, D. L. (1992). Restricted activity days among older adults. *American Journal of Public Health, 82,* 1263–1267.

Krause, N. (1989). Issues of measurement and analysis in studies of social support, aging and health. In K. S. Markides & C. L. Cooper (Eds.), *Aging, stress, and health* (pp. 43–66). Chichester, England: John Wiley & Sons.

Krynski, M. D., Tymchuk, A. J., & Ouslander, J. G. (1994). How informed can consent be? New light on comprehension among elderly people making decisions about enteral tube feeding. *Gerontologist, 34,* 36–43.

Kubler-Ross, E. (1969). *On death and dying.* New York: Macmillan.

Kulis, S. S. (1992). Social class and the locus of reciprocity in relationships with adult children. *Journal of Family Issues, 13,* 482–504.

Kurdek, L. A. (1991). Marital stability and changes in marital quality in newly wed couples: A test of the contextual model. *Journal of Social and Personal Relationships, 8,* 27–48.

Kuypers, J. H., & Bengtson, V. L. (1983). Toward competence in the older family. In T. H. Brubaker (Ed.), *Family relationships in later life* (pp. 211–228). Beverly Hills, CA: Sage.

L

Labouvie-Vief, G. (1992). A neo-Piagetian perspective on adult cognitive development. In R. J. Sternberg & C. A. Berg (Eds.), *Intellectual development* (pp. 197–228). New York: Cambridge University Press.

Labouvie-Vief, G., Hakim-Larson, J., & Hobart, C. J. (1987). Age, ego level, and the life-span development of coping and defense processes. *Psychology and Aging, 2,* 286–293.

Labouvie-Vief, G. V. (1985). Intelligence and cognition. In J. E. Birren & K. W. Schaie (Eds.), *Handbook of the psychology of aging* (2nd ed., pp. 500–530). New York: Van Nostrand Reinhold.

Labus, J. G., & Dambrot, F. H. (1985–1986). A comparative study of terminally ill hospice and hospital patients. *Omega: Journal of Death and Dying, 16,* 225–232.

Lachman, M. E. (1991). Perceived control over memory aging: Developmental and intervention perspectives. *Journal of Social Issues, 47,* 159–175.

Lakatta, E. G. (1987). The aging heart: Myths and realities. In J. W. Elias & P. H. Marshall (Eds.), *Cardiovascular disease and behavior. Series in health psychology and behavioral medicine* (pp. 179–193). Washington, DC: Hemisphere.

Lamb, M. E. (1986). The changing role of fathers. In M. E. Lamb (Ed.), *The father's role: Applied perspectives* (pp. 4–29). New York: Wiley.

Lane, N. E., Bloch, D. A., Jones, H. H., Marshall, W. H., Wood, P. D., & Fries, J. F. (1986). Long-distance running, bone density, and osteoarthritis. *Journal of the American Medical Association, 255,* 1147–1154.

Lang, A. M., & Brody, E. M. (1983). Characteristics of middle aged daughters and help to their elderly mothers. *Journal of Marriage and the Family, 45,* 193–202.

Larson, J. H., & Holman, T. B. (1994). Premarital predictions of marital quality and stability. *Family Relations, 43,* 228–237.

Larson, J. H., Wilson, S. M., & Beley, R. (1994). The impact of job insecurity on marital and family relationships. *Family Relations, 43,* 138–143.

Lauer, R. H., Lauer, J. C., & Kerr, S. T. (1990). The long-term marriage: Perceptions of stability and satisfaction. *International Journal of Aging and Human Development, 31,* 189–195.

Lavee, Y., & Olson, D. H. (1993). Seven types of marriage: Empirical typology based on ENRICH. *Journal of Marital and Family Therapy, 19,* 325–340.

Lawton, L., Silverstein, M., & Bengtson, V. (1994). Affection, social contact, and geographic distance between adult children and their parents. *Journal of Marriage and the Family, 56,* 57–68.

Lawton, M. P. (1975). *Planning and managing housing for the elderly.* New York: Wiley.

Leana, C. R., & Feldman, D. C. (1991). Gender differences in responses to unemployment. *Journal of Vocational Behavior, 38,* 65–77.

Leary, W. E. (1988, February 25). The new hearing aids: Nearly invisible devices filtering sound. *The New York Times,* p. B6.

Lebowitz, B. D. (1993). Mental health and aging: Federal perspectives. *Generations, 17*(1), 65–68.

Lee, G. R., Dwyer, J. W., & Coward, R. T. (1993). Gender differences in parent care: Demographic factors and same gender preferences. *Journals of Gerontology, 48,* S9–S16.

Lee, G. R., & Ellithorpe, E. (1982). Intergenerational exchange and subjective well-being among the elderly. *Journal of Marriage and the Family, 44,* 217–224.

Leiblum, S. R. (1990). Sexuality and the midlife woman. *Psychology of Women Quarterly, 14,* 495–508.

Lemon, B. W., Bengtson, V. L., & Peterson, J. A. (1972). An exploration of the activity theory of aging, activity types and life satisfaction among in-movers to a retirement community. *Journal of Gerontology, 27,* 511–523.

Lesnoff-Caravaglia, G., & Klys, M. (1987). Lifestyle and longevity. In G. Lesnoff-Caravaglia (Ed.), *Realistic expectations for long life.* New York: Human Sciences Press.

Lester, P., & Becker, P. (1992–1993). College students' attitudes toward death today as compared to the 1930's. *Omega: Journal of Death and Dying, 26,* 219–222.

Levant, R. F. (1988). Education for fatherhood. In P. Bronstein & C. P. Cowan (Eds.), *Fatherhood today: Men's*

changing role in the family (pp. 253–275). New York: John Wiley & Sons.

Levenson, R. W., Carstensen, L. L., & Gottman, J. M. (1993). Long-term marriage: Age, gender, and satisfaction. *Psychology and Aging, 8,* 301–313.

Leventhal, H., Leventhal, E. A., & Schaefer, P. M. (1992). Vigilant coping and health behavior. In M. G. Ory, R. P. Abeles, & P. D. Lipman (Eds.), *Aging, health, and behavior* (pp. 109–140). Newbury Park, CA: Sage.

LeVine, R. A., & White, M. (1987). Parenthood in social transformation. In J. B. Lancaster, J. Altmann, A. S. Rossi, & L. R. Sherrod (Eds.), *Parenting across the life span: Biosocial dimensions* (pp. 271–293). Hawthorne, NY: Aldine.

Levitan, S., & Conway, E. (1990). *Families in flux: New approaches to meeting work-force challenges for child, elder, and health care in the 1990's.* Washington, DC: Bureau of National Affairs.

Levitt, M. J., Weber, R. A., & Guacci, N. (1993). Convoys of social support: An intergenerational analysis. *Psychology and Aging, 8,* 323–326.

Lewin-Epstein, N. (1991). Determinants of regular source of health care in black, Mexican, Puerto Rican, and non-Hispanic white populations. *Medical Care, 29,* 543–557.

Lichtenberg, P. A., Ross, T., Millis, S. R., & Manning, C. A. (1995). The relationship between depression and cognition in older adults: A cross-validation study. *Journals of Gerontology, 50,* P25–P32.

Lichter, D. T., McLaughlin, D. K., Kephart, G., & Landry, D. J. (1992). Race and the retreat from marriage: A shortage of marriageable men? *American Sociological Review, 57,* 781–799.

Lieberman, M. A., & Fisher, L. (1995). The impact of chronic illness on the health and well-being of family members. *Gerontologist, 35,* 94–102.

Lieberman, M. A., & Tobin, S. S. (1983). *The experience of old age: Stress, coping and survival.* New York: Basic Books.

Liebowitz, N. R., Kranzler, H. R., & Meyer, R. E. (1990). Pharmacologic approaches to alcoholism treatment. *Alcohol Health and Research World, 14,* 144–153.

Light, K. E., & Spirduso, W. W. (1990). Effects of adult aging on the movement complexity factor of response programming. *Journals of Gerontology, 45,* P107–P109.

Light, L. L. (1991). Memory and aging: Four hypotheses in search of data. *Annual Review of Psychology, 42,* 333–376.

Lindemann, E. (1944). Symptomatology and management of acute grief. *American Journal of Psychiatry, 101,* 141–148.

Lindenberger, U., & Baltes, P. B. (1994). Sensory functioning and intelligence in old age: A strong connection. *Psychology and Aging, 9,* 339–355.

Lipsitz, L. A. (1995–1996). The teaching nursing home: Accomplishments and future directions. *Generations, 19*(1), 47–51.

Litwak, E., & Longino, C. F. (1987). Migration patterns among the elderly: A developmental perspective. *Gerontologist, 27,* 266–272.

Liu, K., & Manton, K. G. (1991). Nursing home length of stay and spend-down in Connecticut, 1977–1986. *Gerontologist, 31,* 165–173.

Loevinger, J. (1976). *Ego development: Conceptions and theories.* San Francisco: Jossey-Bass.

Loevinger, J., & Wessler, R. (1970). *Measuring ego development.* San Francisco: Jossey-Bass.

Lopata, H. (1973). *Widowhood in an American city.* Cambridge, MA: Schenkman.

Lopata, H. (1979). *Women as widows: Support systems.* Cambridge, MA: Schenkman.

Loscocco, K. (1990). Career structures and employee commitment. *Social Science Quarterly, 71,* 54–68.

Loscocco, K. A., & Roschelle, A. R. (1991). Influences on the quality of work and nonwork life: Two decades in review. *Journal of Vocational Behavior, 39,* 182–225.

Lowenthal, M. F., Thurnher, M., Chiriboga, D., & Associates (1975). *Four stages of life: A comparative study of women and men facing transitions.* San Francisco: Jossey-Bass.

Lund, D. A., Caserta, M. S., & Dimond, M. F. (1986). Gender differences through two years of bereavement among the elderly. *Gerontologist, 26,* 314–320.

Luszex, M., & Fitzgerald, M. (1986). Understanding cohort differences in cross generational self and peer perceptions. *Journal of Gerontology, 41,* 234–240.

Lye, D. N., & Biblarz, T. J. (1993). The effects of attitudes toward family life and gender roles on marital satisfaction. *Journal of Family Issues, 14,* 157–188.

Lyness, S. A. (1993). Predictors of differences between Type A and B individuals in heart rate and blood pressure reactivity. *Psychological Bulletin, 114,* 266–295.

Lyness, S., Eaton, E. M., & Schneider, L. S. (1994). Cognitive performance in older and middle-aged depressed outpatients and controls. *Journals of Gerontology, 49,* P129–P136.

M

Maas, H. S., & Kuypers, J. A. (1975). *From thirty to seventy: A forty year study of adult lifestyles and personality.* San Francisco: Jossey-Bass.

Madden, D. J. (1990). Adult age differences in the time course of visual attention. *Journals of Gerontology, 45,* P9–P16.

Maddox, G. L. (1991). Aging with a difference. *Aging Well, 1,* 7–10.

Maddox, G. L., & Clark, D. O. (1992). Trajectories of functional impairment in later life. *Journal of Health and Social Behavior, 33,* 114–125.

Magaziner, J., Simonsick, E. M., Kashner, M., Hebel, J. R., & Kenzora, J. E. (1990). Predictors of functional recovery one year following hospital discharge for hip fracture: A prospective study. *Journals of Gerontology, 45,* M101–M107.

Malcolm, A. T., & Janisse, M. P. (1991). Additional evidence for the relationship between Type A behavior and social support in men. *Behavioral Medicine, 17,* 131–133.

Mallinckrodt, B., & Fretz, B. R. (1988). Social support and the impact of job loss on older professionals. *Journal of Counseling Psychology, 35,* 281–286.

Mancini, J. A. (1984). Research on family life in old age: Exploring the frontiers. In W. H. Quinn & G. A. Hughston (Eds.), *Independent aging: Family and social systems perspectives* (pp. 58–71). Rockville, MD: Aspen.

Manton, K. G. (1990). Population models of gender differences in mortality, morbidity, and disability risks. In M. G. Ory & H. R. Warner (Eds.), *Gender, health, and longevity: Multidisciplinary perspectives* (pp. 201–253). New York: Springer.

Manton, K. G., Patrick, C. H., & Johnson, K. W. (1989). Health differentials between blacks and whites: Recent trends in mortality and morbidity. In D. P. Willis (Ed.), *Health policies and black Americans* (pp. 129–199). New Brunswick, NJ: Transaction.

Manton, K. G., & Suzman, R. (1992). Forecasting health and functioning in aging societies: Implications for health care and staffing needs. In M. G. Ory, R. P. Abeles, & P. D. Lipman (Eds.), *Aging, health, and behavior* (pp. 327–357). Newbury Park, CA: Sage.

Manton, K. G., Wrigley, J. M., Cohen, H. J., & Woodbury, M. A. (1991). Cancer mortality, aging, and patterns of comorbidity in the United States: 1968 to 1986. *Journals of Gerontology, 46,* S225–S234.

Manuck, S. B., Muldoon, M. F., Kaplan, J. R., Adams, M. R., & Polefrone, J. M. (1989). Coronary artery atherosclerosis and cardiac response to stress in cynomolgus monkeys. In A. W. Siegman & T. M. Dembroski (Eds.), *In search of the coronary prone behavior: Beyond Type A* (pp. 207–223). Hillsdale, NJ: Erlbaum.

Mare, R. D., & Winship, C. (1991). Socioeconomic change and the decline of marriage for blacks and whites. In C. J. Jencks and P. E. Peterson (Eds.), *The urban underclass* (pp. 175–202). Washington, DC: Brookings Institution.

Markides, K. S. (Ed.). (1989). *Aging and health: Perspectives on gender, race, ethnicity, and class.* Newbury Park, CA: Sage.

Markides, K. S., & Cooper, C. L. (Eds.). (1989). *Aging, stress, and health.* Chichester, England: John Wiley & Sons.

Markides, K. S., Coreil, J., & Rogers, L. P. (1989). Aging and health among Southwestern Hispanics. In K. S. Markides (Ed.), *Aging and health: Perspectives on gender, race, ethnicity, and class* (pp. 177–210). Newbury Park, CA: Sage.

Markus, H., & Nurius, P. (1986). Possible selves. *American Psychologist, 41,* 954–969.

Marlatt, G. A., & Gordon, J. R. (1985). *Relapse prevention.* New York: Guilford Press.

Martin, C. E. (1981). Factors affecting sexual functioning in 60–79 year old married males. *Archives of Sexual Behavior, 10,* 399–420.

Marx, J. (1991). New clue found to Alztheimer's. *Science, 253,* 857–858.

Marx, J. (1992). Major setback for Alzheimer's models. *Science, 255,* 1200–1202.

Masters, W. H., & Johnson, V. E. (1966). *Human sexual response.* Boston: Little, Brown.

Matthews, S. H., & Sprey, J. (1985). Adolescents' relationships with grandparents: An empirical contribution to conceptual clarification. *Journal of Gerontology, 40,* 621–626.

Mattoon, M. A. (1981). *Jungian psychology in perspective.* New York: Free Press.

Mazess, R. B., & Forman, S. H. (1979). Longevity and age exaggeration in Vilcabamba, Ecuador. *Journal of Gerontology, 34,* 94–98.

McAdams, D. P. (1992). The five-factor model in personality: A critical appraisal. *Journal of Personality, 60,* 329–361.

McAdams, D. P. (1994). *The person: An introduction to personality psychology* (2nd ed). San Diego: Harcourt Brace Jovanovich.

McAdams, D. P., & de St. Aubin, E. D. S. (1992). A theory of generativity and its assessment through self-report, behavioral acts, and narrative themes in autobiography. *Journal of Personality and Social Psychology, 62,* 1003–1015.

McAdams, D. P., de St. Aubin, E., & Logan, R. (1993). Generativity among young, middle aged and older adults. *Psychology and Aging, 8,* 221–230.

McAdoo, J. L. (1988). Changing perspectives on the role of the black father. In P. Bronstein & C. P. Cowan (Eds.), *Fatherhood today: Men's changing role in the family* (pp. 79–92). New York: John Wiley & Sons.

McClearn, G. E. (1993). Behavioral genetics: The last century and the next. In R. Plomin & G. E. McClearn (Eds.), *Nature, nurture, and psychology* (pp. 27–49). Washington, DC: American Psychological Association.

McCrae, R. (1982). Age differences in the use of coping mechanisms. *Journal of Gerontology, 37,* 454–460.

McCrae, R., & Costa, P. T. (1988). Recalled parent-child relations and adult personality. *Journal of Personality, 56,* 417–434.

McCrae, R. R., & Costa, P. T., Jr. (1990). *Personality in adulthood.* New York: Guilford Press.

McCrae, R. R., Costa, P. T., & Piedmont, R. L. (1993). Folk concepts, natural language, and psychological constructs: The California Psychological Inventory and the five-factor model. *Journal of Personality, 61,* 1–26.

McDermid, S., Huston, T., & McHale, S. M. (1990). Changes in marriages associated with the transition to parenthood: Individual differences as a function of sex-role attitudes and changes in the division of household labor. *Journal of Marriage and the Family, 52,* 475–486.

McGonagle, K. A., Kessler, R. C., & Schilling, E. A. (1992). The frequency and determinants of marital disagreements in a community sample. *Journal of Social and Personal Relationships, 9,* 507–524.

McGowen, D. F. (1993). *Living in the labyrinth.* New York: Delacourt Press.

McGrath, E., Keita, G. P., Strickland, B. R., & Russo, N. F. (Eds.). (1990). *Women and* depression: Risk factors and treatment issues. Washington, DC: American Psychological Association.

McGue, M. (1993). From proteins to cognitions: The behavioral genetics of alcoholism. In R. Plomin & G. E. McClearn (Eds.), Nature, nurture, and psychology (pp. 245–268). Washington, DC: American Psychological Association.

McGue, M., Hirsch, B., & Lykken, D. T. (1993). Age and the self-perception of ability: A twin study analysis. Psychology and Aging, 8, 72–80.

McGue, M., Vaupel, J. W., Holm, N., & Harvald, B. (1993). Longevity is moderately heritable in a sample of Danish twins born 1870–1880. Journals of Gerontology, 48, B237–B244.

McIntosh, J. L. (1992). Suicide of the elderly. In B. M. Bongar (Ed.), Suicide: Guidelines for assessment, management, and treatment (pp. 106–124). New York: Oxford University Press.

McKay, J. R., & Maisto, S. A. (1993). An overview and critique of advances in the treatment of alcohol use disorders. Drugs and Society, 8, 1–29.

McLannahan, S., & Adams, J. (1987). Parenthood and psychological well-being. Annual Review of Sociology, 13, 237–257.

Mehdizadeh, S. A., & Luzadis, R. A. (1994). The effect of job mobility on pension wealth. Gerontologist, 34, 173–179.

Mellman, M., Lazarus, E., & Rivlin, A. (1990). Family time, family values. In D. G. Blankenhorn, S. Bayme, & J. B. Elshtain (Eds.), Rebuilding the nest: A new commitment to the American family (pp. 73–92). Milwaukee: Family Service America.

Mental health and aging: Problems and prospects. (1993, Winter/Spring). Generations, 17 (1).

Metts, S., & Cupach, W. R. (1990). The influence of relationship beliefs and problem-solving responses on satisfaction in romantic relationships. Human Communication Research, 17, 170–185.

Meyer, B. J. F., & Rice, G. E. (1989). Prose processing in adulthood: The text, the reader and the task. In L. W. Poon, D. C. Rubin, & B. A. Wilson (Eds.), Everyday cognition in adulthood and late life (pp. 157–194). New York: Cambridge University Press.

Mezey, M., Ramsey, G. C., & Mitty, E. (1994). Making the PSDA work for the elderly. Generations, 18, 13–18.

Michael, R. T., Gagnon, J. H., Laumann, E. O., & Kolata, G. (1994). Sex in America. Boston: Little, Brown.

Michaels, G. Y., & Goldberg, W. (1988). The transition to parenthood: Current theory and research. New York: Cambridge University Press.

Midanik, L. T., Soghikian, K., Ransom, J. J., & Tekawa, I. S. (1995). The effect of retirement on mental health and health behaviors: The Kaiser Permanente Retirement Study. Journals of Gerontology, 50, S59–S61.

Milardo, R. M., Johnson, M. P., & Huston, T. L. (1983). Developing close relationships: Changing patterns of interaction between pair members and social networks. Journal of Personality and Social Psychology, 44, 964–976.

Miller, B., McFall, S., & Montgomery, A. (1991). The impact of elder health, caregiver involvement, and global stress on two dimensions of caregiver burden. Journals of Gerontology, 46, S9–S19.

Miller, M. V., & Hoppe, S. K. (1994). Attributions for job termination and psychological distress. Human Relations, 47, 307–327.

Miller, S., Blalock, J., & Ginsberg, H. (1984–1985). Children and the aged: Attitudes, contact, and discriminative ability. International Journal of Aging and Human Development, 19, 47–53.

Miller, T., & Cugliari, A. M. (1990). Withdrawing and withholding treatment: Policies in long-term care facilities. Gerontologist, 30, 462–468.

Mills, E. S. (1993). The story of Elderhostel. Hanover, NH: University Press of New England.

Miner, A. S., & Robinson, D. F. (1994). Organizational and population level learning as engines for career transitions. Journal of Organizational Behavior, 15, 345–364.

Minkler, M., & Roe, K. (1996). Grandparents as surrogate parents. Generations, 20(1), 34–38.

Minois, G. (1989). History of old age. Chicago: University of Chicago Press.

Mirvis, P. H., & Hall, D. T. (1994). Psychological success and the boundaryless career. Journal of Organizational Behavior, 15, 365–380.

Mitchell, D. B. (1989). How many memory systems? Evidence from aging. Journal of Experimental Psychology—Learning, Memory, and Cognition, 15, 31–49.

Mitchell, V., & Helson, R. (1990). Women's prime of life: Is it the 50s? Psychology of Women Quarterly, 14, 451–470.

Mitchell-Flynn, C., & Hutchinson, R. L. (1993). A longitudinal study of the problems and concerns of urban divorced

men. Journal of Divorce and Remarriage, 19, 161–182.

Moen, P., Robison, J., & Fields, V. (1994). Women's work and caregiving roles: A life course approach. Journals of Gerontology, 49, S176–S186.

Monea, H. E. (1978). The experiential approach in learning about sexuality and aging. In R. L. Solnick (Ed.), Sexuality and aging (pp. 115–131). Los Angeles: University of Southern California Press.

Montgomery, R. J. V., & Kosloski, K. (1994). A longitudinal analysis of nursing home placement for dependent elders cared for by spouses vs. adult children. Journals of Gerontology, 49, S62–S74.

Moon, H. (1975). Coronary arteries in fetuses, infants, and juveniles. Circulation, 15, 366.

Mor, V., Banaszak-Holl, J., & Zinn, J. (1995–1996). The trend toward specialization in nursing care facilities. Generations, 19(1), 24–29.

Moras, K., Craske, M. G., & Barlow, D. H. (1990). Behavioral and cognitive therapies for panic disorder. In M. Roth, R. Noyes, & G. D. Burrows (Eds.), Handbook of anxiety (pp. 311–323). New York: Elsevier.

Morgan, L. (1984). Changes in family interaction following widowhood. Journal of Marriage and the Family, 49, 323–331.

Morgan, L. A. (1989). Economic well-being following marital termination: A comparison of widowed and divorced women. Journal of Family Issues, 10, 86–101.

Morgan, L. A. (1991). After marriage ends: Economic consequences for midlife women. Newbury Park, CA: Sage.

Morris, R., & Bass, S. A. (1988). Toward a new paradigm about work and age. In R. Morris & S. A. Bass (Eds.), Retirement reconsidered (pp. 3–14). New York: Springer.

Morrison, R. S., & Meier, D. E. (1994). Physician assisted dying: Fashion public policy with an absence of data. Generations, 18 (4), 48–53.

Morrow, D., Leirer, V., Altiteri, P., & Fitzsimmons, C. (1994). When expertise reduces age differences in performance. Psychology and Aging, 9, 134–148.

Mote, P. L., Grizzle, J. M., Walford, R. L., & Spindler, S. R. (1991). Influence of age and caloric restriction on expression of hepatic genes for xenobiotic and oxygen metabolizing enzymes in the mouse. Journals of Gerontology, 46, B95–B100.

Mui, A. C. (1995). Caring for frail elderly parents: A comparison of adult sons and daughters. Gerontologist, 35, 86–93.

Multiple Risk Factor Intervention Trial Research Group. (1982). Multiple risk factors intervention trial: Risk factor changes and mortality results. *Journal of the American Medical Association, 248,* 1465–1477.

Munjack, D. J., & Moss, H. B. (1981). Affective disorder and alcoholism in families of agroraphobics. *Archives of General Psychiatry, 38,* 869–871.

Murphy, F. C., & Elders, M. J. (1992). Diabetes and the black community. In R. Braithwaite & S. E. Taylor (Eds.), *Health issues in the black community* (pp. 121–131). San Francisco: Jossey-Bass.

Murray, C. (1984). *Losing ground: American social policy, 1950–1980.* New York: Basic Books.

Murstein, B. (1980). Mate selection in the 1970s. *Journal of Marriage and the Family, 42,* 777–792.

Musante, L., Treiber, F. A., Davis, H., Strong, W. B., & Levy, M. (1992). Hostility: Relationship to lifestyle behaviors and physical risk factors. *Behavioral Medicine, 18,* 21–26.

Myerhoff, B. (1994). *Number our days.* New York: Meridian.

Myers, J. K., Weissman, M. N., Tischler, C. E., Holzer, C. E., III, Orvaschel, H., Anthony, J. C., Boyd, J. H., Burke, J. D., Jr., Kramer, M., & Stoltzman, R. (1984). Six month prevalence of psychiatric disorders in three communities. *Archives of General Psychiatry, 41,* 959–967.

N

Narikiyo, T. A., & Kameoka, V. A. (1992). Attributions of mental illness and judgments about help seeking among Japanese-American and white American students. *Journal of Counseling Psychology, 39,* 363–369.

Nathanson, C. A. (1990). The gender-mortality differential in developed countries: Demographic and sociocultural dimensions. In M. G. Ory & H. R. Warner (Eds.), *Gender, health, and longevity: Multidisciplinary perspectives* (pp. 3–23). New York: Springer.

National Center for Health Statistics. (1995). *Health, United States, 1994.* Hyattsville, MD: U.S. Public Health Service.

National Center for Health Statistics. (1995). *Healthy People 2000: Review, 1994.* Hyattsville, MD: U.S. Public Health Service.

National Institute on Aging. (1989). *Older and wiser* (NIH Publication No. 89-2797).

Bethesda, MD: National Institutes of Health.

National Institute on Aging. (1993). *With the passage of time: The Baltimore Longitudinal Study of Aging* (NIH Publication No. 93-3685). Bethesda, MD: National Institutes of Health.

Neely, A. S., & Backman, L. (1993). Long-term maintenance of gains from memory training in older adults: Two $3\frac{1}{2}$-year follow-up studies. *Journals of Gerontology, 48,* P233–P237.

Neugarten, B. L. (1977). Personality and aging. In J. E. Birren & K. W. Schaie (Eds.), *Handbook of the psychology of aging* (pp. 626–659). New York: Van Nostrand Reinhold.

Neugarten, B. L., & Associates (Eds.). (1964). *Personality in middle and late life.* New York: Atherton.

Neugarten, B. L., & Gutmann, D. L. (1964). Age-sex roles and personality in middle age: A thematic apperception study. In B. L. Neugarten & Associates (Eds.), *Personality in middle and late life* (pp. 58–89). New York: Atherton.

Neugarten, B. L., Havinghurst, R. J., & Tobin, S. S. (1968). Personality and patterns of aging. In B. L. Neugarten & Associates (Eds.), *Middle age and aging: A reader in social psychology* (pp. 173–177). Chicago: University of Chicago Press.

Neugarten, B. L., & Weinstein, K. K. (1964). The changing American grandparent. *Journal of Marriage and the Family, 26,* 199–204.

Nickel, J. T., & Chirikos, T. N. (1990). Functional disability of elderly patients with long-term coronary heart disease: A sex-stratified analysis. *Journals of Gerontology, 45,* S60–S68.

Nickles, R. W., & Hedgespeth, J. (1991). A generic model for divorce mediation. *Journal of Divorce and Remarriage, 17,* 157–169.

Noelker, L. S., & Poulshock, S. W. (1984). Intimacy: Factors affecting its development among members of a home for the aged. *International Journal of Aging and Human Development, 19,* 177–190.

Noell, E. (1995–1996). Design in nursing homes: Environment as a silent partner in caregiving. *Generations, 19*(1), 14–19.

Nuland, S. (1995). *How we die.* New York: Vintage.

Null, R. L. (1988). Model kitchen design for the low vision elderly community. *Journal of Visual Impairment and Blindness, 82,* 240–245.

The nursing home revisited. (1995–1996, Winter). *Generations, 19* (4).

O

O'Bryant, S. L. (1990–1991). Forewarning of a husband's death: Does it make a difference for older widows? *Omega: Journal of Death and Dying, 22,* 227–239.

O'Bryant, S. L., & Straw, L. B. (1991). Relationship of previous divorce and previous widowhood to older women's adjustment to recent widowhood. *Journal of Divorce and Remarriage, 15,* 49–67.

Ogilvie, D. M. (1987). Life satisfaction and identity structure in late middle aged men and women. *Psychology and Aging, 2,* 217–224.

O'Rand, A. M. (1988). Convergence, institutionalization, and bifurcation: Gender and the pension acquisition process. In G. L. Maddox & M. P. Lawton (Eds.), *Annual review of gerontology and geriatrics: Vol. 8. Varieties of aging* (pp. 132–155). New York: Springer.

Orgel, L. (1973). The maintenance of the accuracy of protein synthesis and its relevance to aging. *Proceedings of the National Academy of Science, 67,* 1496.

Ornstein, S., & Isabella, L. A. (1990). Age vs. stage models of career attitudes of women: A partial replication and extension. *Journal of Vocational Behavior, 36,* 1–19.

Orthner, D. K. (1990). The family in transition. In D. G. Blankenhorn, S. Bayme, & J. B. Elshtain (Eds.), *Rebuilding the nest: A new commitment to the American family* (pp. 93–118). Milwaukee: Family Service America.

Ory, M. G., & Warner, H. R. (Eds.). (1990). *Gender, health, and longevity: Multidisciplinary perspectives.* New York: Springer.

Ozer, D. J., & Reise, S. P. (1994). Personality assessment. *Annual Review of Psychology, 45,* 357–388.

P

Palmore, E. (1990). *Ageism: Positive and negative.* New York: Springer.

Palmore, E. B. (1971). Attitudes towards aging as shown by humor. *Gerontologist, 11,* 181–186.

Palmore, E. B., Burchett, B., Fillenbaum, G. G., George, L. K., & Wallman, L. M. (1985). *Retirement: Causes and consequences.* New York: Springer.

Parkes, C. (1972). *Bereavement: Studies of grief in adult life.* New York: International Universities Press.

Parkes, C. M., & Weiss, R. S. (1983). *Recovery from bereavement.* New York: Basic Books.

Patterson, D. G., & Schwartz, P. (1994). The social construction of conflict in intimate same sex couples. In D. D. Cahn (Ed.), *Conflict in personal relationships* (pp. 3–26). Hillsdale, NJ: Erlbaum.

Pearlin, L. (1980). Life strains and psychological distress among adults. In N. J. Smelser & E. H. Erikson (Eds.), *Themes of love and work*. Cambridge: Harvard University Press.

Pearlin, L. I., Mullan, J. T., Semple, S. J., & Skaff, M. M. (1990). Caregiving and the stress process: An overview of concepts and their measures. *Gerontologist, 30,* 583–594.

Pelham, B. W. (1993). The idiographic nature of human personality: Examples of the idiographic self-concept. *Journal of Personality and Social Psychology, 64,* 665–677.

Pellman, J. (1992). Widowhood in elderly women: Exploring its relationship to community integration, hassles, stress, social support, and social support seeking. *International Journal of Aging and Human Development, 35,* 253–264.

Pendlebury, W. W., & Solomon, P. R. (1994). Alzheimer's disease: Therapeutic strategies for the 1990's. *Neurobiology of Aging, 15,* 287–289.

Penning, M. J. (1990). Receipt of assistance by elderly people: Hierarchical selection and task specificity. *Gerontologist, 30,* 220–227.

Perlmutter, M., Kaplan, M., & Nyquist, L. (1990). Development of adaptive competence in adulthood. *Human Development, 33,* 185–197.

Perlmutter, M., & Nyquist, L. (1990). Relationships between self-reported physical and mental health and intelligence performance across adulthood. *Journals of Gerontology, 45,* P145–P155.

Perrucci, C. C., & Targ, D. B. (1988). Effects of a plant closing on marriage and family life. In P. Voydanoff & L. C. Majka (Eds.), *Families and economic distress: Coping strategies and social policy* (pp. 55–71). Newbury Park, CA: Sage.

Perry-Jenkins, M., & Folk, K. (1994). Class, couples, and conflict: Effects of the division of labor on assessments of marriage in dual-earner families. *Journal of Marriage and the Family, 56,* 165–180.

Peterson, C., & Seligman, M. E. P. (1987). Explanatory style and illness. *Journal of Personality, 55,* 237–265.

Peterson, C., Seligman, M. E. P., & Vaillant, G. E. (1994). Pessimistic explanatory style is a risk factor for physical illness: A thirty-five-year longitudinal study. In A. Steptoe & J. Wardle (Eds.), *Psychosocial processes and health: A reader* (pp. 235–246). Cambridge: Cambridge University Press.

Peterson, D., & Coberly, S. (1988). The older worker: Myths and realities. In R. Morris & S. A. Bass (Eds.), *Retirement reconsidered* (pp. 116–129). New York: Springer.

Peterson, P. (1993). *Facing up: How to restore the economy from crushing debt and restore the American dream.* New York: Simon & Schuster.

Phillips, S. D. (1982a). Career exploration in adulthood. *Journal of Vocational Behavior, 20,* 129–140.

Phillips, S. D. (1982b). The development of career choices: The relationships between patterns of commitment and career outcomes in adulthood. *Journal of Vocational Behavior, 20,* 141–152.

Pieper, H. G., Petkovsek, L., & East, M. (1986, November). *Marriage among the elderly.* Paper presented at the 39th Annual Meeting of the Gerontological Society of America, Chicago.

Pillemer, K., & Bachman-Prehn, R. (1991). Helping and hurting: Predictors of maltreatment of patients in nursing homes. *Research on Aging, 13,* 74–95.

Pillemer, K., & Suitor, J. J. (1991). Will I ever escape my child's problems?: Effects of adult children's problems on elderly parents. *Journal of Marriage and the Family, 53,* 585–594.

Pina, D. L., & Bengtson, V. L. (1995). Division of household labor and the well-being of retirement aged wives *Gerontologist, 35,* 308–317.

Pirkl, J. J. (1995). Transgenerational design: Prolonging the American dream. *Generations, 19*(1), 32–36.

Pittman, J. F., Wright, C. A., & Lloyd, S. A. (1989). Predicting parenting difficulty. *Journal of Family Issues, 10,* 267–286.

Planek, T. W., & Fowler, R. C. (1971). Traffic accident problems and exposure characteristics of the older driver. *Journal of Gerontology, 26,* 224–230.

Plomin, R. (1995). Genetics and children's experiences in the family. *Journal of Child Psychology and Psychiatry, 36,* 33–68.

Plomin, R., DeFries, J. C., & McClearn, G. E. (1980). *Behavioral genetics: A primer.* San Francisco: Freeman.

Plomin, R., Lichtenstein, P., Pedersen, N., McClearn, G., & Nesselroade, J. R. (1990). Genetic influence on life events during the last half of the life span. *Psychology and Aging, 5,* 25–30.

Plomin, R., & McClearn, G. E. (1990). Human behavioral genetics of aging. In J. E. Birren & K. W. Schaie (Eds.), *Handbook of the psychology of aging* (3rd ed., pp. 67–77). San Diego: Academic Press.

Plomin, R., & McClearn, G. E. (Eds.). (1993). *Nature, nurture, and psychology.* Washington, DC: American Psychological Association.

Plomin, R., McClearn, G. E., Pedersen, N. L., Nesselroade, J. R., & Bergemen, C. S. (1988). Genetic influence on childhood family environment perceived retrospectively from the last half of the life span. *Developmental Psychology, 24,* 738–745.

Plomin, R., & Nesselroade, J. R. (1990). Behavioral genetics and personality change. *Journal of Personality, 58,* 191–220.

Plomin, R., Owen, M. J., & McGuffin, P. (1994). The genetic basis of complex human behaviors. *Science, 264,* 1733–1739.

Poon, L. W., Rubin, D. C., & Wilson, B. A. (Eds.). (1989). *Everyday cognition in adulthood and late life.* New York: Cambridge University Press.

Popenoe, D. (1988). *Disturbing the nest: Family change and decline in modern societies.* New York: Aldine de Gruyter.

Popenoe, D. (1990). Family decline in America. In D. G. Blankenhorn, S. Bayme, & J. B. Elshtain (Eds.), *Rebuilding the nest: A new commitment to the American family* (pp. 39–51). Milwaukee: Family Service America.

Popenoe, D. (1993). American family decline, 1960–1990: A review and appraisal. *Journal of Marriage and the Family, 55,* 527–555.

Portes, A., & Rumbaut, R. (1990). *Immigrant America.* Berkeley: University of California Press.

Powell, F. C., & Thorson, J. A. (1991). Constructions of death among those high in intrinsic religious motivation: A factor-analytic study. *Death Studies, 15,* 131–138.

Price, V. A. (1988). Research and clinical issues in treating Type A behavior. In B. Kent & C. R. Snyder (Eds.), *Type A behavior pattern: Research, theory, and intervention* (pp. 275–311). New York: John Wiley & Sons.

Proppe, H. (1968). Housing for the retired and aged in southern California: An architectural commentary. *Gerontologist, 8,* 176–179.

Prusank, D. T., Duran, R. L., & DeLillo, D. A. (1993). Interpersonal relationships in women's magazines: Dating and relating in the 1970's and 1980's. *Journal of Social and Personal Relationships, 10,* 307–320.

Q

Qian, Z., & Preston, S. H. (1993). Changes in American marriage, 1972 to 1987: Availability and forces of attraction by age and education. *American Sociological Review, 58,* 482–495.

Quinn, J. F., & Burkhauser, R. V. (1990). Work and retirement. In R. Binstock & L. K. George (Eds.), *Handbook of aging and the social sciences* (3rd ed., pp. 307–323). San Diego: Academic Press.

Quirouette, C., & Gold, D. P. (1992). Spousal characteristics as predictors of well-being in older couples. *International Journal of Aging and Human Development, 34,* 257–269.

R

Rahe, R. H. (1974). Life change and subsequent illness reports. In E. K. Gunderson & R. H. Rahe (Eds.), *Life stress and illness* (pp. 58–78). Springfield, IL: Thomas.

Rakowski, W. (1992). Disease prevention and health promotion with older adults. In M. G. Ory, R. P. Abeles, & P. D. Lipman (Eds.), *Aging, health, and behavior* (pp. 239–275). Newbury Park, CA: Sage.

Rakowski, W. (1994). The definition and measurement of prevention, preventive healthcare, and health promotion, *Generations, 18* (1), 18–23.

Rando, T. A. (1984). *Grief, dying, and death: Clinical interventions for caregivers.* Champaign, IL: Research Press.

Rando, T. A. (1992–1993). The increasing prevalence of complicated mourning: The onslaught is just beginning. *Omega: Journal of Death and Dying, 26,* 43–59.

Rank, M. R. (1986). Family structure and the process of exiting from welfare. *Journal of Marriage and the Family, 48,* 607–618.

Rawson, R. A., Obert, J. L., McCann, M. J., & Marinelli-Casey, P. (1993). Relapse prevention strategies in outpatient substances abuse treatment. Special Series: Psychosocial treatment of the addictions. *Psychology of Addictive Behaviors, 7,* 85–95.

Rea, M. P., Greenspoon, S., & Spilka, B. (1975). Physicians and the terminal patient: Some selected attitudes and behavior. *Omega: Journal of Death and Dying, 6,* 291–302.

Reed, M. (1995). Designs for living and the frustrations of aging. *Generations, 19*(1), 13–14.

Reich, R. (1992). *The work of nations.* New York: Knopf.

Riegel, K. (1977). History of psychological gerontology. In J. E. Birren & K. W. Schaie (Eds.), *Handbook of the psychology of aging* (pp. 7–10). New York: Van Nostrand Reinhold.

Riegel, K. F., & Riegel, R. M. (1972). Development, drop, and death. *Developmental Psychology, 6,* 306–319.

Riegel, K. F., Riegel, R. M., & Meyer, G. (1967). A study of the dropout rates in longitudinal research on aging and the prediction of death. *Journal of Personality and Social Psychology, 5,* 342–348.

Riley, M. W., & Riley, J. W. (1994). Age integration and the lives of older people. *Gerontologist, 34,* 110–115.

Rindfuss, R. R., Morgan, S. P., & Swicegood, G. (1988). *First births in America: Changes in the timing of parenthood.* Berkeley: University of California Press.

Roberto, K. A. (1992). Coping strategies of older women with hip fractures: Resources and outcomes. *Journals of Gerontology, 47,* P21–P26.

Robertson, J. F. (1977). Grandmotherhood: A study of role conceptions. *Journal of Marriage and the Family, 39,* 165–174.

Robinson, I., Ganza, B., Katz, S., & Robinson, E. (1991). Twenty years of sexual revolution, 1965–1985: An update. *Journal of Marriage and the Family, 53,* 216–220.

Rodin, J. (1986). Aging and health: Effects of the sense of control. *Science, 233,* 1271–1276.

Rodin, J., & Langer, E. (1977). Long term effects of a control relevant intervention with the institutionalized aged. *Journal of Personality and Social Psychology, 35,* 897–902.

Rodin, J., & Langer, E. (1980). Aging labels: The decline of control and the fall of self esteem. *Journal of Social Issues, 36,* 12–29.

Rodin, J., & McAvay, G. (1992). Determinants of change in perceived health in a longitudinal study of older adults. *Journals of Gerontology, 47,* P373–P384.

Rodin, J., & Timko, C. (1992). Sense of control, aging, and health. In M. G. Ory, R. P. Abeles, & P. D. Lipman (Eds.), *Aging, health, and behavior* (pp. 174–206). Newbury Park, CA: Sage.

Rogers, A., Rogers, R. G., & Belanger, A. (1990). Longer life but worse health?

Measurement and dynamics. *Gerontologist, 30,* 640–649.

Rosen, J. L., & Neugarten, B. L. (1964). Ego functions in the middle and later years: A thematic apperception study. In B. L. Neugarten & Associates (Eds.), *Personality in middle and late life* (pp. 90–101). New York: Atherton.

Rosenbaum, J. E. (1984). *Career mobility in a corporate hierarchy.* Orlando FL: Academic Press.

Rosenwaike, I., & Dolinsky, A. (1987). The changing demographic determinants for the growth of the extreme aged. *Gerontologist, 27,* 275–280.

Ross, L. M., & Pollio, H. R. (1991). Metaphors of death: A thematic analysis of personal meanings. *Omega: Journal of Death and Dying, 23,* 291–307.

Rossi, A. S. (1987). Parenthood in transition: From lineage to child to self-orientation. In J. B. Lancaster, J. Altmann, A. S. Rossi, & L. R. Sherrod (Eds.), *Parenting across the life span: Biosocial dimensions* (pp. 31–84). Hawthorne, NY: Aldine.

Rossiter, A. B. (1991). Initiator status and separation adjustment. *Journal of Divorce and Remarriage, 15,* 141–155.

Rossman, P. (1977). *Hospice.* New York: Fawcett Columbine.

Roth, M., Tomlinson, B. E., & Blessed, G. (1966). Correlation between scores for dementia and counts of "senile plaques" in cerebral grey matter of elderly subjects. *Nature, 209,* 109–110.

Rowe, J. W., & Kahn, R. L. (1987). Human aging: Usual and successful. *Science, 237,* 143–149.

Rubinstein, L. A., Josephson, K. R., Weiland, G. D., English, P. A., Sayre, J. A., & Kane, R. L. (1984). Effectiveness of a geriatric evaluation unit: A randomized trial. *New England Journal of Medicine, 331,* 1664–1670.

Rubinstein, R. (1986). The construction of a day by elderly widowers. *International Journal of Aging and Human Development, 23,* 161–173.

Rudberg, M. A., Furner, S. E., Dunn, J. E., & Cassel, C. K. (1993). The relationship of visual and hearing impairments to disability: An analysis using the longitudinal study of aging. *Journals of Gerontology, 48,* M261–M265.

Ruiz, P. (1985). Clinical care update: The minority patient. *Community Mental Health Journal, 21,* 208–216.

Rule, B. G., Milke, D. L., & Allen, R. (1992). Design of institutions: Cognitive functioning and social interactions of the aged resident.

Journal of Applied Gerontology, 11, 475–488.

Rumbaut, R. G. (1991). Passages to America: Perspectives on the new immigration. In A. Wolfe (Ed.), America at century's end (pp. 208–244). Berkeley: University of California Press.

Russell, J. E. A. (1994). Career counseling for women in management. In W. B. Walsh & S. H. Osipow (Eds.), Career counseling for women (pp. 263–326). Hillsdale, NJ: Erlbaum.

Ryan, E. B. (1992). Beliefs about memory changes across the adult life span. Journals of Gerontology, 47, P41–P46.

Rybash, J. N., Hoyer, W. J., & Roodin, P. (1986). Adult cognition and aging: Developmental changes in processing, knowing, and thinking. New York: Pergamon Press.

Ryff, C. D., & Heincke, S. G. (1983). Subjective organization of personality in adulthood and aging. Journal of Personality and Social Psychology, 44, 807–816.

Ryff, C. D., Lee, Y. H., Essex, M. J., & Schmutte, P. S. (1994). My children and me: Midlife evaluations of grown children and of self. Psychology and Aging, 9, 195–205.

S

Sabatelli, R. M. (1988). Measurement issues in marital research: A review and critiques of contemporary survey instruments. Journal of Marriage and the Family, 50, 891–915.

Sachs, G. A. (1994). Improving care of the dying. Generations, 18 (4), 19–22.

Salthouse, T. A. (1985). Speed of behavior and its implications for cognition. In J. E. Birren & K. W. Schaie (Eds.), Handbook of the psychology of aging (2nd ed., pp. 400–426). New York: Van Nostrand Reinhold.

Salthouse, T. A. (1990). Cognitive competence and expertise in aging. In J. E. Birren & K. W. Schaie (Eds.), Handbook of the psychology of aging (3rd ed., pp. 310–319). San Diego: Academic Press.

Salthouse, T. A. (1991). Theoretical perspectives on cognitive aging. Hillsdale, NJ: Erlbaum.

Salthouse, T. A. (1992). The information-processing perspective on cognitive aging. In R. J. Sternberg & C. A. Berg (Eds.), Intellectual development (pp. 261–278). New York: Cambridge University Press.

Salzman, C. (1989). Treatment with antianxiety agents. In American Psychiatric Association (Ed.), Treatments

of psychiatric disorders: A task force report of the American Psychiatric Association (Vol. 3, pp. 2036–2051). Washington, DC: American Psychiatric Association.

Savage, D. D., McGee, D. L., & Oster, G. (1989). Reduction of hypertension-associated heart disease and stroke among black Americans: Past experience and new perspectives on targeting resources. In D. P. Willis (Ed.), Health policies and black Americans (pp. 297–321). New Brunswick, NJ: Transaction.

Savin-Williams, R. C. (1995). Lesbian, gay male, and bisexual adolescents. In A. R. D'Augelli & C. J. Patterson (Eds.), Lesbian, gay, and bisexual identities over the lifespan (pp. 165–175). New York: Oxford University Press.

Saxon, S. V., & Etten, M. J. (1978). Physical change and aging: A guide for the helping professions. New York: Tiresias Press.

Schacter, D. L. (1992). Understanding implicit memory: A cognitive neuroscience approach. American Psychologist, 47, 559–569.

Schacter, D. L., Kaszniak, A. W., Kihlstrom, J. F., & Valdiserri, M. (1991). The relation between source memory and aging. Psychology and Aging, 6, 559–568.

Schaie, K. W. (1965). A general model for the study of developmental problems. Psychological Bulletin, 64, 92–107.

Schaie, K. W. (1977–1978). Toward a stage theory of adult cognitive development. International Journal of Aging and Human Development, 8, 129–138.

Schaie, K. W. (Ed.). (1983). Longitudinal studies of adult psychological development. New York: Guilford Press.

Schaie, K. W. (1988). The impact of research methodology in theory building in the developmental sciences. In J. E. Birren & V. L. Bengtson (Eds.), Emergent theories of aging (pp. 41–57). New York: Springer.

Schaie, K. W. (1989). Individual differences in the rate of intellectual change. In V. L. Bengtson & K. W. Schaie (Eds.) The course of later life: Research and reflections (pp. 65–85). New York: Springer.

Schaie, K. W. (1990). Intellectual development in adulthood. In J. E. Birren & K. W. Schaie (Eds.), Handbook of the psychology of aging (3rd ed., pp. 291–309). San Diego: Academic Press.

Schaie, K. W. (1996). Intellectual development in adulthood. In J. E. Birren & K. W. Schaie (Eds.), Handbook of the psychology of aging (4th ed., pp. 266–286). San Diego: Academic Press.

Schaie, K. W., & Willis, S. L. (1993). Age difference patterns of psychometric intelligence in adulthood: Generalizability

within and across ability domains. Psychology and Aging, 8, 44–55.

Scheibel, A. B. (1996). Structural and functional changes in the aging brain. In J. E. Birren & K. W. Schaie (Eds.), Handbook of the psychology of aging (4th ed., pp. 105–128). San Diego: Academic Press.

Scherwitz, L., & Canick, J. C. (1988). Self-reference and coronary heart disease risk. In B. K. Houston & C. R. Snyder (Eds.), Type A behavior pattern: Research, theory, and intervention (pp. 146–167). New York: John Wiley & Sons.

Schiffman, S. (1977). Food recognition by the elderly. Journal of Gerontology, 32, 586–592.

Schiffman, S., & Pasternak, M. (1979). Decreased discrimination of food odors in the elderly. Journal of Gerontology, 34, 73–79.

Schlesinger, M. (1989). Paying the price: Medical care, minorities, and the newly competitive health care system. In D. P. Willis (Ed.), Health policies and black Americans (pp. 270–296). New Brunswick, NJ: Transaction.

Schmidt, D. F., & Boland, S. M. (1986). Structure of perceptions of older adults: Evidence for multiple stereotypes. Psychology and Aging, 1, 255–260.

Schoen, R., & Weinick, R. M. (1993). Partner choice in marriages and cohabitations. Journal of Marriage and the Family, 55, 408–414.

Schoen, R., & Wooldredge, J. (1989). Marriage choices in North Carolina and Virginia, 1969–71 and 1979–81. Journal of Marriage and the Family, 51, 465–481.

Schooler, C. (1990). Psychological factors and effective cognitive functioning in adulthood. In J. E. Birren & K. W. Schaie (Eds.), Handbook of the psychology of aging (3rd ed., pp. 347–358). San Diego: Academic Press.

Schor, J. (1991). The overworked American: The unexpected decline of leisure. New York: Basic Books.

Schram, R. (1979). Marital satisfaction over the family life cycle: A critique and proposal. Journal of Marriage and the Family, 41, 7–12.

Schulz, R., & Schlarb, J. (1987–1988). Two decades of research on dying: What do we know about the patient? Omega: Journal of Death and Dying, 18, 299–317.

Schulz, R., Visintainer, P., & Williamson, G. M. (1990). Psychiatric and physical morbidity effects of caregiving. Journals of Gerontology, 45, P181–P191.

Scribner, S. (1986). Thinking in action: Some characteristics of practical thought. In

R. J. Sternberg & R. K. Wagner (Eds.), *Practical intelligence: Origins of competence in the everyday world* (pp. 13–31). New York: Cambridge University Press.

Seccombe, K., & Ishii-Kuntz, M. (1994). Gender and social relationships among the never married. *Sex Roles, 30*, 585–603.

Sedney, M. A. (1985–1986). Growing more complex: Conceptions of sex roles across adulthood. *International Journal of Aging and Human Development, 22*, 15–29.

Sehgal, A., Galbraith, A., Chesney, M., Schoenfeld, P., Charles, G., & Lo, B. (1992). How strictly do dialysis patients want their advance directives followed? *Journal of the American Medical Association, 267*, 59–63.

Selig, S., Tomlinson, T., & Hickey, T. (1991). Ethical dimensions of intergenerational reciprocity: Implications for practice. *Gerontologist, 31*, 624–630.

Seligman, M. E. P. (1975). *Helplessness: On depression, development and death*. San Francisco: Freeman.

Selye, H. (1976). *The stress of life* (Rev. ed.). New York: McGraw-Hill.

Senchak, M., & Leonard, K. E. (1992). Attachment styles and marital adjustment among newlywed couples. *Journal of Social and Personal Relationships, 9*, 51–64.

Seyler, D. L., Monroe, P. A., & Garand, J. C. (1995). Balancing work and family: The role of employer-supported child care benefits. *Journal of Family Issues, 16*, 170–193.

Shanas, E. (1979a). Social myth as hypothesis: The case of the family relations of old people. *Gerontologist, 19*, 3–9.

Shanas, E. (1979b). The family as a social support system in old age. *Gerontologist, 19*, 169–174.

Shanas, E. (1980). Older people and their families: The new pioneers. *Journal of Marriage and the Family, 42*, 9–15.

Shanas, E. (1984). Old parents and middle-aged children: The four- and five-generation family. *Journal of Geriatric Psychiatry, 17*(1), 7–19.

Sharps, M. J., & Gollin, E. S. (1988). Aging and free recall for subjects located in space. *Journals of Gerontology, 43*, P8–P11.

Sheehy, G. (1993). *The silent passage*. New York: Pocket.

Sheilds, R. R. (1988). *Uneasy endings: Life in an American nursing home*. Ithaca, NY: Cornell University Press.

Sheppard, H. L. (1988). Work continuity versus retirement: Reasons for continuing work. In R. Morris & S. A. Bass (Eds.), *Retirement reconsidered* (pp. 129–148). New York: Springer.

Shneidman, E. S. (1976). Death work and stages of dying. In E. S. Shneidman (Ed.), *Death: Current perspectives* (pp. 443–451). Palo Alto, CA: Mayfield.

Shock, N. W., Greulich, R. C., Andres, R., Arenberg, D., Costa, P. T., Lakatta, E. G., & Tobin, J. D. (Eds.). (1984). *Normal human aging: The Baltimore Longitudinal Study of Aging* (NIH Publication No. 84-2450). Washington, DC: U.S. Public Health Service.

Shore, L. M., & Bleicken, L. M. (1991). Effects of supervisor age and subordinate age on rating congruence. *Human Relations, 44*, 1093–1105.

Shorr, R., & Bauwens, S. F. (1992). Diagnosis and treatment of outpatient insomnia by psychiatric and nonpsychiatric physicians. *American Journal of Medicine, 93*, 78–82.

Shorr, R., Bauwens, S. F., & Landefeld, C. S. (1990). Failure to limit quantities of benzodiazepine hypnotic drugs for outpatients: Placing the elderly at risk. *American Journal of Medicine, 89*, 725–732.

Shorr, R., & Robin, D. (1994). Rational use of benzodiazepines in the elderly. *Drug Therapy, 4*, 9–20.

Shorr, R. I., Fought, R. L., & Ray, W. A. (1994). Changes in antipsychotic drug use in nursing homes during implementation of the OBRA-87 regulations. *Journal of the American Medical Association, 271*, 358–362.

Simon, B. L. (1987). *Never married women*. Philadelphia: Temple University Press.

Simoneau, G. G., Cavanagh, P. R., Ulbrecht, J. S., Leibowitz, H. W., & Tyrrell, R. A. (1991). The influence of visual factors on fall-related kinematic variables during stair descent by older women. *Journals of Gerontology, 46*, M188–M195.

Simoneau, G. G., & Leibowitz, H. W. (1996). Posture, gait, and falls. In J. E. Birren & K. W. Schaie (Eds.), *Handbook of the psychology of aging* (4th ed., pp. 204–217). San Diego: Academic Press.

Simonton, D. K. (1975). Age and literary creativity: A cross cultural and transhistorical survey. *Journal of Cross Cultural Psychology, 6*, 259–277.

Simonton, D. K. (1989). The swan song phenomenon: Last works effects for 172 classical composers. *Psychology and Aging, 4*, 42–47.

Simonton, D. K. (1990a). Creativity in the later years: Optimistic prospects for achievement. *Gerontologist, 30*, 626–631.

Simonton, D. K. (1990b). Creativity and wisdom in aging. In J. E. Birren & K. W. Schaie (Eds.), *Handbook of the psychology of aging* (3rd ed., pp. 320–329). San Diego: Academic Press.

Simonton, D. K. (1991). Emergence and realization of genius: The lives and works of 120 classical composers. *Journal of Personality and Social Psychology, 62*, 829–840.

Simpson, J. A. (1990). Influence of attachment styles on romantic relationships. *Journal of Personality and Social Psychology, 59*, 971–980.

Simpson, J. A., Gangestad, S. W., & Lerma, M. (1990). Perception of physical attractiveness: Mechanisms involved in the maintenance of romantic relationships. *Journal of Personality and Social Psychology, 59*, 1192–1201.

Sinnott, J. D. (1986). Prospective/intentional and incidental everyday memory: Effects of age and passage of time. *Psychology and Aging, 1*, 110–116.

Sinnott, J. D. (1989). Prospective/intentional memory and aging: Memory as adaptive action. In L. W. Poon, D. C. Rubin, & B. A. Wilson (Eds.), *Everyday cognition in adulthood and late life* (pp. 352–372). New York: Cambridge University Press.

Sinnott, J. D. (1991). What do we do to help John? A case study of postformal problem solving in a family making decisions about an acutely psychotic member. In J. D. Sinnott & J. C. Cavanaugh (Eds.), *Bridging paradigms: Positive development in adulthood and cognitive aging* (pp. 203–219). New York: Praeger.

Sloane, P. D., Lindeman, D. A., Phillips, C., Moritz, D. J., & Koch, G. (1995). Evaluating Alzheimer's special care units: Reviewing the evidence and identifying potential sources of study bias. *Gerontologist, 35*, 103–111.

Smith, A. D. (1996). Memory. In J. E. Birren & K. W. Schaie (Eds.), *Handbook of the psychology of aging* (4th ed., pp. 236–250). San Diego: Academic Press.

Smith, J., & Baltes, P. B. (1990). Wisdom-related knowledge: Age/cohort differences in response to life-planning problems. *Developmental Psychology, 26*, 494–505.

Smith, J., Staudinger, U. M., & Baltes, P. B. (1994). Occupational settings facilitating wisdom-related knowledge: The sample case of clinical psychologists. *Journal of Consulting and Clinical Psychology, 62*, 989–999.

Smith, J. R. (1990). Minireview: DNA synthesis inhibitors in cellular senescence. *Journals of Gerontology, 45*, B32–B35.

Smith, P. C., Range, L. M., & Ulmer, A. (1991–1992). Belief in afterlife as a buffer in suicidal and other bereavement. *Omega: Journal of Death and Dying, 24*, 217–225.

Smith, T. W. (1994). Attitudes toward sexual permissiveness: Trends, correlates, and behavioral connections. In A. S. Rossi (Ed.), *Sexuality across the life course* (pp. 63–97). Chicago: University of Chicago Press.

Snyder, D. K., Wills, R. M., & Fletcher-Grady, A. (1991). Long-term effectiveness of behavioral versus insight-oriented marital therapy: A 4-year follow-up study. *Journal of Consulting and Clinical Psychology, 59,* 138–141.

Snyder, D. L., Pollard, M., Wostmann, B. S., & Luckert, P. (1990). Life span, morphology, and pathology of diet-restricted germ-free and conventional lobund-wistar rats. *Journals of Gerontology, 45,* B52–B58.

Social Security Administration. (1994). *Fast facts and figures about Social Security.* Washington, DC: U.S. Government Printing Office.

Soldo, B. J., Wolf, D. A., & Agree, E. M. (1990). Family, households, and care arrangements of frail older women: A structural analysis. *Journals of Gerontology, 45,* S238–S249.

Somers, M. D. (1993). A comparison of voluntarily child-free adults and parents. *Journal of Marriage and the Family, 55,* 643–650.

Song, Y. I. (1991). Single Asian American women as a result of divorce: Depressive affect and changes in social support. *Journal of Marriage and the Family, 53,* 219–229.

Spitze, G., & Logan, J. (1990). More evidence on women (and men) in the middle. *Research on Aging, 12,* 182–198.

Spitze, G., Logan, J. R., Joseph, G., & Lee, E. (1994). Middle generation roles and the well-being of men and women. *Journals of Gerontology, 49,* S107–S116.

Spokane, A. R. (1985). A review of research on person-environment congruence on Holland's theory of careers. *Journal of Vocational Behavior, 26,* 306–343.

Squire, L. R. (1992). Memory and the hippocampus: A synthesis from findings with rats, monkeys, and humans. *Psychological Review, 99,* 195–231.

Stanford, E. P., & Schmidt, M. G. (1995–1996). The changing face of nursing home residents: Meeting their diverse needs. *Generations, 19*(4), 20–23.

Staudinger, U. M., Smith, J., & Baltes, P. B. (1992). Wisdom-related knowledge in a life-review task: Age differences and the role of professional specialization. *Psychology and Aging, 7,* 271–281.

Stearns, L. R., Netting, F. E., Wilson, C. C., & Branch, L. G. (1990). Lessons from the implementation of CCRC regulation. *Gerontologist, 30,* 154–162.

Stearns, P. N. (1991). Fatherhood in historical perspective: The role of social change. In F. W. Bozett & S. M. H. Hanson (Eds.), *Fatherhood and families in cultural context* (pp. 28–52). New York: Springer.

Stephen, D. L. (1991–1992). A discussion of Avery Weisman's notion of appropriate death. *Omega: Journal of Death and Dying, 24,* 301–308.

Stephen, T. D. (1984). A symbolic exchange framework for the development of intimate relationships. *Human Relations, 37,* 393–408.

Sternberg, R. J. (1988a). *The triarchic mind: A new theory of human intelligence.* New York: Viking Press.

Sternberg, R. J. (1988b). Triangulating love. In R. J. Sternberg & M. L. Barnes (Eds.), *The psychology of love* (pp. 119–138). New Haven, CT: Yale University Press.

Sternberg, R. J., & Barnes, M. L. (Eds.). (1988). *The psychology of love.* New Haven, CT: Yale University Press.

Sternberg, R. J., & Berg, C. A. (Eds.). (1992). *Intellectual development.* New York: Cambridge University Press.

Sternberg, R. J., & Wagner, R. K. (Eds.). (1986). *Practical intelligence: Origins of competence in the everyday world.* New York: Cambridge University Press.

Stevens-Ratchford, R. G. (1993). The effect of life review reminiscence activities on depression and self-esteem in older adults. *American Journal of Occupational Therapy, 47,* 413–420.

Stine, E. A. L., Wingfield, H., & Myers, S. D. (1990). Age differences in processing information from television news: The effects of bisensory augmentation. *Journals of Gerontology, 45,* P1–P8.

Stock, R. (1995, July 17). Balancing the needs and risks of older drivers. *The New York Times,* p. B5.

Stone, A. A., Bovbjerg, D. H., Neale, J. M., Napoli, A., Valdimarsdottir, H., Cox, D., Hayden, F. G., & Gwaltney, J. M. (1992). Development of common cold symptoms following experimental rhinovirus infection is related to prior stressful life events. *Behavioral Medicine, 18,* 115–120.

Strawbridge, W. J., Camacho, T. C., Cohen, R. D., & Kaplan, G. A. (1993). Gender differences in factors associated with change in physical functioning in old age: A six year longitudinal study. *Gerontologist, 33,* 603–609.

Strawbridge, W. J., & Wallhagen, M. I. (1991). Impact of family conflict on adult child caregivers. *Gerontologist, 31,* 770–777.

Stroebe, M. (1993). Coping with bereavement: A review of the grief work hypothesis, *Omega: Journal of Death and Dying, 26,* 19–42.

Stump, T. E., Johnson, R. J., & Wolinsky, F. D. (1995). Changes in physician utilization over time among older adults. *Journals of Gerontology, 50B,* S45–S58.

Styron, W. (1990). *Darkness visible.* New York: Vintage.

Sue, S. (1992). Ethnicity and mental health: Research and policy issues. *Journal of Social Issues, 48,* 187–205.

Super, D. E. (1980). A life-span, life-space approach to career development. *Journal of Vocational Behavior, 16,* 282–298.

Super, D. E. (1985). Coming of age in Middletown: Careers in making. *American Psychologist, 40,* 405–414.

Super, D. E. (1957). *The psychology of careers: An introduction to vocational development.* New York: Harper.

Surra, C. A. (1990). Research and theory on mate selection and premarital relationships in the 1980's. *Journal of Marriage and the Family, 51,* 844–865.

Szinovacz, M., & Harpster, P. (1994). Couples' employment/retirement status and the division of household tasks. *Journals of Gerontology, 49,* S125–S136.

T

Talbott, M. M. (1990). The negative side of the relationship between older widows and their adult children: The mothers' perspective. *Gerontologist, 30,* 595–603.

Taylor, R. J., & Chatters, L. M. (1991). Extended family networks of older black adults. *Journals of Gerontology, 46,* S210–S217.

Teachman, J. D., Call, V. R., & Carver, K. P. (1994). Marital status and the duration of joblessness among white men. *Journal of Marriage and the Family, 56,* 415–428.

Technology and aging: Developing and marketing new products for older persons. (1995, Spring). *Generations, 19* (1).

Teri, L., McCurry, S. M., Edland, S. D., Kukull, W. A., & Larson, E. B. (1995). Cognitive decline in Alzheimer's disease: A longitudinal investigation of risk factors for accelerated decline. *Journals of Gerontology, 50A,* M49–M55.

Thomas, C., & Kelman, H. R. (1990). Gender and the use of health services among elderly persons. In M. G. Ory & H. R. Warner (Eds.), *Gender, health, and longevity: Multidisciplinary perspectives* (pp. 137–156). New York: Springer.

Thomas, J. L. (1986). Age and sex differences in perceptions of grandparenting. *Journal of Gerontology, 41,* 417–423.

Thomas, J. L. (1990a). The grandparent role: A double bind. *International Journal of Aging and Human Development, 31,* 169–177.

Thomas, J. L. (1990b). Grandparenthood and mental health: Implications for the practitioner. *Journal of Applied Gerontology, 9,* 464–479.

Thomas, R. M. (1996). *Comparing theories of child development* (4th ed.). Pacific Grove, CA: Brooks/Cole.

Thomasson, H. R., & Li, T. K. (1993). How alcohol and aldehyde dehydrogenase genes modify alcohol drinking, alcohol flushing, and the risk for alcoholism. *Alcohol Health and Research World, 17,* 167–172.

Thompson, J. M. (1995). *A case study analysis of the social behavioral aspects of menopause.* Unpublished master's thesis, Middle Tennessee State University, Murfreesboro.

Thoresen, C. E., & Pattillo, J. R. (1988). Exploring the Type A behavior pattern in children and adolescents. In B. K. Houston & C. R. Snyder (Eds.), *Type A behavior pattern: Research, theory, and intervention* (pp. 98–145). New York: John Wiley & Sons.

Thornton, A., Young–De Margo, L., & Goldscheider, F. (1993). Leaving the parental nest: The experience of a young white cohort in the 1980's. *Journal of Marriage and the Family, 55,* 216–229.

Toole, T., & Abourezk, T. (1989). Aerobic function, information processing, and aging. In A. C. Ostrow (Ed.), *Aging and motor behavior* (pp. 37–66). IN: Benchmark Press.

Treas, J., & VanHilst, A. (1976). Marriage and remarriage rates among older Americans. *Gerontologist, 16,* 132–136.

Troll, L. E. (1983). Grandparents: The family watchdogs. In T. Brubaker (Ed.), *Family relationships in later life* (pp. 63–74). Beverly Hills, CA: Sage.

Tsuang, M. T., & Faraone, S. V. (1990). *The genetics of mood disorders.* Baltimore: John Hopkins University Press.

Tucker, B., & Mitchell-Kernan, C. (1990). New trends in black American interracial marriage: The social structural context. *Journal of Marriage and the Family, 52,* 209–218.

Tulving, E. (1985). How many memory systems are there? *American Psychologist, 40,* 385–398.

Tune, L. (1993). Neuroimaging: Advances and new directions. *Generations, 17,* 79–80.

U

Udry, J. R., & Campbell, B. C. (1994). Getting started on sexual behavior. In A. S. Rossi (Ed.), *Sexuality across the life course* (pp. 187–208). Chicago: University of Chicago Press.

Ullman, A. D., & Orenstein, A. (1994). Why some children of alcoholics become alcoholics: Emulation of the drinker. *Adolescence, 29*(113), 1–11.

Umberson, D. (1989a). Parenting and well being: The importance of context. *Journal of Family Issues, 10,* 427–438.

Umberson, D. (1989b). Relationships with children: Explaining parents' psychological well being. *Journal of Marriage and the Family, 51,* 999–1010.

Umberson, D., & Gove, W. R. (1989). Parenthood and psychological well-being: Theory, measurement, and stage in the family life course. *Journal of Family Issues, 10,* 440–462.

Umberson, D., & Williams, C. L. (1993). Divorced fathers: Parental role strain and psychological distress. *Journal of Family Issues, 14,* 378–400.

Umberson, D., Wortman, C. B., & Kessler, R. C. (1992). Widowhood and depression: Explaining long-term gender differences in vulnerability. *Journal of Health and Social Behavior, 33,* 10–24.

U.S. Bureau of the Census. (1993). *Statistical abstract of the United States 1993.* Washington, DC: U.S. Government Printing Office.

U.S. Bureau of the Census. (1994). *Statistical abstract of the United States 1994.* Washington, DC: U.S. Government Printing Office.

U.S. Bureau of the Census. (1995). *Statistical abstract of the United States 1995.* Washington, DC: U.S. Government Printing Office.

U.S. Department of Health and Human Services. (1989). *Reducing the health consequences of smoking: Twenty-five years of progress: A report of the Surgeon General: Executive summary.* Rockville, MD: Author.

U.S. Department of Health and Human Services. (1990a). *Seventh special report to the U.S. Congress on alcohol and health.* Rockville, MD: National Institute on Alcohol Abuse and Alcoholism.

U.S. Department of Health and Human Services. (1990b). *Health status of the disadvantaged, chartbook 1990.* Washington, DC: U.S. Government Printing Office.

U.S. Department of Health and Human Services. (1991). *Health status of minorities and low income groups.* Washington, DC: U.S. Government Printing Office.

U.S. Department of Health and Human Services. (1994a). *Mental health, United States, 1994.* Rockville, MD: Author.

U.S. Department of Health and Human Services. (1994b). *National Health Care Survey, 1994.* Atlanta: Centers for Disease Control and Prevention.

U.S. Public Health Service. (1995). *Monthly vital statistics report* (Vol. 43, Supplement No. 6). Atlanta: Centers for Disease Control and Prevention.

U.S. Senate Special Committee on Aging. (1991a). *Aging America: Trends and projections* (1991 ed.). Washington, DC: Author.

U.S. Senate Special Committee on Aging. (1991b). *Lifelong learning for an aging society* (DHHS Publication No. 102-J). Washington, DC: U.S. Government Printing Office.

U.S. Senate Special Committee on Aging. (1992). *Lifelong learning for an aging society* (Annotated) (DHHS Publication No. 102-R). Washington, DC: U.S. Government Printing Office.

V

Vaillant, C. O., & Vaillant, G. E. (1993). Is the U-curve of marital satisfaction an illusion?: A 40-year study of marriage. *Journal of Marriage and the Family, 55,* 230–239.

Vaillant, G. (1977). *Adaptation to life.* Boston: Little, Brown.

Valente, S. M. (1993–1994). Suicide and elderly people: Assessment and intervention. *Omega: Journal of Death and Dying, 28,* 317–331.

Van de Water, D. A., & McAdams, D. P. (1989). Generativity and Erikson's "belief in the species." *Journal of Research in Personality, 23,* 435–449.

Veevers, J. E. (1991). Traumas versus strens: A paradigm of positive versus negative divorce outcomes. *Journal of Divorce and Remarriage, 15,* 99–126.

Verbrugge, L. M. (1989). Gender, aging, and health. In K. S. Markides (Ed.), *Aging and health: Perspectives on gender, race, ethnicity, and class* (pp. 23–78). Newbury Park, CA: Sage.

Verbrugge, L. M. (1990). The twain meet: Empirical explanations of sex differences in health and mortality. In M. G. Ory & H. R. Warner (Eds.), *Gender, health, and longevity: Multidisciplinary perspectives* (pp. 159–200). New York: Springer.

Verwoerdt, A., Pfeiffer, E., & Wang, H. S. (1969, February). Sexual behavior in senescence: 2. Patterns of sexual activity and interest. *Geriatrics, 24,* 137–154.

Viney, L. L., Walker, B. M., Robertson, T., Lilley, B., & Ewan, C. (1994). Dying in palliative care units and in hospital: A comparison of the quality of life of terminal cancer patients. *Journal of Consulting and Clinical Psychology, 62,* 157–164.

Viney, L. L., & Westbrook, M. (1986–1987). Is there a pattern of psychological reactions to chronic illness which is associated with death? *Omega: Journal of Death and Dying, 17,* 169–181.

Vinovskis, M. A. (1987). Historical perspectives on the development of the family and parent-child interactions. In J. B. Lancaster, J. Altmann, A. S. Rossi, & L. R. Sherrod (Eds.), *Parenting across the life span: Biosocial dimensions* (pp. 295–312). Hawthorne, NY: Aldine.

Vogt, T. M. (1992). Aging, stress, and illness: Psychobiological linkages. In M. G. Ory, R. P. Abeles, & P. D. Lipman (Eds.), *Aging, health, and behavior* (pp. 207–238). Newbury Park, CA: Sage.

Voydandoff, P., & Majka, L. C. (Eds.). (1988). *Families and economic distress: Coping strategies and social policy.* Newbury Park, CA: Sage.

W

Wagner, R., & Sternberg, R. (1986). Trait knowledge and intelligence in the everyday world. In R. J. Sternberg & R. K. Wagner (Eds.), *Practical intelligence: Origins of competence in the everyday world* (pp. 51–83). New York: Cambridge University Press.

Wagner, R. M. (1993). Psychosocial adjustments during the first year of single parenthood: A comparison of Mexican-American and Anglo women. *Journal of Divorce and Remarriage, 19,* 121–142.

Walford, R. (1969). *The immunologic theory of aging.* Baltimore: Williams & Wilkins.

Walford, R. (1983). *Maximum lifespan.* New York: Norton.

Walker, A. J., Martin, S. S., & Jones, L. L. (1992). The benefits and costs of caregiving and care receiving for daughters and mothers. *Journals of Gerontology, 47,* S130–S139.

Walker, A. J., & Thompson, L. (1983). Intimacy and intergenerational aid and contact among mothers and daughters. *Journal of Marriage and the Family, 45,* 841–848.

Walsh, W. B., & Osipow, S. H. (Eds.). (1994). *Career counseling for women.* Hillsdale, NJ: Erlbaum.

Walz, T. H., & Blum, N. S. (1987). *Sexual health in later life.* Lexington, MA: Heath.

Ward, R. A., Logan, J., & Spitze, G. (1992). Consequences of parent-adult child coresidence: A review and research agenda. *Journal of Family Issues, 13,* 553–572.

Warner, K. E. (1989). Effects of the antismoking campaign: An update. *American Journal of Public Health, 79,* 144.

Warr, P., Jackson, P., & Banks, M. H. (1988). Unemployment and mental health: Some British studies. *Journal of Social Issues, 44,* 47–68.

Wasow, M., & Loeb, M. B. (1978). Sexuality in nursing homes. In R. L. Solnick (Ed.), *Sexuality and aging* (pp. 154–162). Los Angeles: University of Southern California Press.

Watkins, P. L., Ward, C. H., Southard, D. R., & Fisher, E. B. (1992). The Type A belief system: Relationships to hostility, social support, and life stress. *Behavioral Medicine, 18,* 27–32.

Webster, J. D. (1995). Adult age differences in reminiscence functions. In B. K. Haight & J. D. Webster (Eds.), *The art and science of reminiscing: Theory, research, methods, and applications* (pp. 89–102). Washington, DC: Taylor & Francis.

Webster, P. S., & Herzog, A. R. (1995). Effects of parental divorce and memories of family problems on relationships between adult children and their parents. *Journals of Gerontology, 50B,* S24–S34.

Wechsler, D. (1981). *WAIS-R manual* (Rev. ed.). New York: Harcourt Brace Jovanovich.

Wegman, R. (1991). How long does unemployment take? *Career Development Quarterly, 40,* 71–81.

Weindruch, R., & Masoro, E. J. (1991). Concerns about rodent models for aging research. *Journals of Gerontology, 46,* B87–B88.

Weishaus, S., & Field, D. (1988). A half century of marriage: Continuity or change? *Journal of Marriage and the Family, 50,* 763–774.

Weisman, A. D. (1976). Denial and middle knowledge. In E. S. Shneidman (Ed.), *Death: Current perspectives* (pp. 452–469). Palo Alto, CA: Mayfield.

Weisman, A. D., & Worden, J. W. (1975). Psychological analysis of cancer deaths. *Omega: Journal of Death and Dying, 6,* 61–75.

Weiss, R. (1990). *Staying the course: The emotional and social lives of men who do well.* New York: Free Press.

Weissman, M. M., & Klerman, G. L. (1990). Interpersonal psychotherapy for depression. In B. B. Wolman & G. Stricker (Eds.), *Depressive disorders: Facts, theories, and treatment methods* (pp. 379–395). New York: John Wiley & Sons.

Weissman, M. M., Myers, J. K., Tischler, G. L., Holtzer, C. E., Leaf, P. J., Orvascel, H., & Brody, J. A. (1985). Psychiatric disorders (*DSM III*) and cognitive impairment among the elderly in a U.S. urban community. *Acta Psychiatrica Scandinavica, 71,* 366–379.

Weitzman, L. (1985). *The divorce revolution.* New York: Free Press.

Weitzman, L. M., & Fitzgerald, L. F. (1993). Employed mothers: Diverse lifestyles and labor force profiles. In J. Frankel (Ed.), *The employed mother and the family context* (pp. 7–30). New York: Springer.

Welch, C. (1989). Electroconvulsive therapy. In American Psychiatric Association (Ed.), *Treatments of psychiatric disorders: A task force report of the American Psychiatric Association* (Vol. 3, pp. 1803–1813). Washington, DC: American Psychiatric Association.

Welford, A. T. (1977). Motor performance. In J. E. Birren & K. W. Schaie (Eds.), *Handbook of the psychology of aging* (pp. 450–496). New York: Van Nostrand Reinhold.

Wells, B. L., & Horn, J. W. (1992). Stage at diagnosis in breast cancer: Race and socioeconomic factors. *American Journal of Public Health, 82,* 1383–1385.

Wennecker, M. B., & Epstein, A. M. (1989). Racial inequalities in the use of procedures for patients with ischemic heart disease in Massachusetts. *Journal of the American Medical Association, 261,* 253–257.

West, R. L. (1989). Planning practical memory training for the aged. In L. W. Poon, D. C. Rubin, & B. A. Wilson (Eds.) *Everyday cognition in adulthood and late life* (pp. 573–597). New York: Cambridge University Press.

West, R. L., & Crook, T. H. (1990). Age differences in everyday memory: Laboratory analogues of telephone number recall. *Psychology and Aging, 5,* 520–529.

West, R. L., Crook, T. H., & Barron, K. L. (1992). Everyday memory performance across the life span: Effects of age and noncognitive individual differences. *Psychology and Aging, 7,* 72–82.

West, S. G., & Graziano, W. G. (1989). Long-term stability and change in personality: An introduction. *Journal of Personality, 57,* 175–193.

Westman, A. S., & Brackney, B. E. (1990). Relationships between indices of neuroticism, attitudes toward and concepts of death, and religiosity. *Psychological Reports, 66,* 1039–1043.

Wetle, T. (1994). Individual preferences and advance directives. *Hastings Center Report, 24,* S5–S8.

Whitbeck, L. B., Hoyt, D. R., & Huck, S. M. (1994). Early family relationships, intergenerational solidarity, and support provided to parents by their adult children. *Journals of Gerontology, 49,* S85–S94.

White, L., & Edwards, J. N. (1990). Emptying the nest and parental well-being: An analysis of national panel data. *American Sociological Review, 55,* 235–242.

White, L. K. (1990). Determinants of divorce: A review of research in the eighties. *Journal of Marriage and the Family, 52,* 904–912.

Wilks, C., & Melville, C. (1990). Grandparents in custody and access disputes. *Journal of Divorce, 13,* 1–14.

Williams, D. R., Takeuchi, D. T., & Adair, R. K. (1992). Marital status and psychiatric disorders among blacks and whites. *Journal of Health and Social Behavior, 33,* 140–157.

Williams, R., Jr., & Barefoot, J. C. (1988). Coronary-prone behavior: The emerging role of the hostility complex. In B. K. Houston & C. R. Snyder (Eds.), *Type A behavior pattern: Research, theory, and intervention* (pp. 189–211). New York: John Wiley & Sons.

Williams, R. B., Jr. (1989). Biological mechanisms mediating the relationship between behavior and coronary heart disease. In A. W. Siegman & T. M. Dembroski (Eds.), *In search of the coronary prone behavior: Beyond Type A* (pp. 195–206). Hillsdale, NJ: Erlbaum.

Williamson, R. C., Reinhart, A. D., & Blank, T. O. (1992). *Early retirement: Promises and pitfalls.* New York: Plenum.

Willis, D. P. (Ed.). (1989). *Health policies and black Americans.* New Brunswick, NJ: Transaction.

Willis, S. L. (1989). Improvement with cognitive training: Which old dogs learn what tricks? In L. W. Poon, D. C. Rubin, & B. A. Wilson (Eds.), *Everyday cognition in adulthood and late life* (pp. 545–572). New York: Cambridge University Press.

Willis, S. L., & Nesselroade, C. S. (1990). Long-term effects of fluid ability training in old-old age. *Developmental Psychology, 26,* 905–910.

Willis, S. L., & Schaie, K. W. (1986). Practical intelligence in later adulthood. In R. J. Sternberg & R. K. Wagner (Eds.), *Practical intelligence: Origins of competence in the everyday world* (pp. 236–270). New York: Cambridge University Press.

Wilson, G. T. (1989). Behavior therapy. In American Psychiatric Association (Ed.), *Treatments of psychiatric disorders: A task force report of the American Psychiatric Association* (Vol. 3, pp. 2025–2035). Washington, DC: American Psychiatric Association.

Wilson, K. B., & De Shane, M. R. (1982). Legal rights of grandparents: A preliminary discussion. *Gerontologist, 22,* 67–71.

Wilson, W. J. (1987). *The truly disadvantaged.* Chicago: University of Chicago Press.

Wilson, W. J. (1991). Public policy research and the truly disadvantaged. In C. J. Jencks & P. C. Peterson (Eds.), *The urban underclass* (pp. 460–482). Washington, DC: Brookings Institution.

Wingard, D. L., & Cohn, B. A. (1990). Variations in disease-specific sex morbidity and mortality ratios in the United States. In M. G. Ory & H. R. Warner (Eds.), *Gender, health, and longevity: Multidisciplinary perspectives* (pp. 25–37). New York: Springer.

Wingfield, A., Poon, L. W., Lombardi, L., & Lowe, D. (1985). Speed of processing in normal aging: Effects of speech rate, linguistic structure, and processing time. *Journal of Gerontology, 40,* 579–585.

Winnick, A. J. (1988). The changing distribution of income and wealth in the United States, 1960–1985: An examination of the movement toward two societies, "separate and unequal." In P. Voydanoff & L. C. Majka (Eds.), *Families and economic distress: Coping strategies and social policy* (pp. 232–260). Newbury Park, CA: Sage.

Wolfe, A. (Ed.). (1991). *America at century's end.* Berkeley: University of California Press.

Wolinsky, F. D., Callahan, C. M., Fitzgerald, J. F., & Johnson, R. J. (1992). The risk of nursing home placement and subsequent death among older adults. *Journals of Gerontology, 47,* S173–S182.

Wood, V., & Robertson, J. F. (1978). Friendship and kinship interaction: Differential effect on the morale of the elderly. *Journal of Marriage and the Family, 40,* 367–375.

Woollett, A., & Phoenix, A., (1991). Psychological views on mothering. In A. Phoenix, A. Woollett, & E. Lloyd (Eds.), *Motherhood: Meanings, practices and ideologies* (pp. 28–46). London: Sage.

Worden, J. W. (1982). *Grief counseling and grief therapy: A handbook for the mental health practitioner* (2nd ed.). New York: Springer.

Worobey, J. L., & Angel, R. J. (1990). Functional capacity and living arrangements of unmarried elderly persons. *Journals of Gerontology, 45,* S95–S101.

Y

Yeo, G., Ingram, L., Skurnick, J., & Crapo, L. (1987). Effects of a geriatric clinic on functional health and well-being of elders. *Journal of Gerontology, 42,* 252–258.

Z

Zarit, S., Orr, N., & Zarit, J. (1985). *The hidden victims of Alzheimer's disease: Families under stress.* New York: New York University Press.

Zarit, S. H. (1980). *Aging and mental disorders: Psychological approaches to assessment and treatment.* New York: Free Press.

Zelinski, E. M., & Miura, S. A. (1988). Effects of thematic information on script memory in young and old adults. *Psychology and Aging, 3,* 292–299.

Zill, N., & Rogers, C. C. (1988). Recent trends in the well-being of children in the United States and their implications for public policy. In A. J. Cherlin (Ed.), *The changing American family and public policy* (pp. 31–115). Washington, DC: Urban Institute Press.

Zisook, S., & Shuchter, S. R. (1991). Early psychological reaction to the stress of widowhood. *Psychiatry, 54,* 320–333.

Zisook, S., Shuchter, S. R., & Mulvihill, M. (1990). Alcohol, cigarette, and medication use during the first year of widowhood. *Psychiatric Annals, 20,* 318–326.

Glossary

A

Ability-extraneous influences on intelligence Influences apart from intrinsic ability, such as years of formal education, that affect how adults perform on IQ tests.

Active life expectancy Average disease- and disability-free life expectancy.

Activity theory As opposed to disengagement theory, the theory that keeping active is the optimum way to age. (*Contrast with* Disengagement theory.)

Advance directives Specific instructions given in advance about preferences for life-sustaining treatment, should an ill individual be unable to make his or her wishes known.

Affirmative action policies Policies designed to systematically increase minority representation in higher education and the work force by giving preferential treatment to underrepresented groups.

Age changes In developmental research, phrase referring to genuine changes that occur due to advancing age alone. (*Contrast with* Age differences.)

Age differences In developmental research, phrase referring to the differences between age groups obtained when researchers conduct cross-sectional studies. (*Contrast with* Age changes.)

Age discrimination Any form of discrimination in the workplace on the basis of age.

Age-integrated society Ideal society in which people are able to perform any activity at any time of life.

Age-irrelevant society Term referring to an ideal society in which adult roles are no longer linked to being a given age and people can engage in any activity at any time in life.

Ageism Any form of prejudice based on age from stereotyping the elderly as incapacitated to denying older people jobs or excluding them from other activities based on age.

Agoraphobia Most serious phobic condition in which the individual is frightened of a range of situations and, in contrast to other more limited phobias, is typically characterized by panic attacks.

Alcohol dependence and alcohol abuse Mental disorders characterized by the excessive and/or chronic, life-impairing use of alcoholic beverages.

Alcoholics Anonymous Popular self-help intervention for alcohol disorders emphasizing spirituality, confession of one's faults in group sessions, and total abstinence from alcohol. (*Contrast with* Relapse prevention.)

Alzheimer's Association National advocacy, self-help organization for dementing illnesses.

Alzheimer's disease Most common dementing illness of later life, characterized by the deterioration of neurons and their replacement by senile plaques, neurofibrillary tangles, and other pathological changes. (*Contrast with* Vascular dementia.)

Androgenous Having balance between masculine and feminine traits.

Anti-anxiety agents Psychotropic medications that work to reduce anxiety.

Anti-depressant drugs Psychotropic medications that work to eradicate depressive symptoms and block panic attacks.

Appropriate death Term coined by thanatologist Avery Weisman to refer to an ideal death, one in which the dying process is as comfortable and optimal as possible.

Arteriosclerosis Age-related loss of elasticity of artery walls, which impairs blood circulation and can contribute to heart disease and stroke. (*See also* Atherosclerosis.)

Atherosclerosis Fatty deposits that gradually accumulate on the walls of arteries, which, when they result in an artery being severely blocked, produce a heart attack or stroke. (*See also* Arteriosclerosis.)

Attachment theory as applied to adults Theory developed by psychologists Cindy Hazan and Phillip Shaver drawing on the infant concepts of secure versus insecure attachment to describe individual differences in the ability to love.

Autobiographical memory Memory for events in one's life.

Average life expectancy Age to which an individual has a 50/50 chance of living from any given age, typically birth.

B

Baby boom cohort Large group of people born during the two decades immediately after World War II, from 1946 to 1964.

Baltimore Longitudinal Study of Aging Landmark ongoing National Institute on Aging–sponsored study of the aging process, focusing mainly on physical functioning.

Becoming a Family Project Research program conducted by psychologists Phillip and Caroline Cowan, exploring the transition to parenthood among middle-class California couples.

Behavioral genetics Field of study examining the impact that genetics has on any behavioral quality from personality traits, to intelligence, to attitudes, to emotional problems.

Berkeley/Oakland Studies Only longitudinal investigation to span a life span, exploring personality and social development in a cohort born in the late 1920s in Berkeley, California.

Big five personality traits As spelled out by personality psychologists Paul Costa and Robert McCrae, five overarching dimensions of personality encompassing all smaller descriptions and traits.

Biological revolution in psychiatry Advances in medication therapy occurring in the 1970s and 1980s that have led to the use of psychotropic drugs as a major treatment for most mental disorders today.

Biological theories of aging Theories that attempt to explain the underlying biological mechanisms involved in aging and death.

Boundaryless career Career path involving not a stable organizational job, but one in which individuals must engineer their work lives on their own. (*Contrast with* Traditional stable career.)

C

Cardiovascular system Circulatory system comprised of the heart and blood vessels.

Career counseling Field devoted to offering people guidance in selecting or changing careers.

Career maturity In Donald Super's life-span theory of career, phrase referring to the maturity with which one contemplates one's work life.

Cataract Later-life visual disorder in which the normal age-related clouding of the lens of the eye has progressed to such a degree that vision is seriously impaired. (*See also* Lens.)

Chronic diseases Category of illnesses that have an extended duration, are not typically transmitted by infectious agents, often come on slowly, and are either never fatal or cause death only after a considerable period has elapsed. (*Contrast with* Infectious diseases.)

Classic aging pattern Typical age finding on traditional IQ tests of relative stability in performance on verbal measures and steady decline beginning early in adult life on timed, non-verbal scales.

Classical conditioning In behaviorism, the process by which human beings (and animals) learn emotions and physiological reactions in new situations. When a stimulus automatically evoking an emotion or reaction occurs in conjunction with a neutral stimulus, that response becomes associated with the previously neutral situation or event. (*Contrast with* Operant conditioning.)

Cognitive behavioral treatment for depression Treatment for depression developed by psychiatrist Aaron Beck involving identifying and changing depression-producing cognitions. (*Contrast with* Interpersonal therapy for depression.)

Cognitive behaviorism Movement in behaviorism stressing the need to go beyond operant and classical conditioning in explaining behavior. Rather than looking only to events that can be observed and externally measured, cognitive behaviorists attempt to understand and change thought processes, perceptions, and ideas about the world.

Cognitive remediation studies Intervention program conducted by K. W. Schaie and his coworkers demonstrating that, through providing training on the tests, age-related IQ losses can be ameliorated or reversed.

Cohabitation Practice of living together outside of marriage.

Cohort Group of people born within a specified short period of time who travel through life at the same period in history.

Cohort factors In developmental research, the biasing effect of being in a certain cohort on the results of cross-sectional studies.

Comorbidity Coexisting presence of two or more mental (or physical) disorders.

Compression of morbidity hypothesis James Fries's hypothesis that due to the lifestyle movement people will live healthy close to their maximum life span.

Contextualist life-span developmental perspective All-inclusive perspective on life-span development emphasizing the need to adopt a multifaceted, multidimensional, individual-difference-centered orientation when describing, explaining, and improving development during life.

Contextual model of marital happiness Principle that marital happiness depends on multiple interacting variables, emphasizing adopting an individual-situation-centered approach to predicting marital success.

Contextual perspective on intelligence Perspective on intelligence emphasizing the multidirectional and individual-specific nature of age changes in cognition and stressing the need to explore individual differences and the contexts promoting intelligence in adult life.

Continuing care retirement community Type of retirement community providing living arrangements for residents in health and later in disability.

Continuous decline model of marital happiness Idea that marital happiness steadily declines over time. (*Contrast with* U-shaped curve of marital happiness.)

Continuum of care Range of services tailored to the needs of people with different degrees of disability.

Co-residence When the extended family lives in a shared household as adults.

Correlation Statistic describing how closely related two variables are to one another. Correlations can range from ±1, denoting a perfect association, to 0, denoting no relationship.

Cross-sectional studies Developmental research technique involving testing different age groups on a particular dimension of interest at the same time.

Crystallized intelligence Category of intelligence denoting one's knowledge base. (*Contrast with* Fluid intelligence.)

D

Day care Service for disability in which the person gets care during the day at a center outside of the home. (*See also* Respite care *and* Home care.)

Death anxiety Fear of death, both conscious and unconscious.

Decision/commitment pole of love In Robert Sternberg's triangular theory of love, love that involves commitment to a partner for life. (*Contrast with* Passion pole of love *and* Intimacy pole of love.)

Defense mechanisms In psychoanalytic theory, unconscious styles of coping with stressful events that can be rated as either more or less mature. (The Grant Study of personality revealed that defense mechanisms become more mature with age.)

Deinstitutionalization of marriage Phrase describing the fact that, due to rising divorce and cohabitation rates and the increase in unmarried motherhood, in recent decades marriage is no longer the standard adult life path in the United States.

Delirium In contrast to dementia, any gross disturbance of consciousness that has a rapid onset and either abates or quickly leads to death.

Dementia Set of chronic diseases characterized by serious, usually irreversible, deterioration in memory and cognition.

Demography Statistical study of populations and variations within populations. Demographers collect census data or conduct population surveys in order to uncover basic social phenomena and trends.

Depression Broad category of mental disorder involving serious, long-lasting low mood accompanied by specific defined symptoms, such as changes in sleeping or eating, activity level, and motivation.

Diagnostic and Statistical Manual of Mental Disorders **(DSM)** Manual used by mental health workers for categorizing mental disorders.

Disengagement theory Controversial idea growing out of the Kansas City Studies of personality that it is normal and appropriate for older people to withdraw from the world. (*Contrast with* Activity theory.)

Displaced workers Workers who have lost their jobs due to company downsizing.

Division of labor Manner in which a couple divides the chores of their married life, especially household responsibilities.

Divorce mediation Alternative to the adversarial approach in which each member hires a lawyer; a trained mediator works collaboratively with a divorcing couple to resolve their issues.

Divorce revolution Dramatic escalation in divorce rates that has occurred during the last third of the twentieth century.

Do not resuscitate (DNR) orders With regard to life-sustaining care, a document in a impaired person's hospital chart stipulating that CPR not be performed during a medical crisis.

DSM-IV Most current *Diagnostic and Statistical Manual* for labeling mental disorders, published by the American Psychiatric Association in 1994.

Dual-career couples Couples in which both husband and wife have careers.

Durable power of attorney Advance directive designating a specific surrogate to make health care decisions in the case of a person's incapacity.

Dying trajectory Term coined by sociologists Bernard Glaser and Anselem Strauss to describe the illness path that people follow on the way to death.

E

Ecological approach Approach to age-related disabilities that explores the impact of the physical environment on promoting either incapacity or more independent functioning.

Ego integrity According to Erik Erikson, the psychosocial task of later life (65+) involving coming to terms with one's own life in order to accept impending death.

Elderhostel Most well known older-adult education program in which people over age 60 take short-term courses on college campuses or in educational settings around the world.

Electroconvulsive therapy Emergency biological intervention for depression in which an electric current is put through the seriously depressed individual's brain.

Enabling factors Impact of an individual's access to medical care on that person's decision to seek medical help. (*Contrast with* Predisposing factors *and* Need factors.)

Epidemiologic Catchment Area Survey First comprehensive epidemiologic survey of the prevalence of U.S. mental disorders, conducted in the early 1980s by researchers at the National Institute of Mental Health. (*See also* National Comorbidity Study.)

Epidemiologic studies Large-scale surveys designed to reveal the prevalence and incidence of diseases within populations.

Episodic memory In memory systems theory, memory for ongoing, single life events. (*Contrast with* Procedural/Implicit memory *and* Episodic memory.)

Erectile dysfunction In males, the inability to have an erection firm enough to complete intercourse.

Erikson's age-linked psychosocial crises Erik Erikson's idea that specific tasks or developmental issues become salient and must be grappled with at each specific age or phase in the life span.

Everyday intelligence In contrast to academic knowledge, intelligence at negotiating daily life.

Everyday memory tasks In contrast to nonsense syllable learning, memory studies using tasks similar to the memory demands people face in daily life.

Excess disabilities In a disabled person, excessive impairment beyond what is warranted on the basis of that individual's medical state.

Excess mortality Higher-than-average rate of death in a particular subgroup compared to the general population.

Expertise Years of experience or practice in an activity that can help offset biologically based losses in that capacity with age.

Explanatory style Cognitive behavioral term referring to the specific way individuals interpret reinforcing and non-reinforcing events. According to psychologist Martin Seligman, explanatory style not only predicts how people behave after instances of success and failure, but also affects subsequent physical and mental health.

Exposure therapy Behavioral treatment for phobias in which, after devising a hierarchy of fear-related situations, individuals gradually encounter each anxiety-provoking stimulus in steps.

External memory aids External reminders to aid memory, such as calendars.

External validity In research, the ability to generalize accurately from the results of a laboratory study to real life. (*See also* Internal validity.)

Extinguish In behaviorism a term meaning disappear or go away.

F

Family and Medical Leave Act Measure signed into law by President Clinton in 1993, requiring companies with over 50 employees to grant 12 weeks of unpaid leave to take care of a newborn or an ill family member.

Family-friendly policies Employer-sponsored programs or workplace policies designed to improve the quality of employees' family lives.

Family support groups Self-help groups for family members caring for loved ones with dementing disorders.

Family support programs Programs funded by the government and private charities devoted to strengthening and improving family life in the United States.

Family watchdogs Phrase describing the function of grandparents to watch over the younger family and step in when a crisis occurs.

Father as provider Role of father as the breadwinner. (*Contrast with* New nurturer father *and* Father as sex-role model.)

Father as sex-role model Role of father as the teacher of appropriate gender-role behavior. (*Contrast with* New nurturer father *and* Father as provider.)

Fluid intelligence Category of intelligence involving the ability to reason well quickly when presented with novel tasks. (*Contrast with* Crystallized intelligence.)

Formal care-giving supports Community services to help disabled people and care-giving families.

Free radicals Molecules excreted during cellular metabolism that damage the functioning of cells and are thought to contribute to aging and death.

Functional impairment In gerontology, the term for disability.

G

General adaptation syndrome Hans Selye's portrayal of the physiological response to stressors involving an alarm reaction, a phase of resistance, and an exhaustion phase.

Generativity According to Erik Erikson, the psychosocial task of midlife (roughly age 35–65) involving guiding the next generation or, more broadly, feeling a sense of meaning in life through bettering the lives of others.

Geriatric medicine Branch of medicine specializing in the problems of elderly people.

Gerontology Study of the aging process and of older people.

Grant Study Classic longitudinal study of adult personality change in which a select group of Harvard undergraduates was evaluated while in college during the 1930s and followed through middle life.

Graying of America Phrase referring to the changing age composition of the U.S. population, specifically the fact that increasing numbers of Americans are in the aging phase of life.

Grief work With regard to bereavement, the idea that in order to recover from a loved one's death it is necessary to grieve openly and intensely.

H

Health-related facilities Long-term-care facilities (or units) offering care for people who do not require intense services, but need ongoing help functioning.

Heterogamy With regard to courtship and mate selection, the practice of dating and marrying dissimilar others. (*Contrast with* Homogamy.)

Holland's personality trait perspective on career Theory developed by vocational psychologist John Holland that career happiness and success come from matching one's work to one's personality.

Home care Service in which a worker comes into the home to provide care to a disabled person. (*See also* Day care *and* Respite care.)

Homogamy With regard to courtship and mate selection, the practice of dating and marrying similar others. (*Contrast with* Heterogamy.)

Hospice Formal program offering palliative care for the terminally ill and assistance to families who want a loved one to die at home.

House husbands Men who stay at home and do the housework and provide childcare while their wives work.

Hypothalamus Brain structure responsible for orchestrating motivational states and programming sexual development, which, according to one biological theory of aging, may be one "clock" that programs aging and death.

I

Immune system System whose function is to destroy foreign substances which, according to one biological theory of aging, may be one "clock" that programs aging and death.

Infectious diseases Category of illnesses that are transmitted by infectious agents or microorganisms, often characterized by a rapid onset with severe symptoms culminating within days or weeks in either death or full recovery. (*Contrast with* Chronic diseases.)

Information processing perspective Perspective on human cognition that uses the operation of a computer as an analogy to the way the mind operates. Information processing researchers analyze cognition by breaking the process of thinking into components, steps, or processing phases.

Information processing perspective on memory Perspective on memory that uses the information processing framework to spell out three distinct stores or steps that information proceeds through on the way to becoming a memory. (*Contrast with* Memory systems theory.)

Intergenerational equity Policy issue of whether America's government programs are unfairly benefiting the elderly compared to children.

Internal validity In research, an investigator's ability to reach accurate conclusions from a study's results based on the internal quality of the research design. (*See also* External validity.)

Interpersonal therapy for depression Psychoanalytically oriented treatment for depression involving exploring and working to repair relationship disturbances. (*Contrast with* Cognitive behavioral treatment for depression.)

Intimacy According to Erik Erikson, the psychosocial task of young adulthood (roughly age 21–35) involving forming an adult love relationship with another individual.

Intimacy at a distance Phrase reflecting the desire of elderly parents to live near their adult children, but not share a residence.

Intimacy pole of love In Robert Sternberg's triangular theory of love, love that involves truly knowing the other person. (*Contrast with* Passion pole of love *and* Decision/commitment pole of love.)

K

Kansas City Studies of Adult Life Earliest large-scale study of personality change in middle and later life conducted in the 1950s, by researchers at the University of Chicago in which married middle-class middle-aged and elderly Kansas City men and women were given a variety of personality tests.

L

Lens Normally clear, circular structure in the eye that functions to permit close vision and grows more opaque with advancing age.

Life-cycle approach to medical care Daniel Callahan's controversial idea that heroic, costly life-sustaining treatment should not be performed on people at the end of their natural lives.

Life-expectancy revolution Phrase referring to the 30-year increase in average life expectancy that has occurred during the twentieth century.

Life rainbow In Donald Super's Life-span theory of career, counseling strategy in which clients construct arcs to chart the relative amounts of time they plan to spend in different roles at different times of life.

Life review sessions Individual or group treatment designed to foster ego integrity and mental health by encouraging older people to review their lives.

Lifestyle movement Change in health consciousness during the late 1960s and 1970s, emphasizing good health practices, such as exercising and eating a healthful diet, as the key to disease prevention.

Lifetime prevalence Risk of developing a mental disorder (or any illness) at some point in life.

Lifetime risk of placement Individual's risk of going to a nursing home at some point in life.

Living will Advance directive in which a person spells out his or her preferences with regard to life-sustaining treatment in the event that he or she is incapacitated by illness and unable to make these wishes known.

Longitudinal studies Developmental research technique involving selecting one or more cohorts and periodically retesting the same subjects, typically over years.

Long-term memory Third memory stage in the information processing framework; relatively permanent, large-capacity memory store housing everything that has been learned. (*Contrast with* Sensory store *and* Working memory.)

M

Male marriageable pool Term coined by sociologist William Wilson referring to the number of acceptable marital partners for women within a given area.

Marital therapy Treatment for marital problems in which a couple jointly sees a therapist to improve their communication.

Matrifocal orientation to the family Principle that, because women are the relationship preservers, extended families are closer knit on the female side.

Maximum life span Maximum age to which the members of a species can live.

Means-tested Allotted on the basis of need, as when government entitlements are only provided to people under a certain income level.

Measurement reliability In research, the first condition for measurement adequacy; when subjects get roughly the same score on a test if immediately retested using that scale. (*See also* Measurement validity.)

Measurement validity In research, the second important criterion for measurement adequacy; when a measure is accurately measuring the entity or quality that it is supposed to be measuring. (*See also* Measurement reliability.)

Mechanics of intelligence Psychologist Paul Baltes's term for biologically based fluid intellectual skills that decline early on with age. (*Contrast with* Pragmatics of intelligence.)

Medicaid Health care system funded jointly by the federal government and the states in which people below a certain income level get free or reduced-cost health care.

Medicare Universal subsidized health care for the elderly funded by the federal government.

Memory self-efficacy In the elderly, faith in one's capacity to have a good memory.

Memory systems theory Model developed by psychologist Endel Tulving dividing memory into three discrete systems or categories. (*Contrast with* Information processing perspective on memory.)

Menopause On average around age 50, the time in life when estrogen production has waned to practically zero, ovulation and menstruation cease, and a women is unable to conceive a child.

Middle knowledge Term coined by thanatologist Avery Weisman referring to the state of being aware of on some level, yet still denying, the reality that one is terminally ill.

Midlife shift toward maturity Carl Jung's idea that in the middle years it is possible to reach an optimally mature state of psychological integration.

Mills College Study Classic longitudinal study of adult personality change in which Mills College for Women seniors were tested in the late 1950s by researchers at the University of California and then followed through midlife.

Mnemonic techniques Techniques to facilitate memory by making information vivid or meaningful.

Modeling Learning that occurs through watching and imitating other people. Also called *observational learning.*

Morbidity Medical term for illness.

Myth of family uninvolvement Erroneous idea that children are uncaring and uninvolved with elderly parents today.

N

National Comorbidity Study Most recent epidemiologic survey of U.S. mental disorders exploring the incidence and prevalence of emotional problems among people aged 15–54 in 34 states. (*See also* Epidemiologic Catchment Area Survey.)

Need factors Impact of an individual's actual physical symptoms on that person's decision to seek medical help. (*Contrast with* Predisposing factors *and* Enabling factors.)

Neo-Piagetian perspective on intelligence Approach to adult cognition that draws on Jean Piaget's stage theory of mental development to postulate a new, optimally mature form of intelligence that develops during adult life. (*See also* Postformal thought.)

Neurofibrillary tangles Wavy filaments or strands of neural tissue that are one characteristic sign of Alzheimer's disease. (*See also* Senile plaques.)

New nurturer father Late-twentieth-century idea that fathers should be equal participants in childcare. (*Contrast with* Father as provider *and* Father as sex-role model.)

No-fault divorce law Law allowing a couple to end a marriage without having to prove anyone is at fault.

Normal age change Physical change that is deleterious, is progressive, and normally occurs as people age.

Normal mourning Typical predictable symptoms of bereavement that occur after a loved one has died. (*Contrast with* Pathological bereavement or chronic grief.)

Norm of non-interference Unspoken grandparenting rule that in order to have harmonious relationships with the younger family one should refrain from criticizing how grandchildren are raised.

Norm of waning involvement Unspoken family rule that, as children grow older, they need less care and attention from parents.

Nursing home ombudsman Volunteer who regularly visits nursing homes acting as an advocate for residents and mediating their complaints.

Nursing homes Inpatient settings offering care over an extended period to people who cannot function independently due to mental or physical impairments.

O

Occupational segregation Phrase referring to the fact that men and women tend to work in different jobs.

Old-age dependency ratio Ratio of working people to older people collecting Social Security and other benefits.

Older-adult education programs Education programs that specifically cater to people over age 60 or 65.

Old-old People in their late seventies and beyond. (*Contrast with* Young-old.)

Operant conditioning According to behaviorists, the process by which human beings (and animals) acquire voluntary behavior. When a response is reinforced, that action or response will recur. Also called *instrumental conditioning.* (*Contrast with* Classical conditioning.)

Operationalize a concept In research, the process of translating an abstract entity or quality, such as happiness or mental health, into concrete measures or scales.

Osteoarthritis Age-related skeletal disorder in which the cushion insulating the joints wears away.

Osteoporosis Skeletal disorder in which the bones become porous, brittle, and fragile; a major cause of disability in older white women.

Outcome studies Research method used to demonstrate the efficacy of treatments for mental disorders in which subjects suffering from an emotional problem are typically assigned to receive a treatment of interest, an alternate treatment, and/or no treatment, and then after an interval has elapsed, improvement rates for each group are compared.

P

Panic attack Intense storms of anxiety that erupt unpredictably and may produce agoraphobia. (*See also* Agoraphobia.)

Parental imperative Personality theorist David Gutmann's hypothesis that the requirements of parenting evoke defined gender roles during the younger, active child-rearing phase of adult life.

Passionate and companionate love Two types of love spelled out by psychologist Elaine Hatfield: passion, which depends on fantasy and excitement, and love based on knowing and caring about the other's well-being.

Passion pole of love In Robert Sternberg's triangular theory of love, love based on fantasy and intense sexual arousal. (*Contrast with* intimacy pole of love *and* Decision/commitment pole of love.)

Pathological bereavement or chronic grief When a bereaved person still is actively mourning beyond the time when recovery should have occurred. (*Contrast with* Normal mourning.)

Pensions Privately sponsored old-age insurance programs in which an employer or the individual sets aside funds when working to be used during retirement.

Person/environment congruence Strategy to reduce disability and enhance independence in older people by adapting the environment to their altered capacities.

Phobias Intense, irrational, debilitating fears connected to a specific situation or object or range of situations or objects.

Physician-assisted suicide When a physician helps a terminally ill individual who desires to die to end his or her life.

Postformal thought Fifth stage of cognition that, according to Neo-Piagetians, develops during adulthood; involves adopting multiple frameworks, synthesizing competing perspectives, and understanding that in making life decisions there often are no absolute answers.

Practical intelligence Term coined by psychologist Robert Sternberg referring to intelligence at negotiating and managing daily life, especially knowing the optimal way to advance in a career.

Practice effects In longitudinal research, the biasing effect of being familiar with the testing situation on subsequent performance that results in an overly positive view of developmental changes that normally occur as people age.

Pragmatics of intelligence Term coined by psychologist Paul Baltes referring to experience-based crystallized intellectual skills that compensate for losses in biologically based fluid capacities. (*Contrast with* Mechanics of intelligence.)

Predisposing factors Impact of an individual's attitude toward medical help–seeking on that person's decision to seek medical help. (*Contrast with* Enabling factors *and* Need factors.)

Presbycusis Characteristic age-related hearing disorder involving the selective impairment in the ability to hear high-pitched tones.

Presbyopia Universal age-related impairment in the ability to see near objects clearly, caused by the inability of the lens of the eye to bend adequately.

Primary aging Physical changes that are intrinsic to and absolutely inevitable in the aging process. (*Contrast with* Secondary aging.)

Primary prevention Efforts to control illness by preventing risk factors for disease from developing. (*Contrast with* Secondary prevention *and* Tertiary prevention.)

Procedural or implicit memory In Memory systems theory, memory for information that is learned and/or recalled without conscious effort. (*Contrast with* Semantic memory *and* Episodic memory.)

Processing resources Term coined by psychologist Timothy Salthouse denoting the basic mechanisms powering the memory system.

Programmed aging theories Category of biological theory of aging that views the aging process as programmed by a specific timer or clock.

Prospective memory Memory for future actions.

Prospective studies Type of longitudinal study in which people are examined when healthy and followed to see what prior conditions predict premature illness and death.

Prosthetic environments Environments that function as permanent support much like glasses or a hearing aid, to make up for age-related losses.

Psychoanalytic theory Theory developed by Sigmund Freud in the early decades of the twentieth century that stresses the primary importance of unconscious motivations and early childhood experiences in determining adult personality.

Psychotherapy Any treatment for emotional disorders involving exploring one's life experiences and unrealistic pathological perceptions in order to achieve mental health.

Psychotropic medications Medications used to treat mental disorders.

R

Reaction time Person's ability to respond quickly and accurately to a stimulus after a specific signal to act occurs. (Slowed reaction time is a basic characteristic of advancing age.)

Real income Actual buying power of a worker's income.

Reinforce In behaviorism, the term referring to reward.

Relapse prevention Cognitive behavioral treatment developed by psychologist Alan Marlatt for substance abuse involving targeting "high risk situations," developing strategies to cope with these situations, and enhancing feelings of self-efficacy about one's ability to control the addiction. (*Contrast with* Alcoholics Anonymous.)

Reserve capacity Built-in extra capacity of organs and systems used only under conditions when maximum physical performance is required.

Respite care Service in which care is given to a disabled person for a limited period when families go on vacation or need time off. (*See also* Home care *and* Day care.)

Risk factors Prior conditions that raise the probability of premature disease and death.

Role Sociological term referring to the major life activities adults engage in, such as mother or worker or grandparent.

Role overload In working women, having an excessive amount to do in juggling the life roles of homemaker and worker.

S

Seattle Longitudinal Study Classic sequential investigation of cognition in which K. W. Schaie and his colleagues found that IQ loss is more minor and occurs much later than cross-sectional studies revealed.

Secondary aging Non-inevitable, age-related physical deterioration caused by environmental damage. (*Contrast with* Primary aging.)

Secondary prevention Efforts to control illness by treating existing risk factors for disease. (*Contrast with* Primary prevention *and* Tertiary prevention.)

Selective attrition In longitudinal research, the fact that a non-random group of the original sample, the least capable or most poorly functioning subjects, tends to drop out as a study progresses. (This type of bias, also called *experimental mortality*, results in a more positive view of developmental changes than normally occur as the typical person ages.)

Selective optimization with compensation Paul Baltes's theory describing the optimal strategy for coping with age-related changes: Select areas of top priority; work harder to optimize performance in essential areas of life; and, when losses have progressed further, use external props to compensate for deficits.

Self-efficacy Cognitive behavioral concept developed by Albert Bandura referring to the internal sense of being competent in an area of life. According to Bandura, efficacy feelings predict which activities people gravitate to, how long they work at pursuits, and whether they persist at working in the face of obstacles or non-reinforcing events.

Self-efficacy perspective on career Theory that draws on Albert Bandura's concept of self-efficacy to predict career choices, especially for women.

Self-schemas or possible selves concept coined by personality psychologist Hazel Markus referring to salient images of the self in the future that direct much human behavior.

Semantic memory In memory systems theory, memory for basic facts. (*Contrast with* Procedural or implicit memory *and* Episodic memory.)

Senile plaques Thick bodies of protein studding the brain that are one characteristic sign of Alzheimer's disease. (*See also* Neurofibrillary tangles.)

Sensory store First stage in the information processing perspective on memory; a fleeting after-image of a stimulus reaching a sense organ that rapidly decays within a second or less. (*Contrast with* Working memory *and* Long-term memory.)

Sequential strategies Developmental research technique devised by K. W. Schaie to uncover true age changes involving conducting several longitudinal and cross-sectional studies and comparing the results.

Sexual double standard Different norms of appropriate sexual behavior for men and women that allow much more sexual latitude to men; specifically, the fact that men are allowed to have multiple sexual partners and sex outside of marriage, while women are expected to be monogamous or sexually chaste.

Sexual revolution Change in mores, attitudes, and values occurring during the 1960s involving a much more permissive approach to sexual expression.

Skeletal system Body system composed of the network of joints and bones.

Skilled care facilities Long-term-care facilities (or units) offering care tailored to the needs of severely disabled people.

Social learning theory Theory developed by psychologist Albert Bandura emphasizing that learning occurs not just through classical and operant conditioning, but also in a social context by observing and modeling others.

Social Security Government-sponsored old-age insurance program which people pay into when working and get benefits from during their retirement years.

Socio-evolutionary theory of mate selection Idea that biological predispositions developed in evolution drive gender differences in mate-seeking behavior; specifically, women are predisposed to seek dominance and power in a man, while men are driven to seek out youth and physical beauty.

Special care dementia units Units in nursing homes catering to the needs of residents suffering from dementing illnesses.

Stages of death theory Elizabeth Kubler-Ross's hypothesis that terminally ill people go through five stages in coping with the knowledge of impending death.

Sternberg's triangular theory of love Typology of love categorizing intimate relationships into different types based on combining three pure facets of love—passion, intimacy, and decision/commitment.

Stimulus-value-role theory Theory developed by psychologist Bernard Murstein dividing mate selection and courtship into three distinct phases.

Super's life-span perspective on career Theory developed by vocational psychologist Donald Super focusing on career development throughout life.

Swedish Adoption/Twin Study of Aging Classic behavioral genetic study conducted in Scandinavia in which identical and fraternal twins adopted into different families were reunited and compared along a variety of dimensions in late middle-age.

T

Task-based approach to terminal care With regard to the terminally ill, thanatologist Charles Corr's four criteria for an appropriate death.

Tasks of mourning With regard to bereavement, benchmarks that must be reached in order to recover from a loved one's death.

Teaching nursing homes Nursing homes that serve as training sites for medical and other health care personnel.

Terminal drop hypothesis Theory that age loss on IQ tests above and beyond what is typical is a sign of impending death.

Tertiary prevention Efforts to control illness once an individual already suffers from a disease. (*Contrast with* Primary prevention *and* Secondary prevention.)

Thematic Apperception Test Test of unconscious processes used in the Kansas City Studies of personality in which people are supposed to reveal unconscious feelings through telling stories about pictures.

Theories Systematic efforts to explain and interpret behavior within a coherent framework.

Theory of optimally exercised and unexercised abilities Nancy Denny's approach to adult cognition tracing the age path of performance on abilities that are practiced during adult life versus those that are not.

Time of measurement effects In longitudinal research, the biasing effect of societal events occurring around the time of testing on an investigator's ability to chart true age changes.

Tournament model of career advancement Idea in career development that, if people do not get promoted early on in a large organization, they are unlikely to get promoted in further "rounds."

Traditional behaviorism Original precepts of behaviorism specifying that all learning occurs through operant and classical conditioning and that behavior can be totally predicted and explained by charting and measuring external stimuli, reinforcers, and responses.

Traditional psychometric intelligence test Standard intelligence test in which people are given a series of items having correct answers and, based on their scores, ranked as having more or less intelligence compared to others their own age.

Traditional stable career Career path in which people are employed in a single organizational setting for their working lives. (*Contrast with* Boundaryless career.)

Transition to parenthood Transition from being a childless couple to being parents and how a couple negotiates that change.

True experiment Only research strategy that can prove that a specific intervention or prior condition causes a given outcome. A researcher randomly assigns subjects to receive that intervention, no treatment, or another intervention and then compares how the groups behave.

Twin studies Technique used by behavioral geneticists to tease out the impact of nature (or genetics) on behavior in which the behavior of identical twins on a trait or dimension of interest is compared with that of fraternal twins or occasionally with other relatives or unrelated individuals.

Type A behavior pattern Competitive, hard-driving, hostile approach to living that may put an individual at risk of premature heart disease.

U

Unrepresentative sample In research, subjects selected for a study who do not reflect the characteristics of the population that an investigator wants to generalize to.

U-shaped curve of marital happiness Hypothesis that marital happiness declines during the child-rearing years and rises at the empty nest. (*Contrast with* Continuous decline model of marital happiness.)

V

Vascular dementia Cardiovascular dementing illness of later life characterized by small strokes. (*Contrast with* Alzheimer's disease.)

Visual acuity Aspect of vision referring to the ability to see clearly at a distance measured by the eye chart.

Vital marriage Marriage in which the couple is intensely fulfilled in all aspects of their relationship.

W

Wechsler Intelligence Scale for Adults Most widely used intelligence test for adults, which has a verbal and a performance scale.

Widening income disparity Phrase referring to the fact that since the decade of the 1970s the income gap between rich and poor Americans has been growing.

Widowed persons services Supportive services to aid widows and widowers.

Wisdom-related expertise Psychologist Paul Baltes's definition of wisdom involving five dimensions designed to measure expertise or skill at the pragmatics of living.

Women in the middle Phrase referring to women simultaneously caring for two adjacent needy generations at the same time, typically those caring for adult children and grandchildren and for ailing elderly parents.

Working memory Second memory stage in the information processing perspective; the gateway memory system containing the limited amount of information that can be kept in consciousness at one time. (*Contrast with* Sensory store *and* Long-term memory.)

Working poor Full-time workers living in poverty.

Y

Young-old People in their mid-sixties to mid-seventies. (*Contrast with* Old-old.)

Name Index

Subject Index

Photo Credits

Chapter 1
2   *The Choices in Life* by Ashton Hinrichs/Superstock; 6 (left)   UPI/Corbis-Bettmann; (right) UPI/Corbis-Bettmann; 10 (left)   Paul SeQueira/Photo Researchers, Inc.; (right) M. Richards/PhotoEdit; 12   George Bellerose/Stock, Boston; 13 (left)   Corbis-Bettmann; (right) Joe Sohm/Stock, Boston; 17   UPI/Corbis-Bettmann.

Chapter 2
24   *Woman Doing Archery* by Marcus Wittig/Superstock; 37   Louis Goldman/Photo Researchers, Inc.; 44   Jean-Claude Lejeune/Stock, Boston; 47 (left and right)   Courtesy of the author; 49   Spencer Grant/Stock, Boston.

Chapter 3
58   *Head of a Black* by Albrecht Duerer. Charcoal drawing, 1508. Graphische Sammlung Albertina, Vienna, Austria. Foto Marburg/Art Resource, NY; 70   Courtesy of the National Institute on Aging; 71   Reuters/Corbis-Bettmann; 72   Ursula Markus/Photo Researchers, Inc.; 80   Courtesy of the National Heart, Lung, Blood Institute, National Institutes of Health, U.S. Department of Health and Human Services; 81   Robert Brenner/PhotoEdit; 82 (left)   Gale Zucker/Stock, Boston; (right) James Holland/Stock, Boston; 85   Teri Leigh Stratford/Photo Researchers, Inc.

Chapter 4
92   *Circus Girl Rider* by Marc Chagall. Lithograph, 1964. Private collection. Art Resource; 97 (left)   UPI/Corbis-Bettmann; (right) Michael Newman/PhotoEdit; 104   Denis MacDonald/PhotoEdit; 117   A. Glaubeiman/Photo Researchers, Inc.; 119   Courtesy of the Electric Mobility Corporation, Sewell, N.J. (800) 662-4548.

Chapter 5
124   *Ragged peasant with his hands behind him, holding a stick* by Rembrandt Harmensz. van Rijn. Etching. Art Resource, NY.; 130   Andy Levin/Photo Researchers, Inc.; 134 (left)   Mark Richards/PhotoEdit; (right) David Young-Wolff/PhotoEdit; 139   Jonathan Kirn/Liaison International; 141   David Young-Wolff/PhotoEdit; 146   Courtesy of Adam Place, National Health Corporation Murfreesboro, Tennessee; 147   Michael Newman/PhotoEdit; 153   Rick Smolan/Stock, Boston.

Chapter 6
156   Courtesy of Muriel Kaplan; 162   Michael Weisbrot/Stock, Boston; 168 (left)   A. Berliner/Liaison International; (right) Rapho/Photo Researchers, Inc.; 176   Rhoda Sidney/PhotoEdit; 181   Jim Harrison/Stock, Boston.

Chapter 7
184   *Self-portrait with open mouth* by Rembrandt Harmensz. van Rijn. 1630. Location not indicated. Foto Marburg/Art Resource, NY; 189   Hazel Hankin/Stock, Boston; 193   Barbara Rios/Photo Researchers, Inc.; 195   James Shaffer/PhotoEdit; 205   Science Source/Photo Researchers; 207   Courtesy of the Joseph L. Morse Geriatric Center, West Palm Beach, Florida.

Chapter 8
212   *On the roof* by Martin Lewis. C. 1937. Drypoint. Location not indicated. Art Resource, NY; 215   Deborah Kahn Kalas/Stock, Boston; 225   Tony Freeman/PhotoEdit; 237   Addison Geary/Stock, Boston.

Chapter 9
240   Detail of *The Drinker (Woman at a Table)* by Henri de Toulouse-Lautrec. Musee Toulouse-Lautrec, Albi, France. Scala/Art Resource, NY; 247   UPI/Corbis-Bettmann; 249   Bob Daemmrich/Stock, Boston; 254   Robert Brenner/PhotoEdit; 258   *The Scream* by Edvard Munch. Art Resource, NY; 264   Myrleen Ferguson/PhotoEdit.

Chapter 10
272   *In the Land of the Gods: What is Life, What is Pleasure* by Marc Chagall. Lithograph. Private Collection. Art Resource, NY; 274   James Carroll/Stock, Boston; 280   Judy Gelles/Stock, Boston; 290   Allen/Gamma Liaison; 294   Michael Newman/PhotoEdit; 299   John Neubauer/PhotoEdit.

Chapter 11
306   *Mother and Child* by Kaethe Kollwitz. 1931. Charcoal drawing. © Copyright ARS, NY. Private collection. Art Resource, NY; 309   Lewis Hines/Corbis-Bettmann; 315 (left)   Tom McCarthy/PhotoEdit; (right) Mark Richards/PhotoEdit; 324   Robert Brenner/PhotoEdit; 327   Michael Newman/PhotoEdit; 333   J. Berndt/Stock, Boston; 336   Jonathan Nourok/PhotoEdit.

Chapter 12
340   Courtesy of Muriel Kaplan; 346   Barbara Alper/Stock, Boston; 354 (left)   Richard Pasley/Stock, Boston; (right) Frank Siteman/Stock, Boston; 355   David Young-Wolff/PhotoEdit; 366   Jeffrey Myers/Stock, Boston; 369   Courtesy of the AARP Grandparent Information Center, Washington, D.C.; 370   John Eastcott/Yva Momatuk/Photo Researchers, Inc.

Chapter 13
372   *Approaching Storm* by Grant Wood. Ca. 1942. Lithograph. Location not indicated. Art Resource, NY; 375   Superstock; 382 (left)   Superstock; (right) Blair Seitz/Photo Researchers, Inc.; 389   Jonathan Nourok/PhotoEdit; 392   Carol Halebian/The Gamma Liaison Network; 394   Cindy Charles/PhotoEdit; 406 (left)   Billy E. Barnes/PhotoEdit; (right) Peter Menzel/Stock, Boston.

Chapter 14
410   *Standing worker with cap* by Kaethe Kollwitz. 1925. Drawing. Private Collection, Berlin, Germany. Foto Marburg/Art Resource, NY; 416 (left)   James Prince/Photo Researchers, Inc.; (right) Ursula Markus/Photo Researchers; 418   Stephen McBrady/PhotoEdit; 428   Spencer Grant/Liaison International; 430   Jeff Greenberg/PhotoEdit; 434   Tim David/Photo Researchers, Inc.; 436 Nubar Alexanian/Stock, Boston.

Figure 3-4 on page 75 showing atherosclerosis development was rendered by Stan Maddock.